Protecting children and strengthening families is complicated. *The Child Welfare Challenge* does not shrink from that complexity. It continues to be an indispensable tool for policy makers and practitioners alike. This edition is further strengthened by its examination of trauma and early adversity on well-being and development, and the use of evidence-based strategies to increase parenting skills. As a child welfare leader, I struggled to manage all of the demands of the job and often looked for literature to supplement my own training and experience. *The Child Welfare Challenge* is an important contribution to our collective efforts to support families and keep children safe.

—Bryan Samuels, *Executive Director, Chapin Hall at the University of Chicago*

Pecora and colleagues have topped previous editions by adding new and cutting-edge information about the status of one of the nation's most complex human service systems. The book is a must read for students, practitioners, policymakers, and researchers interested in improving the lives of children and families who come into contact with the child welfare system. Highly recommended!

—Jeff Jenson, *PhD, Philip D. and Eleanor G. Winn Endowed Professor for Children and Youth, Graduate School of Social Work, University of Denver*

This book offers an evidence-rich examination of both the cutting edge of child welfare practice and the critical policy and program design context and challenges. Their analysis goes beyond traditional frameworks to employ public health, economic and global lenses through which child welfare's present and future are viewed.

—Crystal Collins-Camargo, *MSW, PhD, Associate Dean for Research and Professor, Kent School of Social Work, University of Louisville*

The Child Welfare Challenge

Using both historical and contemporary contexts, *The Child Welfare Challenge* examines major policy practice and research issues as they jointly shape child welfare practice and its future. This text focuses on families and children whose primary recourse to services has been through publicly funded child welfare agencies, and considers historical areas of service—foster care and adoptions, in-home family-centered services, child-protective services, and residential treatment services—where social work has an important role.

This fourth edition features new content on child maltreatment and prevention that is informed by key conceptual frameworks informed by brain science, public health, and other research. This edition uses cross-sector data and more sophisticated predictive and other analytical processes to enhance planning and practice design. The authors have streamlined content on child protective services (CPS) to allow for new chapters on juvenile justice/cross-over youth, and international innovations, as well as more content on biology and brain science. The fourth edition includes a glossary of terms as well as instructor and student resource papers available online.

Peter J. Pecora is Professor of Social Work at the University of Washington and Managing Director of Research Services for Casey Family Programs.

James K. Whittaker is the Charles O. Cressey Endowed Professor Emeritus in the School of Social Work at the University of Washington.

Richard P. Barth is Dean of the School of Social Work and Professor of Social Work at the University of Maryland.

Sharon Borja is Assistant Professor of Social Work in the Graduate College of Social Work at the University of Houston.

William Vesneski is Assistant Professor of Social Work at Seattle University.

Modern Applications of Social Work
James K. Whittaker, Series Editor

The Child Welfare Challenge (Fourth Edition)
Policy, Practice, and Research
Peter J. Pecora, James K. Whittaker, Richard P. Barth, Sharon Borja, and William Vesneski

Psychotherapeutic Change through the Group Process
Dorothy Stock Whitaker and Morton A. Lieberman

Integrated Ego Psychology (Second Edition)
Norman A. Polansky

Behavioral Methods in Social Welfare
Steven Paul Schinke, editor

Human Behavior Theory and Social Work Practice (Third Edition)
Roberta R. Greene

Social Treatment
An Approach to Interpersonal Helping
James K. Whittaker

Evaluation in Child and Family Services
Comparative Client and Program Perspectives
Tiziano Vecchiato, Anthony N. Maluccio, and Cinzia Canali, editors

Assessing Outcomes in Child and Family Services
Comparative Design and Policy Issues
Anthony N. Maluccio, Cinzia Canali, and Tiziano Vecchiato, editors

Building Community Capacity
Robert J. Chaskin, Prudence Brown, Sudhir Venkatesh, and Avis Vidal

HIV, AIDS, and the Law
Legal Issues for Social Work, Practice, and Policy
Donald T. Dickson

The Child Welfare Challenge

Policy, Practice, and Research

Fourth Edition

Peter J. Pecora, James K. Whittaker,
Richard P. Barth, Sharon Borja,
and William Vesneski

Routledge
Taylor & Francis Group

NEW YORK AND LONDON

Fourth edition published 2019
by Routledge
711 Third Avenue, New York, NY 10017

and by Routledge
2 Park Square, Milton Park, Abingdon, Oxon, OX14 4RN

Routledge is an imprint of the Taylor & Francis Group, an informa business

First edition published by Aldine de Gruyter 1992
Third edition published by Transaction 2009

Library of Congress Cataloging-in-Publication Data
Names: Pecora, Peter J., author.
Title: The child welfare challenge : policy, practice, and research / Peter J. Pecora
    [and four others].
Description: 4th edition. | New York, NY : Routledge, 2018. | Includes bibliographical
    references and index. |
Identifiers: LCCN 2018006826 (print) | LCCN 2018008037 (ebook) | ISBN 9781351141161
    (Master Ebook) | ISBN 9781351141154 (Web pdf) | ISBN 9781351141147 (ePub) |
    ISBN 9781351141130 (Mobipocket) | ISBN 9780815351658 (hardback) |
    ISBN 9780815351665 (pbk.)
Subjects: LCSH: Child welfare—United States.
Classification: LCC HV741 (ebook) | LCC HV741 .C512 2018 (print) | DDC 362.7—dc23
LC record available at https://lccn.loc.gov/2018006826

ISBN: 978-0-8153-5165-8 (hbk)
ISBN: 978-0-8153-5166-5 (pbk)
ISBN: 978-1-351-14116-1 (ebk)

Typeset in Optima
by Apex CoVantage, LLC

Printed and bound by CPI Group (UK) Ltd, Croydon, CR0 4YY

Visit the eResources: www.routledge.com/9780815351665

Our colleague, friend, and mentor Anthony N. ("Tony") Maluccio played a vital and significant role as co-author in all three previous editions of *The Child Welfare Challenge*. His deep knowledge of the terrain of child welfare in all of its complexity helped the author team immeasurably in crafting each successive revision. While matters of health limited his direct participation in this new edition, Tony's vision of a robust and energized child welfare field – guided both by research and profound respect for vulnerable children and families – continues to animate and inform this latest effort.

With profound respect and deep affection, we hereby dedicate this fourth edition of the *Child Welfare Challenge* to Tony.

Peter, Jim, Rick, Sharon, and William
(June 15, 2018)

Contents

Contents

Preface

Purpose and Scope of the Book

Across the United States, many government agencies, child welfare leaders, partners, and policy makers are committing themselves to improving policies and practices to have a more positive impact upon families. Meanwhile, the child welfare field is becoming more research-based, with child welfare workers, judges, and mental health providers seeking better assessment and intervention tools to serve vulnerable children and families. In some states, more evidence-informed interventions are being implemented, while in other communities, agencies are in the process of discontinuing the use of evidence-based practices that are too costly or burdensome to implement. As a result, child welfare (CW) service agencies are collaborating with new and traditional partners to improve the range and quality of services that help more children live in safe, nurturing, and permanent family homes.

Public and private CW agencies have as their primary goal ensuring that all children have safe, stable, and loving families that they can forever call their own. Enabling children to live safely in their family home and community eliminates the additional challenges and risks children face when they are removed from their home of origin. CW system reform strategies can accelerate permanency planning, thereby safely reducing the number of children in foster care. Ideally, savings from reductions in foster care services at the state and county level can be reinvested in high-quality interventions to reduce the need for foster care *and* provide better services for the children who require out-of-home care. The value of developing policy and practice tailored to a local community but drawing ideas and innovations from a wide range of other states and countries is being recognized. CW agency leaders and staff see the value of different *perspectives* (e.g., emotional permanence, trauma-informed care, strong social welfare safety nets), as well as *specific interventions* from the U.S. and other countries. (See discussion of some international innovations in Chapter 10.)

In this book we present the major policies and program design parameters that shape the delivery of CW services, along with the research studies that support this work. Because of their central importance to serving families in child welfare we include content related to child behavioral and emotional health services, juvenile justice, and partner violence – along with a special chapter devoted to international innovations.

Acknowledgments

As with the previous three editions, a large number of academic and professional colleagues, students, and other collaborators have contributed to the development of this fourth edition. The world of child welfare services is growing around the globe and we are fortunate to be in regular contact with leading scholars, program managers, and policy makers in the U.S. and other countries. We have benefited greatly from their example, their advice, their critiques of our work, and their encouragement. In many cases, we have known these colleagues for a substantial part of our careers; with others, they have added new voices to the work.

This book draws from material in the third edition of *The Child Welfare Challenge*. We appreciate the advice from that textbook's co-authors who are not authors in this edition, notably Anthony Maluccio, Diane DePanfilis, and Robert Plotnick. Special thanks go to the policy staff of the American Public Human Services Association, Casey Family Programs, and Child Welfare League of America for the policy briefs and position statements that informed the legislative policy section. Christine Calpin, Tyler Corwin, Erin Maher, Kristen Rudlang-Perman, Barbara Pryor, and Susan Smith of Casey Family Programs provided key ideas and statistical charts. We, of course, take full responsibility for any errors or omissions contained within this volume. We want to acknowledge the passing of three child welfare pioneers: William Meezan, Leroy Pelton, and Barbara Pine, from whom we have learned much over many years. Our colleagues in child welfare service agencies and across academia have also imparted more wisdom than we can remember or include in this volume.

Our students have also taught us much of what should be addressed in a CW course through their reactions to earlier material and to draft versions of this edition. It is they who are the future of child welfare, and we hope this book will contribute to their preparation for excellence in the field. Alumni of foster care, practitioners, and foster parents have taught us much about the real impacts of policy; we appreciate the time they have devoted to improving child welfare services.

Purpose, Goals, Objectives, and Key Policies of Child and Family Social Services, With a Special Focus on Child Welfare

Learning Objectives

1. Understand the purpose, goals, and policy objectives of child and family services.
2. Explore child welfare policy and related legislation through the years.
3. Learn about child welfare policy change strategies.
4. Review policy and program design challenges.

Purpose, Goals, and Policy Objectives of Child and Family Services

Purpose of Child Welfare Services

Child welfare services (CW) provides a variety of child and family social services, including child protective services, in-home services, relative and non-relative family foster care, and various forms of group care – as well as family reunification, adoption, and guardianship as forms of permanency planning. CW services include an array of decision-making and family service programs of last response when more preventive and universal services fail. When educational programs are unable to engage children and families and high truancy rates persist, when public housing and job creation are not sufficient to make safe housing affordable, when children with challenging behavior can no longer live safely with their families, and when maternal and child health does not ensure that mothers are ready and able to parent when they are called on to do so, CW services become engaged. At the time of writing, more and more families are struggling just to get by. We have growing evidence that financial stressors, among many, are a significant determinant of child maltreatment and CW services involvement (Slack, Berger, & Noyes, 2017). The brief list of issues below identifies critical problems facing low- and moderate-income families that must be addressed if CW is to achieve its goals:

- *Child poverty remains unacceptably high and stagnant.* The child poverty rate has been stagnant since it began to rise in the early 2000s. Despite some indications of economic growth, child poverty has not returned to the levels seen in the late 1990s. As of 2015, 21 percent – over one in five children – live in a family that is officially considered poor (U.S. Census Bureau, 2015).

- *Full-time work is not always enough to provide for a family.* Research consistently shows that a full-time job at low wages is not enough to exceed the poverty-level level.

- *Many families do not have access to critical supports and services, such as childcare, paid sick leave, and mental health services.* Many families lack access to affordable, high-quality childcare, and do not have any paid sick leave to care for themselves or for a sick family member, or personal leave to attend events related to special needs of their children. Using 2012 data, a special U.S. Department of Labor (2014, p. 143) study found that fewer than 10 percent of individuals in the lowest 25 percent of earners have access to paid family leave. (See the ALICE [Asset Limited, Income Constrained and Employed] reports done by United Way in 2017, available at www. unitedwayalice.org/reports.php.).

- *A sizable number of children still lack health insurance.* The Affordable Care Act (ACA) has increased substantially the number of children and families covered by health insurance, in part, by extending Medicaid coverage to many low-income individuals in states that have expanded, and providing marketplace subsidies for individuals below 400 percent of poverty. The ACA's major coverage provisions went into effect in January 2014 and have led to significant coverage gains, but this law is being undermined by recent federal legislation. Yet, as of 2015, 3,886,000 children (5.2%) remain uninsured,. Comprehensive health and behavioral health insurance coverage is critical to improving children's access to care as well as to ensuring good health (U.S. Census Bureau, 2016).

- *Too few young children have access to quality early experiences.* Low-income 3- and 4-year-olds are less likely to have access to preschool programs than their more well-off peers, even though there is growing recognition that the impact of the first five years lasts a lifetime. Programs like Early Head Start and Head Start can prepare young children for a productive life, but they are not able to serve every eligible infant and toddler (adapted and updated from the National Center for Children in Poverty, available at http://nccp.org/rel_18.html).

During FFY 2016, CW agencies received an estimated 4.1 million referrals involving approximately 7.4 million children, with 676,000 confirmed victims (U.S. Department of Health and Human Services [U.S. DHHS], 2018). More than one-third of all children will be investigated as victims of child maltreatment during their lifetime (Kim et al., 2016). Notwithstanding these large numbers, there is some evidence that both reporting and incidence rates of child maltreatment have decreased significantly over the past 15 years – but with significant variation among states and counties (Finkelhor & Jones, 2006; Sedlak et al., 2010; U.S. DHHS, 2018).

Overall, the number of children in foster care placement rose steadily between 1980 and 2000. However, as a result of changes in CW policies and programs, the number of children in out-of-home care has slowly decreased since 2000 with a slight increase from 2014 to 2016 (U.S. DHHS, 2016a, 2016b; 2017b, 2017c) which appeared to continue through 2017. In the United States as of September 30, 2016, 437,465 children were in out-of-home protective placements in foster care and non-family settings, and 687,000 children were served by CW agencies (U.S. DHHS, 2017b, 2017c).

Child maltreatment is clearly a major social and health challenge, and a variety of programs have been developed for prevention as well as child treatment and placement. In this field, public policy makers, practitioners, and scholars are working to devise new ways to address child maltreatment and its root causes. Indeed, new resources and ideas are reshaping CW practices across the country. Notably, agencies in Florida, Illinois, New York City, and in other communities are making successful efforts to reduce child length of stay in out-of-home care, reduce the level of restrictiveness of child placements, and increase the proportion of children placed with kin who are not blood relatives. In addition, the number of children being adopted or securing a permanent placement through guardianship has increased over the past 20 years (U.S. DHHS, 2014).

These innovations may expand further with new initiatives designed to reduce the time that children spend in foster care and increase permanency. These initiatives include CW demonstration waivers (www.acf.hhs.gov/cb/programs/child-welfare-waivers), "permanency roundtables" (Rogg, Davis, & O'Brien, 2011), expedited adoptive parent assessments, expedited approvals of subsidy applications, family group conferencing (Connolly & McKenzie, 1999), judicial reforms (American Bar Association, 2017), and heightened attention by the agencies and courts to the need for more timely permanency planning.

Although CW agencies are burdened with yet another significant drug epidemic that is impairing child safety, professionals, families, and advocates across the country are experimenting with new policies and procedures designed to find safe and enduring living arrangements for children.

In this chapter, we review the mission and goals of CW services. Next the major social policies that are directed toward these families will be described. Drawing from innovative projects and programs across the country, we will present some policy change strategies and conclude with an overview of major policy challenges in CW.

Mission and Goals of Child Welfare Services

The mission of CW has long been to respond specifically to the needs of children reported to public child protection agencies as abused or neglected, or at risk of child maltreatment. In this century, there has been more emphasis on looking beyond public and private CW agencies to involve communities as a whole in the protection and nurturing of children, and to formulate collaborative community efforts to prevent and respond to child abuse and neglect. Our knowledge of the interplay of risk and protective factors at the child, parent, family, neighborhood, and community levels has grown to underscore the need to look beyond the parent–child dyad. Although all children have highly individual needs and characteristics, they live in the context of their families; families live in the context of their cultures and communities; and communities in the context of their social, economic, cultural, and political environments (Child Welfare League of America, 2004).

When CW services incorporate and draw upon the richness and strength embodied in this context of family life, they can more effectively respond to the needs of vulnerable children and troubled families. While agency mission statements provide the overall context for service, it is essential that key goals or outcomes are specified to help guide such functions as establishing agency strategic plans, policy formulation, funding decisions, and worker practice within a context of philosophical values and scientific practice (Testa & Poertner, 2010; Wulczyn et al., 2005). System goals and expected outcomes are discussed in the next section.

Early childhood development, neuroscience, and epigenetic research underscore the importance of communities paying careful attention to nurturing children via supporting the adults who raise them (Biglan et al., 2012). Recently, a somewhat broader framework for CW has emerged, and, in the interest of protecting and nurturing children, greater emphasis is being placed on communities as a whole. Consistent with this expanded frame of reference, CW agencies have increased their efforts to engage employers as well as mental health, primary education, healthcare, and higher education institutions to form collaborative community strategies aimed at preventing and responding to child abuse and neglect: "There is no 'children's well-being' system in the United States to which child welfare workers can refer children in need. Instead, we have a siloed set of service systems that may or may not be child-focused" (Berrick, 2018, p. 28).

Child Welfare Service Outcomes

In spite of foundational disagreements on the definition of maltreatment, the field of CW services is gaining clarity and consensus about its primary mission. A primary goal and two secondary goals for CW services have emerged with widespread support. First and foremost, the primary goal is safety – to protect children from harm. The second goal, which is focused on child permanency, is to preserve existing family units, including birth, relative, and adoptive families, as appropriate. The third goal is to promote children's development as adults who can live independently and contribute to their communities. This final goal may enlist a variety of permanency planning alternatives such as family reunification, placement with relatives, different forms of guardianship, adoption, and intentionally planned kinship care with legal safeguards such as guardianship (U.S. DHHS, 2014).

Currently, a challenging and controversial issue facing CW is the disproportionate number of children of color in foster care placements. Of the 117,794 U.S. children awaiting adoption in 2015, nearly 23 percent (26,709) were Black and 22 percent (25,822) were Hispanic (U.S. DHHS, 2017b). In fact, about 54 percent of the foster care population are children of color (i.e., African American/Black, Latino/Hispanic, Asian, Native American/Indigenous, and two or more races), and some of these children will remain in foster care placements until they are emancipated at age 18 (U.S. DHHS, 2014, 2017b). Furthermore, African American children represented 23 percent of the children placed in out-of-home care nationwide in 2016 (U.S. DHHS, 2017b), which is significantly higher than the percentage of African American children in the general population for 2015 (14%) (Annie E. Casey Foundation, 2017). It is well documented that the placement of Native American children is even more disproportionate with their population: Native American children represented 2 percent of the children placed in out-of-home care nationwide in 2016 (U.S. DHHS, 2017b) – double their percentage in the general population in 2015 (1%) (Annie E. Casey Foundation, 2017). The most important contributors to this disproportionality continue to be a matter of significant research and discussion.

There is some debate in the field about the usual legislative language that makes child safety a goal superior to family support (the way that this is framed depends on decisions in each state). Indeed, many family advocates and some researchers have argued that without a simultaneous emphasis on child safety *and* family support, neither goal will be achieved in an equitable manner. Similarly, the capacity of the system to support families and promote positive developmental outcomes for children in custody has been the subject of much criticism and debate (Berrick, 2018; Wulczyn et al., 2005). The key components of each of these major goals (also called *outcome domains*) are summarized next.

Safety of Children

Maltreatment has a detrimental impact on the cognitive, emotional, and physical development of children. Thus, a core goal for CW services is keeping children safe from child abuse and neglect. This goal includes children living with their birth families, children reunited with their families after a maltreatment event, and children placed in out-of-home care when parental custody has been terminated because of maltreatment. In terms of concrete outcomes, the public policies that support CW services are intended (1) to prevent children from being maltreated, and (2) to keep families safely together, including families that may be functioning at a minimum standard of parenting. CW workers operate on the philosophical basis that all children have a right to live in a safe environment that is free from abuse and neglect. There is little or no debate that the first focus of CW services should be to deliver services that are preventive, non-punitive, and geared toward parental rehabilitation through identification and treatment of the factors that underlie maltreatment.

This consensus breaks down in a variety of areas, however, including defining what constitutes child abuse or neglect, establishing standards for agency intervention, and specifying what constitutes a minimum standard of parenting (popularized by the question, "What is a good-enough parent?"). In the face of this widespread disagreement, CW is a policy and practice area that is benefitting from recent research on risk and protective factors in child development.

Standards used in case decision making seriously affect provision of services. Historically, the standard used for CW intervention has been very child-focused. Such a broad and subjective standard skewed CW workers' actions toward frequent removal of children. This approach to practice resulted in an emphasis (and a public expectation) that CW services should be used to improve all areas of family functioning. In addition, child placement was also justified because it was the "best" plan for the child. The best plan was sometimes confused with a *"better"* plan because there were better health and educational resources for the child in an alternative setting. In addition, the public and certain community agencies may have expected that family functioning had to be improved to an unrealistically high level before the case was closed.

That expectation is no longer feasible or ethical. It is not feasible because high caseloads and a shortage of services have forced agencies to target their services to clients most in need. From an ethical standpoint, laws protecting parent rights and family privacy prohibit forcing services upon families whose functioning does not fall below a certain minimum standard of parenting. These families are generally best voluntarily engaged and served by other community agencies. Knowing from research that most youth want to have ongoing contact with their families, whether they are at home or not (Chapman, Wall, & Barth, 2004), we assume that the development of more effective in-home services will be welcomed by youth and parents alike.

Finally, we lack the research data that allow us to predict what is in the child's best interest, beyond protecting children in severe situations. While risk assessment and case decision-making approaches have improved with more refined models and early (but very preliminary) results from some predictive analytic approaches (Putnam-Hornstein, Needell, & Rhodes, 2013; Roberts et al., 2018; Vaithianathan et al., 2013), the CW field is not yet able to predict outcomes for children in relation to determining whether child placement would be superior for many cases. In particular, we can also see that children who remain at home following a relatively low-intensity form of neglect fare at least as well as those who go into foster care and experience foster care instability (Doyle, 2007; Lloyd & Barth, 2011).

CW service agencies are, instead, focusing on *minimum standards of parenting,* with a requirement that involuntary CWS intervention proceed only if there is evidence that children have been harmed or will be at serious risk of maltreatment in the near future. In most states, CW workers are encouraged to focus on minimally adequate care and levels of risk to the child, rather than requiring that all parents provide some "optimal" level of nurturing. The types of services available to help parents meet a minimal standard of parenting heavily influence CW decision making and the case plan to be implemented. No agency has a completely adequate range of services, but within most communities there should be a variety of resources to supplement and support what CW staff can provide, such as crisis nurseries, treatment day care, home-based services and parenting support groups. Finally, perhaps one of the most pivotal determinants is client ability or willingness to use the services. Regardless of what a worker can do for or plan with a family, a successful outcome is dependent upon the ability of family members to benefit from the service and their willingness to work with CW staff and allied service providers required by the court.

Permanency: Preserving Families and Creating Permanent Homes for Children

When the state steps in to protect an abused or neglected child, the CW agency must also consider the child's needs for permanent and stable family ties. In addition to protecting a child, the state should ensure that the child has the opportunity to be brought up by stable and legally secure permanent families, rather than in temporary foster or group care under the supervision of the state.

This principle has been well established in federal law, increasingly so by the Adoption Assistance and Child Welfare Act of 1980, then by the Adoption and Safe Families Act of 1997, and then by the Adoption Promotion Act of 2003. While permanency alone does not guarantee a normal healthy childhood, it is a key factor in the successful upbringing of children for a number of reasons. First, many mental health experts have proposed that stable and continuous caregivers are important to normal child development. Children benefit from secure and uninterrupted positive emotional relationships with adults who are responsible for their care in order to learn how to form healthy relationships later on (Appleyard, Egeland, & Sroufe, 2007). They do not benefit from uninterrupted emotional relationships that traumatize them, result in elevated stress, and may diminish their capacity for learning and social relationships.

Second, children need parents who are fully committed to caring for them, and it is easier for parents (whether biological, foster, or adoptive) to maintain a strong commitment to the child when their role is secure. Children are likely to feel more secure under the care of parents than CW agencies. In addition, fully committed parents are more likely to provide conscientiously for the child's needs. As Rita Pierson said, "Every child deserves a champion – an adult who will never give up on them, who understands the power of connection, and insists that they become the best that they can possibly be" (www.the positiveencourager.global/rita-f-pierson-every-child-needs-a-champion-video/ retrieved July 9, 2017).

Third, having a permanent family adds a critical element of predictability to a child's life, thereby promoting their sense of belonging. Not knowing when and where one might live next can impose great stress on a child. With a permanent family, a child can form a more secure sense of the future and better weather other difficulties and changes in childhood and adolescence (Casey Family Programs, 2003; Kerman, Maluccio, & Freundlich, 2008). This is especially true, as more young people rely on living with family and extended financial support well into their third decade of life.

Fourth, autonomous families are generally more capable of raising children than is the state (Berrick et al., 1998; Goldstein, Freud, & Solnit, 1973). Decision making for children in state-supervised foster care tends to be fragmented and diffuse because it is shared by CW workers, professional therapists and evaluators, foster parents, court personnel, and biological parents. Full-time permanent families, who concentrate far more personal commitment and time on the child than any professional, are best able to make fully informed and timely decisions for a child.

In terms of concrete outcomes, we should be looking to CW services for a number of permanency-related outcomes, including *purposeful case plans* that explicitly address the child's legal status and need for permanency planning. If permanent placement is an important goal for abused and neglected children, it follows that service plans for such children should be designed accordingly. Whether a service plan has been logically designed to achieve a safe and permanent home for the child is a key indicator by which to measure the appropriateness of the plan and, ultimately, to measure the plan's success and that of the CW agency.

Permanency planning is the systematic process of carrying out, within proscribed time frames, a set of goal-directed activities designed to help children live in safe families that offer them a sense of belonging and legal, lifetime family ties (Maluccio, Fein, & Olmstead, 1986). Permanency planning thus refers to the process of taking prompt, decisive action to maintain children in their own homes or place them in legally permanent families. Above all, it addresses a single – but crucial – question: What will this child's family be when he or she grows up? It embodies a family-focused paradigm for CW services, with emphasis on providing a permanent legal family and sensitivity to ensuring family continuity for children across the life span (McFadden & Downs, 1995).

Federal policy mandates the states to promote permanency planning for children and youths coming to their attention through such means as subsidized adoption, procedural reforms, time limits, and, above all, preventive and supportive services to families. Each state, in turn, enacts legislation or policies designed to implement these Acts, resulting in major changes in service delivery and, apparently, changes in outcomes for children in foster care and their families (Barth, Wulczyn, & Crea, 2005; U.S. DHHS, 2014).

As the meaning of permanency planning is considered, one should note that there are different options or routes to it (Kerman et al., 2008). These include maintaining the child in her or his own home; reunification of placed children with their biological families; adoption; and permanent or long-term foster family care in special situations, such as those of older children with ongoing relationships with their birth parents. This hierarchy of options is generally accepted. This does not mean, however, that any one of these options is inherently good or bad for every child. It does mean that in each case there should be careful assessment and extensive work to maintain children with their own families or to make other permanent plans when it has been demonstrated that the parents cannot care for the child. In short, permanency planning encompasses both prevention and rehabilitation and can serve as a framework for CW practice in general. It involves attention not only to children in care but also to those who are at risk of out-of-home placement (see Chapters 5 and 6).

Other outcomes (framed in italics to help distinguish them from one another) include children being *placed in the least restrictive placement* possible, *with siblings* whenever possible, with *minimal placement moves or disruptions*, and with a *timely resolution of their legal status* so that they can be adopted by a caring adult if a birth parent is unable to care for them.

Child and Family Well-being: Meeting Developmental Needs

Achieving child well-being means not only that a child is safe from child abuse or neglect but also that a child's basic needs are being met and that the child is provided with the opportunity to grow and develop in an environment with consistent nurture, support, and stimulation. In this goal area, we include the need for children to develop a healthy sense of identity; an understanding of their ethnic heritage; and skills for coping with racism, sexism, homophobia, and other forms of discrimination that they may experience. CW should promote standards of parenting that, at a minimum, will provide a child with the developmental opportunities and emotional nurturance needed to grow into an adult who can live as independently as possible.

Child well-being is related ipso facto to family well-being. Achieving child well-being means that families must have the capacity to care for children and to fulfill children's basic developmental, health, educational, social, cultural, spiritual, and housing needs. Ensuring family well-being also implies that CW staff members have responsibility for locating these essential services and supports (and that these services are available), and for helping to find community partners to sustain or promote parents in their child-rearing roles.

Family well-being. In earlier editions of this volume we indicated that family well-being was generally not viewed as a central goal of CW but might be thought of as an outcome in a reformulated child and family services program that is concerned not only about the impact of services upon children but also upon each family member. We are pleased to report that new federal outcome standards have now included three child and family well-being indicators. In the new federal usage, children's services workers have some responsibility for locating and securing these essential services and supports for the sake of the family's well-being. These are process indicators rather than quantitative outcome indicators, but, nonetheless, indicate growing support for the idea that family strengthening is fundamental to CW.

The federal outcome standards and child and family service reviews are based on the safety, permanency, and well-being concepts. The CW agency is also responsible for engaging in activities that will result in the provision of education, health, and mental health services that will assist a child who needs them. These "system outcomes" are not presented in this chapter but will be discussed in various chapters, and especially in Chapter 9 on organizational requisites. One of the areas for further development is child and family well-being. For example, on December 14, 2016, final regulations were released by the U.S. Department of Health and Human Services (DHHS) revising the data that child welfare systems will be required to report annually to DHHS as part of the Adoption and Foster Care Analysis and Reporting System (AFCARS), a child welfare data collection system designed to gather uniform and reliable information across states on children who are in foster care and children who have been adopted. Among the many changes under the final rule, child welfare agencies will now be required to report on several elements related to education, including school enrollment, highest grade completed, special education, and whether the child experienced school moves, and the reason for any school moves (see www.federalregister.gov/documents/2016/12/14/2016-29366/adoption-and-foster-care-analysis-and-reporting-system).

System Goals Define Outcome Domains

Each of these goals is related to outcome domains, albeit imperfectly, by federal outcome standards, as shown in Tables 1.1 and 1.2. Using these federal outcome indicators – which have since been updated for a second time (www.acf.hhs.gov/cb/monitoring/child-family-services-reviews/round3) – as a framework for a child and family services review (CFSR), an outside, onsite review team assesses each state's performance by collecting data on two outcome indicators in the domains of safety; five in the area of permanency; and three in the area of child and family well-being. To measure a state's achievement of the outcomes, the review team assesses items (via onsite review) or items and data indicators (via onsite review plus statewide assessment using administrative data). The items or data indicators associated with the outcomes and systemic factors are listed in Tables 1.1 and 1.2, and are in need of further refinement.

Note that the CFSR also assesses systemic factors to ensure that agencies are conducting quality programs and practices (see Table 1.2).

Additional Philosophical Underpinnings of Child Welfare Services

Besides the focus on child safety, permanence, and other well-being areas, we believe that a core set of philosophical principles can be used to inform the selection of key

Table 1.1 National Standards for Child and Family Services Review Round 3 (CFSR R3)

Outcome Area and State Data Indicators	National Standard
Safety Outcome 1: Children are, first and foremost, protected from abuse and neglect (1: Timeliness of Initiating Investigations of Reports of Child Maltreatment)	
• **Maltreatment in foster care** (Of all children in foster care during a 12-month period, what is the rate of victimization per day of foster care?)	8.50 victimizations per 100,000 days in foster care
• **Recurrence of maltreatment** (Of all children who were victims of a substantiated or indicated maltreatment report during a 12-month reporting period, what percentage were victims of another substantiated or indicated maltreatment report within 12 months of their initial report?)	9.1%
Safety Outcome 2: Children are safely maintained in their homes whenever possible and appropriate (2: Services to Family to Protect Child(ren) in the Home and Prevent Removal or Re-entry Into Foster Care; 3: Risk Assessment and Safety Management)	
Permanency Outcome 1: Children have permanency and stability in their living situations (4: Stability of Foster Care Placement, 5: Permanency Goal for Child; and 6. Achieving Reunification, Guardianship, Adoption, or Another Permanent Planned Living Arrangement)	
• **Permanency in 12 months for children entering foster care** (Of all children who enter foster care in a 12-month period, what percentage are discharged to permanency within 12 months of entering foster care? Permanency, for the purposes of this indicator and the other permanency-in-12-months indicators, includes discharges from foster care to reunification with the child's parents or primary caregivers, living with a relative, guardianship, or adoption)	40.5%
• **Permanency in 12 months for children in foster care between 12 and 23 months** (Of all children in foster care on the first day of a 12-month period who had been in foster care (in that episode) between 12 and 23 months, what percentage discharged from foster care to permanency within 12 months of the first day of the period?)	43.6%
• **Permanency in 12 months for children in foster care for 24 months or more** (Of all children in foster care on the first day of a 12-month period who had been in foster care (in that episode) for 24 months or more, what percentage discharged to permanency within 12 months of the first day?)	30.3%

Outcome Area and State Data Indicators	National Standard
• **Re-entry to foster care in 12 months** (Of all children who enter foster care in a 12-month period who were discharged within 12 months to reunification, living with a relative, or guardianship, what percentage re-enter foster care within 12 months of their discharge?)	8.3%
• **Placement stability** (Of all children who enter foster care in a 12-month period, what is the rate of placement moves per day of foster care?)	4.12 moves per 1,000 days in foster care
Permanency Outcome 2: The continuity of family relationships and connections is preserved for children (7: Placement With Siblings; 8: Visiting With Parents and Siblings in Foster Care; 9: Preserving Connections; 10: Relative Placement; 11: Relationship of Child in Care With Parents)	
Child and Family Well-being Outcome 1: Families have enhanced capacity to provide for their children's needs (12: Needs and Services of Child, Parents, and Foster Parents; 13: Child and Family Involvement in Case Planning; 14: Caseworker Visits With Child; 15: Caseworker Visits With Parent(s))	
Child and Family Well-being Outcome 2: Children receive appropriate services to meet their educational needs (16: Educational Needs of the Child)	
Child and Family Well-being Outcome 3: Children receive adequate services to meet their physical and mental health needs (17: Physical Health of the Child; 18: Mental/Behavioral Health of the Child)	

Sources:
U.S. Department of Health and Human Services, Administration for Children and Families, Administration on Children, Youth and Families, Children's Bureau. (2016). *Child and family services reviews procedures manual.* Washington, DC: Author, pp. A-1 – A-4. Retrieved from www.acf.hhs.gov/sites/default/files/cb/round3_procedures_manual.pdf.
U.S. Department of Health and Human Services, Administration for Children and Families, Administration on Children, Youth and Families, Children's Bureau. (2016). *Executive summary of the final notice of statewide data indicators and national standards for child and family services reviews* (amended May, 2015). Washington, DC: Author. Retrieved from www.acf.hhs.gov/sites/default/files/cb/round3_cfsr_executive_summary.pdf.

outcomes for CW and the strategies for achieving them. The principles can also provide useful guideposts for agencies as they design performance-based contracts, implement managed care approaches to service delivery, or design staff development programs. This list is not intended to be exhaustive or definitive.

1. Community supports for families. Families raise children within communities. Family efforts are affected by the community's social and economic health. Communities, therefore,

Table 1.2 Systemic Factors

Systemic Factor and Items	Substantial Conformity Determination
Systemic Factor 1: Statewide Information System Item 19: Statewide Information System	For the systemic factor to be in substantial conformity, the information obtained from the statewide assessment and/or stakeholder interviews, if necessary, must indicate that *the one required item* is functioning as required.
Systemic Factor 2: Case Review System Item 20: Written Case Plan Item 21: Periodic Reviews Item 22: Permanency Hearings Item 23: Termination of Parental Rights Item 24: Notice of Hearings and Reviews to Caregivers	For the systemic factor to be in substantial conformity, the information obtained from the statewide assessment and/or stakeholder interviews, if necessary, must indicate that *no more than one of five items* for this systemic factor fails to function as required.
Systemic Factor 3: Quality Assurance System Item 25: Quality Assurance System	For the systemic factor to be in substantial conformity, the information obtained from the statewide assessment and/or stakeholder interviews, if necessary, must indicate that *the one required item* is functioning as required.
Systemic Factor 4: Staff and Provider Training Item 26: Initial Staff Training Item 27: Ongoing Staff Training Item 28: Foster and Adoptive Parent Training	For the systemic factor to be in substantial conformity, the information obtained from the statewide assessment and/or stakeholder interviews, if necessary, must indicate that *no more than one of the three items* for this systemic factor fails to function as required.

Source: U.S. Department of Health and Human Services, Administration for Children and Families, Administration on Children, Youth and Families, Children's Bureau. (2016). *Child and family services reviews procedures manual.* Washington, DC: Author, pp. A-4–A-5. Retrieved from www.acf.hhs.gov/sites/default/files/cb/round3_procedures_manual.pdf (accessed July 4, 2017).

need to support families in providing a safe and nurturing child-rearing environment. Healthy communities offer both formal and informal supports to families which clearly help prevent harm to children, because prevention efforts are key components of CW programs.

Sound social, economic, and moral reasons compel equal attention and resources to preventive programs and to services that support child well-being and effective family functioning. Basic supports such as jobs, housing, and community economic development are needed so that CW services can stem the causes of child maltreatment, rather than simply responding after children have suffered abuse or neglect. Although CW does not have a principal responsibility for the quality of community life, CW efforts can be implemented, often in concert with other government and civic organizations, to reduce the harms associated with undermining community characteristics and to increase the capacity of communities to support good parenting. Thus, cooperative housing, sober living programs or family support agencies with extended childcare hours may help provide community resources needed to help families under strain.

Locally tailored, preventive, and family supportive services, such as school-based parent resource centers and crisis nurseries that are easily accessible to all children and families in their own communities and integrated with other community support systems (such as housing, health care, education, and early child development) are critical underpinnings for responsive CW services (see, e.g., Institute of Medicine, 2014; DePanfilis & Salus, 2003; Schorr & Marchand, 2007).

2. Family-centered services. Responsive CW approaches offer family-centered services that directly address the needs and interests of individual children and families. When families are actively involved in making key decisions about their children and designing services to meet their needs, the family's capacity to safely parent its children is likely to be increased (Fraser, Pecora, & Haapala, 1991; Schorr & Marchand, 2007). Effective CW agencies work to create an atmosphere in which families feel comfortable in speaking honestly and openly about their strengths and needs. In partnership with families, these agencies strive to construct service responses that support effective family functioning and allow children to remain safely with their families. Most families have the motivation and capacity to be actively involved in providing or creating provisions for their children's safety and well-being, as long as they are properly supported. Indeed, in 2016, of the 4.1 million reports of maltreatment involving 7.4 million children, fewer than 143,866 children entered foster care – most of them to later return home (U.S. DHHS, 2018, p. xii). In 2016 about 84,308 children exited foster care to live with someone other than their parents, relatives, or a guardian (who are often relatives). Thus, the birth family or kinship network is likely to be the continuous parent for the vast majority of maltreated children (U.S. DHHS, 2018, p.3; U.S. DHHS, 2017b). Even when a child's parents cannot be her or his primary caregivers, family members and extended family are a vital part of the caring circle for children and can contribute to the child's growth and development.

When a child has been placed outside of his or her own home, agency workers should strive to maintain relationships of continuity for the child, ideally with birth parents and with kin or previous caregivers. If other out-of-home care is required, the least restrictive, most family-like setting possible, which is responsive to a child's special needs, is the preferred setting for this care. It should be noted, however, that *routinely* making same-race foster care or adoption placements is not allowable under the Multi-ethnic Placement Act and Inter-ethnic Adoption Provisions Act, unless the child has unique cultural needs (e.g., speaks only Spanish).

3. Cultural competence. Children and parents of color represent the largest group served by CW. According to the U.S. Census Bureau, immigrant and refugee families represent the fastest growing proportion of the U.S. population (see www.census.gov/ipc/www/usinterimproj/). A culturally competent CW system is one that develops behaviors, attitudes, and policies to promote effective cross-cultural work. By engaging in a cultural self-assessment process to help both the organization and individual workers clarify their basic cultural values, agencies can address how agency and worker values may affect serving clients with different cultural orientations than those of the agency and its workers and improve the access, availability, acceptance, and quality of services to all cultural groups being served. Providing workers, and the agency or organization as a whole, with a flexible context for gaining and expanding cultural knowledge, understanding the dynamics arising from cultural differences, and promoting the successful adaptation of services to meet unique cultural needs in partnership with community members is the most effective way for agencies to improve their cultural competence (see, e.g., Harper et al., 2006; The Business Council and The Conference Board Partnership for 21st Century Skills, 2006).

Many service reforms – detailed later in the book – are being developed with attention to cultural issues in their implementation. Such attention is critical to the development and use of effective services. Emerging evidence indicates that such interventions are effective (e.g., Chaffin et al., 2012), and rigorous reviews of existing, standard child and adult mental health interventions suggest that their success is robust across racial and ethnic groups (Huey & Polo, 2008; Lau, 2006; Miranda et al., 2005). CW decision making also seems to be influenced more by the conditions that families are in than the race of the CW workers (Font, Berger, & Slack, 2012).

4. System accountability and timeliness. A well-organized service delivery system, accountable to specific performance standards and time frames for service provision, is essential to effectively protect children and strengthen families (Wulczyn et al., 2005). The effectiveness of CW is being measured in terms of its ability to produce defined and visible outcomes for children and families through a continuum of resources. Multiple perspectives on these outcomes are considered in the continuous process of improving services that may be shown to:

- prevent family problems from occurring in the first place;
- increase and maintain children's safety and families' emotional health and ability to care for their children during a stressful time or transition;
- prevent re-victimization or another family problem, or slow progressively deteriorating conditions.

Effective services are those that are timely from a child's perspective; that is, services are provided quickly enough to respond to a child's or youth's developmental and emotional needs. Evidence is piling up that the most important years for intervention are the earliest, as assistance provided to children younger than age 5 has a far greater impact upon lifetime earnings and well-being than investments in adolescents and young adults (see, e.g., Garcia et al., 2016). Nonetheless, there are critical periods for youth who are involved with CW, including such times children face when they reach the age of majority and must leave the custody and care of foster care. Service providers and the system as a whole can recognize the imperative of children's developmental time frames and critical developmental periods and ensure that services are organized to coincide with them. Service provision that is sensitive to a child's sense of time helps: (1) children to remain in or be placed in safe and permanent homes; (2) CW workers to perform their jobs more effectively; and (3) workers and the courts to make wiser decisions (e.g., Berrick et al., 1998).

5. *Coordination of system resources.* A cohesive system of family-centered, community-based, culturally competent, timely, and accountable services and supports for children and families is the CW challenge. Organizing system resources to ensure consistent, reliable coordinated service delivery, along with the availability of informal supports for families in their own communities, will maximize the effectiveness of CW. At the individual family level, formal efforts to coordinate services and supports are necessary among different providers serving the same family. CW workers, and our allies, have a responsibility to act as coordinators by ensuring that all family needs are identified, assessed, and met with a coordinated plan to provide resources that will achieve specific outcomes for children and their families.

At the systems level, formal cooperative agreements or protocols can increase the cohesiveness of related services provided by different agencies. Funding that is not limited to specific service categories or that allows for the provision of a combination of resources to meet individual child and family needs also strengthens a coordinated response to families. This approach to resource allocation may allow communities the flexibility to meet local needs and to provide a holistic array of services, resources, and informal supports for children and families (see, e.g., Daro et al., 2005).

Child Welfare Policy And Related Legislation Through the Years

Key Child Welfare Policy and Legislation

A number of public policies influence CW programs and affect the families receiving CW services. Listed below are some of the key federal policies related to CW. These policies include adoption, child protection, income support, education, early intervention, family support, and foster care. In general, they show a growth of understanding about how to respond to child abuse in a way that aims to provide protection from cradle to young adulthood with lifetime permanency always in mind (for more information, see the policy resource paper – Pecora et al., 2018 - on the publisher's website).

1970 to 1980

- *Child Abuse Prevention and Treatment Act of 1974 (P.L. 93–247):* Provides some financial assistance for demonstration programs for the prevention, identification, and treatment of child abuse and neglect; mandates that states must provide for the reporting of known or suspected instances of child abuse and neglect.

- *Juvenile Justice and Delinquency Prevention Act of 1974 (P.L. 93–415):* Provides funds to reduce the unnecessary or inappropriate detention of juveniles and to encourage state program initiatives in the prevention and treatment of juvenile delinquency and other status offenses (see www.ojjdp.ncjrs.gov/about/ojjjact.txt).

- *Title XIX of the Social Security Act:* Provides healthcare to income-eligible persons and families. One of the sections of this Act established the Early and Periodic Screening, Diagnosis, and Treatment program, which provides cost-effective healthcare to pregnant women and young children (see www.ssa.gov/OP_Home/ssact/title19/1900.htm).

- *The Education for All Handicapped Children Act of 1975 (P.L. 94–142):* This law supports education and social services for handicapped children. The act requires states to (1) offer programs for the full education of handicapped children between the ages of 3 and 18, (2) develop strategies for locating such children, (3) use intelligence testing that does not discriminate against the child racially or culturally, (4) develop an individualized education plan (IEP) for each child, and (5) offer learning opportunities in the *least restrictive educational environment* possible, with an emphasis on mainstreaming – integrating handicapped children into regular classrooms (see www.projectidealonline.org/pub licPolicy.php). (These provisions have remained, usually with expansion, in subsequent federal legislation: No Child Left Behind and the, newer, Every Student Succeeds Act.)

- *The Individuals with Disabilities Education Act (IDEA):* The Individuals with Disabilities Education Act (IDEA) began as the Education for All Handicapped Children Act (EHCA) of 1975 (P.L. 94–142) and gave all children with disabilities the right to a free and appropriate public education. This watershed civil rights law resulted from sustained advocacy by parents of children with disabilities. Special education has been shaped by the six core principles that formed the nucleus of the EHCA: (1) zero reject, meaning schools could not opt to exclude any children with disabilities from instruction; (2) nondiscriminatory evaluation, by which every child receives an individualized, culturally, and linguistically appropriate evaluation before being placed in special education; (3) an Individual Education Plan (IEP) that delineates current performance, progress on past objectives, goals, and services for the school year, and evaluation of outcomes; (4) least restrictive environment, which is in settings with non-disabled children; (5) due process, which codifies the legal steps to ensure a school's fairness and accountability in meeting the child's needs and how parents can obtain relief via a hearing or by second opinions; and (6) parental participation, whereby parents have the right to access their child's education records and participate in IEP planning (Kirk, Gallagher, & Anastasiow, 1993, pp. 51–52).

Another part of IDEA that is important for children served by CW is early intervention, which has as its purpose the provision of prevention and treatment services to improve cognitive, social, and emotional development of the youngest children (under the age of 3). Children receiving early intervention services are either considered at risk for delayed development or have been identified as having a developmental disability (Ramey & Ramey, 1998).

- *The Indian Child Welfare Act of 1978 (P.L. 95–608):* Strengthens the standards governing the removal of Native American children from their families. Provides for a variety of requirements and mechanisms for tribal government overseeing and services for children (see www.nicwa.org/law/; Plantz et al., 1989).

1981 to 1990

- *The Adoption Assistance and Child Welfare Act of 1980 (P.L. 96–272):* This is one of the key laws for CW reform because it uses funding incentives and procedural requirements to implement a wide range of placement prevention and permanency planning (see www.ssa.gov/OP_Home/comp2/F096–272.html; Pine, 1986).

- *Independent Living Initiative (P.L. 99–272):* Provides funding for services to prepare adolescents in foster care for living in the community on an independent basis (Mech, 1988).

1991 to 2000

- *Personal Responsibility and Work Opportunity Reconciliation Act (PRWORA):* Funds the Temporary Assistance to Needy Families (TANF), the largest income transfer program for poor families. This is part of the nation's welfare system, administered by the states and funded jointly by state and federal governments. Low-income families of children with disabilities can also receive income transfers through TANF, which is the limited welfare program enacted in 1996 by PRWORA. TANF replaced Aid to Families with Dependent Children (AFDC), which limits program participation (with some exceptions) to 60 months. TANF allows states to exempt up to 20 percent of their welfare caseload from work requirements, but states have the discretion to establish more strict work participation rules (see www.cbpp.org/cms/?fa=view&id=936).

- *Foster Care Independence Act of 1999 (P.L. 106–169):* Authorized the Education Training Voucher (ETV) program. Congress provided federal funding of $42 million for the first time in fiscal year (FY) 2003 and increased funding to $45 million for FY 2004. In both years, the president requested $60 million in his budget (see www.acf.hhs.gov/programs/cb/laws_policies/cblaws/public_law/p1106_169/p1106_169.htm).

- The voucher program is a component of the Chafee Independent Living Program, which helps older youth leaving foster care to get the higher education, vocational training, and other education supports they need to move to self-sufficiency. Up to $5,000 per year is available to a young person for the cost of attending college or vocational school. ETV funds are distributed to the states using the same formula as the Chafee Independent Living Program under the Foster Care Independence Act. If a state does not apply for funds for the ETV program, the funds are reallocated to other states based on their relative need.

- *Keeping Children and Families Safe Act (P.L. 108–36):* Reauthorizes the Child Abuse Prevention and Treatment Act. Authorizes funds for grants to state CW agencies, competitive grants for research and demonstration programs, and grants to states for the establishment of community-based programs and activities designed to strengthen and support families, all of which support services to prevent and treat child abuse and neglect. The act amends the Adoption Reform Act of 1978 (Adoption Opportunities), focusing on the placement of older foster children in adoptive homes with an emphasis on child-specific recruitment strategies and efforts to improve interjurisdictional adoptions. This Act also includes amendments to the Abandoned Infants Assistance Act, making aid a priority to infants who are infected with the HIV virus, have a life-threatening disease, or have been exposed perinatally to a dangerous drug. The Act also includes an amendment to the Family Violence Prevention and Services Act, extending from FY 2004 through FY 2008 authorization of appropriations for specified family violence prevention programs (see www.naesv.org/Resources/FVPSA.pdf). This represents the first significant investment in providing social services to families involved in partner violence, an area previously funded by the Department of Justice.

2001 to 2010

- *The Adoption Incentive Program (P.L. 108–145):* The Adoption Incentive Program was first enacted as part of the Adoption and Safe Families Act in 1997 to promote permanence for children. In 2003, Congress passed the Adoption Promotion Act of 2003 (P.L. 108–145) to reauthorize the program with modifications. The Adoption Incentive Program is designed to encourage states to finalize adoptions of children from foster care, with additional incentives for the adoption of foster children with special needs. States receive incentive payments for adoptions that exceed an established baseline. The Adoption Promotion Act revises the incentive formula in current law, creating four categories of payment (see www.childwelfare.gov/systemwide/laws_ policies/federal/index.cfm?event=federalLegislation.viewLegis&id=85) so that, basically, improvement in the rate of adoption is rewarded, rather than just the raw number of adoptions.

- *Runaway, Homeless, and Missing Children Protection Act (Title III of the Juvenile Justice and Delinquency Prevention Act of 1974), as Amended by the Runaway, Homeless, and Missing Children Protection Act (P.L. 108–96):* Authorizes funds for the establishment and operation of centers to provide shelter, protection from sexual and other abuse, counseling, and related services to runaway and homeless youth under 18 years of age. The Act authorized local groups to open "maternity group homes" for homeless pregnant teens or for those who have been abused. These homes are required to educate runaway youth about parenting skills, child development, family budgeting, health and nutrition, and related skills to promote long-term independence and the health and well-being of youth in their care (see www.acf.hhs.gov/programs/fysb/content/aboutfysb/RHYComp.pdf; and www.acf.hhs.gov/programs/fbci/progs/fbci_rhyouth.html).

- *Fostering Connections to Success and Increasing Adoptions Act (H.R. 6893/P.L. 110–351) of 2008*: This law helps children and youth in foster care by ensuring permanent placements for them through kinship and adoption and improving educational and healthcare outcomes. It will also extend federal support for youth to age 21. The Act offers for the first time substantial support to American Indian children residing in child protective custody. Key provisions include offering federal support to children who leave foster care to live permanently with relative guardians through a federal subsidized guardianship program. P.L. 110–351 helps relatives connect the children with the services and supports they need by using kinship navigator programs. The Act addresses non-safety licensing requirements that were creating barriers to children living with relatives in foster care. To improve the quality of services, the Act allows states to be reimbursed for training provided to an expanded group of individuals and organizations, including kinship caregivers, court personnel, court-appointed special advocates, and non-agency workers providing CW services. Finally, the Act provides additional support to older youth and increases their opportunities for success by:

- Continuing federal support for children in foster care after age 18: The law allows states, at their option, to provide care and support to youth in foster care until the age of 21.

- Providing transition support: The Act requires CW agencies to help youth make this transition to adulthood by requiring – during the 90-day period immediately before a youth exits from care, the development of a personalized transition plan that identifies options for housing – health insurance, education, local opportunities for mentoring, continuing support services, workforce supports, and employment services.

- Granting qualified tribes direct access to Title IV-E funding for foster care.

- Requiring states to ensure that placement of the child in foster care takes into account the appropriateness of the current educational setting and the proximity to the school in which the child is enrolled at the time of placement.

- Promoting coordinated healthcare for children in out-of-home care by requiring that states develop a plan for the oversight and coordination of health, mental health, and dental services for children in foster care.

2011 to the Present

- The *Patient Protection and Affordable Care Act of 2010 (P.L. 111–148):* This Act makes it easier for some parents to receive preventive or treatment services as part of a "medical home" and changes in payment structures. The Act should also make it easier for foster care alumni to get and keep health insurance coverage, even with pre-existing conditions, and even if they are not a parent of a minor (single low-income adults are eligible for Medicaid in states that accepted Medicaid expansion funds).

- *Child Abuse CAPTA Reauthorization Act of 2010 (P.L. 111–320):* This law amended the Child Abuse Prevention and Treatment Act (CAPTA), the Family Violence Prevention and Services Act, the Child Abuse Prevention and Treatment and Adoption Reform Act of 1978, and the Abandoned Infants Assistance Act of 1988, to reauthorize the Acts, and make other changes to them. In addition to many other provisions, this Act authorized grants to public or private agencies to develop or expand effective collaborations between child protective service (CPS) entities and domestic violence service entities.

It also reauthorized CAPTA, including appropriations, through FY 2015. Amendments to the Act also required further efforts to promote the adoption of older children, minority children, and children with special needs. And it renewed through FY 2014 the authority of DHHS to authorize states to conduct CW program demonstration projects likely to promote the objectives of Title IV-B or IV-E.

- *P.L. 112–34 amended part B of Title IV of the Social Security Act in 2011:* This Act extends the Child and Family Services Program through FY 2016. It included a wide range of provisions, including requiring each state plan for the oversight and coordination of healthcare services for any child in foster care to include an outline of the monitoring and treatment of emotional trauma associated with a child's maltreatment and removal from home, and protocols for the appropriate use and monitoring of psychotropic medications. It also requires each state plan for CW services to describe the activities to reduce the length of time that children under the age of 5 are without a permanent family and activities to address the developmental needs of such children.

- In 2013, the Uninterrupted Scholars Act amended the Family Educational Rights and Privacy Act (FERPA) to allow CW agencies access to the student records of youth in foster care. When FERPA was written in 1974, lawmakers intended to protect parental control over their children's student records. However, the unintended consequence for children in the custody of the state – like those in foster care – was the creation of time-consuming legal hurdles to access to the school records of children in care. This law should address this problem (see www.gpo.gov/fdsys/pkg/PLAW-112publ278/pdf/PLAW-112publ278.pdf).

- *The Family First Prevention Services Act (P.L. 115–123):* In February, 2018, this was signed into law as part of the Bipartisan Budget Act. The new law has a number of key components, such as that it allows states the option to use new open-ended Title IV-E funds to provide prevention services and programs for up to 12 months for children at imminent risk of entering foster care, any parenting or pregnant youth in foster care, and the parents – biological or adopted – as well as kin caregivers of these children. The new Title IV-E prevention services, as well as training and administrative costs associated with developing these services, would have no income test (i.e., they are "delinked" from the AFDC income eligibility requirement). Eligible services would include evidence-based mental health and substance abuse prevention and treatment services, and in-home parent skill-based services. The new option took effect on October 1, 2019; with the federal level of support set at 50 percent; effective October 1, 2026, the federal level of support would be the state's Federal Medical Assistance Percentage (FMAP) rate. Tribes who operate direct Title IV-E programs would also be eligible to choose to operate a prevention program. This allows for Title IV-E foster care maintenance payments to be made for a child in foster care placed with a parent in a licensed residential family-based treatment facility for up to 12 months. No income eligibility test would apply for receipt of these services (see www.congress. gov/115/bills/hr1892/BILLS-115hr1892enr.pdf).

Listed in a special resource paper on the Taylor & Francis website are some of the key federal policies related to CW (Pecora et al., 2018). These policies address adoption, child protection, income support, education, early intervention, family support, and foster care.

Policy Change Strategies

Opportunities for Policy Change

What are the greatest policy challenges before CW? Better targeting seems to be needed for a program that now touches the lives of 37 percent of all children by the time they reach the age of 18, and more than half of all African American children (Kim et al., 2016). There is an urgent need to refine community supports and the front end of CW services (which ironically would be supported partially by recent CW finance reform legislation) in terms of, for example, (1) more carefully matching family needs with prevention and treatment services, (2) reforming who staffs CW agency hotlines and the safety assessments being used; and (3) changing the handling of reports of very young children who are more vulnerable to maltreatment. For example, Franklin County Ohio and other communities respond to hotline calls for 0- to 5-year-olds *differently* in that those reports are always seen by someone such as a public health or community outreach worker, or a CW staff person. Another promising strategy is how New Jersey child welfare leaders refine how they addressed children/teens with behavioral health conditions that cause them to be at risk of placement.

The National Academies of Sciences, Engineering, and Medicine (2016) has recommended that far more attention be paid to strengthening parenting for children aged 0 to 8. One big idea is that CW involvement would not be the major entryway to parenting programs. Some of these programs would be built on the chassis of existing programs such as WIC, well-baby/well-child clinics, and Head Start. Another big idea is that we need more ongoing services for the approximately 10 to 20 percent of children and parents who experience persistent adversities and who are repeatedly reported to CW (Wald, 2014).

STRATEGIES TO STRENGTHEN FAMILIES:
THE CHILDREN'S BUREAU'S VISION FOR CHANGING NATIONAL CHILD WELFARE PRACTICE

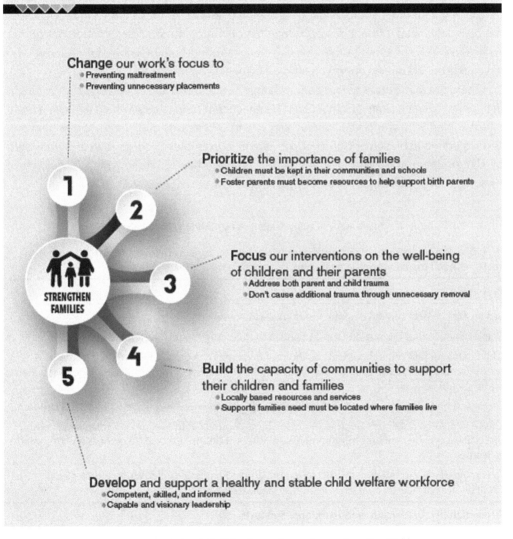

Change our work's focus to
- Preventing maltreatment
- Preventing unnecessary placements

Prioritize the importance of families
- Children must be kept in their communities and schools
- Foster parents must become resources to help support birth parents

Focus our interventions on the well-being of children and their parents
- Address both parent and child trauma
- Don't cause additional trauma through unnecessary removal

Build the capacity of communities to support their children and families
- Locally based resources and services
- Supports families need must be located where families live

Develop and support a healthy and stable child welfare workforce
- Competent, skilled, and informed
- Capable and visionary leadership

Figure 1.1 A Federal Call for Strategies to Strengthen Families
Source: U.S. Children's Bureau.

The "back-end" of the system needs reform as well – in terms of helping groups of children who remain in out-of-home care for a long time. We also have many children who re-enter foster care after going home (some of them also enter juvenile services, which is not the goal), yet there is little attention given to post-reunification services (Goering & Shaw, 2017; Roberts, O'Brien, & Pecora, 2017). What to do about group care and residential treatment programs is another vexing issue. States are reducing the use of group home and residential treatment care for younger children and are also endeavoring to go further in reducing it for older youth. Federal legislation (Family First Prevention and Services Act) has been advanced (but not passed at the time of writing) to provide incentives for further reductions. Yet, some argue that this can be a safe and helpful setting for children who have no other option except psychiatric placement or homelessness.

There are many areas where policy change could improve CW outcomes, so we highlight policy change strategies that could be enacted in more states to help achieve a more effective long-term workforce, careful response to CPS reports, judicious use of foster care, and expedited achievement of legal permanency. Examples of these strategies, clustered by CW program areas, are given in Table 1.3. The chapter closes with a discussion of pressing policy challenges facing CW services.

Table 1.3 Examples of Policy Strategies by Child Welfare Service Phase

(Note that the evidence base supporting each of these strategies varies, and many of these strategies need more evaluation so that we can confirm their impact.)

Prevention

Leadership support and development for a statewide child abuse prevention plan.

Employ some of the innovations recommended in Parenting Matters (described above).

Child behavior problems should *not* be the reason parents "give up" their children to CW as a means to obtain services. Voluntary service programs that support the family and the child in their home should be available.

Blend and braid federal, state, and local funding streams to effectively serve families and children.

Create integrated databases (such as the federally supported Child Welfare Information System) and data-sharing agreements to promote cross-system collaboration and accountability for shared outcomes.

Recommendations offered by the 2016 Commission to Eliminate Child Abuse and Neglect Fatalities are considered by each state and at the federal level.

Accountability, Leadership, and Workforce Supports

Caseload limits and workloads for CW staff are closely monitored and the effects measured to help ensure that families receive the necessary services in a timely manner.

Accountability, Leadership, and Workforce Supports

Create a children's cabinet that helps integrate all of the work of agencies concerned with children.[a]

Create a structure to develop a comprehensive approach for improving services and outcomes for youth in transition. (For example, one state convened an interdepartmental task force to focus on serving at-risk youth transitioning to adulthood. The director of the Department of Human Services and a state Supreme Court justice co-chaired the task force but we need good outcome data about what was accomplished. (see National Governor's Association, Center for Best Practices, 2008).

Supervisors need to be chosen carefully so that they are well qualified for their position and compensated appropriately.

Enable expert CW workers to remain as practitioners with ongoing opportunities for salary increases instead of feeling pressured to apply for supervisory positions to obtain a salary increase.

Establish a CW ombudsman to monitor performance and track concerns raised.

Docket management and judicial caseloads are monitored closely as those can significantly affect timely CPS-related hearings and child achievement of permanency.

Create a data-informed policy to identify which kinds of CW cases need to be teamed (e.g., identify the child abuse and neglect reports and CW cases that are so complex and high risk there should be teaming to achieve effective results.

Invest in the CW workforce by strengthening minimum hiring qualifications, require modern and streamlined hiring processes, as well as by instituting job-sharing and other innovations to attract and retain a highly skilled workforce.

Legal representation of agency staff, parents, and children is mandated and funded adequately.

Performance-based contracting can help improve services effectiveness if designed properly. (It requires accountability and measures progress being made for improving child outcomes but uses a non-punitive continuous quality improvement approach and adequate support of the essential Management Information Systems infrastructure.)

A provider database is established and maintained with Geographic Information System (GIS) mapping of risk factors to help spot gaps in services coverage in relation to service need.

Providers are assessed for their ability to provide the right kinds of high-quality and research-informed practices to achieve key outcomes.

Require regular studies of services access, quality and outcomes to help spot differences in age, gender, and racial disproportionality that are disparately different from other areas to spot areas for improvement.

Support training and specialized staff coaching, including agency–university partnerships.

Examples of Front-end/Child Protective Services Policies

CPS reporting laws changed to: (1) be more specific, such as around emotional or psychological maltreatment or neglect; (2) ban chronic truancy from school as a reason for a CPS response; and (3) include dependent child "Poverty Exception" language.

(*Continued*)

Table 1.3 (Continued)

Examples of Front-end/Child Protective Services Policies

Consider broadening the use of best practices in differential response enacted to increase access to community-based services to low-risk family situations instead of a formal court-driven public CW agency response.

District Attorney and Legal Services Officers receive training on CW policy and practice to minimize unnecessary child removals.

As in New Mexico, state law can mandate cooperation between law enforcement and CW when a child is at risk of child maltreatment so that CW workers can be involved, whenever possible, for any emergency child removal.

Notification of CPS by law enforcement any time there is a domestic violence allegation made that was substantiated by law enforcement in a household where children are residing.

Re-examine how the federal time limits affect parents trying to overcome substance abuse.

Reports for children ages 3 and under are handled differently and by specially trained staff (draw upon the Commission to Eliminate Child Abuse and Neglect Fatalities). They are never to be screened out at the CPS Hotline.

Staff minimum qualifications for hiring requirements are strengthened for CPS Hotline and/or CPS Investigator positions in terms that the job qualifications match what the job requires, and that the agencies help ensure that the applicants have the essential qualifications and are able to learn quickly on the job.

Examples of In-home Services Provision

Research/evidence-based models are incentivized and required for all key CW and behavioral health services, including parent training (with support for selected use of promising models with an evaluation component).

Mobile crisis intervention services for children's mental health mandated for urban areas, with some form of tele-behavioral-health approach for rural areas, with evening and weekend coverage.

Test innovative home-based services ideas with evaluation.

Examples of Foster Care and Permanency Planning Services

While we must prioritize services and supports for youth in cases that lead to timely permanency, we may need to allow a small proportion of youth to remain in foster care longer if that is what it will require for them to achieve legal permanency or emancipate successfully from foster care.

Prioritize placement of children with relatives in their home community to minimize separation from key relatives and a school.

Concurrently license all foster parents as adoptive parents so they can step into that role, if needed.

Court reviews for youth in care are expedited/held more frequently (e.g., Tennessee's CW agency has a very structured process for reviewing permanency progress in individual cases at 9, 12, and 15 months, which includes regional and state leadership).

Examples of Foster Care and Permanency Planning Services

Dedicated staff to work with kin, secure financial and other supports for kin, and monitor and review permanency efforts with kin.

Evidence-based models are incentivized and required for key services (with support for selected use of promising models with an evaluation component).

Enact agreements and technical methods for sharing information among CW, the judiciary, education, mental health, juvenile justice, and other key departments.

Help research to confirm that Medicaid coverage for all youth in foster care and transitioning out of care has in fact been extended until age 26.

Family-Finding (assertive use of this promising practice model) is incentivized.

Family Group Decision Making or Family Team Conferences are incentivized.

Felony expungement laws are changed to more readily apply that process for potential foster, guardianship, or adoptive parents for past offenses that are not related to ensuring child safety.

Group care placement requires executive approval (for all or certain kinds of congregate care placements such as children under the age of 10 or where a congregate care placement is the first placement for a child).

Interjurisdictional placement statutes and processes are improved, such as by using the National Electronic Interstate Compact Enterprise (NEICE).

Keep children in foster care connected to their siblings with regular in-person and social media contacts.

Kinship Navigators are incentivized as part of clearly prioritizing the use of relatives and kinship care whenever child safety can be maintained.

Licensing criteria and processes are amended to better address the circumstances of relatives applying for foster home licensure.

Make permanency for older youth a priority. Restrict the use of APPLA (Another Planned Permanent Living Arrangement). For example, in South Carolina, use of APPLA was reduced when review by a county director was required (Casey Public Policy, 2015a).

Open adoption statutes are clear and do not pose a barrier to the use of this legal form of permanency, when it is appropriate.

Parent–child visitation standards are aligned with what research tells us is needed, along with monitoring, transportation, and coaching supports.

Permanency Roundtables are incentivized for long-stayers in foster care. For example, Arkansas, Colorado, and South Carolina noted that PRTs and related training have contributed to permanency. In Hawaii and Minnesota, permanency values are embedded in the state practice model (Casey Public Policy, 2015b).

Placement moves are closely scrutinized and a higher level of review for those cases is required by administrative rule or statute.

Because trial reunification is allowed under temporary family supervision, with notice to the court but prior to court approval – encourage more cases to be considered for this.

(Continued)

Table 1.3 (Continued)

Examples of Foster Care and Permanency Planning Services

Specialized staff units are authorized in state statute, where needed, for American Indian families, relative foster care, kinship care, and other special service populations.

Subsidized guardianship laws are changed by the state to do one or more of the following (Vesneski et al., 2017):

- Eligibility criteria for guardianship (e.g., some states go beyond not making guardianship contingent upon the termination of parent's rights, but affirm that it can be entered into without terminating these rights).
- Supports to guardianship families – both financial support and services may be increased beyond the federal minimums to encourage guardianship instead of prolonged foster care.
- Parent visitation is to be proactively planned. (Parents may have active roles in their children's lives and the terms of contact should be articulated in the home study leading to a guardianship.)
- States make clear that this obligation is legally distinct from the subsidy payment to guardians. In other words, it appears that parents do not owe the *guardians* child support, but instead must pay support to the *state* (presumably as a reimbursement for the monthly subsidy). At least 31 states variously refer to parents' ongoing child support duties.
- Reunification with parents after establishing guardianship is made possible if family circumstances improve. (Parents may bring a legal action to end a guardianship and seek reunification with their children in much the same way that a non-custodial parent in a divorced family may seek custody of one's children, possibly years after a divorce was finalized. Such actions may be prompted by an improvement in a parent's circumstances. The roots of this finding may be found in policy language from both Oklahoma and New Jersey, as well as Iowa.)

Termination of parental rights (TPR) hearings are expedited (for those family situations where TPR is truly justified).

Waive college tuition at public schools for youth who have spent time in foster care in ways that the college tuition benefit does not incentivize spending time in care or remaining in foster care.

Aftercare/Post-placement Services

Evidence-based models are incentivized and required for key services (with support for selected use of promising models with an evaluation component).

Post-placement and post-adoption support programs are required and supported by federal, state, and local funding.

[a]Approximately 10 states have created children's cabinets to bring together cabinet-level directors from the various departments that provide services to children and families. These cabinets are typically charged with improving program coordination, service delivery, and resource alignment to achieve cross-cutting goals for children and youth. (National Governor's Association, Center for Best Practices, 2008).

Some state CW agencies have recently used a *three-branch* approach to formulating and implementing strategies with partners (Executive, Judicial, Legislative) (see National Governor's Association, 2017), along with forming partnerships with tribal nations – but with a broader perspective that also uses a *Five Sector Approach*. This approach was championed by William C. Bell (2016) of Casey Family Programs and it emphasizes that it takes an entire community – all five sectors – to come together, to work together to raise children, and to create a community of hope for them and their families:

- The public sector – that is, the government, including tribal governments.
- The general public – children, families, neighbors, and everyday citizens living in rural, urban, large, small, wealthy, and poor communities all across this nation.
- The private non-profit sector which provides many services through non-profit agencies.
- The philanthropic sector which provides resources designed to stimulate innovation and to support programs not yet supported by other sectors.
- The business sector which offers technical expertise, employment opportunities, and corporate support for social innovation.

Policy and Program Design Challenges

Overview

This section highlights briefly some CW policy and program design challenges, but note that many of these issues are discussed in more detail in the chapters that follow. We begin with a list in Box 1.1.

Box 1.1   The Top Ten Child Welfare Challenges

It is a major challenge to ensure that:

1. Children do not become involved with CW services when income assistance, job training, and other preventive or remedial social service programs could have prevented caregiver abuse and/or neglect.

---

2. CW services agencies work collaboratively with community resources, including allied agencies such as behavioral health, employment, housing, public assistance, and education to strengthen families that, without special supports, would otherwise need child placement services.

3. Children and families receive services that result in high levels of child safety as well as child well-being.

4. The safety needs of children, and the rights and responsibilities of parents to care for their own children, are balanced so that children are not removed unnecessarily from their parent(s)' care when the children have been abused or neglected.

5. Families of children placed in foster care are given the opportunity to experience timely and effective family reunification services so that they do not remain in care for an undue amount of time or return home prematurely.

6. Children placed in foster care who cannot otherwise go home are able to develop a lifelong connection to a caring adult, including kin or adoptive families.

7. Services are designed and financed so that higher cost programs provide more benefit to children than lower cost programs, and that the child's needs are matched with the right level of care and specific trauma-informed interventions.

8. CW services are delivered fairly and are not biased because of the race, ethnicity, gender, religion, geographical location, or sexual orientation of the child or family.

9. Continuous improvement of CW programs occurs as a result of monitoring services' quality and outcomes and corresponding professional development.

10. CW services allow scrutiny by researchers and the media in ways that maximize public understanding but minimize threats to the confidentiality of clients.

Cross-systems collaboration should be strengthened as a way to overhaul CPS. The risk and protective factors related to child maltreatment bear a remarkable resemblance to risk and protective factors for other social and health problems. This suggests that a more integrated and coordinated approach to family support and children's services could be designed to address common risk factors. Income assistance, education, mental health, public health, intimate partner violence, law enforcement, juvenile justice, and CW agencies need to work more toward a common purpose and minimize operating in isolation from each other (Chahine, Pecora, & Sanders, 2013). Cross-systems collaboration – sometimes called a system of care – is needed to strengthen provision of services to families with concurrent occurrences of child maltreatment, depression, drug abuse, and partner violence (see Chapter 8).

Workforce strengthening. CW worker and supervisor retention rates are relatively low in many (but not all) jurisdictions – which undermines key practice and other reforms. Note that in this text, we will not refer to the CW workforce as social workers because most CW systems do *not* require a social work degree, and less than 50 percent of the CW workforce has a BSW or MSW. Thus the more accurate term is "CW worker." One hypothesis that needs more research is how much CW practice would be improved if agencies hired more people with job-related degrees in social work, psychology, and other closely related fields. There is certainly some evidence to indicate that employing more CW workers with social work training would improve case outcomes (Barbee et al., 2012; McDaniel, 2010).

Foster care should not be the preferred approach. Many children who have used foster care and adoption have done well. But while child safety is paramount in CW, some children are in foster care who should not have been placed, and others are placed for too long at a time. While there is research evidence of positive outcomes for children placed in foster care and certain group care programs, the outcomes for many placed children are not positive. For example, the Casey and Midwest foster care alumni studies reported poor outcomes for some children in care like child re-abuse while in foster care, teen pregnancy, criminal justice involvement, homelessness, inadequately treated behavioral health, and poor education and employment outcomes (Courtney et al., 2007; Pecora et al., 2010). *Keeping children with families and kin should always be the primary goal – given the trauma of removal and the inconsistent outcomes reflected above.*

Child maltreatment prevention services are underfunded and lack federal guidance on what would be a coherent approach. Early intervention services have long been recognized as helping families avoid involvement with the CW system (e.g., Reynolds & Robertson, 2003). Best practices for early intervention programs involve the provision of a range of family-centered services that focus on meeting the needs of the child within the context of the family as well as the larger environment. For example, early intervention might include referring parents to job assistance or adult education, and providing parents with assistance in obtaining housing and healthcare. Child-centered early intervention programs have been linked with improved child development across multiple domains (Garcia et al., 2016; Kilburn & Karoly, 2008). Given advances in prevention science (Jenson & Bender, 2014), it is quite possible that the design, development, and delivery of improved early intervention services could reduce the incidence of child maltreatment.

A risk, resilience, and protective factor perspective undergirds the philosophy supporting early intervention. Early intervention should aim to disrupt risk processes, promote protective mechanisms, and stimulate resilience. Ideally, early intervention services promote well-being and optimal development by providing comprehensive community-based support services to help improve child developmental outcomes. Two examples of such interventions are Point of Engagement (Marts, Lee, McCroy, & McCroskey, 2008) and the Prevention Intervention Development Initiative in Los Angeles (McCroskey et al., 2012). Unfortunately, these types of services are underfunded at the federal level, and without Title IV-E waivers or more permanent federal fiscal reforms, states often lack the flexibility to reallocate federal funds designated for placement services to fund family support programs. Apart from a few exceptions such as the CDC's violence prevention initiatives and papers from the Development Services Group, Inc. (2013) and the Institute of Medicine (IOM and NRC, 2014), the Federal government has not issued a practical framework for guiding child maltreatment prevention.

Differential response approaches to child protective services intake need additional testing. New intake approaches are attempting to refer low-risk families (i.e., those with low risk for a subsequent maltreatment referral) to supportive programs other than child protective services. Although promising, these approaches need further testing and evaluation to clarify the roles of law enforcement; medical, legal, and social services personnel; and voluntary agencies. If new intake procedures accurately distinguish families in which the likelihood of severe maltreatment is low from those in which it is high, these new protocols could complement family support interventions that have been researched and found to be cost-effective, such as Nurse Family Partnership, Safe Care and Triple P. Furthermore, practice, administrative, policy, and other system-reform strategies exist that can improve well-being for children at risk of child maltreatment (e.g., Family Connects) and accelerate permanency planning, such as the Concurrent Planning and Project KEEP. Some of these strategies can safely reduce the number of children in foster care, and those placement cost savings can be reinvested in higher quality services for the children for whom out-of-home care is the most appropriate option. (For additional examples of such programs and their cost-effectiveness, see Pecora, O'Brien, & Maher, 2015; Washington Institute of Public Policy Research, 2017; also www.wsipp.wa.gov/BenefitCost, as this website is periodically updated.)

Finance reform in CW is needed: family support and other child maltreatment prevention services are not funded in alignment with desired outcomes. Family support programs, which include parent hotlines, crisis nursery services, personal assistance, and mental health and crisis interventions are often "lifelines." These services allow families to care for their children at home rather than placing a child in out-of-home care, which is expensive and generally publicly financed (National Academies of Sciences, 2016). The goals of family support services include enabling families to raise children at home by reducing stress and by strengthening and enhancing caregiving capacities (Pew Foundation, 2008; Walton, Sandau-Beckler, & Mannes, 2001). Family caregivers' acceptance and use of formal support services play a significant role in reducing the burdens and stress associated with caring for a child and in helping families obtain services for unmet needs. Across the United States, family support services are usually jointly financed by federal, state, and local governments, often using Medicaid resources, and are typically administered by state or county governments. Not surprisingly, given the differences among the states in the provision of social services, there is vast variability across states in the funding levels for family support and in the types of services available (Parish, Pomeranz, & Braddock, 2003). Consequently, these services are often not only underfunded but also among the first to be cut during periods of economic downturns.

One of the key CW challenges is enacting finance reform that will enable more funds to be spent on prevention and family-strengthening services rather than on out-of-home care. Some of the most substantial improvements in CW outcomes have come about because of federal or state legislation – which produced a change in law, administrative regulations, policy, or funding patterns that governed key areas. For example:

- Personal tax deductions for adoptions, as well as adoption and guardianship subsidy laws, have increased the number of youth achieving legal permanency, along with agency policies requiring frequent visitations between parents and their children in foster care.

- Greater flexibility in licensing regulations for relatives to serve as foster parents have helped more youth minimize the trauma of foster care and in many cases these policies facilitate reunification.

- Agency policy changes that require executive approval of any residential treatment or group home placement for children under the age of 12 have decreased the use of group care for that age group.

- Policies that prohibit foster family placement changes without notice to the family and other safeguards have improved practice.

- Changes in performance contracting policy that require the use of evidence-based practices or incentivize shortened length of stay in foster care can improve systems performance.

There is long-standing agreement among policy makers, advocates, and state CW directors that comprehensive CW finance reform should align federal funding and policies to incentivize and ensure the safety, permanency, and well-being of children and their families. There are a number of proposals that would allow states to use Title IV-E foster care funds to support children in out-of-home care and also allow their use to support child abuse prevention and post-adoption services.

These proposals may be seen as efforts to address the family support issue. However, the downside to these proposals is that the overall budget for children's services would decrease if all the areas under proposed legislation are considered. Based on what occurs with the federal block grant process for Medicaid and the Supplemental Nutrition Assistance Program (SNAP: formerly the food stamp program), families would no longer have an entitlement. Therefore, educational efforts are needed to inform the public and policy makers of the importance of policies that preserve the open-ended entitlement to key CW programs. In addition, child and family advocates need to raise awareness among policy makers and the public that program funds should be tied to performance. Results should be rewarded, and savings due to lowered rates of foster care should be reinvested to improve the quality of CW services (Annie E. Casey Foundation, 2014; Annie E. Casey Foundation and the Jim Casey Youth Opportunities Initiative, 2013). The following principles outline what is important to address to achieve this vision:

- Federal funding targeted for CW should be available for any child or his or her family on the basis of risk rather than an income standard but should also be available for a limited time period and for a specific set of services.

- Federal funding for CW should be flexible enough to allow states to address their unique challenges and issues (thus there should be some exceptions to the time limits identified above).

- Federal funding should further incentivize and encourage better outcomes for children and their families by encouraging performance-based contracting and supporting states to meet the Child and Family Service Review (CFSR) standards (Casey Family Programs and the Brookings Institution, 2013)

Policies and funding to treat mental health and substance abuse problems must be coordinated with CW services. Fragmented funding streams and policies for mental health, substance abuse, developmental disabilities, and CW services unduly complicate the treatment of parents and children with co-morbid conditions (Kessler & Magee, 1993). Depending on the community, 30 percent or more of the families with children who have been placed in out-of-home care may also have substance abuse problems (Child Welfare

Information Gateway, 2014; Traube, 2012). To serve the dual needs of these families, many agency administrators are diverted from other activities while trying to "braid" or cobble together sources of funding to cover the costs of drug treatment and other programs. Such efforts highlight the need for increased program coordination at all levels to maximize the effectiveness of existing resources (Johnson, Knitzer, & Kaufmann, 2003). This type of increased coordination may be facilitated by a system of care approach. (For a discussion of systems of care in mental health, see Chapter 8, this volume.)

Policies should increase the likelihood that youth will achieve and maintain permanency in a reasonable period through foster care, reunification, relative placement, guardianship, or adoption. In many states, a substantial number of children have a case goal of *alternative planned living arrangement* (APLA), such as emancipation from foster care at age 18 or exit before age 18 via independent living. For many children, little effort is made to keep them in touch with their kin so that they have a solid path back to family life after emancipation. Reforms that are needed include crafting policies to ensure that kinship care families have access to resources that allow them to raise healthy children in stable home environments.

Policy makers need to recognize the seriousness of, and make changes to reduce, racial and ethnic disproportionality and disparity if unrelated to the level of safety concerns. Although the disproportionate numbers of children of color in the CW system, and the disparities in the outcomes of those children, have been recognized as ethical, policy, and program issues, continued efforts are needed. First, we need to promote the investment of public resources into gathering accurate data about African American, Native American, Asian American, and Hispanic children who are involved in the CW. This information ranges from the level of access to services of birth parents for children of color in the CW system to data concerning use of substance abuse and mental health services both before entering and during their contact with the system (Fluke et al., 2011). Second, using this information, officials must enhance national awareness of the disproportionate number of children of color in foster care and pinpoint the reasons for this disproportionality. Finally, communities should launch efforts to reduce disparities, as was recently accomplished in Sacramento County (Ellis et al., 2013). The goal of these efforts should be to remove race and ethnicity as a predictor of outcome in CW services. For example, Marts et al. (2008) provide an example of a Point of Engagement strategy used in Los Angeles to reduce racial and ethnic disparities in CW. Most importantly, this should be accomplished while also reducing the proportionately high rate of preventable injury deaths which are more than three times higher for African American children (by age 5) after they come to the attention of CW than they are for other children (Putnam-Hornstein, 2012).

Kinship care funding, licensing, and practice policies need to be aligned. Some 5.7 million children under age 18 were living with a grandparent householder in 2013 (U.S. Census

Bureau, 2013). The number of children raised in relative-headed households has increased significantly. U.S. Census data show that 2.4 million grandparents are taking primary responsibility for the basic needs of their grandchildren. Furthermore, for every child in the foster care system with relatives, another 20 children are being raised by grandparents or other relatives outside of formal foster care systems (Generations United, 2016).

Kinship caregivers often lack the information and range of supports they need to fulfill their parenting role. The Fostering Connections legislation (P.L. 110–351) authorizes federal support for *kinship navigators* to advise these parents. However, more work needs to be done to help resolve the policy inconsistencies in licensing and support of these families.

Tribal access to federal CW services funding should be increased and existing infrastructure improved. Consistent with their cultures, Native American tribes have exercised jurisdiction over their children, but most tribes have seriously underdeveloped services. Tribal entities need to build a variety of service infrastructures such as management information systems and quality improvement programs. The Fostering Connections legislation enables American tribes to access Federal Title IV-E funds directly but is still little used because of the challenges for tribes of becoming IV-E eligible.

Agency policies should promote better assessment and support of gay, lesbian, bisexual, and transgender youth in out-of-home care. More CW agencies are now encouraging staff members and foster parents to protect and nurture gay, lesbian, bisexual, and transgendered (GLBT) youth. Such youth are vulnerable to victimization, depression, and suicide. Because of their sexual orientations, GLBT youth have a higher risk of placement disruption. Special efforts are needed both to assess the needs of these youths and to devise supportive services for them (Mallon, 2014). In 2016, the Children's Bureau funded its first Quality Improvement Center on Tailored Services, Placement Stability and Permanency for LGBTQ Children in Foster Care which will conduct four to six demonstration projects, in partnership with public CW, to identify effective services and supports for LGBTQ youth (www.qiclgbtq2s.org/).

Transition policies and support for emancipating youth must be overhauled. Too many graduates of the foster care system are undertrained and underemployed. Many youth and young adults are part of a large group of marginalized youth who age out of the system without adequate skills for independent living and without a support system. Children placed in foster care vary widely in their level of preparation for emancipation from foster care in terms of education and income (Courtney et al., 2007; Valentine, Skemer, & Courtney, 2015).

Programmatically, CW should promote investment in culturally relevant services, support, and opportunities to ensure that every youth in foster care makes a safe, successful transition to adulthood. Preparation for independent living must be redesigned to start as early as the age of 10 (even if children will be reunified or adopted). A comprehensive transition plan should be developed for every child. It should include planning for support-ive relationships, community connections, education, life skills assessment and develop-ment, identity formation, housing, employment, physical health, and mental health (Casey Family Programs, 2001; Los Angeles County Departments of Children and Family Services/ Probation, Youth Development Service, 2013). Employment training and work experience should be expanded for many youth while they are in care. Policies and incentives should ensure that no young person leaves foster care without housing, access to healthcare, employment skills, and permanent connections to at least one adult.

Policies should provide fiscal incentives to improve high-school graduation rates and to support post-secondary education and training for children and youth in foster care. Recent changes in the federal Higher Education Act, reauthorized in 2008 as the Higher Education Opportunity Act (HEOA; P.L. 110–315), provide more consideration of the spe-cial needs of children and youth in foster care. Continuous policy innovation and systems change is needed to strengthen elementary and secondary education programs, includ-ing special education initiatives. In addition, federal and state policies must maintain the financial viability and array of services within the Medicaid and State Children's Health Insurance Program (SCHIP) programs for youth in foster care and ensure that no young per-son leaves foster care without access to appropriate healthcare. All youth in high school while in foster care should receive the experiential life skills, tutoring, and employment preparation and experiences that build work-related skills.

Performance-based contracting should be fully implemented. Attempts to implement state and county policies to promote performance-based contracting have been hampered by a lack of knowledge of baseline conditions, concrete target goals, and infrastruc-ture funding gaps. Clear performance criteria, cohort-based and longitudinal data anal-yses, and quality improvement systems must be in place to enable agencies to improve performance-based contracting and the implementation of evidence-based practice mod-els (Mordock, 2002; Wulczyn et al., 2009).

Conclusion

The Road Ahead

This chapter has summarized the major goals, intended outcomes, and policies that guide CW services in the United States, while discussing a wider range of policy and program challenges, some of which have been inspired by work in other countries. Child welfare services are ever evolving. As we write, states are passing legislation to address certain policy gaps or needs, such as instituting alternative response systems to support families, reducing length of stay in therapeutic residential care, requiring stronger preparation for youth to transition from foster care, extending the length of time youth can remain in foster care and can receive Medicaid. Some have advocated for Federal CW funding reform because the Title IV-E waiver legislation has enabled over 25 jurisdictions to engage in a variety of service reform activities.

The Grand Challenges for Social Work, an important initiative that also addresses challenges for the social work profession, has been underway since 2012 (and was formally launched in early 2016: see Box 1.2; Uehara et al., 2017; Fong, Lubben, & Barth, 2018). The Grand Challenges are being developed under the auspices of the American Academy for Social Work and Social Welfare (where more information is available). Although there was not a Grand Challenge that explicitly addressed a CW program area, among the 12 challenges identified, the accomplishment of each of these challenges will intersect with those of the CW challenges. We encourage readers to look at these challenges and engage in thinking about how to bring the benefits of progress on them to bear for CW-involved families and social workers.

Box 1.2   The Grand Challenges

1. Ensure healthy development for all youth: http://aaswsw.org/grand-challenges-initiative/12-challenges/ensure-healthy-development-for-all-youth/.

2. Close the health gap: http://aaswsw.org/grand-challenges-initiative/12-challenges/close-the-health-gap/.

3. Stop family violence: http://aaswsw.org/grand-challenges-initiative/12-challenges/stop-family-violence/.

4. Advance long and productive lives: http://aaswsw.org/grand-challenges-initiative/12-challenges/advance-long-and-productive-lives/.

5. Eradicate social isolation: http://aaswsw.org/grand-challenges-initiative/12-challenges/eradicate-social-isolation/.

6. End homelessness: http://aaswsw.org/grand-challenges-initiative/12-challenges/end-homelessness/>.

7. Create social responses to a changing environment: http://aaswsw.org/grand-challenges-initiative/12-challenges/create-social-responses-to-a-changing-environment/.

---

8. Harness technology for social good: http://aaswsw.org/grand-challenges-initi ative/12-challenges/harness-technology-for-social-good/.

9. Promote smart decarceration: http://aaswsw.org/grand-challenges-initiative/12-challenges/promote-smart-decarceration/.

10. Reduce extreme economic inequality: http://aaswsw.org/grand-challenges-ini tiative/12-challenges/reduce-extreme-economic-inequality/.

11. Build financial capability for all: http://aaswsw.org/grand-challenges-initiative/12-challenges/build-financial-capability-for-all/.

12. Achieve equal opportunity and justice: http://aaswsw.org/grand-challenges-ini tiative/12-challenges/achieve-equal-opportunity-and-justice/.

Source: http://aaswsw.org/grand-challenges-initiative/12-challenges/. Join the Grand Challenges for Social Work: http://aaswsw.org/grand-challenges-initiative/join/.

For More Information

Child Trends for key statistical summaries, child and family trend data and issue summaries, www.childtrends.org.

National Academies of Sciences, Engineering, and Medicine. (2016). *Parenting Matters: Supporting Parents of Children Ages 0–8.* Washington, DC: The National Academies Press. doi:10.17226/21868. Retrieved from www.nap.edu/read/21868/chapter/1#ii.

U.S. Children's Bureau for state outcomes and foster care statistics, www.acf.hhs.gov/programs/cb/publications.

Bibliography

American Bar Association. (2017). Court improvement projects. Retrieved from www.ameri canbar.org/groups/child_law/what_we_do/projects/rclji/courtimp.html.

American Humane Association, Children's Division; American Bar Association, Center on Children and the Law; Annie E. Casey Foundation; The Casey Family Program; Casey Family Services; and Institute for Human Services Management. (1998). *Assessing outcomes in child welfare services: Principles, concepts, and a framework of core indicators.* Englewood, CO: The Casey Outcomes and Decision-making Project. Retrieved from www.aecf.org/upload/publicationfiles/assessing%20framework.pdf.

Annie E. Casey Foundation. (2014). *The cost of doing nothing.* Retrieved from www.aecf.org/~/media/Pubs/Topics/Child%20Welfare%20Permanence/Other/CostofDoingNothingInfo/CostOfDoingNothingInfo.pdf.

Annie E. Casey Foundation. (2017). *National KIDS COUNT.* Baltimore, MD: Author. Retrieved from http://datacenter.kidscount.org/data/tables/103-child-population-by-race?loc=1&loct=1#detailed/1/any/false/573/68,72/423,424.

Annie E. Casey Foundation and the Jim Casey Youth Opportunities Initiative. (2013). *When child welfare works: A working paper.* Baltimore, MD: Author. Retrieved from www.aecf.org/KnowledgeCenter/Publications.aspx?pubguid={2437146B-7A85-4E9F-9524-94114F185106}.

Appleyard, K., Egeland, B., & Sroufe, A. (2007). Direct social support for young high risk children: Relations with behavioral and emotional outcomes across time. *Journal of Abnormal Child Psychology, 35*(3), 443–457.

Barbee, A.P., Antle, B.F., Sullivan, D., Dryden, A.A., & Henry, K. (2012). Twenty-five years of the Children's Bureau investment in social work education. *Journal of Public Child Welfare, 6*, 376–389.

Barth, R.P., Wulczyn, F., & Crea, T. (2005). From anticipation to evidence: Research on the Adoption and Safe Families Act. *Journal of Law and Social Policy*, 371–399.

Bell, W.C. (2016). Speech for the Fourteenth Annual Together We Can Conference Building Community, Creating Hope. Lafayette, Louisiana, October 24.

Berrick, J.D. (2018). *The impossible imperative – Navigating the competing principles of child protection.* Oxford and New York City: Oxford University Press.

Berrick, J.D., Needell, B., Barth, R.P., & Jonson-Reid, M. (1998). *The tender years: Toward developmentally sensitive child welfare services for very young children.* New York: Oxford University Press.

Biglan, A., Flay, B.R., Embry, D.D., & Sandler, I.N. (2012). The critical role of nurturing environments for promoting human well-being. *American Psychologist, 67*(4), 257–271. doi:10.1037/a0026796.

Casey Family Programs. (2001). *It's my life – A framework for youth transitioning from foster care to successful adulthood.* Seattle, WA: Casey Family Programs.

Casey Family Programs. (2003). *Family, community, culture: Roots of permanency – A conceptual framework on permanency from Casey Family Programs.* Seattle, WA: Author.

Casey Public Policy. (2015a). *Public policy levers for increasing exits from out of home care.* Seattle, WA: Casey Family Programs.

Casey Public Policy (2015b). *State policy levers to increase timely permanency: Interviews with high-performing states.* Seattle, WA: Author.

Casey Family Programs and the Brookings Institution. (2013). *Working paper: Child protection reform principles to achieve improved outcomes* (mimeograph). Seattle, WA: Casey Family Programs.

Chaffin, M., Bard, D., Bigfoot. D.S., & Maher, E.J. (2012). Is a structured, manualized, evidence-based treatment protocol culturally competent and equivalently effective among American Indian parents in child welfare? *Child Maltreatment, 17*, 242–252.

Chahine, Z., Pecora, P.J., & Sanders, D. (2013). Special foreword: Preventing severe maltreatment-related injuries and fatalities: Applying a public health framework and innovative approaches to child protection. *Child Welfare, 92*(2), 13–18.

Chapman, M.V., Wall, A., & Barth, R.P. (2004). Children's voices: The perceptions of children in foster care. *American Journal of Orthopsychiatry, 74*(3), 293.

Child Welfare Information Gateway. (2014). *Parental substance use and the child welfare system.* Washington, DC: U.S. Department of Health and Human Services, Children's Bureau. Retrieved from www.childwelfare.gov/pubPDFs/parentalsubabuse.pdf.

Child Welfare League of America. (2004). *Making children a national priority: A framework for community action.* Washington, DC: Author.

Connolly, M., & McKenzie, M. (1999). *Effective participatory practice: Family group conferencing in child protection.* Piscataway, NJ: Aldine-Transaction Books.

Courtney, M.E., Dworsky, A., Cusick, G.R., Keller, T., Havlicek, J., Perez, A., Terao, S., & Bost, N. (2007). *Midwest evaluation of adult functioning of former foster youth: Outcomes at age 21.* Chicago, IL: University of Chicago, Chapin Hall Center for Children.

Daro, D., Budde, S., Baker, S., Nesmith, A., & Harden, A. (2005). *Creating community responsibility for child protection: Findings and implications from the evaluation of the community partnerships for protecting children initiative.* Chicago, IL: University of Chicago, Chapin Hall Center for Children.

DePanfilis, D., & Salus, M.K. (2003). *Child Protective Services: A guide for caseworkers* (Guide). Washington, DC: U.S. DHHS, Administration for Children and Families, Administration on Children, Youth and Families, Children's Bureau, Office on Child Abuse and Neglect.

Development Services Group, Inc. (2013). *Protective factors for populations served by the administration on children, youth, and families. A literature review and theoretical framework: Executive summary.* Washington, DC: U.S. Department of Health and Human Services, Administration for Children and Families, Children's Bureau. Retrieved from www.dsgonline.com/acyf/DSG%20Protective%20Factors%20Literature%20Review%20 2013%20Exec%20Summary.pdf.

Doyle, J.J. (2007). Child protection and child outcomes: Measuring the effects of foster care. *The American Economic Review, 97*(5), 1583–1610.

Ellis, M.L., Eskenazi, S., Bonnell, R., & Pecora, P.J. (2013). *Taking a closer look at the reduction in entry rates for children in Sacramento County with an emphasis on African American children: A spotlight on practice.* Seattle, WA: Casey Family Programs, www.Casey.org.

Finkelhor, D., & Jones, L. (2006). Why have child maltreatment and child victimization declined? *Journal of Social Issues, 62*, 685–716.

Fluke, J., Jones-Harden, B., Jenkins, M., & Ruehrdanz, A. (2011). *Research synthesis on child welfare disproportionality and disparities.* Denver, CO: American Humane Association and the Annie E. Casey Foundation.

Fong, R., Lubben, J., & Barth, R.P. (Eds) (2018). *Grand Challenges for Social Work.* NY: Oxford and NASW Press.

Font, S.A., Berger, L.M., & Slack, K.S. (2012). Examining racial disproportionality in child protective services case decisions. *Children and Youth Services Review, 34*(11), 2188–2200.

Fraser, M.W., Pecora, P.J., & Haapala, D.A. (1991). *Families in crisis: The impact of intensive family preservation services.* Hawthorne, NY: Aldine de Gruyter.

Garcia, J.L., Heckman, J.J., Leaf, D.E., & Prados, M.J. (2016). *The lifecycle benefits of an influential early childhood program.* Chicago, IL: The University of Chicago. Retrieved from https://heckmanequation.org/resource/lifecycle-benefits-influential-early-childhood-program/.

Generations United. (2016). *Raising the children of the opioid epidemic: Solutions and support for grandfamilies.* Washington, DC. Retrieved from www.gu.org/Portals/0/documents/Reports/16-Report-State_of_Grandfamiles.pdf.

Goering, E.S., & Shaw, T.V. (2017). Foster care reentry: A survival analysis assessing differences across permanency type. *Child Abuse & Neglect, 68,* 36–43.

Goldstein, J., Freud, A., & Solnit, A. (1973). *Beyond the best interests of the child.* New York: The Free Press.

Harper, M., Hernandez, M., Nesman, T., Mowery, D., Worthington, J., & Isaacs, M. (2006). Organizational cultural competence: A review of Assessment Protocols. Retrieved from http://rtckids.fmhi.usf.edu/publications, www.acf.hhs.gov/programs/cb/resource/trends-in-foster-care-and-adoption.

Huey, S.J., & Polo, A.J. (2008). Evidence-based psychosocial treatments for ethnic minority youth. *Journal of Clinical Child and Adolescent Psychology, 37*(1), 262–301.

IOM (Institute of Medicine) and NRC (National Research Council). (2014). *New directions in child abuse and neglect research.* Washington, DC: The National Academies Press. Retrieved from www.nap.edu/catalog/18331/new-directions-in-child-abuse-and-neglect-research.

Jenson, J.M., & Bender, K.A. (2014). *Preventing child and adolescent problem behavior: Evidence-based strategies in schools, families and communities.* New York: Oxford University Press.

Johnson, K., Knitzer, J., & Kaufmann, R. (2003). *Making dollars follow sense: Financing early childhood mental health services to promote healthy social and emotional development in young children.* New York: Columbia University, National Center on Children in Poverty.

Kerman, B., Maluccio, A.N., & Freundlich, M. (2008). *Achieving permanence for older children and youth in foster care.* New York: Columbia University Press.

Kessler, R.C., & Magee, W.J. (1993). Childhood adversities and adult depression: Basic patterns of association in a US national survey. *Psychological Medicine, 23,* 679–690. doi:10.1017/S0033291700025460.

Kilburn, M.R., & Karoly, L.A. (2008). *The economics of early childhood policy: What the dismal science has to say about investing in children* (RAND Doc. No. OP-227-CFP). Santa Monica, CA: RAND Corporation.

Kim, H., Wildeman, C., Jonson-Reid, M., & Drake, B. (2016). Lifetime prevalence of investigating child maltreatment among US children. *American Journal of Public Health, 107*(2), 274–280.

Kirk, S., Gallagher, J., & Anastasiow, N. (1993). *Educating exceptional children* (7th edn). Boston, MA: Houghton Mifflin.

Lau, A.S. (2006) Making the case for selected and directed cultural adaptations of evidence-based treatments: Examples from parent training. *Clinical Psychology: Science and Practice, 13*(4), 295–310.

Lloyd, E.C., & Barth, R.P. (2011). Developmental outcomes after five years for foster children returned home, remaining in care, or adopted. *Children and Youth Services Review, 33*, 1383–1391.

Los Angeles County Departments of Children and Family Services/Probation. (2013). *Los Angeles County Departments of Children and Family Services/Probation, Youth Development Service (YDS) Individualized Transition Skills Program (ITSP) fact sheet.* Retrieved from http://dcfsilp.co.la.ca.us/documents/ITSPPromotionalFACTSHEET2013.pdf.

Mallon, G.P. (2014). *Lesbian, gay, bisexual and trans foster and adoptive parents: Recruiting, assessing, and supporting an untapped resource for children and youth* (2nd edn). Washington, DC: Child Welfare League of America.

Maluccio, A.N., Fein, E., & Olmstead, K.A. (1986). *Permanency planning for children: Concepts and methods.* London and New York: Routledge, Chapman and Hall.

Marts, E.J., Lee, R., McCroy, R., & McCroskey, J. (2008). Point of engagement: Reducing disproportionality and improving child and family outcomes. *Child Welfare, 87*(2), 335–358.

McCroskey, J., Pecora, P.J., Franke, T., Christie, C.A., & Lorthridge, J. (2012). Strengthening families and communities to prevent child abuse and neglect: Lessons from the Los Angeles Prevention Initiative Demonstration Project. *Child Welfare, 91*(2), 39–60.

McDaniel, N. (2010). *Connecting the dots: Workforce selection and child welfare outcomes.* National Child Welfare Workforce Institute. Presented at the 2010 Florida Coalition for Children Annual Conference.

McFadden, J.E., & Downs, S.W. (1995). Family continuity: The new paradigm in permanence planning. *Community Alternatives: International Journal of Family Care, 7*, 39–59.

Mech, E.V. (Ed.). (1988). *Independent-living services for at-risk adolescents.* Washington, DC: Child Welfare League of America.

Miranda, J., Guillermo, B., Lau, A., Kohn, L., Wei-Chin, H., & LaFromboise, T. (2005) State of the science on psychosocial interventions for ethnic minorities. *Annual Review of Clinical Psychology, 1*, 113–142.

Mordock, J.B. (2002). *Managing for outcomes: A basic guide to the evaluation of best practices in the human services.* Washington, DC: Child Welfare League of America Press.

National Academies of Sciences, Engineering, and Medicine. (2016). *Parenting matters: Supporting parents of children ages 0–8.* Washington, DC: The National Academies Press. doi:10.17226/21868. Retrieved from www.nap.edu/read/21868/chapter/1#ii.

National Conference of State Legislatures, National Governor's Association & Casey Family Programs. (2017). Three Branch Institute on Improving Child Safety and Preventing Child Fatalities. Retrieved from www.ncsl.org/research/human-services/ncsl-and-nga-three-branch-institute.aspx.

National Governor's Association, Center for Best Practices. (2008). *Nine Things Governors Can Do to Build a Strong Child Welfare System.* Washington, DC: Author.

Parish, S.L., Pomeranz, A.E., & Braddock, D. (2003). Family support in the United States: Financing trends and emerging initiatives. *Mental Retardation, 41,* 174–187. doi:10.1352/0047-6765(2003)41<174:FSITUS>2.0.CO;2.

Pecora, P.J., O'Brien, K., & Maher, E. (2015). *Levels of research evidence and benefit-cost data for Title IV-E waiver interventions: A Casey research brief* (3rd edn). Seattle, WA: Casey Family Programs. Retrieved from www.casey.org/media/Title-IV_E-Waiver-Interventions-Research-Brief.pdf.

Pecora, P.J., Whittaker, J.K., Barth, R.P., Vesneski, W., & Borja, S., (2018). *Child welfare policy and related legislation through the years: A resource paper.* New York: Taylor and Francis.

Pecora, P.J., Kessler, R.C., Williams, J., Downs, A.C., English, D.J., White, J., & O'Brien, K. (2010). *What works in family foster care? Key components of success from the Northwest foster care alumni study.* New York and Oxford: Oxford University Press.

Pew Foundation. (2008). *Time for reform: Investing in prevention: Keeping children safe at home.* Philadelphia, PA: Author. Retrieved from http://kidsarewaiting.org/tools/reports/files/0011.pdf.

Pine, B.A. (1986). Child welfare reform and the political process. *Social Service Review, 60,* 339–359. doi:10.1086/644381.

Plantz, M.C., Hubbell, R., Barrett, B.J., & Dobrec, A. (1989). Indian Child Welfare Act: A status report. *Children Today, 18,* 24–29.

Putnam-Hornstein, E. (2012). Preventable injury deaths: A population-based proxy of child maltreatment risk in California. *Public Health Reports, 127*(2), 163–172.

Putnam-Hornstein, E., Needell, B., & Rhodes, A.E. (2013). Understanding risk and protective factors for child maltreatment: The value of integrated, population-based data. *Child Abuse & Neglect, 37*(2–3), 930–936.

Ramey, C.T., & Ramey, S.L. (1998). Early intervention and early experience. *American Psychologist, 53,* 109–120. doi:10.1037/0003–066X.53.2.109.

Reynolds, A.J., & Robertson, D.L. (2003). School-based early intervention and later child maltreatment in the Chicago longitudinal study. *Child Development, 74,* 3–26.

Roberts, Y.H., O'Brien, K., & Pecora, P.J. (2017). *Supporting lifelong families ensuring long-lasting permanency and well-being.* Seattle, WA: Casey Family Programs. Retrieved from www.casey.org/supporting-lifelong-families/

Roberts, Y.H., O'Brien, K., & Pecora, P.J. (2018). *Can predictive analytics make a difference in child welfare?* Seattle, WA: Casey Family Programs. Retrieved from www.casey.org/implementing-predictive-analytics/.

Rogg, C.S., Davis, C.W., & O'Brien, K. (2011). *Permanency roundtable project: 12-month outcome evaluation report.* Seattle, WA: Casey Family Programs. Retrieved from www.casey.org/resources/publications/pdf/garoundtable_12 month_FR.pdf.

Schorr, E., & Marchand, V. (2007). *Pathway to the prevention of child abuse and neglect.* Washington, DC: Project on Effective Interventions, Pathways Mapping Initiative. Retrieved from www.cssp.org/uploadFiles/PCANPDFFI NAL11–14–07.pdf.

Sedlak, A.J., Mettenburg, J., Basena, M., Petta, I., McPherson, K., Greene, A., & Li, S. (2010). *Fourth National Incidence Study of Child Abuse and Neglect (NIS-4): Report to Congress.* Washington, DC: U.S. Department of Health and Human Services, Administration for Children and Families. Retrieved from www.acf.hhs.gov/programs/opre/abuse_neglect/natl_incid/nis4_ report_congress_full_pdf_jan2010.pdf.

Slack, K.S., Berger, L.M, & Noyes, J.L. (2017). Introduction to the special issue on the economic causes and consequences of child maltreatment. *Children and Youth Services Review, 72,* 1–4.

Testa, M.F., & Poertner, J. (2010). *Fostering accountability: Using evidence to guide and improve child welfare policy.* Oxford and New York: Oxford University Press.

The Business Council and The Conference Board Partnership for 21st Century Skills, Corporate Voices for Working Families, and Society for Human Resource Management. (2006). *The business council survey of chief executives: CEO survey results, February 2006.* The Business Council and the Conference Board.

Traube, D. (2012). The missing link to child safety, permanency, and well-being: Addressing substance misuse in child welfare. *Social Work Research, 36*(2), 83–87.

Uehara, E.S., Barth, R.P., Coffey, D., Padilla, Y., & McClain, A. (2017). An introduction to the special section on grand challenges for social work. *Journal of the Society for Social Work and Research, 8*(1), 75–85.

U.S. Census Bureau. (2013). *American Community Survey, Table B10001.* Retrieved from http://factfinder.census.gov/bkmk/table/1.0/en/ACS/13_1YR/B10001>.

U.S. Census Bureau, 2015 American Community Survey 1-Year Estimates. (2016). *Table S1701: Poverty status In the past 12 months.* Washington, DC: United States Census Bureau. Retrieved from http://factfinder.census.gov/faces/tableservices/jsf/pages/productview.xhtml?pid=ACS_15_1YR_S1701&prodType=table.

U.S. Census Bureau. (2016). *2016 CPS Health Insurance Table: HI-08. Health insurance coverage status and type of coverage by selected characteristics for children under 18 (all children): 2015.* Retrieved July 3, 2017 from www.census.gov/data/tables/2016/demo/cps/hi-08.html.

U.S. Department of Health and Human Services, Administration for Children and Families, Administration on Children, Youth and Families, Children's Bureau. (2014). *Child Welfare Outcomes 2010–2013: Report to Congress.* Washington, DC: Author.

U.S. Department of Health and Human Services, Administration for Children and Families, Administration on Children, Youth and Families, Children's Bureau. (2016a). *The AFCARS*

Report No. 23. Washington, DC: Author. Retrieved from www.acf.hhs.gov/cb/resource/afcars-report-23.

U.S. Department of Health and Human Services, Administration for Children and Families, Administration on Children, Youth and Families, Children's Bureau. (2016b). *Trends in foster care and adoption*. Washington, DC.: Author. Retrieved from www.acf.hhs.gov/cb/resource/trends-in-foster-care-and-adoption-fy15.

U.S. Department of Health and Human Services, Administration for Children and Families, Administration on Children, Youth and Families, Children's Bureau. (2017a). *Child maltreatment 2015*. Washington, DC: Author. Retrieved from www.acf.hhs.gov/programs/cb/research-data-technology/statistics-research/child-maltreatment.

U.S. Department of Health and Human Services, Administration for Children and Families, Administration on Children, Youth and Families, Children's Bureau. (2017b). *Preliminary FY' 2016 estimates as of October 20, 2017. No. 24*. Washington, DC: Author. Retrieved from /www.acf.hhs.gov/sites/default/files/cb/afcarsreport24.pdf.

U.S. Department of Health and Human Services, Administration for Children and Families, Administration on Children, Youth and Families, Children's Bureau. (2017c). *Trends in foster care and adoption*. Washington, DC: Author. Retrieved from www.acf.hhs.gov/cb/resource/trends-in-foster-care-and-adoption.

U.S. Department of Health and Human Services, Administration for Children and Families, Administration on Children, Youth and Families, Children's Bureau. (2018). *Child maltreatment 2016*. Retrieved from www.acf.hhs.gov/cb/research-data-technology/statistics-research/child-maltreatment.

U.S. Department of Labor. (2014). *A paper series celebrating the 50th anniversary of American women. Report on the President's Commission on the Status of Women*. Retrieved from www.dol.gov/asp/evaluation/reports/WBPaperSeries.pdf#page=147.

U.S. General Accounting Office. (1995). *Foster care: Health needs of many young children are unknown and unmet* (GAO/HEHS-95–114). Washington, DC: Author.

U.S. General Accounting Office. (2004). *Child and family services reviews: Better use of data and improved guidance could enhance HHS's oversight of state performance* (GAO-04–333). Washington, DC: Government Printing Office. Retrieved from www.gao.gov/cgi-bin/getrpt?GAO-04–333.

U.S. Government Accountability Office. (2007). *African American children in foster care: Additional HHS assistance needed to help states reduce the proportion in care* (GAO 07–816). Washington, DC: Author. Retrieved from www.gao.gov/new.items/d07816.pdf.

Vaithianathan, R., Maloney, T., Putnam-Hornstein, E., & Jiang, N. (2013). Children in the public benefit system at risk of maltreatment: Identification via predictive modeling. *American Journal of Preventive Medicine, 45*(3), 354–359.

Valentine, E.J., Skemer, M., and Courtney, M.E. (2015). *Becoming adults: One-year impact findings from the Youth Villages Transitional Living Evaluation*. New York: MDRC.

Vesneski, W., Killos, L., Pecora, P.J., & McIntire, E. (2017). An analysis of state law and policy regarding subsidized guardianship for children: Innovations in permanency. *Journal of Juvenile Law & Policy, 21*(1), 26–75. University of California at Davis Law School.

Wald, M.S. (2014). Beyond child protection: Helping all families provide adequate parenting. In K. McCartney, H. Yoshikawa, & L.B. Forcier (Eds), *Improving the odds for America's children: Future directions in policy and practice* (pp 135–148). Cambridge, MA: Harvard Education Press.

Walton, E., Sandau-Beckler, P., & Mannes, M. (Eds) (2001). *Balancing family-centered services and child well-being: Exploring issues in policy, practice, and research.* New York: Columbia University Press.

Washington State Institute for Public Policy. (2017). *Benefit–Cost Results.* Olympia, WA: Author. Retrieved from www.wsipp.wa.gov/BenefitCost.

Wulczyn, F.H., Orlebeke, B., & Haight, J. (2009). *Finding the return on investment: A framework for monitoring local child welfare agencies.* Chicago, IL: Chapin Hall at the University of Chicago. Retrieved from www.chapinhall.org/sites/default/files/Finding_Return_On_Investment_07_20_09.pdf.

Wulczyn, F., Barth, R.P., Yuan, Y-Y.T., Jones-Harden, B., & Landsverk, J. (2005). *Beyond common sense: Child welfare, child well-being, and the evidence for policy reform.* Piscataway, NJ: Aldine Transaction.

Child Maltreatment

Nature, Prevalence, and the Implications for Social Policy

Learning Objectives

1. Be able to define various forms of child abuse and neglect.

2. Understand the scope and complexity of measuring the prevalence of child maltreatment.

3. Identify the risk and protective factors for child maltreatment, building on conceptual frameworks for Adverse Childhood Experiences (ACEs) and trauma such as NEAR (Neuroscience, Epigenetics, ACEs and Resilience).

4. Know about Federal and state policy governing child protective services.

Introduction

Types of Child Abuse and Neglect

In this chapter, in addition to defining the four major types of child maltreatment and the incidence of child maltreatment, we review risk and protective factors related to the reasons why children and their families become involved in the child welfare system, as well as the major social policies directed toward these families. In addition, we examine the ways in which the concepts of risk and protection are implemented in those policies. Drawing from innovative efforts across the United States and other countries, we outline key policy and program design issues for the child welfare agency response to this problem through child protective services.

We conclude with a discussion of current policy issues and recommendations for improving child protective services. But we begin with a concise set of definitions of the major types of child maltreatment.

The term *child maltreatment* encompasses four major types of child abuse and neglect: (1) physical abuse; (2) neglect; (3) sexual abuse; and (4) psychological maltreatment (see Table 2.1). Many other threats to the health and safety of children are subsumed under these four types, including: prenatal drug exposure, chronic truancy, exposure to domestic violence, and untreated chronic health conditions. Definitions of child maltreatment are partially derived in federal law, but unfortunately vary substantially across states. Originally passed in 1974 by the U.S. Congress, the Federal Child Abuse Prevention and Treatment Act (CAPTA) (42 U.S.C.A. §5101and §5106g) as amended by the Keeping Children and Families Safe Act of 2003 (P.L. 93–247) and as amended by the CAPTA Reauthorization Act of 2010 (P.L.111–320), provides a foundation for national definitions of child abuse and neglect. They provide a national definition of child abuse and neglect as, at a minimum: "Any recent act or failure to act on the part of a parent or caretaker which results in death, serious physical or emotional harm, sexual abuse or exploitation; or an act or failure to act, which presents an imminent risk of serious harm" (U.S. DHHS, 2018, p. 15).

Table 2.1 Child Abuse and Neglect Defined

Neglect or deprivation of necessities. A type of maltreatment that refers to the failure by the caregiver to provide needed, age-appropriate care although financially able to do so or offered financial or other means to do so.[a]

Physical abuse. Type of maltreatment that refers to physical acts that caused or could have caused physical injury to a child.[a]

Sexual abuse. A type of maltreatment that refers to the involvement of the child in sexual activity to provide sexual gratification or financial benefit to the perpetrator, including contacts for sexual purposes, molestation, statutory rape, prostitution, pornography, exposure, incest, or other sexually exploitative activities.[a]

Psychological or emotional maltreatment. A type of maltreatment that refers to acts or omissions, other than physical abuse or sexual abuse, that caused, or could have caused, conduct, cognitive, affective, or other mental disorders. Includes emotional neglect, psychological abuse, mental injury, etc. Frequently occurs as verbal abuse or excessive demands on a child's performance and may cause the child to have a negative self-image and disturbed behavior.[b]

---

[a]U.S. Department of Health and Human Services, Administration for Children and Families, Administration on Children, Youth and Families, Children's Bureau. (2016). *Child maltreatment 2014.* Retrieved from www.acf. hhs.gov/programs/cb/research-data-technology/statistics-research/child-maltreatment

[b]U.S. Department of Health and Human Services, Administration for Children and Families, Administration on Children, Youth and Families, Children's Bureau. (2010). *National Child Abuse and Neglect Data System (NCANDS) Glossary.* Washington, DC: Author, p. 12. Retrieved from www.acf.hhs.gov/sites/default/files/cb/ncands_glossary.pdf.

CAPTA provides minimum standards for defining physical child abuse, child neglect, and sexual abuse that states must incorporate into their statutory definitions in order to receive federal funds. Under CAPTA, child abuse and neglect means: (1) any recent act or failure to act on the part of a parent or caretaker which results in death, serious physical or emotional harm, sexual abuse, or exploitation; or (2) an act or failure to act, which presents an imminent risk of serious harm. While federal legislation sets minimum definitional standards, each state is responsible for providing its own definitions of child abuse and neglect within civil and criminal laws. Definitions of child abuse and neglect are located primarily in three places within each state's statutory code:·

- Mandatory child maltreatment reporting statutes (civil laws) provide definitions of child maltreatment to guide those individuals mandated to identify and report suspected child abuse. These reports activate the child protection process.

- Criminal statutes define the forms of child maltreatment that are criminally punishable. In most jurisdictions, child maltreatment is criminally punishable when one or more of the following statutory crimes have been committed: homicide, murder, manslaughter, false imprisonment, assault, battery, criminal neglect and abandonment, emotional and physical abuse, pornography, child prostitution, computer crimes, rape, deviant sexual assault, indecent exposure, child endangerment, and reckless endangerment.

- Juvenile or family court jurisdiction statutes provide definitions of the circumstances necessary for the court to have jurisdiction over a child alleged to have been abused or neglected. When the child's safety cannot be ensured in the home, these statutes allow the court to take custody of a child and to order specific intervention and treatment services for the parents, child, and family; recent statutes also allow agencies to forgo the provision of services to some families based on the type and severity of maltreatment.

Together, these legal definitions of child maltreatment determine the minimum standards of care and protection for children and serve as important guidelines for professionals who are required both to report and respond to reports of child abuse and neglect. The next section describes the four major types of child maltreatment in more detail. Each state defines the types of child abuse and neglect in its statutes and policies. Child welfare (CW) agencies determine the appropriate response for the alleged maltreatment based on those statutes and policies. In most states, the majority of reports receive an investigation. (Note: many child welfare agencies continue to have a division called "CPS," standing for Child Protective Services, which handles child abuse and neglect screening and investigations.)

An investigation response results in a determination (also known as a disposition) about the alleged child maltreatment. The two most prevalent dispositions are: (1) *Substantiated*: An investigation disposition which concludes that the allegation of maltreatment or risk of maltreatment was supported or founded by state law or policy; and (2) *Unsubstantiated*: An investigation disposition which concludes that there was not sufficient evidence under state law to conclude or suspect that the child was maltreated or at risk of being maltreated. Less commonly used dispositions for investigation responses include the following:

- *Indicated*: A disposition which concludes that maltreatment could not be substantiated under state law or policy, but that there was a reason to suspect that at least one child may have been maltreated or was at risk of maltreatment. This is applicable only to states that distinguish between substantiated and indicated dispositions.

- *Intentionally false*: A disposition which concludes that the person who made the allegation of maltreatment knew the allegation was not true.

- *Closed with no finding:* A disposition that does not conclude with a specific finding because the CPS response could not be completed. This disposition is often assigned when CPS is unable to locate the alleged victim.

- *Other*: States may use the category of "other" if none of the above is applicable. Several states use this disposition when the results of an investigation are uncertain, inconclusive, or unable to be determined (U.S. DHHS, 2018, pp. 15–16).

Types of Child Maltreatment

Child Physical Abuse

Child physical abuse may be defined as "physical acts that caused or could have caused physical injury to a child" (U.S. DHHS, 2018, p. 107). The public CW system becomes involved in cases of child physical abuse when the act has been inflicted by a parent or other person responsible for the child's care. The types of acts that may result in injury or a serious risk of harm include: punching, beating, kicking, biting, shaking, throwing, stabbing, burning, choking, or hitting with a hand, stick, strap, or other object (Goldman & Salus, 2003).

It is important to distinguish between corporal punishment and physical abuse. While many oppose the practice of spanking children, corporal punishment is still commonly practiced and is not against the law in any state. In general, hitting for the purpose of punishment or discipline is not usually considered abuse unless more than a temporary redness results. Infants are an exception and any hitting of an infant may be construed as abuse (Dubowitz, 2000b). In addition, some cultural practices that may hurt children (e.g., circumcision, cupping, and coining therapy) are not defined as abuse. And, while many state laws suggest the need to consider culture in the investigations of abuse reports, definitions of physical abuse in each state law provide the actual guidance of when an act on the part of a parent or other caregiver that has resulted in harm to a child is actually considered to be abuse. Growing scholarship suggests the harms that spanking does and that it may encourage more serious abuse of children by condoning physical strategies for solving family problems (Lee, Grogan-Kaylor, & Berger, 2014). Yet, spanking is still legal in the United States (but not in many other countries).

Child Sexual Abuse

Child sexual abuse is defined as a type of maltreatment that refers to the "involvement of the child in sexual activity to provide sexual gratification or financial benefit to the perpetrator, including contacts for sexual purposes, molestation, statutory rape, prostitution, pornography, exposure, incest, or other sexually exploitative activities" (U.S. DHHS, 2017, p. 110). Child sexual abuse includes a range of behaviors between an adult and a child, such as: oral, anal, or genital penile penetration; anal or genital digital or other penetration; genital contact with no intrusion; fondling of a child's breasts or buttocks; indecent exposure; inadequate or inappropriate supervision of a child's voluntary sexual activities; and use of a child in prostitution, pornography, internet crimes, or other sexually exploitative activities (Goldman & Salus, 2003).

CW agencies are usually only involved in cases of child sexual abuse within the family (i.e., biological, foster, adoptive, and stepfamilies), as distinguished by sexual assault by a non-relative. Sexual abuse within the family is most often committed by adults in a father's relationship to the child; however, it is also committed by other relatives or caregivers, such as mothers, aunts or uncles, grandparents, cousins, or the boyfriend or girlfriend of a parent.

Psychological Maltreatment

Psychological maltreatment, also described as emotional abuse and neglect, is defined as "acts or omissions – other than physical abuse or sexual abuse – that caused or could have caused – conduct, cognitive, affective, or other behavioral or mental disorders. Frequently occurs as verbal abuse or excessive demands on a child's performance" (U.S. DHHS, 2018, p. 108). It includes a caregiver's *actions* (abuse) or *omissions* (neglect) which convey to children that they are worthless, flawed, unloved, unwanted, endangered, or only of value in meeting another's needs (Brassard & Hart, 2000) (see Table 2.2). The decision about whether to charge a parent with psychological maltreatment typically turns on whether they agree to stop their harmful conduct and assist in their child's treatment of any emotional or behavioral health problems that have arisen.

Table 2.2 Types of Psychological Maltreatment

Types of Psychological or Emotional *Abuse*

Spurning (hostile rejecting, and degrading)	Verbal and nonverbal acts toward a child, including belittling, degrading, shaming or ridiculing a child for showing normal emotions, public humiliation, consistently singling out a child to criticize or punish (American Professional Society on the Abuse of Children, 1995; Brassard & Hart, 2000).
Terrorizing	Caregiver behavior that threatens to hurt, kill, abandon, or place the child or child's loved ones or objects in dangerous situations (American Professional Society on the Abuse of Children, 1995; Brassard & Hart, 2000).
Exploiting or corrupting	Encouraging or modeling for the child to develop antisocial behavior such as participation in criminal activities (American Professional Society on the Abuse of Children, 1995; Brassard & Hart, 2000).

Types of Psychological or Emotional *Neglect*

Delay in obtaining needed mental health care	A child is not provided needed treatment for an emotional or behavioral impairment (Zuravin & DePanfilis, 1996).
Inadequate nurturance or affection	Marked inattention to the child's needs for affection, emotional support, attention, or competence; being detached or uninvolved, interacting only when absolutely necessary, failing to express affection, caring, and love for the child. This includes cases of nonorganic failure to thrive as well as other instances of passive emotional rejection of a child or apparent lack of concern for a child's emotional well-being or development (American Professional Society on the Abuse of Children, 1995; U.S. Department of Health and Human Services, 1996).

(Continued)

Table 2.2 (Continued)

Types of Psychological or Emotional *Neglect*

Isolating	The child is consistently denied opportunities to meet needs for interacting/communicating with peers or adults inside or outside the home; markedly overprotective restrictions that foster immaturity or emotional overdependency; chronically applying expectations clearly inappropriate in relation to the child's age or level of development; and inattention to the child's developmental/emotional needs. (Adapted from American Professional Society on the Abuse of Children, 1995; U.S. Department of Health and Human Services, 1996)
Permitting alcohol or drug use	Encouraging or permitting of drug or alcohol use by a child. At the seriously inadequate level, there is a pattern of this condition and the child has suffered physical or emotional consequences (U.S. Department of Health and Human Services, 1996).
Permitting other maladaptive behavior	Encouraging or permitting of other maladaptive behavior (e.g., severe assaults, chronic delinquency) under circumstances where the caregiver had reason to be aware of the existence and seriousness of the problem but did not attempt to intervene. At the seriously inadequate level, the child has suffered physical or emotional consequences (U.S. Department of Health and Human Services, 1996).
Witnessing violence	A child witnesses violence in the home, (e.g., partner abuse or violence between other persons who visit the home on a regular basis). At the seriously inadequate level, the level of violence is escalating and negatively affecting the child (U.S. Department of Health and Human Services, 1996).

Child Neglect

Child neglect is the most common and yet it is the least researched form of child maltreatment – with a shortage of attention paid to cost-effective prevention and practice strategies. In general, neglect refers to (1) acts of omission of care to meet a child's basic needs that (2) result in harm or a threat of harm to children (DePanfilis, 2006; Dubowitz, 2000a). In the National Child Abuse and Neglect Data System (NCANDS), the annual national study of child abuse and neglect reports, the definition of neglect takes into consideration that conditions should not be classified by neglect if they are solely influenced by poverty. In that study (U.S. DHHS, 2018, p. 106), neglect is referred to as "the failure by the caregiver to provide needed, age-appropriate care although financially able to do so or offered financial or other means to do so."

Despite its ubiquity in the CW system, neglect is not well defined in CW law, policy, or practice (Hearn, 2011; Vesneski, 2011; Tanner & Turney, 2003). Research also clearly suggests a connection between neglect and poverty, but the exact nature of this linkage is unclear (Slack et al., 2004; Eamon & Kopels, 2004). How neglect is defined shapes the types of situations that professionals may report to Child Protective Services (CPS), CW and it defines the CPS's response. Because the goal of defining neglect is to protect children and to support families to meet the basic needs of their children, definitions help determine if an incident or pattern of behaviors or conditions qualifies as neglect and therefore should prompt a CW response.

Recent attempts at refining neglect definitions have sought to align them with the various subtypes of maltreatment found in the National Incidence Survey (NIS-4) (Rebbe, 2017). Researchers have also used case record classification systems (Barnett, Manly, & Cicchetti, 1993; Trocme, 1996; Zuravin & DePanfilis, 1996) or self-report measures with children and/or parents (Harrington et al., 2002; Straus, Kinard, & Williams, 1995). While the field is far from reaching a consensus on the best way to define neglect and classify the various ways in which a child's basic needs are unmet, for the purposes of this chapter we categorize various types of child neglect based on failures to provide for physical, supervisory, cognitive-educational, or emotional needs (see Table 2.3). Note that the failure to meet a child's *emotional* needs has already been described in the section on psychological maltreatment and the types are defined in Table 2.3.

Table 2.3 Types of Neglect

Physical Neglect	
Drug-exposed newborn	A newborn infant has been exposed to drugs because the mother has used one or more illegal substances during her pregnancy. Exposure may have resulted in negative physical consequences to the infant's health. At the seriously inadequate level, the caregivers are unable or unwilling to meet the special needs of the infant at birth (Dunn et al., 2002; National Council of Juvenile and Family Court Judges, 1992).
Inadequate clothing	Chronic inappropriate clothing for the weather or conditions. At the seriously inadequate level, a child has suffered consequences such as illness or threat of illness (Magura & Moses, 1986).

(Continued)

Table 2.3 (Continued)

Physical Neglect

Inadequate/delayed health care	Failure of a child to receive needed care for physical injury, acute illnesses, physical disabilities, or other medical need that if left untreated could result in negative consequences for the child (Jenny, 2007; U.S. Department of Health and Human Services, 1996; Zuravin & DePanfilis, 1996).
Inadequate nutrition	Failure to provide a child with regular and ample meals that meet *basic* nutritional requirements or when a caregiver fails to provide the necessary rehabilitative diet to a child with particular types of physical health problems. At the seriously inadequate level, caregivers may intentionally withhold food or water from children and/or children are observed as malnourished or dehydrated (Magura & Moses, 1986; Trocme, 1996; Zuravin & DePanfilis, 1996).
Insufficient household furnishings	Family lacks essential household and furniture or functions (e.g., no working sink, no beds for sleeping, no table for holding family meals, etc.), and the absence of these essential items strains the relationships in the family and jeopardizes a child's safety (Mennen et al., 2010; Magura & Moses, 1986).
Poor personal hygiene	Failure to attend to cleanliness of the child's hair, skin, teeth, and clothes. At the seriously inadequate level, a child has suffered consequences such as physical illness (Magura & Moses, 1986; Zuravin & DePanfilis, 1996).
Environmental neglect	Presence of obvious hazardous physical conditions in the home that could result in negative consequences for the child(ren). Examples include leaking gas from stove or heating unit, peeling lead-based paint, dangerous substances or objects in unlocked lower shelves or cabinets; no guards on open windows; broken or missing windows; rodent infestation or rotting food. At the seriously inadequate level, there are multiple household hazards that have resulted in physical injury to a child or the child may be ill (Mennen et al., 2010; Magura & Moses, 1986; Zuravin & DePanfilis, 1996).
Unstable living conditions	Moves of residence due to eviction or lack of planning at least three times within a six-month period or homelessness due to the lack of available, affordable housing or the caregiver's inability to manage finances. At the seriously inadequate level, a child has suffered negative consequences (Zuravin & DePanfilis, 1996).

Supervisory Neglect

Abandonment	When a parent's identity or whereabouts are unknown, the child has been left by the parent in circumstances in which the child suffers serious harm, or the parent has failed to maintain contact with the child or to provide support for a specified period of time (Child Welfare Information Gateway, 2016a).
Inadequate supervision	Child left unsupervised or inadequately supervised for extended periods of time, or allowed to remain away from home overnight without the caregiver knowing the child's whereabouts. At the seriously inadequate level, the lack of supervision includes exposing the child to dangerous conditions, which may have resulted in negative consequences (Knutson et al., 2005; Trocme, 1996; U.S. Department of Health and Human Services, 1996).
Inappropriate substitute caregiver	Failure to arrange for safe and appropriate substitute childcare when the caregiver leaves the child with an inappropriate caregiver. At the seriously inadequate level, the child may experience other forms of maltreatment as a result of being left with an inappropriate caregiver (Knutson et al., 2005; Magura & Moses, 1986; Zuravin & DePanfilis, 1996).
Shuttling and lack of continuity of parenting	The child is repeatedly left at one household or another due to apparent unwillingness to maintain custody, or chronically and repeatedly leaving a child with others for days/weeks at a time. At the seriously inadequate level, a child has suffered negative consequences (Magura & Moses, 1986; U.S. Department of Health and Human Services, 1996; Zuravin & DePanfilis, 1996).

Cognitive-educational Neglect

Chronic absence or truancy	Failing to enroll a child of mandatory school age in school and permitting chronic absence from school (in excess of 20 days); at the seriously inadequate level, the child has experienced negative consequences that could have long-standing effects (Stoltenborgh, Bakermans-Kranenburg, & van IJzendoorn, 2013; U.S. Department of Health and Human Services, 1996; Zuravin & DePanfilis, 1996).

(Continued)

Table 2.3 (Continued)

Cognitive-educational Neglect	
Inadequate parental teaching/ stimulating	Children have few, if any, games, toys, or play materials; parents may ignore children or think children a bother, children may have no place to do their homework, may not be assisted with their homework, and may not be exposed to natural opportunities to learn within the home. Consequences may include poor academic school performance problems or acting out or participating in status offenses, or more serious criminal behavior as the child gets older (Magura & Moses, 1986; Straus, Kinard, & Williams, 1995).
Unmet special education needs	A child fails to receive recommended special or remedial educational services, or treatment for a child's diagnosed learning disorder or other special educational needs or problems of the child (Stoltenborgh, Bakermans-Kranenburg, & van IJzendoorn, 2013; American Professional Society on the Abuse of Children, 1995; U.S. Department of Health and Human Services, 1996).

Impact of Child Maltreatment

From a child development perspective, maltreatment often results in delayed physical growth, neurological damage, and mental and emotional/psychological problems, such as violent behavior, depression, and posttraumatic stress disorders. Research has shown that maltreatment is positively associated with a variety of social and health problems, including substance abuse, eating disorders, obesity, depression, suicide, and risky sexual behavior in transition to adulthood (e.g., Chen et al., 2010; Dunn et al., 2013; Kendall-Tackett, 2013; Institute of Medicine and National Research Council, 2014, ch. 4).

Not surprisingly, child maltreatment is a costly problem, with detrimental consequences that follow the initial trauma of neglect or abuse and continue throughout development to adult emotional and physical adaptation. For example, using 2008 maltreatment data as the base, the estimated average lifetime cost per victim of non-fatal child maltreatment is $210,012 in 2010 dollars. The total lifetime economic burden resulting from new cases of fatal and non-fatal child maltreatment in the United States in 2008 is approximately $124 billion – with some estimates nearly three times higher (Fang et al., 2012). The economic cost of first-time child maltreatment in the U.S. in 2014 includes almost $5.9 trillion in lifetime spending, $2.7 trillion in lost gross domestic product, and 27.9 million person-years of employment.

While many of the prior efforts to quantify economic aspects of child maltreatment reflect excellent and careful scholarship that is highly useful, they only measure certain aspects of the total cost. Incremental outlays for excessive and avoidable health care and education is largely a net withdrawal of resources from the economy that could otherwise be used in more productive ways. Moreover, when the earnings of individuals are diminished, society is deprived of productive capacity and spending potential which results in both losses in output throughout the supply chain and reductions in the demand for consumer goods. The effects of these withdrawals, which have not previously been quantified in a comprehensive manner, cascade through all aspects of business activity.

(The Perryman Group, 2015, p. 9)

We also now know that children who grow up exposed to abuse and neglect are more likely to end up having significant difficulty when they become parents (Ben-David et al., 2015; Putnam-Hornstein et al., 2015).

The Current CPS Approach to Responding to Child Maltreatment

Identifying and Reporting Child Maltreatment

As of 2015, approximately 48 States, the District of Columbia, American Samoa, Guam, the Northern Mariana Islands, Puerto Rico, and the Virgin Islands designate professions whose members are mandated by law to report child maltreatment. A *mandatory reporter* is a person who is required by law to make a report of child maltreatment under specific circumstances. Individuals typically designated as mandatory reporters have frequent contact with children. Such individuals may include social workers, school personnel, healthcare workers, mental health professionals, childcare providers, medical examiners or coroners, and law enforcement officers. Some other professions frequently mandated across the states include commercial film or photograph processors (in 12 states, Guam, and Puerto Rico) and computer technicians (in 6 States). Substance abuse counselors are required to report in 14 states, and probation or parole officers are mandatory reporters in 17 states. Directors, employees, and volunteers at entities that provide organized activities for children, such as camps, day camps, youth centers, and recreation centers, are required to report in 13 states.

Six states and the District of Columbia include domestic violence workers on the list of mandated reporters, while six other states and the District of Columbia include animal control or humane officers. Illinois includes both domestic violence workers and animal control or humane officers as mandatory reporters. Court-appointed special advocates are mandatory reporters in 11 states. Members of the clergy are now required to report in 27 states and Guam. Eleven states now have faculty, administrators, athletics staff, and other employees and volunteers at institutions of higher learning, including public and private colleges and universities and vocational and technical schools, designated as mandatory reporters.

In approximately 18 states and Puerto Rico, any person who suspects child abuse or neglect is required to report. Of these 18 states, 16 states and Puerto Rico specify certain professionals who must report, but also require all persons to report suspected abuse or neglect, regardless of profession. New Jersey and Wyoming require all persons to report without specifying any professions. In all other states, territories, and the District of Columbia, any person is permitted to report. These *voluntary reporters of abuse* are often referred to as "permissive reporters" (Child Welfare Information Gateway, 2016b, p. 2).

The term "institutional reporting" refers to those situations in which the mandated reporter is working (or volunteering) as a staff member of an institution, such as a school or hospital, at the time he or she gains the knowledge that leads him or her to suspect that abuse or neglect has occurred. Many institutions have internal policies and procedures for handling reports of abuse, and these usually require the person who suspects abuse to notify the head of the institution that abuse has been discovered or is suspected and needs to be reported to child protective services or other appropriate authorities. Statutes in 33 states, the District of Columbia, and the Virgin Islands provide procedures that must be followed in those cases.

In 18 states, the District of Columbia, and the Virgin Islands, any staff member who suspects abuse must notify the head of the institution when the staff member feels that abuse or possible abuse should be reported to an appropriate authority. In nine states, the District of Columbia, and the Virgin Islands, the staff member who suspects abuse notifies the head of the institution first, and then the head or his or her designee is required to make the report. In nine states, the individual reporter must make the report to the appropriate authority first and then notify the institution that a report has been made. Laws in 15 states make clear that, regardless of any policies within the organization, the mandatory reporter is not relieved of his or her responsibility to report. In 17 states, an employer is expressly prohibited from taking any action to prevent or discourage an employee from making a report (Child Welfare Information Gateway, 2016b, p. 3).

In all jurisdictions, the initial report of child abuse or neglect may be made orally to either the CPS program within the CW agency or to a law enforcement agency. As discussed earlier in this chapter, reporting laws provide definitions of child abuse and neglect to guide the reporter in knowing what circumstances should be officially reported to the CW agency. Guidelines to define the circumstances a mandatory reporter should consider when making a report vary from state to state.

> Typically, a report must be made when the reporter, in his or her official capacity, suspects or has reason to believe that a child has been abused or neglected. Another standard frequently used is in situations in which the reporter has knowledge of, or observes a child being subjected to, conditions that would reasonably result in harm to the child. In Maine, a mandatory reporter must report when he or she has reasonable cause to suspect that a child is not living with the child's family.
>
> Mandatory reporters are required to report the facts and circumstances that led them to suspect that a child has been abused or neglected. They do not have the burden of providing proof that abuse or neglect has occurred. Permissive reporters follow the same standards when electing to make a report.
>
> (Child Welfare Information Gateway, 2016b, p. 3)

Child Maltreatment's Extent and Form

Estimating the Extent of Child Maltreatment

The scope of child maltreatment impacts the resources needed to respond to the problem. There are three basic approaches to estimating the scope of the problem. The first is to estimate the prevalence or incidence of child abuse or neglect through a "sentinel study" that surveys people who are designated as the official reporters of child abuse or neglect: social services, educational, medical, daycare, law enforcement, and other mandated or those thought to be the most suitable reporters. Based on precise definitions of child abuse or neglect, this method attempts to estimate the actual number of children known by the sentinels to have experienced child abuse or neglect, whether or not a report was made to a CW agency.

A second approach is to survey a general population of adults and/or youth directly to determine if they have been maltreated. The advantage of this approach is that it collects data directly from those who may have experienced the problem and, depending on any response bias or hesitancy to identify themselves as victims, may provide the most accurate data. However, these studies are often compromised owing to low response rates and because it is difficult to derive an estimate that generalizes to the nation as a whole unless sophisticated sampling procedures have been implemented.

The third way to understand the scope of the problem is to examine the extent of *reported* incidents of child abuse or neglect, with a focus on suspected and substantiated/confirmed/founded/indicated reports. Some drawbacks with this approach are that definitions vary across jurisdictions about what these determinations mean, and, most importantly, this approach does not include all of the incidents of child abuse or neglect that may actually have occurred but were never officially reported – a substantial number according to the findings of the other two methods. However, the advantage of examining reporting is that these are the children and families reported to the public CW agency from which a formal societal response may result.

National Incidence Study of Child Abuse and Neglect: Overview

The National Incidence Study (NIS) of child abuse and neglect is a congressionally mandated, periodic research effort to assess the incidence of child abuse and neglect in the United States (Sedlak, 2001). The National Incidence Studies have been conducted approximately once each decade, beginning in 1974, in response to requirements of the Child Abuse Prevention and Treatment Act (CAPTA). Although the U.S. DHHS Children's Bureau collects annual state-level administrative data on official reports of child maltreatment, the NIS studies are designed to estimate more broadly the incidence of child maltreatment in the United States by including both cases that are reported to the authorities as well as those that are not. A unique contribution of the NIS has been the use of a common definitional framework for classifying children according to types of maltreatment as well as the severity of maltreatment.

The NIS gathers information from multiple sources to estimate the number of children who are abused or neglected and to provide information about the nature and severity of the maltreatment; the characteristics of the children, perpetrators, and families; and the extent of changes in the incidence or distribution of child maltreatment since the time of the last national incidence study. Because key demographic characteristics of maltreated children and their families are collected, NIS results provide information about which children are most at risk for child maltreatment.

The NIS design assumes that the maltreated children who are investigated by child protective services (CPS) represent only the "tip of the iceberg," so although NIS estimates include children investigated by CPS they also include maltreated children who are identified by professionals in a wide range of agencies in representative communities. These professionals, called "sentinels," are asked to remain on the lookout for children they believe are maltreated during the study period. Children identified by sentinels and those whose alleged maltreatment is investigated by CPS during the same period are evaluated against standardized definitions of abuse and neglect. The data are unduplicated, so a given child is counted only once in the study estimates. Four national incidence studies have been implemented to date (Sedlak et al., 2010). Using an elaborate sampling methodology, the NIS selects nationally representative samples of counties to represent the U.S. population and weights the estimates based on this multi-tiered sampling methodology. Consistent with findings from the first three incidence studies, the NIS-4 indicates that the actual incidence of child maltreatment is much greater than the number of cases cited in published studies of "official" reports of child abuse and neglect. The nature of reporting skews estimates of the incidence of maltreatment because allied professionals, on average, report less than half of the cases of suspected maltreatment that they are aware of. The findings from national incidence studies over time have contributed to the conclusion that reports of child maltreatment are only the tip of the iceberg.

In examining the incidence of child maltreatment, different levels of official recognition or public awareness must be delineated. The methodology used for all four of the National Incidence Studies was based on a model that used five levels of official recognition or public awareness of abuse or neglect. These levels are illustrated in Figure 2.1.

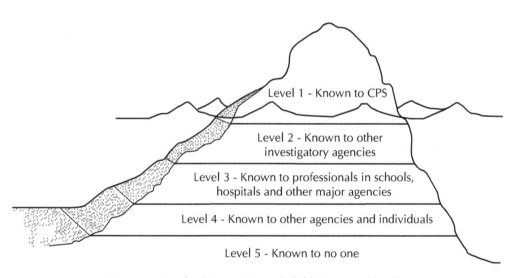

Figure 2.1 Levels of Recognition of Child Abuse and Neglect
Source: NCCAN (1988).

In addition to the main study, the NIS-4 included several supplementary studies to help interpret the main study findings. Two were surveys of CPS agencies; the first on their overall policies, procedures, and practices and the second on their screening standards, to determine how they would treat referrals concerning the uninvestigated cases that sentinels identified. The third supplementary study was a survey of sentinels on their (a) backgrounds and (b) definitions of child abuse and neglect (c) and standards for reporting suspected maltreatment to CPS or submitting data on maltreated children to the NIS (Sedlak et al., 2010, p. 4).

National Incidence Study No. 4 of Child Abuse and Neglect: Findings

The findings of the fourth National Incidence Study of Child Abuse and Neglect (NIS-4) show an overall decrease in the incidence of maltreatment since the NIS-3, as well as decreases in some specific maltreatment categories and increases in others. The fourth National Incidence Study (NIS-4) also updated the set of risk factors for child maltreatment in key areas:

- **Employment.** Compared to children with employed parents, those with no parent in the labor force had two to three times the rate of maltreatment overall.

- **Family structure and living arrangement.** Compared to children living with married biological parents, those children whose single parent had a live-in partner had more than eight times the rate of maltreatment overall, over ten times the rate of abuse, and nearly eight times the rate of neglect.

- **Grandparents as caregivers.** Children cared for by a grandparent had lower rates of physical abuse compared to those with no identified grandparent caregiver.

- **Socioeconomic status.** Children in low socioeconomic status households had significantly higher rates of maltreatment. They experienced some types of maltreatment at more than five times the rate of other children; they were more than three times as likely to be abused and about seven times as likely to be neglected.

- **Family size.** The general pattern was nonlinear. The incidence rates were highest for children in the largest families (those with four or more children), intermediate for singleton children (i.e., "only" children) and those in households with three children, and lowest among children in families with two children (see the NIS-4 report for more details).

- **Child's age.** In most cases, 0- to 2-year-old children had significantly lower maltreatment rates than older children.

- **County metropolitan status.** On balance, the incidence of maltreatment was higher in rural counties than in urban counties.

- **Perpetrator's relationship to the child.** Biological parents were the most closely related perpetrators, accounting for 71 percent of physically abused children and for 73 percent of emotionally abused children. The pattern was distinctly different for sexual abuse, with 42 percent of sexually abused children victimized by someone other than a parent (whether biological or non-biological) or a parent's partner, whereas just over one-third (36%) were sexually abused by a biological parent. In addition, the severity of harm from physical abuse varied by the perpetrator's relationship to the child. A physically abused child was more likely to sustain a serious injury when the abuser was not a parent.

- **Perpetrator's alcohol use, drug use, and mental illness.** Alcohol use and drug use contributed approximately equally to maltreatment, each applying to 11 percent of the countable children, whereas mental illness was a factor in the maltreatment of 7 percent of the children. All three factors were more often involved in maltreatment when the perpetrator was a biological parent (Sedlak et al., 2010, pp. 14–15).

Unlike previous NIS cycles, the NIS-4 found strong and pervasive race differences in the incidence of maltreatment. In nearly all cases, the rates of maltreatment for Black children were significantly higher than those for White and Hispanic children. These differences occurred under both definitional standards in rates of overall maltreatment, overall abuse, overall neglect, and physical abuse and for children with serious or moderate harm from their maltreatment. They also occurred in the incidence of Harm Standard sexual abuse, in the incidence of children who were inferred to be harmed by Harm Standard maltreatment, and in Endangerment Standard rates for physical neglect, emotional maltreatment, and children who were endangered but not demonstrably harmed by their maltreatment (Sedlak et al., 2010). Race is confounded by the other factors listed above such as employment, socioeconomic status, and community characteristics, for example, so we are not listing it as a risk factor per se.

Child Maltreatment Statistics

Most states recognize four major types of maltreatment: neglect, physical abuse, psychological maltreatment, and sexual abuse. Although any of the forms of child maltreatment may be found separately, they can occur in combination. This section presents key findings which stem from data which states provide through the National Child Abuse and Neglect Data System (NCANDS). NCANDS was established in 1988 as a voluntary national data collection and analysis program to make available state child abuse and neglect information. Data have been collected every year since 1991 and NCANDS now annually collects maltreatment data from child protective services agencies in the 50 states, the District of Columbia, and the Commonwealth of Puerto Rico (sometimes referred to as "52 states"). Key findings from the 2016 NCANDs data (U.S. Department of Health and Human Services, 2018) include the following (with some statistics also included in Figure 2.2):

1. *How many allegations of maltreatment were reported and received an investigation or assessment for abuse and neglect?* During FFY 2016, CPS agencies received an estimated 4.1 million referrals involving approximately 7.4 million children. Among the 45 states that reported both screened-in and screened-out referrals, 58.0 percent of referrals were screened in and 42.0 percent were screened out. For FFY 2016, 2.3 million referrals were screened in for a CPS response and received a disposition. The national rate of screened-in referrals (reports) was 31.3 per 1,000 children in the national population (p. ix).

2. *Who reported child maltreatment?* For 2016, professionals submitted (64.9%) reports alleging child abuse and neglect. The term professional means that the person had contact with the alleged child maltreatment victim as part of his or her job. This term includes teachers, police officers, lawyers, and social services staff. The highest percentages of reports were from education personnel (18.9%), legal and law enforcement personnel (18.4%), and social services personnel (11.2%) (p. ix).

3. *How many referrals are screened in?* Screened-in referrals are called reports. In most states, the majority of reports receive an investigation. This response includes assessing the allegation of maltreatment according to state law and policy. The primary purpose of the investigation is twofold: (i) to determine whether the child was maltreated or is at risk of being maltreated; and (ii) to determine whether services are needed and which services to provide. In some states, reports (screened-in referrals) may receive an alternative response.

   This response is usually reserved for instances where the child is at a low or moderate risk of maltreatment. The primary purpose of the alternative response is to focus on the service needs of the family. In the National Child Abuse and Neglect Data System (NCANDS), both investigations and alternative responses receive a CPS finding also known as a disposition. In the National Child Abuse and Neglect Data System

(NCANDS), both investigations and alternative responses receive a CPS finding known as a disposition. Nationally for FFY 2016, an estimated 2.3 million reports (screened-in referrals) received dispositions. This is a 10.7 percent increase from the 2012 national rounded number of 2.1 million reports that received dispositions (p. 7).

4. *How many children were victims?* For FFY 2016, there were a nationally estimated 676,000 victims of child abuse and neglect. The victim rate was 9.1 victims per 1,000 children in the population (p. x). Three-quarters (74.8%) of victims were neglected, 18.2 percent were physically abused, and 8.5 percent were sexually abused. In addition, 6.9 percent of victims experienced such "other" types of maltreatment as threatened abuse or neglect, drug/alcohol addiction, and lack of supervision. States may code any maltreatment as "other" if it does not fit into one of the NCANDS categories. In this analysis, a victim who suffered more than one type of maltreatment was counted for each maltreatment type, but only once per type (pp. x, 20).

5. *Who were the child victims?* Children in their first year of life had the highest rate of victimization at 24.8 per 1,000 children of the same age in the national population. Most victims were of three races or ethnicities: White (44.9%), Hispanic (22.0%), and African-American (20.7%). The racial distributions for all children in the population are 51.1 percent White, 13.8 percent African American, and 24.9 percent Hispanic. For FFY 2016, American Indian or Alaska Native children had the highest rate of victimization at 14.2 per 1,000 children in the population of the same race or ethnicity; and African American children had the second highest rate at 13.9 per 1,000 children. The FFY 2016 data show a reduction in the African American rate per 1,000 children and an increase in the American Indian or Alaska Native rate per 1,000 children when compared with the FFY 2015 rates (p. 20).

6. For all victims younger than 1 year, percentages of victims with the alcohol abuse child risk factor increased from 3.1 in 2012 to 4.8 in 2016. The rates per 1,000 children of the same age increased from 0.7 to 1.2, respectively. For all victims younger than 1 year, percentages of victims with the drug abuse child risk factor increased from 12.3 in 2012 to 15.2 in 2016. The rates per 1,000 children of the same age increased from 2.6 to 3.9, respectively (p. x).

7. *Do children receive services?* CPS agencies provide services to children and their families, both in their homes and in foster care. Approximately 1.3 million children received post-response services from a CPS agency. Two-thirds (60.6%) of victims and one-third (29.7%) of non-victims received post-response services (p. xi).

8. *Who maltreated the children?* A perpetrator is the person who is responsible for the abuse or neglect of a child. Fifty states reported 518,136 perpetrators. According to the analyses performed on the perpetrators for whom case-level data were obtained:

   - More than four-fifths (83.4%) of perpetrators were between the ages of 18 and 44 years.

   - More than half (53.7%) of perpetrators were women, 45.3 percent of perpetrators were men, and 1.0 percent were of unknown sex.

   - The three largest percentages of perpetrators were White (49.8%), African American (20.0%), or Hispanic (18.8%).

9. *How many children died from abuse or neglect?* For FFY 2016, 49 states reported 1,700 fatalities. Based on these data, a nationally estimated 1,750 children died from abuse and neglect. According to the analyses performed on the child fatalities for whom case-level data were obtained the national rate of child fatalities was 2.36 deaths per 100,000 children (p. x). This is likely an undercount, as there are many problems in how child fatalities are counted (Commission to Eliminate Child Abuse and Neglect Fatalities, 2016; Schnitzer, Gulino, & Yuan, 2013).

Child Fatalities

As documented by many studies, infants and young children are most at risk of fatalities and serious injuries from child abuse or neglect. They comprise a large proportion of children for whom out-of-home placement is necessary to keep them safe. Analyses conducted by the United States Administration for Children, Youth and Families on the child fatalities for whom case-level data were obtained found that:

- Seventy percent of all child fatalities were younger than 3 years, and the child fatality rates mostly decreased with age. Children who were younger than 1 year died from maltreatment at a rate of 20.63 per 100,000 children in the population younger than 1 year. This is three times the fatality rate for children who were 1 year old (6.50 per 100,000 children in the population of the same age). Younger children are the most vulnerable to death as the result of child abuse and neglect.

- Boys had a higher child fatality rate than girls: 2.87 per 100,000 boys in the population, compared with 2.11 per 100,000 girls in the population. Eighty-seven percent (87.4%) of child fatalities were White (45.1%), African American (28.5%), and Hispanic (13.8%). Using the number of victims and the population data to create rates highlights some racial disparity. The rate of African American child fatalities (4.65 per

100,000 African American children) is 2.2 times greater than the rate of White children (2.08 per 100,000 White children), and nearly 3 times greater than the rate of Hispanic children (1.58 per 100,000 Hispanic children).

- Of the children who died, 74.6 percent suffered neglect and 44.2 percent suffered physical abuse either exclusively or in combination with another maltreatment type. Because a victim may have suffered from more than one type of maltreatment, every reported maltreatment type was counted, and total more than 100.0 percent.

- Most perpetrators were caregivers of their victims. More than three-quarters (78.0%) of child fatalities involved parents acting alone, together, or with other individuals. Fewer (16.7%) fatalities did not have a parental relationship to their perpetrator. Child fatalities with unknown perpetrator relationship data accounted for 5.3 percent (U.S. Department of Health and Human Services, 2018, pp. 54–56).

The NCANDS death stats substantially undercount the number of child fatalities due to differences in how states track these cases, the cases that are misclassified, and because near-fatality cases are not tracked sufficiently (U.S. GAO, 2011). We now also have data from California that follow children from birth to their fifth birthday and determine the level of preventable injury deaths for children who are involved with CW vs. those who are not and how that differs by race. Black children had twice the child maltreatment substantiation rate of White and Hispanic children and more than twice the death rate (Putnam-Hornstein, 2012).

Nature of Child Maltreatment Differs by Age

One of the key insights that can be gleaned from the NCANDS and national foster care data is how various forms of child maltreatment drive foster care placements (see Figure 2.3 and Table 2.4). Note that many states do not use the substance abuse reason; and in some states it is not even a statutorily acceptable removal reason. In addition, the increase over time of substance abuse as placement reason in some states may be more about reporting than about actual change (personal communication, Susan Smith, January 26, 2018).

Race, Ethnicity, Income, and Maltreatment

Poverty and race/ethnicity are related in the United States, and both are correlated with maltreatment. Indeed, as reported above, the racial and ethnic distribution of perpetrators in a substantiated case is similar to the race and ethnicity of victims. These proportions have changed little over recent years (U.S. DHHS, 2013, p. 61). Although the literature

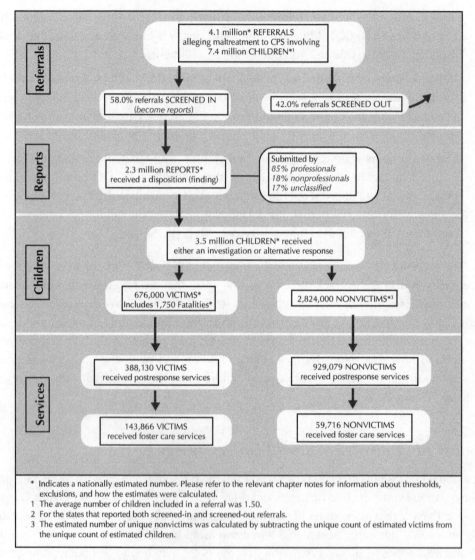

Figure 2.2 Key Child Maltreatment Statistics from the NCANDS Report

Source: U.S. Department of Health and Human Services, Administration for Children and Families, Administration on Children, Youth and Families, Children's Bureau (2018, p. xii).

is sparse, differences by race and ethnicity should be understood in the context of other known risk factors, especially poverty. The NIS-4 also found significant differences in child abuse rates based on socioeconomic factors. Poor children were three times more likely than other children to experience abuse (Sedlak et al., 2010). When income was controlled

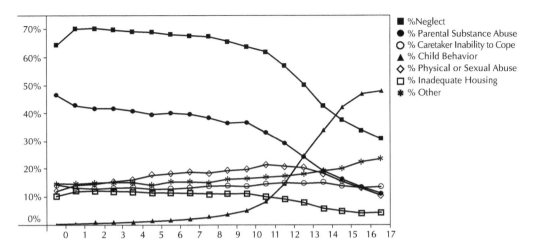

Figure 2.3 Removal Reason by Age Group in Federal Fiscal Year 2015

Children enter care for many reasons. These categories represent the standard removel resons states provide as part of their required AFCARS submission. How states utilize these standard fields, and whether or not they use all fields, is impacted by two key things: 1) how the removal reasons in their case management system are mapped to these categories; and 2) how caseworkers are instructed to determine removal reasons for a child. State policy and practice vary.

Data source: AFCARS national data, available from the National Data Archive on Child Abuse & Neglect Data (NDACAN), Cornell University. Produced by Data Advocacy, Casey Family Programs.

in analyses, the differences found in maltreatment rates between White and Black children in low-income families were negligible. In fact, larger differences were observed in the "not low income" classification, in which higher rates were observed for African American families as compared to White families.

Racial differences in risks to safe parenting are large, as evidenced by a higher infant mortality rate for Black children than for other children (Drake et al., 2011). Thus, it is predictable that the need for CW services would be greater.

The complex interplay of race, poverty, and CW system involvement has challenged the field for many years and has spurred critical assessments of the system. Legal scholar Dorothy Roberts (2002, 2003), for example, has argued that the overrepresentation of poor African American youth is not only unjust but is tantamount to a civil rights violation. Others have suggested that the overrepresentation of children of color may be rooted in different system responses at different moments in the life of a CW case (Hines et al., 2004), and some argue that institutional discrimination is likely a significant factor (Rodenborg, 2004). Regardless of the specific mechanism at play, it is clear that service provision and quality must meet the needs of African American families and take into account the more challenging environments posed by racialized poverty (Lorthridge et al., 2011).

Table 2.4 Removal Reason by Age Group in Federal Fiscal Year 2015

	0	1	2	3	4	5	6	7	8	9	10	11	12	13	14	15	16	17
% Neglect	65%	70%	70%	70%	69%	69%	68%	68%	68%	66%	64%	62%	57%	50%	43%	38%	34%	31%
% Parental Substance Abuse	47%	43%	42%	42%	41%	40%	40%	40%	38%	37%	37%	33%	29%	24%	19%	16%	13%	11%
% Other	15%	15%	15%	15%	15%	14%	16%	16%	15%	16%	17%	17%	18%	18%	19%	20%	23%	24%
% Caretaker Inability to Cope	14%	13%	13%	13%	14%	13%	13%	13%	14%	14%	14%	15%	15%	15%	15%	14%	13%	14%
% Inadequate Housing	11%	12%	12%	12%	12%	12%	12%	12%	11%	11%	11%	10%	9%	8%	6%	5%	4%	5%
% Physical or Sexual Abuse	12%	14%	14%	16%	16%	18%	19%	19%	19%	20%	20%	22%	21%	21%	18%	16%	13%	10%

Notes: Children enter care for many reasons. These categories represent the standard removal reasons states provide as part of their required AFCARS submission. How states utilize these standard fields, and whether or not they use all fields, is impacted by two key things: 1) how the removal reasons in their case management system are mapped to these categories; and 2) how caseworkers are instructed to determine removal reasons for a child. State policy and practice vary.

Data source: AFCARS national data, available from the National Data Archive on Child Abuse and Neglect Data (NDACAN), Cornell University. Produced by Data Advocacy, Casey Family Programs.

Cumulative Rates of Child Maltreatment

Child maltreatment is a risk factor for poor health throughout the life course. Existing estimates of the proportion of the U.S. population maltreated during childhood are based on retrospective self-reports. Records of officially confirmed maltreatment have been used to produce annual rather than cumulative counts of maltreated individuals. Wildeman et al. (2014) estimated the proportion of U.S. children with a report of maltreatment (abuse or neglect) that was indicated or substantiated by Child Protective Services (referred to as confirmed maltreatment) by 18 years of age. The National Child Abuse and Neglect Data System (NCANDS) Child File includes information on all U.S. children with a confirmed report of maltreatment, totaling 5,689,900 children (2004–2011). They developed synthetic cohort life tables to estimate the cumulative prevalence of confirmed childhood maltreatment by 18 years of age. The cumulative prevalence of confirmed child maltreatment was analyzed by race/ethnicity, sex, and year.

At 2011 rates, 12.5 percent (95% CI, 12.5–12.6%) of U.S. children will experience a confirmed case of maltreatment by 18 years of age. Girls have a higher cumulative prevalence (13.0% [95% CI, 12.9–13.0%]) than boys (12.0% [12.0–12.1%]). Black (20.9% [95% CI, 20.8–21.1%]), Native American (14.5% [14.2–14.9%]), and Hispanic (13.0% [12.9–13.1%]) children have higher prevalence rates than White (10.7% [10.6–10.8%]) or Asian/Pacific Islander (3.8% [3.7–3.8%]) children.

The risk for maltreatment is highest in the first few years of life; 2.1 percent (95% CI, 2.1–2.1%) of children have confirmed maltreatment by 1 year of age, and 5.8 percent (5.8–5.9%), by 5 years of age. Estimates from 2011 were consistent with those from 2004 through 2010. What does this mean? Annual rates of confirmed child maltreatment dramatically understate the cumulative number of children confirmed to be maltreated during childhood. Their findings indicate that maltreatment will be confirmed for 1 in 8 U.S. children by 18 years of age, far greater than the 1 in 100 children whose maltreatment is confirmed annually. For Black children, the cumulative prevalence is 1 in 5; for Native American children, 1 in 7 (Wildeman et al., 2014). These figures show that CW services are now a major influence on the outcomes of a large proportion of American children. This creates an even greater burden on those designing and staffing these services.

Recurrence of Child Abuse and Neglect

The recurrence of child maltreatment following a report to the CPS hotline and response by the CW agency is one index of the effectiveness of the public CW system. Experts have expressed concern that CPS programs across the country are faced with problems of such magnitude that their ability to protect children and prevent recurrences is severely compromised (Commission to Eliminate Child Abuse and Neglect Fatalities, 2016; Sanders, 2017b). The movement to adopt risk assessment and safety evaluation systems to assess the likelihood of recurrence, to evaluate the potential safety of maltreated children, and to guide decision making in CW is an example of a policy movement that has evolved from this concern (Chahine et al., 2013).

For many victims who have experienced repeated maltreatment, the efforts of the CW system have not been successful in preventing subsequent victimization. Through the Child and Family Services Reviews (CFSR) (see Chapter 1), the Children's Bureau has established the current national standard for recurrence of child maltreatment as 94.6 percent, defined as: "Absence of Maltreatment Recurrence. Of all children who were victims of substantiated or indicated abuse or neglect during the first 6 months of the reporting year, what percent did not experience another incident of substantiated or indicated abuse or neglect within a 6-month period?" The national average percentage of children without a new substantiated incident of child maltreatment increased from 91.9 during 2004 to 94.6 in 2013 with considerable state variation – ranging from 87.1 to 99.2 percent (U.S. DHHS, 2013, p. iii).

Summary

As presented above, the cumulative rates of child abuse and neglect when children are followed from birth are substantial (1 in 8 U.S. children by 18 years of age). Based on recent research by Putnam-Hornstein and key findings from the NSCAW I and II studies, it appears that current CW services, while having positive intentions and achieving decreasing rates of repeat child maltreatment, may be failing to protect many of the 3 million children at risk of child maltreatment in America due to constraints in policy, program design, practice, and funding. These children who are at risk have not received effective prevention services. Even children placed in foster homes and group care are not immune to this risk: studies have found that child maltreatment and child abuse-related fatalities occurring in foster care appeared to be occurring with two to three times the frequency of that in the general population (Nunno & Motz, 1988; Uliando & Mellor, 2012).

Risk and Protective Factors for Child Maltreatment

Risk Factors

A variety of biological, psychological, and environmental factors converge to create the conditions in which maltreatment occurs, and a somewhat similar set of factors influences a child's recovery from maltreatment. The application of a risk and resilience perspective to CW falls into two areas. The first has to do with factors that elevate the odds for maltreatment, and the second has to do with factors that promote recovery from the experience of maltreatment. As summarized in many research studies and the textbook resource paper (Pecora, 2018), the factors correlated with maltreatment include poverty, parental substance abuse, parental mental illness, parental history of child maltreatment, social isolation, lack of employment resources in the community, and neighborhood gangs and crime. However, none of these factors alone is sufficient to produce maltreatment. Nevertheless, maltreatment becomes more likely as the number of risk factors increases. At the same time, we now know that a number of factors operate protectively and can reduce the likelihood of maltreatment in the presence of risk.

As presented earlier, the fourth National Incidence Study (NIS-4) also updated the set of risk factors for child maltreatment in key areas. Indeed, across all children, the NIS-4 and other research by Putnam-Hornstein (2011) suggest that developmental outcomes are influenced by individual and environmental risk factors as well as by a host of cultural resources and practices that may both act as a buffer against risk and promote recovery from negative life events. One of the most frequently discussed risk factors is poverty. Low-income families are less likely to have adequate food, safe housing, and prenatal or other medical care. Households that are living near or below the poverty line tend to have few social supports and experience more stress in child rearing, all of which can increase the risk of child maltreatment. Generally, poverty has a direct negative influence on maternal behavior and subsequently on the quality of parenting that children receive (Brooks-Gunn, Klebanov, & Liaw, 1995). For children, living in poverty is associated with a host of negative consequences, including poor physical health, diminished cognitive abilities, reduced educational attainment, increased emotional and behavioral problems, and higher risk of maltreatment (Brooks-Gunn & Duncan, 1997; Ridge, 2009; Sedlak et al., 2010). Due to persistent racial disparities in wealth and income in the United States, families of color contend with more poverty-related risk factors, including an overburdened social support system.

The relationship of poverty to maltreatment and other negative child developmental outcomes appears mediated in part by stress. Using global data, Wilkinson and Pickett (2009) charted the level of health and social problems against the level of income inequality in 20 of the world's richest nations and in each state of the United States. They found that mental illness, drug and alcohol abuse, obesity, and teenage pregnancy were more common in states and countries with a big gap between the incomes of rich and poor households. Moreover, areas with a large income gap also had higher homicide rates, shorter life expectancies, and lower scores for children's educational performance and literacy. The Scandinavian countries and Japan consistently scored at the positive end of this spectrum, and these countries have the smallest differences between higher and lower incomes and the best record of psychosocial health. The countries with the widest gulf between rich and poor, and the highest incidence of health and social problems, were Britain, the United States, and Portugal.

The Wilkinson and Pickett (2009) data and recent reviews of families living in "deep poverty" (Urban Institute, 2013) suggest that poverty creates not only physical hardship but also a stressful environment that exacerbates social and health problems. Commenting on Wilkinson and Pickett's analysis, Crary (2009, p. 1) argued:

> It is not only the poor who suffer from the effects of inequality, but the majority of the population. For example, rates of mental illness are five times higher across the whole population in the most unequal than in the least unequal societies in their survey. One explanation [.] is that inequality increases stress right across society, not just among the least advantaged. Much research has been done on the stress hormone cortisol, which can be measured in saliva or blood, and it emerges that chronic stress affects the neural system and in turn the immune system. When stressed, we are more prone to depression and anxiety, and more likely to develop a host of bodily ills including heart disease, obesity, drug addiction, liability to infection and rapid aging.

Although it is far beyond the capacity of service providers to influence national income differentials, these data suggest that health promotion and child safety may be associated with poverty and stress. In seeking to reduce stress, researchers are increasingly looking at protective factors, including cultural rootedness and family resources – both of which act as a buffer against stress related to poverty and other adversities such as racial discrimination. In addition to African American youth and their families, immigrant families constitute an increasing part of the population served by CW. In designing more effective services for these children, data suggest that it is important to understand how the experiences of immigration, immigration stress, and acculturation affect family dynamics, strengths, and risk and protective factors (e.g., Dalla et al., 2009).

Protective Factors

Although the available research on protective factors associated with child maltreatment is limited, this research has been growing (e.g., Development Services Group, Inc., 2013) and has been informed by the larger body of literature on protective factors. Several studies have outlined factors that differentiate resilient children from children who experience serious adjustment problems. Protective factors appear to fall into three general categories: individual characteristics, family characteristics, and the presence of supportive others (Garmezy, 1985; Rutter, 1990; Werner, 1989). Individual characteristics include attributes such as self-sufficiency, high self-esteem, and altruism. Family characteristics include supportive relationships with adult family members, harmonious family relationships, expressions of warmth between family members, and the ability to mobilize supports in times of stress. Finally, community supports refer to supportive relationships with people or organizations that are external to the family. As also described in the child maltreatment risk and protective factors resource paper (Pecora, 2018), these external supports provide positive and supportive feedback to the child and act to reinforce and reward the child's positive coping abilities (Hodges, 1994).

Consistent with this perspective, the American Psychological Association's Task Force on Resilience and Strength in Black Children and Adolescents (hereafter, APA Task Force) called for reframing research to better conceptualize adaptive and protective processes for African American children. With the intent of providing researchers, policy makers, educators, practitioners, and the public with a useful lens through which to view the design of services for African American youth, the report explored how themes of resilience cut across five widely accepted developmental domains of functioning:

- *Identity development.* A positive racial identity is essential to the well-being of African American youth. Children should be encouraged to develop a positive sense of self in a society that often devalues them through negative stereotypes.

- *Emotional development.* Coping with emotions effectively is directly related to self-esteem and better mental health. African American youth need to be made aware of how their emotional expressions resonate across all situations and circumstances.

- *Social development.* Family and community interaction is crucial to African American youths' social development. This interaction includes having access to high-quality childcare, after-school programs, and faith-based institutions.

- *Cognitive development.* African American youth must believe in their abilities in the classroom. Parents should avoid harsh parenting styles, and schools should continue to look at ways to infuse culturally relevant themes into the classroom as a way to improve academic performance.

- *Physical health and development.* Access to healthcare must be improved. A wide range of health conditions disproportionately affect African American youth, including obesity, poor oral health, asthma, violent injury, sickle-cell anemia, diabetes, and HIV/AIDS (APA Task Force, 2008).

Child protection has always been a key aspect of CW services, but the literature on risk and resilience has provided new insights for child protection policy and program design. For many children, prevailing over the adversity of maltreatment involves strengthening protective processes in the family and community context. These strengthening efforts include building parental competence and teaching positive disciplinary approaches; enhancing the racial and ethnic identities of children; and engaging caregivers, advocates, peer networks, and extended family members in providing culturally anchored social support. Other critical protective characteristics involve inclusion of families in community activities and the availability of medical, educational, and financial resources that allow parents to provide appropriate care for their children.

Summary

We have reported the major statistical approaches to estimating the prevalence of child abuse and neglect. The lack of service and funding integration were noted as well as many policy developments that illustrate how risk-reduction strategies could improve CW services. To disrupt the risk mechanisms that lead to child maltreatment and that complicate recovery from victimization, CW agencies need adequate funding, as well as new and more effective ways to link funding to effective programs.

CW policy, performance incentives, and practices lack alignment (e.g., Wulczyn et al., 2009). Critics argue that the CW system needs to be overhauled to better address risk factors leading to child abuse and neglect (Roberts, 2009; Edna McConnell Clark Foundation, 2004; Lindsey, 2004; Whittaker & Maluccio, 2002). In addition, the emerging literature on protective processes, which buffer children from risk and promote recovery from victimization, holds potential to influence policy and practice.

To underscore the complexity of the challenges incumbent in reform, a case study is presented in Box 2.1. The case describes a family in which multiple forms of child neglect are present. This family situation illustrates how child neglect can have serious consequences for child development. The complexity of this family situation is evident; it is the too frequent situation in which genuine love for children is interwoven with mental health problems, partner violence, poverty, and deficits in parenting skills. In this scenario, the concepts of risk, resiliency, and protective factors have utility for guiding case decision making and the choice of interventions.

Box 2.1   Children Who Are Not Headliners

Introduction

This case example involves multiple forms of child neglect. An intergenerational cycle may be at work here: a "passing on of infantilism, mother to daughter, through processes of deprivation leading to detachment (the deprivation-detachment hypotheses), failure to provide stimulation, and the child's identification with an inadequate role model. Hence the cycle of neglect might be said to derive from a cycle of infantilism" (Polansky et al., 1981, p. 43). Although it must be emphasized that generalizing these families is not wise because of their diversity, some of the research data depict a group of neglectful caregivers who are generally (1) less able to love; (2) less capable of working productively; (3) less open about feelings; (4) more prone to living planlessly and impulsively; (5) susceptible to psychological symptoms and to phases of passive inactivity and numb fatalism; (6) more likely to live in a situation of family conflict, to be less organized and more chaotic; (7) less verbally expressive; and (8) less positive and more negative in affect (Gaudin et al., 1996; Polansky et al., 1981; Polansky, Gaudin, & Kilpatrick, 1992). Although many families involved with substance abuse never come to the attention of child welfare agencies, when they do they are very often identified as having problems related to child neglect (U.S. Department of Health and Human Services, 1996).

In a sense, the parenting/nurturing instinct has been weakened or distorted in its aim, or overwhelmed by the parent's struggle in personal survival. This stunting or crippling of parenting or nurturing is not often an emergent response to current stress but is predictable from the social history of the parent and the lack of nurturance in his or her childhood (Polansky et al., 1981, pp. 147–157). Some of those risk factors (and family strengths and resources) are illustrated by the following case example.

The family comprises Mona Stay, aged 23, and her common-law husband Frank Brown, aged 26. There are three children: Frank Stay, 3, Sylvia Stay, 18 months, and Wilma, 7 months. The Stay-Browns have been together for over five years. Although they quarrel and separate periodically, they seem very mutually dependent and likely to remain a couple.

Their original referral was from a nurse who had become aware of the eldest child's condition. He was difficult to discipline, was eating dirt and paint chips, and seemed hyperactive. Although over 2 years old, he was not speaking. His father reacted to him with impatience. He was often slapped, and hardly ever spoken to with fondness. The caseworker got Mona to cooperate in taking young Frank in for a test for lead poisoning, and for a full developmental evaluation. This child had had several bouts with impetigo, had been bitten through the eyelid by a stray dog, and had a series of ear infections resulting in a slight hearing loss. Although physically normal, he appeared already nearly a year delayed.

Often this child was found outside the house alone when the caseworker came to see the family. On one occasion he was seen hanging from a broken fire escape on the second floor. The worker was unable to rouse his mother, or to enter the house until she got help from the nearby landlord, after which she ran upstairs and rescued the child. Only then did the sleeping Mona awaken.

With much effort having been expended on his behalf, this child had been attending a therapeutic nursery. His speech is already improved after four or five months, and his hyperactivity has calmed. He comes through as a lovable little boy.

Sylvia is surprisingly pale [.] and indeed suffers from severe anemia. This child has had recurrent eye infections, and had a bout with spinal meningitis at age 3 months which, fortunately, seems to have left no residual effects. Much effort has gone into working with Mona concerning Sylvia's need for proper diet and iron supplement. After a year of contact this is still a problem.

The baby was born after the family had become known to the agency. Despite the agency's urging, Mona refused to go for prenatal care until she was in her second trimester, but she did maintain a fairly good diet, helped by small "loans" from the agency when her money for food ran out. When Wilma was born, she had to remain for a time at the hospital for treatment of jaundice. After she went home, she was left to lie most of the time in her bassinet, receiving very little attention from either parent. At 4 months of age, Wilma weighed only 5 pounds and was tentatively diagnosed as exhibiting "failure to thrive" by the hospital. Thereafter the mother avoided going to the clinic, and the caseworker spent much effort concerning the feeding and sheer survival of Wilma. The baby is now slowly gaining weight but is still limp and inactive.

In addition to an active caseworker, a homemaker was assigned to this family for months. Much more was involved than trying to help Mona learn to organize her day: she had almost no motivation to get started. Rather than learning how to manage, she tried to manipulate the homemaker into doing her housework for her. However, with time and patience, Mona has been persuaded to go with the caseworker on shopping trips, is learning how to buy groceries to best advantage, and from time to time manages to get the laundry into and out of the laundromat. So far as her plans for herself, Mona has talked of seeking training as a beauty operator, but has never followed through on this or on other positive plans.

The family's sole support is public assistance. Frank Brown, the father, was on drugs earlier in their relationship, but managed to get off them. Now, however, he drinks heavily, and although he manages to work, he never contributes to the household.

Mona, apparently, was herself a neglected child, and was removed from her parents in infancy. Placed with an adoptive family, there was constant friction during her growing up, and she ran away from home several times. During her teens, she was placed in an institution for incorrigible girls. Later she spent a period in a mental hospital during which she was withdrawn from heroin addiction. It is a commentary on her life that she regards this period in the adolescent ward as one of her happiest ever. Her adoptive mother is now dead, and her father wants nothing more to do with her, so she was more or less living on the streets when she met Frank and set up their present establishment.

Frank and Mona, despite his obvious exploitativeness, seem to love each other and their children, and to want to keep the family together. They are able to relate to those who try to help them, so at least one is not operating constantly against hostile resistance. Mona is an intelligent woman and now shows adequate ability to handle the children. She can be an excellent cook – when there is food available. Yet this remains a disorganized household. Bills are never paid, clothes are thrown around, the children never sleep on clean sheets, trash is piled around the house so that flies and maggots abound. Mona still leaves the youngsters quite alone for brief periods. There is no heat in the house, and the family will soon have to move, with neither any idea where to go nor funds for rent deposits and the like. Mona, at least, is currently wearing an IUD.

The Stay-Brown ménage was not invented, although of course we have altered names and some facts to protect all concerned. These are real people, and they are clearly involved in child neglect. The failures center on poor feeding, uncleanliness, extremely bad housing, filthy circumstances which make the children prone to infections, lack of medical care, inadequate supervision and protections from danger, lack of intellectual stimulation, inattentiveness to the children bordering on rejection – one could go on. The fine staff trying to help Mona improve her childcare finally gave up and closed her case after about 15 months of effort. The care was improving slowly, if at all, and there were recurrent instances of regression.

Frank proved superficially amenable to suggestions when he could be seen, but in fact evaded any real responsibility for the household. The time, money, and – more importantly – motivation for hard work with such families are chronically in short supply. So the decision was made to try to help someone else who might be more treatable.

Meanwhile these children are with their parents. Since they have not literally been abandoned, it is uncertain whether a local judge would decide the home is so bad that the children must be removed. If a catastrophe were to occur, if one were to read that these three children had burned to death in a fire, one would be saddened but not greatly surprised. If one of the three were to die of an infectious disease or an undiagnosed appendicitis, one would not be surprised either. For the present, however, they are among the group which child protection workers know well, but which the public does not, because they do not make headlines – or at least not yet.

Source: Polansky et al. (1981, pp. 5–7). Copyright © 1981. Reprinted with permission of the University of Chicago Press.

Child Protective Services Policy and Program Design Issues

Federal and State Policy Governing Child Protective Services

As described in Chapter 1 and mentioned at the beginning of this chapter, one of the key federal CPS policies is the Child Abuse Prevention and Treatment Act (CAPTA), (42 U.S.C. §5101), as amended by the CAPTA Reauthorization Act of 2010, which defines child abuse and neglect as well as funding key services. In 2010, the Child Abuse CAPTA Reauthorization Act of 2010 (P.L. 111–320) amended the Child Abuse Prevention and Treatment Act (CAPTA), the Family Violence Prevention and Services Act, the Child Abuse Prevention and Treatment and Adoption Reform Act of 1978, and the Abandoned Infants Assistance Act of 1988, to reauthorize the Acts, and make other changes to them. In addition to many other provisions, this Act authorized grants to public or private agencies to develop or expand effective collaborations between child protective service (CPS) entities and domestic violence service entities. It also reauthorized the Child Abuse Prevention and Treatment and Adoption Reform Act of 1978, including appropriations, through FY 2015. Amendments to the Act also required efforts to promote the adoption of older children, minority children, and children with special needs.

Broadening Who is Responsible for Protecting Children

CW agencies are charged with investigating or assessing reports of child maltreatment and intervening to protect children from harm or risk of harm. A variety of options can be taken, including referring families to voluntary community services, providing judicially mandated in-home services, and placing children in out-of-home care. However, the current CW system and CPS function are designed and funded primarily to provide out-of-home care. The "child rescue" orientation/framework continues to serve as the basis for public child protection policy and practice in this country. Currently, the media, policy makers, and the public continue to equate child removals with child safety, especially when responding to child maltreatment deaths. This fundamental belief drives too much of the CW funding, public policy, and practice.

Protecting children from maltreatment cannot be achieved without a fundamental paradigm shift away from "child rescue" as the primary societal response. Children need strong, healthy families and families need strong, healthy communities for children to be safe and to thrive. This change would set the stage for a broader framework that sees child maltreatment as a public health problem that requires the active involvement of multiple systems and communities to promote child safety and well-being and to prevent maltreatment from occurring in the first place. Improving the safety, permanency, and well-being of children requires multiple systems and community partners to address the underlying issues that impact the families and communities. The increasing availability and integration of data from across systems provides unique opportunities for communities to share information and to focus on place-based preventive strategies. In order to achieve sustainable changes, efforts need to reach beyond the CW agency toward government and non-government systems (philanthropy, businesses, faith-based, etc.) and the community at large. With this shift, the public CW agency plays an important role in partnering with other systems to keep children safe (Pecora & Chahine, 2016).

Recently, David Sanders (who led one of the largest public CW agencies in the country for Los Angeles in the early 2000s) spoke about the need for a twenty-first-century public health approach to child safety that includes a broad spectrum of community agencies and systems to identify, test, and evaluate strategies to prevent harm to children. "A public health approach for child safety is one that promotes the healthy development and well-being of children," he said.

> It starts with changing attitudes, beliefs and behaviors, and then focuses on prevention and support of community conditions. Rather than focusing on treating individuals or targeting interventions in ways that can seem punitive, a public health model works on a population level to look at, and to shape, patterns across the entire community.
>
> (Sanders, 2017a)

Sanders also said that constituent voices, particularly those of birth parents, are critical to changing public perceptions about how and why neglect takes place, and in discussions about how we can make sure parents have the support and resources they need to take care of their children.

The underlying societal values and beliefs about child maltreatment drive policies and the allocation of funding to address social problems. Policies that promote a comprehensive preventive community approach and integration across systems are believed to be more effective than those policies designed to address problems after the fact. Policies should include a level of accountability to the outcomes but not be overly proscriptive on how to accomplish the goals. It is also about advocating for policies that lead to effective outcomes by creating a continuum of care and moving from "program" thinking to "social" and "systems" change thinking.

This paradigm shift would also entail a fundamental change in funding allocations and more effective use of resources. The public funding streams (federal, state, and local) tend to be categorical and deficit-oriented. Each funding stream is targeted to address a particular problem or condition (e.g., child maltreatment) usually intervening only *after* the problem has occurred. The majority of government funding has been focused on intervention rather than prevention. Funding is targeted to fixing particular problems rather than promoting well-being. At a minimum, the public sector must work better to integrate funds across health and human services systems (e.g., Medicaid, TANF, Titles IV-B and IV-E) and to focus more efforts on what works to create high impact in lives of families, children, and communities beyond the provision of services. Jurisdictions have access to multiple sources of funding and resources including public/private/non-profit sector businesses and communities at large. Maximizing access and effective utilization as well as leveraging resources are all keys to promoting the well-being of families and communities – partnering across public and private systems. Pooled government funding across departments, pay for success, or social impact bonds are examples of these more integrated finance strategies.

Brain Science and Trauma Treatment

CW policy is slowly but steadily being shaped by research related to risk, resilience, protection, neuroscience, and epigenetics. New materials from the Harvard Center on the Developing Child and landmark books such as *Neurons to Neighborhoods* reinforce infant and young child stimulation principles outlined by earlier pioneers, and make scientific knowledge accessible to a broad audience (Shonkoff & Phillips, 2000). Other CW researchers such as Berrick and colleagues (1998) and Maier (1978) have emphasized the importance of paying attention to child development fundamentals (e.g., attachment theory and social learning) in designing CW policy and programs. Advances in the treatment of child abuse and neglect have emphasized how children with varied psychological compositions and differing amounts of social support respond differently to various healing approaches (Briere & Scott, 2006; Cohen et al., 2003; Kendall-Tackett, 2013).

Community Supports and Permanency

Because children who are separated from parents and other birth family members experience trauma, families should be supported and preserved whenever possible. The field has also recognized the simultaneous needs of moving every child placed in out–of-home care (irrespective of background and age) to permanent family situations – while also being cognizant of the need to nurture the child development of children who remain involved in the CW service system beyond a three-month protective services intervention (Kerman, Maluccio, & Freundlich, 2008). As part of this process, racial and ethnic disproportionality in the provision of services and achievement of permanency outcomes must be acknowledged where it is occurring and, if it indicates poor service provision, addressed (e.g., Derezotes, Poertner, & Testa, 2005; Fluke et al., 2011; Hines et al., 2004). Finally, as mentioned earlier in terms of broadening who is responsible for child safety, leaders in child protective services, family support, and foster care have identified community collaborations as essential for effective services (Morgan, Spears, & Kaplan, 2003; Pew Foundation, 2008; Schorr & Marchand, 2007).

ACEs and Community Development Approaches to Preventing ACEs as an Anti-Poverty Approach

Adverse Childhood Experiences (ACEs) are stressful or traumatic experiences, and they are surprisingly prevalent, as exemplified by the national statistics shown in Table 2.5.

Table 2.5 National ACEs Prevalence Data

ACE Category	National Prevalence (1995–1997)[a]
Physical abuse	28%
Alcoholic or drug-addicted caregiver	27%
Loss of a parent to death, abandonment, or divorce	23%
Sexual abuse	21% (25% of women and 16% of men report sexual abuse during childhood)
Mentally ill, depressed, or suicidal person in the home	19%
Emotional neglect	15%
Witnessing domestic violence against a parent or guardian	13% witnessed domestic violence against the *mother or stepmother*
Emotional abuse	11%
Physical neglect	10%
Incarceration of any family member	5%
At least one ACE	**64%**
Three or more ACEs	**22%**

[a]*Source:* www.cdc.gov/ace/prevalence.htm. Collected between 1995 and 1997, the prevalence rates (%) presented are estimated from the entire ACE Study sample (n = 17,337). Individual research papers that use only Wave 1 data or Wave 2 data will contain slightly but not significantly different prevalence estimates for individual ACEs.

ACEs tend to occur in clusters, and those children who experience more ACEs have more health and social problems. Washington State is the first state in the nation to have detailed information about the prevalence of ACEs and its relationship to mental, physical, and behavioral health, as well as other factors that affect worker performance, parenting, and intergenerational transmission of trauma. Categorical approaches to the health and social problems caused by ACEs are generally not effective. The current "siloed" approaches in some human service systems are understandable from a historical perspective, but for future success a coordinated effort that links existing human service systems and improves community capacity to reduce ACEs is needed.

Community and service improvements should include information about ACEs and their effect on human development, along with the latest scientific findings on brain science and early child development. This creates a common framework for change that will contribute to community norms that effectively build the foundations of healthy development, more meaningful diagnoses, earlier and improved treatment of exposed children and their families, and better integration of healthcare, prevention, social services, juvenile justice, public school systems, and legal venues. For example, the Community Public Health and Safety Networks (CPHSN) in Washington State to reduce ACEs have been evolving to become *total community* approaches. Some of these networks are now at a stage where they can better document how their strategies are improving family and child functioning over time through linked community efforts. Other ACEs, resilience, and trauma-informed approaches have been developed in other communities, and these deserve careful evaluation. See, for example, staff, program, and budget shifts in Waupaca (Meyer et al., 2017), the *Fostering Futures* initiative in Wisconsin, and a three-part *New York Times* series by Bornstein (2016).

Systems Complexities

Systems thinking has been adopted in the child protection field both in the United States and globally. As Wulczyn and colleagues (2010) note, the systems approach fits well with a major theoretical model in the field of child development: that of Bronfenbrenner (1979). From any perspective, children can be considered in terms of the nested and interacting

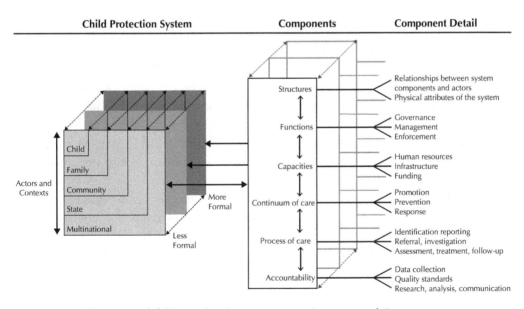

Figure 2.4 Child Protection Systems: Actors, Contexts, and Components
Source: Wulczyn et al. (2010). Reprinted with permission.

structures (e.g., families, communities) that affect them. Conversely, considering any child-related issue without taking such a perspective will be an incomplete exercise. From the perspective of the child protection system, all the systems that deal with children are highly enmeshed and must work in concert to achieve effective results (Wulczyn et al., 2010). Figure 2.4 depicts the interplay among the actors, contexts, and components of child protection systems as described by Wulczyn et al. (2010).

Child Protective Services Program Design

Overview

Child Protective Services (CPS) agencies are charged with investigating or assessing reports of maltreatment and intervening to protect children from further maltreatment. Safety and risk assessment are central to decision making regarding what actions should be taken to protect children from maltreatment. They are the "gateways" of CPS practice upon which most important decisions are predicated. Thus, effective safety and risk assessments depend on the ability of CPS professionals to obtain accurate and timely factual information, as well as processes that promote critical analysis of that available information.

In the area of child protective services, many states and counties are refining how they approach safety and risk assessment to make the process more transparent, more comprehensive, *and* more child/family-centered. Despite a steady set of setbacks due to leadership turnover, child deaths, and swings in funding availability (among other factors), in some communities there is evidence that clinical decision making can be improved, unnecessary foster care placements are being reduced, and children are achieving legal permanence without large increases in child maltreatment recurrence rates or foster care re-entry (e.g., Casey Family Programs, 2013; Ellis et al., 2013; Marts et al., 2008; McCroskey et al., 2010). This section highlights just a few of the many key program design areas for CPS.

Fortunately, knowledge about what works in child protection has increased over time, in part because of research related to risk factors and characteristics of families whose children have died due to maltreatment or suffered non-accidentally inflicted severe head injuries (Berger, Fromkin, & Stutz, 2011). For example, it is well understood that babies and other very young children are at highly elevated risk of a maltreatment-related fatality: in 2015 over three-quarters (78.4%) of all child maltreatment fatalities were children younger than 3 years old (U.S. DHHS, 2018, p. 53). Nevertheless, our understanding of the causal processes resulting in serious injuries or death related to maltreatment is incomplete.

As an expert in the field once stated, "working in child protection is not rocket science, it is harder." Three types of problems have been identified: (1) simple problems, (2) complicated problems, and (3) complex problems. Sending a rocket to the moon is considered to be only a "complicated problem" because once the steps necessary to send a rocket to the moon are specified, the steps can be replicated with precision (Gawande, 2009). Decisions about complex problems are characterized by ambiguity, inconsistent goals, complexity of decisions and systems, severe time constraints, and inherent unpredictability (Dörner & Wearing, 1995; Funke, 1991).

While there are situations in child protection where routine processes have been well established, there are many aspects of CPS where precise replication is difficult. For instance, safety and risk assessment tools generally contain discrete factors, yet it is the interactions of these factors, such as parent–child interactions or the interactions of risk and safety factors from disparate domains, that are likely to figure in the causal processes leading to lethal assaults of young children. Hence, there are limits to the ability of professionals, no matter how competent, to assess the safety of a child or to predict the likelihood of future maltreatment. At best, decision making is subject to errors related to "false negatives" (risk or safety threat is thought not to be present but children are maltreated) and "false positives" (risk or safety threat is identified but children are not maltreated). Supporting a family to safely remain together or deciding to remove a child from a family are critical decisions, are subject to these types of errors, and can potentially have life-and-death consequences.

CPS systems have increasingly adopted assessment tools to improve safety and risk decision making in child protection cases. This next section highlights the most current models used in child protection to assess safety and risk, and discusses implications of these approaches for predicting or estimating the likelihood of severe and fatal child maltreatment.

Major Safety and Risk Approaches

The issues of safety and risk assessment are central to effective CW practice and yet the field continues to struggle in this area (Pecora, Chahine, & Graham, 2013). For a review of how difficult a challenge this is, see Munro (2010) and Turnell, Murphy, and Munro, (2013). There are several approaches to safety and risk assessment that are being used currently in CW in the United States. There are consensus-based safety assessment tools such as those developed by Action for Child Protection (ACTION for Child Protection, n.d.) and individual states, and there are evidence-based risk assessment tools such as those in the Structured Decision Making® (SDM) system developed by the Children's Research Center

(Children's Research Center, 1999; Wagner & Bogie, 2010). More recently, an approach called Signs of Safety® (SofS) has been implemented in several states (Turnell & Murphy, 2017) and other countries; it also has a well-defined approach to mapping harm, danger, and complicating factors.

Each of the three methods summarized uses slightly different conceptualizations of important concepts related to danger, safety, risk, need, and complicating factors. In any given jurisdiction, clarity about these terms and implications for decision making is vital. Unfortunately, there is not as yet universal agreement on these terms or concepts. The intent of this section is *not* to compare and contrast the three approaches, nor to argue for the use of one approach over the others. All of these approaches are designed to help identify immediate safety threats, estimate the risk of child maltreatment, and safeguard child safety across a broad range of situations.

The ACTION for Child Protection SAFE Model. The ACTION for Child Protection SAFE model is a decision-making support tool, which structures the assessment of danger threats, child vulnerability and caregiver protective capacities to arrive at a decision about whether a child is safe or unsafe. A unique feature of the ACTION framework is the clear distinction between *"Present danger"* (present danger is an immediate, significant, and clearly observable threat to a child occurring in the present), and *"Impending danger"* (impending danger refers to threatening family conditions that are not obvious or active or occurring in your presence but are out of control and likely to have a severe effect on a child in the near future). This distinction provides a clear focus for the decision maker at first contact with the family (*is the child unsafe right now and does something have to be done before the caseworker leaves the home?*), and also provides guidance as the caseworker proceeds through her investigation and learns more about the daily life of the family, which may also reveal current safety threats or emotional and physical harm which has already occurred.

Addressing safety threats is a key concern, which requires the caseworker to develop a plan to control the behaviors and conditions which are often seen in child fatality and near-fatality cases, such as violent behavior, incapacitating substance abuse, extreme environmental hazards, and serious mental health conditions. The SAFE model is focused strictly on safety assessment, safety management, and enhancing the caregiver protective capacity that results in improved child safety. This safety-focused intervention approach may be embraced by agencies which want to prioritize or serve only families in which children are currently assessed as unsafe. The safety focus is maintained through the life of the case so that all key decisions are safety-based: screening, response time, case opening, removal, visitation, reunification, and case closure (ACTION for Child Protection, n.d.). This approach facilitates thorough collection of information through the establishment of specific information collection standards in six domains: child maltreatment; surrounding circumstances of the maltreatment; child functioning; general parenting; parenting discipline; and adult functioning (personal communication, Theresa Costello, January 10, 2013).

Structured Decision Making (SDM). The Structured Decision Making (SDM) system is a decision support system that provides standardized and tailored assessments for key decision points in the life of a case. It is designed to help guide these key decisions, and uses assessments designed to help increase the consistency and accuracy of decisions. A distinguishing feature of the SDM system is the amount of research and evaluation data available about these tools. The SDM risk assessment is created through an actuarial research method. Other SDM assessments begin as consensus-based tools or a combination of actuarial and consensus-based tools, and then an evaluation is conducted to test and improve their reliability and validity. Importantly, an organization that uses the SDM system is directing its scarce resources toward the highest risk families, and those families where there is current danger.

While the SDM system is designed to reduce the recurrence of any future abuse or neglect by targeting the highest risk families for services, there are several ways that the system can be expected to reduce severe incidents. These include: (1) response priority assessment when children are most likely to be unsafe, (2) clarity about the threshold for danger, (3) use of a checklist to assure that dangers not mentioned in the CPS referral are identified and assessed, (4) identification of children who have a substantially higher probability of future maltreatment and when the family can continue safely on their own, and (5) reunification assessment.

Of course, no set of assessment tools can keep children safe merely by use of checklists or ratings. The SDM system is designed to be used in the context of strong social work practices, including relationship building, good interviewing skills, participatory assessment, and planning with parents. The results of each SDM assessment tool should be reviewed using professional judgment and consideration of a family's readiness to participate in specific services. Assessment tools are not a substitute for caseworker knowledge in areas such as trauma, mental health, substance abuse, child development, and building on family strengths. Assessments alone will not keep a child safe. However, having reliable, valid, and equitable assessments to inform professional judgment is prudent practice (Children's Research Center, 1999; personal communication, Raelene Freitag, January 25, 2013).

Signs of Safety®. One of the more recent efforts to improve CW practice with families is Signs of Safety®, a strengths-based, safety-focused approach to CPS. The approach was created by Andrew Turnell, social worker and family therapist, and Steve Edwards, Child

Protection practitioner, in partnership with 150 Child Protection caseworkers in Western Australia during the 1990s. The approach has evolved over time based on the experiences and feedback of Child Protection practitioners. It is currently being implemented in at least 32 jurisdictions in 11 countries around the world (Turnell & Murphy, 2017, www. signsofsafety.net).

Signs of Safety® draws upon brief solution-based casework, and was designed to give CPS practitioners a framework for engaging all persons involved in a CPS case, including professionals, family members, and children. The primary goal for Signs of Safety® is the safety of children, which is viewed as a continuum that can be scaled. Turnell identifies three core principles of the Signs of Safety® approach (Western Australian Department for Child Protection, 2011):

1. Establishing constructive working relationships between professionals and family members, and between professionals themselves.
2. Engaging in critical thinking and maintaining a position of inquiry.
3. Staying grounded in the everyday work of CPS practitioners.

Signs of Safety® uses an assessment framework that involves "mapping" four components with families: (1) harm, danger and complicating factors, or worries; (2) existing strengths and safety factors; (3) agency and family goals for regarding future child safety, and (4) a safety judgment. Practitioners complete the map with the family so that it is understandable to them. It is a way to help both practitioners and family members think through a situation involving risk of child maltreatment, and to guide the case from beginning to end. Signs of Safety® also offers concrete tools and strategies for engaging children in the risk assessment and safety planning process. Signs of Safety® is a guided professional judgment approach to risk and safety based on caseworker/family interactions, in contrast to an actuarial model that assesses the presence or absence of specific risk factors. Some states and counties utilize a combination of Signs of Safety® and SDM.

Predictive Risk Modeling Using Administrative Data

The use of administrative data collected on individuals in CW and other service fields to inform decision making and improve outcomes has grown substantially (e.g., Cuccaro-Alamina et al., 2017). Such data can be linked within and across systems for predicting future events, which is often referred to as Predictive Risk Modeling (PRM). Although the methods and understanding continue to evolve, predictive analytics may usefully be defined as *"the practice of extracting information from data sets to determine patterns and predict outcomes and trends"* (adapted from www.webopedia.com/TERM/P/predictive_analytics.html). PRM is a form of predictive analytics that focuses on risk of a particular outcome (e.g., risk of re-abuse, risk of re-entering care). Effective PRM requires: (1) a sufficient sample size; (2) comprehensive and timely administrative data on risk factors; (3) risk scores that can be easily generated, and (4) risk scores that can be predicted with sufficient accuracy, and ethical and transparent use of the data (Roberts, O'Brien, & Pecora, 2018; Vaithianathan et al., 2012, 2013) (see Figure 2.5).

PRM is a tool which takes information from many cases to identify patterns in the data that could not otherwise be observed. It is a tool to support clinical judgment that can help make sense of how all the information collected on a population of youth may be used to better serve individual youth. Thus, PRM is intended to be an efficient process which identifies cases that have factors indicating elevated risk in in a timely manner. Ground-breaking work in applying PRM in CW has been done by researchers in Allegany County, California, Florida, New Zealand, and Texas (e.g., Daley et al., 2017). For example, research undertaken in New Zealand demonstrates that administrative data from a linked

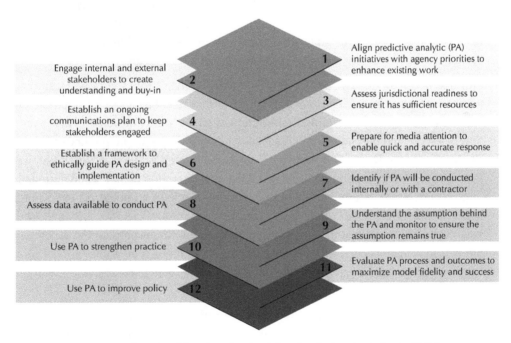

Figure 2.5 Twelve Considerations for Applying Predictive Analytics in Childcare
Source: Roberts, O'Brien, & Pecora (2018). Reprinted with permission.

set of public benefit, health, CPS, and justice records can be used to make reasonably accurate predictions about which children will have contact with CPS and subsequently be found to be victims of substantiated maltreatment (Vaithianathan et al., 2012, 2013).

In California, linked birth and child maltreatment records have been shown to be useful in stratifying children in a birth cohort based on the likelihood of being reported for maltreatment before the age of 5 (Putnam-Hornstein, Needell, & Rhodes, 2013). In addition, analysis from Missouri suggests that the accuracy of PRM is improved by including administrative data from multiple sources (e.g., benefits) as opposed to only CPS data (personal communication, John Fluke).

Typical characteristics of predictive analytics include the following (from O'Brien, 2015, p.4):

- *The use of a variety of statistical methods*. Many methods fall under the predictive analytics umbrella, including those typically taught in graduate statistics classes (regression, hierarchical linear modeling) and some that require more advanced programming (machine learning, which is a type of artificial intelligence (AI) that provides computers with the ability to learn without being explicitly programmed). Some predictive analytic projects employ algorithms, which is following a set of procedures to solve a problem. Understandably, there is significant complexity involved when a computer algorithm is created to solve a problem related to children in care, such as: "What are the characteristics of youth who age out of foster care?"

- *Multiple predictors of an outcome(s)*. Predictive analytics looks at how a combination of predictors impacts an outcome alone and in relationship to other predictors. When the prediction involves analysis of more than one outcome variable at the same time, then it is multivariate in nature. The key here is that multiple predictors have to be involved; otherwise results reflect a correlation, which is the association between two variables. A correlation does not provide any information on the relative strengths of predictors when examining their combined influence on an outcome. We want to know which variables are more important for predicting a specific outcome. Child welfare has made great strides over the past decade in understanding the youth who are served, what services they receive, and the outcomes they achieve. Less progress has been made in examining the influence of variables in combination with one another and from multiple data sources.

- *Opportunities to integrate data from multiple sources for greater depth and understanding*. Combining information from several data sources creates deeper knowledge to support critical decisions in a timely manner. Thus, data integration, for example, could assist child welfare in further describing and understanding youth in the context of the broader population of youth in a community by linking sources from mental health, pediatrics, juvenile justice, and other systems. Integration not only alleviates the burden of duplicating data- gathering efforts, but can also enable the extraction of information that it would otherwise be impossible to obtain (Subrahmanian, et al., 1996).

- **Re-branding of existing methods**. Many of the methods used are not new. Re-branding has helped make predictive analytics a buzzword and has provided an opportunity for statistical software companies to take advantage of the excitement around this buzz. Predictive analytics does not replace, but rather requires, substantive expertise to produce meaningful results and a strategic course of action. Thus, the most appropriate and desired practice would be for a statistical software company to team with child welfare experts in order to create and test a predictive model aimed at improving child outcomes.

Policy and Program Design Challenges in Child Protective Services

Clarifying the Mission of CPS

An agency mission that places priority on a family-centered approach is also being promoted because of the "ideological fit" of such an agency mission with the standards of the Federal Child and Family Services Review (see Chapter 1) and of allied agencies involved with children's mental health. Many CW agencies are also reconsidering the agency mission in order to respond to the requirements of the CFSR to deepen their community partnerships so that they can show that they are working with education, juvenile justice, mental health, and the courts to achieve services to promote child well-being (see Chapters 3 and 8).

As mentioned earlier in this chapter, definitions of what constitutes child maltreatment and how to respond are inconsistent across states. This includes improving the consistency of CPS reporting laws – ensuring that state laws regarding how to handle child maltreatment reports allow for agency discretion. While this process often requires changes in state law, it can improve the targeting of services and lower unreasonably high worker caseloads. These administrators may believe that CW staff should not act as public health enforcers, school attendance enforcement agents, or family therapists for local school systems in cases that do not very clearly involve child abuse or neglect. Other agencies are attempting to limit their child protection types of cases because of concern for abrogating parent rights and the need to try to allocate scarce resources to primary and secondary prevention programs rather than to the administrative costs of pursuing court-supervised interventions. Innovative program designs have been developed, along with a call for family-centered and outcome-oriented services (Testa & Poertner, 2010; Wulczyn, Orlebeke, & Haight, 2009). See Box 2.2.

Box 2.2   Inspiration from the Federal Commission to Prevent Child Fatalities

Imagine

Imagine a society[.]

[.]where children do not die from abuse or neglect.

[.] where children are valued, loved, and cared for first and foremost by their parents.

[.]where the safety and well-being of children are everyone's highest priority, and federal, state, and local agencies work collaboratively with families and communities to protect children from harm.

[.]where leaders of child protective services agencies do not stand alone but share with multiple partners a responsibility to keep children safe long before families reach a crisis.

Imagine a society[.]

[.]where research and integrated data are shared in real time in order to identify children most at risk for abuse or neglect fatalities and make informed and effective decisions about policies, practices, and resources.

[.]where state and local agencies charged with child safety have the resources, leaders, staff, funds, technology, effective strategies, and flexibility to support families when and how it is most helpful.

Imagine a society[.]

[.]where every child has a permanent and loving family, and young parents who grew up in foster care get the support they need to break the cycle of abuse and neglect.

[.]where all children are equally protected and their families equally supported, regardless of race, ethnicity, income, or where they live.

Imagine child welfare in the twenty-first century[.]

where children are safe and families are strong and where prevention

of child abuse and neglect deaths is a reality.

What Will It Take to Get There?

Source: Commission to Eliminate Child Abuse and Neglect Fatalities. (2016, p. 2).

CPS Hotline Design and Staffing Needs Urgent Attention

We need to enable CPS hotline staff members to use well-designed safety and risk assessment strategies to screen cases properly. This is complicated by the fact that often these staff do not receive special training and compensation – and that one of the key functions of CPS is risk assessment and yet how risk and protective factors may operate is non-linear – despite the use of risk assessment tools where it is sometimes implied that adding up the risk factor scores is applying a valid *linear understanding* (Stevens & Cox, 2008).

Improving Safety Planning and Use of Safety Networks

CPS agencies are charged with assessing reports of child maltreatment and intervening to protect children from harm. A variety of options can be taken, including referring families to voluntary community services, providing judicially mandated in-home services, and placing children in out-of-home care. In order to meet the needs of their families, jurisdictions are turning to new strategies that utilize a less adversarial approach to increase family engagement by actively partnering with them in case planning and decision making. One of the tools that has been increasingly highlighted is a safety plan (ACTION for Child Protection, Inc., 2003; Bunn, 2013). As described in more detail in Chapter 3, the development of a safety plan often involves working in partnership with the family to create a safety network. Child protection workers help families identify and list all the potential adults – including relatives, friends, and other professionals – who work together to support the family and ensure the safety of their children (Rothe, Nelson-Dusek, & Skrypek, 2013).

The goal of safety plans and safety networks is to identify specific people and strategies that will help keep the children safe. An important but unanswered question in the field is the extent to which these safety networks endure and are useful beyond case closure. More and more jurisdictions worldwide are adopting this approach in their work with families in child protection, but little research has been devoted to this topic (Bunn, 2013; Rothe et al., 2013).

CPS Staff Retention

As will be discussed in more detail in Chapter 9, we need to retain CW and CPS staff because effective safety and risk assessments depend on the ability of CPS professionals to obtain accurate and timely factual information, as well as agency processes that promote critical analysis of that available information. Increased leadership attention to staffing, career ladders, and staff development is essential because the new practice models and evidence-based interventions require a more highly skilled workforce.

An Array of Community-based Services Is Essential

To be successful, CW programs need an adequate supply of the community-based services that are most needed by families at risk of child maltreatment such as behavioral health, domestic violence, home visiting, housing, parent coaching, and prenatal services. This involves improving collaboration among the police, judges, and other community agencies, including having judges and law enforcement staff who understand the complexities of CPS practice and who prioritize family preservation as long as child safety can be maintained. For example, in 2016, the Keizer Police Department and Oregon Department of Human Services (DHS) embarked on a pilot project to place two child protective services (CPS) case managers at the Keizer police station. The program's successes are already changing the way DHS assigns case workers and smoothing relationships between public safety officers and case managers (see www.keizertimes.com/2017/08/16/closing-the-gaps/)

CPS Agency Leadership Continuity

CW organizations and CPS staff need consistent and enduring leaders. We need to improve continuity in agency policy and practice models as politically appointed leadership changes – as well as to better resist the knee-jerk reaction to terminate the CW agency leader just because a practice mistake has been made that resulted in the serious injury or death of a child. The child protection agency has an important role to play as part of a broader network of a CW system. However, it must move beyond the crisis responses to tragic events which include firing employees, writing new policies, or retraining staff. These reactions can often distract or derail careful planning and implementation

Causes and Consequences	Services in Complex Systems and Policy
• Improve understanding of the separate and synergistic consequences of different forms of child abuse and neglect. • Initiate high-quality longitudinal studies of child abuse and neglect. • Target innovative research on the causes of child abuse and neglect. • Improve understanding of the behavioral and neurobiological mechanisms that mediate the association between child abuse and neglect and its sequelae.	• Explore highly effective delivery systems. • Develop and test new programs for underserved children and families. • Identify the best means of replicating effective interventions and services with fidelity. • Identify the most effective ways to implement and sustain evidence-based programs in real-world settings. • Investigate the longitudinal impacts of prevention. • Encourage research designed to provide a better understanding of trends in the incidence of child abuse and neglect. • Evaluate the impact of laws and policies that address prevention and intervention systems and services for child abuse and neglect at the federal, state, and local levels.

Disentangle the role of cultural processes, social stratification influences, ecological variations, and immigrant/acculturation status.

Apply multidisciplinary, multimethod, and multisector approaches.

Leverage and build upon the existing knowledge base of child abuse and neglect research and related fields, as well as research definitions, designs, and opportunities.

Figure 2.6 Research Priorities in Child Abuse and Neglect

Source: IOM (Institute of Medicine) and NRC (National Research Council) (2014, pp. 264–265) (www.nap.edu/catalog/18331/new-directions-in-child-abuse-and-neglect-research). Reprinted with permission.

of reforms, as well as intimidate staff to place more children if the crises are not handled well by agency leaders (Turnell, Murphy, & Munro, 2013). These approaches have poor results when it comes to making systems safer.

Additional Research Is Needed

As shown in Figure 2.6, in 2014 a national scientific panel outlined a set of key research priorities for child abuse and neglect.

Conclusions

Most protective services should be supported to build "upstream" networks of collaboration and services because CW alone cannot keep children safe. Strong communities can lead to strong families which then produce healthy children. Keeping children safe requires a community-wide multi-systems approach (e.g., compassionate schools, housing, public assistance, public health, and other partners), and yet we continue to struggle with how to build public will and community capacity (Commission to Eliminate Child Abuse and Neglect Fatalities, 2016; Pecora et al., 2013). CW and community advocacy organizations can be excellent allies and sources of new ideas if communication is clear and flows both ways. Legislators and legislative policy research centers can provide objective analyses to help inform and drive change (see the Washington Institute of Public Policy for examples of insightful reports at www.wsipp.wa.gov/)

The field of child protection must evolve from outdated models of safety commonly used today. The use of predictive analytics and safety science in other fields, such as aviation and healthcare, has transformed these systems and led to improved outcomes. Models of safety have progressed and become more systemic in nature (Oster, Strong, & Zorn, 2013; Wachter, 2010). In contrast, relatively few strategies have been developed and evaluated to prevent child fatalities and severe child injuries related to child maltreatment – especially for children who at least initially are thought to be low risk and are diverted from the CW system. This occurs despite the very recent data that shows that children under the age of 5 (and especially aged 3 or under) are at much higher risk of severe injury due to child maltreatment, and thus reports regarding these children need to be handled differently. Fortunately, there are efforts underway to help reduce infant mortalities and child injuries across a range of sectors. See, for example, Alabama's use of "baby boxes" to promote infant safe sleeping, as well as Delaware's and Michigan's efforts to reduce infant mortality rates (http://dhss.delaware.gov/dph/files/infantmortalityreport.

pdf and www.michigan.gov/infantmortality/0,5312,7-306-64191-296542–,00.html). And the field of "injury control" in public health (formerly known as accident prevention) has been making key strides in a variety of areas, including the use of bicycle helmets, infant car seats, and baby boxes for safe sleeping (e.g., Rivara & Grossman, in press). Chapter 3 will outline policy and program design approaches for strengthening families to better protect children.

Discussion Questions

1. What would you do to improve the effectiveness of CPS?

2. What inconsistencies in state law regarding child maltreatment reporting most urgently need to be addressed?

3. What policy gaps, if addressed, would most increase CPS program effectiveness?

For Further Information

Hurley, D. (2018). Can an algorithm tell when kids are in danger? *New York Times*, January 2. Retrieved from www.nytimes.com/2018/01/02/magazine/can-an-algorithm-tell-when-kids-are-in-danger.html?smprod=nytcore-iphone&smid=nytcore-iphone-share. A very balanced and insightful story about using predictive analytics in child welfare.

Putnam-Hornstein, E., Needell, B., & Rhodes, A. E. (2013). Understanding risk and protective factors for child maltreatment: The value of integrated, population-based data. *Child Abuse & Neglect, 37*(2–3), 930–936. An insightful research study based on a broad array of data.

Turnell, A., Murphy, T., & Munro, E. (2013). Soft is hardest: Leading for learning in child protection services following a child fatality. *Child Welfare, 92*(2), 199–216. The importance of establishing a learning culture in child protection and for leaders to support workers in a time of crisis.

Bibliography

ACTION for Child Protection, Inc. (2003). *The safety plan*. Aurora, CO: Author. Retrieved from http://actionchildprotection.org/documents/2003/pdf/Dec2003TheSafetyPlan.pdf.

ACTION for Child Protection. (n.d.) *The CPS safety intervention system*. Retrieved from www.actionchildprotection.org/the-cps-safety-intervention-system/the-cps-safety-intervention-system/ (accessed February 15, 2013).

American Professional Society on the Abuse of Children. (1995). *Psychosocial evaluation of suspected psychological maltreatment in children and adolescents*. Chicago, IL: Author.

American Psychological Association Task Force on Resilience and Strength in Black Children and Adolescents. (2008). *Resilience in African American children and adolescents: A vision for optimal development*. Washington, DC: Author. Retrieved from www.apa.org/pi/families/resources/resiliencerpt.pdf.

Barnett, D., Manly, J.T., & Cicchetti, D. (1993). Defining child maltreatment: The interface between policy and research. In D. Cicchetti, & S. L. Toth (Eds), *Child abuse, child development, and social policy* (pp. 7–73). Norwood, NJ: Ablex Publishing Corporation.

Baumann, D.J., Fluke, J., Dalgleisch, L., & Kern, H. (2014). The decision-making ecology. In *From Evidence to Outcomes in Child Welfare: An International Reader* (pp. 24–40). New York: Oxford University Press.

Beck, U. (1992) *Risk society: Toward a new modernity*. London: Sage.

Ben-David, V., Jonson-Reid, M., Drake, B., & Kohl, P.L. (2015). The association between childhood maltreatment experiences and the onset of maltreatment perpetration in young adulthood controlling for proximal and distal risk factors. *Child Abuse & Neglect, 46*, 132–141. doi:10.1016/j.chiabu.2015.01.013.

Berger, R.P., Fromkin, J., Herman, B., Pierce, M.C., Saladino, R.A., Flom, L., Tyler-Kabara, E.C., McGinn, T., Richichi, R., & Kochaneck, P.M. (2016). Vlidation of the Pittsburgh Infant Brain Injury Score for abusive head trauma. *Pediatrics, 138*(1), pii. doi:10.1542/peds.2015-3756.

Berger, R.P., Fromkin, J.B., Stutz, H., Makoroff, M., & Scribano, P.V. (2011). Abusive head trauma during a time of increased unemployment: A multicenter analysis. *Pediatrics, 128*, 637–643.

Berrick, J.D., Needell, B., Barth, R.B., & Jonson-Reid, M. (1998*). The tender years: Toward developmentally sensitive child welfare services for very young children*. New York: Oxford University Press.

Bornstein, D. (2016). Putting the power of self-knowledge to work. *New York Times*, Article series on August 10, 17, and 23, 2016. Retrieved from www.nytimes.com/2016/08/23/opinion/putting-the-power-of-self-knowledge-to-work.html?rref=collection%2Fcolumn%2Ffixes&action=click&contentCollection=opinion&region=stream&module=stream_unit&version=latest&contentPlacement=1&pgtype=collection.

Brassard, M.R., & Hart, S. (2000). What is psychological maltreatment? In Dubowitz, H. & DePanfilis, D. (Eds), *Handbook for child protection practice* (pp. 23–27). Thousand Oaks, CA: Sage.

Briere, J., & Scott, C. (2006). *Principles of trauma therapy: A guide to symptoms, evaluation, and treatment*. Newbury Park, CA: Sage.

Bronfenbrenner, U. (1979). *The ecology of human development*. Cambridge, MA: Harvard University Press.

Brooks-Gunn, J., & Duncan, G.J. (1997). The effects of poverty on children. *The Future of Children, 7*(2), 55–71.

Brooks-Gunn, J., Klebanov, P.K., & Liaw, F. (1995). The learning, physical, and emotional environment of the home in the context of poverty: The Infant Health and Development program. *Children and Youth Services Review, 17*, 251–276.

Bunn, A. (2013). *Signs of Safety® in England.* London: National Society for the Prevention of Cruelty to Children. Retrieved from www.nspcc.org.uk/services-and-resources/research-and-resources/signs-of-safety-model-england/ (accessed July 3, 2015).

Casey Family Programs. (2013). *Traditions renewed: The Mill Lacs Band of Ojibwe improves Its Indian Child Welfare Programs by incorporating tribal family values.* Seattle, WA: Author. Available at: www.casey.org/Resources/Publications/MilleLacs.htm.

Chahine, Z., Pecora, P.J., Sanders, D., & Wilson, D. (Eds) (2013). Preventing severe maltreatment-related injuries and fatalities: Applying a public health framework and innovative approaches to child protection. *Child Welfare, 92*(2), 1–253.

Chen, L.P., Murad, M.H., Paras, M.L., Colbenson, K.M., Sattler, A L., Goranson, E.N., Elamin, M B., Seime, R.J., Shinozaki, G., Prokop, L.J., & Zirakzadeh, A. (2010). Sexual abuse and lifetime diagnosis of psychiatric disorders: Systematic review and meta-analysis. *Mayo Clinic Proceedings, 85*(7), 618–629.

Child Welfare Information Gateway. (2016a). *Definitions of child abuse and neglect.* Retrieved from www.childwelfare.gov/topics/systemwide/laws-policies/statutes/define/ (accessed September 26, 2017).

Child Welfare Information Gateway. (2016b). *Mandatory reporters of child abuse and neglect.* Washington, DC: U.S. Department of Health and Human Services, Children's Bureau, Child Welfare Information Gateway. Retrieved from www.childwelfare.gov/emailBtn/?emailsent=yep&redirectURLvar=https://www.childwelfare.gov/topics/systemwide/laws-policies/statutes/manda/&isHuman=1.

Children's Research Center. (1999). *The improvement of child protective services with Structured Decision Making: The CRC Model.* Madison, WI: Author.

Cohen, J.A., Mannarino, A.P., Zhitova, A.C., & Capone, M.E. (2003). Treating child abuse-related posttraumatic stress and comorbid substance abuse in adolescents. *Child Abuse & Neglect, 27* (2003), 1345–1365.

Commission to Eliminate Child Abuse and Neglect Fatalities. (2016). *Within our reach: A national strategy to eliminate child abuse and neglect fatalities.* Washington, DC: Government Printing Office. Retrieved from www.acf.hhs.gov/programs/cb/resource/cecanf-final-report.

Crary, J. (2009). *The spirit level: Why more equal societies almost always do better* by Richard Wilkinson and Kate Pickett [Book review]. *London Sunday Times*, March 9. Retrieved from http://entertainment.timesonline.co.uk/tol/arts_and_entertainment/books/non-fiction/article5859108.ece.

Cuccaro-Alamina, S. Foust, R., Vaithianathan, R., & Putnam-Hornstein, E. (2017). Risk assessment and decision making in child protective services: Predictive risk modeling in context. *Children and Youth Services Review, 79*, 291–298.

Daley, D., Bachmann, M., Bachmann, B., Pedigo, C., Bui, M., & Coffman, J. (2017). Risk terrain modeling predicts child maltreatment. *Child Abuse & Neglect, 62*, 29–38.

Dalla, R.L., Defrain, J., & Johnson, J.M. (Eds) (2009). *Strengths and challenges of new immigrant families: Implications for research, education, policy and service.* New York: Lexington Books.

DePanfilis, D. (2006). *Child neglect: A guide for prevention, assessment, and intervention.* Washington, DC: U.S. Department of Health and Human Services, Administration on Children and Families, Administration for Children, Youth, and Families, Children's Bureau, Office on Child Abuse and Neglect.

Derezotes, D., Poertner, J., & Testa, M. (Eds) (2005). *Race matters in child matters in child welfare: The overrepresentation of African American children in the system.* Washington, DC: Child Welfare League of America.

Development Services Group, Inc. (2013). *Protective factors for populations served by the Administration on Children, Youth, and Families. A literature review and theoretical framework: Executive summary.* Washington, DC: U.S. Department of Health and Human Services, Administration for Children and Families, Children's Bureau, p. 6. Retrieved from www.dsgonline.com/acyf/DSG%20Protective%20Factors%20Literature%20Review%20 2013%20Exec%20Summary.pdf.

Dörner, D., & Wearing, A. (1995). Complex problem solving: Toward a (computer-simulated) theory. In P.A. Frensch & J. Funke (Eds), *Complex problem solving: The European Perspective* (pp. 65–99). Hillsdale, NJ: Lawrence Erlbaum Associates.

Drake, B., Jolley, J.M., Lanier, P., Fluke, J., Barth, R.P., & Jonson-Reid, M. (2011). Racial bias in child protection? A comparison of competing explanations using national data. *Pediatrics, 127*(3), 471–478. doi:10.1542/peds.2010–1710. Retrieved from www.pediatrics.org (accessed April 25, 2013).

Dubowitz, H. (2000a). What is neglect? In H. Dubowitz & D. DePanfilis (Eds), *Handbook for child protection practice* (pp. 10–14). Thousand Oaks, CA: Sage.

Dubowitz, H. (2000b). What is physical abuse? In H. Dubowitz & D. DePanfilis (Eds), *Handbook for child protection practice* (pp. 15–17). Thousand Oaks, CA: Sage.

Dunn, E.C., McLaughlin, K.A., Slopen, N., Rosand, J., & Smoller, J.W. (2013). Developmental timing of child maltreatment and symptoms of depression and suicidal ideation in young adulthood: Results from the national longitudinal study of adolescent health. *Depression and Anxiety, 30*(10), 955–964.

Dunn, M., Tarter, R., Mezzich, A., Vanyukov, M., Kirisci, L. & Kirillova, G. (2002). Origins and consequences of child neglect in substance abuse families. *Clinical Psychology Review, 22*, 1063–1090.

Eamon, M., & Kopels, S. (2004). For reasons of poverty: Court challenges to child welfare practices and mandated programs. *Child and Youth Services Review, 26*, 821–836.

Edna McConnell Clark Foundation. (2004). *Theory of change behind the program for children.* New York: Author. Retrieved from www.emcf.org/programs/children/indepth/theory.htm.

Ellis, M.L., Eskenazi, S., Bonnell, R., & Pecora, P.J. (2013). *Taking a closer look at the reduction in entry rates for children in Sacramento County with an emphasis on African American children: A spotlight on practice.* Seattle, WA: Casey Family Programs.

Fang, X., Brown, D.S., Florence, C.S., & Mercy, J.A. (2012). The economic burden of child maltreatment in the United States and implications for prevention. *Child Abuse & Neglect, 36*(2), 156–165.

Fluke, J., Jones-Harden, B., Jenkins, M., & Ruehrdanz, A. (2011*). Research synthesis on child welfare disproportionality and disparities.* Denver, CO: American Humane Association and the Annie E. Casey Foundation. Retrieved from www.cssp.org/publications/child-welfare/alliance/Disparities-and-Disproportionality-in-Child-Welfare_An-Analysis-of-the-Research-December-2011.pdf.

Funke, J. (1991). Solving complex problems: Human identification and control of complex systems. In R.J. Sternberg & P.A. Frensch (Eds), *Complex problem solving: Principles and mechanisms* (pp. 185–222). Hillsdale, NJ: Lawrence Erlbaum Associates.

Garmezy, N. (1985). Stress resistant children: The search for protective factors. In J.E. Stevenson (Ed.), *Recent research in developmental psychopathology* (pp. 76–93). Oxford: Pergamon Press.

Gateway. (2016). *Mandatory reporters of child abuse and neglect.* Washington, DC: U.S. Department of Health and Human Services, Children's Bureau. Retrieved from www.childwelfare.gov/pubPDFs/manda.pdf.

Gaudin, J.M., Polanksy, N.A., Kilpatrick, A.C., & Shilton, P. (1996). Family functioning in neglectful families. *Child Abuse & Neglect, 20*, 363–377. doi:10.1016/0145-2134(96)00005-1.

Gawande, A. (2009). *The checklist manifesto: How to get things right.* New York: Metropolitan books (Division of Macmillan).

Giddens, A. (1994) *Beyond left and right: The future of radical politics.* Cambridge: Polity Press.

Glisson, C. (2007). Assessing and changing culture and climate for effective services. *Research on Social Work Practice, 17*(6), 736–747.

Glisson, C., & Hemmelgarn, A. (1998). The effects of organizational climate and interorganizational coordination on the quality and outcomes of children's service systems. *Child Abuse & Neglect, 22*(5), 401–421.

Goldman, J., & Salus, M.K. (2003). *A coordinated response to child abuse and neglect: The foundation for practice.* Washington, DC: U.S. Department of Health and Human Services, Administration on Children and Families, Administration for Children, Youth, and Families, Children's Bureau, Office on Child Abuse and Neglect.

Government of Western Australia, Department of Child Protection. (2011). *The Signs of Safety Child Protection Practice Framework.* Retrieved from www.dcp.wa.gov.au/Resources/Documents/Policies%20and%20Frameworks/SignsOfSafetyFramework2011.pdf.

Harrington, D., Zuravin, S.J., DePanfilis, D., Ting, L., & Dubowitz, H. (2002). The Neglect Scale: Confirmatory factor analysis in a low-income sample. *Child Maltreatment, 7*, 359–368.

Hearn, J. (2011). Unmet needs in addressing child neglect: Should we go back to the drawing board? *Children and Youth Services Review, 33*, 715–722.

Hines, A., Lemon, K., Wyatt, P., & Merdinger, J. (2004). Factors related to the disproportionate involvement of children of color in the child welfare system: A review and emerging themes. *Children and Youth Services Review*, 507–527.

Hodges, V. (1994). Assessing for strengths and protective factors in child abuse and neglect: Risk assessment with families of color. In P.J. Pecora & D.J. English (Eds), *Multi-cultural guidelines for assessing family strengths and risk factors in child protective services* (pp. II–1–11). Seattle, WA: University of Washington School of Social Work, and Washington State Department of Social Services.

Institute of Medicine and National Research Council. (2014). *New directions in child abuse and neglect research.* Washington, DC: The National Academies Press. Retrieved from www.nap.edu/catalog/18331/new-directions-in-child-abuse-and-neglect-research.

Jenny, C. (2007). Recognizing and responding to medical neglect. *Pediatrics, 120*, 1385–1389.

Kendall-Tackett, K. (2013). *Treating the lifetime health effects of childhood victimization* (2nd edn). Kingston, NJ: Civic Research Institute.

Kerman, B., Maluccio, A.N., & Freundlich, M. (Eds) (2008). *Achieving permanence for older children and youth in foster care.* New York: Columbia University Press.

Knutson, J., DeGarmo, D., Koeppl, G., & Reid, J. (2005). Care neglect, supervisory neglect, and harsh parenting in development of children's aggression: A replication and extension. *Child Maltreatment, 10*, 92–107.

Lee, S.J., Grogan-Kaylor, A., & Berger, L.M. (2014). Parental spanking of 1-year-old children and subsequent child protective services involvement. *Child Abuse & Neglect, 38*(5), 875–883. doi:10.1016/j.chiabu.2014.01.018.

Lindsey, D. (2004). *The welfare of children* (2nd edn). New York: Oxford University Press.

Lorthridge, J., McCroskey, J., Pecora, P.J., Chambers, R., & Fatemi, M. (2011). Strategies for improving child welfare services for families of color: First findings of a community-based initiative in Los Angeles. *Children and Youth Services Review, 34*, 281–288.

Magura, S., & Moses, B.S. (1986). *Outcome measures for child welfare services.* Washington, DC: Child Welfare League of America.

Maier, H.W. (1978). *Three theories of child development* (Third edn). New York: Harper and Row.

Marts, E.J., Lee, R., McCroy, R., & McCroskey, J. (2008). Point of engagement: Reducing disproportionality and improving child and family outcomes. *Child Welfare, 87*(2), 335–358.

McCroskey, J., Franke, T, Christie, T., Pecora, P.J., Lorthridge, J., Fleischer, D., & Rosenthal, E. (2010). *Prevention Initiative Demonstration Project (PIDP): Year two evaluation summary report.* Los Angeles, CA: LA County Department of Children and Family Services and Seattle, WA: Casey Family Programs. www.casey.org.

Mennen, F., Kim, K., Sang, J., & Trickett, P. (2010). Child neglect: Definition and identification of youth's experiences in official reports of maltreatment. *Child Abuse & Neglect, 34*, 647–658.

Meyer, A.F., Beyer, C., Miller, K., & Kelly, S. (2017). *Becoming a trauma informed agency: The Waupaca story.* Waupaca, WI: Department of Health and Human Services (DHHS).

Morgan, L.J., Spears, L.S., & Kaplan, C. (2003). *A framework for community action: Making children a national priority.* Washington, DC: Child Welfare League of America.

Morris, K., & Burford, G. (2016). Engaging families and managing risk in practice. In M. Connolly (Ed.), *Beyond the risk paradigm: Debates and new directions in child protection* (Ch. 7). Basingstoke: Palgrave-Macmillan.

Munro, E. (2010). *Munro review of child protection part one: A systems analysis.* London: Secretary of State, Department of Education. Product Reference: DFE-00548-2010. Retrieved from www.education.gov.uk.

Munro, E. (2011). *Munro review of child protection: Final report – a child-centred system.* Department of Education. Ref: ISBN 9780101806220, Cm 8062.

National Council of Juvenile and Family Court Judges. (1992). *Protocol for making reasonable efforts to preserve families in drug-related dependency cases.* Reno, NV: Author.

NCCAN. (1988). *Study findings: Study of national incidence and prevalence of child abuse and neglect – 1988* (p. 2.2). Washington, DC: U.S. Department of Health and Human Services.

Nunno, M.A., & Motz, J.K. (1988). The development of an effective response to the abuse of children in out-of-home care. *Child Abuse & Neglect, 12*, 521–528.

O'Brien, K. (2015). What is predictive analytics? *Casey Practice Digest*, January, Issue 7, pp. 4–6.

Oster, C., Strong, J., & Zorn, C. (2013). Analyzing aviation safety: Problems, challenges, opportunities. *Research in Transportation Economics, 43*, 148–164.

Pecora, P.J. (2018). *Risk and protective factors for child abuse and neglect: A resource paper.* New York: Taylor and Francis.

Pecora, P.J., & Chahine, Z. (2016). Catalysts for child protection reform. *CW360 – Child Welfare Reform*. A publication of the University of Minnesota, p. 11. Retrieved from http://cascw.umn.edu/wp-content/uploads/2016/05/CW360_Spring2016_WEB.pdf.

Pecora, P.J., Chahine, Z., & Graham, C. (2013). Safety and risk assessment frameworks: Overview and implications for child maltreatment fatalities. *Child Welfare, 92*(2), 139–156.

Pecora, P.J., Whittaker, J.K., Maluccio, A N., Barth, R.P., & DePanfilis, D. (2009). *The child welfare challenge* (3rd edn) (ch. 13). Piscataway, NJ: Aldine-Transaction Books.

Pew Foundation. (2008). *Life chances: The case for early investment in our kids.* Retrieved from www.pewtrusts.org/uploadedFiles/American_Prospect_1207_EarlyEdSpecialRep.

Polansky, N. A., Gaudin, J.M., Jr., & Kilpatrick, A.C. (1992). Family radicals. *Children and Youth Services Review, 14*, 19–26. doi:10.1016/0190–7409(92)90010-S.

Polansky, N. A., Chalmers, M.A., Buttenweiser, E., & Williams, D.P. (1981). *Damaged parents: An anatomy of child neglect.* Chicago, IL: University of Chicago Press.

Putnam-Hornstein, E. (2011). Report of maltreatment as a risk factor for injury death: A prospective birth cohort study. *Child Maltreatment, 16*, 163–174.

Putnam-Hornstein, E. (2012). Preventable injury deaths: A population-based proxy of child maltreatment risk in California. *Public Health Reports, 127*(2), 163–172.

Putnam-Hornstein, E., Needell, B., & Rhodes, A.E. (2013). Understanding risk and protective factors for child maltreatment: The value of integrated, population-based data. *Child Abuse & Neglect, 37*(2–3), 930–936.

Putnam-Hornstein, E., Cederbaum, J.A., King, B., Eastman, A.L., & Trickett, P.K. (2015). A population-level and longitudinal study of adolescent mothers and intergenerational maltreatment. *American Journal of Epidemiology, 181*, 496–503. doi:10.1093/aje/kwu321.

Rebbe, R. (2017). *What is neglect? A comparative analysis of state definitions in the U.S.* (unpublished paper). Seattle, WA: University of Washington, School of Social Work.

Ridge, T. (2009). *Living with poverty: A review of the literature on children's and families' experiences of poverty.* Department for Work and Pensions Research Report No. 594. London: Department for Work and Pensions.

Rivara, F.P., & Grossman, D.C. (2016). Injury control. In R.M. Kliegman, B.F. Stanton, J.W. St. Geme, N.F. Schor, & R.E. Behrman (Eds), *Nelson textbook of pediatrics* (pp. 5.1-41– 5.1-47). Philadelphia, PA: Elsevier Publishers.

Roberts, D. (2002). *Shattered bonds.* New York: Basic Civitas Books.

Roberts, D. (2003). Child welfare and civil rights. *University of Illinois Law Review*, 171–182.

Roberts, D. (2009). Keynote, "Why ending racial disparity will transform child welfare," 30th National Adoption Conference, Adoption Network, Cleveland, OH, April 23.

Roberts, Y.H., O'Brien, K., & Pecora, P.J. (2018). *Considerations for applying predictive analytics in child welfare.* Seattle, WA: Casey Family Programs.

Rodenborg, N. (2004). Services to African American children in poverty: Institutional discrimination in child welfare? *Journal of Poverty, 8*, 109–130.

Rothe, M.I., Nelson-Dusek, S., & Skrypek, M. (2013). *Innovations in child protection services in Minnesota: Research chronicle of Carver and Olmsted Counties.* St. Paul, MN: Wilder Research. Retrieved from: www.co.olmsted.mn.us/cs/cspublications/Documents/CFSPublications/WilderReportSignsOfSafety1-13.pdf.

Rutter, M. (1990). Psychosocial resilience and protective mechanisms. In J. Rolf (Ed.), *Risk and protective factors in the development of psychopathology* (pp. 42–73). New York: Cambridge University Press.

Sanders, D. (2017a). It's going to take all of us. Presentation for the Idaho Children's Trust Fund Annual Training Institute, Boise, March 21.

Sanders, D. (2017b). Policy and practice changes form around national strategy to reduce fatalities and improve child safety. *Chronicle of Social Change.* Retrieved from https://chronicleofsocialchange.org/opinion/policy-and-practice-changes-form-around-national-strategy-to-reduce-child-maltreatment-fatalities-and-improve-child-safety/25095.

Schnitzer, P.G., Gulino, S.P., & Yuan, Y.Y. (2013). Advancing public health surveillance to estimate child maltreatment fatalities: Review and recommendations, *Child Welfare, 92*, 77–98.

Schorr, E., & Marchand, V. (2007). *Pathway to prevention of child abuse and neglect.* California Department of Social Services, Children and Family Services Division Office of Child Abuse Prevention. The Pathways Mapping Initiative is also supported by the Annie E. Casey Foundation and the W.K. Kellogg Foundation. Retrieved from www.Pathways ToOutcomes.org.

Sedlak, A.J. (2001). *A history of the National Incidence Study of Child Abuse and Neglect.* Rockville, MD: Westat, Inc. Retrieved from www.nis4.org/NIS_History.pdf (accessed February 15, 2008).

Sedlak, A.J., Mettenburg, J., Basena, M., Petta, I., McPherson, K., Greene, A., and Li, S. (2010). *Fourth National Incidence Study of Child Abuse and Neglect (NIS–4): Report to Congress.* Washington, DC: U.S. Department of Health and Human Services, Administration for Children and Families. Retrieved from www.acf.hhs.gov/sites/default/files/opre/nis4_report_ congress_full_pdf_jan2010.pdf.

Shonkoff, J., & Phillips, D. (2000). *From neurons to neighborhoods: The science of early childhood development.* Washington, DC: National Research Council and Institute of Medicine.

Signs of Safety® (n.d.). *Signs of Safety.* Retrieved from www.signsofsafety.net/signs-of-safety/

Slack, K., Holl, J., McDaniel, M., Yoo, J., & Bolger, K. (2004). Understanding the risks of child neglect: An exploration of poverty and parenting characteristics. *Child Maltreatment, 9,* 395–408.

Stevens, I. & Cox, P. (2008). Complexity theory: Developing new understandings of child protection in field settings and in residential child care. *British Journal of Social Work, 38*(7), 1320–1336.

Stoltenborgh, M., Bakermans-Kranenburg, M., & van IJzendoorn, M. (2013). The neglect of child neglect: A meta-analytic review of the prevalence of neglect. *Social Psychiatry and Psychiatric Epidemiology, 48,* 345–355.

Straus, M.A., Kinard, E.M., & Williams, L.J. (1995). The Neglect Scale. Paper presented at the Fourth International Conference on Family Violence Research, Durham, NH, July 23.

Subrahmanian, V.S., Adali, S., Brink, A., Lu, J.J., Rajput, A., Rogers, T.J., Ross, R. & Ward, C. (1996). *HERMES: A Heterogeneous Reasoning and Mediator System.* Retrieved from www. cs.umd.edu/projects/hermes/overview/paper/section1.html.

Tanner, K., & Turney, D. (2003). What do we know about child neglect? A critical review of the literature and its application to social work practice. *Child & Family Social Work, 8,* 25–34.

Testa, M.F., & Poertner, J. (2010). *Fostering accountability: Using evidence to guide and improve child welfare policy.* Oxford and New York: Oxford University Press.

The Perryman Group. (2015). *Suffer the little children: An assessment of the economic cost of child maltreatment.* Retrieved from www.perrymangroup.com/wpcontent/uploads/Perry man_Child_Maltreatment_Report.pdf (accessed April 7, 2016).

Trocme, N. (1996). Development and preliminary evaluation of the Ontario Neglect Index. *Child Maltreatment, 1,* 145–155.

Turnell, A. (in press). *Building safety in child protection practice: Working with a strengths and solution-focus in an environment of risk*. New York: Palgrave-Macmillan.

Turnell, A., & Murphy, T. (2017). *Signs of Safety Comprehensive Briefing Paper*. Perth, Australia: Signs of Safety. Retrieved from www.signsofsafety.net/shop/.

Turnell, A, Murphy, T., & Munro, E. (2013). Soft Is hardest: Leading for learning in child protection services following a child fatality. *Child Welfare, 92*(2), 199–216.

U.S. Department of Health and Human Services, Administration for Children and Families. (2008). *Issue brief: Differential response to reports of child abuse and neglect*. Washington, DC: Child Information Gateway. Retrieved from www.childwelfare.gov/pubs/issue_briefs/differential_response/differential_response.pdf.

U.S. Department of Health and Human Services, Administration for Children and Families, Administration on Children, Youth and Families, Children's Bureau. (2013). *Child Welfare Outcomes 2010–2013 – Report to Congress*. Washington, DC: Author. Retrieved from www.acf.hhs.gov/programs/cb/resource/cwo-10-13.

U.S. Department of Health and Human Services, Administration for Children and Families, Children's Bureau. (2015). *Child maltreatment 2013*. Retrieved from www.acf.hhs.gov/programs/cb/research-data-technology/statistics-research/child-maltreatment.

U.S. Department of Health and Human Services, Administration for Children and Families, Administration on Children, Youth and Families, Children's Bureau. (2016). *Child maltreatment 2014*. Retrieved from www.acf.hhs.gov/programs/cb/research-data-technology/statistics-research/child-maltreatment.

U.S. Department of Health and Human Services, Administration for Children and Families, Administration on Children, Youth and Families, Children's Bureau. (2017). *Child maltreatment 2015*. Washington, DC: Author.

U.S. Department of Health and Human Services, Administration for Children and Families, Administration on Children, Youth and Families, Children's Bureau. (2018). *Child maltreatment 2016*. Retrieved from www.acf.hhs.gov/cb/research-data-technology/statistics-research/child-maltreatment.

U.S. Department of Health and Human Services, National Center on Child Abuse and Neglect. (1996). *Study findings: Study of national incidence and prevalence of child abuse and neglect (NIS-3)*. Washington, DC: Author.

Uliando, A., & Mellor, D. (2012). Maltreatment of children in out-of-home care: A review of associated factors and outcomes. *Children and Youth Services Review, 34*, 2280–2286.

United States Government Accountability Office. (2011). *Child maltreatment: Strengthening national data on child fatalities could aid in prevention* (Report No. GAO-11-599). Washington, DC: Author.

Urban Institute. (2013). Addressing deep and persistent poverty. A framework for philanthropic planning and investment. Washington, DC: Author. Retrieved from www.urban.org/UploadedPDF/412983-addressing-deep-poverty.pdf.

Vaithianathan, R., Maloney, T., Putnam-Hornstein, E., & Jiang, N. (2013). Children in the public benefit system at risk of maltreatment: Identification via predictive modeling. *American Journal of Preventive Medicine, 45*(3), 354–359.

Vaithianathan, R., Maloney, T., Jiang, N., De Haan, I., Dale, C., & Putnam-Hornstein, E. (2012). *Vulnerable children: Can administrative data be used to identify children at risk of adverse outcomes?* Report Prepared for the Ministry of Social Development. Auckland: Centre for Applied Research in Economics (CARE), Department of Economics, University of Auckland.

Vesneski, W. (2011). State law and the termination of parental rights. *Family Court Review, 49,* 364–378.

Wachter, R. (2010). Patient safety at ten: Unmistakable progress, troubling gaps. *Health Affairs, 29*(1), 165–173.

Wagner, D., & Bogie, A. (2010*). California Department of Social Services validation of the SDM® reunification reassessment.* Retrieved from www.nccdglobal.org/sites/default/files/publication_pdf/crr_validation_report.pdf (accessed May 11, 2013).

Werner, E.E. (1989). High-risk children in young adulthood: A longitudinal study from birth to 32 years. *American Journal of Orthopsychiatry, 59,* 72–81.

Western Australian Department for Child Protection. (2011). *The Signs of Safety Child Protection Practice Framework.* Perth: Department for Child Protection.

Whittaker, J.K., & Maluccio, A.N. (2002). Rethinking "child welfare": A reflective essay. *Social Service Review, 76,* 107–134. doi:10.1086/324610.

Wildeman, C., Emanuel, N., Leventhal, J., Putnam-Hornstein, E., Waldfogel, J., & Lee, H. (2014). The prevalence of confirmed maltreatment among American children, 2004–2011. *JAMA Pediatrics, 168*(8), 706–713 [PMID: 24887073].

Wilkinson, R., & Pickett, K. (2009). *The spirit level: Why more equal societies almost always do better.* London: Allen Lane.

Wulczyn, F.H., Orlebeke, B., & Haight, J. (2009). *Finding the return on investment: A framework for monitoring local child welfare agencies.* Chicago, IL: Chapin Hall at the University of Chicago. Retrieved from www.chapinhall.org/sites/default/files/Finding_Return_On_Investment_07_20_09.pdf.

Wulczyn, F., Daro, D., Fluke, J., Feldman, S., Glodek, C., & Lifanda, K. (2010). *Adapting a systems approach to child protection: Key concepts and considerations.* New York: United Nations Children's Fund.

Zuravin, S., & DePanfilis, D. (1996). *Child maltreatment recurrences among families served by Child Protective Services.* Final report to the National Center on Child Abuse and Neglect [Grant #90CA1497].

3 | Protecting Children from Child Abuse and Neglect by Strengthening Families and Communities

Learning Objectives

1. Understand the value of conceptual frameworks and principles from the Centers of Disease Control, the Center for the Study of Social Policy, and the Harvard Center on the Developing Child.

2. Review issues and strategies for preventing child fatalities and severe injuries.

3. Explore child maltreatment prevention strategies such as Differential Response, Family-based services, Family Connections, Family Group Conferencing, Family Finding, Family Preservation Services, Home visiting, and safety networks.

4. Understand the many policy challenges and areas for innovation.

Introduction

While there are many innovations underway in child welfare, fundamental reforms are needed, especially in child protective services and related services. Child welfare (CW) should make fundamental design changes to enable it to marshal greater public will and community resources to improve child safety, permanency, and well-being. However, substantial improvements can be made now to keep more children safe from child maltreatment. In fact, some jurisdictions are considering radical changes to the design of their child welfare and related systems. Against this backdrop, this chapter will present strategies for keeping children safe from maltreatment.

Chapter 2 described the scope of the problem in terms of overall child maltreatment, child fatalities, and the cost to children and society. Strategies to address poverty and its association with child maltreatment are addressed in Chapter 4. With that foundation, this chapter will address the following topics:

1. Outline research-based theoretical and conceptual frameworks for understanding and preventing child maltreatment.

2. Present research-informed and evidence-based strategies for preventing child fatalities and severe injuries due to child abuse and neglect.

3. Highlight strategies for preventing other forms of child abuse and neglect.

4. Discuss policy and program design issues and challenges, including gaps in research and policy.

Research-based Theoretical and Conceptual Frameworks

Context

Theoretical and other conceptual frameworks help us understand the contributing factors, protective factors, complexities, and strategies for preventing child abuse and neglect. For example, Urie Bronfenbrenner's landmark work on the social ecology of child development showcased how forces at micro, mezzo and macro levels (including child maltreatment) affect child development (Bronfenbrenner, 1979; Bronfenbrenner & Morris, 1998). Risk and protective factors associated with various types of child abuse and neglect are described in resource papers for the textbook (Pecora, 2018b). Human ecology, social justice, and social diversity perspectives underscore the vital roles that broad community networks and environments play in services and healing. A major Institute of Medicine report described a growing array of evidence-based programs for preventing emotional, behavioral, and substance abuse disorders in children and young adults (O'Connell et al., 2009). Beyond being protected from physical harm, safety for children requires that they are provided with care that meets their physical and emotional health and well-being, and that they receive age-appropriate support for their development (de Haan & Manion, 2011). But in many respects, as some of the child maltreatment theoretical frameworks from Belsky (1980) and Cicchetti (1994) have emphasized, child safety begins with healthy parent functioning.

The Centers for Disease Control Frameworks

Research on the *social determinants of health* uses a health equity lens publicized by the World Health Organization that stresses how important it is to understand the social conditions which are risk factors for child abuse and neglect (e.g., domestic violence, parental substance abuse, poverty) and to further understand the social norms, policies, and structures that place certain population groups in these conditions and thus at higher risk. Examining what has the largest public health impact (Figure 3.1) has led some in the field to endorse:

> policy-oriented approaches that have the potential to impact multiple forms of violence by addressing gender, racial, and socioeconomic inequalities, social and cultural norms, and other community and societal risks (e.g., economic supports for children and families, economic empowerment and development schemes, urban upgrading, equal pay and other employment-based policies to improve opportunities and economic stability for women).
>
> (Centers for Disease Control and Prevention, 2016, p. 8)

The CDC public health impact pyramid (see Figure 3.1) underscores the potentially greater impact of targeting socioeconomic and community factors, including broad

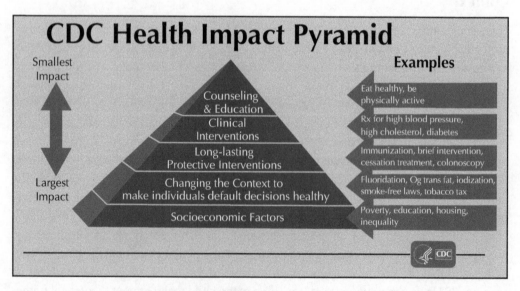

Figure 3.1 CDC Health Impact Pyramid

supports for parents, as compared to individual treatment efforts. Safe, stable, nurturing relationships and environments are essential for preventing child abuse and neglect, and to ensure that all children reach their full potential. These relationships receive support from an environment that includes housing stability, income supports, and accessible and evidence-based behavioral healthcare.

Many experts and the CDC believe that young children:

experience their world through their relationships with parents and other caregivers. Safe, stable, nurturing relationships and environments between children and their caregivers provide a buffer against the effects of potential stressors such as [child maltreatment] CM and are fundamental to healthy brain development. They also shape the development of children's physical, emotional, social, behavioral, and intellectual capacities, which ultimately affect their health as adults. As a result, promoting safe, stable, nurturing relationships and environments can have a positive impact on a broad range of health problems and on the development of skills that will help children reach their full potential.

(Centers for Disease Control, 2014, p. 7)

Building on this work, the CDC proposed the *Essentials for Childhood* Framework to assist communities committed to the positive development of children and families, and specifically to the prevention of child abuse and neglect. As shown in Figure 3.2, the framework has four goal areas and suggests steps based on the best available evidence to achieve each goal. While child abuse and neglect is a significant public health problem, it is also a preventable one, where a broad commitment to preventing child abuse and neglect can help create communities in which every child can thrive.

The Protective Factors Framework from the Center for the Study of Social Policy (CSSP)

There are other frameworks that help establish a values and research-driven foundation for strengthening families and communities so that children can be protected and nurtured. One of the most widely known was developed by the Center for the Study of Social Policy

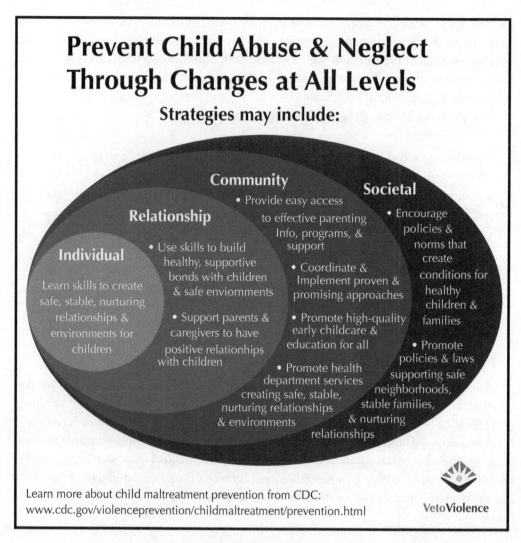

Prevent Child Abuse & Neglect Through Changes at All Levels

Strategies may include:

Community
• Provide easy access to effective parenting Info, programs, & support
• Coordinate & Implement proven & promising approaches
• Promote high-quality early childcare & education for all
• Promote health department services creating safe, stable, nurturing relationships & environments

Societal
• Encourage policies & norms that create conditions for healthy children & families
• Promote policies & laws supporting safe neighborhoods, stable families, & nurturing relationships

Relationship
• Use skills to build healthy, supportive bonds with children & safe enviornments
• Support parents & caregivers to have positive relationhips with children

Individual
Learn skills to create safe, stable, nurturing relationships & environments for children

Learn more about child maltreatment prevention from CDC:
www.cdc.gov/violenceprevention/childmaltreatment/prevention.html

VetoViolence

Figure 3.2 Preventing Child Abuse and Neglect by Targeting All Levels
Source: Centers for Disease Control and Prevention. (n.d.).

(CSSP) based on a comprehensive review of the research literature and conversations with many community stakeholders over the years (see Table 3.1). It focuses on five key factors that need to be present to help provide a nurturing environment for children (see also Harper-Browne, 2014.)

Table 3.1 Core Meanings of the Strengthening Families Protective Factors

Protective Factor	Core Meaning
Parental Resilience	*Resilience Related to General Life Stress*

a. managing the stressors of daily life and functioning well even when faced with challenges, adversity and trauma;
b. calling forth the inner strength to proactively meet personal challenges, manage adversities, and heal the effects of one's own traumas;
c. becoming more self-confident and self-efficacious;
d. having faith, feeling hopeful;
e. believing that one can make and achieve goals;
f. solving general life problems;
g. having a positive attitude about life in general;
h. managing anger, anxiety, sadness, feelings of loneliness, and other negative feelings;
i. seeking help for self when needed.

Resilience Related to General Parenting Stress

a. calling forth the inner strength to proactively meet challenges related to one's child;
b. not allowing stressors to keep one from providing nurturing attention to one's child;
c. solving parenting problems;
d. having a positive attitude about one's parenting role and responsibilities;
e. seeking help for child when needed.

Social Connections

a. Building trusting relationships; feeling respected and appreciated.
b. Having friends, family members, neighbors, and others who provide emotional support (e.g., affirming parenting skills):

- provide instrumental support/concrete assistance (e.g., transportation);
- provide informational support/serve as a resource for parenting information;
- provide spiritual support (e.g., hope and encouragement);
- provide an opportunity to engage with others in a positive manner;
- help solve problems;
- help buffer parents from stressors;
- reduce feelings of isolation;
- promote meaningful interactions in a context of mutual trust and respect.

c. Having a sense of connectedness that enables parents to feel secure, confident, and empowered to "give back" to others.

(Continued)

Table 3.1 (Continued)

Protective Factor	Core Meaning
Knowledge of Parenting and Child Development	Seeking, acquiring, and using accurate and age/stage-related information about:

a. parental behaviors that lead to early secure attachments;
b. the importance of:

- being attuned and emotionally available to one's child;
- being nurturing, responsive and reliable;
- regular, predictable, and consistent routines;
- interactive language experiences;
- providing a physically and emotionally safe environment for one's child;
- providing opportunities for one's child to explore and to learn by doing.

c. appropriate developmental expectations;
d. positive discipline techniques;
e. recognizing and attending to the special needs of a child.

Concrete Support in Times of Need

a. being resourceful;
b. being able to identify, find, and receive the basic necessities everyone deserves in order to grow (e.g., healthy food, a safe environment), as well as specialized medical, mental health, social, educational or legal services;
c. understanding one's rights in accessing eligible services;
d. gaining knowledge of relevant services;
e. navigating through service systems;
f. seeking help when needed;
g. having financial security to cover basic needs and unexpected costs.

Children's Social and Emotional Competence

Regarding the parent:

a. having a positive parental mood;
b. having positive perceptions of and responsiveness to one's child;
c. responding warmly and consistently to a child's needs;
d. being satisfied in one's parental role;
e. fostering a strong and secure parent–child relationship;
f. creating an environment in which children feel safe to express their emotions;
g. being emotionally responsive to children and modeling empathy;
h. talking with the child to promote vocabulary development and language learning;
i. setting clear expectations and limits;
j. separating emotions from actions;

Protective Factor	Core Meaning
	k. encouraging and reinforcing social skills such as greeting others and taking turns;
	l. creating opportunities for children to solve problems.
	Regarding the child:
	a. developing and engaging in self-regulating behaviors;
	b. interacting positively with others;
	c. using words and language skills;
	d. communicating emotions effectively.

Source: Center for the Study of Social Policy. (2013). *Core meanings of the strengthening families protective factors*. Retrieved from: www.cssp.org/reform/strengthening-families/2013/Core-Meanings-of-the-SF-Protective-Factors.pdf. Reprinted with permission.

Preventing Child Fatalities and Severe Injuries[1]

Infants and Young Children Have Special Vulnerability

As documented by many studies and summarized in Chapter 2, infants and young children are most at risk of fatalities and serious injuries from child abuse or neglect. Based on recent research, including key findings from the National Commission to Eliminate Child Abuse and Neglect Fatalities and the NSCAW I and II studies, it appears that despite positive intentions, current child welfare services may be failing to protect many of the 3 million children at risk of child maltreatment in the United States due to constraints in policy, program design, practice, and funding (Commission to Eliminate Child Abuse and Neglect Fatalities, 2016b; Miyamoto et al., 2016; Putnam-Hornstein et al., 2013). These children who are at risk have not received effective prevention services. While child fatality reviews have been conducted and there has been a slightly increased use of multi-sector data to identify families most at risk, relatively little research exists with regard to understanding the services that families receive prior to a maltreatment fatality, as discussed by Douglas (2016, p. 240):

> A descriptive study which asked child welfare workers to recount the services that families received prior to a fatality showed that never more than one third of families were receiving services (Douglas, 2013). About one third of families completed parenting education and were receiving counseling or psychotherapy.

A much smaller percentage, 14%, were receiving in-home services when the child died. Further 40% indicated that even though the parents were referred for services, they were not using them regularly.

With no claim that the information is exhaustive or that each domain or particular strategy is mutually exclusive, Pecora (2017) used the diagram in Figure 3.3 to organize some approaches to preventing child fatalities and severe injuries. With respect to the "practice quadrant" highlighted in the lower right-hand side, evidence-based and promising practices that have been found to prevent child fatalities and severe child injuries are summarized in one of the textbook's resource papers (Pecora, 2018a). For example, Nurse–Family Partnership (described next) is one of the few strategies associated with measurable decreases in child fatalities.

Nurse–Family Partnership

Nurse–Family Partnership (NFP) is a well-developed home-visiting program that has helped prevent child fatalities and hospitalization of children with severe injuries. Developed by Dr. David Olds, the goal is to promote the child's development, and to provide support and instructive parenting skills to parents. The program is designed to serve young, unmarried, first-time mothers from economically disadvantaged backgrounds or households. Women voluntarily enroll as early in their pregnancy as possible, with nurse home visits beginning ideally by the sixteenth week of pregnancy, and continuing through the first two years of the child's life.

Nurses visit participants at home to listen to their concerns, identify needs, provide information on available resources, and help the mothers set and meet goals. The visits focus on personal health, environmental health, "life course" development, the maternal role, family and friends, and health and human services. Funding sources typically include Federal Title 19, state, and county funds. NFP has achieved the following consistent program effects across multiple trials:

- Improved prenatal health.
- Fewer childhood injuries, including child maltreatment.
- Fewer subsequent pregnancies.
- Increased intervals between births.
- Increased maternal employment.

(See www.nursefamilypartnership.org/index.cfm?fuseaction=home.) A 15-year follow-up study found effects for the entire sample, while a shorter follow-up study found differences only in certain subgroups (e.g., Eckenrode et al., 2000; Olds et al., 1998; Olds et al., 2007). Note that more recent NFP reports (e.g., Heckman et al., 2017) have described the short-term child abuse prevention benefits of this program in contrast with earlier publications that showed these effects when youth were followed up at age 15 (e.g., Zielinski, Eckenrode, & Olds, 2009; Olds et al., 1998) or older (Olds et al., 2014).

Nurse–Family Partnership typically costs approximately $4,500 per family per year, with a range of $2,914 to $6,463 per family per year. Contrary to common perceptions, the Nurse–Family Partnership nurse home visitors are sometimes but not always more expensive than the professionals, paraprofessionals, and parents used in other leading home-visitation programs. Due to variations in the type of staff employed, caseloads, and variations in training, supervision, and worker turnover costs, there may or may not be a cost differential between Nurse–Family Partnership and other home-visitation programs (abstracted from www.nursefamilypartnership.org/resources/files/PDF/Fact_Sheets/NFP CostBrief.pdf).

While the feasibility of scaling this intervention is an issue because it relies on using professional nurses and only targets first-time mothers, it has the strongest evidence base of any home-visiting model and should be considered wherever this kind of approach is possible. In fact, the U.S. government has invested significantly in this program's expansion through the Maternal, Infant, and Early Childhood Home Visiting Program (MIECHV Program). Nurse–Family Partnership sites range in size and location from large agencies in major urban areas serving hundreds of families to small programs in rural, remote areas. Some agencies focus their work in several neighborhoods of an inner city, while other sites cover an entire county or several counties in a rural area. Most are implemented through local, county, or state health departments, although some are implemented through independent non-profits and hospitals (see www.nursefamilypartnership.org/content/index. cfm?fuseaction=showMap&navID=17).

Other Prevention Strategies

Back to Sleep Campaigns have documented effectiveness for reducing Sudden Infant Death Syndrome cases. Other promising programs with less research evidence of effectiveness are those intended to reduce shaken baby syndrome/abusive head trauma (SBS/AHT) through education about the dangers of shaking babies and about alternative calming strategies such as Kohl's Shaken Baby Syndrome Prevention Campaign and the Period of PURPLE Crying Education Campaign. These are briefly described in Pecora (2017).

In relation to preventing severe child inquiries due to child maltreatment, the Healthy Start Program – Enhanced Model and the Positive Parenting Program (Triple P) are two of the few programs that found positive outcomes in parent and child behavior, and that reduce the likelihood of physical abuse (e.g., Poole, Seal, & Taylor, 2014). Triple P is a multi-level parenting support program that has a media campaign as Level 1 and intensive parent treatment as Level 4. It is intended to have the kind of widespread reach and effect that we need. One of the strongest studies of Triple P was a population-based study that provided parenting education at all levels of prevention to a random selection of 18 counties (Prinz et al., 2009). The research team found 340 fewer cases post-intervention of substantiated child maltreatment, 240 fewer foster care placements, and 60 fewer injuries caused by child maltreatment, as determined by hospitals and emergency rooms – as compared with the counties without the intervention. Replication of this study and an examination of the sustainability of this model in other communities are needed. As promising as this work is, the National Academy of Science, Engineering, and Medicine recently

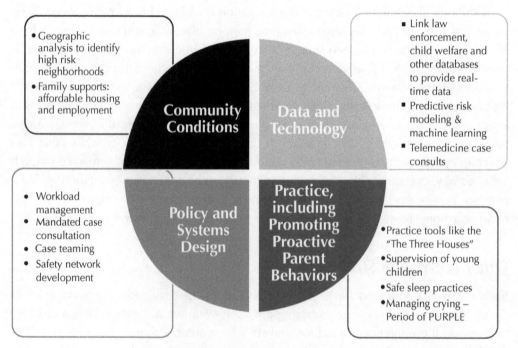

Figure 3.3 Examples of Varied Approaches to Keeping Children Safe from Severe Injuries or Fatalities

Source: Adapted from Pecora (2017).

failed to fully endorse Triple P as a highly recommended practice (Parenting Matters, IOM/ NASEM report of 2016).

Other Interventions to Consider for Which Rigorous Child Fatality and Injury Data Do Not Yet Appear to be Available

Promising strategies that need more evidence of effectiveness for preventing child fatalities and severe child injuries related to child maltreatment are briefly summarized in Pecora (2018a) and other resources. These include Crisis Nurseries, SafeCare, certain substance abuse treatment programs, TRAIN (Timely Recognition of Abusive Injuries), and Child Welfare Birth Match. Some of these programs have been rated according to their effectiveness for maltreatment prevention more generally, and specific data regarding their ability to prevent child fatalities and severe injuries are needed.

In addition, some more general types of services are associated with lowering the risk of child fatalities. Douglas (2016) found that receiving family support services, court-appointed representation, foster care, and case management services all significantly reduce the risk for a child fatality, with odds ratios (OR) ranging from .25–.69 (p < .001– .046). There was also a trend toward significance for family preservation services (OR =.69, p = .092). But more research is needed about specific models, as well as information about intensity, duration, and combinations of services.

Parent coaching can also be effective. Helping new parents understand the importance of adequate sleep for themselves and coaching them through feeding or infant crying challenges can also make a difference (Hurley et al., 2013; Olds et al., 2014). A recent study used NCANDS data to examine the impacts of services upon child fatalities over a five-year period. It underscores the impact of child welfare and family support services. One judicial-related finding from this study is worth exploring further: children with legal representation were less likely to experience a child maltreatment fatality (Douglas, 2016).

Community and System Design Prevention Strategies

It is important to step back and consider the larger ecological context in which severe child injuries and fatalities due to maltreatment occur, and the risk and protective factors that have been associated with child maltreatment (see Figures 3.1, 3.2, and 3.4, as well as Pecora, 2018).

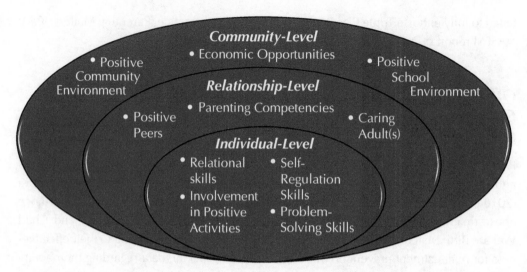

Figure 3.4 Major Parent Support and Child Protective Factors for Children in Child Welfare
Source: Development Services Group, Inc. (2013).

With this wider frame, some experts recognize the value of the following:

- *Geographic analysis* to identify neighborhoods where the most vulnerable children live. For example, Daley and her colleagues have used Risk Terrain Modeling to predict child maltreatment at the small neighborhood level (400 x 400 square feet) to distribute resources more cost-effectively (Daley et al., 2016). Wildeman (2017) is using NCANDS and AFCARS data to map cumulative risk of child maltreatment and foster care placement by state and county.

- *Promoting community norms that protect children*, such as not using corporal punishment, promoting social connections among neighbors, and not leaving children in the care of other children who lack the capacity for childcare of their siblings. See, for example, some of the broad Triple P tier one strategies (www.triplep.net/glo-en/home/) as well as new ACEs prevention and mitigation initiatives (http://resiliencetrumpsaces.org/).

- *Other public health-informed policies to increase community capacity to support families,* such as "Family Action Councils" or "Neighborhood Action Groups" where parents develop social supports to reduce their sense of isolation and learn practical tips for raising their children (Hargreaves et al., 2015; McCroskey et al., 2012).

- *Income and housing supports* that improve parental capacity to care for their children by increasing key resources, and by reducing the stress that can contribute to greater risk of child maltreatment.

- *Implementing an agency-wide "culture of safety."* Child welfare leaders and other experts in Tennessee have focused on this area for the past few years, drawing ideas from continuous quality improvement as well as aviation, nuclear power, and maritime safety research. They have made a series of strategic policy and organizational systems shifts that bode well (Vogus et al., 2016). This includes child welfare leaders focusing on all the factors that contribute to a service failure instead of placing the blame on workers or their supervisors (Turnell, Murphy, & Munro, 2013).

- *Workload management* is essential because large caseloads may prevent caseworkers from making essential kinds of collateral contacts. It may also rush decision making because not enough time has been invested in safety assessment, outreach to other family members, and development of a safety network (Nelson-Dusek et al., 2017).

- *Case consultation mandates* can help ensure that staff get "just-in-time" case review and consultation for certain kinds of higher risk cases. For example, the Federal Commission to Eliminate Child Abuse and Neglect Fatalities recommended that "every state should review their policies on screening reports of abuse and neglect to ensure that the children most at risk for fatality – those under age three – receive the appropriate response, and they and their family are prioritized for services, with heightened urgency for those under the age of 1" (Commission to Eliminate Child Abuse and Neglect Fatalities, 2016a, p.1).

- In that vein, the Los Angeles Board of Supervisors requested that the County Department pair CPS investigators with a nurse for all child maltreatment cases for children under 2 years old. From a different perspective, physical abuse cases with multiple fractures and other indicators, genetic testing may be needed for Osteogenesis Imperfecta (a genetic condition that makes children much more susceptible to bone fractures) (Pepin & Byers, 2015). Finally, the Eckerd Rapid Safety Feedback approach mandates case review with quality assurance staff for cases identified as high risk by a regularly refreshed predictive risk model (see www.eckerd.org/programs-services/system-of-care-management/eckerd-rapid-safety-feedback/).

- *Telemedicine strategies* can help workers in rural areas or those working weekends and late night shifts to have access to high-quality consultation from a variety of medical, developmental, substance abuse, behavioral health, and other specialists.

Summary

While well-intentioned, current child welfare services may be failing to protect children from fatal and serious injuries due to constraints in policy, program design, practice, and funding. Drawing from new advances in the injury control field, we found relatively few evidence-based practices for preventing child fatalities and severe child injuries related to child maltreatment. But there are promising interventions and a wide range of community, policy, and systems change strategies that could be tested further.

Federal agencies, state agencies, and foundations could also collaborate with other stakeholders to evaluate upstream prevention and support services for families where risks for maltreatment are particularly high (e.g., families with certain risk factors such as a previous severe child injury, where parents' rights have been terminated for a previous child, infants with a previous CPS referral, children born to young mothers where no paternity has been recorded) (Putnam-Hornstein & Needell, 2011). For CW services, this means creating a strategy for engaging families who we predict to have a high likelihood of poor child outcomes even though they have not, yet, harmed a child. This is new territory for CW but we see the need to cross a significant cultural bridge into this area. This may be facilitated by teaming with other fields where primary prevention is a major priority, and those who have experience working with at-risk families more generally, such as the field of public health.

Strategies for Preventing Less Serious Child Injuries

Prevention Strategies with Some Evidence for Certain Child Maltreatment Types

While certain types of child maltreatment like physical abuse are being addressed by proven and promising interventions, other child maltreatment types have received less attention and fewer interventions have been developed for them. This section and Table 2 in the resource paper (Pecora, 2018a) describe interventions for which there is moderate to strong evidence of effectiveness; and they are listed in alphabetical order grouped by the child maltreatment types and subtypes. A few additional strategies are highlighted in the sections that follow. (We recognize that these ratings may change as the CEBC4CW gets new information; see cebc4cw.org.)

Differential Response and Alternative Response

Some intake approaches are attempting to divert low-risk families to supportive programs other than child protective services. Initial research data indicate either no differences or that families in alternative response systems receive more services (U.S. Department of Health and Human Services, 2005). As highlighted by the National Governor's Association and others, reporting by CW administrations indicates that these alternatives to conventional child protective services can be powerful ways to divert families from more formal child welfare services involvement, especially when the links to community-based support services are strong (e.g., National Governor's Association Center for Best Practices, 2008; Wright, Ticklor, & Vernor, 2008). These systems, however, need continued evaluation because without additional research data how will the field know, for example, which families benefit most from these system designs, which children are most vulnerable, and what different roles should be fulfilled by law enforcement, medical, legal, and voluntary social services personnel?

There is a growing and somewhat controversial body of research on this approach. Some studies have examined the relationships between alternative response systems and incidence of child maltreatment – the main outcome of interest. Other studies have measured family safety, family engagement, and future interaction with the CW agency. For example, a study of the multiple response system in North Carolina found "that its implementation appeared to reduce substantiations of child maltreatment, and had no adverse impact on the rate of assessments, response time, or case decision-making, and families responded positively to the approach" (Center for Child and Family Policy, 2004). The evaluation was not able to determine whether there were changes in the overall level of harms to children.

A review of Minnesota's alternative response system found different results, concluding that the alternative response approach resulted in services that are more responsive and engaged families. (See assessments by the Institute of Applied Research atwww.iarstl. org/papers/FinalMNFARReport.pdf and at www.iarstl.org/papers/ARFinalEvaluationRe port.pdf.) This RCT study found that the Minnesota AR program both saved money and led to better outcomes for children and families, including reduced child out-of-home placements and fewer subsequent maltreatment referrals. A review of data from the National Child Abuse and Neglect Data System (NCANDS) revealed that services are more frequently provided to alternative response families than to families that have a traditional investigation, possibly because some investigated cases are not substantiated. The study also determined that families served through the alternative response are not necessarily at a greater risk for subsequent reports of child victimization than families that were investigated (Zielewski et al., 2006, pp. 1–2).

In the Compton community of Los Angeles, Point of Engagement (POE) has a long enough history to show impact. One of the main community-based agencies (Shields for Families) that has partnered with the public child welfare agency has completed approximately 2,700 assessments over the years with fewer than 50 child removals. Kathy Icenhower, the Shields agency director, believes that without the assessments and the resulting services these families received, most of these children would have been removed. She noted: "That's about 5,000 children over the last four years who have stayed in their homes because of Up-Front Assessments" (Edgar, 2009, p. 11). Looking at Los Angeles Department of Child and Family Services (DCFS) data, the detentions in Compton have decreased 51 percent since FY 2002. DCFS leaders estimated savings of almost $5 million, given a monthly cost of foster care of $1,802 per child or an annual cost of $21,624 per child. This trend cannot be solely attributed to POE or upfront assessments, of course; it is part of a county-wide decrease in placement rates. But the Compton child welfare staff believe that these special assessments and services help families keep their children at home (Marts et al., 2008).

Yet recent critiques and discussions of Differential Response reveal different understandings of the approach and its level of effectiveness (e.g., Baird, Park, & Lohrbach, 2013; Drake, 2013; Fluke et al., 2016; Hughes et al., 2013; Loman & Siegel, 2013). For these reasons, this approach to assessment and services allocation requires close monitoring in the years ahead.

Family Group Conferences

As discussed in Chapter 10, one of the first models of family-centered meetings that has been commonly adopted in CW is the family group conference (FGC). First introduced and legislated in 1989 in New Zealand, the FGC was based on Maori traditional decision-making processes and in response to the disproportionate representation of Maori children and families in various public systems, including child welfare, youth justice, and corrections (Huntsman, 2006).

Family Preservation Services: Homebuilders'® Program

The Homebuilders'® model of Intensive Family Preservation Services (IFPS) is a prevention intervention that consists of short-term, in-home, intensive family-based services targeted at families facing child removal (see www.institutefamily.org/ and www.cebc4cw.org/program/homebuilders/detailed). Previous IFPS evaluations have questioned the ability of the intervention to prevent foster care placements. Research experts, however, have pointed to some of the methodological challenges of these earlier studies, which included problems with model fidelity, and the difficulty systems have with identifying families in imminent risk of child removal. A few recent studies have shown more positive results (e.g., Schweitzer et al., 2015). In fact the Washington State Institute of Public Policy (WSIPP) noted that IFPS programs that adhere closely to the Homebuilders'® Program standards have multiple positive effects for children and families, including:

- Significant reductions in subsequent reports of child abuse and neglect.

- Total net benefits of $17,832 (society and family).

- Netting $6.16 in benefits per dollar of cost (WSIPP, 2016a, p. 4).

Not all intensive family preservation programs will achieve these outcomes. Programs with demonstrated fidelity to the Homebuilders'® model (13 or more of 16 identified components) reduced out-of-home placement by 31 percent. In those that did not follow the Homebuilders'® model closely, there was no significant reduction in placement in the intervention group (WSIPP, 2016b).

Family Preservation Services: Multisystemic Therapy for Child Abuse and Neglect (MST-CAN)

As also mentioned in Chapter 8, MST-CAN is described by its originators as: "an intensive, time-limited, home and family focused treatment approach [. . .] that targets directly for change those factors within the youth's family, peer group, school and neighborhood that are contributing his or her antisocial behavior" (Schoenwald, Borduin, & Henggeler, 1998, pp. 486–487). Consistent with many features of intensive family preservation services (low caseloads, delivery of services in home, school and community settings, time limits, 24-hour availability, comprehensive services), MST has been used extensively, though not exclusively, in work with antisocial youth within the juvenile justice systems. But recent efforts have extended the model into child welfare – hence the use of this program name: Multisystemic Therapy for Child Abuse and Neglect (MST-CAN). MST-CAN is an adaptation of MST that was developed to treat families who:

- Have come to the attention of Child Protective Services due to physical abuse and/or neglect.

- Have a target child in the age range of 6 to 17.
- Have had a new report of abuse or neglect in the past 180 days.

MST-CAN works with families to keep children at home with increased safety. The focus is providing treatment to the whole family with special attention given to parents to overcome some of the parenting challenges they face. It is very common for parents in MST-CAN programs to have experienced a traumatic event and treatment is provided to help overcome the impact of trauma. A great deal of safety planning is included in addition to treatment for anger management difficulties, parental or youth substance abuse, and family problem solving and communication problems. The MST-CAN team delivers treatment in the family's home at flexible times, with a 24/7 on-call service to help the family manage crises after hours. Treatment lasts for six to nine months. Because of the complexity of the issues which families face, in addition to Master's degree therapists, the team includes a full-time crisis caseworker and a part-time psychiatrist with capacity to treat adults and children (abstracted from Multisystemic Therapy Institute, 2017).

MST and MST-CANS appears to be a well-validated set of treatment models – with an impressive corpus of outcome research, including several clinical trials (Burns & Hoagwood, 2002). Studies are examining the infrastructure necessary to assure treatment fidelity, an "Achilles' Heel" of much earlier family preservation demonstrations. In a five-year clinical trial, MST-CAN was proven to be more effective than enhanced outpatient treatment.

Box 3.1

Across 16 months, youth who received MST-CAN showed the following effects:

- Significantly greater reductions in internalizing problems, such as anxiety and dissociation, total behavior problems, and PTSD symptoms.
- Significantly fewer out-of-home placements.
- Significantly fewer changes in placement.

Parents evidenced the following:

- Significantly greater reductions in psychological distress.
- Significantly greater reductions in parenting problems, such as neglectful parenting, minor and severe assault of the child, and psychological aggression.

- Significantly fewer decreases in non-violent discipline.
- Significantly greater increases in natural social support.
- Significantly greater treatment satisfaction.

Source: www.mstcan.com/research/.

An analysis of data from one agency (Youth Villages), which has been supervised by MST for many years and has MST Clinical Services approved teams, is also showing an impact upon non-MST approved child welfare cases. The evaluation is based on services data – and not based on a randomized clinical trial – but indicates that MST may result in better outcomes for CW-involved youth than placement into a Re-Ed model residential program. This study, using propensity score matching to risk adjust the characteristics of youth served at home with MST or served in residential care, shows that the one-year outcomes were nearly significantly better ($p < .06$) for the CW-involved youth who received MST than those who were in residential treatment (Barth et al., 2007).

MST is currently receiving considerable attention in many states in North America and elsewhere around the world as a model "evidence-based" ecologically oriented treatment program (see) http://mstconference.com/e-newsletter/spring06/ (accessed April 12, 2008). This interest continues despite a rigorous meta-analysis completed by Littell (2005) that raised questions about the methodology of the many positive findings of MST (e.g., that the studies were not independent, and they did not account for all the children who started the study and dropped out).

MST - Building Stronger Families (MST-BSF) is a similar program that developed from the MST-CAN model which is currently being implemented in Connecticut. MST-BSF is a comprehensive treatment program for families who are experiencing co-occurring parental substance abuse and child maltreatment, and who are involved in the child protective service system. MST-BSF utilizes a specialized version of the MST-CAN treatment model that includes a weekly social club component and an enhanced focus on substance abuse issues (Multisystemic Therapy Institute, 2017). MST-BSF integrates two models with empirical support for their effectiveness: MST-CAN for child maltreatment (Swenson et al., 2010) and RBT for adult substance abuse (Tuten et al., 2012) into one comprehensive treatment package. The major interventions within the MST-BSF arm include safety planning and implementation, functional analysis of the abuse incident, cognitive behavioral interventions for PTSD symptomatology and low anger management, family communication and problem solving, abuse clarification, and Reinforcement Based Treatment (RBT) for adult substance abuse. RBT is an incentive-based drug treatment program for adults who abuse opiates, cocaine, or other illicit drugs.

Home-visiting Programs

Overview. Part of the theoretical underpinning for nursing and public health-based family support services is research demonstrating that successful caregiver–infant relationships may be highly important for preventing future parenting problems, including child maltreatment. Parents are helped to deal with the inevitable stresses that a new infant brings to a family, and are helped to feel comfortable in caring for that child. Thus, a promising approach to child abuse prevention has been the voluntary use of home visitors for families with newborns and young children at risk. Not until the late 1970s, when David Olds conducted the now landmark Elmira nurse home visitation study, did these programs gain traction in the U.S. (Olds et al., 1986). Since then, evidence of effectiveness has begun to emerge through rigorously conducted research. Mostly funded by states and foundations, in 2008, the Federal government made its first significant investment in funding home-visitation programs (Olds, Sadler, & Kitzman, 2007). (For a recent systematic review of home-visiting programs, see http://homvee.acf.hhs.gov/homvee_executive_summary.pdf.)

High-quality home-visiting programs can help strengthen parent functioning in ways that reduce child abuse and neglect. There are also important longer term economic savings:

- *Education costs* associated with developmental delays and learning disorders.

- *Medical costs* associated with fetal growth retardation, pre-eclampsia, and prematurity-related problems such as respiratory distress syndrome.

- *Social services spending* for public assistance, child abuse, and neglect and foster care.

- *Spending for emotional and psychological problems* including aggressive behavior and conduct disorders.

- *Financial burdens on families* that result from limited economic, social, and emotional support of non-resident fathers; productivity losses among caregivers and injured children later in life; and permanent disability by injury (abstracted from www.nursefamilypartnership.org/resources/files/PDF/Fact_Sheets/Cost-BenefitOverview.pdf.)

Not all home visiting programs, however, are created equal. Most focus on caregivers considered to be at risk for parenting problems, based on factors such as maternal age, marital status and education, low household income, lack of social supports, or, in some programs, mothers testing positive for drugs at the child's birth. Depending on the program, the content of the home visits consists of instruction in child development and health, referrals for service, or social and emotional support. Some programs provide additional services, such as preschool (Burwick et al., 2014; see also WSIPP, 2017 at http://wsipp.wa.gov/BenefitCost). Program design, program cost, implementation requirements in terms of staff characteristics, degree of teaming, supervision, and cost-effectiveness vary across home-visiting program models (e.g., Avellar et al., 2013; Burwick et al., 2014).

One recent evaluation of a modified *Healthy Families America* program used a model that emphasized cognitive appraisal theory to reduce risks for abuse and neglect as well as better implementation practices. This model yielded considerably more favorable results compared with both the unenhanced *Healthy Families America* program and a control group that did not receive any home-visiting services. These positive findings were especially evident for medically vulnerable infants, such as those born prematurely or those with low APGAR scores at birth (Bugental et al., 2002). Thus the evidence for the effectiveness of this approach with families at risk of child maltreatment remains promising but mixed as researchers attempt to determine an optimum service composition, length, intensity, and other additional factors. Because home visiting is only one part of a system of supports, and as such may not be effective without other pieces in place, the efficacy of the network of available community-based services should be evaluated instead of testing one individual program (Marcenko & Staerkel, 2006).

The outcomes of home visiting have varied considerably. Information is accumulating about program components that may be most beneficial and program costs. For example, treatment duration and/or intensity may indeed be key factors. Parents feel that their relationships with the home visitor was crucial to the program (Krysik, LeCroy, & Ashford, 2008). But it may be time to consider the purposeful pairing of home-visiting programs with "parent mentor" models where parents who have had experience with child welfare services go on to coach parents newly reported to CW (Cohen & Canan, 2006; Leake et al., 2012). Community-based substance abuse treatment services and other key interventions are also being added to these service models. With the shortage of nurses, use of parent aides has been attempted with varied results. Some programs have decreased the rate of subsequent occurrence of child abuse and neglect.

SafeCare. SafeCare is an in-home parenting model program that provides direct skill training to parents in child behavior management and planned activities training, home safety training, and child healthcare skills to prevent child maltreatment. It uses weekly sessions at approximately 1.5 hours each for 18 to 20 weeks (see www.safecare center.org and www.cachildwelfareclearinghouse.org/program/76/detailed). Like many interventions, it is most effective if intensive supervision is provided to help the practitioner properly deliver the intervention (Lutzker & Bigelow, 2002, cited in Barth, 2008). It has also been shown to be effective with American Indian families involved with CW (Chaffin et al., 2012).

Utah HomeWorks. Utah's Division of Child and Family Services (DCFS) piloted a home-visiting program that emphasizes up-front, in-home services designed to keep families together. Called "HomeWorks," the program was launched in 2013 under a Federal Title IV-E demonstration waiver to provide families with services and tools to improve functioning and well-being, including addiction treatment, relapse prevention support, mental health therapy, and financial support for housing and other necessities. According to KIDS COUNT, Utah has one of the lowest rates of children in foster care in the United States, despite having the highest proportion of children per capita (KIDS COUNT Data Center, n.d.). DCFS estimated that for the annual costs of placing a single child in foster care, 11 families could receive in-home services (Utah Child and Family Services, Department of Human Services, DCFS, 2014).

Safety Networks

As discussed by Nelson-Dusek et al. (2017), two of the tools used to increase family engagement, case planning, and decision making that have been increasingly highlighted are safety plans and safety networks (ACTION for Child Protection, Inc., 2003; Bunn, 2013). Safety planning is grounded in family violence literature and requires practitioners to take into account the overall needs of women and children – with plans reliant on interagency understanding of the issues and collaboration. It is further described as "a pragmatic approach to working with women that acknowledges and builds on women's own perceptions and responses to their partner's power and control" (Waugh & Bonner, 2002, p. 293).

Research by Thompson (1995) and Wahler (1980) demonstrated how damaging social insularity (lack of social networks and support) is for parents and their ability to care for their children. Consequently, Nelson-Dusek et al. (2017) define safety networks as a group of adults (e.g., relatives, friends, and other professionals) that parents in child protection can rely on to support them and in turn help ensure the safety of their children. Safety plans are defined as a plan developed by the parent, worker, children (depending on their age), and network members to ensure the safety of their children. Within child welfare, it is recognized that the earlier we can intervene to ensure a child's safety, the better (Munro, 2011). A safety plan is not a product, but rather a journey requiring a focus on relationships (Turnell & Essex, 2006). Waugh and Bonner (2002, p. 283) highlight two key aspects of safety planning: first, that it is a practical, down-to-earth process; second, that it recognizes that when people have problems, their own knowledge of their situation is fundamental to finding solutions.

Research on the prevention of child abuse and neglect stresses the importance of informal social supports (which can act as safety networks) as a key factor in effective prevention and intervention efforts (e.g., Thompson, 1995; Heller et al., 1999). Specifically, extra-familial support has been shown to mitigate the relationship between abuse experiences in childhood and later mental health (see Heller et al., (1999) for review), including anxiety and depression (Sperry & Widom, 2013), and life satisfaction, feelings of nervousness, hopelessness, restlessness, depression, worthlessness, and distress (Nurius et al., 2015). Extra-familiar support has also been shown to act as a buffer against re-abuse within a family (Thompson, 1995), and help stop the cycle of intergenerational child abuse (Caliso & Milner, 1994).

Family members and fictive kin often comprise an important safety net surrounding a child. With this in mind, the development of a safety plan often involves working in partnership with the family to create a safety network. Within the model, child protection workers help families identify and list all of the potential adults – including relatives, friends, and other professionals – who work together to support the family to help ensure the safety of their children. Sometimes this group of people meet to form a safety network for the child. The goal of safety plans and safety networks is to identify specific people and strategies. In some safety networks, a member or members of that network are the persons who children are encouraged to call if they are concerned about the behavior of their parents. Typically, these are grandparents or an aunt.

A recent pilot study in Minnesota used interviews with parents and safety network members to explore respondents' perceptions, use of a safety plan and safety network, and use of core components of the Signs of Safety framework. Findings from this pilot investigation included insights about how safety plans and safety networks are established, how they function, and opportunities for enhancing their use with families with the goal of providing supports that increase the likelihood of continued safety for children following case closure. While additional research is needed, preliminary results also suggest that these tools may contribute to reduced re-reports to child protection (Nelson-Dusek et al., 2017).

Family Connections

Family Connections was developed in 1996 to reduce risk factors associated with neglect and to enhance protective factors that may help families more adequately meet the basic needs of their children resulting in improved outcomes for their children. Its target population is families with children (birth to 18) who meet risk criteria (criteria are adapted based on geographic differences). This program has a growing evidence base of effectiveness (e.g., DePanfilis, 2015; DePanfilis, Dubowitz, & Kunz, 2008; Filene, Brodowski, & Bell, 2014; www.cebc4cw.org/program/family-connections/). The core intervention components are as follows:

1. Intake – which involves screening against risk factors for child maltreatment.
2. Outreach and engagement.
3. Concrete/emergency services.
4. Comprehensive family assessment (including the use of standardized clinical assessment instruments).
5. Outcome-driven case plans with SMART goals (Specific, Measurable, Attainable, Realistic, Timely).
6. Minimum of one hour per week of purposeful change-focused interventions.
7. Evaluation of change using standardized instruments.
8. Case closure – which involved verifying outcomes and goals achieved and risk of maltreatment reduced.

Adaptations of Family Connections include the following:

*   Grandparent Family Connections (GFC) – works with informal kinship families (community or public child welfare agency).
*   Trauma Adapted-Family Connections (TA-FC) – targets families where parents and/or children screen with trauma symptoms at intake (community agency) (Collins et al., 2011).
*   SAFE–Family Connections (SAFE–FC) – targets families with children who have been evaluated as unsafe following a report of child abuse or neglect (public child welfare agency) (abstracted from Filene, DePanfilis, and Smith, 2010).

Poverty and Child Maltreatment

There are several reasons why we should care about poverty and its relationship to child maltreatment:

1. The research is clear. There are strong associations between poverty and need for child welfare services, especially child neglect (see Figure 3.5).

2. Families who are poor, or deeply poor, and are also involved with child welfare reflect a high degree of vulnerability that deserves attention.

3. The more we understand about this association between child welfare and poverty, the more we can address the unique needs of families, and interrupt the intergenerational transmission of both poverty and child welfare involvement.

4. If we develop systematic solutions to address poverty, there is great potential for having a long-term positive impact upon individuals and on cross-sector human service system involvement, including societal well-being and cost savings (Maher, Corwin, & Pecora, 2017).

Poverty deserves special attention, as noted by Jonson-Reid et al. (2010, p. 272):

> It can be argued that the majority of the risk factors mentioned in maltreatment studies are somehow intertwined with poverty, although the exact pathway between poverty and chronic maltreatment has proven to be elusive. Even before children are born, parenting for the poor becomes a challenge due to poor maternal nutrition and lack of prenatal care. These prenatal factors may affect the development of the child, which in turn, may put the child at a higher risk of maltreatment (Kaiser & Delaney, 1996). It can also be argued that poverty can create chronic stress, psychological distress, and depression, which may in turn lead to substance abuse and marital strife, also risk factors for maltreatment. Berger (2004) used data from the National Longitudinal Survey of Youth and found that income insufficiency retains some association with maltreatment (measured indirectly) even after family characteristics are controlled for.

Slack, Berger, and Noyes (in press) reviewed an array of studies, using varied methods, which suggest a strong relationship between policies that change family income – based on changes to child support enforcement, monthly stipends for foster parents, and other policy manipulations – and child maltreatment. This very promising area of work involves providing financial coaching and income assistance (e.g., Project GAIN in Wisconsin); and it deserves further testing to determine the extent to which providing families with greater financial resources, as a complement or substitute for services, affords greater advantages in ensuring child safety.

Redesigning Child Welfare Using Brain Science Concepts

A recent monograph summarized how some of the key concepts from the Center and the National Scientific Council on the Developing Child about the effects of trauma on the

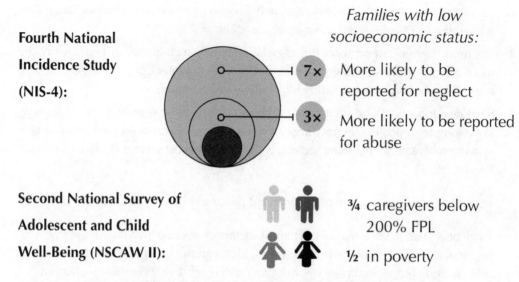

Fourth National Incidence Study (NIS-4):

Families with low socioeconomic status:

7× More likely to be reported for neglect

3× More likely to be reported for abuse

Second National Survey of Adolescent and Child Well-Being (NSCAW II):

¾ caregivers below 200% FPL

½ in poverty

Figure 3.5 The Relationship between Poverty and Child Maltreatment
Source: Maher, Corwin, & Pecora (2017).

brain, healing pathways, and building protective capacities and resilience may be applied to CW. The authors focus "on the ways that developmental science points to changes that could improve the child welfare system, and better support the children, families, and communities that it serves."

Many of their concepts deserve review but we will highlight just two of them to illustrate their power and applicability to CW. The authors mention that a pile-up of adversity makes it difficult to develop and use core foundational skills. According to the Center team, three interlocking problems stand in the way (as depicted in Figure 3.6):

First, serious early adversity overdevelops the "fear circuitry" in the brain, making people more likely to perceive and focus attention on potential threats throughout life. Second, severe and frequent stress experienced as an adult overloads our ability to use the skills we do have. Chaotic, threatening, or unpredictable environments activate the "fight or flight" response and make it difficult to engage executive functions. The same individual, faced with significant financial stress, is likely to show diminished cognitive capacity, compared to when he or she has sufficient resources available [Mani et al., 2013]. Third, frequently experiencing circumstances that seem beyond our control can lead to a low sense of self-efficacy – the belief that we can be agents in improving our own lives – which is needed to engage in planning, goal-oriented behaviors,

(Center on the Developing Child, 2016, p. 8)

Another area to emphasize is building healthy relationships:

For children, healthy relationships confer a double benefit, both stimulating brain development and providing the buffering protection that can keep even very challenging experiences from producing toxic stress effects. Healthy relationships are also essential for adults who need to make substantial changes in their own lives, as is typically the case for adults involved with the child welfare system. These relationships are a source of emotional and practical support for adults, and knowing that another person cares about them helps build hope and the possibility of change.

(Center for the Developing Child, 2016, p. 12)

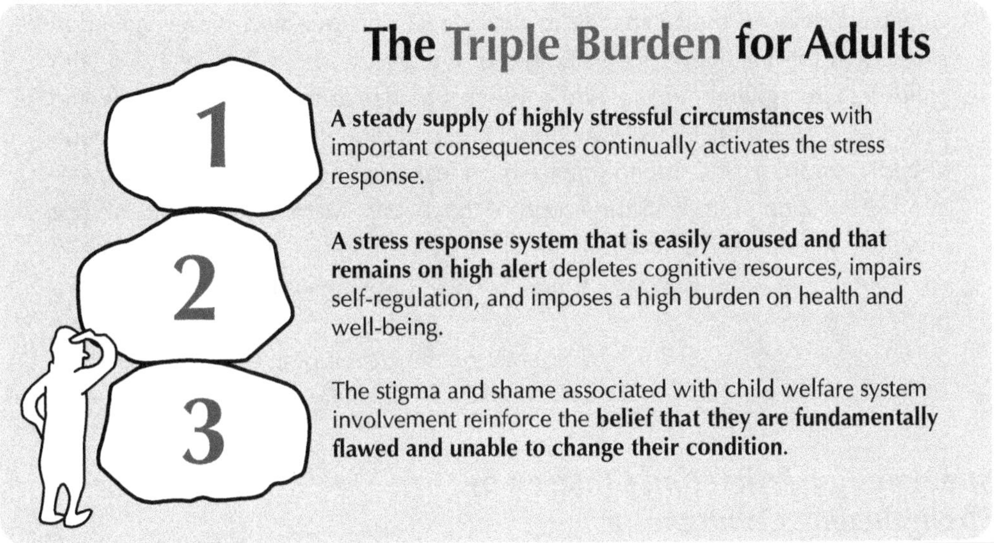

The Triple Burden for Adults

1 A steady supply of highly stressful circumstances with important consequences continually activates the stress response.

2 A stress response system that is easily aroused and that remains on high alert depletes cognitive resources, impairs self-regulation, and imposes a high burden on health and well-being.

3 The stigma and shame associated with child welfare system involvement reinforce the belief that they are fundamentally flawed and unable to change their condition.

Figure 3.6 Three Key Challenges Facing Many Parents Involved with the Child Welfare System
Source: Center on the Developing Child at Harvard University. (2016, p. 8). Reprinted with permission.

Helping to build and support strong relationships should therefore be an essential element of all CW work, along with strengthening core life skills such as being able to work, manage household finances, and ensure that children eat and are well supervised (see Figure 3.7).

The Center monograph closes by calling for improvements in how we can support families more broadly:

> [S]cientists define child neglect as the persistent absence of responsive caregiving. This is very different from the legal definition of neglect, which focuses on the absence of sufficient food, clothing, shelter, or supervision. Many children who have not been neglected in a legal sense could nevertheless benefit if their caregivers were better able to provide the kinds of responsive interactions that support healthy development. This is, emphatically, not a call to expand the jurisdiction of child welfare systems, which are not well-positioned to help this larger population of children and their parents. Those systems are already overburdened, and the fact that they exercise a police power makes it exceedingly difficult for families to trust them as helpers.
>
> Instead, we should consider this issue more broadly: How can we build a universal understanding of responsive caregiving, and help parents and other caregivers develop their capacity to provide it? This question directs attention away from the relatively small number of children and families involved with child welfare systems and toward a much broader array of social norms and practices. It also shifts focus away from unhelpful dichotomies (are parents good or bad?) toward a more useful emphasis on learning and improvement. Answering this question is beyond the scope of this paper; we note only that the first principle set out above – advancing an understanding of the science of child development in order to open up new ways of thinking and acting – is surely a piece of the answer.
>
> (Center on the Developing Child, 2016, p. 16)

Strategies for Protecting Children by Strengthening Communities

As highlighted earlier in this chapter and by one of the dimensions in Figure 3.7, a supportive community plays a key role in strengthening families. William C. Bell (2016) of Casey Family Programs emphasizes that it takes an entire community – all five sectors – to

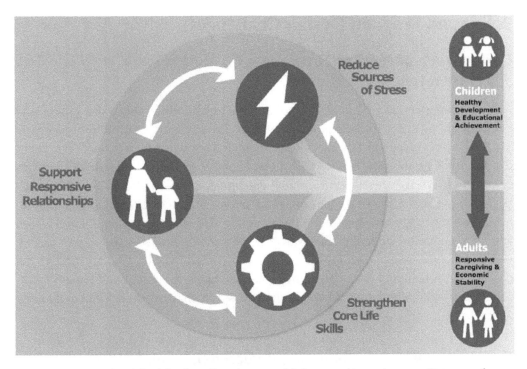

Figure 3.7 Design Principles from Developmental Science to Use to Improve Outcomes for Children and Families

Source: Center on the Developing Child at Harvard University (2017, p. 1). Reprinted with permission.

come together, to work together to raise children, and to create a community of hope for them and their families:

- The public sector that is the government, including tribal governments.
- The general public – children, families, neighbors, and everyday citizens living in rural, urban, large, small, wealthy and poor communities all across this nation.
- The private non-profit sector which provides many services through non-profit agencies.
- The philanthropic sector which provides resources designed to stimulate innovation and to support programs not yet supported by other sectors.
- The business sector which offers technical expertise, employment opportunities, and corporate support for social innovation.

Policy and Program Design Challenges

Current Federal Funding Encourages Child Placement and Not Prevention

A small proportion of federal CW funding goes toward child abuse prevention and intervention. In 2016, for example, only about 3.8 percent ($668 million) of nearly $17.378 billion in federal CW allocations originated from Title IV-B of the Social Security Act, which states may use to fund supports and services for children and families (Stoltzfus, 2017, p. 1). Most of the remaining federal funds derive from Title IV-E, which largely goes toward foster care subsidies, adoption assistance, CW training, and independent living programs. Some states have addressed the lack of funding for prevention and intervention by launching CW waiver demonstration projects, which permit Title IV-E funds to be reallocated toward services supported by Title IV-B so long as the project is cost-neutral. Nevertheless, most states struggle to support and sustain therapeutic services for children and families in the CW system (Government Accountability Office, 2013).

Policy Changes for Encouraging Research-informed Practice and Pay for Performance

State and federal policies, such as Family First, that support states to improve outcomes for all children who have entered or are at risk of entering the CW system should be implemented. First, state agencies should make use of research-informed practice approaches. Legislators and agency leaders need to demand that the services provided directly by public agencies or purchased by them use evidence-informed practices whenever possible. Such mandates must, however, be tempered with an understanding of the current research limitations; the practical considerations of implementation related to model fidelity, cost, and geographic distribution; and the need to support the evaluation of innovations and adaptations (Bond et al., 2009; Fixsen et al., 2005).

Second, increase federal and state fiscal support for new business models. States should have the flexibility to use federal funds to provide more prevention-oriented family support services. Additional reforms should also include performance-based contracts with private providers and Medicaid payments for clinical services needed by children or parents – even when the child is not living with the family. Support should follow the child to ensure that families have what they need to ensure healthy child development and reduce the likelihood that the child will re-enter care.

Systems Need to be Redesigned

Child maltreatment prevention depends on intervening earlier with an emphasis on community-based and home-based services. But we should not underestimate the power of a positive relationship. For example, therapeutic relationships are critical in helping parents struggling with child maltreatment. While concrete assistance with life tasks is often not part of the typical treatment, research has found that families whose treatment focused exclusively on parent training and child behavior dropped out more often than families who had opportunities to discuss life concerns beyond child management, particularly among families facing greater adversity (Prinz & Miller, 1994). The parents seemed to appreciate the therapists who provided them with help in their "real lives," beyond the limited therapeutic milieu.

In contrast to short-term parenting education programs, prevention programs that serve children and families over several years are based on different theories regarding how and why behavior change occurs. Short-term parenting programs aim to develop specific skills and achieve a narrow range of well-defined goals. Long-term prevention programs aim to improve parental functioning, broadly considered, and to support families in ongoing efforts to promote child development and school readiness. Ongoing relationships and sustained parental participation are important factors in long-term prevention programs.

Individual programs/interventions can be very helpful but are not, by themselves, the answer. Parents who find themselves connected to the CW system are typically experiencing multiple troubles. They are likely to have been raised in families and housing environments where their own needs were not met and, in fact, where they experienced harsh parenting, and victimization, in one or more ways. While staff may focus on domestic violence, substance abuse, and depression, these conditions may in fact be only the symptoms of far more pervasive and painful problems that may be generational in nature. What these parents need is nurturing relationships and the possibility of staying connected to their children – whether they are able to retain custody or not. They need to find respect in the way the CW workers, lawyers, judges, foster parents, and treatment providers interact with them. They need to be seen as the experts on their children. The specific interventions may be less important than the context in which they are offered. The programs listed in this chapter can be important parts of the system's response to these parents. However, unless we reconfigure the way the system interacts with parents, the individual programs cannot hope to achieve long-term repair for these families (Mann, Kretchmar, & Worsham, 2011; personal communication, Lucy Hudson, April 22, 2011).

Carrying forward and building on the conclusions of the 2014 Institute of Medicine study group and the 2017 Parenting Matters report from the IOM, may be useful (Box 3.2).

Box 3.2

**Key Points Raised by Individual Speakers at the
2012 IOM Study Workshop**

- Universal prevention efforts, especially when focused on new parents, provide evidence of altering parental behaviors and improving outcomes. However, these positive impacts from early intervention programs are inconsistent across models and populations.

- Home visits targeted at mothers with depression can reduce child maltreatment and the transmissions of those behaviors across generations.

- Brief, focused interventions can substantially reduce child maltreatment recurrence rates compared with more typical and higher dose parenting programs.

- A variety of evidence-based prevention models for child maltreatment are now available for dissemination, implementation, and evaluation in community settings (IOM (Institute of Medicine) and National Research Council (NRC), 2012, p. 55).

**Key Points Raised in the Parenting Matters Report of the
National Academy of Sciences/IOM**

- CW is not designed to address those families who have many and chronic needs by virtue of the brief and discontinuous way in which services are delivered.

- New models of service are needed that include periodic checking in with families (perhaps based on contacts with health providers or via collaboration with schools) so that families view services as reliable, positive, and accessible prior to needing CW.

Use Concepts from the Injury Control Field

While addressing a broader set of circumstances other than maltreatment that put children at risk, there are many insights and strategies we can learn from the injury control experts in public health and medicine:

> Injuries have defined risk and protective factors that can be used to define prevention strategies. The term *accident* implies an event occurring by chance, without

pattern or predictability. In fact, most injuries occur under fairly predictable circumstances to high-risk children and families. Most injuries are preventable. The reduction of morbidity and mortality from injuries can be accomplished not only through primary prevention (averting the event or injury in the 1st place), but also through secondary and tertiary prevention.

(Rivara & Grossman, 2015, p.1.41)

Improve Surveillance and Assessment

As the recent Commission to Eliminate Child Abuse and Neglect Fatalities (2016a, 2016b) and others (e.g., Smith et al., 2011) have documented, one of the key areas of work involves using more consistent definitions, measures, monitoring, and case review procedures of child deaths and near deaths – "surveillance" – across states. Vital records data such as child birth certificates, law enforcement (911 and domestic violence calls), hospital emergency room visits, public health data (such as the Women and Infants Care program – WIC), and other data could be more readily merged to learn more about key risk factors. For example, Cook Children's Medical Center in Fort Worth is working on a records-merging project with the University of Texas and the Texas Advanced Computing Center. While breakthroughs are being made in using cross-sector data to identify children most at risk, limitations in policy and practice retard improvement (Barth et al., 2016, p. 5):

> Covington and Petit (2013) identified some of the factors that continue to plague child welfare services. These factors include failure to properly assess the well-being of children in the home and to recognize imminent danger, failure to complete safety and risk assessments correctly or at all, failure to remove children subsequently born into a household after the death of a child or after the parent's custodial rights to another child have been terminated, failure to address the mental health needs of parents, and failure to recognize and respond to parents' clear, repeated indications that they do not want their children. Policies that largely fail to follow up with mothers who have previously shown dangerous parenting – mothers whose parental rights to another child have been previously terminated – create an unnecessary risk for children (Shaw, Barth, Mattingly, Ayer, & Berry, 2013). Assessment tools may aid workers in ascertaining the potential for a child to be harmed in the future. The failure to properly invest in and rigorously test such tools also contributes to risk.

Workforce Development and Support

To implement effective family support strategies, agencies are learning that they need to supplement traditional training workshops with ongoing coaching and clinical support of line staff and supervisors. Organizational culture, climate, and rewards for using effective practices need to be aligned to ensure full implementation and maintenance of high-fidelity practice approaches.

Dissemination of research findings to practitioners is a part of this work. As important as it is to supplement current knowledge regarding what services are effective in reducing child maltreatment and maltreatment recurrence, it is equally important to develop means of systematically communicating findings from research to CW caseworkers and supervisors (DuMont, 2013; Roberts et al., 2017). The Administration for Children, Youth and Families (ACYF), universities, policy think-tanks, and foundations might consider joining together to produce a series of "lessons from research" papers on various CW subjects, or working with universities to produce these papers utilizing the United Kingdom model of making knowledge available to CW practitioners. For more than two decades, the Department of Health (the United Kingdom's counterpart to ACYF) has produced research summaries on foster care and child protection written for practitioners by distinguished scholars. Apart from an occasional practitioner-oriented research review paper and some federal "user guides," there are few publications that are similar to these reports in American scholarship – especially those where high standards of methodological rigor are used as the rubric for study inclusion.

To help address the knowledge gaps, more child maltreatment researchers, CW agency–university partnerships, and innovative funding mechanisms are needed (Institute for the Advancement of Social Work Research, 2008). Especially with the passage of P.L. 115–23 in early 2018, the Federal government should make CW research a higher priority and encourage high standards for methodological rigor, with recognition that mixed-methods studies may be essential.

Organizational Capacity-building

Current CW prevention programs may benefit from a stronger focus on key principles of effectiveness such as higher intensity and/or longer duration, professional and well-trained staff, and comprehensive family services. As mentioned earlier, some interventions may also require specialized contract providers, while others require the participation of allied agencies such as Public Health or Mental Health.

Program implementation has varied substantially due to such factors as inadequate planning, variation from the core model parameters, and jurisdiction or contextual uniqueness. Program administrators and evaluators need to monitor fidelity to the program model, and should employ randomized control groups or other rigorous research designs to determine program impact. Concerns have been raised about the scaling up of innovative services and their implementation without ensuring fidelity. Obstacles to implementation of models originally developed in university settings must be considered. These are becoming core principles in the development of evidence-based and research-informed interventions for CW services (Fixsen et al., 2005).

Finally, we need to support innovative forms of practice. This can be accomplished by setting a policy goal of eliminating intergenerational transmission of child maltreatment, paying greater attention to helping parents and children heal, and by reforming CW federal finance mechanisms (Casey Family Programs, 2010, 2016; Samuels, 2011; Wilson, 2010).

Effective Substance Abuse Treatment Programs Need to be Expanded

The prevalence of substance abuse among caregivers who have maltreated their children is substantial – with rates ranging from about 29 percent (2015 AFCARS data; Wilson et al., 2012; Samuels, 2011) to 79 percent or higher (Young & Gardner, 2002). An epidemiological study published in the *American Journal of Public Health* in 1994 found 40 percent of parents who had physically abused their child, and 56 percent who had neglected their child met lifetime criteria for an alcohol or drug disorder (Kelleher et al., 1994).

While some promising and evidence-based programs exist (e.g., Addiction Policy Forum, 2017; Eienbinder, 2010; Grant et al., 2011; Hall et al., 2015; Maher & Grant, 2013), the field needs more community-based models for working with CW-involved parents with substance abuse issues – a leading cause of neglect and chronic neglect – that have sustainable funding sources. Timely access to these programs is often a challenge (National Institute on Drug Abuse, 2010), and there are many gaps in implementing in practice what we know from good research in this area.

Some interventions that have evidence of effectiveness, and that families and caseworkers view as culturally competent, are ready to take the next step in intervention refinement by incorporating a strong substance abuse treatment component. For example, researchers have determined that the SafeCare intervention is effective with American Indian families involved with CPS (Chaffin et al., 2012). The SafeCare developers are also planning to integrate a substance abuse treatment component into their home-visiting intervention. Research is needed regarding how and for which groups of families to combine or sequence substance abuse treatment, whole family treatment approaches, or domestic violence interventions with parenting skill programs with strong evidence of effectiveness.

One of the promising interventions that may increase parents' willingness to engage in substance abuse treatment is motivational interviewing. Motivational interviewing (MI) is defined as "a client-centered, directive method for enhancing intrinsic motivation to change by exploring and resolving ambivalence" (Miller, Rollnick, & Conforti, 2002, p. 25). It includes a combination of philosophical and clinical aspects that together make up the whole of MI. Three primary aspects include the "spirit" of MI, which forms the foundation for all of the clinical strategies; four general principles to guide the clinical practice; and five early methods for establishing rapport and eliciting motivational statements.

The strategies are designed to help the parents and children examine their ambivalence about change, with the goal of increasing their desire for change, their recognition of the importance of change, and their belief in their ability to make the change. As clients voice these arguments for change, their intention to change increases, which in turn leads to subsequent behavior change. This treatment strategy has been credited with boosting the effectiveness of substance abuse treatment and inducing discouraged parents to engage in counseling (Institute for Family Development, 2008).

One randomized controlled trial studied 71 young mothers involved with CPS and (in most cases) the juvenile court due to substance use and abuse during pregnancy. Half of the mothers were assigned to MI and half to an educational intervention prior to entry into a comprehensive 12-month treatment program. In this study no differences were found between the MI and an education control condition, but for both the MI and EC conditions, the more intervention sessions they attended, the better their treatment engagement and retention. The authors speculated that MI may not provide any additional benefit when the population is coerced. Coercion in and of itself may be the necessary component in treatment engagement and retention, with MI exerting little additional effect (Mullins et al., 2004). This study provided some data on the effectiveness of MI with parents who are involved with CPS and the courts, but additional research and possible model refinement for use in CPS are needed. Students preparing for careers in CW are increasingly likely to be trained in the skilled use of motivational interviewing (Hohman, Pierce, & Barnett, 2015; Pecukonis et al., 2016), although CW agencies are still struggling to determine when a more authoritative approach is needed.

Addressing Other Gaps in Practice Regarding Effective Interventions

There are key gaps in research-based evidence, and a lack of effective widespread implementation, even where we have such evidence. The good news is that there are more promising and research-based practices. While the promising practices have yet to be fully evaluated to qualify as an evidence-based practice, they are gaining recognition among practitioners as being helpful. In addition, there are programs that have been proven effective but have not been validated with evidence using a CW population. However, many models with existing evidence of effectiveness lack an analysis of benefit/cost, and how that might affect a jurisdiction's ability to reinvest foster care savings. In addition, sample sizes in many studies limit our understanding about how programs may have differentially beneficial effects for families facing different kinds of challenges.

A substantial fraction of families with open CW cases have histories of multiple types of child maltreatment and/or have multiple co-occurring risk factors such as substance abuse, depression, family violence, parenting skill deficits, inadequate income, and substandard housing. Effective treatment plans in these cases must address concrete needs as well as underlying conditions that affect parenting such as substance abuse, mood disorders, and parenting skill deficits. As mentioned earlier, caseworkers must address two core dilemmas when working with these hard-to-serve families: (1) where to begin with child safety, supportive and therapeutic interventions; and (2) how to organize a sequence of interventions that does not overwhelm family members (Turnell et al., 2017; Wilson, 2010).

As discussed by Pecora et al. (2014), while there has been encouraging progress in the development and testing of evidence-based interventions in recent years, there continues to be a dearth of effective interventions for some groups of maltreating parents in relation to the following areas:

1. *Child neglect:* Chronic child neglect remains an under-researched area in terms of what can make a difference in these families, particularly when accompanied by substance abuse and mental health disorders.

2. *Develop and evaluate a CW practice model for infants and toddlers:* This may include evaluating one or more approaches that have a population-level effect. This may also involve more widespread use of practice innovations like Three Houses (see http://bayareaacademy.org/wp-content/uploads/2013/05/parker-handout-prompts.pdf) for interviewing children to identify family risk factors and needed strategies.

3. *Combating poverty as a major risk factor:* The potential benefits of various poverty-related services for addressing neglect have not been adequately tested, even though the experimental evaluations of differential response systems in Minnesota and Ohio have provided encouraging evidence that concrete services can have a direct effect in reducing maltreatment recurrence rates and out-of-home placement of children referred to CPS. Promising results have also been found in a community network-based

approach to preventing child abuse recurrence and accelerating permanency in Los Angeles (McCroskey et al., 2010).

4. *Domestic violence:* While there has been slow but steady progress in understanding the link between domestic violence and child maltreatment, and the need for cross-systems collaboration, other than the *Nurse–Family Partnership*, there is little or no research evidence of programs for perpetrators of domestic violence that also reduce child maltreatment recurrence rates (see Hovmand & Ford, 2009; MacMillan et al. 2009; and www. nij.gov/topics/crime/intimate-partner-violence/interventions/batterer-intervention.htm).

5. *Maternal depression and co-morbid disorders:* Are there cognitive behavioral treatment strategies proven to be effective that could be combined with group work interventions and then scaled up for more widespread use in CW? Group work models of treatment have been shown to be cost-effective across a number of areas (Cohen, Phillips, & Hanson, 2008; Macgowan, 2009). But what programs are most effective for parents with co-occurring substance abuse and mental health disorders? Certain innovations such as the combined SafeCare family behavior therapy substance abuse treatment approach may be able to shed some light on the extent of this co-occurrence, and the effectiveness of the home-visiting approaches. But these models have not yet been tested sufficiently for these types of situations to know their true value.

6. *Parent trauma treatment:* There continues to be a dearth of evidence-based interventions for some groups of parents who are struggling with their own victimization (see Box 3.3). For example, trauma-focused cognitive behavioral treatment for parents with PTSD can help speed healing and improve parent functioning. For more information about trauma-focused cognitive behavioral treatment (TF-CBT), see http://tfcbt.musc.edu/. Note that there is also a National Center for Trauma Informed Care (a center within SAMHSA) that offers training on trauma-informed care to states that agree to commit to a trauma-informed approach (see www.samhsa.gov/nctic/training.asp). This is becoming a more widely available intervention because of the research evidence and multiple ways for practitioners to become trained in the model, but we did not locate any evidence that TF-CBT can reduce child maltreatment recurrence.

Box 3.3   Resilience Trumps ACES

The local Walla Walla County Community Network invited Dr. Anda to town in March, 2008 and 165 participants attended his morning seminar [on Adverse

Childhood Experiences (ACES)] at our local community college. At the end of the seminar, one participant, a mother of three, was so moved by Dr. Anda's information, that she stood up, in front of the largely professional organizations of social service providers, health, education and law enforcement entities attending, and said, "For the first time in my life I now know I am not a bad person or a bad parent. I have all 10 ACEs. I just heard Dr. Anda say, My childhood is not my fault." Her willingness to speak so publicly about something as private as her ACE score was inspirational from the standpoint that if a parent, in her first exposure to this information, was so moved by the message of hope and healing that this movement is truly about, then wouldn't the *whole* community want to know this?

Source: The executive director of the Walla Walla Community Resilience Initiative recounting how a parent from Walla Walla recognized that the negative impacts of Adverse Childhood Experiences do not define you as a person. See https://resiliencetrumpsaces.org/about-us/our-story/.

7. *Parents with cognitive impairment:* The research literature regarding programs for severely cognitively impaired parents who are struggling with child maltreatment is scant. Front-line caseworkers urgently need a range of interventions effective for working with developmentally disabled parents. Sometimes interventions like those based on cognitive behavioral techniques will only be effective if special modifications are made for parents with limited cognitive functioning.

8. *Multiple forms of maltreatment:* There has been little or no research in recent years concerning therapeutic interventions for parents engaged in multiple types of child maltreatment; for example, neglect combined with physical abuse and/or sexual abuse. What sequence of interventions would be most cost-effective? Can they address family dynamics and parents' early histories?

9. *Increase research about chronic high-risk families:* We need to increase the research base about chronic high-risk families (Wald, 2014) and what works to prevent maltreatment (see Figure 3.8). N'SCAW-II and other data about what kinds of services children living at home are receiving and how the youth are functioning could be analyzed further. The analysis should include the high percentage of children at home and not receiving services for comparison purposes.

Causes and Consequences	Services in Complex Systems and Policy
• Improve understanding of the separate and synergistic consequences of different forms of child abuse and neglect. • Initiate high-quality longitudinal studies of child abuse and neglect. • Target innovative research on the causes of child abuse and neglect. • Improve understanding of the behavioral and neurobiological mechanisms that mediate the association between child abuse and neglect and its sequelae.	• Explore highly effective delivery systems. • Develop and test new programs for underserved children and families. • Identify the best means of replicating effective interventions and services with fidelity. • Identify the most effective ways to implement and sustain evidence-based programs in real-world settings. • Investigate the longitudinal impacts of prevention. • Encourage research designed to provide a better understanding of trends in the incidence of child abuse and neglect. • Evaluate the impact of laws and policies that address prevention and intervention systems and services for child abuse and neglect at the federal, state, and local levels.

Disentangle the role of cultural processes, social stratification influences, ecological variations, and immigrant/acculturation status.

Apply multidisciplinary, multimethod, and multisector approaches.

Leverage and build upon the existing knowledge base of child abuse and neglect research and related fields, as well as research definitions, designs, and opportunities.

Figure 3.8 Key Research Priorities for Understanding and Preventing Child Maltreatment

Source: Institute of Medicine and National Research Council (2014, p. 392). Permission granted by the National Academy of Sciences, Courtesy of the National Academies Press, Washington, DC.

Summary

Practitioners need to embrace a child development perspective and consider which child well-being goals are most important to address first. In addition, carefully target families that can truly benefit from skill-focused parenting education programs that are evidence-based. It is also important to collaborate with substance abuse and mental health agencies to sustain long-term case management programs for parents with substance abuse and mental health problems. Finally, support early childhood education programs or therapeutic child development programs for children aged 0 to 5 in low-income families referred to CPS.

Evidence-based parenting interventions such as The Incredible Years teach a fairly narrow range of skills in a limited time frame (e.g., 12 to 20 weeks is typical for many programs). A key question that must be answered for effective case planning is whether family members can benefit from skills-based programs before making significant progress in substance abuse or mental health treatment, and/or before domestic violence has ceased. Some parents with substance abuse disorders or depression can benefit from skill-based programs in an early phase of treatment while others need to be in recovery before they are able to apply new parenting skills. As a practical matter, family assessments that address when and how to initiate skill-based parenting interventions for families with substance abuse, mental health, and family violence issues are needed to effectively align interventions with the capacity of parents to benefit from these programs. Research is also needed on how and for which families to combine or sequence substance abuse treatment, mental health services, or domestic violence interventions with evidence-based parenting skills programs.

Treatment planning for multiple forms of child maltreatment must also consider the erosion of social norms around parenting among many at-risk families. It is not enough to teach parenting skills to parents who have lost touch with widely accepted community norms around parenting (e.g., recognizing that preschool children must be consistently supervised and nurtured). Additional research that accounts for family dynamics, cultural and ethnic norms, and the early history of the parents that may itself have involved multiple forms of child abuse and neglect is needed to inform treatment planning for families engaged in multiple forms of maltreatment.

Interventions and prevention programs are needed that not only help maltreating parents develop individual knowledge and skills, strengthen support networks, and provide concrete services, but also that influence deeply ingrained caregiver cultural norms or values that may contribute to child maltreatment. For example, some Samoan families use severe corporal punishment to enforce household rules (Dubanoski & Snyder, 1980). The Nurturing Parents Program has been adapted to specialized populations such as the Hmong, and Triple P has shown strong results in influencing whole communities made up of different ethnic groups. Can some of the existing evidence-based interventions be successfully adapted to other cultures? If so, which ones should we consider? What would a culturally competent and evidence-based intervention or prevention program look like? How do we move beyond intervening in a superficial "culturally responsive manner" to providing truly culturally competent, evidence-based interventions and programs? While reviews of evidence-based interventions for children's mental health are showing that most EBPs do indeed work well across various ethnic groups, these are questions that researchers and practitioners still need to address more extensively (Barrera et al., 2013; Huey & Polo, 2008). Finally, EBP purveyors need to set affordable pricing structures and feasible fidelity assessment processes so that CW agencies can implement EBPs, or scale-up of EBPs will remain sparse in CW.

Conclusions

Besides using the broad-scale but focused prevention efforts referenced earlier, the systems change strategies should be actively supported by government agencies responsible for CW, community supports, health, employment, housing, public assistance, and public health. Note that over 30 states participated in the Casey safety forum discussions, and jurisdictions are already implementing some of these strategies (Chahine et al., 2013; Sanders, 2017). Additional actions are discussed below.

The best of what we know about screening, risk assessment, and decision making from aviation safety, medicine, law enforcement, maritime safety, cognitive psychology, legal risk management, and other fields could be synthesized better and applied more systematically. For example, safety predictors in terms of the leading causes of death among infants, young children, and adolescents have been summarized by the CDC and others. But the risk factors for severe injury and death for those groups of children, including but not limited to injuries and fatalities due to child maltreatment, could be analyzed in more sophisticated ways (see, e.g., Barth et al. (2016) for a summary of domestic and international methodological advances that could be used). Nearly three-quarters (74.8%) of all child fatalities were younger than 3 years old. How could the CW field use "capture-recapture," signal detection, and machine-learning child abuse prediction models (e.g., Schwartz et al., 2017), frequently refreshed predictive analytic algorithms such as those used by the New Zealand model of predictive analytics in Alleghany County (Vaithianathan et al., 2013), Eckerd Rapid Safety Feedback, and other advances to learn more about how to spot and respond better to these families?

The strategies and programs described in this chapter and a recent federal report (Child Welfare Information Gateway, 2017) demonstrate that there are currently a limited number of proven and promising practices that can help prevent child maltreatment and help parents safely avoid child placement. Thus it may be useful to consider these conclusions from the 2014 full report *New directions in child abuse and neglect research* shown in Box 3.4.

Box 3.4   The Bottom Line: Gauging the Current Status of Child Maltreatment Prevention

Investments in preventing child abuse and neglect are increasingly being directed to evidence-based interventions that target pregnant women, new parents, and young children. Since the 1993 NRC report was issued, the prevention field has become stronger and more rigorous both in how it defines its services and in its commitment to evaluative research. And although greater attention is being paid to the development of home-visiting interventions, the field embraces a plethora of prevention strategies. Communities and public agencies continue to demand and support broadly targeted primary prevention strategies such as school-based violence-prevention education, public awareness campaigns, and professional practice reforms, as well as a variety of parenting education strategies and support services for families facing particular challenges.

None of these program approaches is perfect, and they often fail to reach, engage, and retain their full target population successfully. Notable gaps exist in service capacity, particularly in communities at high risk and among populations facing the greatest challenges. And a substantial proportion of those families that do engage in intensive, long-term early intervention programs will exit the services before achieving their targeted program goals. That said, the committee finds the progress in prevention programming to be impressive but the strategies employed to be underdeveloped and inadequately researched.

Finding: A broad range of evidence-based child abuse and neglect prevention programs are increasingly being supported at the community level to address the needs of different populations. Strategies such as early home visiting, targeting pregnant women and parents with newborns are well researched and have demonstrated meaningful improvements in mitigating the factors commonly associated with an elevated risk for poor parenting, including abuse and neglect. Promising prevention models have also been identified in other areas, including school-based violence-prevention education, public awareness campaigns, parenting education, and professional practice reforms.

Finding: Despite substantial progress in the development of effective prevention models, many of these models require more rigorous evaluation. Research is needed to devise strategies for reaching, engaging, and retaining target populations better, as well as to develop the capacity to deliver services to communities at high risk and among populations facing the greatest challenges.

Source: Institute of Medicine and National Research Council (2014). Permission granted by the National Academy of Sciences, Courtesy of the National Academies Press, Washington, DC.

Discussion Questions

1. What would stronger collaboration between CW, CPS, pediatricians, and public health look like?

2. How could a broader array of community supports be brought to bear to prevent child maltreatment?

3. What child maltreatment prevention strategies need to be scaled up most urgently?

Note

1   Abstracted from Pecora, P.J. (2017). *Evidence-based and promising interventions for preventing child fatalities and severe child injuries related to child maltreatment.* Austin, TX: Upbring. Retrieved from www.upbring.org/wp-content/uploads/2017/04/Evidence_based_and_Promising_042617.pdf.

For Further Reading

Committee on Supporting the Parents of Young Children; Board on Children, Youth, and Families; Division of Behavioral and Social Sciences and Education; National Academies of Sciences, Engineering, and Medicine. (2016). *Parenting matters: Supporting parents of children ages 0–8.* Washington, DC: The National Academies Press. Retrieved from www.nap.edu/21868. Comprehensive review of issues and strategies related to strengthening parenting.

Heckman, J., Holland, M.L., Makino, K.K., Pinto, M.L., & Rosales-Rueda, M. (2017). *An analysis of the Memphis Nurse–Family Partnership Program*. Cambridge, MA: National Bureau of Economic Research. Retrieved from https://heckmanequation.org/assets/2017/07/NFP_Final-Paper.pdf. Reanalysis of the Memphis Nurse–Family Partnership data to better identify short- and long-term outcomes and economic benefits.

Bibliography

ACTION for Child Protection, Inc. (2003). *The safety plan*. Author: Aurora, CO. Retrieved from http://actionchildprotection.org/documents/2003/pdf/Dec2003TheSafetyPlan.pdf (accessed July 3, 2015).

Addiction Policy Forum. (2017). *Spotlight series*. Retrieved from www.addictionpolicy.org/spotlightseries.

Avellar, S., Paulsell, D., Sama-Miller, E., & Del Grosso, P. (2013). *Home visiting evidence of effectiveness review: Executive summary*. Washington, DC: Office of Planning, Research and Evaluation, Administration for Children and Families, U.S. Department of Health and Human Services.

Baird, C., Park, K., & Lohrbach, S. (2013). Response to the Hughes et al. paper on Differential Response. *Research on Social Work Practice, 23*(5), 535–538.

Barrera, M., Jr., Castro, F.G., Strycker, L.A. & Toobert, D.J. (2013) Cultural adaptations of behavioral health interventions: A progress report. *Journal of Consulting and Clinical Psychology, 81*, 196–205. 10.1037/a0027085, Retrieved from www.ncbi.nlm.nih.gov/pmc/articles/PMC3965302/.

Barth, R.P. (2008). The move to evidence-based practice: How well does it fit child welfare services? *Journal of Public Child Welfare, 2*, 145–172.

Barth, R.P., Putnam-Hornstein, E., Shaw, T.V., & Dickinson, N.S. (2016). *Safe children: Reducing severe and fatal maltreatment* (Grand Challenges for Social Work Initiative Working Paper No. 17). Cleveland, OH: American Academy of Social Work and Social Welfare. Retrieved from http://aaswsw.org/wp-content/uploads/2015/12/WP17-with-cover.pdf (accessed December 20, 2015).

Barth, R.P., Greeson, J.K.P., Guo, S., Green, R.L., Hurley, S., & Sisson, J. (2007). Outcomes for youth receiving intensive in-home therapy or residential care: A comparison using propensity scores. *American Journal of Orthopsychiatry, 77*, 497–505.

Bell, W.C. (2016). *Together we can*. Speech for the fourteenth annual Together We Can Conference: Building community, creating hope, October 24, Lafayette, Louisiana.

Belsky, J. (1980). Child maltreatment: An ecological integration. *American Psychologist, 35*, 320–335.

Berger, L.M. (2004). Income, family structure, and child maltreatment risk. *Children and Youth Services Review, 26*(8), 725–748.

Bond, G.R., Drake, R.E., McHugo, G.J., Rapp, C.A., & Whitley, R. (2009). Strategies for improving fidelity in the National Evidence-based Practices Project. *Research on Social Work Practice, 19*(5), 569–581.

Bronfenbrenner, U. (1979). *The ecology of human development.* Cambridge, MA: Harvard University Press.

Bronfenbrenner, U., & Morris, P.A. (1998). The ecology of developmental processes. In W. Damon (Ed.), *Handbook of child psychology, fifth edition* (pp. 993–1028). New York: John Wiley & Sons, Inc.

Bugental, D.P., Ellerson, P.C., Lin, E.K., Rainey, B., Kokotovic, A., & O'Hara, N. (2002). A cognitive approach to child abuse prevention. *Journal of Family Psychology, 16*, 243–258.

Bunn, A. (2013) *Signs of Safety® in England.* National Society for the Prevention of Cruelty to Children, London. Retrieved from /www.nspcc.org.uk/services-and-resources/research-and-resources/signs-of-safety-model-england/.

Burns, B.J. and Hoagwood, K. (2002). *Community treatment for youth: Evidence-based interventions for severe emotional and behavioral disorders.* New York: Oxford University Press.

Burwick, A., Zaveri, H., Shang, L., Boller, K., Daro, D., & Strong, D.A. (2014). *Costs of early childhood home visiting: An analysis of programs implemented in the supporting evidence-based home visiting to prevent child maltreatment initiative.* Princeton, NJ: Mathematica Policy Research, Inc.

Caliso, J.A., & Milner, J.S. (1994). Childhood physical abuse, childhood social support, and adult child abuse potential. *Journal of Interpersonal Violence, 9*, 27–44.

Casanueva, C., Wilson, E., Smith, K., Dolan, M., Ringeisen, H., & Horne, B. (2012). *NSCAW II. Wave 2 Report: Child Well-being.* OPRE Report #2012-38, Washington, DC: Office of Planning, Research and Evaluation, Administration for Children and Families, U.S. Department of Health and Human Services. Retrieved from www.acf.hhs.gov/sites/default/files/opre/nscaw_report_w2_ch_wb_final_june_2014_final_report.pdf.

Casey Family Programs. (2010). *Ensuring safe, nurturing and permanent families for children: The need for federal finance reform.* Seattle, WA: Author. Retrieved from www.casey.org/Our Work/PublicPolicy/WhitePapers/

Casey Family Programs. (2016). *7 to 1: Federal investments in child welfare.* Seattle, WA: Author. Retrieved from www.casey.org/federal-investments-in-child-welfare/.

Center for Child and Family Policy. (2004). *Multiple response system evaluation report to the North Carolina Division of Social Services.* Durham, NC: Author.

Center on the Developing Child at Harvard University. (2016). *Applying the Science of child development in child welfare systems.* Retrieved from www.developingchild.harvard.edu.

Center on the Developing Child at Harvard University. (2017). *Three principles to improve outcomes for children and families.* Boston, MA: Author. Retrieved from www.developing child.harvard.edu, p.1.

Centers for Disease Control and Prevention. (2014). *Essentials for childhood: Steps to create safe, stable, nurturing relationships and environments.* Retrieved from www.cdc.gov/viol enceprevention/pdf/essentials_for_childhood_framework.pdf.

Centers for Disease Control and Prevention. (2016). *Preventing multiple forms of violence: A strategic vision for connecting the dots*. Atlanta, GA: Division of Violence Prevention, National Center for Injury Prevention and Control, Centers for Disease Control and Prevention. Retrieved from www.cdc.gov/violenceprevention/pdf/strategic_vision.pdf.

Centers for Disease Control and Prevention. (n.d.). *Social-ecological models for specific types of violence prevention* (web page of resources). Retrieved from https://vetoviolence.cdc.gov/violence-prevention-basics-social-ecological-model.

Chaffin, M. (2004). Is it time to rethink Healthy Start/Healthy Families? *Child Abuse and Neglect, 28*, 589–595.

Chaffin, M., Bard, D, Bigfoot, D.S., & Maher, E.J. (2012). Is a structured, manualized, evidence-based treatment protocol culturally competent and equivalently effective among American Indian parents in child welfare? *Child Maltreatment, 17*, 242–252.

Chahine, Z., Pecora, P.J., Sanders, D., & Wilson, D. (Eds) (2013). Preventing severe maltreatment-related injuries and fatalities: Applying a public health framework and innovative approaches to child protection. *Child Welfare, 92*(2), 9–253.

Child Welfare Information Gateway. (2017). *Child maltreatment prevention: Past, present, and future*. Washington, DC: U.S. Department of Health and Human Services, Children's Bureau. Retrieved from www.childwelfare.gov/pubPDFs/cm_prevention.pdf.

Cicchetti, D. (1994). Advances and challenges in the study of the sequelae of child maltreatment. *Development and Psychopathology, 6*, 1–3.

Cohen, C.S., Phillips, M.H., & Hanson, M. (Eds). (2008). *Strength and diversity in social work with groups: Think group*. New York: Routledge.

Cohen, E., & Canan, L. (2006). Closer to home: Parent mentors in child welfare. *Child Welfare, 85*, 867–884.

Collins, K.S., Strieder, F., DePanfilis, D., Tabor, M., Freeman, P., Linde, L., & Greenberg, P. (2011). Trauma Adapted Family Connections (TA-FC): Reducing developmental and complex trauma symptomatology to prevent child abuse and neglect. *Child Welfare, 90*, 29–47.

Commission to Eliminate Child Abuse and Neglect Fatalities. (2016a). *FACT SHEET – Within our reach: A national strategy to eliminate child abuse and neglect fatalities*. Washington, DC: Government Printing Office, p.1.

Commission to Eliminate Child Abuse and Neglect Fatalities. (2016b). *Within our reach: A national strategy to eliminate child abuse and neglect fatalities*. Washington, DC: Government Printing Office. Retrieved from www.acf.hhs.gov/programs/cb/resource/cecanf-final-report.

Covington, T.M., & Petit, M. (2013). Prevention of child maltreatment fatalities. In K. Briar-Lawson, M. McCarthy, & N. S. Dickinson (Eds), *The Children's Bureau: Shaping a century of child welfare practices, programs, and policies* (pp. 141–165). Washington, DC: NASW Press.

Daley, D., Bachmann, M., Bachmann, B.A., Pedigo, C., Bui, M., & Coffman, J. (2016). Risk terrain modeling predicts child maltreatment. *Child Abuse & Neglect, 62*, 29–38.

De Haan, I., & Manion, K. (2011) Building safety and deepening our practice. *Social Work Now, 47*, 35–43.

DePanfilis, D. (2015). Family Connections: Using collaborative partnerships to support dissemination. *New Directions for Child and Adolescent Development, 2015*(149), 57–67.

DePanfilis, D., Dubowitz, H., & Kunz, J. (2008). Assessing the cost-effectiveness of Family Connections. *Child Abuse & Neglect, 32*, 335–351.

Development Services Group, Inc. (2013). *Protective factors for populations served by the administration on children, youth, and families. A literature review and theoretical framework: Executive summary*. Washington, DC: U.S. Department of Health and Human Services, Administration for Children and Families, Children's Bureau, p. 6. Retrieved from www.dsgonline.com/acyf/DSG%20Protective%20Factors%20Literature%20Review%20 2013%20Exec%20Summary.pdf (accessed May 20, 2016).

Douglas, E.M. (2013). Case, service and family characteristics of households that experience a child maltreatment fatality in the United States. *Child Abuse Review, 22*, 311–326.

Douglas, E.M. (2016). Testing if social services prevent fatal child maltreatment among a sample of children previously known to child protective services. *Child Maltreatment*, pp. 1–11. doi:10.1177/1077559516657890 cmx.sagepub.com.

Drake, B. (2013). Differential response: What to make of the existing research? A response to Hughes et al. *Research on Social Work Practice, 23*(5), 539–544.

Dubanoski, R.A., & Snyder, K. (1980). Patterns of child abuse and neglect in Japanese- and Samoan-Americans. *Child Abuse & Neglect, 4*(4), 217–225. See also how advocates are emphasizing non-violent child-rearing aspects of the Samoan culture: www.samoaob server.ws/index.php?option=com_content&view=article&id=1357%3Achild-abuse-not-part&Itemid=85.

DuMont, K. (2013). *Realizing the potential of research in child welfare*. New York: William T. Grant Foundation. Retrieved from http://wtgrantfoundation.org/library/uploads/2017/03/ 2017-URE-Supplemental-Guidance.pdf.

Eckenrode, J., Ganzel, B., Henderson, C.R., Jr., Smith, E., Olds, D.L., Powers, J., Cole, R., Kitzman, H., & Sidora, K. (2000). Preventing child abuse and neglect with a program of nurse home visitation: The limiting effects of domestic violence. *JAMA, 284*, 1385–1391.

Edgar, J. (2009). Stories of prevention on Los Angeles County, DCFS and community agencies join hands to support families and children. Retrieved from www.casey.org/Resources/Pub lications/StoriesOfPreventionLA.htm.

Eienbinder, S.D. (2010). A qualitative study of Exodus graduates: Family-focused residential substance abuse treatment as an option for mothers to retain or regain custody and sobriety in Los Angeles, California. *Child Welfare, 89*(4), 29–45.

Filene, J.H., Brodowski, M.L., & Bell, J. (2014). Using cost analysis to examine variability in replications of an efficacious child neglect prevention program. *Journal of Public Child Welfare, 8*(4), 375–396. doi:10.1080/15548732.2014.939249.

Filene, J.H., DePanfilis, D., & Smith, E.G. (2010). *Paper 1: Cultural adaptations and assessment of fidelity*. Presentation for a Symposium: Multi-site Findings from the Replication of a Family Strengthening Program with Diverse Populations to Prevent Child Maltreatment. The IVIII ISPCAN International Congress: Strengthening Children and Families Affected by Personal, Intrapersonal, and Global Conflict. Honolulu, Hawaii, September 26–29.

Fixsen, D.L., Naoom, S.F., Blase, K A., Friedman, R.M., & Wallace, F. (2005). *Implementation research: A synthesis of the literature*. Tampa, FL: University of South Florida, Louis de la Parte Florida Mental Health Institute, The National Implementation Research Network (FMHI Publication #231).

Fluke, J.D., Harlaar, N., Heisler, K., Darnell, A., Brown, B., & Merkel-Holguin, L. (2016). *Differential response and the safety of children reported to child protective services: A tale of six states*. Washington, DC: U.S. Department of Health and Human Services, Office of Assistant Secretary for Planning and Evaluation. Retrieved from https://aspe.hhs.gov/system/files/pdf/204981/DifferentialResponse.pdf.

Government Accountability Office. (2013). Child welfare: States use flexible federal funds, but struggle to meet service needs (GA-13-170). Retrieved from www.gao.gov/assets/660/651667.pdf.

Grant, T., Huggins, J., Graham, J.C., Ernst, C., Whitney, N., & Wilson, D. (2011). Maternal substance abuse and disrupted parenting: Distinguishing mothers who keep their children from those who do not. *Children and Youth Services Review, 33*, 2176–2185.

Hall, M.T., Huebner, R.A., Sears, J.S., Posze, L., Willauer, T., & Oliver, J. (2015). Sobriety treatment and recovery teams in rural Appalachia: Implementation and outcomes. *Child Welfare, 94*(4), 119–138.

Hargreaves, M., Verbitsky-Savitz, N., Penoyer, S., Vine, M., Ruttner, L., & Davidoff-Gore, A. (2015). *APPI cross-site evaluation: Interim report*. Cambridge, MA: Mathematica Policy Research. Retrieved July 15, 2017 from www.appi-wa.org or www.mathematica-mpr.com (accessed July 15, 2017 (keyword: APPI).

Harper-Browne, C. (2014). *The Strengthening Families Approach and Protective Factors Framework: Branching out and reaching deeper*. Washington, DC: Center for the Study of Social Policy, September.

Heckman, J., Holland, M.L., Makino, K.K., Pinto, M.L., & Rosales-Rueda, M. (2017). *An analysis of the Memphis Nurse–Family Partnership Program*. Cambridge, MA: National Bureau of Economic Research. Retrieved from https://heckmanequation.org/assets/2017/07/NFP_Final-Paper.pdf.

Heller, S.S., Larrieu, J.A., D'Imperio, R., & Boris, N.W. (1999). Research on resilience to child maltreatment: Empirical considerations. *Child Abuse & Neglect, 23*(4), 321–338.

Hohman, M., Pierce, P., & Barnett, E. (2015). Motivational interviewing: An evidence-based practice for improving student practice skills. *Journal of Social Work Education, 51*(2), 287–297. doi:10.1080/10437797.2015.1012925.

Hovmand, P.S., & Ford, D.N. (2009). Sequence and timing of three community interventions to domestic violence. *American Journal of Community Psychology, 44*, 261–272. doi:10.1007/s10464-009-9264-6.

Huey, S.J., & Polo, A. (2008). Evidence-based psychosocial treatments for ethnic minority youth. *Journal of Clinical Child & Adolescent Psychology, 37*(1), 262–301.

Hughes, R.C., Rycus, J.S., Saunders-Adams, S.M., Hughes, L.K., & Hughes, K.N. (2013). Issues in differential response. *Research on Social Work Practice, 23*(5), 493–520.

Huntsman, L. (2006). *Family group conferencing in a child welfare context.* New South Wales, Australia: Centre for Parenting & Research.

Hurley, K.M., Pepper, M.R., Candelaria, M., Wang, Y., Caulfield, L.E., Latta, L., Hager, E.R., & Black, M.M. (2013). Systematic development and validation of a theory-based questionnaire to assess toddler feeding. *Journal of Nutrition, 143*(12), 2044–2049. doi:10.3945/jn.113.179846.

Institute for the Advancement of Social Work Research. (2008). *Strengthening university/agency research partnerships to enhance child welfare outcomes: A toolkit for building research partnerships.* Seattle, WA: Casey Family Programs.

Institute for Family Development. (2008). *Motivational interviewing in the Homebuilders® Model.* Federal Way, WA: Author. Retrieved from www.institutefamily.org/pdf/Motivation alInterviewingHOMEBUILDERS.pdf (accessed March 1, 2008).

Institute of Medicine and National Research Council. (2012). *Child maltreatment research, policy, and practice for the next decade: Workshop summary.* Washington, DC: The National Academies Press.

Institute of Medicine and National Research Council. (2014). *New directions in child abuse and neglect research.* Washington, DC: The National Academies Press. Retrieved from www.nap.edu/catalog/18331/new-directions-in-child-abuse-and-neglect-research.

Jonson-Reid, M., Emery, C.R., Drake, B., & Stahlschmidt, M.J. (2010). Understanding chronically reported families. *Child Maltreatment, 15*(4), 271–281.

Kaiser, A., & Delaney, E. (1996). The effects of poverty on parenting young children. *Peabody Journal of Education, 71*(4), 66–85.

Kelleher, K., Chaffin, M., Hollenberg, J., & Fischer, E. (1994). Alcohol and drug disorders among physically abusive and neglectful parents in a community-based sample. *American Journal of Public Health, 84*, 1586–1590.

Krysik, J., LeCroy, C.W., & Ashford, J.B. (2008). Participants' perceptions of healthy families: A home visitation program to prevent child abuse and neglect. *Child and Youth Services Review, 30*, 45–61.

Leake, R., Longworth-Reed, L. Williams, N., & Potter, C. (2012). Exploring the benefits of a parent partner mentoring program in child welfare, *Journal of Family Strengths, 12*(1). Retrieved from http://digitalcommons.library.tmc.edu/jfs/vol12/iss1/6.

Littell, J.H. (2005). Lessons from a systematic review of effects of multisystemic therapy. *Children and Youth Services Review, 27*(4), 445–463.

Loman, L.A., & Siegel, G.L. (2013). Hughes et al. Science or promotion? *Research on Social Work Practice, 23*(5), 554–559.

Lutzker, J.R., & Bigelow, K.M. (2002). *Reducing child maltreatment: A guidebook for parent services.* New York: Guilford Press.

Macgowan, M.J. (2009). *Group work across populations, challenges, and settings.* Oxford bibliographies online paper. Retrieved from www.oxfordbibliographiesonline.com/view/document/obo-9780195389678/obo-9780195389678-0032.xml.

MacMillan, H.L., Wathen, C.N., Barlow, J., Fergusson, D.M., Leventhal, J.M., & Taussig, H.N. (2009). Interventions to prevent child maltreatment and associated impairment. *Lancet, 373*, 250–266.

Maher, E., Corwin, T., & Pecora, P.J. (2017). *Poverty and child welfare.* Presentation for the Birth Parent Advisory Committee, Casey Family Programs, May 15.

Maher, E.J., & Grant, T. (2013). *Parent–Child Assistance Program outcomes suggest sources of cost savings for Washington State* (Research brief). Seattle, WA: Casey Family Programs. Retrieved from http://depts.washington.edu/pcapuw/inhouse/PCAP_Cost_Savings_Brief_Feb_2013.pdf. Also see: http://depts.washington.edu/pcapuw/.

Mani, A., Mullainathan, S., Shafir, E., & Zhao, J. (2013). Poverty impedes cognitive function. *Science, 341*(6149), 976–980.

Mann, J.C., Kretchmar, M.D., & Worsham, N.L. (2011). Being in relationship: Paradoxical truths and opportunities for change in foster care. *Zero to Three, 31*(3), 11–16.

Marcenko, M., & Staerkel, E. (2006). Home visiting for parents of pre-school children in the US. In C. McCauley, P.J. Pecora, & W.E. Rose (Eds), *Enhancing the well being of children and families through effective interventions – UK and USA evidence for practice* (p. 89). London, and Philadelphia, PA: Jessica Kingsley.

Marts, E.J., Lee, R., McCroy, R., & McCroskey, J. (2008). Point of engagement: Reducing disproportionality and improving child and family outcomes. *Child Welfare, 87*(2), 335–358.

McCroskey, J., Pecora, P.J., Franke, T., Christie, C.A., & Lorthridge, J. (2012). Strengthening families and communities to prevent child abuse and neglect: Lessons from the Los Angeles Prevention Initiative Demonstration Project. *Child Welfare, 91*(2), 39–60.

McCroskey, J., Franke, T., Christie, C.A., Pecora, P.J., Lorthridge, J., Fleischer, D., & Rosenthal, E. (2010). *Prevention Initiative Demonstration Project (PIDP): Year two evaluation summary report.* Los Angeles, CA: Los Angeles County Department of Children and Family Services and Seattle, WA: Casey Family Programs.

Miller, W.R., Rollnick S., & Conforti, K. (2002). *Motivational interviewing: Preparing people for change.* New York: The Guilford Press.

Miyamoto, S., Romano, P.S., Putnam-Hornstein, E., Thurston, H., Dharmar, M., & Joseph, J.G. (2016). Risk factors for fatal and non-fatal child maltreatment in families previously investigated by CPS: A case-control study. *Child Abuse & Neglect, 63*, 222–232.

Mullins, S.M., Suarez, M., Ondersma, S.J., & Page, M.C. (2004). The impact of Motivational Interviewing on substance abuse treatment retention: A randomized control trial of women involved with child welfare. *Journal of Substance Abuse Treatment, 27*, 51–58.

Multisystemic Therapy Institute. (2017). *MST-Child Abuse and Neglect (CAN).* Retrieved from: http://mstservices.com/target-populations/chld-abuse-and-neglect.

Munro, E. (2011). *Munro review of child protection: Final report – a child-centred system*. London: Department of Education.

National Governor's Association Center for Best Practices. (2008). *Nine things Governors can do to build a strong child welfare system*. Washington, DC: Author.

National Institute on Drug Abuse. (2010). *Strategic plan 2010*. Retrieved from www.nida.nih. gov/StrategicPlan/StratPlan10/Index.html.

Nelson-Dusek, S., Idzelis Rothe, M.I., Humenay Roberts, Y.H., & Pecora, P.J. (2017). Assessing the value of family safety networks in child protective services: Early findings from Minnesota. *Child & Family Social Work, 22*(4), 1365–1373.

Nurius, P.S., Green, S., Logan Greene, P., & Borja, S. (2015). Life course pathways of adverse childhood experiences toward adult psychological well-being: A stress process analysis. *Child Abuse & Neglect, 45*, 143–153.

O'Connell, M.E., Boat, T., & Warner, K.E. (Eds) (2009). *Preventing mental, emotional, and behavioral disorders among young people: Progress and possibilities*. Committee on Prevention of Mental Disorders and Substance Abuse Among Children, Youth, and Young Adults: Research Advances and Promising Interventions. National Research Council and Institute of Medicine. Board on Children, Youth, and Families, Division of Behavioral and Social Sciences and Education. Washington, DC: The National Academies Press. Retrieved from www.nap.edu/catalog.php?record_id=12480.

Olds, D.L., Sadler, L., & Kitzman, H. (2007). Programs for parents of infants and toddlers: Recent evidence from randomized trials. *Journal of Child Psychology and Psychiatry, 48*, 355–391. doi:10.1111/j.1469-7610.2006.01702.x.

Olds, D.L., Henderson, C.R., Chamberlin, R., & Tatelbaum, R. (1986). Preventing child abuse and neglect: A randomized trial of nurse home visitation. *Pediatrics, 78*, 65–78.

Olds, D.L., Kitzman, H., Knudtson, M.D., Anson, E., Smith, J.A., & Cole, R. (2014). Effect of home visiting by nurses on maternal and child mortality: Results of a 2-decade follow-up of a randomized clinical trial. *JAMA Pediatrics, 168*(9), 800–806. doi:10.1001/jamapediatrics.2014.472.

Olds, D., Henderson, C.R. Jr., Cole, R., Eckenrode, J., Kitzman, H., Luckey, D., Pettitt, L., Sidora-Arcoleo, K., Morris, P., & Powers, J. (1998). Long-term effects of nurse home visitation on children's criminal and antisocial behavior: 15-year follow-up of a randomized controlled trial. *JAMA, 280*, 1238–1244.

Olds, D.L., Kitzman, H., Hanks, C., Cole, R., Anson, E., Sidora-Arcoleo, K., Luckey, D.W., Henderson, C.R., Jr., Holmberg, J., Tutt, R.A., Stevenson, A.J., & Bondy, J. (2007). Effects of nurse home visiting on maternal and child functioning: Age-9 follow-up of a randomized trial. *Pediatrics, 120*, e832–845.

Pecora, P.J. (2017). A Road Map from Research to Practice: Upbring's second Annual Conference on Child Maltreatment, *Evidence-based and Promising Interventions for Preventing Child Fatalities and Severe Child Injuries Related to Child Maltreatment*. Austin, TX: April 10. Retrieved from www.upbring.org/wp-content/uploads/2017/04/Evidence_based_and_Promising_042617.pdf.

Pecora, P.J., (2018a). *Preventing child fatalities and serious injuries due to child abuse and neglect: A resource paper.* New York: Taylor and Francis.

Pecora, P.J. (2018b). *Risk and protective factors for child abuse and neglect: A resource paper.* New York: Taylor and Francis.

Pecora, P.J., Sanders, D., Wilson, D., English, D., Puckett, A., & Rudlang-Perman, K. (2014). Addressing common forms of child maltreatment: Intervention strategies and gaps in our knowledge base. *Child & Family Social Work, 19*(3), 321–332. doi:10.1111/cfs.12021.

Pecukonis, E., Greeno, E., Hodorowicz, M., Park, H., Ting, L., Moyers, T., Burry, C., Linsenmeyer, D., Strieder, F., & Wade, K. (2016). Teaching motivational interviewing to child welfare social work students using live supervision and standardized clients: A randomized controlled trial. *Journal of the Society for Social Work and Research, 7*(3), 479–505. doi:10.1086/688064.

Pepin, M.G., & Byers, P.H. (2015). What every clinical geneticist should know about testing for osteogenesis imperfecta in suspected child abuse cases. *American Journal of Medicine and Genetics Part C: Seminars in Medical Genetics, 169,* 307–313.

Poole, M.K., Seal, D.W., & Taylor, C.A. (2014). A systematic review of universal campaigns targeting child physical abuse prevention. *Health Education Research, 29*(3), 388–432.

Prinz, R.J., & Miller, G. (1994). Family-based treatment for childhood antisocial behavior: Experimental influences on dropout and engagement. *Journal of Consulting and Clinical Psychology, 62,* 645–50. doi:10.1037//0022-006X.62.3.645.

Prinz, R.J., Sanders, M.R., Shapiro, C.J., Whitaker, D.J., & Lutzker, J.R. (2009). Population-based prevention of child maltreatment: The U.S. Triple P System Population Trial. *Prevention Science, 10,* 1–13.

Putnam-Hornstein, E., & Needell, B. (2011). Predictors of child welfare contact between birth and age five: An examination of California's 2002 birth cohort. *Children and Youth Services Review, 33*(11), 2400–2407.

Putnam-Hornstein, E., Cleves, M., Licht, R., & Needell, B. (2013). Risk of fatal injury in young children following abuse allegations: Evidence from a prospective, population-based study. *American Journal of Public Health, 103*(10), e39–e44.

Rivara, F.P., & Grossman, D.C. (2015). Injury control. In R.M. Kliegman, B.F. Stanton, J.W. St. Geme, N.F. Schor, & R.E. Behrman (Eds), *Nelson textbook of pediatrics* (pp. 1–41 to 1–47). Philadelphia, PA: Elsevier Publishers.

Roberts, Y.H., Killos, L.F., Maher, E., O'Brien, K., & Pecora, P.J. (2017). *Strategies to promote research use in child welfare.* Seattle, WA: Casey Family Programs. Retrieved from www.casey.org/media/strategies-promote-research.pdf.

Samuels, B. (2011). *Promoting social and emotional well-being: A new narrative for the future of child welfare.* Presented at the Carter Center Symposium on Mental Health, Atlanta, GA, October.

Sanders, D. (2017). Policy and practice changes form around national strategy to reduce fatalities and improve child safety. *Chronicle of Social Change.* Retrieved from https://chronicleofsocialchange.org/opinion/policy-and-practice-changes-form-around-national-strategy-to-reduce-child-maltreatment-fatalities-and-improve-child-safety/25095.

Schoenwald, S.K., Borduin, C.K., & Henggeler, S.W. (1998). Multisystemic therapy: Changing the natural and service ecologies of adolescents and families. In M.H. Epstein, K. Kutash, & A. Duchnowski (Eds), *Outcomes for children and youth with emotional and behavioral disorders and their families: Programs and evaluation best practice.* Austin, TX: Pro-Ed. (pp. 485–511). Quotation from pp. 486–487.

Schwartz, I.M., Nowakowski, E., Ramos-Hernandez, A., & York, P. (2017). Predictive and prescriptive analytics, machine learning and child welfare risk assessment: The Broward County experience. *Children and Youth Services Review. 81*, 309–320. doi:10.1016/j.childyouth.2017.08.020.

Schweitzer, D., Pecora, P.J., Nelson, K., Walters, B., & Blythe, B. (2015). Building the evidence base for intensive family preservation services. *Journal of Public Child Welfare, 9*, 423–443.

Shaw, T.V., Barth, R.P., Mattingly, J., Ayer, D., & Berry, S. (2013). Child welfare birth match: Timely use of child welfare administrative data to protect newborns. *Journal of Public Child Welfare, 7*(2), 217–234.

Slack, K.S., Berger, L.M., & Noyes, J.L. (in press). Poverty and child maltreatment: What we know and what we still need to learn. *Children and Youth Services Review.*

Smith, L.R., Gibbs, D., Wetterhall, S., Schnitzer, P.G., Farris, T., Crosby, A.E., & Leeb, R.T. (2011). Public health efforts to build a surveillance system for child maltreatment mortality: Lessons learned for stakeholder engagement. *Journal of Public Health Management and Practice, 17*(6), 542–549. doi:10.1097/PHH.0b013e3182126b6b.

Sperry, D.M., & Widom, C.S. (2013). Child abuse and neglect, social support, and psychopathology in adulthood: A prospective investigation. *Child Abuse & Neglect, 37*(6), 415–435.

Stoltzfus, E. (2017). *Child welfare: An overview of federal programs and their current funding.* Washington, DC: Congressional Research Service. Retrieved from https://fas.org/sgp/crs/misc/R43458.pdf.

Swenson, C.C., Schaeffer, C.M., Henggeler, S.W., Faldowski, R., & Mayhew, A.M. (2010). Multisystemic therapy for child abuse and neglect: A randomized effectiveness trial. *Journal of Family Psychology, 24*(4), 497–507. Retrieved from http://dx.doi.org/10.1037/a0020324.

Thompson, R.A. (1995) *Preventing child maltreatment through social support: A critical analysis.* Thousand Oaks, CA: Sage.

Turnell, A., & Essex, S. (2006) *Working with situations of "denied" child abuse: The resolutions approach.* Buckingham: Open University Press.

Turnell, A, Murphy, T., & Munro, E. (2013). Soft is hardest: Leading for learning in child protection services following a child fatality. *Child Welfare, 92*(2), 199–216.

Turnell, A., Pecora, P.J., Roberts, Y.H., Caslor, M., & Koziolek, D. (2017). Signs of safety as a promising comprehensive approach for reorienting CPS organizations' work with children, families and their community supports. In M. Connolly (Ed.), *Beyond the risk paradigm in child protection.* London: Palgrave Macmillan Education (pp. 130–146). Retrieved from https://he.palgrave.com/page/detail/beyond-the-risk-paradigm-in-child-protection-marie-connolly/?sf1=barcode&st1=9781137441300.

Tuten, M., Jones, H.E., Schaeffer, C.M., Wong, C.J., & Stitzer, M.L. (2012). *Reinforcement-based treatment (RBT): A practical guide for the behavioral treatment of drug addiction*. Washington, DC: American Psychological Association.

University of Maryland Medical Center. (n.d.). SEEK Project, University of Maryland Medical Center. Retrieved from.www.umm.edu/pediatrics/seek_project.htm.

U.S. Department of Health and Human Services. (2005). *Alternative responses to child maltreatment: Findings from NCANDS*. Washington, DC: US Department of Health and Human Services, Office of the Assistant Secretary for Planning and Evaluation.

U.S. Department of Health and Human Services, Administration for Children and Families, Administration on Children, Youth and Families, Children's Bureau. (2016). *Child Maltreatment 2015,* pp. 52–55. Retrieved from www.childrensrights.org/wp-content/uploads/2017/01/cm2015.pdf (accessed January 28, 2017).

U.S. Department of Health and Human Services, Administration for Children and Families, Administration on Children, Youth and Families, Children's Bureau. (2018). *Child maltreatment 2016*. Retrieved from www.acf.hhs.gov/cb/research-data-technology/statistics-research/child-maltreatment.

Utah Child and Family Services, Department of Human Services. (2014). *HomeWorks: Social Services Appropriations Subcommittee update*. Retrieved from http://le.utah.gov/interim/2014/pdf/00005436.pdf.

Vaithianathan, R., Maloney, T., Putnam-Hornstein, E., & Jiang, N. (2013). Children in the public benefit system at risk of maltreatment: Identification via predictive modeling. *American Journal of Preventive Medicine, 45*(3), 354–359.

Vogus, T.J., Cull, M.J., Hengelbrok, N.E., Modell, S.J., & Epstein, R.A. (2016). Assessing safety culture in child welfare: Evidence from Tennessee. *Children and Youth Services Review, 65,* 94–103.

Wahler, R.G. (1980). The insular mother: Her problems in parent–child treatment. *Journal of Applied Behavior Analysis, 13,* 207–219.

Wald, M.S. (2014). Beyond child protection: Helping all families provide adequate parenting. In K. McCartney, H. Yoshikawa, & L.B. Forcier (Eds), *Improving the odds for America's children: Future directions in policy and practice* (pp. 135–148). Cambridge, MA: Harvard Education Press.

Washington State Institute for Public Policy (WSSIP). (2004). *Benefit–Cost results*. Olympia, WA: Author.

Washington State Institute for Public Policy (WSSIP). (2016a). *Benefit–Cost results*. Olympia, WA: Author.

Washington State Institute for Public Policy (WSSIP). (2016b*) Intensive Family Preservation Services: Program Fidelity Influences Effectiveness – Revised*. Retrieved from www.wsipp.wa.gov/Reports/168.

Waugh, F., & Bonner, M. (2002) Domestic violence and child protection: Issues in safety planning. *Child Abuse Review, 11,* 282–295.

Wildeman, C. (2017). *Geographic variation in the cumulative risk of maltreatment and foster care placement.* Presentation to Casey Family Programs, Seattle, Washington, March 8.

Wilson, D. (2010). *Mustering resources to prevent child neglect: Reflections and strategies.* Presentation for the Center for Advanced Studies in Child Welfare, School of Social Work, University of Minnesota, Minneapolis, MN, June 9.

Wilson, E., Dolan, M., Smith, K., Casanueva, C., & Ringeisen, H. (2012). *NSCAW child well-being spotlight: Caregivers of children who remain in-home after maltreatment need services.* Washington, DC: Office of Planning, Research and Evaluation, U.S. Department of Health and Human Services. Retrieved from www.acf.hhs.gov/programs/opre/resource/nscaw-iichild-well-being-spotlight-caregivers-of-children-whoremain-in.

Wright, M., Ticklor, S. & Vernor, K. (2008). *California child welfare services eleven-county pilot project evaluation report.* Santa Rosa, CA: The Results Group.

Young, N.K., & Gardner, S.L. (2002). *Navigating the pathways: Lessons and promising practices in linking alcohol and drug services with child welfare* (SAMHSA Publication No. SMA 02-3752). Rockville, MD: Substance Abuse and Mental Health Services Administration, Center for Substance Abuse Treatment.

Zielewski, E.H., Macomber, J., Bess, R., & Murray, J. (2006). *Families' connections to services in an alternative response system.* Washington, DC: Urban Institute press. Retrieved from www.urban.org/UploadedPDF/311397_Families_Connections.pdf.

Zielinski, D.S., Eckenrode, J., & Olds, D.L. (2009). Nurse home visitation and the prevention of child maltreatment: Impact on the timing of official reports. *Development and Psychopathology, 21,* 441–453.

Strengthening Families through Anti-poverty Efforts[1]

Learning Objectives

1. Understand the definitions, extent, and contributors to poverty in the USA.

2. Explore strategies for reducing poverty, including international innovations.

3. Understand where the anti-poverty field may be headed.

Introduction

Why Should We Care about Child and Family Poverty?

As discussed in Chapter 2 and the risk and protective factors resource paper for this textbook (Pecora, 2018), poverty is a major risk factor for child maltreatment, as it hampers positive parenting and healthy family functioning in many ways. The consequences for health and well-being of poverty are immeasurable and experienced by children through higher rates of parental violence toward each other, substance abuse, homelessness, and mental illness. Although we have long resisted, as a field, the notion that these problems are not equally distributed across all economic groups, the findings have become increasingly clear, over the course of our four volumes, that poverty does not only increase the likelihood of having these problem detected; the differences are real.

Poverty Rates

Poverty can be measured in many ways. More than one-third of households in the U.S. meet the official federal poverty level rate or are asset limited, income constrained, and employed (see the ALICE project at http://unitedwayalice.org/). Whereas the official poverty rate indicates that 10.4 percent of households lived in poverty in 2015 we recognize that many more families are finding that their incomes are being outpaced by the cost of housing and transportation, and that they have insufficient savings to manage even a small financial crisis. Together, these represent more than one-third of the population, even in more prosperous states like Maryland and New Jersey (U.S. Census Bureau, 2016a).

But one in five children in the U.S. lives below the federal poverty level (FPL) and nearly half of children in America are classified as poor or near poor (DeNavas-Walt & Proctor, 2015). Most of these children have parents who work, but low wages, part-time work hours, a lack of benefits, and unstable employment leave their families struggling to make ends meet (National Center on Children in Poverty, 2014).

This is important as a growing body of research is establishing the connection between family income and child maltreatment, notably physical child neglect (Berger et al., 2013; Sedlack et al., 2010). The NIS 3 study found that the incidence of neglect was more than 40 times higher in families with incomes under $15,000 per year vs. families with incomes over $30,000 per year (U.S. DHHS, 1996). Children from these families were over 22 times more likely to experience some form of maltreatment that fit the Harm Standard [the NIS more serious maltreatment category] and over 25 times more likely to suffer some form of maltreatment as defined by the Endangerment Standard [the NIS less serious maltreatment category]. Children from the lowest income families were 18 times more likely to be sexually abused, almost 56 times more likely to be educationally neglected, and over 22 times more likely to be seriously injured from maltreatment as defined under the Harm Standard than children from the higher income families (Sedlak & Broadhurst, 1996, pp. xvii, 8–7). In NIS-4, families deemed to have low socioeconomic status continued to be more likely to experience child maltreatment than families of higher socioeconomic status (Sedlak et al., 2010), although the ratios were smaller than NIS-3 (perhaps because the sample was larger and, thus, the variation was less).

Racial and ethnic differences. African American (28.1%), Native American (26.6%: Proctor, Semega, & Kollar, 2016), and Hispanic American (any race – 25.0%), families have the highest poverty rates, in that order compared to White-only families (14.3%) (U.S. Census Bureau, 2016f). Statistics showing the large poverty gap between Black, Native American, and Latino children – compared to Whites and Asians – do not adequately capture the far greater disparities that occur when there is concentrated poverty (Drake & Rank, 2009).

Prevention of racial disproportionality in actual and reported child maltreatment may only be successful by addressing the poverty in which Black children live (Drake & Jonson-Reid, 2011); Latino maltreatment rates are less closely tied to poverty rates.

Extreme Poverty

Deep or extreme poverty exists profoundly in America. Deep poverty is defined as having a household income below half of the federal poverty line. So, for a family of three (a parent with two children), this would be defined as having a household income of less than $10,390 in 2018 dollars (see https://aspe.hhs.gov/poverty-guidelines). In 2015, about 6.6 percent of Americans (20.3 million) lived in deep poverty (Proctor, Semega, & Kollar, 2016; U.S. Census Bureau, 2016b). This percentage is higher for children. About 11 percent of all U.S. children under the age of 9 live in deep poverty: that means more than one in ten children (Ekono, Jiang, & Smith, 2016). *Put another way, 3 million children in the U.S. are living in households with incomes of less than $2 per day per person in the household.* Since the passage of TANF in 1996, the number of families living in $2-a-day poverty has more than doubled, reaching 1.5 million households in early 2011 (Edin & Shaefer, 2015). There is also a strong relationship between rates of deep poverty and African American and Native American racial ethnic identity.

Health Insurance Coverage

Health insurance coverage is another key indicator of family deprivation. The Affordable Care Act has increased health insurance coverage for millions of Americans, but the cost of the insurance plans and prescription drug co-pays remains too expensive. For example, between 2014 and 2015, the percentage and number of people without health insurance coverage decreased by 1.3 percentage points. In 2015, the percentage of people without health insurance coverage for the entire calendar year was 9.1 percent, or 29.0 million (see Figure 1 and Table 1 in a report at www.census.gov/data/tables/2016/demo/health-insurance/p60-257.html). Over time, changes in the rate of health insurance coverage and the distribution of coverage types may reflect economic trends, shifts in the demographic composition of the population, and policy changes that impact access to healthcare. Several such policy changes occurred in 2014, when many provisions of the Patient Protection and Affordable Care Act went into effect. In 2015, the uninsured rate for children younger than age 19 was down to 5.3 percent, but we still need to do more for children in poverty: in 2015, the uninsured rate for children younger than age 19 in poverty (7.5%) was higher than the uninsured rate for children not in poverty (4.8%) (U.S. Census Bureau, 2016a).

Economic Disconnection

Despite the high numbers of U.S. families in poverty and deep poverty, there are a high number of poor families that are not receiving economic assistance. Families that neither work nor receive economic assistance are called "economically disconnected" families. Nationally, only about 23 percent of poor families actually receive cash assistance or cash transfers (other than food stamps). This number has gone down significantly since 1996 before welfare reform. This is due to time limits, work requirements, and administrative hurdles (Clark, 2016).

For example, researchers examined this issue in a child welfare sample, and found that one in five (20%) of the child welfare-involved families in Washington State can be classified as economically disconnected. Over four out of five (84%) of these caregivers report an unmet need such as housing, medical care, or help with finding employment. They report higher levels of alcohol and substance abuse and are the least engaged in services. They are the most likely to have children in out-of-home care. This group obviously represents a target population with unmet economic needs, social and economic isolation, and significant challenges in successfully parenting and engaging in services that might be of assistance. Given that Washington and many other states struggle with long-stayers in foster care, we need to identify a way to better work with them, since 20 percent is not a small segment of the child welfare population (Partners for Our Children, 2016).

Nationally, only *23 percent* of poor families receive cash assistance or cash transfers (nationwide). This has important implications because welfare benefits are (1) one way to reach and identify families who may need more help or where children are at risk; and (2) these families may also be more socially isolated than other families – and social isolation is a risk factor for maltreatment (see Chapter 2, this volume, and Pecora, 2018).

Why Should We Care about Family Poverty?

As discussed in Chapter 2, one of the textbook resource papers (Pecora, 2018), and other research (e.g., Slack, Berger, & Noyes, in press), family poverty remains one of the strongest factors associated with child maltreatment because of the deprivation and stress it places on families:

Poverty involves at least 3 types of disadvantage: income poverty, severe material hardship, and adult health problems such as family illness or disability that threaten economic security. Material hardship is related to finances, utilities, food, housing, and medical care, as evidenced by running out of money before the next paycheck, utilities turned off because of lack of payment, food insecurity, moving in with others or moving to a shelter, or foregoing medical services because of lack of money.

(Dreyer et al., 2016a, p. S2)

Poverty is an underlying factor in some of the most common reasons for a child maltreatment report: child deprivation, insufficient food, clothing, shelter, inadequate hygiene, or sometimes just general "neglect." *But the vast majority of the poor do not abuse or neglect their children*, and not all child maltreatment occurs in poor families. But parenting in poverty, especially deep poverty, becomes an act of heroism (personal communication, Erin Maher, September 20, 2016). To reduce maltreatment associated with poverty, we must substantially reduce poverty and ameliorate the worst of its impacts upon families.

One Wisconsin study merged state-level administrative data on CPS investigations and substantiations with foreclosure filings. The researchers found that in the year before and after a foreclosure filing there was a 70 percent greater risk for a family to be investigated or substantiated for maltreatment (Berger et al., 2015). This is key data about one of the economic stressors for families.

Another study used admissions data from several hospitals and saw a correlation between the timing of the recession and hospital admissions for abusive head trauma. The Abusive Head Trauma (AHT) rates were highest during the recession, but remained higher than prior to the recession for the three years following, suggesting a lingering effect. In fact, they found a 60 percent increase in AHT during the recession than before it. Their analysis, however, did not point to unemployment rates as a major contributor (Berger et al., 2015, 2011).

Because of their large economic and social costs, minimizing child maltreatment and other Adverse Childhood Experiences (ACEs) is crucial to a healthy and productive society. When we look at poverty's association with known risk factors for child maltreatment, we start to get at some of the mechanisms by which poverty and maltreatment are related. For example, the following are primary risk factors for maltreatment *other than poverty*:

- substance abuse
- mental health

- parenting stress
- domestic violence
- a combination of these factors.

While the causal pathways are complex and not fully mapped, it is clear that decreasing family poverty will substantially reduce child neglect and – to a lesser but still significant degree – physical abuse. And because of the heart-breaking emotional toll which child maltreatment has on children, and because of the huge economic costs that we discussed previously, this persistent problem needs to be addressed. Research has also confirmed the negative effects of poverty on a host of child well-being, long-term school and health outcomes, and most indicators of success across the life span. For example, researchers have shown the impact of poverty upon the brain in terms of how socioeconomic status is linked with gray matter: it is correlated with a smaller brain surface area and gray matter volumes are 8 to 10 percent lower (see, e.g., https://morgridge.wisc.edu/documents/Brain_Drain_A_Childs_Brain_on_Poverty.pdf).

Poverty has also been shown to impair *executive function* – the critical building blocks for successful life outcomes – flexibility, adaptability, self-regulation, memory, and self-control. Children gain these skills as a product of nurturing relationships with their caregivers and others. This video highlights the importance of executive function and how that is impaired by toxic stress such as poverty (see www.youtube.com/watch?v=efCq_vHUMqs for a video on this topic of executive function: Center on the Developing Child at Harvard University, 2012).

Poverty is not listed specifically as an adverse experience but, as this chapter has discussed, at least in the case of child maltreatment, many of these experiences are associated with poverty. And, the more poor one is, the more likely one's children are to experience more adverse experiences, as illustrated by Figure 4.1.

Poverty and mental health. The relationship between adult mental health and poverty has been examined rather more extensively. For example, 55 percent of low-income mothers suffer from depression, and yet only about one-third of poor mothers with severe depression receive treatment for it (Chester et al., 2016). As depicted in Figure 4.2, in general, adults in poverty are four to five times more likely to experience depression than the highest income group, though it is a linear relationship across incomes (National Center for Health Statistics, 2012). Suicidal ideations are almost twice as high among the poor than among the non-poor.

The field would benefit from more discussion of the mechanisms by which poverty undermines competent functioning and leads to higher rates of mood disorders. For example, any social condition that reduces control over life circumstances increases rates of

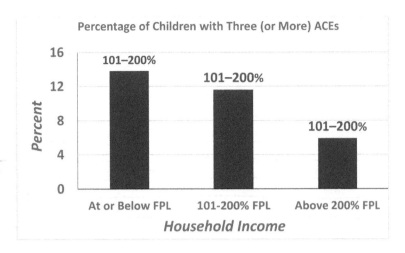

Figure 4.1 Poverty and ACES

Note: FPL = Federal Poverty Level.

Source: Analysis of 2011–2012 National Survey of Children's Health Data, Child Trends (2013). Retrieved from www.childtrends.org/wp-content/uploads/2013/07/124_fig3.jpg.

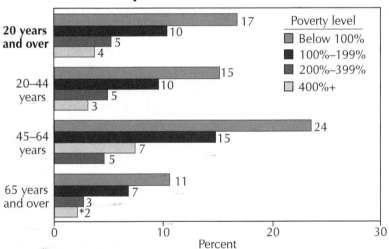

Figure 4.2 Poverty and Mental Health in Terms of Depression

Note: *Estimates unreliable (relative standard error of 20 to 30 percent).

Source: Health, United States, 2011 (fig. 33), CDC/NCHS. Retrieved from www.samhsa. gov/data/sites/default/files/Health_Equity_National_BHB_1-27-16_508.pdf.

depression (e.g., old age, female gender, trauma, and poverty). Child welfare agencies serve many families in which multiple factors have disempowered parents and children, as well as removed their hope for positive change. Poverty combined with substance abuse and depression, domestic violence, criminal justice involvement, and poor health leads to demoralization and helplessness when facing challenges (Marmot, 2005; personal communication, Dee Wilson, October 6, 2016).

Domestic violence. Poor women are also more likely to be victims of domestic violence. Women with household incomes of less than $7,500 are seven times as likely as women with household incomes over $75,000 to experience domestic violence. It is actually shown to be a linear relationship (ACLU Women's Rights Project, 2006). As household income goes up, domestic violence likelihood goes down. Community conditions matter as well: poor women who reside in distressed communities, with higher levels of community violence, are more likely to experience violence in their homes than poor women in more affluent neighborhoods. Domestic violence is a cause of homelessness for women and children. It is also a cause of lateness and absenteeism from work, lost productivity at work, and job loss (www.vawnet.org/applied-research-papers/print-document. php?doc_id=2187).

Another study by Renner, Slack, and Berger (2008) found that income level has more of an effect on risk of neglect than abuse, in part because risk of abuse is influenced strongly by family climate; for example, by the presence or absence of domestic violence. One of the mechanisms that explains the relationship of poverty and neglect suggested by their research is the buffering effect – or lack of same – of ample space, i.e., less housing space for large families is associated with more domestic violence (Renner, Slack, & Berger, 2008).

Poverty and parenting stress. Chronic maltreatment (the combination of neglect and physical abuse and/or sexual abuse) is common and not the exception in families with three or more screened in CPS reports. The underlying dynamic in chronic neglect and chronic maltreatment includes (1) erosion or collapse of social norms around parenting, and (2) loss of self-efficacy. In chronically referring families with four or more CPS reports, poverty combined with other disempowering factors lead to demoralized responses to life circumstances in which control over every domain of life is being gradually erased, including self-care, maintaining home conditions, control of children, basic security, intimate relationships, and protection from danger. Deep poverty greatly accelerates this process, which can eventually lead to the collapse of parenting standards (personal communication, Dee Wilson, October 6, 2016).

In addition, shifts in parenting styles have been associated with economic status. Parenting styles (authoritarian, authoritative, permissive, or uninvolved) are often examined in the context of their impact upon child development, not necessarily maltreatment. Studies have shown that economic hardship impacts parenting practices, but poor parenting practices as an outgrowth of economic stress (disrupted parenting) could be mitigated by strong social support networks, marital quality, etc. (see, e.g., Yoshikawa, Aber, & Beardslee, 2012). Similarly, another landmark longitudinal study found that the stress of poverty caused depression (rather than the reverse), and that depression was likely to result in harsher or more inconsistent parenting. The logic model hypothesized here is that family stress from harsh economic conditions leads to depression, which leads to poor parenting quality (less warmth, developmentally inappropriate expectations, no clear rules or routines, harsh discipline, etc.) (Katz et al., 2007). In fact, one study which used a commonly used index (the Parenting Stress Index) found that parent distress and parent child dysfunction are higher in low-income families (Reitman, Currier, & Stickle, 2002). So, by examining some of the risk factors that are correlated with child welfare involvement or the need for foster care and their correlations with poverty, we are getting at some of the mechanisms, or at least intersections between these different risk factors, and perhaps a clustering and compounding effect that leads to reports of neglect or abuse (personal communication, Tyler Corwin, August 20, 2016).

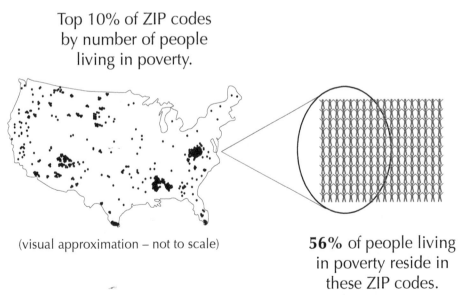

Top 10% of ZIP codes
by number of people
living in poverty.

(visual approximation – not to scale)

56% of people living
in poverty reside in
these ZIP codes.

Figure 4.3 Geographic Concentration of Poverty

Source: Analyses undertaken by the Geographic Analysis Team, Casey Family Programs.

In addition, some of the best studies on co-occurring disorders (Newmann & Sallman, 2004) have found that a very high proportion of low-income women with co-occurring substance abuse and behavioral health disorders have extensive histories of early trauma (e.g., physical abuse and sexual abuse in childhood and then domestic violence in young adulthood). One plausible causal sequence for the development of co-occurring disorders is that when long-term poverty in childhood is combined with early trauma, early onset of behavioral health problems can occur, which are then managed through the use of drugs or alcohol. This research found that extreme poverty and an epidemic of violence characterized these women's lives.

Community characteristics and associations with child maltreatment. First, it is important to look at the clustering and concentration of risk. Figure 4.3 shows that a majority of children in poverty are clustered in a small number of communities. Other geographic analyses show the high correlation between child poverty and a host of other indicators of community health (e.g., Coulton et al., 2007).

But, as alluded to earlier, we also need to look at community factors, which have been shown to independently influence rates of child maltreatment within a community. Zip codes characterized by high rates of abuse and neglect are often also characterized by higher rates of poverty, lower educational attainment, more single-parent households, or greater population turnover.

Strategies for Reducing Family Poverty

Overview

We need to get to a place where affordable housing, affordable healthcare, and living wage jobs are viewed as essential for a healthy and productive society, and where the multi-billion-dollar costs of child maltreatment and trauma are fully recognized to a point where people are willing to invest in community and family supports. To achieve this aim we will need to change spending priorities, shift the tax code so that it reduces the high levels of income inequality, and look for savings where social services funds could be redirected to more effective programs and other strategies.

Besides increasing the number of jobs paying a living wage and maximizing use of the Earned Income Tax Credit, what anti-poverty strategies have strong research evidence? When a cross-section of the studies is examined, it appears that a small number of anti-poverty strategies have some research evidence, and an additional set of strategies have promise. Ten Key Anti-Poverty Strategies are summarized in Table 4.1. Experts

Table 4.1 Ten Key Anti-poverty Strategies

1. A strong economy that emphasizes living-wage jobs (and the childcare, training, and other supports that may be necessary to match people with potential employers).

2. Incentivize communities to foster collective efficacy (informal social control and social cohesion), intergenerational closure (the extent to which families know each other's children), diversity, affordable housing, neighborhood social networks (nearby friends and relatives), and discourage physical and social disorder (e.g., graffiti, vacant houses).

3. Maximize access for eligible people to receive federal tax policies such as the Earned Income Tax Credit (EITC), Social Security Disability and Survivor's Benefits, Medicaid, and SCHIP.

4. Maximize coverage of public health insurance, including CHIP and Medicaid for children and Medicaid for parents through the Affordable Care Act (ACA).

5. Create greater access to financial capital through increasing one's credit score and other strategies.

6. Help eligible parents access the Supplemental Nutrition Assistance Program (SNAP) and Special Supplemental Nutrition Program for Women, Infants, and Children (WIC), which also reduce poverty rates.

7. Expunge more felonies and establish eligibility for reduction in convictions so that people who have grown beyond past transgressions or have been victimized by unjust sentencing policies can qualify for a broader range of jobs.

8. Institute *paid* family leave for adoption, childbirth, and family caregiving in times of poor health.

9. Strengthen public assistance program offices because a positive organizational culture and worker behavior in income assistance programs can positively influence recipient outcomes (Godfrey & Yoshikawa, 2012).

10. Expand financial eligibility assessment, financial counseling and one-time emergency funds for utilities, appliance repair, security deposits, etc. (e.g., Project GAIN in Wisconsin and a similar project in Colorado).

caution that multiple anti-poverty strategies need to be implemented simultaneously to have enough power to affect this deeply ingrained social condition (see, e.g., Agnone & Corwin 2013; Duncan & Magnuson, 2004; Plotnick, 2009; Urban Institute, 2013; U.S. Census Bureau, 2013).

Pfingst (2012) emphasizes that both history and recent research show that prosperity "happens when we deliberately invest in the foundations of a strong economy – broad and equal opportunity to build knowledge and skills, adequate compensation and support for workers, and adequate investments in conditions that foster economic growth" (p.1). But as shown in Table 4.2, enabling families to avoid being poor or escaping poverty is not just about helping citizens get jobs that pay a living wage with benefits, but "access to the

Table 4.2 Strategies to Build Shared Prosperity[a]

Goal: Opportunity for All	**Provide a high-quality basic education:** • Provide high-quality, universal pre-school. • Target resources to close the K-12 racial achievement gap. • Invest in public universities and community and technical colleges. **Support economic security of children and families during tough times:** • Increase access to food, housing, and support services.	**Protect public health and the natural environment:** • Fully implement the Affordable Care Act. • Strengthen investments in clean air, water, and land. **Reprioritize state spending to build thriving communities:** • Implement more stringent cost-benefit analysis of tax breaks.
Goal: Better Jobs	**Invest in public works jobs:** • Fix infrastructure and build human capital.	**Make work pay:** • Strengthen workers' rights and work supports. • Fully fund the Working Families Tax Rebate.
Goal: A Productive, Equitable Revenue System	**Modernize the tax system:** • Expand the sales tax to include more services.	**Make the tax system equitable:** • Shift greater tax responsibility to those most able to pay.

Source: Pfingst, L. (2012). *In pursuit of prosperity: Eight strategies to rebuild Washington State's economy.* Olympia, WA: Washington State Public Policy Center, p. 8.

opportunities that built a strong middle class – attending quality public schools, access to health care and transportation, affording a home and growing up in safe, healthy neighborhoods" (Pfingst, 2012, p. 1).

Major anti-poverty strategies that have some research support are briefly described below:

Maximize access for eligible people to receive federal tax policies such as the Earned Income Tax Credit (EITC), Social Security Disability and Survivor's Benefits, Medicaid, and SCHIP. Without government assistance in 2010, poverty would have been twice as high: nearly 30 percent of the population (Sherman, 2011). Thus this strategy focuses on strengthening and expanding the current set of publicly funded anti-poverty programs – making full systems more adaptive and responsive to the needs of the population. For example, EITC programs appear to be very effective work incentives because of their phase-in and phase-out structure (Berger et al., 2013).

Tax credits such as the Earned Income Tax Credit (EITC) and the Child Tax Credit (CTC) deliver critical work supports for employees earning low to moderate wages (see Table 4.3). Claiming these tax credits can put an eligible worker on the path to securing better housing, obtaining dependable transportation, paying for quality child-care, or pursuing higher education. To benefit from any tax credit, eligible workers must file a tax return. Preparing a tax return can be complicated and may seem overwhelming. That is why it is so important to promote free tax filing along with working family tax credits. The importance of income supports was recognized years ago by Dr. Martin Luther King (1967):

> In addition to the absence of coordination and sufficiency, the programs of the past all have another common failing – they are indirect. Each seeks to solve poverty by first solving something else. I'm now convinced that the simplest approach will prove to be the most effective – the solution to poverty is to abolish it directly by a now widely discussed measure: the guaranteed income.

The benefits of EITC are substantial and multi-faceted: tax credits for working families have been shown not only to decrease child poverty but to lead to higher birth weight, better school outcomes, and increased employment in adulthood. Likewise, the Supplemental Nutrition Assistance Program (SNAP, or food stamps) has been shown to have similar positive impacts. It is likely that these programs work by reducing family stress due

Table 4.3 Income Levels and EITC Benefits

Children	Single	Married	EITC up to
None	$14,880	$20,430	$506
1	$39,296	$44,846	$3,373
2	$44,648	$50,198	$5,572
3 or more	$47,955	$53,505	$6,269

Source: The Earned Income Tax Credit Estimator (Tax Year 2016). Retrieved from www.eitcoutreach. org/learn/tax-credits/earned-income-tax-credit/eligibility/ and www.eitcoutreach.org/.

to financial difficulties, and by preventing neuroendocrine and biochemical changes that affect long-term child outcomes (Dreyer et al., 2016b).

But some workforce system resources are not coordinated and fail to reach low-skill and low-wage workers, people struggling in deep poverty, undocumented residents, and people with multiple problems (Urban Institute, 2013). Through targeted outreach and simplifying application processes, families are given assistance in receiving the benefits for which they are eligible. Potentially billions of dollars in assistance go unused or unclaimed because of the inability of struggling families to gain access to these benefits (Waters-Boots, 2010). Removing the barriers to access for many benefits (e.g., by revising eligibility requirements) and improving awareness through outreach will help lift many families out of poverty (Agnone & Corwin, 2012, pp. 2–3).

Another caution with respect to public assistance (TANF) is that there is some evidence that while the welfare reform efforts of the 1990s improved the well-being of some low-income groups, primarily single-parent mothers (Meyer & Sullivan, 2004), those reforms resulted in *greater* material hardship for the more deeply poor families. Material hardship consists of measures of food hardship, difficulty paying for housing, unmet medical needs, and problems with paying for essential household expenses such as rent or utilities (Shaefer & Ybarra, 2012). In addition, there is insufficient information about what particular clusters of services might be most effective for families of different compositions and at different developmental stages.

No singular benefit package seems to stand out across the existing research as "the" economic safety net, and benefit packaging appears to change over time, as family structure, children's ages, and family circumstances change. There is currently little understanding of how low-income families with minor-aged children create economic safety nets using a broader array of cash and in-kind programs, in combination with child support and employment, particularly during the post-welfare reform era (Slack et al., 2014, p. 4).

Finally, new research indicates that the organizational culture and worker behavior in income assistance programs can influence recipient outcomes. One study found that three aspects of the public assistance office emerged as influential: *personalized client attention* and *emphasis on employment* were found to increase average yearly earnings relative to the control group, whereas *larger staff caseload size* was found to decrease it (Bloom, Hill, & Riccio, 2003). A more recent study confirmed these effects:

- Mothers in welfare offices characterized by high support from caseworkers had steeper increases in earnings and income.

- On the other hand, mothers in offices with a high caseload size had greater decreases in their income and welfare receipt over time.

- Finally, mothers in offices with a stronger emphasis on employment had higher initial levels of welfare receipt but experienced a larger decrease in the amount of their welfare receipt over time. These associations were evident even after controlling for an array of potentially confounding individual- and office-level characteristics (Godfrey & Yoshikawa, 2012, p. 394).

Help eligible parents access SNAP and Special Supplemental Nutrition Program for Women, Infants, and Children (WIC), which also reduce poverty rates. For example, in some states, public assistance/TANF/SNAP program leaders and their counterparts in child welfare are discovering how they can join forces to serve families before child placement may be needed (e.g., Project GAIN in Wisconsin). The Family Check Up program is also bringing family coaching to WIC recipients and improving child outcomes in the long term (Dishion et al., 2008), although these effects were lost by age 9.5 in the extreme deprivation neighborhoods, unless the parents markedly improved parent–child interactions during the toddler period (Shaw et al., 2016).

Maximize coverage of public health insurance, including CHIP and Medicaid for children and Medicaid for parents through the Affordable Care Act (ACA). This has offered significant financial benefits to families. These benefits have included reduced out-of-pocket medical expenses, increased financial stability, and improved material well-being. Child poverty in measures like the SPM can be decreased when out-of-pocket medical expenses are reduced (Wherry, Kenney, & Sommers, 2016). For example, as depicted in Figure 4.4, many people who are eligible for key programs are not aware of them.

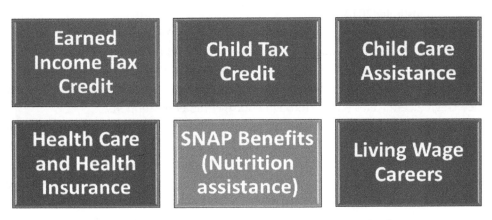

Figure 4.4 Examples of Programs Where Boosting Awareness Should Increase Usage by Eligible Persons

Source: Maher, Corwin, & Pecora (2017).

Pair public assistance programs with more effective employment requirements and employment supports. Commissioned by ACF, Office of Planning, Research and Evaluation and conducted by Mathematica Policy Research, this project highlighted 180 programs with strong evidence and positive employment outcomes (see http://employmentstrategies. acf.hhs.gov/).

While the evidence is mixed and dependent partially on the *quality* of the employment program, a Minnesota study demonstrated the benefits of this approach. Researchers measured the effectiveness of social benefits and work mandates by randomly assigning families into three groups to receive: (1) status quo social benefits, (2) the Minnesota Family Investment Program (MFIP) incentives, or (3) the MFIP incentives and work mandates (which required employment and training activities). They found that the MFIP included higher earnings disregards, reduced upfront costs of childcare, employment training for single parents, and simplified public assistance procedures. Unlike some other welfare-to-work programs, MFIP included a financial incentive that incentivized working. Long-term MFIP recipients were more likely to be employed, have higher earnings, and have higher incomes than long-term AFDC recipients. MFIP recipients also demonstrated improved family outcomes, such as reduced incidences of domestic abuse that may be directly tied to economic and family stability (Gennetian & Miller, 2002).

Help low-income citizens build assets and social capital. These capital assets can cushion people "from financial shocks and hardship in the short term, and allow them to invest in education, training, or housing in the long term. Examples include individual development accounts (IDAs), child development accounts (CDAs), and 'small dollar credit' options that can take the place of expensive payday and auto title loans" (Sherraden et al., 2015; Urban Institute, 2013, p. 15).

Increase GED class access and support, particularly at a time when GED standards are being toughened. Economists have documented the added earning power of a GED, diploma and a college degree, with greater income earned with higher levels of education (Tyler, 2003). As important is to help adults obtain high school diplomas or General Equivalency Degree certificates (GEDs) through course completion supports.

Create greater access to financial capital through increasing individual credit scores and other strategies. Shonkoff and Fisher (2013) have argued that asset-building beyond parenting skills is needed. Special coaching for how to work with financial institutions like banks and mortgage companies is valuable. Micro-lending and other partnership strategies create access to capital and can generate revenue for residents and their neighborhoods (see Annie E. Casey (2017) at www.aecf.org/work/economic-opportunity/financial-well-being/; McKernan & Ratcliff, 2009).

Help parents reduce stress, think more clearly, and increase their nurturing behavior. Several studies show that family interventions which help parents become more nurturing have a beneficial impact upon *family income*. For example, a program that reduced parents' harsh and inconsistent parenting practices and increased their positive parenting practices led to subsequent improvements in mothers' incomes and reduced the likelihood of the mother being arrested. Patterson, Forgatch, and DeGarmo (2010) reported a detailed analysis of the impact of the Oregon Parent Management program. They found that the program reduced parents' harsh and inconsistent parenting practices and increased their positive parenting practices. Reductions in coercive parenting practices caused by the intervention led to subsequent improvements in mothers' incomes and reduced the likelihood of the mother being arrested. Thus the study provides evidence that reducing harsh parenting practices contributes to improving mothers' ability to earn income rather than increased income contributing to improve parenting (personal communication, Anthony Biglan, February 27, 2014; see also Patterson, Forgatch, & DeGarmo, 2010).

The *Incredible Years* program reduced maternal use of public assistance, and that effect was linked with fewer reports of child maltreatment. Eckenrode and Ganzel (1999) found that mothers who were randomly assigned to the NFP subsequently had fewer children and were less likely to be on welfare over the next 15 years. In a mediation analysis, they found that the impact of the program in reducing child maltreatment could be explained by the fact that it reduced the number of subsequent children and dependency on welfare – both of which were associated with lower rates of child maltreatment. Recently, Babcock, of EMPath, shared information about a new approach to working with the poor that addresses this dynamic: people in poverty tend to get stuck in vicious cycles where stress leads to bad decision making, compounding other problems and reinforcing the idea that they cannot improve their own lives.

> "What we're trying to do is create virtuous cycles where people take a step and they find out they can accomplish something that they might not have thought they could accomplish, and they feel better about themselves," Babcock said. Maybe that step helps them earn more money, solves a child-care problem that leads to better child behavior, or simply establishes a sense of control over their own lives. All of these things reduce stress, freeing up more mental bandwidth for further positive steps.
>
> (Elizabeth Babcock, cited in Mathewson, 2017, p. 2)

Use the latest science to inform community development and housing to reduce poverty. Four community development strategies hold great promise: *incentivize communities to foster collective efficacy* (informal social control and social cohesion), *intergenerational closure* (the extent to which families know each other's children), *neighborhood social networks* (nearby friends and relatives), and *discourage physical and social disorder* (e.g., graffiti, vacant houses) (Molnar et al., 2016). (See also www.slate.com/blogs/xx_fac tor/2016/04/08/getting_poor_kids_out_of_poor_neighborhoods_helps_even_more_than_ we_thought.html.)

Families are still struggling to secure housing. The housing stock has increased, but in many cities there is a shortage of *affordable* housing. Unlike France, Italy, and Japan, with current levels of immigration and birth rates, the United States is above the population replacement level. But the "baby boomers" born in the 1950s who are now beginning to retire will put a strain on the economy, and so we need every younger citizen to be productive.

Targeted housing strategies may produce the largest benefits (see Box 4.1). For example, the initial evaluations of MTO (*Moving to Opportunity*) showed little differences among the families in the various comparison group conditions. But when the data were reanalyzed using more sophisticated techniques, they found that moving to a lower poverty neighborhood significantly improves college attendance rates and earnings for children who were young (below age 13) when their families moved. These children also live in better neighborhoods themselves as adults and are less likely to become single parents:

> The treatment effects are substantial: children whose families take up an experimental voucher to move to a lower-poverty area when they are less than 13 years old have an annual income that is $3,477 (31%) higher on average relative to a mean of $11,270 in the control group in their mid-twenties. In contrast, the same moves have, if anything, negative long-term impacts on children who are more than 13 years old when their families move, perhaps because of the disruption effects of moving to a very different environment. The gains from moving fall with the age when children move, consistent with recent evidence that the duration of exposure to a better environment during childhood is a key determinant of an individual's long-term outcomes. The findings imply that offering vouchers to move to lower-poverty neighborhoods to families with young children who are living in high poverty housing projects may reduce the intergenerational persistence of poverty and ultimately generate positive returns for taxpayers.
>
> (Chetty, Hendren, & Katz, 2015, Abstract)

Thus, housing programs should be designed with those effects in mind, and with a broader mindset, as discussed by Sutton and Kemp, (2011a, p.3):

> We believe that today's social and environmental challenges demand an alternative to the city/suburb, black/white, rich/poor dichotomies of the post-Civil Rights

era. Future scholars and professionals must be able to conceive a metropolitan landscape that enhances the quality of life for an economically and culturally diverse population while conserving natural resources and embracing the full participation of previously marginalized communities of color.

Box 4.1   Can Neighborhood Gentrification Help Certain Impoverished Neighborhoods?

While the *Moving to Opportunity* study highlighted the value of paying attention to mobility out of a neighborhood, insightful historical analyses have highlighted the damaging effects of social policies that discouraged people from employment, and encouraged the movement out by White and Black families as their income increased. These case studies cite the lack of income diversity, and reduction of ethnic diversity as incredibly destructive to communities and families – including worsening racial tensions, dropping educational performance, and a maintenance of social isolation that hampers upward mobility in all racial groups.

Historical analyses like those that have been done for the Brownsville neighborhood in Brooklyn provide powerful stories of how well-intentioned liberal policies such as relaxing resident eligibility rules and unfettered community control of schools resulted in a concentration of poverty and a host of negative effects. These authors make a strong case for encouraging or preserving some diversity in income levels and ethnicity in communities, including, where needed, some gentrification to bring back in key community assets like grocery stores with fresh food, banks, and other resources (Hymowitz, 2017).

Radner and Shonkoff (2013, pp. 338–339) in Box 4.2 offer both cautions and strategies about using community development efforts to combat poverty.

Box 4.2   Community-based Efforts to Combat Entrenched Poverty

[G]enerations of efforts that began during the War on Poverty of the 1960s and continue to the present day have underscored both the promise and the challenges of community-based efforts to combat entrenched poverty. As we ponder the future of place-based approaches to social change, four themes provide a promising framework for fresh thinking about the challenges. The first is the *complexity* of neighborhood poverty, whose diffuse burdens (such as jobs shortages, social and racial exclusion, transportation gaps, violent crime, poor public health, and deficient educational opportunities) all affect each other and demand simultaneous attention.[a] The second theme is *conflict*, which is fueled by disagreements among key stakeholders about objectives, resources, time horizons, and messaging (among others) that can result in deeply entrenched positions that block innovation.[b] For example, the War on Poverty's community action program quickly encountered tensions among public officials and neighborhood leaders over the extent to which the purpose was policy change or program implementation.

The third theme is *context*, which refers to the challenge of widely applying innovations developed in a particular community that depend on its unique aspects and are therefore difficult to incorporate into sustainable, large-scale policies.[c] The fourth and final theme is *time*, which is reflected in the simple reality that effective community development requires patience for listening and relationship building, while it faces intense pressure for rapid results.[d]

Notes

a. This challenge was recognized in the 1960s as policy makers worked to improve on early War on Poverty results; Robert Kennedy famously called it the need to "grasp the web whole."

b. For a recent account of pitfalls and strategies in this arena, see Xavier de Souza Briggs. (2007). *Networks, power, and a dual agenda: New lessons and strategies for old community building dilemmas*. Boston, MA: MIT Press, 2007. Retrieved from http://web.mit.edu/ workingsmarter/ media/pdf-ws-kia-brief-0703.pdf (accessed March, 2012).

c. For an insightful review of this challenge, see Lisbeth B. Schorr (1997). *Common purpose*. New York: Anchor Doubleday.

d. This challenge was also encountered by community efforts in the 1960s, as Schorr (1997, p. 311) notes.

Source: Radner & Shonkoff (2013).

Sutton and Kemp (2011b) have compiled a series of essays on how certain strategies can reduce inequality and transform marginalized communities, particularly in urban areas. For example:

We believe that today's social and environmental challenges demand an alternative to the city/suburb, black/white, rich/poor dichotomies of the post-Civil Rights era. Future scholars and professionals must be able to conceive a metropolitan landscape that enhances the quality of life for an economically and culturally diverse population while conserving natural resources and embracing the full participation of previously marginalized communities of color.

(Sutton and Kemp, 2011a, p. 3)

Better integrate the multiple but fragmented services in communities that can target the complex needs of people suffering from deep and persistent poverty. The federal Promise Neighborhoods Program (modeled on the highly regarded Harlem Children's Zone) is an example of this approach, as well as the HOST initiative, which delivers intensive support services to the most disadvantaged families living in public housing developments (Urban Institute, 2013, p. 4). Place-based community initiatives may be some of the most powerful ways to address these barriers, as exemplified by the Harlem Children's Zone, Los Angeles Prevention Initiative Demonstration Project (McCroskey et al., 2012), and the Durham Family Initiative (Dodge et al., 2014) (for community-based strategies see Daro & Dodge, 2009; Dodge et al., 2004).

In addition, Slack and Berger in their study of a multi-strategy economic support intervention in Milwaukee (Project GAIN) have preliminary findings showing increases in family income and a 25 percent reduction in child maltreatment re-reports to CPS:

Key features of GAIN include (1) a comprehensive eligibility assessment for an array of public and private economic supports and assistance accessing these resources, (2) collaborative work with a GAIN financial support specialist to identify financial goals and steps to achieve them, and improve financial decision-making, and (3) in some cases, access to one-time emergency cash supplements to alleviate immediate financial stressors. The combination of these three "pillars" of the model are predicted to increase family financial stability and income level, which in turn are predicted to improve family functioning overall (e.g., reduced parenting stress and mental health problems, improved parenting skills and self-efficacy).

(Slack & Berger, 2014, pp. 1–2)

The authors note that there is no reason why this model, if proven effective, should be limited to families deflected from the front-end of CPS. If efficacious, it could easily be transferred to other child welfare populations, such as reunified families, youth aging out of care, and adoptive families.

191

Children's allowance. Michael Wald, Professor Emeriti of Stanford Law School, is deeply concerned about the 15 percent of American families who have the most extensive and multi-generational level of difficulty:

> One possibility is the adoption of a "children's allowance" for low-income families, perhaps conditional on certain parental behaviors. For example, the allowance might be accessed at pediatrician's offices or provided at home visits and conditioned on regular pediatric visits or involvement with the home visitor. This would address the incentive issue, as well as the poverty problem. Such an allowance could build upon New York City's current experiments with Conditional Transfers.
>
> (Personal communication, Michael Wald, March 1, 2014; see also Wald, 2014, 2015)

Strategically link housing assistance programs with other anti-poverty strategies. Biglan (personal communication, February 27, 2014) cautions that housing programs, by themselves, have not been shown to be effective anti-poverty strategies:

> Perhaps the most extensive effort has been the federal government's Hope VI program, administered by the Department of Housing and Urban Development. It sought to reduce the concentration of poverty in public housing by replacing large high-rise buildings that housed only families below the poverty line with neighborhoods consisting of a mix of family incomes and lower density. Popkin, Theodos, Getsinger, and Parilla (2010) reviewed the evidence for this program's impact. The hope was that creating neighborhoods with a greater diversity of family incomes would contribute to economic wellbeing of poorer families by, for example, providing models of working parents or by making information about available jobs available to poorer families. However, Popkin et al. (2010) found no evidence that HOPE VI was associated with improvements in the income of the poorest residents.
>
> (Popkin et al., 2004, 2010)

Expand financial eligibility assessment, financial counseling and one-time emergency funds for utilities, appliance repair, security deposits, etc. (e.g., Project GAIN in Wisconsin and a similar project in Colorado). Society should be willing to invest as much to keep a family together as we spend to tear them apart by placing their children in out-of-home care.

Expunge criminal records, establish eligibility for reduction in convictions, and expand programs that provide certificates of rehabilitation (McCroskey et al., 2012).

Additional Strategies for Reducing Poverty

There are other promising strategies, but the following have modest amounts of research evidence:

A. Better match people who need work with living-wage jobs that fit their skill set.

B. Increase access to career pathways and job mobility (Agnone & Corwin, 2012, 2013).

C. Support small business development.

D. Target job training programs to the careers that are most strategically needed, and have living-wage salary levels.

E. Expand financial literacy and computer literacy classes.

F. Reduce duplication in order to invest anti-poverty funds more effectively and efficiently. For example, the Urban Institute has begun to analyze these programs according to four areas: (1) *Whom* does the approach help? (2) *Where* does the approach operate or deliver help? (3) *How* does the approach help?, and (4) *When* does the approach help? (Urban Institute, 2013, Table 2).

G. Engage and empower poor people to advocate effectively for themselves, as exemplified by the work of the Marguerite Casey Foundation and others (see, e.g., http://caseygrants.org/equalvoice/).

H. Combine child protective services' differential response with other anti-poverty approaches. For example, the long-term effects of providing material or anti-poverty services to families with reports of child maltreatment were examined in a field experiment in a Midwestern state in which differential response (DR) had been implemented. Significant increases were found in anti-poverty services to low SES experimental families. Proportional hazards analyses indicated that these changes were associated with reductions of later reports and placements of children. From a pool of families determined to be appropriate for DR family assessments, 2,605 randomly assigned experimental families that received family assessments were compared to 1,265 randomly assigned control families that received traditional investigations. Families were tracked for eight to nine years. Formal service case openings increased for experimental families. In addition, by controlling for service differences, the analyses demonstrated significant effects of the non-adversarial, family-friendly approach of DR family assessments (Loman & Siegel, 2012).

I.   Educate the broader community to build public will for changes in public policy or the social contract.

J.   Explore food-related platforms. For example, one particular zip code in Jacksonville, Florida with poor outcomes on a wide range of key child and family indicators also suffers from a lack of major grocery stores or pharmacies in the community.

Finally, the Aspen Institute (http://ascend.aspeninstitute.org/pages/the-two-generation-approach), the Urban Institute, and others have emphasized taking a two-generational approach by focusing on the future of young children in persistently poor families. Thus, society needs to look beyond jobs and subsidized jobs to address mental illness, criminal justice history, disabilities, and other personal challenges that often stand in the way of work. Wald (2014) and Golden et al. (2013) have stressed that there needs to be more flexibility in the Temporary Assistance to Needy Families (TANF) program to allow parenting activities to count as "work" activity in families with children under age 3; other poverty-related programs also need to be modified to provide easier access and coverage. And, as mentioned earlier, we should address the intersection of poverty and environmental health by, for example, focusing on the social determinants of health as they relate to place (environment) and economic well-being (poverty/opportunity) (Urban Institute, 2013. p. 5).

For example, in Virginia the Comprehensive Health Investment Project (CHIP) uses the Parents as Teachers curriculum in home visits with new parents but goes beyond the usual focus on maternal and infant health. In addition to the quarterly visits from a registered nurse, a parent educator helps parents develop important skills, such as creating routines, managing their families, and bolstering their children's health – all of which help parents become employed. The educators also assist families with achieving self-sufficiency goals, such as getting a driver's license, earning a GED or certification, or pursuing higher education. CHIP has seen a nearly 40 percent increase in the number of families with one or both parents working at least part-time after a year in the program (see www.chipofvir ginia.org/outcomes.asp as featured in the Annie E. Casey Foundation, 2014).

Policy and Program Design Issues

Cautions and Complexities with Respect to Anti-poverty Programs

Political battles have been preventing major reforms from occurring that, when implemented together, would make a significant difference toward addressing some key challenges. For example, women who work full-time are paid less than men in comparable jobs (Rosin, 2013). Eighty percent of all single-parent families are headed by women (U.S. Census Bureau, 2016e). Today one in four children under the age of 18 – a total of about 17.4 million – are being reared without a father (U.S. Census Bureau, 2016d), and 40 per cent live below the poverty line (U.S. Census Bureau, 2016c) (see also Lee, 2017).

Worried about displaced workers, former President Barack Obama proposed the American Jobs Act, a $447 billion package of economic actions, including construction jobs to improve crumbling infrastructure and cuts in payroll taxes. Congress did not support it. The president then proposed help for working parents through higher tax credits for childcare. Congress did not support it. As economist and Wall Street executive Steven Rattner documented, some members of Congress blocked plans for expansion of the earned income tax credit, new rules to allow retirement plans to be portable, tax credits for manufacturing communities, and community college investments. But some states have expanded Medicaid payments to take care of the poor and working poor who need operations, medicine, and other treatment. But 19 states have refused federal money to help impoverished residents. To be denied proper health just because of the state you live in is unfair (McFeatters, 2016).

The poor, and especially the persistent poor, defy easy description and prescriptions. The families and individuals suffering from deep and persistent poverty are diverse. Their circumstances defy one-dimensional characterizations and their needs reflect multiple and interacting disadvantages. They include the homeless, people with physical or mental disabilities, single mothers, single men, ex-offenders, and undocumented immigrants. About half of those living in deep poverty are under the age of 25. Wald (2015) has written about the need to reconceptualize how we assist these families to grow and develop over a long period of time. African Americans and Hispanics are disproportionately represented among those in deep poverty. Most deeply poor adults are not working.

> Poverty is, by definition, a lack of income, but deep and persistent poverty reflects profound personal challenges and systemic barriers. These in turn require intensive and sustained engagement that cuts across conventional policy and programmatic silos. Work requirements and other conditions imposed by many of today's federal programs may be beneficial for the working poor or for people experiencing short spells of poverty and unemployment, but they do not address the needs of people in deep and persistent poverty.
>
> (Urban Institute, 2013, p. 3)

Using multiple strategies is important, and their effectiveness has been demonstrated in other states and countries. For example, the United Kingdom was able to reduce child poverty by over 50 percent in the ten years between 1999 and 2009 through similar areas of reform. Making work pay through tax credits for working families and welfare-to-work programs, raising income for families with children through child tax credits and increasing welfare for families with children, and investing in children through expanded maternity/paternity leave and universal preschool drove this significant reduction in poverty (Center for Law and Social Policy, 2011). The U.K.'s original goal was to implement U.S.-originated poverty policies, but to implement them with better funding and operational approaches. "This indicates that the system of benefits in the U.S. is not broken, but rather in need of revitalization" (Agnone & Corwin, 2013, p. 4).

The constellation of antipoverty efforts in the United States is vast, complex, and fragmented.

> A multiplicity of programs and initiatives provide various forms of assistance or support to different groups of poor people at different points in their lives. In the case of federally funded programs, one study documents over 80 need-based programs that provide cash benefits, food assistance, medical benefits or insurance, housing, education, child care, job training, energy aid, and a wide variety of other services.
>
> (Urban Institute, 2013, p. 1)

In addition, variations in eligibility and the nature of support undermine its effectiveness and reach:

> The type and level of help varies and depends, in part, on program funding, where a recipient lives, and his/her characteristics (such as age, size of family, or disability). Because some programs are capped, not all eligible families receive assistance. Moreover, eligibility rules for some programs vary across states or localities so that two families with identical needs can receive different benefits. Finally, many individuals and families who are eligible for government assistance do not apply for benefits, and therefore receive no help.
>
> (Urban Institute, 2013, p. 3)

Major investments in children and families take time to pay off. Some of the most successful anti-poverty interventions, including the MTO housing project discussed earlier, have had disappointing results in the early stages of implementation, but achieved a surprising amount of long-term effects on a range of outcomes, including graduation rates, rates of incarceration, rates of employment, and overall income into the twenties and thirties. Reducing poverty in a major way through our current array of strategies takes a generation (personal communication, Dee Wilson, October 6, 2016).

Other strategies may show results more quickly. For example, Jane Costello's landmark Smoky Mountains study found that through increasing by $6,000 the income of poor Native American families through casino revenue a number of key developmental benefits were realized. When the researchers compared the psychiatric profiles of the tribe's children during the four years before and the four years after the casino opened, they discovered that the frequency of psychiatric symptoms had decreased among the children of families who had moved out of poverty and become comparable to that of children whose families had never been poor. "So just as environmental stresses can create mental illness," Costello says, "so environmental interventions can remove them" (Brain and Behavior Research Foundation, 2010, p. 1). Thus, within a few years, the children in these families had less depression and better school performance.

The unit of analysis and focus may need to shift back and forth. One challenge with thinking about strategies for poor neighborhoods is that the neighborhood itself is unlikely to be the *exclusive* entity of interest. Rather, we will often need both neighborhood- and individual-focused efforts – such as strategies that help individuals living in distressed resource-poor areas increase their income.

Conclusions

What Are the Implications of These Statistics and Observations?

Public child welfare leaders such as Susan Dreyfus, President and CEO of the Alliance for Strong Families and Communities, have pointed out that the capacity of professional social services will never be sufficient to meet current levels of demand. She and others, such as the Institute of Medicine prevention panel, believe that the answers lie upstream in supportive communities and strong families (National Research Council, & Institute of Medicine of the National Academies, 2009).

Research has shown that neighborhood factors, including structural characteristics such as rates of poverty, residential instability, and household composition, are related to rates of child abuse and neglect (Ernst, 2000; Freisthler, Bruce, & Needell, 2007; Klein & Merritt, 2014; Morton, Simmel, & Peterson, 2014). As mentioned earlier, one recent study adds a new dimension by examining neighborhood social characteristics, including *collective efficacy* (informal social control and social cohesion), *intergenerational closure* (the extent to which families know each other's children), *neighborhood social networks* (nearby friends and relatives), and *physical and social disorder* (e.g., graffiti, vacant houses) (Molnar et al., 2016). The full range of social characteristics, as well as structural measures of poverty and crime, strongly predicted substantiated findings of child neglect, physical abuse, and substance-exposed infants. Structural and social characteristics were less strongly associated with rates of substantiated sexual abuse. This study is important in part because its authors have focused on "modifiable" structural and social characteristics, factors that communities can, at least in theory, change in order to improve outcomes for children and families.

This underscores the potential of Promise Neighborhoods, modeled after the Harlem Children's Zone; programs to reduce violence, particularly among youth; and targeted efforts to strengthen communities by increasing collective efficacy, such as the Strong Communities program (Corwin, Pecora, & Ostrum, 2016). To support this work there are two community assessment tools that may be useful:

- Sandel and colleagues have recently highlighted mobility assistance programs to move low-income children to higher opportunity neighborhoods, but they focus primarily on three case studies of neighborhood-level interventions. They describe the Child Opportunity Index, a tool that integrates multiple indicators of child-relevant neighborhood opportunities and risks in three domains: education, health and environmental, and social and economic. The Child Opportunity Index may be used to track change over time and to understand the impact of interventions. Note that the Child Opportunity Index was developed by Diversity Data Kids (www.diversity datakids.org/) at Brandeis University and the Kirwan Institute on Race and Ethnicity at Ohio State University (see Sandel et al., 2016).

- The Community Capacity-Building Survey (ARC3) that was built by ACES Public Private Initiative, Community Science and Mathematica to assess multiple dimensions of community capacity that are necessary for effective community action (Hargreaves et al., 2017).

All children deserve to be raised in a supportive environment that seeks to create the opportunities they need to achieve their potential and prepare the way for the next generation. As emphasized by William C. Bell (2015):

> To build strong communities is to strengthen the people living in them. It's creating viable opportunities. It's showing vulnerable children, youth, families and other

populations that they too have a reason to hope. If we want to secure the well-being of every woman, girl, boy and man in the United States, we have to secure the well-being of their communities. We have to make sure that the communities they live in have the resources and environment that support their needs and their dreams for a better life

A number of Foundations such as the Annie E. Casey Foundation, Casey Family Programs, the Doris Duke Charitable Foundation, Kresge, and the W. K. Kellogg Foundation recognize the importance of improving community-based efforts to prevent child abuse and neglect through engaging at-risk families and the role that a safe, stable, and permanent family plays in the lives of all children. The "rescue" mentality in the current child welfare system has led to treating the issue of child safety in isolation from all of the other challenges facing at-risk families. In turn, the challenges facing those families have been treated in isolation from the condition of the communities in which they live. Unless that reality is changed, any gains made on behalf of vulnerable children are likely to be short-lived in the face of family and community despair that exists for far too many people.

There is evidence to be cautiously optimistic. The hope is that the U.S. will reach a *"tipping point"* in culture and norms that may substantially reduce institutional racism. Research has demonstrated that tax credits allow workers to keep more of their earned income; social benefit programs provide a basic quality of life and short-term sustainability for many living in poverty; job training and employment opportunities create higher skilled, in-demand workers, which can strengthen the economy in the long term; supporting families and investing in children promote long-term well-being and prosperity; efforts to reduce inequality and grow assets provide security and stability for struggling families (Agnone & Corwin, 2012, pp. 2–4). In addition, we could correct the broad inequality of wealth and income through a variety of innovative means related to wages and tax benefits associated with capital gains, retirement accounts, and homeownership. Greater lifelong access to education will also provide broader economic opportunities (Hooper (2016), in describing the paper by Lein, Romich, and Sherraden (2016)).

In conclusion, it appears that a modest number of anti-poverty strategies have strong research evidence, and an additional set of strategies have promise. Experts caution that multiple anti-poverty strategies need to be implemented simultaneously to have enough power to affect this serious social problem, and that a careful multi-systems analysis should be undertaken to identify which particular strategy combinations will be most effective for that particular community.

Discussion Questions

1. What well-intentioned public policies have inadvertently worsened conditions for the poor in the U.S.?

2. What do you think are the most powerful anti-poverty strategies? Which research-based strategies can reduce poverty among families living in the poorest neighborhoods? Who should we prioritize within that group? For example, eliminating deep poverty and child homelessness would make a huge difference in child welfare.

3. At this current time in terms of the economy and federal politics, what strategies to lessen poverty do you think are most feasible?

Note

1   Thanks to *Tyler Corwin*, *Dave Danielson* and *Erin Maher* of Casey Family Programs; and the national experts who contributed key ideas and research: *Jon Agnone* (Northwest Research Group), *Lonnie Berger* (University of Wisconsin-Madison School of Social Work), *Anthony Biglan* (Oregon Research Institute), *Shannon Harper* (University of Washington, Evans School of Public Affairs), *Mark C. Long* (University of Washington, Evans School of Public Affairs), *Kristen Shook Slack* (University of Wisconsin-Madison School of Social Work), and *Michael Wald* (Stanford Law School).

For Further Information

Urban Institute. (2013). *Addressing deep and persistent poverty. A framework for philanthropic planning and investment.* Washington, DC: Author. Retrieved from www.urban.org/UploadedPDF/412983-addressing-deep-poverty.pdf (see page 9 in this report for a concise table summarizing the main federal means-tested programs and tax credits).

Bibliography

ACLU Women's Rights Project. (2006). *Domestic violence and homelessness.* Washington, DC: Author. Retrieved from www.aclu.org/sites/default/files/pdfs/dvhomelessness032106.pdf.

Agnone, J., & Corwin, T. (2012). *Blueprint for reducing child poverty in Washington State – Executive summary. Prepared for the* WA St. Budget and Policy Center, Seattle, WA.

Agnone, J., & Corwin, T. (2013). *Blueprint for reducing child poverty in Washington State.* Seattle, WA: Northwest Research Group.

Annie E. Casey Foundation. (2014). *Creating opportunity for families: A two-generation approach*. Baltimore, MD: Author, p. 11. Retrieved from www.aecf.org/resources/creating-opportunity-for-families.

Annie E. Casey (2017). Financial well-being. (Web posting). Baltimore: Author. Retrieved from www.aecf.org/work/economic-opportunity/financial-well-being/.

Bell, W.C. (2015, June). *A declaration of hope: Building a stronger community foundation*. Keynote address from a forum of New England Blacks in Philanthropy, Boston, MA, June. Retrieved from www.casey.org/building-stronger-community-foundation/.

Berger, L., Font, S.A., Slack, K.S., & Waldfogel, J. (2013). *Income and child maltreatment: Evidence from the earned income tax credit*. Paper prepared for presentation at the 2013 Annual Meeting of the Association of Public Policy Analysis and Management, Washington, DC, November 7–9.

Berger, L.M., Collins, J.M, Font, S.A., Gjertson, L., Slack, K.S., & Smeeding, T. (2015). Home foreclosure and child protective services involvement. *Pediatrics, 136*(2), 299–307. Retrieved from http://pediatrics.aappublications.org/content/early/2011/09/15/peds.2010-2185.

Berger, R.P., Fromkin, J.B., Stutz, H., Makoroff, K., Scribano, P.V., Feldman, K., Tu, L.C., & Fabio, A. (2011). Abusive head trauma during a time of increased unemployment: A multicenter analysis. *Pediatrics, 128*, 637–643. Retrieved fromwww.ncbi.nlm.nih.gov/pubmed/26183000.

Bloom, H.S., Hill, C., & Riccio, J. (2003). Linking program implementation and effectiveness: Lessons from a pooled sample of welfare-to-work experiments. *Journal of Public Policy Analysis and Management, 22*, 551–575.

Brain and Behavior Research Foundation. (2010). *Jane Costello: What the Great Smoky Mountains Study is telling us about mental illness among children*. New York: Author. Retrieved from www.bbrfoundation.org/content/jane-costello-what-great-smoky-mountains-study-telling-us-about-mental-illness-among.

Center for Law and Social Policy. (2011). *Reducing child poverty: Tips for the U.S. from across the Pond*. Washington, DC: Author.

Center on the Developing Child at Harvard University. (2012). *InBrief: Executive Function: Skills for Life and Learning* (Video). Retrieved from www.youtube.com/watch?v=efCq_vHUMqs.

Chester, A., Schmit, S., Alker, J., & Golden, O. (2016). *Medicaid expansion promotes children's development and family success by treating maternal depression*. Washingon, DC: Center for Children and Families, Health Policy Institute, Georgetown University and the Center for Law and Social Policy. Retrieved from www.clasp.org/resources-and-publications/publication-1/Treating-Maternal-Depression.pdfg.

Chetty, R., Hendren, N., & Katz, L. (2015). *The effects of exposure to better neighborhoods on children: New evidence from the Moving to Opportunity Experiment*. Washington, DC: National Bureau of Economic Research. Retrieved from www.equality-of-opportunity.org/images/mto_paper.pdf.

Clark, K. (2016). *The Disconnected: Two decades after "welfare to work," some women are navigating life without either welfare or work*. Retrieved from www.slate.com/articles/

news_and_politics/moneybox/2016/06/_welfare_to_work_resulted_in_neither_welfare_nor_work_for_many_americans.html.

Corwin, T., Pecora, P.J., & Ostrum, P. (2016). *Community-based family support strategies: Exemplars with implementation and evaluation strategies.* Seattle, WA: Casey Family Programs. See www.Casey.org.

Coulton, C.J., Crampton, D.S., Irwin, M., Spilsbury, J.C., & Korbin, J.E. (2007). How neighborhoods influence child maltreatment: A review of the literature and alternative pathways. *Child Abuse & Neglect, 31,* 1117–1142.

Daro, D., & Dodge, K.A. (2009). Creating community responsibility for child protection: Possibilities and challenges. *Future of Children, 19*(2), 67–93.

DeNavas-Walt, C., & Proctor, B.D. (2015). *Income and poverty in the United States: 2014.* Washington, DC: US Government Printing Office (pp. 60–252). Washington, DC: US Census Bureau, Current Population Reports.

Dishion, T.J., Shaw, D., Connell, A., Gardner, F., Weaver, C., & Wilson, M. (2008). The Family Check-Up with high-risk indigent families: Preventing problem behavior by increasing parents' positive behavior support in early childhood. *Child Development, 79*(5), 1395–1414. doi:10.1111/j.1467–8624.2008.01195.x.

Dodge, K.A., Goodman, W.B., Murphy, R., O'Donnell, K., Sato, J., & Guptill, S. (2014). Implementation and randomized controlled trial evaluation of universal postnatal nurse home visiting. *American Journal of Public Health, 104*(S1), S136–143.

Dodge, K., Berlin, L.J., Epstein, M., Spitz-Roth, A., O'Donnell, K., Kaufman, M., Amaya-Jackson, L., Rosch, J., & Christopoulos, C. (2004). The Durham Family Initiative: A preventive system of care. *Child Welfare, 83*(2), 109–128.

Drake, B., & Jonson-Reid, M. (2011). NIS interpretations: Race and the National Incidence Studies of child abuse and neglect. *Children and Youth Services Review, 33,* 16–20.

Drake, B., & Rank, M. (2009). The racial divide among American children in poverty: Assessing the importance of neighborhoods. *Children and Youth Services Review, 31*(12), 1264–1271.

Dreyer, D., Chung, B., Szilagyi, P., & Wong, S. (2016a). Child poverty in the United States today: Introduction and executive summary. *Academic Pediatrics, 16,* S1–S5.

Dreyer, D., Chung, B., Szilagyi, P., & Wong, S. (2016b). Boosting low-income children's opportunities to succeed through direct income support. *Academic Pediatrics, 3*(Suppl), S90–S97.

Duncan, G., & Magnuson, K. (2004). Individual and parent-based strategies for promoting human capital and positive behavior. In P.L. Chase-Lansdale, K. Kiernan, & R. Friedman (Eds), *Human development across lives and generations: The potential for change.* (pp. 93–138) Cambridge: Cambridge University Press.

Eckenrode, J., & Ganzel, B. (1999). *Preventing child maltreatment through a program of nurse home visitation: Mediating and moderating effects in a long-term follow-up study.* Paper presented at American Psychological Association meetings, August 20–24, Boston, MA.

Edin, K.J., & Shaefer, H.L. (2015). *$2 per day: Living on almost nothing in America*. New York: Houghton Mifflin Harcourt.

Ekono, M., Jiang, Y., & Smith, S. (2016). *Young children in deep poverty* (Fact Sheet). National Center for Children in Poverty, Retrieved from www.nccp.org/publications/pdf/text_1133.pdf.

Ernst, J.S. (2000). Mapping child maltreatment: Looking at neighborhoods in a suburban county. *Child Welfare, 79*(5), 555–572.

Federal Poverty Level (FPL). Retrieved from www.healthcare.gov/glossary/federal-poverty-level-FPL/.

Freisthler, B., Bruce, E., & Needell, B. (2007). Understanding the geospatial relationship of neighborhood characteristics and rates of maltreatment for Black, Hispanic, and White children. *Social Work, 52*(1), 7–16.

Gennetian, L.A., & Miller, C. (2002). Children and welfare reform: A view from an experimental welfare program in Minnesota. *Child Development, 73*, 601–620.

Godfrey, E.B., & Yoshikawa, H. (2012). Caseworker–recipient interaction: Welfare office differences, economic trajectories, and child outcomes. *Child Development, 83*(1), 382–398.

Golden, O., McDaniel, M., Loprest, P., & Stanczyk, A. (2013). *Disconnected mothers and the well-being of children: A research report* (Working paper). Washington, DC: Urban Institute.

Hargreaves, M.B., Verbitsky-Savitz, N., Coffee-Borden, B., Perreras, L., White, C.R., Pecora, P.J., Morgan, G.J., Barila, T., Ervin, A., Case, L., Hunter, R., & Adams, K. (2017). Advancing the measurement of collective community capacity to address adverse childhood experiences and resilience. *Children and Youth Services Review, 76*, 142–153. Retrieved from http://dx.doi.org/10.1016/j.childyouth.2017.02.021.

Hooper, D. (2016). The top twelve grand challenges facing society today. *Social Work Helper*, January 14, 2016. Retrieved from www.socialworkhelper.com/2016/01/14/top-twelve-grand-challenges-facing-society-today/.

Hymowitz, K.S. (2017). *The new Brooklyn*. Lanham, MD: Rowman & Littlefield.

Katz, I., Corylon, J., La Placa, V., & Hunter, S. (2007). *The relationship between parenting and poverty*. York: Joseph Rowntree Foundation. Retrieved from www.jrf.org.uk/sites/default/files/jrf/migrated/files/parenting-poverty.pdf.

King, M.L. Jr. (1967). *Where do we go from here: Chaos or community?* New York: Harper & Row.

Klein, S., & Merritt, D.H. (2014). Neighborhood racial and ethnic diversity as a predictor of child welfare system involvement. *Children and Youth Services Review, 41*, 95–105.

Lee, J. (2017). *Single mother statistics*. Retrieved from https://singlemotherguide.com/single-mother-statistics/#footnote_2_13.

Lein, L. Romich, J.L., & Sherraden, M. (2016). *Reversing extreme inequality*. A grand challenges paper from the American Academy of Social Work and Social Welfare. Retrieved from https://swhelper-wpengine.netdna-ssl.com/wp-content/uploads/2016/01/WP16-with-cover-2.pdf.

Loman, L.A., & Siegel, G.L. (2012). Effects of anti-poverty services under the differential response approach to child welfare. *Children and Youth Services Review, 34*, 1659–1666.

Maher, E., Corwin, T., & Pecora, P.J. (2017). *Poverty and child welfare.* Seattle, WA: Casey Family Programs, Research Services (presentation materials).

Marmot, M. (2005). *The status syndrome: How social standing affects our health and longevity.* New York: Henry Holt and Company, LLC.

Mathewson, T.G. (2017). How poverty changes the brain: The early results out of a Boston non-profit are positive. *The Atlantic*, April 19. Retrieved from www.theatlantic.com/education/archive/2017/04/can-brain-science-pull-families-out-of-poverty/523479/.

McCroskey, J., Pecora, P.J., Franke, T., Christie, C.A., & Lorthridge, J. (2012). Strengthening families and communities to prevent child abuse and neglect: Lessons from the Los Angeles Prevention Initiative Demonstration Project. *Child Welfare, 91*(2), 39–60.

McFeatters, A. (2016). Hey, Donald, want to know what's not fair? *Savannahnow* news, April 16. Retrieved from http://sav-cdn.com/opinion-columns/2016-04-14/ann-mcfeatters-hey-donald-want-know-whats-not-fair# (accessed April 17, 2016).

McKernan, S-M., & Ratcliff, C. (2009). Asset building for today's stability and tomorrow's security. *New England Community Development*. Boston, MA: Federal Reserve Bank of Boston. Retrieved from www.urban.org/sites/default/files/publication/28041/1001374-Asset-Building-for-Today-s-Stability-and-Tomorrow-s-Security.PDF.

Meyer, B.D., & Sullivan, J.X. (2004). The effects of welfare and tax reform: The material well-being of single mothers in the 1980s and 1990s. *Journal of Public Economics, 88*(7–8), 1387–1420.

Molnar, B.E., Goerge, R.M., Gilsanz, P., Hill, A., Subramanian, S.V., Holton, J.K., Duncan, D.T., Beatriz, E.D., & Beardslee, W.R. (2016). Neighborhood-level social processes and substantiated cases of child maltreatment. *Child Abuse & Neglect, 51*, 41–53.

Morton, C.M., Simmel, C., & Peterson, N.A. (2014). Neighborhood alcohol outlet density and rates of child abuse and neglect: Moderating effects of access to substance abuse services. *Child Abuse & Neglect, 38*(5), 952–961.

National Center for Health Statistics. (2012). *Health, United States 2011: With special feature on socioeconomic status and health.* Hyattsville, MD: Author. Retrieved from www.cdc.gov/nchs/data/hus/hus11.pdf.

National Center on Children in Poverty. (2014). See http://nccp.org/about.html and http://nccp.org/publications/pub_1087.html.

National Research Council, & Institute of Medicine of the National Academies. (2009). *Preventing mental, emotional, and behavioral disorders among young people: Progress and possibilities.* Washington, DC: National Academies Press.

Newmann, J.P., & Sallman, J. (2004). Women, trauma histories and co-occurring disorders. *Social Service Review, 78*, 466–499.

Office of the Assistant Secretary for Planning and Evaluation. (2018). *U.S. federal poverty guidelines used to determine financial eligibility for certain federal programs.* Washington, DC: Author. Retrieved from https://aspe.hhs.gov/poverty-guidelines.

Partners for Our Children. (2016.) *Poverty and involvement in the child welfare system.* Retrieved from file:///W:/Research/Poverty/Poverty%20and%20Child%20Welfare%20Involvement%205-3-16.pdf.

Patterson, G.R., Forgatch, M.S., & DeGarmo, D.S. (2010). Cascading effects following intervention. *Development and Psychopathology, 22*, 949–970.

Pecora, P.J. (2018). *Risk and Protective Factors for Child Abuse and Neglect: A resource paper.* New York City: Taylor and Francis.

Pfingst, L. (2012). *In pursuit of prosperity: Eight strategies to rebuild Washington State's economy.* Olympia, WA: Washington State Public Policy Center.

Plotnick, R. (2009). Economic security for families with children. In P.J. Pecora, J.K. Whittaker, A.N. Maluccio, R.P. Barth, & D. DePanfilis, *The child welfare challenge* (3rd edn). Piscataway, NJ: Aldine-Transaction Books.

Popkin, S.J., Theodos, B., Getsinger, L., & Parilla, J. (2010). *An overview of the Chicago Family Case Management Demonstration: Supporting vulnerable public housing families Brief 1.* Washington, DC: The Urban Institute.

Popkin, S.J., Levy, D.K., Harris, L.E., Comey, J., Cunningham, M.K., & Buron, L.F. (2004). The HOPE VI program: What about the residents? *Housing Policy Debate, 15*, 385–414.

Proctor, B.D., Semega, J.L., & Kollar, M.A. (2016). *Income and poverty in the United States: 2015 current population reports.* Retrieved from www.census.gov/content/dam/Census/library/publications/2016/demo/p60-256.pdf (accessed September 16, 2016).

Radner, J.M., & Shonkoff, J.P. (2013). Mobilizing science to reduce intergenerational poverty. In Nancy O. Andrews & David J. Erickson (Eds), *Investing in what works for America's communities: Essays on people, place & purpose.* San Francisco, CA: Federal Reserve Bank of San Francisco and the Low Income Investment Fund. Retrieved from www.whatworksforamerica.org/ideas/mobilizing-science-to-reduce-intergenerational-poverty/#.WA7jo5AzX3i.

Reitman, D., Currier, R.O., & Stickle, T.R. (2002). A critical evaluation of the Parenting Stress Index-Short Form (PSI-SF) in a head start population. *Journal of Clinical Child Adolescent Psychology, 31*(3), 384–392.

Renner, L.M., Slack, K.S., & Berger, L.M. (2008). A descriptive study of intimate partner violence and child maltreatment: Implications for child welfare policy. In Duncan Lindsey & Aron Shlonsky (Eds), *Child welfare research* (pp. 154–172). New York: Oxford University Press.

Rosin, H. (2013). The gender wage gap is a lie. *Slate.* Retrieved from www.slate.com/articles/double_x/doublex/2013/08/gender_pay_gap_the_familiar_line_that_women_make_77_cents_to_every_man_s.html.

Sandel, M., Faugno, E., Mingo, A., Cannon, J., Byrd, K., Garcia, D.A., Collier, S., McClure, E., & Boynton Jarrett, R. (2016). Neighborhood-level interventions to improve childhood opportunity and lift children out of poverty. *Academic Pediatrics, 3*(Suppl), S128–S135.

Sedlak, A.J., & Broadhurst, D.D. (1996). *Third national incidence study of child abuse and neglect: Final report.* Washington, DC: U.S. Department of Health & Human Services.

Sedlack, A.J., Mettenburg, J., Basena, M., Petta, I., McPherson, K., Greene, A., & Li, S. (2010). *Fourth National Incidence Study of Child Abuse and Neglect (NIS-4): Report to Congress.* Washington, DC: U.S. Department of Health and Human Services, Administration for Children and Families.

Shaefer, H.L., & Ybarra, Y. (2012). The welfare reforms of the 1990s and the stratification of material well-being among low-income households with children. *Children and Youth Services Review, 34*(9), 1810–1817.

Shaw, D.S., Sitnick, S.L., Brennan, L.M., Choe, D.E., Dishion, T.J., Wilson, M.N., & Gardner, F. (2016). The long-term effectiveness of the Family Check-Up on school-age conduct problems: Moderation by neighborhood deprivation. *Development and Psychopathology, 28*(4), 1471–1486. doi:10.1017/S0954579415001212.

Sherman, A. (2011). *Poverty and financial distress would have been substantially worse in 2010 without government action, new census data show.* Retrieved from www.cbpp.org/cms/index.cfm?fa=view&id=3610 (accessed March 3, 2014).

Sherraden, M.S., Huang, J., Frey, J.J., Birkenmaier, J., Callahan, C., Clancy, M.M., & Sherraden, M. (2015). *Financial capability and asset building for all.* Grand Challenges for Social Work Initiative Working Paper No. 13. Cleveland, OH: American Academy of Social Work and Social Welfare. Retrieved from http://aaswsw.org/grand-challenges-initiative/12-challenges/build-financial-capability-for-all/.

Shonkoff, J.P., & Fisher, P.A. (2013). Rethinking evidence-based practice and two-generation programs to create the future of early childhood policy. *Development and Psychopathology: A Vision Realized, 25*(4), part 2, 1635–1653. doi:10.1017/S0954579413000813.

Slack, K., & Berger, L. (2014). *Does economic support play a role in preventing child maltreatment? An experimental evaluation of Project GAIN: Summary of project goals and needs.* Madison, WI: University of Wisconsin-Madison, School of Social Work.

Slack, K.S., Berger L.M., & Noyes J.L. (in press). Poverty and child maltreatment: What we know and what we still need to learn. *Children and Youth Services Review.*

Slack, K.S., Kim, B., Yang, M.Y., & Berger, L.M. (2014). *The new economic safety net for low-income families.* Working Paper. Madison, WI: Institute for Research on Poverty, University of Wisconsin-Madison.

Sutton, S.E., & Kemp, S.P. (2011a). Introduction: Place as marginality and possibility. In S.E. Sutton & S.P. Kemp (Eds), *The paradox of urban space: Inequity and transformation in urban communities* (pp. 3–10). New York: Palgrave Macmillan.

Sutton, S.E., & Kemp, S.P. (Eds) (2011b). *The paradox of urban space: Inequity and transformation in urban communities.* New York: Palgrave Macmillan.

Tyler, J.H. (2003). The economic benefits of the GED: Lessons from recent research. *Review of Educational Research, 73*(3), 369–403.

Urban Institute. (2013). *Addressing deep and persistent poverty. A framework for philanthropic planning and investment.* Washington, DC: Author. Retrieved from www.urban.org/UploadedPDF/412983-addressing-deep-poverty.pdf.

U.S. Census Bureau. (2013). The Research SUPPLEMENTAL POVERTY MEASURE: 2012 (Current Population Reports). Washington, DC: Author. Retrieved from www.census.gov/prod/2013pubs/p60-247.pdf (accessed March 2, 2014).

U.S. Census Bureau. (2016a). *Income, poverty and health insurance coverage in the United States: 2015* (Press release, September 13, 2016). Retrieved from www.census.gov/news room/press-releases/2016/cb16-158.html (accessed September 16, 2016).

U.S. Census Bureau. (2016b). *Income and poverty in the United States: 2015*. Retrieved from www.census.gov/library/publications/2016/demo/p60-256.html.

U.S. Census Bureau. (2016c). Table C8. Poverty Status, Food Stamp Receipt, and Public Assistance for Children Under 18 Years by Selected Characteristics: 2016. Retrieved from www.census.gov/data/tables/2016/demo/families/cps-2016.html.

U.S. Census Bureau. (2016d). Table C2. Household Relationship and Living Arrangements of Children Under 18 Years, by Age and Sex: 2016. Washington, DC: Author. Retrieved from www.census.gov/data/tables/2016/demo/families/cps-2016.html.

U.S. Census Bureau. (2016e). Table FG10. Family Groups: 2016. Washington, DC: Author. Retrieved from www.census.gov/data/tables/2016/demo/families/cps-2016.html.

U.S. Census Bureau. (2016f). Table 4. Poverty Status of Families, by Type of Family, Presence of Related Children, Race, and Hispanic Origin: 1959 to 2015. Washington, DC: Author. Retrieved from www.census.gov/data/tables/2016/demo/income-poverty/p60-256.html.

U.S. Department of Health and Human Services, National Center on Child Abuse and Neglect. (1996). *Study findings: Study of national incidence and prevalence of child abuse and neglect (NIS-3)*. Washington, DC: Author.

Wald, M. (2014). Beyond child protection: Helping all families provide adequate parenting. In K. McCartney, H. Yoshikawa, & L.B. Forcier (Eds), *Improving the odds for America's children: Future directions in policy and practice* (pp. 135–147). Cambridge, MA: Harvard Education Press.

Wald, M.S. (2015). Beyond CPS: Developing an effective system for helping children in "neglectful" families. *Child Abuse & Neglect, 41*, 49–66.

Waters-Boots, S. (2010). *Improving access to public benefits: Helping eligible individuals and families get the income supports they need*. Ford Foundation.

Wherry, L.R., Kenney, G.M., & Sommers, B.D. (2016). The role of public health insurance in reducing child poverty. *Academic Pediatrics, 3*(Suppl): 8–S104.

Yoshikawa, H., Aber, J.L., & Beardslee, W. (2012). The effects of poverty on the mental, emotional, and behavioral health of children and youth: Implications for prevention. *American Psychologist, 67*(4), 272–284. doi:10.1037/a0028015.

Family Foster Care and Kinship Care

5

Learning Objectives

1. Learn about the purpose, goals, and scope of foster care.

2. Understand the evolution of family foster care, polices over the years, and what we have learned from the past.

3. Appreciate the value and complexities of kinship care.

4. Understand the potential of treatment foster care as a specialized resource that may also be delivered by specially trained relatives of the child.

Purpose, Goals, and Scope of Foster Care

Purpose and Goals

Family foster care, a phenomenon with ancient origins, continues to affect the lives of millions of children, youths, and their families. Following a brief review of its evolution, this chapter examines contemporary foster care in the United States. The major areas to be covered in this chapter are (1) Evolution, definition, and the policy context for foster care; (2) Types of family foster care (including kinship care and treatment foster care); (3) Foster care statistics and recent trends; (4) Recruitment, training, and support of foster parents; (5) Effectiveness of services; and (6) Policy and program design challenges in foster care. The chapter will conclude with consideration of where family foster care is headed. Content pertaining to family reunification, guardianship, and adoption will be covered in Chapter 6; and residential treatment will be discussed in Chapter 8 (Specialized Treatment Services).

Evolution of Family Foster Care

Early History

Family foster care in one form or another has a long history (cf. Chambers, 1963; Hacsi, 1995; Kadushin & Martin, 1988). Kinship care, probably the most common precursor to family foster care, may have origins "under ancient Jewish laws and customs, children lacking parental care became members of the household of other relatives, if such there were, who reared them for adult life" (Slingerland, 1919, p. 27). Children from every culture continue to be raised by their kin when parents are unwilling or unable to fulfill the parental role.

In modern times in the United States, family foster care has been marked by a number of developmental milestones and federal laws. Family foster care began as an effort to "rescue" children who were "dependent" or whose parents were "inadequate" and relying on charity; the movement was substantially stimulated by the Reverend Charles Loring Brace and the Placing Out System of the New York Children's Aid Society. Brace and his associates planned and promoted the transfer by train of tens of thousands of children from the streets of New York to the west or south, where they were placed with farming families in which they would work and grow up (Brace, 1872). While many children were orphans, others had one or both parents living. Most came from recently arrived immigrant families from Southern Europe.

The transfer of those children eventually created much controversy, including opposition of the Catholic Church to placement of Catholic children with Protestant families, as well as resistance from child welfare professionals who were concerned about uprooting so many young people. As a result of these and other developments in child welfare services this approach eventually declined, and Children's Aid Societies were established to administer foster care programs within each state. These changes presage the current movement to provide children's care close to home.

By the 1950s, a range of out-of-home care options had emerged, including the following:

- receiving or shelter homes – in which children were cared for on an emergency, time-limited basis;
- wage (or free) homes – particularly for older children who contributed some work in return for receiving care;

- boarding homes – for which the agency or parents paid a board rate to the foster parents;

- group homes – for small groups of unrelated children;

- larger residential homes (large campuses serving many children).

In each of the above options, the emphasis was on providing a family setting for every child. Indeed, as early as 1909, the first White House Conference on Children proclaimed:

> Home life [.] is the highest and finest product of civilization. It is the great molding force of mind and character. Children should not be deprived of it except for urgent and compelling reasons.
>
> (Bremner, 1971, p. 352)

In the efforts to achieve the goal of a "secure and loving home," following the 1909 conference a complex set of child welfare (CW) services evolved encompassing both governmental and voluntary agencies. Gradually, family foster care, which had emerged in the latter part of the nineteenth century as a means of rescuing children from their "inadequate" parents, came to be considered a temporary service whose purpose was to reunite children with their families or place them, if necessary, in another family in which they could grow up. The evolution of foster care as a temporary service, however, often occurred more at the policy and philosophical levels than in practice. Many children remained in foster care for lengthy periods of time up through to the end of the twentieth century. Especially since the 1950s, it became apparent that the goal of a "secure and loving home" was not being realized for many children, despite the proliferation of new agencies and additional resources.

Foster Care and Permanency Planning Evolves

Practice experiences; research findings from landmark studies such as those by Fanshel and Shinn (1978), Maas and Engler (1959), and Shyne and Schroeder (1978); and critiques of foster care in the 1950s, 1960s, and 1970s underscored a number of points:

- Despite its temporary purpose, foster care placement had become a permanent status for many children entering the services.

- Many children were drifting in foster care – going from one placement to another, with little sense of stability or continuity in their living arrangements.

- Children were often inappropriately moved out of their homes – with little effort to help the parents to care for them.

- Most of the children came from poor families – often families that were barely managing to survive on limited income from public welfare.

- Although some children were effectively helped through placement in foster care, for others the experience of separation from their families had adverse aspects, including losing track of siblings and other disrupted relationships.

As a result of these and other findings, as well as the rapid increase in the numbers of children going into foster care, questions were raised about the effectiveness of CW services. At the same time, there were other pertinent developments, such as the growth of the civil rights movement, which led to the child advocacy movement and to growing concern about the rights of children and parents. As discussed in Chapter 2, there was also the discovery (or rediscovery) of physical abuse of children by their parents or other family members, which led to a tremendous expansion of child protection services and, inevitably, to an increase in the numbers of children going into out-of-home care.

In addition, the family became respectable again as a social unit to be supported rather than blamed (Lasch, 1977). For example, in the 1970s there emerged conviction at the federal and state levels that needy people – including children – should be cared for in the least restrictive environment.

Legal and Policy Framework

Foster care practice and programs are governed by an intricate – and not necessarily coherent – set of policies and laws at the federal, state, and local levels. These are described in Chapter 1, the policy resource paper on the Routledge website (Pecora et al., 2018) and considered throughout this book. For example, at the federal level, policies that directly affect foster family care are embedded primarily in major laws enacted by the U.S. Congress during the past four decades.

Perhaps the most controversial and sensitive issue is balancing the rights of parents with those of children, especially children placed in foster care because of parental abuse or neglect (Annie E. Casey Foundation, 2015; Wald, 2015). Despite the proliferation of statutes, policies, and legal procedures, decision making in this area is heavily influenced by a number of idiosyncratic factors. These include, among others, availability of prevention and placement resources; values and biases of service providers; presence of strong advocates for the parents or children; attitudes of juvenile court judges toward placement; rigor of the screening process; ambiguities in definition of abuse, neglect, and child protection; and the imprecise nature of information about human behavior and the impossibility of predicting the future. The consequences of such an idiosyncratic approach to decision making can be negative, as seen, for example, in some cases in which termination of parental rights is accomplished legally, but the child is then left to drift in foster care without any family connection or other permanent plan. Yet, discretion and flexibility can also be used for the greater good. For this reason, as suggested in Chapters 2 and 3, sound decision making in child protective services, foster care, and in CW in general, requires not only partnership between the family and service providers but also active collaboration among community agencies, CW workers, judges, attorneys, and others working with children and their parents.

Definition and Purpose of Family Foster Care

Foster care is generally used as a term encompassing not only family foster care, but also placement of children and youths in group homes and residential settings, a topic covered later in this chapter. Family foster care, the focus of this chapter, has been defined as:

> the provision of planned, time-limited, substitute family care for children who cannot be adequately maintained at home, and the simultaneous provision of social services to these children and their families to help resolve the problems that led to the need for placement.
>
> (Blumenthal, 1983, p. 296)

The above definition reflects various principles that are well accepted in the field of child welfare, as exemplified by the "CWLA Standards of Excellence for Family Foster Care" (Child Welfare League of America, 1995), although not fully realized in policy or practice. First, family foster care is conceptualized as a comprehensive family support service, and the family is regarded as the central focus of attention. Second, family foster care is carefully planned to be short term and to provide access to time-limited services and opportunities that can help families become rehabilitated and children to grow up and develop.

The major functions of family foster care include emergency protection, crisis intervention, assessment and case planning, reunification, preparation for adoption, and preparation for independent living. To implement such functions, diverse forms of foster care are required, including emergency foster care, kinship foster care, placement with unrelated foster families, treatment foster care, foster care for medically fragile children, shared family foster care, and small family group home care. In addition, long-term family foster care is an option for a *very* small number of youths for whom family reunification, kinship care, or adoption are not viable permanency planning options.

In addition, there are indications that family foster care is responding to the substantial behavioral health needs of the children in care and becoming more treatment oriented. Specialized family foster care programs – particularly treatment foster care – for children and youths with special needs in such areas as emotional disturbance, behavioral problems, and educational underachievement, are gaining significant use (e.g., Chamberlain, 2003; Family-based Treatment Association, 2013, 2015). In most communities, family foster care is a multi-faceted service, including specialized or therapeutic services for some children, temporary placements for children in "emergency" homes, and supports to relatives raising children through kinship care. Despite the NSCAW (Dolan et al., 2011) and recent studies of "superutilizers" of services in child welfare (e.g., Weigensberg et al., 2018), and other studies, we still lack adequate descriptive data on services to children in foster care and their specific effectiveness. Furthermore, we believe that much of foster care is delivered without significant services for children other than referral to health and mental health agencies for treatment.

Types of Foster Care

Kinship Care

History. Kinship care is an ancient phenomenon. In many cultures, the practice whereby grandparents, older siblings, aunts and uncles, or other adults or elders assume responsibility for children unable to live with their parents is a time-honored tradition (Child Welfare League of America, 1994; Scannapieco & Hegar, 1999; Testa & Shook-Slack, 2002). Kinship care for children who must be separated from their biological parents is attractive for many reasons, since it:

- enables children to live with persons whom they know and trust;
- reduces the trauma children may experience when they are placed with persons who are initially unknown to them;
- reinforces children's sense of identity and self-esteem, which flows from their family history and culture;

- facilitates children's connections to their siblings;
- strengthens the ability of families to give children the support they need (Wilson & Chipungu, 1996, p. 387).

Although it is not a new phenomenon, kinship care may be viewed as a new child placement paradigm due to "its recent embrace by the child welfare field, social work, and public policy" as a "model governing thought and practice" (Scannapieco & Hegar, 1999, p. 225). In recent years, it has become the first choice – rather than the last resort – in the continuum of services for children requiring out-of-home care (McDaniel, 2014). Decision making and planning in CW require listening to the voices of children. The poem in Box 5.1 reflects children's yearnings for security in their lives, and especially for connections with their kin and with their familiar environments.

Box 5.1   A Child's Yearning for Placement with Her Grandmother

Grandma's House
By Chiemi T. Davis*

I'm scared. Yesterday they came and got me.
I'm scared. My mom's using again and nobody's home.
I'm scared. Where they going to put me?
I'm scared. Who's going to take care of me?

I want to go to Grandma's house
Where I know the smells.
She'll cook my food and do up my hair.
She'll sing my songs, I can sleep in her bed,
She'll hold and rock me all night long.

I want to go to Grandma's house
Where I can go to my store.
Ms. Robinson, she'll be there
She'll yell and tell me to "git"
but first she'll give me a free soda and some "sugar" to go.

I want to go to Grandma's house
Cause my mom will know where I am.

She'll say "sorry baby" and kiss my hand.
Grandma will tell her "enough is enough"
She'll know she can't smoke here
She'll get straight and do what's right.

I'm scared and I want to go to Grandma's house.

Note:
*Chiemi T. Davis is Senior Director of Social Services, Liliuokalani Trust. Reprinted with permission.

Definition and scope of kinship care. The Child Welfare League of America's Kinship Care Policy and Practice Committee defined kinship care as: "the full-time nurturing and protection of children who must be separated from their parents by relatives, members of their tribes or clans, godparents, stepparents, or other adults who have a kinship bond with a child" (Child Welfare League of America, 1994, p. 2). Scannapieco and Hegar (1999, p. 3) further explain that there are different perspectives on what constitutes kinship care, a phrase originally inspired by Carol Stack (1974) in her work on extended kinship networks in the African American community. In particular, they note that kinship care includes both care entered into by private family arrangement and care provided through auspices of a public child welfare agency with legal custody of a child.

According to Nisivoccia (1996, p. 1), kinship foster care may be regarded as "a form of extended family preservation that offers continuity of family ties and maintains culture and ethnic identity while cushioning the trauma of foster care placement for children." Whether provided through informal or formal arrangements, it can be a culturally sensitive response that respects the child's and family's origins (Crumbley & Little, 1997, pp. 65–71).

Kinship care under ASFA. Kinship care was a relatively unobserved part of child welfare services when the first major child welfare reform law was passed in 1980 (P.L. 96–272). By 1997, however, when the Adoption and Safe Families Act (ASFA) was passed, almost as many children were in kinship care as in any other kind of care. Whereas Congress decided not to become involved in a major analysis of kinship care at the time when ASFA was debated, ASFA does include language about kinship care that is crucial to understand.

ASFA requires that states file or join a petition to terminate parental rights and responsibilities when a child has been abandoned (in foster care for 15 of the most recent

22 months), or the parent has been convicted of a very serious crime against his or her own child. Yet, there are three exceptions and the first one mentioned is that the child is placed with a relative (at the option of the state). This is an acknowledgment that being in the care of kin may provide a permanent plan with many desirable features.

At the same time, state and county agencies are re-examining their use of long-term kinship foster care because children who enter kinship care have such long stays and are dominating their caseloads. In many jurisdictions (e.g., Alleghany County, Illinois, Los Angeles County, New York City) renewed efforts are being made to explain the options of legal guardianship and adoption to kin in order to encourage them to follow those paths to permanency if appropriate. Several states (e.g., Illinois and California) are also using the flexibility provided by Title IV-E waivers to allow children to "exit" from the formal reunification or permanency planning program by giving the foster family a payment that is higher than the TANF payment but lower than a full foster care payment and will help kinship caregivers care for the child but not requiring that they continue to have a child welfare worker or go to court on behalf of their child. We may expect to see considerably more innovation regarding reunification and kinship care in the years ahead.

Increase in kinship care. Although kinship care has long been used on an informal basis, there are an increasing number of children not only living with grandparents but also being placed with relatives who become their permanent or long-term primary caregivers. Consider some of these recent statistics from the U.S. Census Bureau American Community Survey (www.census.gov/newsroom/facts-for-features/2017/grandparents-day.html):

- *7.3 million:* The number of *grandparents* whose grandchildren under age 18 were living with them in 2015 (source: 2015 American Community Survey, Table B10050).

- *5.9 million:* The number of *children* under age 18 living with a grandparent householder in 2015. Nearly half, or 2.6 million, were under age 6 (source: 2015 American Community Survey, Table B10001).

- *2.6 million:* The number of grandparents responsible for the basic needs of one or more grandchildren under age 18 living with them in 2015. Of these caregivers, 1.6 million were grandmothers and 1.0 million were grandfathers (source: 2015 American Community Survey, Table B10056).

- *509,922:* The number of grandparents responsible for grandchildren under age 18 whose income was below the poverty level in the past 12 months, compared with the

2.1 million grandparent caregivers whose income was at or above the poverty level (source: 2015 American Community Survey, Table B10059).

- *$51,448:* The median income for families with grandparent householders responsible for grandchildren under age 18. Among these families, where a parent of the grandchildren was not present, the median income was $37,580 (source: 2015 American Community Survey, Table B10010).

- *642,852:* The number of grandparents who had a disability and were responsible for their grandchildren (source: 2015 American Community Survey, Table B10052).

- *8.7 percent:* The percentage of Native Hawaiian and Other Pacific Islanders who lived with grandchildren in 2015. This is followed by American Indian and Alaska Natives and those of Some Other Race, which were not statistically different from each other at 7.3 and 7.4 percent, respectively, Hispanics at 6.9 percent, Asians at 6.1 percent, and African Americans at 5.6 percent. Non-Hispanic Whites are the group least likely to have grandparents living under the same roof as their grandchildren at 2.5 percent (source: 2015 American Community Survey, Selected Population Profile S0201).

More than one in three youth in out-of-home care in the United States (3 percent or 139,017) were served in kinship (relative) foster homes versus 45 percent (196,446) were placed in a non-relative home as of September 30, 2016. Another positive aspect of the trend toward greater use of kinship care is that it may indicate that child welfare agencies are becoming more sensitive to family, racial, ethnic, and cultural factors and the importance of family continuity in child development. Given that out-of-home care, whether family foster care, kinship care, or group care, needs to be both "child centered and family affirming" rather than solely child focused – use of kinship care may represent an improvement in the quality and efficacy of these services (Generations United, ChildFocus, and American Bar Association Center on Children and the Law, 2017). Less positively, the trend may be a response to the increasing difficulty in recruiting and retaining foster families. This long-standing difficulty and the rise in the number of children entering care, especially adolescents, indicate that without a growth in kinship care the child welfare system, in recent years, would have experienced an even greater placement-finding crisis.

Kinship care policy issues. Conway and Hutson (2007) discuss some powerful myths surrounding kinship care that may have an impact upon policies or programs. For example, *"The apple doesn't fall far from the tree."* In fact, research shows that children living with relatives are no more likely – and are perhaps less likely – than children living with non-kin foster parents to experience abuse or neglect after being removed from their homes.

A second myth is, *"It's your moral responsibility as a relative to care for these children."* By the very fact that they are providing this care, kinship caregivers agree with this statement.

> They take the responsibility of raising their grandchildren, nieces, and nephews when the children's parents, for a variety of reasons, cannot. These caregivers lack neither morals nor a sense of responsibility; they do, however, lack resources. They may be living on a fixed income or be retired; whatever the reason, it is highly unlikely that they planned financially for raising a relative's child.
>
> (Conway & Hutson, 2007, p. 3)

Furthermore, the vast majority of children living with relative caregivers are eligible for the Temporary Assistance for Needy Families (TANF) child-only grant. However, most relative caregivers do not access TANF or any other public financial assistance. Even when caregivers access TANF child-only grants, this assistance amounts to about half of the anticipated cost of raising a child.

As discussed above, kinship caregivers often lack the information and range of supports they need to fulfill their parenting role. That is why some states and county CW agencies hire "kinship navigators" to advise these parents. However, more work needs to be done to help resolve the policy inconsistencies in the licensing and support of these families, and much remains to be learned about the best ways to help ensure the success of kinship care placements for children (Geen, 2003).

Kinship care, as previously noted, has traditionally been provided for children separated from parents due to family impoverishment, neglect, abuse, or abandonment. A re-emphasis on kinship care is of course in line with the emergence of the political rhetoric associated with conservative family values. This rhetoric is also associated with efforts to reduce the influence and cost of governmental services. Kinship care appears to fit this political paradigm, as it may be cheaper than non-relative foster care, especially if support services, including financial payments to kinship families, are less than those provided to non-relative foster parents. This may be so even though the pattern of service to kinship carers by comparison to non-relative foster carers indicates that kinship caregivers often receive low levels of service (Berrick, Barth, & Needell, 1994). Yet children in care with relatives – especially if the latter are paid the same as foster parents – stay much longer than other children, which means that kinship care is becoming more costly in many places (see AFCARS trend data: Berrick et al., 1998). As a result, some states try to move children in kinship care to non-foster care status or to guardianship – which maintains the reimbursements to the kin, but reduces the court and case management costs (Children's

Defense Fund, Child Trends, American Bar Association Center on Children and the Law, Casey Family Programs, Child Focus, & Generations United, 2012).

A precise analysis of the entire range of foster parent costs – including, for example, higher costs for wear and tear on the home – was completed by a team of social workers and economists; and it clarifies the minimum adequate care rate, adjusted for state costs of living. This report shows that nearly every state is failing to adequately reimburse foster parents – even while struggling to recruit enough foster parents to serve the children in their care (DePanfilis et al., 2007).

The role that the state should play in support and supervision of relatives as caregivers remains controversial in some ways. For instance, should support be primarily financial or also service-related? Should relatives be required to receive counseling or other services if they simply request financial assistance? Should relatives be formally assessed, as with unrelated foster parent applicants?

Practice standards. Although the use of kinship care has greatly increased, there is a modest but growing set of protocols to guide decisions about placing and serving children with kinship carers, such as standards from the Child Welfare League of America (CWLA) (2000), Council on Accreditation (2013), National Association of Social Workers (2013), and guidelines from ChildFocus (2009). The recommendations from the CWLA Kinship Care Policy and Practice Committee (1994), as outlined below, are as relevant today as they were over 24 years ago:

- *Assess:* "the willingness and ability of kin to provide a safe, stable, nurturing home and meet the child's developmental needs" (p. 44).

- *Approval/licensing of kinship homes:* approval and licensing are necessary to ensure "a basic level of care for children in the custody of the state" (p. 47).

- *Services for children:* "kinship services must meet the range of needs of children cared for by kin" (p. 51).

- *Services for parents:* "child welfare agencies should provide the services that parents need for support, rehabilitation, and enhancement of their functioning as parents" (p. 53).

- *Services to kinship families:* "child welfare agencies should provide kin with the supports and services they need to meet the child's needs, assist the child's parents, and meet their own needs as caregivers" (p. 54).

- *Financial supports:* financial supports for children in kinship care should be provided "at a level appropriate to meet the children's physical, mental health, and developmental needs" (p. 56).

- *Monitoring and supervision:* there should be "regular and frequent contacts between the agency social worker and the child and kinship parent to continually address the health, safety, and well-being of the child and the service needs of the kinship family" (p. 62).

- *Permanency planning:* the "child welfare agency should arrange the most appropriate permanent plan for the child – that is, reunification with parent, adoption by relatives, subsidized guardianship by kin, long-term kinship care, or nonrelative adoption" (pp. 63–71).

Outcomes of kinship care. The combination of a decline in the availability of non-relative foster care placements and a re-emergence of conservative family values is not a good omen for children who need out-of-home care. Kinship carers, at least in the U.S., appear to be older and less well off financially (see 2015 American Community Survey, Table B10059 and 2015 American Community Survey, Table B10010*)*, and to have more health and mental health problems than non-relative foster parents. Yet, despite these conditions, analyses from the NSCAW study find few differences between children in kinship and non-kinship care with regard to their developmental outcomes (Barth, Guo, Green, & McRae, 2007).

Besides cost savings, there are many other benefits of placing children, whenever possible, with relatives. First, *it helps keep families together.* Placing children with grand-parents helps maintain healthy connections to the family and its traditions. In many cases, kinship caregiving enables sibling groups to remain intact. Children who are cared for by kin are able, to a greater extent, to maintain relationships with their birth parents and other family members (Annie E. Casey Foundation, 2005). Children who reunify with their birth parent(s) after kinship care are less likely to re-enter foster care than those who had been in non-relative foster placements or in group care facilities (Courtney & Needell, 1997). In addition, kinship caregivers provide stability to children and youth with incarcerated parents. Not only are some of these children not placed in foster care, the incarceration of a parent is often traumatic on a variety of levels for children, and living with family members can provide some measure of stability (Conway & Hutson, 2007).

Second, kinship care placements are more stable living situations. Children in kinship care have more stability in their living situation than they have in a non-kin foster care placement. Children placed with kin by the child welfare system are less likely to experience multiple placements, which has been linked by recent research to less involvement with the juvenile justice systems (Ryan & Testa, 2005), and more positive adult mental health, financial and other outcomes (see the research summary below). It bears repeating, however, that some studies of children placed into kinship care indicate that they have fewer problems to start with than children placed into non-kinship care.

Third, children in kinship care report more positive perceptions of their placements and have fewer behavioral problems. Compared to children in non-relative foster care and those in group care, children in kinship care are:

- More likely to report liking those with whom they live (93 percent versus 79 percent [non-relative foster care] and 51 percent [group care]) (NSCAW, 2005).

- More likely to report wanting their current placement to be their permanent home (61 percent versus 27 percent and 2 percent) (NSCAW, 2005).

- Less likely to report having tried to leave or run away (6 percent versus 16 percent and 35 percent) (NSCAW, 2005).

- More likely to report that they "always felt loved" (94 percent versus 82 percent [non-relative foster care]) (Wilson & Chipungu, 1996).

Yet, it is important to understand that, in terms of scores in physical, cognitive, emotional, and skill-based domains, children in kinship care have scores, at their entry into care, that are much more like those of children who are able to remain at home following a child abuse and neglect investigation than do children in foster or group care, who have more extreme scores (NSCAW data as cited in U.S. Department of Health and Human Services (2005)). The problems of children who enter kinship care are also less than those who go into non-relative foster care.

Fourth, kinship families utilize and preserve cultural values. Historically, families of color, especially African American, Native American, and Hawaiian families, have offered care to children in the extended family, providing culturally specific care that maintains the child's connection to the cultural norms and practices that inform his or her identity. Finally, kinship care may bolster states' ability to comply with federal requirements by providing children with stability and permanency, although this is difficult to say because children who enter kinship care have fewer problems at the time of placement and even the best analyses have difficulty controlling for these differences (Rubin et al., 2007).

In summary, in her review of kinship care and guardianship research, Killos (2017) highlighted that studies in this area consistently indicate that children in relative kinship care or relative guardianship experience improved outcomes when compared with children placed in non-kinship foster care (Winokur, Holtan, & Batchelder, 2014). These improved outcomes include the following:

- Greater placement stability and fewer school changes (Helton, 2011; Park & Helton, 2010; Testa, Bruhn, & Helton, 2010).

- Higher levels of permanency (Falconnier et al., 2010; Zinn et al., 2006).

- Better behavioral and mental health outcomes (Cheung et al., 2011; Garcia et al., 2014; Rubin et al., 2008).

However, some studies are limited by methodological and design weaknesses (Winokur, Holtan, & Batchelder, 2014), including the absence of a national representative sample of children and families in the CW system. Further, we do not have strong evidence regarding whether these benefits and positive outcomes are consistent for children and youth of all ages (Lutman, Hunt, & Waterhouse, 2009; Wu, White, & Coleman, 2015); and which guardianship policies are associated with the most positive outcomes for children and families in guardianship.

Non-relative Care

This form of foster care remains the most commonly used form of out of home care – with 45 percent of children placed in such homes as of September 30, 2016 (U.S. DHHS, 2017). Non-relative foster care will likely remain a significant placement option, despite the use of aggressive family finding and emphasis on placing children with relatives, tribal clan members, and fictive kin. Program and policy design issues that will be discussed later in the chapter, such as recruitment, retention, support, and prevention of maltreatment, also apply to this type of care.

Treatment Foster Care as a Specialized Form of Out-of-home Care

One form of foster care that has emerged over the past 20 years is more of a treatment-oriented service. It involves systematic evaluation and selection of prospective foster parents, more adequate compensation, greater foster parent training and supervision, lower caseloads for workers, substantial participation of foster parents as members of the agency's service team, and more frequent involvement of foster parents in helping biological parents. The above characteristics, along with others, are described in reports and in the "Program

Standards for Treatment Foster Care" promulgated by the Foster Family-based Treatment Association (2013). These standards provide a guide to quality programming and include a "Standard Review Instrument" that agencies can use to conduct a self-assessment.

Despite its growing acceptance at the philosophical level, treatment foster care is not well implemented in some communities and not all treatment foster parents are professionalized. However, there are many exemplary programs, such as Pressley Ridge School's PRYDE program in Pennsylvania, Treatment Foster Care Oregon-Adolescents (TFCO-A), and BoysTown treatment foster care (Meadowcroft & Trout, 1990). Interventions that have a strong evidence base are increasing, such as *Attachment and Biobehavioral Catch-up (ABC)* (Lewis et al., in press); Parent Child Interaction Therapy (PCIT) (Timmer et al., 2006), Trauma-Focused Cognitive-Behavioral Treatment (Cohen & Mannarino, 2004), and others.

Statistics about Children in Family Foster Care and their Families

Who is in Foster Care?

Although there has been a recent upward trend in the number of children in care, overall there has been a significant decline in the out-of-home care population since 2000. This decline has resulted in nearly 25 percent fewer children in care – with total numbers of such children under the age of 18 at just over 424,000 (Conn et al., 2013; U.S. DHHS, 2013, 2017). A total of 437,465 children of all ages were placed in out-of-home care as of September 31, 2016 (a 2.3 percent increase since 2015). In the 1990s there was a steady increase in children in foster care, including children in family foster care or group care (see Figure 5.1). For example, over three in four states (37 in total) had an increase of 1 percent or more (Federal AFCARS statistics). For further details on numbers of children in care, see the U.S. Children's Bureau website for state and national AFCARS data (www. acf.dhhs.gov/programs/cb/stats/afcars).

Planning and delivery of foster family care should be informed by information that helps us to answer the following questions: *What are the risk factors that most place a child at risk of child maltreatment? What child and family protective factors and resources can be brought to bear to address those risk factors? What qualities of foster families and what mix of services do children and families need in order to promote the success of families in resuming their parenting and the development of children's behavioral and educational success?* In response to the above questions, we should first understand

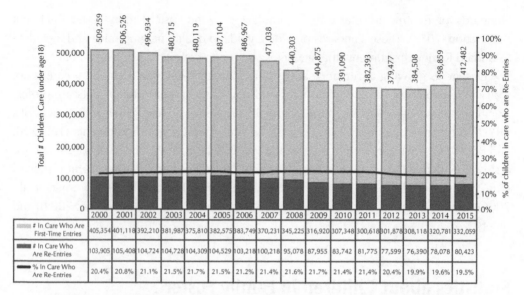

	2000	2001	2002	2003	2004	2005	2006	2007	2008	2009	2010	2011	2012	2013	2014	2015
# In Care Who Are First-Time Entries	405,354	401,118	392,210	381,987	375,810	382,575	383,749	370,231	345,225	316,920	307,348	300,618	301,878	308,118	320,781	332,059
# In Care Who Are Re-Entries	103,905	105,408	104,724	104,728	104,309	104,529	103,218	100,218	95,078	87,955	83,742	81,775	77,599	76,390	78,078	80,423
% In Care Who Are Re-Entries	20.4%	20.8%	21.1%	21.5%	21.7%	21.5%	21.2%	21.4%	21.6%	21.7%	21.4%	21.4%	20.4%	19.9%	19.6%	19.5%

Figure 5.1 The Number of Children in All Forms of Out-of-home Care and
the Re-entry Rate since 2000

Source: AFCARS National File; available from NDACAN at Cornell University; data accessed
April 21, 2017 by Data Advocacy, Casey Family Programs. Note that some states include
juvenile justice foster care placements in these statistics.

the situations of children and families coming to the attention of child welfare services, especially in regard to their numbers, reasons for placement, age distribution, and race and ethnicity

Gradually we are obtaining better data regarding children in out-of-home care nationally, even with some state gaps in reporting. But there are complexities and limitations to these data. For example, while available statistics tend to focus on children placed in out-of-home care through child welfare services and neglect, the data include those placed for mental health reasons and some youth placed via juvenile justice services, as well as those in informal foster care. Consequently, some states are tracking juvenile justice involved youth as a special group. And because some parents may allow the transfer of custody of their child to the state agency because they cannot afford the level of care necessary to treat a child who is severely emotionally disturbed, these youth enter foster care – but some states like Texas have passed legislation to preclude the use of foster care for that reason.

While the federal government is now collecting data from most states through the Adoption and Foster Care Analysis and Reporting System (AFCARS), not all states are reporting on all items. For these reasons, we have reasonable but not precise estimates of the numbers of children in family foster care or in out-of-home placement in general.

These certainly underrepresent the total number of children living away from their parents due to concerns about their well-being. For the latest national and state AFCARS data, see www.afc.dhhs.gov/programs/CB/stats.

Reasons for Placement

Although some of the variable definitions could be more precise, reports from the field document changes in the kinds of children entering placement. Most children still enter foster care owing to the consequences of parent-related problems, largely child neglect and abuse. But as one can see in Figures 5.2 and 5.3, a considerable number of children (especially adolescents) enter care owing to parent substance abuse and child behavioral problems. Note the high rate of Native American children entering care owing to parent substance abuse (nearly all of which is alcohol) – as a call to action for communities to

Neglect and parental substance abuse lead the list of reasons children enter care
(*Note:* multiple reasons may be selected for a single child, FY2015)

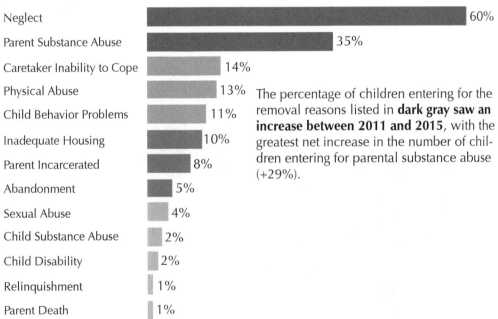

Neglect	60%
Parent Substance Abuse	35%
Caretaker Inability to Cope	14%
Physical Abuse	13%
Child Behavior Problems	11%
Inadequate Housing	10%
Parent Incarcerated	8%
Abandonment	5%
Sexual Abuse	4%
Child Substance Abuse	2%
Child Disability	2%
Relinquishment	1%
Parent Death	1%

The percentage of children entering for the removal reasons listed in **dark gray saw an increase between 2011 and 2015**, with the greatest net increase in the number of children entering for parental substance abuse (+29%).

Figure 5.2 Reasons Why Children Entered Out-of-home Care

Data source: AFCARS national data, available from the National Data Archive on Child Abuse and Neglect Data (NDACAN), Cornell University. Produced by Data Advocacy, Casey Family Programs.

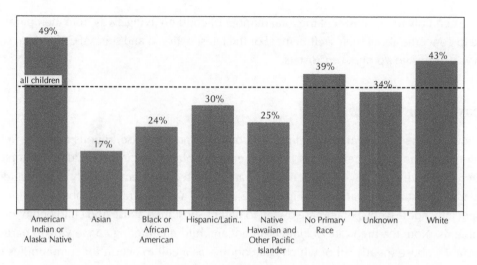

Figure 5.3 Variation by Race among Children Entering for Parental Substance Abuse in Federal Fiscal Year 2015

Note: dotted line is the rate for all children.

Data source: AFCARS national data, available from the National Data Archive on Child Abuse and Neglect Data (NDACAN), Cornell University. Produced by Data Advocacy, Casey Family Programs.

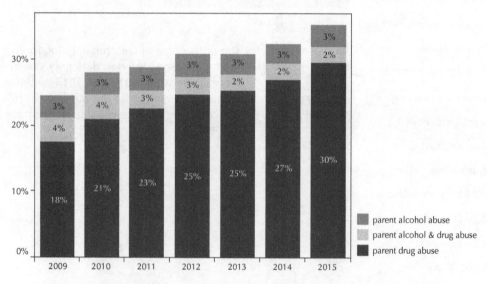

Figure 5.4 Types of Substance Abuse as Reasons for Out-of-home Placement in Federal Fiscal Year 2015

Data source: AFCARS national data, available from the National Data Archive on Child Abuse and Neglect Data (NDACAN), Cornell University. Produced by Data Advocacy, Casey Family Programs.

improve their prevention strategies and treatment services. Across all families, as shown in Figure 5.4, drug abuse remains the predominant type of substance abuse necessitating child placement. Some examples of child placements follow:

- Gloria, 3-month-old daughter of a 16-year-old developmentally disabled girl without any family supports, has been placed in an emergency foster home since birth.

- Tyrone, aged 2, was placed in a pre-adoptive foster home following the mother's death due to HIV-AIDS. No known relatives or family friends could be located who could care for him.

- Bobby and Gerry, aged 8 and 2, were removed from their family due to physical abuse of both boys by their father, who visits them occasionally in the foster home.

- Lucy, aged 10, and her family have been referred to the child protection unit of a county welfare department following a teacher's complaint that Lucy was neglected at home and an investigation showing that she was sexually abused by her mother's boyfriend.

- Steven, aged 12, has been in a treatment foster home following seven days of intensive assessment and stabilization in a psychiatric hospital ever since his widowed father was hospitalized over a year ago for a psychiatric disturbance; the father had severely beaten Steven on at least two occasions for "misbehaving."

There has been an increase in the number and percentage of children entering as a result of parental substance abuse. Most of this increase has been among children who have a parent who is abusing drugs. In addition, there is an indication of increasing proportions of children entering care – and remaining there – from these groups: children with special health or developmental needs, children living in families with severe domestic violence, drug-exposed infants, children from multi-problem families and severely dysfunctional families, children from substance-abusing families, and adolescents with serious behavioral and/or emotional problems (NSCAW data, cited in U.S. DHHS, 2005; Wald, 2015). Furthermore, now as in the past, most children in foster care come from poor families – families with multiple problems in such areas as housing, employment, health, and education (Barth, Wildfire, & Green, 2006; Pelton, 2015; Slack, Berger, & Noyes, in press). Research has also shown that high proportions of children in foster care have major learning problems in school (Turney & Wildeman, 2016) and multiple health problems (Goemans et al., 2016; Turney & Wildeman, 2016). Also, children entering foster care have a history of difficult birth circumstances: exceptionally high rates of low birth weight, birth abnormality, no prenatal care, and families with three or more children (National Survey of Child and Adolescent Well-Being data, cited in U.S. DHHS, 2005).

Age Distribution

We should also note the changing age distribution of children in out-of-home care and the consequent impact upon service delivery. The proportion of adolescents in care, in particular, increased rapidly in the 1980s, as the permanency planning movement initially resulted in keeping younger children out of care, reuniting them with their biological families following placement, or placing them in adoption or other permanent plans (Maluccio et al., 1990, p. 6). Adolescents still constitute a major group in the foster care population and they represent three different groups: those who were placed at an early age and have remained in the same foster home; those who were placed at an early age and have been moving from one placement to another; and those who were placed for the first time as teenagers, usually because of their behavioral or relationship problems.

Many youth enter foster care as adolescents – now, only a small but worrisome group grow up in foster care. In recent years, the greatest growth in foster care has resulted from an influx of very young children. Children from birth to age 1 are the single largest group of children entering foster care – 26 percent of all children placed in foster care were 1 year of age or younger in 2016 (U.S. DHHS, 2017). As Berrick and colleagues (1998) explain in their extensive analysis of data from a range of studies, and reinforced by the Commission to Eliminate Child Abuse and Neglect Fatalities (2016), CW services, policies, and laws have historically paid limited attention to the unique developmental needs and characteristics of preschool children, especially infants; the emphasis has been on school-aged children and on undifferentiated services and programs. This pattern has been reflected in federal and state laws, notably the Adoption Assistance and Child Welfare Act of 1980 (Public Law 96–272). For example, this pioneering federal legislation set a maximum of 18 months for making a permanent plan for a child coming to the attention of CW services, thus overlooking the potentially destructive impact of temporary foster care placement upon infants and other young children. (Conversely, the tighter time limits in the more recently enacted ASFA may not adequately address the needs of older children and youths who enter foster care.)

When the above legislation was enacted nearly two decades ago, the greatest concern was about the plight of older children who had traditionally been placed in unstable, unplanned, long-term foster care that failed to promote their development. Understandably, the emphasis then was on the need of many of these youths for stability and permanence. In recent years, as mentioned above, there has also been a dramatic increase in the number of very young children coming to the attention of the CW services, including infants placed in foster care, as a result of such societal problems as poverty, homelessness, family violence, child abuse and neglect, and substance abuse.

Such an increase has served to underscore the inadequacy of existing laws, policies, and services. As a result, researchers, practitioners, administrators, and policy makers have been challenged to serve young children in a more discriminating and responsive fashion and in accordance with their developmental needs. In particular, there has been further attention to the following question, which Wald raised over three decades ago: "How can we build in *developmental knowledge* to make the laws more sophisticated and more likely to serve the best interests of children?" (Wald, 1976, p. 678). To that end, Berrick et al. (1998), Harvard Center on the Developing Child (2017), and the National Child Traumatic Stress Network have formulated ways of improving CW services by explicitly building a brain science, developmental and trauma perspective into CW research, policy, and practice; effectively using knowledge about child development to propose laws and policies pertaining to child protection; and leading the way toward redesigning CW services for very young children by taking into account their unique needs and qualities and developmental processes. Some of this emphasis is slowly bearing policy fruit, as the Child Abuse Prevention and Treatment Act reforms of 2001 called for the referral of children who experience substantiated maltreatment to be referred to early intervention (a.k.a. IDEA Part C) services so that they could receive developmental screening and intervention, and the Children's Bureau (U.S. DHHS, 2012) has underscored the importance of paying attention to child well-being.

Trends in Foster Care

Trends in foster care were recently summarized by the federal government (see Box 5.2).

Box 5.2   Trends in Out-of-home Care

Numbers of Children in Foster Care: After declining by nearly 19 percent between FY 2007 and FY 2012 to a low of 397,000, the number of children in foster care on the last day of each fiscal year since has shown an increase; however, the percent increase from 2015 to 2016 was 2.3 which is lower than FY 2014's 3.2 increase and FY 2015's 3.1 increase.

Entries into and Exits from Foster Care: Trends for children entering the system follow a similar pattern. Beginning with FY 2007, numbers of entries to care generally declined through FY 2012 to 251,000, increased slightly to 255,000 in FY 2013, and continued to rise to 274,000 in FY 2016. The number of exits, which reached a peak most recently in FY 2007 at 295,000, had been on a continual decline to 237,000 in FY 2014 before increasing to 250,000 in FY 2016.

Children Waiting to be Adopted: The numbers of children waiting to be adopted are a subset of those in care on the last day. As numbers of children in care were

---

declining, the numbers waiting for adoption declined, as well. Similarly, in the past four years a slight increase in the numbers of children waiting for adoption has been observed, moving from a low in FY 2012 of 102,000 up to 118,000 in FY 2016. The percentage of children who are defined as waiting to be adopted has remained stable over the past decade, averaging between 26 and 27 percent of children in care on the last day.

Children Waiting to be Adopted Whose Parents' Rights Were Terminated: The percentage of children waiting to be adopted whose parents' parental rights had been terminated has shown a continuous decline, from nearly 63 percent in FY 2009 to 55 percent in FY 2016; however, the decrease in the percentages has been minimal since FY 2013 in particular (much less than one percentage point per year). Each FY since 2013 there has been an increase in the absolute numbers of children whose parent's rights were terminated, increasing from 58,700 in FY 2013 to 65,300 in FY 2016.

Children Adopted: The number of adoptions that are finalized each year has remained relatively flat (ranging between 50,700 to 53,600) over the last decade, with the exception of FY 2009, when the numbers rose to over 57,000. Since then, the numbers have leveled off again, similar to the two years prior to FY 2009, to nearly 51,000 in FY 2013 and FY 2014, and 53,600 in FY 2015 and FY 2016 represents a second year of increases in adoptions to 57,200, matching the number of adoptions in FY 2009. As a proportion of the exits, adoption has remained very stable, making up about 21 percent of the discharges each year since FY 2009.

Source: U.S. Department of Health and Human Services, Administration for Children and Families, Administration on Children, Youth and Families, Children's Bureau. (2017). *Trends in foster care and adoption.* Washington, DC: Author. Retrieved from www.acf.hhs.gov/sites/default/files/cb/trends_fostercare_adoption_07thru16.pdf (see pp. 2 and 3 for technical information and data definitions).

Recruitment, Training, and Support of Foster Parents

Resource Family Recruitment

Resource families – which include foster parents, foster-to-adopt families, and kinship caregivers – are critical partners for child welfare professionals because they provide care for children who cannot live with their parents, and they can play a supportive role in reunification. A broad range of resource families are needed to support the many needs of children and youth involved in out-of-home care (Gateway, 2017b).

As part of a broader effort to reform foster care (e.g., Annie E Casey Foundation, 2015) resource family recruitment is an evolving area with an increasing number of public and private agencies collaborating in terms of recruitment campaigns and refining their marketing methods, such as the use of psychographic marketing to locate promising foster parents. For example, the Florida Intelligent Recruitment Project (IRP) is a collaborative initiative between DCF and three Florida Community Based Care Lead Agencies. The project's major focus is the implementation of a values- and behavior-based multi-layered strategic marketing process to target and attract quality foster and adoptive parents for youth in the target population. Thus, the more innovative CW agencies are deploying multiple recruitment strategies such as (1) *Using data to update child and placement resources* (continuous updating of children in care using AFCARS data, ongoing analysis of the pool of children available for adoption and adoptive placement resources); (2) *Community collaboration* to identify available placement resources; and (3) *General, targeted, and child-specific marketing*, including relationship mining. But most foster parent recruitment approaches can be bolstered in at least four ways:

1. By using information gathered by marketing firms to identify the most appropriate market segments (groups of people who share certain specific characteristics) to talk with and recruit from (psychographic marketing – see www.predict-align-prevent.org/).

2. By using a common database for tracking foster parent capacity and availability and text messaging (see BIT North America) so that multiple agencies can better match a child with a foster parent. One such database is ECAP – Every Child A Priority – a database co-created by TFI Family Services and the University of Kansas School of Social Welfare (see https://fostercaretech.com/).

3. By paying attention to any unique networking or cultural issues, such as for American Indian and other groups of color (e.g., Killos et al., 2017).

4. By *retaining* the foster parents currently licensed by supporting them with intensive but then graduated reductions to monthly visitation upon the initial placement of a child (as is required in New Jersey), timely caseworker response, pertinent training and clinical coaching (e.g., KEEP - Keeping Foster and Kin Parents Supported and Trained, Functional Family Therapy), and the use of "navigators" to help foster parents access services for the children in their care (for additional information and state examples of resource family recruitment strategies, see Gateway, 2017b, 2017c).

Foster Parent Training and Ongoing Support

Another issue concerns the education and training of social workers and foster parents. It is now widely recognized in the CW field that foster parents and social workers, as well as other service providers, need specialized training for practice in case situations involving family foster care. While in many agencies initial training has been improved with the help of a curriculum from the Child Welfare League of America and the National Child Traumatic Stress Network, ongoing training tends to be fragmented and irregular. Extensive discussion of the purposes, content, and methods of necessary training is beyond the scope of this book. We would, however, like to stress several themes.

First, social workers (Gateway, 2017a), as well as foster parents, can best be helped to enhance their skills through a competency-based or performance-based approach to education and training (e.g., Child Welfare League of America PRIDE training: www.cwla. org/pride-training/). Such an approach stresses the development of practice-based competences in the design, delivery, and evaluation of training in a specialized area of practice. There is considerable attention to the selection of appropriate instructional methods, which typically include self-instructional materials, coaching, use of learning contracts, experiential exercises, and small-group interactions. Curriculum development is organized around what practitioners need to know and is based on a thorough analysis of the knowledge, skills, and attributes required of staff members. Moreover, training is developed concerning areas identified as having the highest priority for effective practice.

Second, training opportunities need to be offered within a supportive agency environment: an environment that encourages professional development; treats "trainees" as adult learners, and involves them in assessment of their training needs and selection of appropriate learning opportunities; and offers incentives and rewards such as career ladders, certification, and salary increments corresponding with increased knowledge and skills.

Third, foster care practice requires that social workers and foster parents have knowledge and competences in a range of areas, including the following:

- child development;
- philosophy and practice of permanency planning;
- impact of separation and placement upon children and their families;
- behavior management;
- appreciation of human diversity and sensitivity to issues of ethnicity, race, gender, sexual orientation, and sociocultural aspects;
- involvement of children and their biological parents in decision making and goal planning.

Fourth, as practice in family foster care has evolved during the past decade, training programs have had to address a range of newer practice strategies and principles, in such areas as ecologically oriented assessment; goal planning that emphasizes contracting with clients and service providers; use of behaviorally specific, time-limited case plans; and case management. In addition, training materials are increasingly available in relation to practice with children and parents having special needs in such areas as HIV/AIDS, substance abuse, and family violence (see, e.g., Gateway (2017a), NSCAW data as featured in U.S. DHHS (2005) and training materials for domestic violence from the National Conference of Juvenile and Family Court Judges (2006)).

Foster Care Outcomes

The federal CFSR case reviews, NSCAW study, and various studies of youth emancipating from care and foster care alumni have underscored the need to improve services. In Table 5.1 we report the CFSR data and in Table 5.2 we present a concise summary of some foster care outcome data, which underscore the effects of key risk factors like previous child maltreatment, chronic medical problems, and school changes, but also highlights how many youth in care plan to attend college and their outcomes as adults. Note that how youth in foster care develop and how they function as they leave foster care and live more independently varies greatly – from those who are very successful to those who are struggling in many areas – so distinct subgroups exist (Courtney, Hook, & Lee, 2012).

Table Overview and Cautions

This table presents outcome data on a range of areas related to foster care, including education experience and achievements of youth in foster care, with some comparisons with the general population. Note that we have used national estimates, where available, but there are many gaps in national data in this area, which we attempt to back-fill with multi-state or single-state studies. When comparing youth in foster care with other groups, it is important to note that most studies do not control for other factors like age, race, and gender. For example, The Northwest Foster Care Alumni Study, when comparing emotional and behavioral health conditions, used propensity score matching to align the foster care alumni sample and the "general population" sample by

Table 5.1 Foster Care Outcomes Measured in the Federal Child and Family Service Reviews (CFSRs)

Outcome Dimension	Results
IN-CARE DATA	
Children in foster care who have chronic medical problems.	50%[a]
Proportion of 17–18 year olds in foster care who experienced five or more school changes (K-12) while in foster care, as reported by foster care alumni.	34%[b]
CFSR Outcome 2: Reduce the incidence of child abuse and/or neglect in foster care Between 2010 and 2013, national performance fluctuated with regard to the maltreatment of children in foster care (measure 2.1). While 27 states declined in performance between 2010 and 2013, 16 improved. Although the national median exhibited a slight overall increase from .33 in 2010 to .34 in 2013, it declined between 2010 and 2012, and the percent change was not significant (3.0 percent increase).	During 2013, state performance regarding the maltreatment of children while in foster care (measure 2.1) ranged from 0.00 to 1.34 percent, with a median of 0.35 percent.
CFSR Outcome 3: Increase permanency for children in foster care States that were generally successful in achieving permanency for children at the time of exit from foster care (measure 3.1) were also successful in achieving permanency for children who are in foster care for long periods of time (measure C3.1). This is demonstrated by the fact that there is a moderate positive correlation (Pearson's r = .56) between these two measures in 2013. In many states, a considerable percentage of children who were emancipated from foster care in 2013 were in foster care for long periods of time before they were emancipated (measures 3.4 and C3.3). In about half of the states, 22.1 percent or more of the children emancipated from foster care were age 12 or younger when they entered foster care (measure 3.4), and 38.6 percent or more of the children emancipated from foster care, or who turned age 18 while in care, were in care for three years or longer (measure C3.3). However, it is encouraging to note that between 2010 and 2013, 31 states showed improved performance on measure 3.4, and 32 states showed improvement on measure C3.3.	In 2013, states were relatively successful in achieving a permanent home for all children exiting foster care (measure 3.1, median = 88.8 percent). However, states were less successful in achieving permanent homes for children exiting foster care who had a diagnosed disability (measure 3.2, median = 79.3 percent), and even less successful in finding permanent homes for children exiting foster care who entered care when they were older than age 12 (measure 3.3, median = 66.3 percent). For children who had been in foster care for long periods of time (measure C3.1), defined as 24 months or longer, only 32.9 percent (median) of these children had permanent homes by the end of 2013. Between 2010 and 2013, 32 states exhibited an improvement in performance, and the national median for this measure increased from 29.8 percent to 32.8 percent (a 10.1 percent change).

CFSR Outcome 4: Reduce time in foster care to reunification without increasing re-entry

Between 2010 and 2013, there was a significant decline in performance in the percentage of reunifications occurring in less than 12 months of the child's entry into foster care for children entering care for the first time (measure C1.3). For this measure, the national median dropped from 42.1 percent in 2010 to 37.2 percent in 2013 (an 11.6 percent decrease). Furthermore, 24 states declined in performance on this measure, while only 8 improved during this period.

Overall, states with a relatively high percentage of children entering foster care who were age 12 or older at the time of entry also had a relatively high percentage of children re-entering foster care (measure C1.4) (Pearson's r = .53).

Overall, states with relatively high foster care entry rates (measure C1.4) also had relatively high percentages of reunifications occurring in less than 12 months (measure C1.1) (Pearson's r = .41).

CFSR Outcome 5: Reduce time in foster care to adoption

Thirty-three states showed improvement in the percentage of children in foster care for 17 months or longer on the first day of the year who became legally free for adoption in the first 6 months of the year (measure C2.4). The median for this measure increased from 11.8 percent in 2010 to 14.3 percent in 2013, a 21.2 percent change.

Thirty-one states showed improved performance in the children in foster care for 17 months or longer on the first day of the year who were adopted by the end of the year (measure C2.3). Consistent with this finding, the national median for this measure increased from 24.9 percent in 2010 to 27.9 percent in 2013 (a 12.0 percent change).

CFSR Outcome 6: Increase placement stability

The proportions of children who moved placement settings more than once increased with more time spent in foster care. The median across states was 64.8 percent for children who have been in foster care for between 12 to 24 months, and 34.8 percent for children who have been in foster care for 24 months or longer.

The 2013 data suggest that, in many states, a majority of children discharged to reunification were reunified in a timely manner. Across states, the median percentage of reunifications occurring in less than 12 months was between 67.2 and 70.0 percent (measures 4.1 and C1.1). The median length of stay in foster care for reunified children was 7.9 months (measure C1.2).

Between 2010 and 2013, there were overall declines in performance on nearly all of the reunification measures. While two measures, C1.1 and C1.4, showed slight improvements in their national medians over time, more states declined than improved in performance on all five of the reunification measures.

In 2013, the percentage of adoptions occurring in less than 24 months from a child's entry into foster care was fairly low (measure C2.1, median = 35.5 percent). However, it is encouraging to note that, between 2010 and 2013, 31 states improved in their performance on this measure.

In this report, adequate placement stability is defined as limiting the number of placement settings for a child to no more than two for a single foster care episode. Among children with less than 12 months of time spent in foster care, the majority remained in stable placements during that time, having no more than two placement settings (median = 85.6 percent in 2013).

(Continued)

Table 5.1 (Continued)

Outcome Dimension	Results
IN-CARE DATA	
For children in care for between 12 and 24 months, the percentage of children experiencing two or fewer placement settings (measure 6.1b) increased from 61.4 percent in 2010 to 64.8 percent in 2013 (a 5.5 percent increase). For this measure, 19 states improved in performance while only 4 declined.	In about half of the states, 4.0 percent or less of children entering foster care under the age of 12 were placed in group homes or institutions in 2013. Data also indicate that there were only two states (Arkansas and California) where the percentage of young children placed in group homes or institutions was above 10 percent.
There was an even greater improvement in performance on measure 6.1c, the percentage of children in care for 24 months or longer who experienced two or fewer placement settings. For this measure, the median increased from 32.0 in 2010 to 34.7 in 2013, an 8.4 percent increase. Furthermore, 32 states demonstrated improvement on this measure, while only 9 declined in performance.	
CFSR Outcome 7: Reduce placements of young children in group homes or institutions	
Previous reports have shown significant improvements over time on measure 7.1, and this trend continued between 2010 and 2013 when the median decreased from 4.5 to 4.0 percent (an 11.1 percent decrease). During the 4-year span, 26 states showed improved performance on this measure, and 12 declined in performance.	

[a]Leslie, L.K., Gordon, J.N., Meneken, L., Premji, K., Michelmore, K.L., & Ganger, W. (2005). The physical, developmental, and mental health needs of young children in child welfare by initial placement type. *Journal of Developmental & Behavioral Pediatrics, 26*(3), 177–179. For a careful comparison between youth in foster care and youth in the general population, see Turney, K. & Wildeman, C. (2016). Mental and physical health of children in foster care. *Pediatrics*, 1–11, doi:10.1542/peds.2016-1118.

[b]Courtney, M.E., Terao, S., & Bost, N. (2004). *Midwest evaluation of the adult functioning of former foster youth: Conditions of youth preparing to leave state care.* Chicago, IL: Chapin Hall Center for children at the University of Chicago, p. 42. In a more recent study in Colorado, students in foster care typically change schools three or more times after initially entering ninth grade. They found that only 10 percent of students did not change high school at all, while 59 percent changed high schools three or more times. See Clemens, E.V. & Sheesley, A.P. (2016). *Educational stability of Colorado's students in foster care: 2007–2008 to 2013–2014.* Retrieved from www.unco.edu/cebs/foster-care research/pdf/reports/Every_Transition_Counts_V.1_Interactive.pdf.

Source: CFSR outcome data from U.S. Department of Health and Human Services, Administration for Children and Families, Children's Bureau. (2016). *Child welfare outcomes 2010–2013: Report to Congress.* Retrieved from www.acf.hhs.gov/cb/resource/cwo-10-13, pp. iii–iv.

Table 5.2 Selected Youth and Foster Care Alumni Outcomes

Outcome Dimension	Results
Physical health conditions	Youth in foster care appear to have more physical health conditions that require treatment than youth in the general population.[a]
Percent of 17- to 18-year-olds who have experienced 5 or more school changes	34.2%[b]
Likelihood of 17- to 18-year-old youth in foster care having an out-of-school suspension	About twice that of other students (Courtney, Terao, & Bost, 2004, p. 42) (In one study the rate was 24% versus a national general population rate of 7%) (Scherr, 2006, pp. 1547–1563)
Alumni of foster care who suffer from post-traumatic stress disorder	25%[c] (This lifetime prevalence rate is similar to that of many U.S. war veterans)
Percent of youth in foster care who complete high school by age 18 (via a diploma or GED)	74%[c] (Compared with 84% in the general population ages 25 to 34[d]) Colorado: 41.8%[k] Midwest Study (age 19): 63%)
Percent of youth in foster care who complete high school by age 21 (via a diploma or GED)	65% by age 21[m] (National data) (Compared with 86% among all youth ages 18–24[n])
Youth emancipating from foster care who plan to attend college	70%–84%[e]
Alumni who enrolled in college	31.8%–45.3%[i] (As compared with a national college enrollment rate of 69.2% in 2015, which is slightly below the national record high of 70.2% in 2009)
Alumni who completed a Bachelor's degree	3%–11%[f] (Compared with 28% for 25- to 34-year-olds in the general population[d])

(Continued)

Table 5.2 (Continued)

Outcome Dimension	Results
Alumni who were employed at age 21	52%[g]
	(Compared with 64.6% employment rate for ages 20–24 in 2016[h])
Alumni who became homeless for one day or more after emancipating from foster care	22%[c]
	(Compared with range of 2.6% to 6.8% for ages 18 to 24 who are homeless in the U.S. in any given year[i])

Notes:

[a]See Rubin, D., Halfon, N., Raghavan, R. & Rosenbaum, S. (2005). *Protecting children in foster care: Why proposed Medicaid cuts harm our nation's most vulnerable children.* Seattle, WA: Casey Family Programs. See also

Halfon, N., Mendonca, A., & Berkowitz, G. (1995). Health status of children in foster care. The experience of the Center for the Vulnerable Child. *Archives of Pediatrics & Adolescent Medicine, 149*(4), 386–392.

Simms, M.D. (1989). The foster care clinic: A community program to identify treatment needs of children in foster care. *Journal of Developmental & Behavioral Pediatrics, 10*(3), 121–128.

Takayama, J.I., Wolfe, E., & Coulter, K.P. (1998). Relationship between reason for placement and medical findings among children in foster care. *Pediatrics, 101*(2), 201–207.

U.S. General Accounting Office. (1995). *Foster care: Health needs of many young children are unknown and unmet* (GAO/HEHS-95–114). Washington, DC: Author.

[b]Courtney, M.E., Terao, S., & Bost, N. (2004). *Midwest evaluation of the adult functioning of former foster youth: Conditions of youth preparing to leave state care.* Chicago, IL: Chapin Hall Center for Children at the University of Chicago, p. 42. Pecora, P.J., Kessler, R.C., Williams, J., O'Brien, K., Downs, A.C., English, D., Hiripi, E., White, C.R., Wiggins, T., & Holmes, K. (2005). *Improving family foster care: Findings from the Northwest Foster Care Alumni Study.* Seattle, WA: Casey Family Programs. In terms of school changes, one-third of the alumni in another recent study had attended more than five elementary schools, averaging a change in schools nearly every year. See Pecora, P.J., Williams, J., Kessler, R.C., Downs, A.C., O'Brien, K., Hiripi, E., & Morello, S. (2003). *Assessing the effects of foster care: Early results from the Casey National Alumni Study.* Seattle, WA: Casey Family Programs, p. 28. Both studies may be downloaded from www.casey.org.

[c]This statistic was derived by averaging the results of a representative set of foster care alumni studies that interviewed older alumni, who had more time to complete high school via a diploma or a GED, attend a post-secondary educational program, and/or complete a Bachelor's degree than younger alumni. The studies were then weighted by study sample size so the larger studies carried more weight in the average. For more information contact Peter J. Pecora at ppecora@casey.org. Examples of studies included in the analysis for the high school completion rate include the following:

Blome, W.W. (1997). What happens to foster kids: Educational experiences of a random sample of foster care youth and a matched group of non-foster care youth. *Child and Adolescent Social Work Journal, 14*(1), 41–53.

Buehler, C., Orme, J.G., Post, J., & Patterson, D.A. (2000). The long-term correlates of family foster care. *Children and Youth Services Review, 22*(8), 595–625.

Casey Family Services. (1999). *The road to independence: Transitioning youth in foster care to independence.* Shelton, CT: Author (www.caseyfamilyservices. org).

Cook, R., Fleishman, E., & Grimes, V. (1989). *A national evaluation of Title IV-E Foster Care Independent Living Programs for Youth* (Phase 2 final report, Volume 1). Rockville, MD: Westat, Inc.

Courtney, M., Piliavin, I., Grogan-Kaylor, A., & Nesmith, A. (2001). Foster youth transitions to adulthood: A longitudinal view of youth leaving care, *Child Welfare, 80,* 685–717.

Festinger, T. (1983). *No one ever asked us [.] A postscript to foster care.* New York: Columbia University Press.

Pecora, P.J., Williams, J., Kessler, R.C., Downs, A.C., O'Brien, K., Hiripi, E., & Morello, S. (2003). *Assessing the effects of foster care: Early results from the Casey National Alumni Study.* Seattle, WA: Casey Family Programs. (www.casey.org).

Pecora, P.J., Kessler, R.C., Williams, J., O'Brien, K., Downs, A.C., English, D., White, C.R., Hiripi, E., Wiggins, T., & Holmes, K. (2005). *Improving family foster care: Findings from the Northwest Foster Care Alumni Study.* Seattle, WA: Casey Family Programs. (www.casey.org).

Reilly, T. (2003). Transition from care: Status and outcomes of youth who age out of foster care. *Child Welfare, 82*(6), 727–746.

[d]U.S. Census Bureau. (2000). Educational Attainment by Sex: 2000 (Table QT-P20). Retrieved from http://factfinder.census.gov/servlet/SAFFPeople?_submenuId=people_5&_sse=on. Click on the "Educational Attainment" table. Note that a more conservative estimate of national high school completion rate of 70 percent has been published by Greene and Forster (2003). They believe that completion statistics are sometimes overstated because they underestimate dropouts, and because they exclude military personnel, prisoners, and institutionalized populations. See Greene, J.P. & Forster, G. (2003). *Public high school graduation and college readiness rates in the United States.* New York: Center for Civic Innovation, Manhattan Institute.

[e]McMillen, C., Auslander, W., Elze, D., White, T., & Thompson, R. (2003). Educational experiences and aspirations of older youth in foster care. *Child Welfare, 82*(4), 475–495. And it was 84 percent in this study: Courtney, Terao, & Bost (2004, p. 39).

[f]According to a weighted average of foster care alumni studies (see reference note c), the college completion rate was 3 percent. College completion rates, however, are higher when follow-up studies include older adults. For example, the college completion rate was three times greater (at 10.8%) in a recent study of foster care alumni ages 20 to 51 (mean age 30.5 years at the time of the interview) who were served by a voluntary child welfare agency. See Pecora, P.J., Williams, J., Kessler, R.C., Downs, A.C., O'Brien, K., Hiripi, E., & Morello, S. (2003). *Assessing the effects of foster care: Early results from the Casey National Alumni Study.* Seattle, WA: Casey Family Programs, pp. 12 and 28.

[g]Courtney, M.E., Dworsky, A., Cusick, G.R., Keller, T., Havlicek, J., Perez, A. et al. (2007). *Midwest evaluation of adult functioning of former foster youth: Outcomes at age 21.* Chicago, IL: University of Chicago, Chapin Hall Center for Children.

(Continued)

Table 5.2 (Continued)

Outcome Dimension	Results

[h] Bureau of Labor Statistics. (2017). Labor Force Statistics from the Current Population Survey, Table 3. Employment status of the civilian noninstitutional population by age, sex, and race. Retrieved from www.bls.gov/cps/cpsaat03.htm.

[i] Ammerman, S.D., Ensign, J., Kirzner, R., Meininger, E.T., Tornabene, M., Warf, C.W., Zerger, S., & Post, P. (2004). *Homeless young adults ages 18–24: Examining service delivery adaptations*. Nashville, TN: National Health Care for the Homeless Council, Inc. U.S. Census Bureau. (2004). *Estimates of the resident population by selected age groups for the United States and States and for Puerto Rico: July 1, 2004 (SC-EST2004–01RES)*. Retrieved from www.census.gov/popest/states/asrh/SC-est2004-01.html (accessed July 7, 2010).

[j] The 31.8 percent rate was found by Courtney, M.E., Dworsky, A., Lee, J., & Raap, M. (2010). *Midwest evaluation of the adult functioning of former foster youth: Outcomes at age 23 and 24*. Chicago, IL: Chapin Hall at the University of Chicago, p. 24. The proportion of alumni aged 25 and older in the Northwest Foster Care Alumni Study that has completed any postsecondary education (45.3%) is substantially lower than that (57%) of the general population in the same age group who completed some college coursework (U.S. Census Bureau, 2000). (Note that the alumni group statistic includes vocational training, while the general population statistic does not. Therefore, the difference between the two groups is underestimated.) See Pecora et al. (2010, p. 125); and U.S. Census Bureau. (2000). Profile of selected social characteristics – 2000 (Table DP-2.). Washington, DC: Author. Retrieved from http://factfinder.census.gov/bf/_lang+en_vt_name+DEC_2000_SF3_U_DP2_geo_ id=01000US.html (accessed March 10, 2005). For the general population statistic see Bureau of Labor Statistics data at www.bls.gov/news.release/hsgec.nr0.htm for 2015 data and National Center for Education Statistics data for 2009 at www.bls.gov/news.release/hsgec.nr0.htm.

[k] Parra, J., & Martinez, J. (2015). *2013–2014 state policy report: Dropout prevention and student engagement*. Denver, CO: Colorado Department of Education, p. 20. Retrieved from www.cde.state.co.us./dropoutprevention/2014statepolicyreport31215.

[l] Courtney, M.E., Dworsky, A., Ruth, G., Keller, T., Havlicek, J., & Bost, N. (2005). *Midwest evaluation of adult functioning of former foster youth: Outcomes at age 19*. Chicago, IL: University of Chicago, Chapin Hall Center for Children, p. 21.

[m] National Youth in Transition Database. Unpublished analyses (April 2016). Administration on Children, Youth and Families, HHS. As cited in U.S. Department of Education and U.S. Department of Health and Human Services. (2016, p. 3). *Non-regulatory guidance: Ensuring educational stability for children in foster care*. Retrieved from www2.ed.gov/policy/elsec/leg/essa/edhhsfostercarenonregulatorguide.pdf.

[n] National Center for Education Statistics. (2014). Digest of education statistics, 2014, table 104.40. Retrieved from https://nces.ed.gov/programs/digest/d15/tables/dt15_104.40.asp?current=yes.

age, race and gender. (See Pecora et al., 2010). The Midwest study used a sample from the Adolescent Health national study that was of the same age range as the comparison group (see Courtney, Terao, & Bost, 2004). But few studies control for key variables such as family income, housing instability or insecurity, food insecurity, English language proficiency, child maltreatment that did not result in out-of-home placement, and other Adverse Childhood Experiences like parent divorce, substance abuse, emotional/behavioral health issues, and incarceration. These factors can outweigh the negative or positive effects of placement and enrollment in a poor or high-quality school.

Education Study Method Cautions

When comparing youth in foster care with other groups, it is important to note that most studies do not control for other factors like age, race, and gender. The Northwest Foster Care Alumni Study, when comparing emotional and behavioral health conditions, adjusted the foster care alumni sample and the "general population" sample by age, race, and gender (Pecora et al., 2010). The Midwest study used a sample from the Adolescent Health study that was of the same age range (Courtney, Terao, & Bost, 2004). Frerer and colleagues' (2013) study matched the youth by grade level, school year, gender, ethnicity, English Language Learner (ELL) status, National School Lunch Program (NSLP), primary disability, district or school, state rank, and baseline California Standardized Test level. In the math sample, youth in foster care and youth not in foster care were additionally matched by math course level for older youth.

Even fewer studies control for key variables such as family income, housing instability or insecurity, food insecurity, English language proficiency, child maltreatment that did not result in out-of-home placement, and other adverse childhood experiences like parent divorce, substance abuse, emotional/behavioral health issues, and incarceration. These factors can outweigh the negative or positive effects of placement and enrollment in a poor or high-quality school. For example, in one recent study in California, education at-risk factors for youth in foster care that were present prior to placement were more reliable predictors of academic performance over time than the majority of child welfare case characteristics. Similar to other at-risk students, youth in foster care who were poor, non-White, and had disabilities (i.e., special education status) struggled on standardized tests more than others. But the association among school quality, placement changes, school transfers, and academic performance is complex.

> While remaining in the same school has potential benefits for some students, it may not support the educational best interest for many foster youth. Remaining in

the same school after entry into foster care may mitigate the number of changes a youth experiences. However, having foster students remain in low-performing schools may impede long-term academic achievement.

(Frerer et al., 2013, p. 3)

Another study that controlled for many of these non-placement factors and that tracked children in out-of-home care and other children in grades 3 to 8 found that out-of-home placement itself does not appear to be causally related to school achievement. Children involved with Child Protective Services (CPS), however, were shown to have consistently low average math and reading standardized test scores. For example, the difference in Wisconsin Knowledge and Concepts Examinations (WKCEs) scores between children in foster care and those receiving Supplemental Nutrition Assistance Program (SNAP) assistance, who are more similar to children in foster care than are children in the general population, is considerably smaller than that between children experiencing placement and all other children. In addition, there are relatively few differences in achievement test scores between children in foster care and other children involved with CPS but not placed out of the home. No differences in achievement by level of CPS involvement were found.

Because all children involved with CPS performed similarly in this study, it suggests that out-of-home care by itself may not be the major factor affecting academic achievement among children involved with CPS. However, whereas they found no evidence of a causal relationship between out-of-home care and achievement, the researchers did find consistent evidence of low average math and reading achievement among children involved with CPS (Berger et al., 2015). Thus, caregivers and service providers should be concerned about the cognitive development of all children experiencing maltreatment, with the caution that we do have other studies which show that changes in living situation/placement and school changes do negatively affect children in out-of-home care as well as other children.

A higher proportion of these youth than youth in the general population are involved in the criminal justice system (e.g., Courtney et al., 2001), and they are at higher risk of teen pregnancy and parenting (National Conference on State Legislatures, 2017). Because most youth in foster care have changed schools multiple times, many have lower reading and math skills, as well as lower high school graduation rates (e.g., National Working Group on Foster Care and Education, 2018). (Note that many of these comparisons must be viewed with caution, as maltreated children and children from families in poverty would be more appropriate comparison groups.) In addition, youth transitioning from foster care are more likely to experience homelessness (Pecora et al., 2003, 2010; Courtney et al., 2001, 2005). In fact, two studies found that one in eight foster care alumni who were never before homeless in their lives, did not have a place to call home for at least a week sometime after age 18 (Pecora et al., 2003, 2010). Other studies show that foster care alumni tend to have higher rates of alcohol and other drug abuse (Courtney et al., 2005; Pecora et al., 2003, 2010) and higher rates of unemployment and likelihood of dependence on public assistance (e.g., Courtney et al., 2001, 2005; Pecora et al., 2010).

Readers should recall that the problems of children who enter foster care, and the family resources they have to rely on when they are in trouble, are not the same as those of youth in the general population – so these findings do not indicate that foster care makes youth worse off than they would have been. Indeed, many of them have indicated that they are grateful to have escaped a life of degradation and desperation (Barth, 1990; Courtney, et al., 1998; Pecora et al., 2010). In fact, a study of foster care alumni aged 20 to 33 (Pecora et al., 2010) found the following examples of successful functioning:

1. Mental Health

   - 45.6 percent have *no* 12-month mental health diagnosis

   - 50.6 percent have SF-12 mental health score of 50 or above.

2. Education

   - 84.8 percent had completed high school via a diploma or GED (Graduate Equivalency Diploma)

   - 20.6 percent had received any degree or certificate past high school.

3. Employment/Finances

   - 67 percent have health insurance

   - 21.3 percent have household income at least three times the poverty level

   - 83.2 percent do not currently receive cash public assistance

   - 74 percent are now working or in school.

However, an examination of youth employment in three states suggests a more complex picture, with many youth aging out of foster care being underemployed, large variations in patterns of employment by state, and a greater likelihood of employment when youth begin work before the age of 18. In all three states, youth were more likely to earn income for the first time during the four quarters prior to and the quarter of their eighteenth birthday than in the two years following (Goerge et al., 2002). Follow-up alumni studies using state public assistance databases are much less expensive and have more complete data by avoiding non-participation rates (e.g., The Urban Institute, 2008).

In a recent study (Goemans et al., 2016), a series of meta-analyses were performed to compare the cognitive, adaptive, and behavioral functioning of 2,305 children placed in foster care with 4,335 children at risk who remained with their biological parents and children from the general population (4,971). Results showed that children in foster care had generally lower levels of functioning than children from the general population. No clear differences were found between children in foster care and children at risk who remained at home, but both groups experienced developmental problems.

To provide more information about education outcomes, Table 5.3 compares the results of three foster care alumni studies involving young adults in their mid-twenties with general population youth of the same age range represented in the United States National Adolescent Health study. For example, the Northwest Alumni Study involved 479 foster care

Table 5.3 Education and Training Outcomes of Three Foster Care Alumni Studies in Comparison with the National Adolescent Health Study

Education and Training	Michigan	Midwest Study	Northwest Study	Add Health
Mean age at time of the interview	24.1	23.9	24.2	**23.1**
Currently enrolled in school	16.9	16.6	15.7	**23.1**
Has high school diploma	35.4		56.3	
Has high school diploma or GED	69.2	75.6	84.8	**92.7**
Any education beyond high school	26.2	31.8	42.7	**61.2**
Any diploma or certificate beyond high school	13.8	6.2	20.6	**33.6**
Completed college (Bachelor's degree)	7.7	3.0	1.8	**24.2**
Sample size	*65*	*602*	*479*	***1,486***

Source: Abstracted from White, C.R., O'Brien, K., Pecora, P.J., Kessler, R.C., Sampson, N. Hwang, I., & Buher, A. (2011). *The Michigan Foster Care Alumni Study: Outcomes at age 23 and 24*. Seattle, WA: Casey Family Programs. For more information about the Casey Northwest Alumni study, see www.casey.org. For more information about the Chapin Hall Midwest Study, see www.chapinhall.org/research/areas/Child-Welfare-and-Foster-Care-Systems. The National Longitudinal Study of Adolescent Health (Add Health) is a longitudinal study of a nationally representative sample of adolescents in grades 7–12 in the United States during the 1994/1995 school year. See www.cpc.unc.edu/projects/addhealth. Note that if you include youth with a broader age range (18–51 years old) served in foster care by Casey Family Programs, a study of those foster care alumni served for at least one year in care between 1966 and 1998 found a college completion rate of 10.8 percent (Pecora et al., 2010, p. 126).

alumni from the states of Oregon and Washington, along with alumni from the Casey Family Programs foster care offices in both of these states. This study found that although two in five alumni received some education beyond high school, less than half of these (20.6%) completed a degree or certificate. One in six completed a vocational/technical degree, and only one in 20 completed a Bachelor's or higher degree. For alumni aged 25 and older, the Bachelor's completion rate (2.7%) was much lower than for the general population in a similar age range of 25 to 34 years (24.4%) (U.S. Census Bureau, 2000, p. 1). Yet, at the time of interview, over one in ten alumni (11.9%) were enrolled in college. Note that if you include youth with a broader age served in foster care for at least one year in care, a college completion rate of 10.8 percent was found for alumni ages 20 to 51 (mean age 30.5 years at the time of the interview) (Pecora et al., 2003, p. 12; Pecora et al., 2010, p. 126). Among the lessons learned are that many youth in care do complete high school in substantial numbers, and college completion statistics are age-dependent – so studies of alumni older than 22 are necessary to gather the most accurate college completion rates. But a wide range of recent data from various states indicate that most schools, CW agencies, and their partners need to do more to boost high school completion rates of youth in care, especially those where a diploma is granted (National Working Group on Foster Care and Education, 2018).

Finally, Salazar (2012) identified the predictors of post-secondary retention and success using survey data from a cross-sectional sample of 329 foster care alumni who received a national scholarship to various colleges provided by the Orphan Foundation of America Foster Care to Success or Casey Family Scholarship Program post-secondary scholarships. All 14 factors that had a statistically significant bivariate relationship with school disengagement were included in the second phase of the analysis. Of the 14 included factors, 3 had a statistically significant association and 1 had a trend-level association with disengagement:

- Ever had a mental health diagnosis
- Satisfaction with college
- Housing support was not needed (curiously, students reporting no need for help with securing housing were significantly more likely than those who received sufficient help to disengage from college)
- Average number of hours worked per week (trend level association).

Summary of Foster Care Outcomes

There are enough methodological concerns with past research (such as a lack of adequate comparison groups and low study response rates) that the results noted above need to be viewed with caution. Furthermore, several studies have found more mixed results, with some youth doing very well, while others struggle to complete classes and learn the skills necessary to succeed as young adults living more independently. For example, some studies show that youth placed in foster care tend to have disproportionately high rates of physical, developmental, and mental health problems, but at least two large alumni studies have found that their average physical health and some areas of mental health functioning are on par with the general population (with alumni having more chronic physical health disorders) (Courtney et al., 2005; Pecora et al., 2005, 2010).

Not only do the study methods vary in type and rigor, but youth outcomes are also affected by variables outside the control of those providing services, including characteristics of the child, the birth family, other relatives, and foster parents; ecological factors before services were begun (such as schooling, neighborhood environment); and the child's degree of resiliency (e.g., Jones-Harden, 2004; Kerman, Wildfire, & Barth, 2002; Development Services Group, Inc., 2013). In addition, because of the lack of "strengths-oriented" research and the media preoccupation with negative effects, the many success stories of older youth in foster care are often not publicized (Bernstein, 2000; Fisher, 2002; Moore, 2010). Stereotypes of poor foster care conditions abound, even though conditions are mostly not deplorable and youth who are interviewed about their circumstances often report liking the foster family with which they live and feeling close to their foster parents – at the same time, they very often report wanting to go home (Chapman, Wall, & Barth, 2004).

Further research on youth outcomes is needed to identify the nature and extent of supports required, the types of skill-building different groups of youth need, and the most promising strategies for delivering those services. Of equal importance is the need to link good outcomes to the cost of achieving them. Until the cost data are more available, including transparent reporting of appropriately co-mingled funding streams, child welfare organizations are not adequately accountable for the "real" costs of obtaining good results and are therefore less likely to make a winning case for the additional resources from either public or private funders.

Key Foster Care Program Components

Reunification

As discussed in more detail in Chapter 6, reunification that does not result in entry back into foster care is not the sole goal of the foster care program. Foster care and reunification are tools to be used to protect the safety and well-being of children. There is evidence that stays in foster care may have beneficial effects and that reunification can result in risks far greater than re-entry to foster care. In two studies in California using different samples and methods, investigators found that children of color who were reunified from foster care had higher mortality rates (Barth & Blackwell, 1998) and a higher likelihood of transitioning to juvenile justice programs (Jonson-Reid & Barth, 2000) than children who remained in foster care. Taussig, Clyman, & Landsverk (2001) followed 149 youths in San Diego over a six-year period. They found that children who are reunified with families following a brief stay in foster care were more likely to abuse drugs, get arrested, drop out of school, and have lower grades than those who stayed in foster care. Although these studies do not present a reason to change dramatically the course of what we do, they are a cautionary note that reunification decisions need to be made carefully, and in some situations follow-up services are essential.

In order to sharply accelerate reunifications, we would first need to be sure that (1) funding mechanisms are there to support post-reunification services; (2) that service models are in place to adequately assist families; and (3) that monitoring is sufficient to look after the safety needs of children following foster care. This has been one of the strongest reasons for passing Family First – so that the Title IV-E funding mechanism, which heretofore only provided federal support under Title IV-E when a child was placed in foster care, and can now help pay for services to prevent placement and after the child returns home.

Transition and Independent Living Services

Preparation for Adult Living is a National Challenge for Youth in Foster Care and Others

Trend data show that the overall rate of children in child welfare-supervised out-of-home care has been slowly decreasing until a few years ago. Of the 273,539 children who *entered* foster care in 2016, 28 percent were aged 11 to 18, while the 35 percent of the 250,248 *exiting* care that year were youth aged 11 to 18 (U.S. DHHS, 2017). Thus over one in three youth in exiting foster care are adolescents.

Adolescents represent three different groups in out-of-home care: (1) those placed at an early age and who have remained in the same foster home; (2) those placed at an early age and who have been moving from one placement to another; and (3) those placed for the first time as teenagers, usually because of their behavioral or relationship problems. Each of these groups has different careers in placement and after placement. As such, they require different approaches, resources, and plans in terms of permanency planning and life skills development. And note that many adolescents are not in family foster care – they are in group care – which has its own set of challenges in terms of helping youth find permanency and learn life skills (Whittaker, del Valle, & Holmes, 2015).

Over 20,000 youth exited/"emancipated" from foster care in 2016 without finding a more permanent living situation such as reunification, guardianship, or adoption – with less than 1 percent (n = 881) leaving care as runaways (U.S. DHHS, 2017). Youth who emancipate from out-of-home care have typically had relatively short stays there, with very few children actually growing up in foster care (see AFCARS data). A large proportion entered care as adolescents but, nonetheless, were unable to achieve an official CW-approved reunification with their biological family.

Under pressure from private and public agencies, juvenile court judges, class action lawsuits, birthparents, and other stakeholder groups, foster care systems are beginning to be held accountable for the effects of their services (Annie E. Casey Foundation, 2015; United States General Accounting Office, 2014, 2015). As a result, although data are sparse, foster care service delivery systems have begun tracking a core set of outcomes encompassing the developmental needs of older youth outlined above (see Tables 1.1 and 1.2). Very few programs, however, track other crucial elements such as employment experience while in foster care, decision-making skills, cultural identity, and social networking. The category of services designed to prepare youth to live as productive, stable adults following their stay in foster care is called independent living services. Even with the development of this service category, there are still serious concerns about the level of readiness and preparation for adults living among this population.

Foster parents and social workers have consistently reported that most adolescents approaching emancipation are unprepared for independent living (U.S. DHHS, 2008). For example, follow-up studies of young persons who grew up in out-of-home placement have also pointed to their lack of preparation for life after foster care. Foster care alumni have consistently highlighted their needs in the following areas: interpersonal and social skills, money management, planning a budget, job training, finding a job, finding housing, maintaining a household, learning to shop, and maintaining family ties (Courtney et al., 2012; Nollan & Downs, 2001; Pecora et al., 2010). Also, in a longitudinal study, Courtney et al. (2007) found that children leaving care at age 18 face a difficult future, as they suffer from emotional problems, are without financial help from relatives, and become vulnerable to homelessness and other problems (see Tables 5.1 and 5. 2).

Thus, much can be done to better serve older children while they are in care and to provide them with better opportunities as they transition out of the system. Programs that draw upon community resources, promote a system of care, link children to mentors, and teach them life skills hold promise for improving the lives of these children. As a result, more than 15 states have changed their laws to cover youth until age 21, and federal legislation was passed that enables states to elect to provide Medicaid coverage to all former foster youth until age 21 and to extend the federal entitlement to age 21 (the Fostering Connections to Success and Increasing Adoptions Act (P.L. 110–351) of 2008). Until all states adopt this legislation, many children in the U.S. who leave foster care will do so at age and will have less of a chance to gain the benefits that in terms of social support, adult guidance, housing, healthcare, and income assistance support being documented for youth who stay in care past age 18 in California (Courtney et al., 2016, 2017) and Illinois (Dworskey & Courtney, 2010). The next sections of this chapter review the purpose of these kinds of policies, and provide examples of promising programs. A more extensive discussion of this area may be found in one of the textbook resource papers (Crume & Pecora, 2018) and new reports by the Los Angeles Division of Child and Family Services (Rivas et al., 2017) and MDRC/Youth Villages (Skemer & Valentine, 2016).

Developmental Needs of Older Youths in Foster Care

Youth development is a lifelong process and part of child welfare's mission to improve child well-being (U.S. DHHS, 2012). According to the U.S. Department of Health and Human Services (DHHS), positive youth development means that adolescents receive the services and opportunities necessary to develop a sense of competence, usefulness, belonging, and empowerment. For older youths in care (and especially for children who have survived abuse and neglect), needed supports include stable living situations; healthy friendships with peers their own age; stable connections to school; educational skills remediation; dental, medical, and vision care; mental health services; consistent, positive adults in their lives; and networks of social support. Life-skills preparation is also very important, covering such areas as daily living tasks, self-care, social development, career development, study skills, money management, self-determination, self-advocacy, and housing and community resources (U.S. DHHS, 2007).

Stimulated in part by federal enactment of the Independent Living Initiative of 1986 (P.L. 99–272) and the subsequent infusion of federal funds, agencies have been developing services focusing on the preparation of young people in care for "emancipation" or "independent living" (Kerman, Maluccio, & Freundlich, 2008). The weak empirical foundation for independent living programs and the concept of independent living, however, has been criticized as having various negative connotations or consequences, such as creating unrealistic and unfair expectations of adolescents, foster parents, and practitioners; regarding the need of adolescents for connectedness with other human beings as a sign of weakness; and placing the burden for preparation for adulthood largely on adolescents themselves (Courtney & Bost, 2002; Montgomery, Donkoh, & Underhill, 2006).

Helping adolescents in family foster care prepare for interdependent living and competent adulthood requires a range of services, strategies, and skills, as highlighted by Moore (2010, pp. 179–180):

> When we're young, it sometimes seems as if the world doesn't exist outside our city, our block, our house, our room. We make decisions based on what we see in that limited world and follow the only models available. The most important thing that happened to me was not being physically transported – the moves from Baltimore to the Bronx to Valley Forge didn't change my way of thinking. What changed was that I found myself surrounded by people – starting with my mom, grandparents, uncles, and aunts, and leading to a string of wonderful role models and mentors – who kept pushing me to see more than what was directly in front of me, to see the boundless possibilities of the wider world and the unexplored possibilities within myself. People who taught me that no accident of birth – not being black or relatively poor, being from Baltimore or the Bronx or fatherless – would ever define or limit me. In other words, they help me to discover what it means to be free. [.] it's up to us, all of us, to make a way for them.

The central thrust of practice should be to help adolescents develop qualities such as the following, through the combined efforts of foster parents, biological parents, social workers, and other service providers:

- competence and mastery of a range of tangible and intangible skills
- satisfying and mutually gratifying relationships with friends and kin
- ability to nurture their own children
- responsibility for their sexuality
- contribution to, and participation in, the community
- making essential connections with others
- positive sense of self.

(Cook, 1994; Youth Villages LifeSet, 2017: www.youthvillages.org/
what-we-do/yvlifeset#sthash.Z6gkW2zd.dpbs)

Yet, personal qualities alone are not sufficient: supportive services are also needed. New initiatives at the state and local levels are generating tutoring, scholarships, transitional supervised living, housing preference in county and local governments, and advocacy organizations for former foster youths, to name a few. In fact, siblings and relatives become a very crucial resource for older youth in foster care, especially if kinship care (or guardianship with relatives) is heavily used as a mode of caregiving.

Key Federal Policies and Promising Programs
Related to Transition Services

A variety of policies and programs have been developed that address the needs of older youth in placement, either directly or indirectly. For example, the Adoption and Safe Families Act attempts to improve the safety of children, to promote adoption and other permanent homes for children who need them, and to support families. The Independent Living Initiative and, subsequently, the Foster Care Independence Act of 1999 provide funding for services to prepare adolescents in foster care for independent living (see Box 5.3 and the text resource paper – Crume & Pecora, 2018 at www.routledge.com/).

Box 5.3   The Foster Care Independence Act 1999

On December 14, 1999, Congress enacted the Foster Care Independence Act to expand services for youth transitioning from foster care. Although an earlier Independent Living Initiative had been authorized in 1985, many service providers, youth advocates, and researchers expressed the opinion that a broader effort was necessary if these youth were to make a successful transition from foster care to independent living. To meet this need, the Act created the Chafee Foster Care Independence Program (named in honor of Senator John H. Chafee as a testimonial to his long-standing leadership for children in foster care) and made several important changes in the provision of transitional services for youth in foster care, including the following:

- Extended eligibility for transition assistance to former foster care children up to age 21, three years longer than previously.

- Doubled the funding for independent living services to $140 million, and established a $500,000 minimum allotment for states.

- Permitted states to use federal funds to support a variety of financial, housing, counseling, employment, education, and other appropriate supports and independent living services for all children who are likely to remain in foster care until 18 years of age and to help these children make the transition to self-sufficiency.

- Clarified that independent living activities should not be seen as an alternative to adoption for children and may occur concurrently with efforts to find adoptive families for these children.

- Allowed states to use up to 30 percent of the funds for room and board for youths ages 18 to 21 transitioning from foster care.

- Gave states the option to extend Medicaid to older youths transitioning from foster care.

- Added adoptive parents to the groups to receive training with federal foster care funds to help them understand and address the issues confronting adolescents preparing for independent living.

- Mandated that states make benefits and services available to Native American children in each state on the same basis as other children.

- Required child welfare agencies to document the effectiveness of their efforts to help their former charges become self-sufficient.

- Added achievement of a high school diploma and incarceration to the list of outcomes to be developed by the Secretary of the U.S. Department of Health and Human Services to assess the performance of states in operating independent living programs.

- Required the secretary to develop a plan for imposing penalties upon states that do not report data as required.

Although states have a great deal of flexibility in deciding how to use their CFCIP funds, the legislation suggests services that include assistance in obtaining a high school diploma; career exploration; vocational training; job placement and retention; training in daily living skills; training in budgeting and financial management skills; substance abuse prevention; and preventive health activities such as smoking avoidance, nutrition education, and pregnancy prevention. The Chafee legislation also specifies that funding may be used to provide personal and emotional support to children aging out of foster care, through mentors and the promotion of interactions with dedicated adults. Despite the importance of independent living services to help youth transitioning from foster care to become self-sufficient, many states have either not drawn down the funds or are not using the funds as effectively as they could.

Advocates believe states will need to use these funds more "boldly, creatively, and effectively" to substantially improve outcomes for youth leaving foster care.

Source: Adapted from Jim Casey Youth Opportunity Initiative. *Opportunity passports for youth in transition from foster care – A vision statement.* St. Louis, MO: JCYOI, April 2002, available online at www.jimcaseyyouth.org/docs/passport.pdf. U.S. Children's Bureau website at www.acf.hhs.gov/programs/cb/programs/; Child Welfare League of America. (1997). *Summary of the Adoption and Safe Families Act of 1997.* Washington, DC: Author.

Other policies that can provide services for homeless and emancipating youth include the U.S. Department of Housing and Urban Development's Family Unification and Youthbuild programs, and the DHHS's Transitional Living Program for Homeless Youth, Survivor's Insurance, and welfare programs, such as Temporary Assistance for Needy Families. The Chafee Education and Training Vouchers (ETVs) are available to help college students from foster care pay for the cost of attending an approved post-secondary education or training program. They provide up to $5,000 per student per year for former foster youth participating in a post-secondary education and training program. Federal ETV funds are allocated annually to each state based on the state's percentage of youth in foster care nationally. ETV funds can pay for expenses used to compute the total cost of post-secondary attendance. Examples of eligible expenses include tuition, application fees, books and supplies, room and board, dependent child care, transportation, and health insurance.

Other amendments to Title IV-E of the Social Security Act attempted to support improvements for this population by increasing the amount of funds available to states for services and by compelling states to better address the needs of youth who are designated for independent living (Leathers & Testa, 2006). For example, youth aged 16 to 21 otherwise eligible for services under a state's Chafee Foster Care Independence Program are eligible to receive an ETV. Youth adopted from foster care after age 16 are also eligible. Students may be eligible to age 23 if they received an ETV by the age of 21. Individual states may further restrict eligibility for ETV services (see www.natl-fostercare.org).

In summary, since an analysis of transition service-related policies in 31 states in 2002 (Zweibel & Strand, 2002), the scope and quality of services provided to current and former foster youth, and the eligibility requirements for these services, still vary widely. More states are providing assistance with education, employment, and housing, but fewer states provide youth with adequate health and mental health services or assistance in developing support networks. For example, while more states need to expand Medicaid coverage to youth aged 18 to 21, many states provide daily living skills instruction and financial assistance. While many states provide mentoring services, they generally do not utilize other methods of enhancing the support networks of youth.

Key barriers that states have identified include staff turnover, transportation problems, lack of coordination among the various services, limited involvement of foster parents, lack of youth employment opportunities, scarcity of housing and supervised living arrangements, lack of affordable education services, and shortage of mentors/volunteers (Annie E. Casey Foundation, 2017; Kerman, Wildfire, & Barth, 2002). The Fostering Connections to Success and Increasing Adoptions Act (P.L. 110–351) promotes permanent families for children through relative guardianship and adoption, and improving education and healthcare. The law also provides additional supports to older youth who reach the age of majority without a permanent family by extending federal support for youth to age 21 (the main provisions of this law are listed in the text policy resource paper – Crume & Pecora, 2018). Two key transition services needing further emphasis to help youth transition successfully from foster care – mentoring and life-skills development – are discussed in the following sections.

Life Skills Development

As mentioned above, with few exceptions, the field lacks research-based life-skills development programs, but more comprehensive life-skills development strategies and programs can better prepare youth for interdependent living. In Box 5.4 we highlight four promising strategies: (1) youth and caregiver involvement, (2) systematic skills assessment and planning, (3) life-skills training, and (4) developing healthy connections with foster parents, birth family members, and the greater community (Sheehy et al., 2002). A system that incorporates the first three strategies is available online for free at www.caseylifeskills. org. The skills learned in this system will help in forming social support networks.

Box 5.4 Life Skills Development Strategies

1. *Youth and Caregiver Involvement.* Youth and caregivers are more invested in the life skills learning process when they are involved in all aspects of it, which is the first effective strategy for preparing youth to live on their own (Nollan et al., 2002). Involving youth as integral players in the development and implementation of their Independent Living Plans can have far-reaching effects. Using

---

caregivers as the primary life skills teachers provides several advantages. For example, caregivers can coach and model appropriate behaviors in real-life situations; skills can be taught incrementally and can be tailored to the youth's unique strengths and needs; skills can be practiced in a safe environment; and progress can be regularly reinforced (Ryan et al., 1988).

2. *Systematic Skills Assessment and Planning.* This is critical to the development of a transition plan based on the individual's strengths and deficits (Skemer & Valentine, 2016). Assessment and planning should start when youth are young (e.g., ages 6 to 8) and involve youth, foster parents, and birth parents (if possible). It is recommended that a developmental, comprehensive assessment with known psychometric properties be used. Assessment is the first step in preparing youth for independent living. Assessment results can inform an overall transition plan, including goal setting and instruction. Planning is followed by learning and skill application. Measurement of progress completes the cycle.

3. *Independent Living Skills Training.* Focused skills training occurs after assessment and planning and is positively related to job maintenance, high school completion, adequate healthcare, economic independence, and general satisfaction with life (e.g., McMillen & Tucker, 1999; Pecora et al., 2010; Valentine, Skemer, & Courtney, 2015). As with assessment and planning, skills training needs to begin when youth are young (e.g., around ages 6 to 8). The most effective training experiences build on existing knowledge and provide real-world practice and experience. It is helpful to have tutors or mentors to reinforce these skills (Mech, Pryde, & Rycraft, 1995; Skemer & Valentine, 2016).

There are a variety of areas on which to focus life skills training. They include the broad categories of career planning, communication, daily living, housing, money management, self-care, social relationships, and work and study skills. As an example, consider GEAR UP, which is based on successful models for increasing the college enrollment rate of at-risk students, especially low-income and first-generation college students. Initial program results suggest that GEAR UP programs have been successful in increasing the percentage of students taking on a more challenging course load, better preparing these students for future college enrollment (see www2.ed.gov/programs/gearup/index.html).

4. *Developing Connections.* Developing connections with foster and birth family members and with the greater community is the fourth strategy. Social support networks for youth are often disrupted by placement (and events leading to

placement) and need to be rebuilt (Greeson et al., 2014). One way to promote connections is to consider a range of permanency options like guardianship, a birth family placement, adoption (even for older youth), and maintaining connections with foster and birth families. While in care, it is important to promote strong foster family, birth family, and social support networks to buffer stress and provide support for finishing education, obtaining housing, finding employment, and receiving financial and other advice. Having a positive, strong relationship with an adult in and after care is related to positive adult outcomes (Cook, 1994; Sheehy et al., 2002). Caregivers can be a vital part of a young person's support network because many youth stay in contact with their foster parents after leaving care (Courtney et al., 2001). Relationships with foster parents also ease the transition to independent living. Yet, there may need to be a specific discussion about the ways in which foster families can support foster youth when they leave – because foster parent licensing may prohibit some activities (e.g., returning home for the weekend) and foster care resources may prohibit others. Community connections also help replace youth's reliance on the agency and can help youth address and resolve feelings of grief, loss, and rejection (Sheehy et al., 2002).

Source: The material for this table was contributed by Dr. Kimberly A. Nollan. For a more complete discussion of these strategies and how they have are making a positive difference, see Nollan (2006), the Los Angeles ITPS program (Rivas et al., 2017), and the Youth Villages research (Skemer & Valentine, 2016).

Examples of Transition Programs

Chelsea Foyer. Another life skills program with an innovative housing component is the Chelsea Foyer program, which serves young people in their late teens and early twenties who are "aging out" of foster and residential care, homeless youth, and other young adults who lack the independent living and employment skills necessary to obtain affordable housing in New York City. Based on a successful European model and the first of its kind in the United States, the Chelsea Foyer is an innovative, supported, housing-based, job-training program for young adults in their late teens and early twenties. Participants live in a congregate setting and participate in an 18- to 24-month personalized program, receiving onsite case management services and linkages to rigorous job training and placement, educational, and life-skills development resources.

The Chelsea Foyer is a collaboration between Common Ground Community and Good Shepherd Services. Good Shepherd has overall responsibility for the program, including provision of intake, case management, youth development, mentoring, and other services. Common Ground provides facility management and building-wide security, as well as linkages to employment training. A third-party study of the Foyer's inaugural year indicates that the majority of residents were making progress in achieving their educational, employment, and independent living goals (see https://goodshepherds.org/program/chelsea-foyer/).

First Star. One transition program – First Star – focuses on building the academic, social skills, life skills, and social support necessary to attend a post-secondary education. A program with 13 sites in the United States and 1 site in London houses and educates high school-aged youth in foster care in the summer on major college campuses. This program has over a 90 percent success rate in helping twelfth graders become admitted to two-year and four-year colleges – with half of the youth admitted to four-year colleges (see www.firststar.org) but a more rigorous evaluation needs to be conducted involving control or comparison groups.

Youth Villages LifeSet. Currently, the most comprehensive transition program with the strongest research base is the Youth Villages LifeSet program. Working with youth aged 17 to 22, specially trained YVLifeSet specialists meet with YVLifeSet participants at least once a week – and more often when needed – in community settings, including their homes, at school or on the job, at a doctor's office, or wherever is most convenient for the young person. Specialists are available 24 hours a day, 7 days a week to help the young adult. Young people typically participate in the program for 6 to 12 months, based on individual needs.

The intensity and comprehensiveness of Youth Villages' YVLifeSet services set this program apart from other services. YVLifeSet specialists use evidence-based practices and research-driven interventions such as trauma-informed care and trauma-focused cognitive behavioral therapy to help participants overcome their challenges and meet their goals. A randomized controlled study of YVLifeSet – the largest study of this population to date – showed that the program is one of the only services that benefits young people in many areas of their lives (Skemer & Valentine, 2016; Valentine, Skemer, & Courtney, 2015). Core components that distinguish the YVLifeSet program and help ensure its success include the following:

- *Intensity:* Small caseloads of eight to ten young adults per specialist with a minimum of one face-to-face session per week as well as other communication throughout the week.

- *Comprehensive services:* Specialists help youth achieve their goals with education, employment, housing, permanency, and basic independent living skills.

- *Youth-driven:* Young adults have input into their service plans, goal development, and group activities.

- *Training and supervision:* Staff receive extensive on-the-job training as well as weekly group supervision and consultation with quarterly boosters and other training as needed.

- *Formalized program model* that uses evidence-based interventions as clinically necessary.

- *Program evaluation:* Youth Villages checks in with young people 6, 12, and 24 months after they have completed the YVLifeSet program.

- *Philosophy:* Staff espouse to "do whatever it takes." Specialists are expected to achieve success with a high percentage of the young adults; the case outcomes are the specialists' responsibility.

- *Collaboration:* The YVLifeSet program works closely with other support systems to help ensure that consistent and effective services are provided (see www.youthvill ages.org/what-we-do/yvlifeset/about-yvlifeset#sthash.d3U1butu.dpbs).

Summary of Independent Living Challenges and Future Directions

The challenges in regard to preparation for independent living include preparing youths earlier in their placement, obtaining flexible funding for work study programs, offering better vocational assessment and training, providing adequate healthcare, and maintaining supports to these young people as they move into adulthood. Such panoply of services is required because adolescents in foster care generally have limited supports in their families and social networks and are often emotionally, intellectually, and physically delayed from a developmental perspective.

Reviews of programs show a high degree of focus on clinical and rehabilitation services, while more universal or normative activities – school, recreation, making and keeping social contacts with peers, work skills, and job experience – are not emphasized strongly enough. A more balanced approach is necessary, particularly for placement of older children, who have a much shorter time to learn to be responsible for themselves. Being problem-free does not equate to being fully prepared (Pittman, 2002). Witness the testimony of Terry (foster care alumnus): "Aging out of foster care shouldn't mean being totally on your own. The end of foster care cannot mean the end of a community's caring" (Hormuth, 2001, p. 30).

Despite the plethora of policies and programs, older children in foster care continue to experience substantial challenges, and foster care agencies struggle to keep older children in a stable foster home, to teach them life skills as early as possible, and to assist them to think seriously about life after foster care. In general, it is impossible to know how well the programs are working because most lack rigorously collected evaluation data. Moreover, one of the challenges of providing a sufficient "dosage" of service is that many youth do not stay for a long time in foster care; in such cases, ensuring a child's safety may be the only realistic outcome to be measured, unless you believe in the value of follow-up services and education supports for foster care alumni under the age of 18 such as First Star academies. Yet, of the 250,248 children leaving out-of-home care in 2016, 28 percent – including many older youth – had been in care for two years or more, enough time to have derived some possible benefit from a social service program (U.S. DHHS, 2017).

Transition policies and support for emancipating youth must be overhauled. As shown by the research findings discussed at the beginning of this chapter, too many graduates of the foster care system are under-trained and underemployed. Society needs to promote investment in culturally relevant services, support, and opportunities to ensure that every youth in foster care makes a safe, successful transition to adulthood. Independent living preparation must be redesigned to start very early at age 10, not at age 17. A comprehensive transition plan should be developed for every child. It should include planning for supportive relationships, community connections, education, life-skills assessment and development, identity formation, housing, employment, physical health, and mental health (Youth Villages, 2017). Employment training and experience should be expanded for many youth while they are in care. Extending the age limit to allow youth to remain in foster care appears to be a promising approach (Courtney et al., 2017) and seems to have growing momentum at the state and federal levels.

Policies and incentives should ensure that no young person leaves foster care without housing, access to healthcare, employment skills, and permanent connections to at least one adult. Systems change is essential. The recent work in extending the age of emancipation from foster care, and improving services in California, Illinois, Washington, and other states, are some of the ways in which the country is responding to the concerns raised by the MacArthur Foundation transition scholars, who documented how major American institutions have not kept pace with societal changes that require new ways of working to remove barriers to youth as they transition to adulthood (Carnegie Council on Adolescent Development, 1989; Courtney et al., 2017).

Policy and Program Design Issues and Challenges

Overview

There are many other challenges facing foster care, as illustrated by the recent news article shown in Box 5.5 discussing five states where increases in foster care have been a concern:

Box 5.5 Five States Struggle with Surging Numbers of Foster Children

NEW YORK (AP) – The number of U.S. children in foster care is climbing after a sustained decline, but just five states account for nearly two-thirds of the recent increase. Reasons range from the creation of a new child-abuse hotline to widespread outrage over the deaths of children who had been repeatedly abused. Addictions among parents are another major factor.

The most dramatic increase has been in Georgia, where the foster care population skyrocketed from about 7,600 in September 2013 to 13,266 last month. The state is struggling to provide enough foster homes for these children and to keep caseloads at a manageable level for child protection workers.

Along with Georgia, the states with big increases are Arizona, Florida, Indiana, and Minnesota. According to new federal figures, the nationwide foster care population rose from 401,213 to 427,910 between September 2013 and September 2015, and these five states accounted for 65 percent of that rise.

In all five states, a common factor driving the increase has been a surge of substance abuse by parents. In Florida, for example, officials said that a crackdown on the abuse of prescription drugs has prompted more parents to turn to heroin and other illegal opioids, leading to the removal of their children from home. Florida's foster care population increased by 24 percent between 2013 and 2015; nationally the increase was less than 7 percent.

In Georgia, parental substance abuse now accounts for about 38 percent of foster care entries. That was the focus of a recent briefing in the state Senate, where a county child welfare official reported, "We recently rescued an 8-year-old boy who graphically disclosed being raped on a regular basis in his home where he lived with his father in a 'drug house'."

Georgia child welfare officials cite two factors beyond drugs. One is a centralized statewide child abuse hotline, created in 2013 to replace the 159 different hotline numbers that were used in Georgia's counties. Since then, abuse reports have

---

increased by 30 percent to more than 110,000 per year, and the number of abuse investigations has nearly doubled.

Another factor has been public outrage following some highly publicized cases in which children died from severe abuse even though caseworkers had prior indications that they were at risk. Heaven Woods, for example, was the subject of an abuse report in May 2014 – the ninth involving her family in the 5-year-old's lifetime – but there was only a cursory investigation, and she was beaten to death three weeks later.

Bobby Cagle, who took over Georgia's Division of Family and Child Services following that incident, toughened up the procedure for investigating alleged abuse. He also helped add more than 600 new positions for his agency, but division spokeswoman Susan Boatwright said personnel problems persist because of high turnover linked in part to starting salaries for caseworkers that range as low as $28,000.

"They're leaving because they can make more money," she said. "If we could hang onto people, we'd be in better shape."

As in Georgia, the surge of the foster care population in Minnesota is due in part to a high-profile child fatality – a 4-year-old boy named Eric Dean who died in 2013 after repeated abuse by his stepmother. In 2014, the *Minneapolis Star-Tribune* ran an in-depth story reporting how Eric's plight drew little scrutiny, despite 15 separate abuse reports being lodged with social workers. In response, Governor Mark Dayton ordered closer oversight of child protection decisions and formed a task force that recommended dozens of steps to place more emphasis on child safety.

As a result, Minnesota is now formally investigating a higher percentage of the child abuse reports received by its hotlines. According to the state Department of Human Services, the volume of those reports has increased by 50 percent since early 2014, and the state's foster care population has risen by about 33 percent. "Now we're erring on the side of removing the child from home, rather than doing everything we can to preserve the family," said Lilia Panteleeva, Executive Director of the Children's Law Center of Minnesota.

She said there were good reasons for the shift, but expressed concern about a dearth of resources to be sure the children removed from their families were being cared for by well-trained foster parents and getting access to quality support services.

"We're dealing with this huge tsunami with very little direction from the legislature," she said. According to the new federal figures, Indiana had the second biggest surge in foster children after Georgia – rising by 37 percent from 12,382 in 2013 to 17,023 in 2015.

James Wide of Indiana's Department of Child Services said parental substance abuse was a major factor. "The increase in heroin, meth, cocaine and prescription medication abuse, compounded by mental health issues, has brought many more children into our system," he said in an email. "Sadly, many adults are addicted, and their disease is keeping them from caring for their children."

In Arizona, where the foster care population has been rising steadily for six years, the child welfare system has been buffeted by a series of major problems – including burdensome caseloads for child protection workers, cutbacks in services to vulnerable families, and a sharp increase in the number of reports of child maltreatment.

Source: David Crary, National Writer, The Associated Press. Published November 24, 2016. Retrieved from http://wjtv.com/2016/11/24/five-states-struggle-with-surging-numbers-of-foster-children/. Reprinted with permission.

Foster Parent Recruitment and Retention

In the face of expanding need, recruitment as well as retention of foster parents is becoming increasingly difficult (see, e.g., Gateway, 2016, 2017b/c). The continuing shortage of foster families results from many factors, including the aging of current foster parents and the growing dropout rate of foster families, many of which are typically dissatisfied with CW services. The "volunteer" labor pool, of which foster parenting is part, has been decreasing because of the increase in single-parent families and the movement of women out of the home and into the paid workforce. In addition, the demands on foster families have increased substantially, because they are called upon to deal with children with special problems and needs; moreover, foster parents increasingly experience a lack of support and rewards in the face of the difficult job they carry out. Where projects have provided additional support, foster parent retention has improved (Price et al., 2009).

Additional demonstration projects are needed to disseminate knowledge about foster parenting in the context of the contemporary crisis in child welfare. Much more remains to be done to recognize explicitly the central roles of foster parents in achieving the goals of foster care. Foster parents must be involved more fully as an integral part of the services team, as partners with agencies and social workers, and society must be more willing to provide them with the supports and services they need to do the job. It is a national tragedy that we spend more per day to house our pets in kennels than we allocate to caring for our next generation of citizens.

Placement Disruption and Other Forms of Placement Change

How many youth experience placement changes in the foster care system? Disruption of a foster home placement – that is, the need to replace a child – can be a traumatic event. Research in this area is limited but has grown in the past 20 years. In the past two decades, multiple studies have been published to determine how many placements youth in foster care are experiencing. The results indicate that there is high variability in the number of placement changes.

One particular study indicated that while approximately one-third (31.9%) of youth experienced three or fewer placements, an equal number (32.3%) experience eight or more placements in the course of their foster care experience. The cumulative percent line in Figure 5.5 indicates that approximately 95 percent of the sample had 15 or fewer placements,

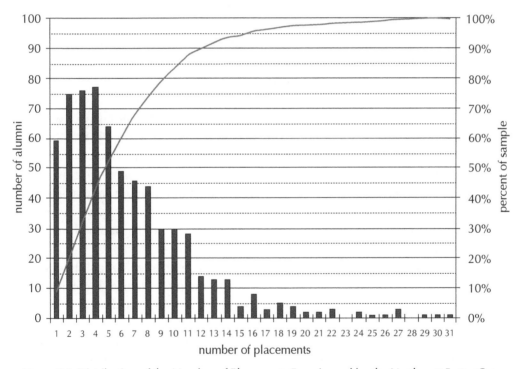

Figure 5.5 Distribution of the Number of Placements Experienced by the Northwest Foster Care Alumni, with Cumulative Percent and Range Groupings

Source: Williams et al. (2009).

while the remaining 5 percent had as many as 31 placements (Pecora et al., 2010). Nationally, on average, 64.8 percent of children who were in foster care for 12 to 24 months have had a placement change more than once (U.S. DHHS, 2016). These variations illustrate the need to account for the amount of time spent in care when comparing the number of placements across samples.

Although we do not believe that all of these placements are necessary, it is difficult to know what these findings mean. Indeed, how should we view the breakdown of a placement? Some placements are useful for such reasons as reuniting children with their siblings, finding potential adoptive homes, and attaining a better fit between children and families. Also, even unplanned changes may not always be an experience with drastic and negative consequences, as generally assumed. Aldgate and Hawley (1986) contend that foster home breakdown should be redefined as a disruption in the placement and constructively exploited in the process of arriving at a long-term plan for the child. For example, according to these authors, workers can help the child, birth parents, and foster parents learn more about themselves as well as learn new skills through the experience of disruption.

This is an important dynamic to monitor closely because placement stability *maximizes continuity in services, decreases foster parent stress, and lowers program costs.* Placement changes disrupt services provision, stress foster parents (thereby lowering retention rates), take up precious worker time, and create administrative-related disruptions. Because we know so little about what causes placement change, with few exceptions (e.g., Weigensberg et al., 2018) the field is less able to predict and therefore prevent them. And yet the dynamics of these changes are important for other reasons. For example, adolescents who were placed alone after a history of joint sibling placements were at greater risk for placement disruption than those who were placed with a consistent number of siblings while in foster care. This association was mediated by a weaker sense of integration and belonging in the foster home among youth placed alone with a history of sibling placements (Leathers, 2005).

Placement stability also increases the likelihood that a child will establish an enduring positive relationship with a caring adult. Clearly, the more stability a child has, the more likely it is that the child will be able to establish a stronger and more varied network of social support and enduring relationships with adults who care about him or her. While more research is needed about the cause and preventive mechanisms for placement change, there is growing evidence that we should minimize placement change for at least five reasons, as outlined in Box 5.6.

Box 5.6   Why Does Placement Stability Matter?

Physical and Behavioral Health

- Children perceive placement changes as unsettling and confusing.[a]

- A child's satisfaction with the foster care system is inversely correlated with the number of placements he or she has had.[b]

- Placement changes can increase the risk of adolescent deviance (delinquency, drug use, alcohol use, school dropout, and status offenses).[c]

- Twenty-three percent of males in placement have a delinquency petition, compared with 11 percent who remain in the family home, further indicating correlation between placement instability and delinquency.[d]

- Over one-third (38%) of youth with two or more placements made visits to a hospital emergency department the following year.[e]

Child Attachment and Emotional and Behavioral Disorders

- Each change in placement reduces the opportunities for a child to attach to an adult and increases the chance that a child will develop emotional and behavioral disorders. But in another study that used a comparison group of low-income youth of the same age (17), while attachment disorders and anxiety were no higher, PTSD symptoms were worse among the youth in care.[f]

- Children who have low to medium rates of placement change are 1.7 and 1.4 times more likely to have had no major mental health symptoms in the past 12 months compared with youth who have a high rate of placement changes.[g]

- Beyond an eight-month period in foster care, placement disruptions are associated with psychological deterioration.[h]

School Mobility and Academic Achievement

- One study indicated that students who have changed schools more than four times lose about one year of educational growth by their sixth school year.[i]

- High school students who change schools at least once are less than half as likely to graduate as their peers who do not change schools.[j]

- Children who change schools score 16 to 20 percent lower on standardized tests than children who do not change schools.[k]

Continuity of Services, Foster Parents' Stress, and Program Costs

- Placement changes disrupt service provision, stress foster parents (thereby lowering retention rates), take up precious caseworker time, and create administrative-related disruptions.[l, m]

- Children moved to placements without siblings are at higher risk of experiencing placement disruption than if they have a history of joint sibling placements.[n]

Potential for Child to Establish a Relationship With Caring Adult

- The more stability a child has, the more likely it is that he or she will be able to develop enduring positive relationships with adults who care about him or her.[o]

Sources: Pecora, P.J. & Boling, S.C. (2017). *Improving placement stability in the foster care system.* Seattle, WA: Research Services, Casey Family Programs; Pecora, P.J., & Huston, D. (2008). Why should child welfare and schools focus on minimizing placement change as part of permanency planning for children? *Social Work Now,* pp. 19–27.

[a]Festinger, T. (1983). *No one ever asked us. A postscript to foster care.* New York: Columbia University Press.
[b]Pecora & Huston (2008, pp. 19–27).
[c]Herrenkohl, E., Herrenkohl, R., & Egolf, B. (2003). The psychosocial consequences of living environment instability on maltreated children. *American Journal of Orthopsychiatry, 73*(4), 367–380.
[d]Ryan, J., & Testa, M. (2004). *Child maltreatment and juvenile delinquency: Investigating the role of placement and placement instability.* Champaign-Urbana, IL: University of Illinois at Urbana-Champaign School of Social Work, Children and Family Research Center.
[e]Rubin, D.M., Alessandrini, E.A., Feudtner, C., Localio, A.R., & Hadley, T. (2004). Placement changes and emergency department visits in the first year of foster care. *Pediatrics, 114*(3), 354–360.
[f]Pecora & Huston (2008, pp. 19–27). The comparison group study that revealed higher rates of PTSD symptoms was by Bederian-Gardner, D. et al. (2018). Instability in the lives of foster and nonfoster youth: Mental health impediments and attachment insecurities. *Children and Youth Services Review, 84,* 159–167.

[g]O'Brien, K., Kessler, R.C., Hiripi, E., Pecora, P.J., White, C.R., & Williams, J. (2008). Working Paper No. 7: *Effects of foster care experiences on alumni outcomes: A multivariate analysis*. Seattle, WA: Casey Family Programs.

[h]Barber, J., & Delfabbro, P. (2004). *Children in foster care*. New York: Routledge.

[i]Kerbow, D. (1996). Patterns of urban student mobility and local school reform. *Journal of Education for Students Placed at Risk, 1*(2), 147 169.

[j]Rumberger, R., & Larson, K.A. (1998). Student mobility and the increased risk of high school dropout. *American Journal of Education, 107*, 1 35.

[k]Calvin, E.M. (2000). *Make a difference in a child's life: A manual for helping children and youth get what they need in school: Advocating for children and youth who are out of home or in foster care*. Seattle, WA: TeamChild and Casey Family Programs.

[l]Flower, C., McDonald, J., & Sumski, M. (2006). *Review of turnover in Milwaukee County private agency child welfare ongoing case management staff*. Milwaukee, WI: Milwaukee County Department of Social Services.

[m]James, S. (2004). Why do foster care placements disrupt? An investigation of reasons for placement change in foster care. *The Social Service Review*, pp. 601 627.

[n]Leathers, S.J. (2005). Separation from siblings: Associations with placement adaptation and outcomes among adolescents in long-term foster care. *Children and Youth Services Review, 27*, 793–819.

[o]Pecora & Huston (2008, pp. 19–27).

What factors lower the risk of placement change? It starts with careful assessment of the child needs and strengths – and matching those with the capacity of the available foster parents. We need foster parents who can welcome and accept the child in times of distress, which encourages more secure child attachment. Matching of foster parent with child is a key process that is hampered when too many children are placed in foster care who could have been served in their birth family or who linger in foster care as "legal orphans" because the parental rights of both parents have been terminated and the case goal is adoption or guardianship – and yet no effective actions are being taken to help them find permanency. Those children overload a system and help create a shortage of foster parents.

In addition, high-quality foster parent caregiving provided by motivated and well-supported foster parents can reduce placement changes. The ability of foster parents to address the behavioral and emotional needs of the children is a key part of this and can be enhanced through specialized training and coaching such as through Project KEEP, Multisystemic Treatment, and Parent–Child Interaction Therapy.

But it also requires prompt foster family support from caseworkers, including during nights and weekends; along with recognition that often a child's relatives are in the picture or should be encouraged to be involved to help support the child. To ensure an adequate pool of foster parents, community awareness of the value of fostering is essential – along with the provision of tangible support of foster parents (e.g., product discount programs such as IFoster.org, "foster parent network" models with a supportive "hub home" like the Mockingbird Family Model: www.mockingbirdsociety.org/index.php/what-we-do/mockingbird-family-model).

Foster Care Re-entry

Nearly one in five children currently in care was in care previously. While recent trends have seen an increase in the number of children coming into care, the percentage in care who are re-entries has not changed. Between 2000 and 2015, almost 97,000 fewer children were in out-of-home care in the U.S. (Figure 5.2). Meanwhile, the percentage of children in care who are re-entries has remained stable at nearly 20 percent. In other words, 80,000 children who are currently in out-of-home care have previously been in care. These re-entry numbers clearly demonstrate that community conditions and service delivery systems are not providing the supports necessary for a significant number of children and families to remain together safely.

Children who exit care as infants have particularly high re-entry rates – and there also appears to be a higher rate of re-entry among minority adolescents. While these data do support the concern that some children are going home and returning to care, determining the ideal re-entry rate is not a simple matter. While every discharge from care should be expected to be successful, a reunification program may not be giving any families the benefit of the doubt and only sending children home when there is evidence beyond a reasonable doubt that the reunification will succeed. Such a standard would prevent many children who could be successfully reunified from going home. Low re-entries into foster care following reunification may also show that there are insufficient follow-up services to detect the need for re-entry and could mean that children who went home were remaining there unsafely. The ideal reunification program has the resources to provide ongoing support to families that have a reasonable chance of re-entry and, coincidentally, provides the vigilance necessary to see that post-reunification harms are rapidly observed and addressed. If child welfare information systems captured the distinction between children who came back into care in a planned way following a monitored reunification failure and could contrast those situations from those in which a child was re-abused, we would have more useful information for improving reunification.

Parental Visiting

During the placement period, it is also crucial to sustain and enhance connections between children and their families, particularly parents or other caregivers. While not without certain critics (e.g., Delfabbro, Barber, & Cooper, 2002), parent–child visiting in foster care has been described as a crucial determinant of the outcome of foster care services, and as the "heart of family reunification" (Warsh, Maluccio, & Pine, 1994, p. 49). In an extensive follow-up investigation of permanency planning for children in foster care, Davis et al. (1996) examined the relationship between parental visiting and reunification. The majority of children who had visited with their parents at the level recommended by the courts were reunified with their families. However, there was no significant relationship between parent–child visiting and whether the child remained in the biological home at a follow-up point a year after the reunification.

The findings of the above study and more recent research (e.g., Gateway, 2013; Partners for our Children, 2011) suggest that explicit policies and practices should be instituted to facilitate parent–child visiting throughout the placement process and to use visiting deliberately as a therapeutic vehicle in preparation for reunification. Visiting helps maintain family ties and provides opportunities for family members to learn and practice new behaviors and patterns of communicating with each other, with the assistance of social workers and foster parents. Yet, visiting continues to be an underdeveloped aspect of practice in foster care, with at best ambivalent attitudes by some foster parents toward birth parents. Moreover, in many cases parent–child visiting is infrequent, irregular, or non-existent.

Such authors as Kemp et al. (2007) offer guidelines for employing parent–child visiting as a strategy for reuniting children in out-of-home care with their families of origin. These authors emphasize that visiting should be carefully planned and implemented, with attention to its different purposes during each phase of the foster care placement. These purposes include: providing reassurance to the child and the family that the agency is concerned with reuniting them, if at all possible; assessing the children's and parents' capacity for reunification; offering opportunities for staff members to help parents and children reconnect with each other and learn or relearn skills for being together; and documenting the progress of children and parents in becoming reunited. As Warsh, Pine, and Maluccio (1996, p. 133) note, "Whether or not children are able to return home, visiting maintains family ties which may contribute to a child's healthy development." The natural bonds between children in foster care and their parents continue to be prominent for parents as well as for children long after they are physically separated.

269

Researchers have identified a number of pertinent strategies for facilitating visitation and promoting connectedness between children in placement and their families (Leathers, 2002; National Family Preservation Network, 2012; Partners for our Children, 2011; Jones, 2011):

- placing children near their parents and other significant kin;

- placing siblings together, unless otherwise indicated (also see Leathers, 2002);

- encouraging foster parents to allow family visits in the foster home, unless contraindicated;

- requiring written visiting plans that specify such aspects as the purposes, frequency, length, and location of each visit;

- selecting visiting activities that provide children and parents with opportunities to learn more effective patterns of interaction;

- preparing children, families, and foster parents for visits and giving them opportunities to work through their reactions before and after each visit.

Gay and Lesbian Children and Youths

Nearly three decades ago, a special committee of the Child Welfare League of America called attention to the needs of gay and lesbian children and youths in the foster care services: "Because of negative societal portrayals, many gay and lesbian youths live a life of isolation, alienation, depression and fear. As a result, they are beset by recurring crises disproportionate to their numbers in the child welfare services" (Child Welfare League of America, 1991, p. 2). Although there is increasing attention to their situations and needs, gay and lesbian children and youth continue to be poorly understood and underserved. Ongoing challenges for practitioners include appreciating the uniqueness of gay and lesbian adolescent development; helping the adolescents to negotiate life within a hostile environment; helping them confront the consequences of breakdown of the family services and the lack of family support; and understanding the rights of lesbian and gay parents in regard to child custody and visitation (Mallon, 2017; Wilber, Ryan, & Marksamer, 2006).

While many of these young people have a remarkable capacity for resilience, in an in-depth study of 54 gay and lesbian young people placed in out-of-home care in Los Angeles, New York, and Toronto, Mallon (1998) found that most were marginalized and struggling to function in society. On the basis of this study as well as other investigations, Mallon (2015, 2017) offers a number of recommendations for meeting the needs of these young people, including family foster care with gay and lesbian adults as foster parents and group homes designed for gay and lesbian adolescents for whom existing group home programs are not adequate.

Licensing lesbians or gay men as foster parents remains a controversial topic in child welfare in certain states, and some state legislation allows agencies to favor certain kinds of families without being at risk of a lawsuit. The Child Welfare League of America recommends ongoing education and training for foster parents, child welfare workers, and often professionals (Wilber et al., 2006). Mallon (2015, 2017) notes that these and other groups need to have a good understanding of the impact of societal stigmatization of gay and lesbian individuals and their families, and to develop basic competence for preserving and supporting families and for the establishment of appropriate gay/lesbian-affirming child welfare services.

Children and Families of Color: Racial Disparity, Disproportionality, and Other Practice Issues in Foster Care

On September 30, 2016, approximately 54 percent of the 437,465 children living in foster care were children of color (Asian, Black/African American, Native Hawaiian/Other Pacific Islander, Hispanic of any race; U.S. DHHS, 2017). This topic has become a central concern of child welfare programs and related advocates and funders because of the possibility that the disproportionality of some ethnic groups may indicate that the CW policies, decision making, or service provision related to placement into out-of-home care are biased and unfair. Further, the hope is that by identifying patterns of ethnic and racial involvement in out-of-home care, additional strategies for providing more culturally competent services will be found so that children of all races and ethnicities will have equal access to family-sensitive, safe, and permanent service. This includes studying the different kinds of dynamics also found for the other decision-making stages (Dunbar & Barth, 2007), such as decision to place, reunify, or adopt a child (Hill, 2007; Kohl, 2007; Wulczyn & Lery, 2007).

In this section, we discuss why there is disproportionality of placement into out-of-home care for three major ethnic/racial groups in relation to their representation in the general population. African American and Native American children are over-represented and White non-Hispanic, and Asian children are underrepresented. Hispanic children when viewed nationally are represented in out-of-home care at about the rate of their representation in the general population, but in certain states and communities are over-represented in foster care.

What are the reasons for disproportional representation of children of color in the child welfare services? What is the "most appropriate" representation of any group of children in the child welfare services? Theories about causation may be classified into three types: parent and family risk factors, community risk factors, and organizational and systemic factors (McCrory, Ayers-Lopez, & Green, 2006; National Association of Public Child Welfare Administrators, 2006). The following sections describe each major reason, but it is important to note that risk factors, community factors, organizational factors, and services factors are often interrelated and do not operate in isolation.

According to theories about *parent and family risk factors*, children of color are over-represented in the child welfare services because they have disproportionate needs. Their parents are more likely to have risk factors, such as unemployment, teen parenthood, poverty, substance abuse, incarceration, domestic violence, mental illness, etc. that result in high levels of child maltreatment (Barth, 2005; Chaffin, Kelleher, & Hollenberg, 1996; Drake et al., 2011). For example, the NIS-4 found strong and pervasive race differences in the incidence of maltreatment. In nearly all cases, the rates of maltreatment for Black children were significantly higher than those for White and Hispanic children. These differences occurred under both definitional standards in rates of overall maltreatment, overall abuse, overall neglect, and physical abuse and for children with serious or moderate harm from their maltreatment. They also occurred in the incidence of Harm Standard sexual abuse, in the incidence of children who were inferred to be harmed by Harm Standard maltreatment, and in Endangerment Standard rates for physical neglect, emotional maltreatment, and children who were endangered but not demonstrably harmed by their maltreatment (Sedlak et al., 2010).

Proponents of *community factors* assert that overrepresentation has less to do with race or class and more with the association of child maltreatment with poverty and lack of adequate housing (Slack, Berger, & Noyes, in press), residing in neighborhoods and communities that have many risk factors, such as high levels of poverty, welfare assistance, unemployment, homelessness, single-parent families, and crime and street violence that make residents more visible to surveillance from public authorities (Coulton & Pandey, 1992; Drake & Pandey, 1996; Garbarino & Sherman, 1980). In contrast, theories about *organizational and systemic factors* contend that racial overrepresentation results from: the decision-making processes of CPS agencies, cultural insensitivity, and biases of workers, governmental policies, and institutional or structural racism (Bent-Goodley, 2003; Everett, Chipungu & Leashore, 1991; McRoy, 2004; Morton, 1999; Roberts, 2002).

In summary, much more needs to be accomplished, however, in the field of child welfare in response to the needs and qualities of African Americans, Native Americans, and other ethnic minority children and families. For instance, greater attention must be paid to the use of flexible program funds to address housing and other environmental needs that prevent family reunification or provide a reason for child removal. Agencies also need to take a closer look at their cultural or ethnic competency, both as organizational cultures and in terms of staff recruitment and training. In this regard, the Child Welfare League of America has developed a guide to assist agencies in their move toward cultural competence (CWLA, 2002). There also needs to be more extensive use of certain forms of other family-based services that are showing promise for meeting the special needs of ethnic minority and other families through the provision of clinical and concrete services in the home setting (Fong, 1994; Kirk & Griffith, 2008).

Maltreatment of Children in Out-of-home Care

The occasional publicity about the abuse of foster children by foster parents creates considerable controversy, yet little is known about the extent and nature of such maltreatment. Allegations of maltreatment involving foster families are worrisome, due to the need to protect already vulnerable children from mistreatment; agency and worker concern regarding legal liability; perceived problems of recruitment and retention of foster homes; and perceived harm to foster children, foster parents, and other foster family members owing in large part to how maltreatment allegations are handled. However, this subject has received relatively little attention from researchers, even though it has been identified as an emerging problem since at least the mid-1980s by foster parent organizations and others (Child Welfare League of America, 2003; Miller et al., 2011; Uliando & Mellor, 2012).

Reports of maltreatment in foster homes comprise a minuscule portion – 1.1 percent – of all maltreatment reports; but foster homes are at much higher risk of report than the general population; and stricter definitions of maltreatment in foster care may influence report and substantiation rates. The National Survey of Child and Adolescent Well-Being finds that children in foster care have substantiated abuse report rates of about 9 percent during an 18-month period, but that the abuse was rarely by the foster parent or in the foster home, per se (it was more often by a parent during a pre-reunification visit or by another adult away from the foster home). Substantiated maltreatment by foster parents occurred in 0.75 percent of cases (Kohl, Gibbons, & Green, 2005). In light of the limited information and controversial nature of maltreatment of children in foster care, it is clear that further research is needed on its nature, extent, and impact. There is, in particular, a need to support the well-being of foster children and their foster families when abuse is alleged. Otherwise, seasoned foster parents will give up their career choice because of frustration with the agency response to them following an allegation against them by a youth in foster care.

Re-entry of Children into Foster Care

As will be discussed in Chapter 6, re-entry of children back into foster care following reunification has not improved much and remains a major challenge for CW. Fortunately, there are strategies that can be implemented – especially with recent shifts in financing because of Family First (Roberts, O'Brien, & Pecora, 2017).

Conclusion

Current Status of Family Foster Care

As a result of many developments, by the 1970s there was much pressure to reform child welfare services, in large measure as a result of the landmark Oregon Project, which contributed greatly to the promotion of *permanency planning* as a large-scale national movement (Pike, 1976), a movement that has continued to evolve with attention to reunification and close examination of the path to impermanence and a broad range of alternatives (Annie E. Casey Foundation, 2015). But despite the enactment of public policies such as the federal permanency planning law of 1980 (P.L. 96–272) and the Adoption and Safe Families Act of 1997 (P.L. 105–89) as well as the infusion of federal, state, and private funds, the number of children in foster care and the extent and complexity of the problems faced by them and their families continue to grow. It is, therefore, no exaggeration to note that foster care needs new ideas, resources, and personnel. Some authors even speak of a crisis in foster care – a crisis of children staying too long in care, being abused in care, and a shortage of high-quality foster parents – that is reported in the mass media and argued in professional circles (e.g., Annie E. Casey Foundation, 2015; Casey Family Programs, 2016).

Yet, foster care must be understood as having several parts, some of which show positive indicators of a more family-focused approach to services. In several of the major states and cities (e.g., California, Illinois, New York City) the number of children in conventional foster care had decreased, with increasing proportions of children in kinship foster care and treatment foster care. This does not mean that there are not massive challenges ahead for providers of out-of-home care for children. Recruiting and retaining quality foster parents is a necessity for effective child welfare services; having well-trained child welfare workers who understand the importance of permanency for children and options for achieving it is essential; flexibility in funding and approach is central to responding to so many diverse child and family needs is critical; and so is having adequate resources to help families and to accommodate a rapidly changing work environment for child welfare workers.

The challenges are evidenced in such areas as the typical pattern of dealing mostly with emergencies while the situations of other children and families deteriorate; the attrition rates of child welfare personnel, including foster parents; the substantial number of children who are further abused by the very foster care services in which they were placed because of maltreatment in their own homes; and the call for returning to a previously discontinued orphanage care. At a time that work with birth families and relatives is being re-emphasized, some foster care workers and foster parents are too overwhelmed to respond. One tragic indicator of this crisis is the high proportion of children in placement whose unmet cognitive, affective, and physical needs are interfering with their ability to learn and develop in a positive manner, as indicated earlier in this chapter.

Foster care services have improved in many ways over recent years, yielding more family-focused care, shorter lengths of stay, higher adoption rates, and practical approaches to working in a more preventive capacity with children in care and permanency planning being developed (e.g., the *3-5-7* model summarized by Henry (2005); treating maltreated preschool-aged children: Fisher et al. (2000)). Yet, the problems embedded in child welfare services are evident in many places throughout the country, consistent with what Kamerman and Kahn (1990) argued from their national study of social services to children, youths, and families. While noting that there are some exemplary programs and practices, these authors found that the efforts of social services remain largely inadequate throughout the country – observations that are sadly pertinent today – which underscore our perspective that the current financing and design of child welfare services is seriously flawed and must be reformed:

> Available delivery systems, interventive methods, and line staffs are not equal to the legitimate and appropriate tasks which lie ahead for the social services. There is a need – on the basis of adequate resource commitments – for innovation and testing, for sharing and exchange, and for ongoing efforts to respecify mission and infrastructure.
>
> (Kamerman and Kahn, 1990, p. 147)

Future Directions

In reflecting about the evolution and status of family foster care, readers may find themselves wishing for a set of more straightforward responses and solutions. Realities, such as resource limitations and the complexities of human behavior, make such solutions less viable, but high-quality family foster care for a small and appropriate group of children is still worth pursuing. A body of knowledge and clinical insights exists and can be applied so that the services may serve vulnerable children and families more effectively than at present, especially as we listen to – and learn from – parents and children themselves.

Some state and voluntary agencies are striving to address these concerns with innovative strategies such as family-based services and special reunification programs supported by a mix of public and private funding, but a more concerted effort at the legislative, policy, and programmatic levels must be made to maximize the quality of family foster care. Can we, as a society, rise to the challenge? As we reform our services, it is important that we listen to the perspectives of birth families and their kin, as discussed in the next chapter on permanency planning.

To do so, however, family foster care must become an integral part of a comprehensive network of services. These must include extensive family supports, especially concrete services such as housing, employment opportunities, healthcare, schooling, income assistance, and recreational services, and substance abuse counseling, mental health services, and education for parenting must also be part of the network. As addressed in this chapter and Chapters 4, 6, and 8, such services would complement a more variegated, flexible network of out-of-home programs that can support families for varying periods of time by providing respite and a safe haven for children. If we are committed to the principle that no child's future is expendable, we have no choice but to be part of the efforts to improve family foster care services.

In addition, foster care must attract, support, and encourage adequately trained, supervised, and rewarded personnel, especially foster parents – our front line of help for many children and families. The major goal of child development within a family setting must be articulated and reinforced through program, policy, and supervision. And organizational supports must be maintained, particularly by providing family-centered services, placing emphasis on services to clients while reducing paperwork and other bureaucratic constraints, and advocating for flexible and sufficient funding at the federal and state levels.

Summary

Our understanding of the perils of short foster care episodes combined with no or brief post-reunification services calls for careful use of who is placed and for how long. Wald (2015) and others have argued that brief CW services are not sufficient for some families and that we must think long term for a small but special set of families. California as part of its Residentially Based Services group care reform (www.cdss.ca.gov/inforesources/Residentially-Based-Services) and other municipalities encourage reunification and allow agencies to provide necessary aftercare services without incurring new costs by paying a fixed rate per case.

Even if the use of a capitated rate is not feasible, local funds, along with new funds available under the Family First Prevention and Support Program, could be used to provide post-reunification services. We should aim to establish a minimum length of combined out-of-home and in-home aftercare. However, since, each year in the U.S., as many as 25,000 children are reunified from foster care after stays of less than six months, Title IV-B funds would not be sufficient to extend post-placement services for these families unless funds were available to supplant nearly all other uses of IV-B (i.e., placement preservation). Clearly, Title IV-E funds must also be brought to bear if we are to routinely provide in-home post-reunification services. Support for these much-needed services could be enabled by allowing Title IV-E funds to pay for case management for up to one year after reunification of children younger than 5 at the time of exit from care. Failing that, states may want to experiment with extended post-placement services under the new Title IV-E waiver provisions underway in over 30 jurisdictions and one Tribal nation (see www.childwelfarepolicy.org /resources?id=0006).'

Programs that guarantee extended periods of case management have been developed in lean fiscal times and have been shown to be cost-effective. In general, a dose–response relationship does exist for services, and longer services are better for those families facing severe or multiple challenges (Barth, 1993; Wald, 2015). The current clientele in child welfare is younger and more vulnerable than ever before. Their child protection needs are extensive, and so must be the services they receive.

As reflected in Chapter 6 and throughout this book, attention to well-planned foster care that prioritizes the use of relatives (kinship care), and timely achievement of permanency are but one expression of the emphasis in child welfare and related fields on preserving families while also protecting children and maintaining their safety (e.g. Rolock et al., 2017). The unique challenges of preserving families that have been separated through placement, however, require new thinking, informed policy changes, supportive programs, revised practice strategies, systematic attention to developing the competence of family reunification practitioners, collaboration among service providers, and emphasis on hope and compassion.

Discussion Questions

1. From your review of current data about who is placed in foster care and the permanency outcomes being achieved, what group of children need more special attention?

2. What strategies do you think would most improve the child well-being outcomes of youth placed in foster care? Their permanency outcomes?

3. How would you help ensure that there is an adequate number and quality of foster parents?

For Further Information

Gateway. (2017c) *Recruiting and retaining resource families*. Washington, DC: U.S. Department of Health and Human Services. Retrieved from www.childwelfare.gov/topics/permanency/recruiting/. Timely summary of useful ideas and resources for foster parent recruitment.

Osgood, D., Foster, E., Flanagan, C., & Ruth, G. (Eds) (2005). *On your own without a net: The transition to adulthood for vulnerable populations*. Chicago, IL: University of Chicago Press. Examines policy and program challenges facing various vulnerable populations such as youth placed in juvenile justice and foster care programs, only one of which is foster youth.

Bibliography

Aldgate, J., & Hawley, D. (1986). *Recollections of disruptions: A study of foster care break-downs*. London: National Foster Care Association.

Annie E. Casey Foundation. (2005). *Elders as resources: Basic data: Kinship care*. Baltimore, MD: Author.

Annie E. Casey Foundation. (2015). *A movement to transform foster parenting*. Baltimore, MD: Author.

Annie E. Casey Foundation. (2017). *The economic well-being of youth transitioning from foster care. Opportunity passport participant survey results show employment helps many thrive*. Baltimore, MD: Author. Retrieved from www.aecf.org/m/resourcedoc/aecf-theeconomic wellbeingofyouth-2017.pdf.

Barth, R.P. (1990). On their own: The experience of youth after foster care. *Child and Adolescent Social Work Journal, 7*(5), 419–446.

Barth, R.P. (1993). Long-term in-home services. In D. Besharov (Ed.), *When drug addicts have children: Reorienting child welfare's response* (pp. 175–194). Washington, DC: Child Welfare League of America.

Barth, R.P. (2005). Child welfare and race: Models of disproportionality. In D. Derezotes, J. Poertner, & M.F. Testa (Eds), *Race matters in child welfare; The overrepresentation of African American children in the system*. Washington, DC: CWLA Press.

Barth, R.P., & Blackwell, D.L. (1998). Death rates among California's foster care and former care populations. *Children and Youth Services Review, 20*(7), 577–604.

Barth, R.P., Wildfire, J., & Green, R. (2006). Placement into foster care and the interplay of urbanicity, child behavior problems, and poverty. *American Journal of Orthopsychiatry, 76*(3), 358–366.

Barth, R.P., Guo, S., Green, R.L., & McRae, J.S. (2007). Developmental outcomes for children in kinship and nonkinship care: Findings from the National Survey of Child and Adolescent Well-Being. In R. Haskins, F. Wulczyn, & M.B. Webb (Eds), *Child protection: Using research to improve policy and practice* (pp. 187–206). Washington, DC: Brookings.

Bent-Goodley, T.B. (Ed.). (2003). *African-American social workers and social policy*. New York: The Haworth Press.

Berger, L.M., Cancian, M., Han, E., Noyes, J., & Rios-Salas, V. (2015). Children's academic achievement and foster care. *Pediatrics, 135*, e109–e116.

Bernstein, N. (2000). A rage to do better: Listening to young people from the foster care system. Retrieved from www.pacificnews.org.

Berrick, J.D., Barth, R.P., & Needell, B. (1994). A comparison of kinship foster homes and foster family homes: Implications for kinship foster care as family preservation. *Children and Youth Services Review, 16*(1–2), 33–63.

Berrick, J.D., Needell, B., Barth. R.P., & Jonson-Reid, M. (1998*). The tender years: Toward developmentally sensitive child welfare services for very young children*. New York: Oxford University Press.

Blumenthal, K. (1983). Making foster family care responsive. In B. McGowan & W. Meezan (Eds), *Child welfare: Current dilemmas – Future directions* (pp. 299–344). Itasca, IL: F. E. Peacock.

Brace, C.L. (1872). *The dangerous classes of New York*. New York: Wyncoop & Hallenback.

Bremner, R. (Ed.) (1971). *Children and youth in America: A documentary history, 1865–1965* (Vol. 2). Cambridge, MA: Harvard University Press.

Carnegie Council on Adolescent Development. (1989). *Turning points: Preparing youth for the 21st century*. Washington, DC: CCAD.

Casey Family Programs. (2016). *Annual report*. Seattle, WA: Author.

Center on the Developing Child at Harvard University (2017). *Three principles to improve outcomes for children and families*. Boston: Author. Retrieved from www.developingchild.harvard.edu.

Chaffin, M., Kelleher, K., & Hollenberg, J. (1996). Onset of physical abuse and neglect: Psychiatric, substance abuse and social risk factors from prospective community data. *Child Abuse & Neglect, 20*, 191–200.

Chamberlain, P. (2003). *Treating chronic juvenile offenders: Advances made through the Oregon multidimensional treatment foster care model*. Washington, DC: American Psychological Association.

Chambers, C.A. (1963), *Seedtime of reform: American social service and social action, 1918–1933*. Minneapolis, MN: University of Minnesota Press.

Chapman, M.V., Wall, A., & Barth, R.P. (2004). Children's voices: The perceptions of children in foster care. *American Journal of Orthopsychiatry, 74*(3), 293.

Cheung, C., Goodman, D., Leckie, G., & Jenkins, J.M. (2011). Understanding contextual effects on externalizing behaviors in children in out-of-home care: Influence of workers and foster families. *Children and Youth Services Review, 33*, 2050–2060.

Child Welfare League of America. (1991). *Serving the needs of gay and lesbian youths – Recommendations to a colloquium – Jan. 25–26 1991*. Washington, DC: Author.

Child Welfare League of America. (1994). *Kinship care: A natural bridge*. Washington, DC: Child Welfare League of America.

Child Welfare League of America. (1995). *Standards of excellence for family foster care.* Washington, DC: Child Welfare League of America.

Child Welfare League of America. (2000). *CWLA standards of excellence for kinship care services.* Washington, DC: Author.

Child Welfare League of America. (2002). *Cultural Competence Agency Self-Assessment Instrument.* Washington, DC: Author. Retrieved from www.cwla.org/pubs.

Child Welfare League of America. (2003). *Child maltreatment in foster care: CWLA Best Practice guidelines.* Washington, DC: CWLA. Retrieved from www.hunter.cuny.edu/socwork/nrcfcpp/downloads/policy-issues/maltreatment-guidelines.pdf.

ChildFocus. (2009). *Ten steps public child welfare agencies can take to support children in safe and stable kinship families.* Retrieved from http://affcny.org/wp-content/uploads/10Kinship Steps.pdf.

Children's Defense Fund, Child Trends, American Bar Association Center on Children and the Law, Casey Family Programs, Child Focus, & Generations United. (2012). *Making It work: Using the Guardianship Assistance Program (GAP) to close the permanency gap for children in foster care.* Seattle, WA, and Washington, DC: Authors. Retrieved from www.childrensdefense.org/library/data/making-it-work-using-the.pdf.

Cohen, J.A., & Mannarino, A.P. (2004). Treatment of childhood traumatic grief. *Journal of Clinical Child and Adolescent Psychology, 33*(4), 819–831.

Commission to Eliminate Child Abuse and Neglect Fatalities. (2016). *Within our reach: A national strategy to eliminate child abuse and neglect fatalities.* Washington, DC: Government Printing Office. Retrieved from www.acf.hhs.gov/programs/cb/resource/cecanf-final-report.

Conn, A.M., Szolagyi, M.A., Franke, T.M., Albertin, C.S., Blumkin, A.K., & Szilagyi, P.G. (2013). Trends in children protection and out-of-home care. *Pediatrics, 132,* 712. doi:10.1542/peds.2013–0969.

Conway, T., & Hutson, R.S. (2007). *Is kinship care good for kids?* Washington, DC: Center for Law and Social Policy.

Cook, R.J. (1994). Are we helping foster care youth prepare for their future? *Children and Youth Services Review, 16*(3–4), 213–229.

Coulton, C.J., & Pandey, S. (1992). Geographic concentration of poverty and risk to children in urban neighborhoods. *American Behavioral Scientist, 35,* 238–257.

Council on Accreditation. (2013). New Family Foster Care and Kinship Care Standards. Retrieved from http://coanet.org/about/whats-new/news-detail/article/62/.

Courtney, M.E., & Bost, N. (2002). *Review of literature on the effeciveness of independent living programs.* Chicago: University of Chicago, Chaplin Hall.

Courtney, M.E., Dworsky, A., Ruth, G., Keller, T., Havlicek, J., & Bost, N. (2005). *Midwest evaluation of adult functioning of former foster youth: Outcomes at age 19.* Chicago, IL: University of Chicago, Chapin Hall Center for Children.

Courtney, M.E., & Needell, B. (1997). Outcomes of kinship care: Lessons from California. In J.D. Berrick, R.P. Barth, & N. Gilbert (Eds), *Child welfare research review* (Vol. 2, pp. 130–149). New York: Columbia University Press.

Courtney, M.E., Hook, J.L., & Lee, J.S. (2012) Distinct subgroups of former foster youth during young adulthood: Implications for policy and practice. *Child Care in Practice, 18*, 409–418.

Courtney, M.E., Terao, S., & Bost, N. (2004). *Midwest evaluation of the adult functioning of former foster youth: Conditions of youth preparing to leave state care.* Chicago, IL: Chapin Hall Center for Children at the University of Chicago.

Courtney, M., Piliavin, I., Grogan-Kaylor, A., & Nesmith, A. (1998). *Foster youth transitions to adulthood: Outcomes 12 to 18 months after leaving out-of-home care.* Madison, WI: School of Social Work and Institute for Research on Poverty, University of Wisconsin-Madison.

Courtney, M., Piliavin, I., Grogan-Kaylor, A., & Nesmith, A. (2001). Foster youth transitions to adulthood: A longitudinal view of youth leaving care. *Child Welfare, 80*(6), 685–717.

Courtney, M.E., Harty, J., Kindle, B., Dennis, K., Okpych, N.J., & Torres García, A. (2017). *Findings from the California Youth Transitions to Adulthood Study (CalYOUTH): Conditions of youth at age 19: Los Angeles County report.* Chicago, IL: Chapin Hall at the University of Chicago.

Courtney, M.E., Dworsky, A., Cusick, G.R., Keller, T., Havlicek, J., Perez, A., Terao, S., & Bost, N. (2007). *Midwest evaluation of adult functioning of former foster youth: Outcomes at age 21.* Chicago, IL: University of Chicago, Chapin Hall Center for Children.

Courtney, M.E., Okpych, N.J., Charles, P., Mikell, D., Stevenson, B., Park, K., Kindle, B., Harty, J., & Feng, H. (2016). *Findings from the California Youth Transitions to Adulthood Study (CalYOUTH): Conditions of Youth at Age 19.* Chicago IL: Chapin Hall at the University of Chicago.

Crumbley, J., & Little, R.L. (Eds) (1997). *Relatives raising children: An overview of kinship care.* Washington, DC: CWLA Press.

Crume, H.J., & Pecora, P.J. (2018). *Transition and independent living services for youth in foster care: A Resource Paper.* New York: Taylor and Francis.

CW 360. (2010). *Promoting placement stability.* Entire issue, pp. 1–48. Minneapolis, MN: Center for Advanced Studies in Child Welfare (CASCW), School of Social Work, College of Education and Human Development, University of Minnesota.

Davis, I.P., Landsverk, J., Newton, R., & Ganger, W. (1996). Parental visiting and foster care reunification. *Children and Youth Services Review, 18*(4–5), 363–382.

Delfabbro, P.H., Barber, J.G., & Cooper, L. (2002). The role of parental contact in substitute care. *Journal of Social Service Research, 28*(3), 19–39.

DePanfilis, D., Daining, C., Frick, K., Farber, J., & Levinthal, L. (2007). *Hitting the M.A.R.C. Establishing foster care minimum adequate rates for children, technical report.* New York: Children's Rights, Inc. Retrieved from http://childrensrights.org/wp-content/uploads/2008/06/hitting_the_marc_summary_october_2007.pdf.

Development Services Group, Inc. (2013). *Protective factors for populations served by the administration on children, youth, and families. A literature review and theoretical framework: Executive summary.* Washington, DC: U.S. Department of Health and Human Services, Administration for Children and Families, Children's Bureau. Retrieved from www.dsgonline.com/acyf/DSG%20Protective%20Factors%20Literature%20Review%20 2013%20Exec%20Summary.pdf.

Dolan, M., Smith, K., Casanueva, C., & Ringeisen, H. (2011). *NSCAW II baseline report: Case-worker characteristics, child welfare services, and experiences of children placed in out-of-home care.* OPRE Report #2011–27e, Washington, DC: Office of Planning, Research and Evaluation, Administration for Children and Families, U.S. Department of Health and Human Services. Retrieved from www.acf.hhs.gov/sites/default/files/opre/nscaw2_cw.pdf.

Drake, B., & Pandey, S. (1996). Understanding the relationship between neighborhood poverty and specific types of child maltreatment. *Child Abuse & Neglect, 20,* 1003–1018.

Drake, B., Jolley, J.M., Lanier, P., Fluke, J., Barth, R.P., & Jonson-Reid, M. (2011). Racial bias in child protection? A comparison of competing explanations using national data. *Pediatrics.* Retrieved from www.pediatrics.org.doi:10.1542/peds.2010-1710.

Dunbar, K., & Barth, R.P. (2007). *Racial disproportionality, race disparity, and other race-related findings in unpublished works derived from the Natural Survey of Child and Adolescent Well-Being.* Seattle, WA: Casey Family Programs.

Dworskey, A. & Courtney, M.E. (2010). Does extending foster care beyond age 18 promote postsecondary educational attainment? Retrieved from www.chapinhall.org/sites/default/files/publications/Midwest_IB1_Educational_Attainment.pdf.

Everett, J.E., Chipungu, S.S., & Leashore, B.R. (Eds) (1991). *Child welfare: An Africentric perspective.* New Brunswick, NJ: Rutgers University Press.

Falconnier, L.A., Tomasello, N.M., Doueck, H.J., Wells, S.J., Luckey, H., & Agathen, J.M. (2010). Indicators of quality in kinship foster care. *Child Welfare and Placement, 91,* 4.

Fanshel, D., & Shinn, E.B. (1978). *Children in foster care: A longitudinal investigation.* New York: Columbia University Press.

Fisher, A. (2002). *Finding fish.* New York: Harper Collins.

Fisher, P.A., Gunnar, M.R., Chamberlain, P., & Reid, J.B. (2000). Preventive intervention for maltreated preschool children: Impact on children's behavior, neuroendocrine activity, and foster parent functioning. *Journal of the American Academy of Child & Adolescent Psychiatry, 39*(11), 1356–1364.

Fong, R. (1994). Family preservation: Making it work for Asians. *Child Welfare, 73,* 331–341.

Foster Family-based Treatment Association. (2013). *Program Standards for Treatment Foster Care* (Revised). Hackensack, NJ: Author. Retrieved from: https://ffta.imiscloud.com/New_FFTA_Content/Learn/Program_Standards.aspx.

Foster Family-based Treatment Association. (2015). *The Kinship Treatment Foster Care Initiative Toolkit.* Hackensack, NJ: Author. Retrieved from https://ffta.imiscloud.com/FFTA/Resources/FFTA_Publications/New_FFTA_Content/Learn/FFTA_Publications.aspx?hkey=97869752-e618-428e-84d8-9f7420262570.

Frerer, K., Sosenko, L.D., Pellegrin, N., Manchik, V., & Horowitz, J. (2013). *Foster youth stability: A study of California foster youths' school and residential changes in relation to educational outcomes.* Berkeley, CA: University of California at Berkeley, Center for Social Services Research, p. 2. Retrieved from www.iebcnow.org/wp-content/uploads/2016/12/pub_foster_youth_stability_2013.pdf.

Garbarino, J., & Sherman, D. (1980). High-risk neighborhoods and high-risk families. *Child Development, 51*, 188–189.

Garcia, A., O'Reilly, A., Matone, M., Kim, M., Long, J., & Rubin, D. (2014). The influence of caregiver depression on children in non-relative foster care versus kinship care placements. *Maternal and Child Health Journal*, June.

Gateway. (2013). *Supporting parent/child visits*. Washington, DC: U.S. DHHS. Retrieved from www.childwelfare.gov/topics/permanency/reunification/parents/visiting/

Gateway. (2016). *Diligent recruitment of families for children in the foster care system*. Washington, DC: U.S. DHHS. Retrieved from www.childwelfare.gov/pubPDFs/diligentrecruitment.pdf.

Gateway. (2017a). *Core/foundation training for caseworkers: Out-of-home care*. Washington, DC: U.S. Department of Health and Human Services. Retrieved from www.childwelfare. gov/topics/management/training/curricula/caseworkers/core/outofhomecare/.

Gateway. (2017b). *Diligent recruitment*. Washington, DC: U.S. Department of Health and Human Services. Retrieved from www.childwelfare.gov/topics/permanency/recruiting/ diligent-recruitment/.

Gateway. (2017c). *Recruiting and retaining resource families*. Washington, DC: U.S. Department of Health and Human Services. Retrieved from www.childwelfare.gov/topics/permanency/ recruiting/.

Geen, R. (2003). *Kinship foster care: Making the most of a valuable resource*. Washington, DC: Urban Institute Press.

Generations United, ChildFocus, and American Bar Association Center on Children and the Law. (2017). *wikiHow for Kinship Foster Care*. Washington, DC. Retrieved from http:// grandfamilies.org/Portals/0/KinshipCareWikiHow_V1R5-2.pdf.

Goemans, A., van Geel, M., Beem, M., & Vedder, P. (2016). Developmental outcomes of foster children: A meta-analytic comparison with children from the general population and children at risk who remained at home. *Child Maltreatment, 21*(3), 198–217.

Goerge, R.M., Bilaver, L.A., Lee, B.J., Needell, B., Brookhart, A., & Jackman, W. (2002). *Employment outcomes for youth aging out of foster care*. Chicago, IL: University of Chicago, Chapin Hall Center for Children.

Greeson, J.K.P., Garcia, A.R., Kim, M., & Courtney, M.E. (2014). Foster youth and social support: The first RCT of independent living services. *Research on Social Work Practice*. doi:10.1177/1049731514534900.

Hasci, T. (1995). From indenture to family foster care: A brief history of child placing. *Child Welfare, 74*, pp.162–180.

Hegar, R.L., & Scannapieco, M. (Eds) (1999). *Kinship foster care – Policy, practice, and research*. New York: Oxford University Press.

Helton, J. (2011). Children with behavioral, non-behavioral, and multiple disabilities and the risk of out-of-home placement disruption. *Child Abuse & Neglect, 35*, 956–964.

Henry, D.J. (2005). *The 3-5-7 Model: A practice approach to permanency*. Harrisburg, PA: Darla L. Henry & Associates, Inc.

Hill, R.B. (2007). *Analysis of racial/ethnic disproportionality and disparity at the national, state and county levels.* Washington, DC: The Casey–CSSP Alliance for Racial Equity, Center for the Study of Social Policy.

Hormuth, P. (2001). *All grown up, nowhere to go: Texas teens in foster care transition.* Austin, TX: Center for Public Priorities.

Institute for Research on Poverty. (2015). Does Foster Care Lower School Achievement? *Focus on Policy,* No. 5. Madison, WI: Author.

Jones, A.S. (2011). Virtual visitation and child welfare, *CW360,* spring, p. 19. Retrieved from http://cascw.umn.edu/wp-content/uploads/2013/12/CW360_2011.pdf.

Jones-Harden, B. (2004). Safety and stability for foster children: A developmental perspective. *Future Child, 14*(1), 30–47.

Jonson-Reid, M., & Barth, R.P. (2000). From maltreatment report to juvenile incarceration: The role of child welfare services. *Child Abuse & Neglect, 24*(4), 505–520.

Kadushin, A., & Martin, J.A. (1988). *Child welfare services.* (4th edition). New York: Macmillan.

Kamerman, S.B., & Kahn, A.J. (1990). Social services for children, youth and families in the United States. *Children and Youth Services Review, 12*(1–2), 184.

Kemp, S., Marcenko, M., Vesneski, W., & Hoagwood, K. (2007). *Parent empowerment and engagement in child welfare: Promising practices and policy opportunities.* Presented at the Casey Foster Care Clinical R&D Project Consensus conference, Washington, DC.

Kerman, B., Maluccio, A.N., & Freundlich, M. (2008). *Achieving permanence for older children and youth in foster care.* New York: Columbia University Press.

Kerman, B., Wildfire, J., & Barth, R.P. (2002). Outcomes for young adults who experienced foster care. *Children and Youth Services Review, 24*(5), 319–344.

Killos, L. (2017). *Children in kinship care: A summary and annotated bibliography.* Seattle, WA: Casey Family Programs.

Killos, L., Lucero, N., Kauffman, M., Brammer, M.J., Freemont, S., & Maher, E. (2017). *Strategies for successfully recruiting and retaining preferred-placement foster homes for American Indian children.* Retrieved from www.casey.org/icwa-recruitment-retention.

Kirk, R.S., & Griffith, D.P. (2008). Impact of intensive family preservation services on disproportionality of out-of-home placement of children of color in one state's child welfare system. *Child Welfare, 87*(5), 87–105.

Kohl, P.L. (2007). *Unsuccessful in-home child welfare service plans following a maltreatment investigation: Racial and ethnic differences.* Washington, DC: Casey – CSSP Alliance for Racial Equality in Child Welfare.

Kohl, P.L., Gibbons, C.B., & Green, R.L. (2005, January 16). *Findings from the National Survey of Child and Adolescent Well-Being (NSCAW): Applying innovative methods to understanding services and outcomes for maltreated children; safety of children in child welfare services: Analysis of reported and undetected maltreatment over 18-months.* Paper presented at the Society for Social Work and Research, Miami, FL.

Lasch, C. (1977). *Haven in a heartless world: The family besieged.* New York: Basic Books.

Leathers, S.J. (2002). Separation from siblings: Associations with placement adaptation and outcomes among adolescents in long-term foster care. *Children and Youth Services Review, 27*, 793–819.

Leathers, S.J., & Testa, M.F. (2006). Youth emancipating from care: Caseworkers' reports on needs and services. *Child Welfare, 85*(3), 463–498.

Lewis, E., Dozier, M., Knights, M., & Maier, M. (in press). Intervening with foster infants' foster parents: Attachment and biobehavioral catch-up. In R.E. Lee & J. Whiting (Eds), *Handbook of relational therapy for foster children and their families.* Washington, DC: Child Welfare League of America.

Lutman, E., Hunt, J., & Waterhouse, S. (2009). Placement stability for children in kinship foster care: A long-term follow-up of children placed in kinship care thorough care proceedings. *Adoption and Fostering, 33*(3), 28–39.

Maas, H.S., & Engler, R.E. (1959). *Children in need of parents.* New York: Columbia University Press.

Mallon, G. (1998). *We don't exactly get the welcome wagon: The experiences of gay and lesbian adolescents in child welfare systems.* New York: Columbia University Press.

Mallon, G.P. (2015). *Lesbian, gay, bisexual and trans foster and adoptive parents: Recruiting, assessing, and supporting untapped family resources for children and youth* (2nd edn). Washington, DC: Child Welfare League of America.

Mallon, G.P. (Ed.) (2017). *Social work practice with lesbian, gay, bisexual, and transgender people* (3rd Edition.). New York: Routledge.

Maluccio, A.N., Krieger, R., & Pine, B.A. (Eds) (1990). *Preparing adolescents for life after foster care: The central role of foster parents.* Washington, DC: Child Welfare League of America.

McCrory, J., Ayers-Lopez, S., & Green, D. (2006). Disproportionality in Child Welfare. *Protection Connection, 12*(4).

McDaniel, S. (2014). *On my way home – A memoir of kinship, grace, and hope.* Pittsburgh, PA: A Second Chance, Inc.

McMillen, J., & Tucker, J. (1999). The status of older adolescents at exit from out-of-home care. *Child Welfare, 78*(3), 339–362.

McRoy, R.G. (2004). The color of child welfare policy. In K. Davis & T. Bent-Goodley (Eds), *The color of social policy* (pp. 37–64). Washington, DC: Council on Social Work Education.

Meadowcroft, P., & Trout, B.A. (Eds) (1990). *Troubled youth in treatment homes: A handbook of therapeutic foster care.* Washington, DC: Child Welfare League of America.

Mech, E.V., Pryde, J.A., & Rycraft, J.R. (1995). Mentors for adolescents in foster care. *Child & Adolescent Social Work Journal, 12*(4), 317–328.

Miller, E., Green, A., Fettes, D., & Aarons, G. (2011). Prevalence of maltreatment among youths in public sectors of care. *Child Maltreatment, 16*(3), 196–204.

Montgomery, P., Donkoh, C., & Underhill, K. (2006). Independent living programs for young people leaving the care system: The state of the evidence. *Children and Youth Services Review, 28*, 1435–1448.

Moore, W. (2010). *The other Wes Moore*. New York: Random House, Spiegel & Grau.

Morton, T. (1999). The increasing colorization of America's child welfare system: The overrepresentation of African American children. *Policy and Practice, 57*(4), 23–30.

National Association of Public Child Welfare Administrators. (2006). *Disproportionate representation in the child welfare system: Emerging promising practices survey*. American Public Human Services Association.

National Association of Social Workers. (2013). *NASW standards for practice in child welfare*. Washington, DC: Author. Retrieved from www.socialworkers.org/LinkClick.aspx?fileticket=_Flu_UDcEac%3d&portalid=0.

National Conference of Juvenile and Family Court Judges. (2006). *Children's exposure to domestic violence: A guide to research and resources*. Reno, NV: Author.

National Conference on State Legislatures. (2017). *Teen pregnancy prevention*. Retrieved from www.ncsl.org/research/health/teen-pregnancy-prevention.aspx#Foster_Care.

National Family Preservation Network. (2012). *Best practice for father–child visits in the child welfare system*. Author. Retrieved from http://centerforchildwelfare.fmhi.usf.edu/kb/Family CenteredPractice/father_child_visits.pdf.

National Foster Care Awareness Project (NFCAP). (2000). Frequently asked questions II: About the Foster Care Independence Act of 1999 and the John H. Chafee Foster Care Independence Program. Seattle, WA: Casey Family Programs. Retrieved from www.casey.org.

National Working Group on Foster Care and Education. (2018). *Fostering success in education: Educational outcomes of students in foster care*. Washington, DC: American Bar Association.

Nisivoccia, D. (1996). Working with kinship foster families: Principles for practice. *Community Alternatives: International Journal of Family Care, 8*(1), 1–21.

Nollan, K., & Downs, A. (2001). *Preparing youth for long-term success: Proceedings from the Casey Family Program National Independent Living Forum*. Washington, DC: CWLA Press.

Nollan, K.A. (1996). *Self-sufficiency skills among youth in long-term foster care* – Doctoral dissertation. Seattle, WA: University of Washington.

Nollan, K.A. (2006). Support for young people leaving care in the USA. In C. McAuley, P.J. Pecora, & W. Rose (Eds), *Enhancing the well-being of children and families through effective interventions: International evidence for practice* (pp. 24–252). London: Jessica Kingsley.

Nollan, K.A., Horn, M., Downs, A.C., Pecora, P.J., & Bressani, R.V. (2002). *Ansell-Casey Life Skills Assessment (ACLSA) and Lifeskills Guidebook Manual*. Seattle, WA: Casey Family Programs.

Park, J.M., & Helton, J. (2010). Transitioning from informal to formal substitute care following maltreatment investigation. *Children and Youth Services Review, 32*, 998–1003.

Partners for our Children. (2011). *Family visitation in child welfare: Helping children cope with separation while in foster care*. Seattle, WA: Author. Retrieved from https://partnersforourchildren.org/resources/briefs/family-visitation-child-welfare-helping-children-cope-separation-while-foster-care.

Pecora, P.J., Whittaker, J.K., Barth, R.P., Vesneski, W., & Borja, S. (2018). *Child welfare policy and related legislation through the years: A resource paper*. New York: Taylor and Francis.

Pecora, P.J., Williams, J., Kessler, R.C., Downs, A.C., O'Brien, K., Hiripi, E., & Morello, S. (2003). *Assessing the effects of foster care: Early results from the Casey National Alumni Study*. Seattle, WA: Casey Family Programs.

Pecora, P.J., Kessler, R.C., Williams, J., Downs, A.C., English, D.J., White, J., & O'Brien, K. (2010). *What works in family foster care? Key components of success from the Northwest Foster Care Alumni Study*. New York and Oxford: Oxford University Press.

Pecora, P.J., Kessler, R.C., Williams, J., O'Brien, K., Downs, A.C., English, D., Hiripi, E., White, C.R., Wiggins, T., & Holmes, K. (2005). *Improving family foster care: Findings from the Northwest Foster Care Alumni Study*. Seattle, WA: Casey Family Programs. Retrieved from www.casey.org.

Pelton, L.H. (2015). The continuing role of material factors in child maltreatment and placement. *Child Abuse & Neglect, 41*, 30–39.

Pike, V. (1976). Permanent families for foster children: The Oregon Project. *Children Today, 5*, 22–25.

Pittman, K. (2002). Keeping our eyes on the prize. *Youth Today, 9*(2), 63.

Price, L.M., Chamberlain, P., Landsverk, J., & Reid, J. (2009). KEEP foster-parent training intervention: Model description and effectiveness. *Child & Family Social Work, 14*(2), 233–242.

Rivas, C., Pecora, P., DeTata, W., & Hernandez, R. (2017). *Transitioning to adulthood: Assessing life skills outcomes for Los Angeles County foster youth*. Los Angeles, CA: Department of Children and Family Services.

Roberts, D.E. (2002). *Shattered bonds: The color of child welfare*. New York: Civitas Books.

Roberts, Y.H., O'Brien, K., & Pecora, P.J. (2017). *Supporting lifelong families ensuring long-lasting permanency and well-being*. Seattle, WA: Casey Family Programs. Retrieved from www.casey.org/supporting-lifelong-families/.

Rolock, N., Pérez, A.G., White, K.R., & Fong, R. (2017). From foster care to adoption and guardianship: A 21st century challenge. *Child & Adolescent Social Work Journal*. doi:10.1007/s10560-017-0499-z.

Rubin, D.M., O'Reilly, A.L.R., Luan, X.Q., & Localio, A.R. (2007). The impact of placement stability on behavioral well-being for children in foster care. *Pediatrics, 119*(2), 336–344.

Rubin, D.M., Downes, K.J., O'Reilly, A.L.R., Mekonnen, R., Luan, X., & Localio, R. (2008). Impact of kinship care on behavioral well-being for children in out-of-home care. *Archives of Pediatric and Adolescent Medicine, 162*(6), 550–556.

Ryan, J.A., & Testa, M.F. (2005). *Child maltreatment and juvenile delinquency: Investigating the role of placement and placement instability*. Urbana-Champagn, IL: University of Illinois at Urbana-Champaign School of Social Work, Children and Family Research Center.

Ryan, P., McFadden, E.J., Rice, D., & Warren, B.L. (1988). The role of foster parents in helping young people develop emancipation skills. *Child Welfare, 67*(6), 563–572.

Salazar, A.M. (2012). Supporting college success in foster care alumni: Salient factors related to post-secondary retention. *Child Welfare, 91*(5), 139–167.

Scannapieco, M., & Hegar, R.L. (Eds) (1999). *Kinship foster care – Policy, practice, and research*. New York: Oxford University Press.

Scherr, T. (2006). Best practices in working children living in foster care. In A. Thomas & J. Grimes (Eds), *Best practices in school psychology V* (pp. 1547–1563). Bethesda, MD: National Association of School Psychologists.

Sedlak, A.J., Mettenburg, J., Basena, M., Petta, I., McPherson, K., Greene, A., and Li, S. (2010). *Fourth National Incidence Study of Child Abuse and Neglect (NIS–4): Report to Congress.* Washington, DC: U.S. Department of Health and Human Services, Administration for Children and Families. Retrieved from www.acf.hhs.gov/sites/default/files/opre/nis4_ report_congress_full_pdf_jan2010.pdf.

Sheehy, A.M., Oldham, E., Zanghi, M., Ansell, D., Correia, P., & Copeland, R. (2002). *Promising practices: Supporting transition of youth served by the foster care system.* Baltimore, MD: The Annie E. Casey Foundation.

Shyne, A., & Schroeder, A.W. (1978). *National study of social services to children and their families.* Rockville, MD: Westat.

Skemer, M., & Valentine, E.J. (2016). Striving for independence: *Two-year impact findings from the Youth Villages Transitional Living Evaluation.* New York: MDRC. Retrieved from www. mdrc.org/sites/default/files/Youth%20Villages_2016_FR.pdf.

Slack, K.S., Berger L.M., & Noyes J.L. (in press). Poverty and child maltreatment: What we know and what we still need to learn. *Children and Youth Services Review.*

Slingerland, W.H. (1919). *Child-placing in families.* New York: Russell Sage Foundation.

Stack, C. (1974). *All our kin: Strategies for survival in the Black community.* New York: Harper and Row.

Taussig, H.N., Clyman, R.B., & Landsverk, J. (2001). Children who return home from foster care: A 6-year prospective study of behavioral health outcomes in adolescence. *Pediatrics, 108*(1) 1–7. Retrieved from http://pediatrics.aappublications.org/content/108/1/e10.full.

Testa, M.F, & Shook-Slack, K. (2002). The gift of kinship foster care. *Children and Youth Services Review, 24*(1–2), 79–108.

Testa, M., Bruhn, C.M., & Helton, J. (2010). *Child welfare and child well-being: New perspectives from the National Survey of Child and Adolescent Well-Being.* New York: Oxford University Press.

The Annie E. Casey Program. (2015). *EVERY KID NEEDS A FAMILY: Giving children in the child welfare system the best chance for success.* A KIDSCOUNT policy report. Baltimore, MD: Author. Retrieved from www.AECF.org.

The Urban Institute, University of California Berkeley, & University of North Carolina at Chapel Hill. (2008). *Coming of age: Employment outcomes for youth who age out of foster care through their middle twenties.* Retrieved from http://aspe.hhs.gov/hsp/08/fosteremp/index. html (accessed April 18, 2008).

Timmer, S.G., Urquiza, A.J., Herschell, A.D., McGrath, J.M., Zebell, N.M., Porter, A.L, & Vargas, E.C. (2006). Parent–Child interaction therapy: Application of an empirically supported treatment to maltreated children in foster care. *Child Welfare, 85*(6), 919–940.

Turney, K., & Wildeman, C. (2016). Mental and physical health of children in foster care. *Pediatrics, 138*(5), e20161118.

Uliando, A., & Mellor, D. (2012). Maltreatment of children in out-of-home care: A review of associated factors and outcomes. *Children and Youth Services Review, 34*(12), 2280–2286.

U.S. Census Bureau, Current Population Survey, & Bureau (2000). *Special tabulations of the supplementary survey*. Washington, DC: Author.

U.S. Department of Health and Human Services. (2005). *National Survey of Child and Adolescent Well-Being (NSCAW) CPS sample component wave 1 data analysis report*. Retrieved from www.acf.hhs.gov/programs/opre/abuse_neglect/nscaw/reports/cps_sample/cps_report_revised_090105.pdf.

U.S. Department of Health and Human Services. (2007). *Putting positive youth development into practice: A resource guide*. Washington, DC: Author. Retrieved from https://ncfy.acf.hhs.gov/sites/default/files/PosYthDevel.pdf.

U.S. Department of Health and Human Services, Administration for Children and Families. (2008). *Evaluation of the early start to emancipation preparation tutoring program: Los Angeles County*. Washington, DC: Author.

U.S. Department of Health and Human Services, Administration for Children and Families, Administration on Children, Youth and Families, Children's Bureau. (2012). *Promoting the social and emotional well-being of children and youth receiving child welfare services*. Memorandum No. ACYF-CB-IM-12–04. Washington, DC: Author. Retrieved from www.hhs.gov/secretary/about/blogs/childhood-trauma-recover.html.

U.S. Department of Health and Human Services, Administration for Children, Youth and Families, Children's Bureau. (2013). *Recent demographic trends in foster care*. (DHHS). Washington, DC: U.S. Government Printing Office.

U.S. Department of Health and Human Services, Administration for Children and Families, Children's Bureau. (2016a). *Child welfare outcomes 2010–2013: Report to Congress*. Retrieved from www.acf.hhs.gov/cb/resource/cwo-10-13.

U.S. Department of Health and Human Services, Administration for Children and Families, Administration on Children, Youth and Families, Children's Bureau. (2016b). *The AFCARS report No. 23*. Washington, DC: Author. Retrieved from www.acf.hhs.gov/cb/resource/afcars-report-23.

U.S. Department of Health and Human Services, Administration for Children and Families, Administration on Children, Youth and Families, Children's Bureau. (2017). *Preliminary FY 2016 Estimates as of October 20, 2017. No. 24*. Washington, DC: Author. Retrieved from www.acf.hhs.gov/sites/default/files/cb/afcarsreport24.pdf.

U.S. General Accounting Office. (1999). *Foster care: Effectiveness of independent living services unknown* (GAO/HEHS-00–13). Washington, DC: USGAO.

United States General Accounting Office. (2014). *HHS needs to improve oversight of Fostering Connections Act implementation* (Report No. GAO-14–347). Retrieved from www.gao.gov/products/GAO-14-347.

United States General Accounting Office. (2015). *HHS could do more to support states' efforts to keep children in family-based care* (Report No. GAO-16–85). Retrieved from www.gao.gov/products/GAO-16-85.

Valentine, E.J., Skemer, M., & Courtney, M.E. (2015). *Becoming adults: One-year impact findings from the Youth Villages Transitional Living Evaluation.* New York: MDRC.

Wald, M. (1976). State intervention on behalf of "neglected" children: Standards for removal of children from their homes, monitoring the status of children in foster care, and termination of parental rights. *Stanford Law Review, 28,* 623, 645.

Wald, M.S. (2015). *Beyond CPS: Developing an effective system for helping children in neglectful families.* Stanford, CA: Stanford University, Stanford Law School. Retrieved from http://ssrn.com/abstract=2554074.

Warsh, R., Maluccio, A.N., & Pine, B.A. (1994). *Family reunification – A sourcebook.* Washington, DC: Child Welfare League of America.

Warsh, R., Pine, B.A., & Maluccio, A.N. (1996). *Reconnecting families – A guide to strengthening family reunification services.* Washington, DC: CWLA Press.

Weigensberg, E., Leininger, L., Stagner, M., LeBarron, S., MacIntyre, S., Chapman, R., Cornwell, D., Maher, E., Pecora, P.J., & O'Brien, K. (2018). *Superutilization of child welfare, Medicaid, and other services among those in the child welfare system.* Washington, DC and Seattle, WA: Mathematica Policy Research and Casey Family Programs.

Whittaker, J.K., del Valle, J.F., & Holmes, L. (2015). *Therapeutic residential care for children and youth: Developing evidence-based international practice.* London: Jessica Kingsley.

Wilber, S., Ryan, C., & Marksamer, J. (2006). *Best practice guidelines: Serving LGBT youth in out-of-home care.* Washington, DC: Child Welfare League of America.

Williams, J., Herrick, M., Pecora, P.J., & O'Brien, K. (2009). *Working paper No. 4: Placement history and foster care experience.* Seattle, WA: Casey Family Programs.

Wilson, D.B., & Chipungu, S.S. (1996). Introduction. Special issue on kinship care. *Child Welfare, 75,* 387–662.

Winokur, M., Holtan, A., & Batchelder, K. (2014). Kinship care for the safety, permanency and well-being of children removed from the home for maltreatment. *Campbell Collaboration, 10*(2).

Wu, Q., White, K., & Coleman, K. (2015). Effects of kinship care on behavioral problems by child age: A propensity score analysis. *Child and Youth Services Review,* 1–8.

Wulczyn, F., & Lery, B. (2007). *Racial disparity in foster care admissions.* Chicago, IL: University of Chicago, Chapin Hall.

Youth Villages. (2017). *Frequently asked questions about YVLifeSet.* Nashville, TN: Author. Retrieved from www.youthvillages.org/what-we-do/yvlifeset/yvlifeset-faqs#sthash.3i76XGIT.dpbs.

Zinn, A., DeCoursey, J., Goerge, R.M., & Courtney, M.E. (2006). A study of placement stability in Illinois. Chicago, IL: University of Chicago, Chapin Hall.

Zweibel, C., & Strand, C. (2002). *How states are helping foster care youth "age out": An assessment of state plans for use of Chafee funds.* St. Louis, MS: Jim Casey Youth Opportunities Initiative.

6

Achieving Permanency through Family Reunification, Adoption, and Guardianship

Learning Objectives

1. To understand the various dimensions of permanency planning: especially, ages of children and the availability of each form of permanence.

2. To explore policy and program design issues with respect to family reunification, adoption, and guardianship for children of different ages.

3. To recognize the trade-offs between the characteristics of each form of permanency.

4. To learn about why foster care re-entry remains a challenge and the importance of strengthening post-permanency family support.

5. To understand options for policy reform that might reduce federal support for services that do not achieve permanence in a timely way.

Introduction

What is Permanency Planning?

Permanency planning is the process of assisting the transition of children from a state in which it is unclear who their permanent legal parent(s) will be to one in which this standing is legally clarified. As a result, children obtain a safe, stable environment in which to grow up and have a nurturing caregiver who is in a lifelong supportive relationship with them. As discussed in Chapter 1, the optimal permanent placement (assuming that safety can be reasonably assured) is with birth parent(s) and then with kin. If no relatives are available to care for a child then the preference for permanency placements aligns with adoption as the next priority, with guardianship (which only calls for a commitment until the age of majority) and, then, independent living. If relatives will only accept the child in a guardianship status, rather than adoption, this is often considered sufficient to preclude placement of children into adoption with non-kin because the connection to the birth family is considered to have the likelihood of developing other supportive life-time ties (although this is a matter of discretion affected by the views of the child welfare agency and the courts). This chapter will address the major ways that children placed in out-of-home care achieve legal permanency, including various service strategies such as Family Group Conferencing, which is highlighted below but discussed in more detail in Chapter 10.

Box 6.1 Family Group Conferencing as a Permanency Strategy

In most jurisdictions, permanency planning begins when a child needs to be placed into foster care. CW agencies generally recognize that the first hours and days of placement often have a significant long-term impact upon the ultimate course of permanency. This is especially true because many judges are reluctant to move children who have been placed satisfactorily with foster parents who are willing to adopt them, even if other family resources emerge. CW agencies are, therefore, increasingly inclined to begin casework services by engaging family members through services like family group decision making (FGDM, also referred to as family involvement meetings) from the very outset of a case in order to make the best possible first placement (Xu, Ahn, & Bright, 2017). Although the overall impact of family group decision making on permanency outcomes is not unequivocally clear (Dijkstra et al., 2016), the approach is highly regarded because it increases children's and families' relational power, self-responsibilities, and social capital, which improve children's removal, placement, and permanency decisions and promote children's long-term well-being (Berzin, Thomas, & Cohen, 2007). The variation in results of studies of FGDM on outcomes (including no apparent benefit) is very possibly due to great variation in ways that the approach is implemented. Best practice may involve having specialists facilitating the meetings rather than asking every CW worker to organize their own – a condition relatively rarely met in practice (Xu, Ahn, & Bright, 2017).

Concurrent Planning May Be Used to Support Permanency Planning

A continuing innovation in child and family welfare is concurrent planning; that is, working "towards family reunification while, at the same time, developing an alternative permanent plan" (Katz, 1999, p. 72). The concurrent planning model was specifically designed for very young children who were drifting in foster care because of their family's continuing challenges and difficulty achieving safety and stability. As explained by Katz (1999, p. 72), one of its originators, the model "addresses this difficult-to-treat family constellation by combining vigorous family outreach, expedited timelines, and potentially permanent family foster care placements to improve the odds of timely permanency for very young children."

At its best, concurrent planning represents team decision making involving professionals, as well as the child, the child's caregivers, birth parents, and extended family members. Its central purpose is accomplished through comprehensive assessment of the parent–child relationship, parental functioning and support systems; front loading of services in such areas as financial assistance, parenting skills, health and mental health, substance abuse, and domestic violence; and frequent staffing, including child, family, caregivers, and service providers.

Katz (1999) delineates strategies for implementing this model, particularly by completing an early assessment of the family's likelihood of being reunited; establishing with the family clear timelines for timely permanency; vigorously promoting frequent parental visiting; and using written agreements. Katz also calls attention to a number of pitfalls in implementation, including failing to consider cultural differences; equating concurrent planning with adoption while minimizing reunification efforts; designing case plans that are not family centered; providing insufficient training to social workers, foster parents, and family members; and not collaborating adequately with other community agencies.

There have been calls for research to better assess the results, and unintended consequences, of this casework approach (D'Andrade, Frame, & Duerr-Berrick, 2006). Handling conflicting loyalties in children, increased tensions between workers and birth parents, scarcity of foster adoption homes, and other challenges must be addressed if concurrent planning is to achieve its goals (D'Andrade, Frame, & Duerr-Berrick, 2006). Practice that has high fidelity to the concurrent planning model is also important. An assessment which included observation and statistical analysis shows that concurrent planning benefits were, indeed, associated with desired outcomes; for example, discussion of voluntary relinquishment options with parents were associated with adoption as an outcome and the full disclosure of the risk that the agency will move for adoption if parents do not comply with the treatment plan resulted in a lower rate of reunification (D'Andrade, 2009). Although this appears to be supportive of the concurrent planning model, the timing of these frank discussions is critical so that they do not imply that one particular path (e.g., adoption or reunification) is destined to be taken and, thereby, undermine the motivation of the parents. Discussions with parents need to be carefully timed and social workers need to engage in "full disclosure" or clearly explain that all options for resolving the case are on the table (including reunification, placement with relative or kin, adoption, or customary adoption with a tribal member) (D'Andrade, Frame, & Duerr-Berrick, 2006).

One of the other significant changes that has resulted from the broad acceptance of the concurrent planning concept is that virtually every foster family is now also considered a resource for adoption. This is now built into home studies; many states are now using home studies like SAFE (Structured Analysis of Family Environments) for all foster and adoptive parents, recognizing that their children need families who can be cleared for adoption should reunification fail (Crea et al., 2009). Although not universally accepted language, many states are now calling foster and adoptive parents "resource families" because they view their greatest value to be their availability to assist with permanency planning rather than because they are going to commit to foster care or to adoption. The era when foster families were told not to get attached to a child because they would not be considered appropriate for adoption because waiting adoptive parents were preferable appears to have finally come to a close.

Intensive Family Preservations Services as a Permanency Strategy

Intensive services can help families reunify or find another permanency option. For example, Fraser and colleagues (1996) completed one of the few experimental evaluations of a state program established to reunify children in foster care with their biological families. These researchers randomly assigned the cases of foster children to: (1) a control group of 53 children whose families received routine agency services as a component of an overall foster care plan, and (2) an experimental group of 57 children whose families received intensive reunification services, with the goal of family preservation. The experimental group receiving intensive services were most likely to be reunited successfully with their families than those in the control group receiving routine services. These differences proved to be statistically significant at the conclusion of treatment as well as during the follow-up period. In particular, relatively brief but intensive, in-home, family-based services positively affected reunification rates and outcomes. Such services involved building strong worker alliances with family members, providing skills training to parents, and meeting the concrete needs of the children and other family members. The findings suggested that reunification is promoted through in-vivo family strengthening. After six years, the experimental group required less supervision time, lived at home for longer, and were in less restrictive placements than those in the control group (Walton, 1998).

Family Finding as a Permanency Support Strategy

Another relatively recent breakthrough receiving much attention is a set of techniques developed to locate relatives of children who are at risk of being placed in foster care or children who are already in care. *Family Finders* is an intensive relative search model with the ultimate goals of achieving permanency and supporting enduring family connections for children in the foster care system. *Family Finders* was conceived by Kevin Campbell in 1999 and is modeled after family-tracing techniques used by agencies such as the Red Cross to reunite families separated by international conflicts and natural catastrophes (see www.nysccc.org/Conferences/2006Conf/Hndout2006.htm). Through the *Family Finders* program, foster care workers are trained to use various search tools including genealogical archives and commercial Internet-based services to find family members of children placed in out-of-home care settings. Since Campbell began training foster care workers in 2000, this model has spread throughout the country and is nationally and internationally recognized as a promising approach for finding permanent homes and family connections for many youth in the foster care system for who traditional attempts at finding permanent placements had failed. The *Family Finders* model is comprised of six stages, which are summarized in Table 6.1.

Table 6.1 Family Finders Model

Stage	Summary
1) Discovery	Identify at least 40 family members for the child or youth
2) Engagement	Involve and provide information to individuals who know the child best, including family and other important connections
3) Planning	Set the stage for a successful future for the child with participation of family members and other important connections
4) Decision Making	Specify the legal and emotional permanency plan while accounting for the child's safety and well-being
5) Evaluation	Assess the permanency plan
6) Follow-up Supports	Ensure that the child and family can secure needed informal and formal supports necessary to maintaining the plan

For more information see www.familyfinding.org/ and www.childtrends.org/research/research-by-topic/evaluating-family-finding/.

Data collected through non-experimental evaluations, as well as anecdotal information, have provided evidence that the *Family Finders* model is successful in making family connections and finding permanent placements for children in the foster care system. However, *Family Finders* has yet to undergo a rigorous evaluation using an experimental design. Given the success of this program and the extent to which the model is currently being replicated on a national scale, experimental evaluations such as the study being conducted by Child Trends are critical for determining the efficacy and effectiveness of the model (www.nationalservice.gov/impact-our-nation/evidence-exchange).

Permanency Roundtables as a Permanency Support Strategy

Permanency Roundtables (PRTs) are structured professional case consultations designed to expedite legal permanency (reunification, adoption, or guardianship) for youth in care through innovative thinking, the application of best practices, and the "busting" of systemic barriers. While the goal of PRTs is to expedite legal permanency, the roundtable process can produce additional outcomes, including the following:

1. increasing *staff competencies* (attitudes, knowledge, skills) related to expediting permanency;

2. assessing *training needs* related to competences related to expediting permanency;

3. strengthening *local capacity to sustain* the process;

4. building capacity to *spread the process geographically*;

5. gathering data to *address systemic and cross-systems barriers* to permanency (policies/protocols/procedures).

Many youth in care could likely benefit from the PRT process. Jurisdictions have completed roundtables on the following target populations:

- Youth with a permanency goal of OPPLA/APPLA (other planned permanent living arrangement/another planned permanent living arrangement) (see www.casey.org/permanency-roundtables/).

- Youth who will "age out" within the next year.

- All youth who have been in care for more than 24 months.

- The "longest waiting" youth who have spent the most time in care.

- Youth whose cases are identified by their caseworkers as being "most difficult" or "stuck."

A PRT team is formed to do the review and consists of a facilitator, one or two clinical consultants skilled in permanency planning, the case manager, and the supervisor. The process involves reviewing the child's case summary (half an hour), conducting a PRT focused primarily on practice and values (two hours), and then holding monthly follow-ups to monitor progress on plan implementation and to provide coaching (half an hour per case). For example, nearly 500 youth went through the initial PRT process in Georgia in 2009. Just over half were male (57%) and over nine in ten (92%) were African American. At the start of the roundtables, the median age was 13, and the median length of stay in foster care was 52 months. Two years after their roundtable, 50 percent of the nearly 500 children had achieved legal permanency (Davis et al., 2013). Some states have modified the PRT process by conducting a second PRT meeting to include youth and families.

Rapid Permanency Reviews as a Permanency Support Strategy

Rapid Permanency Reviews (RPRs) involve a quick and intensive review of a case's movement through a child welfare agency and the court. The purpose is to simultaneously identify and mitigate case-level and system-level bottlenecks and barriers to legal permanency. The RPR strategy is focused on completing processes and eliminating procedural barriers to legal permanency. The RPR process is conducted by a two-person review team, case manager, supervisor, and next-level manager intended to quickly identify and address bottlenecks, system, and/or court barriers in the process toward legal permanency. The team conducts the meeting using a review tool to focus on completion of milestones and amelioration of system-level bottlenecks to achieving legal permanency (half an hour). Then a "Cadence of Accountability" review meeting is held at case, executive, and system levels monthly to follow up on action steps from meetings (one hour each).

This process is for children in care who are close to achieving legal permanency, defined as children with goals of adoption, guardianship, or who live with relatives who have been in their current family-based placement one year or longer; children with an adoption goal who have had parental rights terminated and are in a family-based placement of any length; and children with a reunification goal who are currently on a trial home visit. While RPR is designed for children closest to permanency, some children who appear close to permanency according to their descriptive data may actually not be close to permanency in real life for a variety of reasons. These children may be better suited for a more intensive review process such as PRTs. A latent class analysis is one avenue used to identify those children not close to permanency to determine the underlying cluster of characteristics they possess to determine the best approaches to help them achieve permanency. This approach has been used in Houston, New York City, Sacramento, and other communities – and while the initial results are positive, more rigorous evaluation is needed (Casey Family Programs, 2016).

Family Reunification

Family reunification is typically viewed as the most desired outcome of out-of-home placement of children and youths. Successful family reunification, however, requires a full range of efforts that are supported by well-grounded theory and that respond carefully to the needs of children and their families. This section offers a definition of reunification; outlines program design principles; reviews evaluative research; and examines the increasing use of formal and informal kinship care.

The theory, policy, and practice of family reunification have traditionally been based on the premise that children and youth in out-of-home care need to be either returned to their families of origin or placed in another permanent setting. We challenge this binary premise here, even though this either-or orientation is supported by the legal framework of federal laws that have been reviewed in previous chapters. In particular, termination of parental rights is expected to be sought when families have been unable to care for children in their own homes, even though there may be a potentially beneficial relationship between parents and children and even when no other permanent family has been, or was likely to be, found.

There are, however, many parents who love their children and want a relationship with them, but who are unable to be full-time caregivers. The children may also want a relationship with their biological parents even though they cannot live safely with them (Chapman, Wall, & Barth, 2004). The CW services response to these parents has often been to test them beyond their limits by returning their children home without significant after-care services or to terminate their parental rights and forever sever their family bonds. Such an either-or orientation is too simplistic and not always in the best interests of the child or the families involved in foster care. In its place, a family reunification orientation is needed that embodies a time-limited but flexible approach to working with children in out-of-home care and their families – an approach that recognizes and meets children's and families' individual needs. This rethinking of family reunification has led to the development of the following expanded definition:

> Family reunification is the planned process of safely reconnecting children in out-of-home care with their families by means of a variety of services and supports to

the children, their families, and their foster parents or other service providers. *It aims to help each child and family to achieve and maintain, at any given time, their optimal level of reconnection – from full re-entry of the child into the family system to other forms of contact, such as visiting, calling, or corresponding, that affirm the child's membership in the family, and to contact with the family even following termination of parental rights and responsibilities.*

(Modified from Maluccio, Warsh, & Pine, 1993)

Such a view of family reunification suggests a flexible approach to preserving family bonds by responding to each child's and family's individual qualities and needs. In particular, it calls for fully respecting human diversity, especially culture, race, and ethnicity, and involving the family and its kin through such approaches as family group decision making and the provision of "wrap-around" services, as considered in later chapters.

It should, of course, be acknowledged that there are situations in which children must be protected through temporary, or even permanent, separation from their parents and that families that adopt or become guardians must also be able to inform the nature and circumstances of a child's contact with biological family members. Since the passage of ASFA, every state must have legally mandated guidelines that identify such situations, including those where a child has previously died due to abuse or neglect; cases involving sexual abuse when the abuser continues to reside in the child's home; and situations in which parents refuse to recognize the need for services, such as substance abuse treatment, despite repeated efforts on the part of agencies (Berrick et al., 2008). Even in these extreme cases, however, attention paid to preserving as much contact with the child's family as possible may help support the child's well-being. In short, reunification can occur in a variety of ways – and to differing degrees – beyond physical reconnection.

Reunification Practice Principles and Strategies

Redefining family reunification leads to a number of principles and guidelines for family reunification policies, programs, practices, and training (Warsh, Maluccio, & Pine, 1994, pp. 3–4). As a form of preserving families, reunification embodies: (1) a conviction about the role of the birth family as the preferred child-rearing unit, if at all possible; (2) recognition of the potential of most families to care for their children if properly assisted; (3) awareness of the impact of separation and loss upon children and parents; and (4) ongoing involvement, as appropriate, of any and all members of the child's family. This also includes members of the extended family or others who, while not legally related, are considered by the child and themselves to be "family."

A commitment to early and consistent contact between the child and family is an essential ingredient in preparing for and maintaining a successful reunification. This begins with a family involvement meeting (perhaps through the family group decision-making approach) as early as possible in the placement. Child–family contact can serve as a laboratory in which both parties work on the problems that may have contributed to the need for placement and it can serve as a venue for learning new ways to be together again safely. Finally, family reunification services should be offered for as long as they are needed to maintain the reconnection of a child with the family. For many families, intensive family reunification services may need to be followed by less intensive services. For a few families, some level of service may be necessary until the child is ready for independent living.

The reunification of children and their families is more likely to be successful when an agency articulates its mission through a comprehensive framework of policies, in line with the principles and guidelines delineated above. In addition, effective reunification programs involve the commitment of agency administrators to hiring social workers with a range of family reunification competences, empowering them through appropriate decision-making authority and opportunities to further develop their skills, facilitating all aspects of service delivery, and continually seeking new directions and pursuing program improvements.

An agency context that supports family reunification practice needs to address numerous aspects in relation to agency policy, direct practice with children and families, collaboration with other systems, and staff development. As considered in detail elsewhere (Kerman, Maluccio, & Freundlich, 2009; Pine, Spath, & Gosteli, 2005; Warsh, Pine, & Maluccio, 1996, pp. 71–180), such a supportive context includes agency policies that, among other aspects, provide adequate resources for supporting practitioners in their outreach to children and families; promote collaboration with other community systems, including other child and family agencies, judicial and legal personnel, state and local legislators, and schools of social work; and offer ongoing staff development programs focusing on family reunification and directed not only to its workers but also to other service providers and community representatives. We need to consider, in particular, how to provide effective services for vulnerable families such as those coming to the attention of CW agencies, including parents who are very likely to be battling co-morbid conditions such as substance abuse and poverty or housing difficulties and mental health problems (Committee on Supporting the Parents of Young Children; Board on Children, Youth, and Families; Division of Behavioral and Social Sciences and Education; National Academies of Sciences, Engineering, and Medicine, 2016; Wald, 2015).

There is also growing concern about post-permanency stability for children discharged from foster care to adoption or legal guardianship (Rolock et al., 2017). Indeed, the Children's Bureau entered into a significant project in late 2017, with the Research Triangle Institute in the lead, to find new ways to count and understand post-permanency implementation (Research Triangle Institute, 2017). After a long hiatus in trying to develop adoption preservation services, new efforts to improve post-permanency outcomes are emerging (Liao & Testa, 2016; Roberts et al., 2017).

Kinship Foster Care

Kinship foster care falls between reunification and other permanent outcomes. One long-standing critique of paying for kinship foster care is that relatives get more help with parenting of children than do the children's own parents (given that there is no post-reunification payment). This creates unfairness and a potential bias toward placing children with kin rather than leaving them at home. (The hope is, of course, that the courts would not disrupt family life and remove the child from parents unless there were significant safety concerns.) Indeed, as discussed in Chapter 5, the history of kinship care has been replete with policy variations that try to address these concerns, some of which remain unresolved. For example, family members providing kinship care may still receive a significantly lower payment than other foster families, such as only a TANF payment for taking care of a single child.

The amount of a kinship care payment does appear to be linked to the relative's ability to maintain a stable living arrangement for the child (Pac, 2017). An exceptionally rigorous study that drew upon the detailed data collection of NSCAW II shows that just a 1 percent increase in the stipend is associated with a 27 percent decrease in the likelihood of disruption of the placement. Further, when the kinship family says that the payment is adequate, the risk of disruption decreases by 45 percent. Given our understanding that foster care payments vary greatly and are often not even remotely adequate to meet the actual costs of caring for a child (Ahn et al., 2018), this is a highly salient policy problem.

Guardianship

One of the most pressing goals of public CW services is to ensure that children achieve permanency rapidly and safely; in other words, be permanently placed with a safe and loving family. For the majority of children, reunification with their parents is the primary goal. However, when reunification is determined to be unsafe or not in a child's best interest, adoption and guardianship are the primary alternatives (U.S. Department of Health and Human Services, 2016a, 2016b).

Relative care is a centuries-old practice, where "children lacking parental care became members of the household of other relatives, if such there were, who reared them to adulthood" (Slingerland, 1919, p. 27) Today, children from every culture continue to be raised by relatives when their parents are unable to meet their responsibilities. For example, in our chapter on International Innovations, we describe the extensive use of long-term relative care in Spain.

In the U.S., relative care has become a preferred option for many CW systems and is the preference under federal law, when children are placed into foster care because they cannot safely remain with their parents (Children's Defense Fund, Child Trends, American Bar Association Center on Children and the Law, Casey Family Programs, Child Focus, & Generations United, 2012; Generations United, 2016). In fact, 10 percent of the approximately 250,000 children exiting foster care in 2016 were released to permanent care with a relative guardian. Similarly, exit to guardianship was a case plan goal for 3 percent of all children in care in 2016. For another 3 percent, the goal was identified as "live with other relative(s)"; however, it should be noted that these children and their caregivers were not receiving the legal or financial benefits of guardianship (U.S. DHHS, 2017). Just as important, for every child in the foster care system placed with relatives, another 20 children are being raised by grandparents or other relatives outside of formal foster care systems (Generations United, 2016).

Several studies and systematic reviews have evaluated permanency outcomes for children who exit from kinship placements, as well as subsidized guardianships (Howard et al., 2006; Koh, 2010). These studies show a variety of outcomes across the states, though they tend to focus on limited numbers of jurisdictions (one and five states) rather than national data. Despite these limits, many of these studies found that children in kinship care had fewer placement changes (Winokur et al., 2014). Further, rates of re-entry into foster care may be even lower when children are placed with legal guardians. For example, in a systematic scoping review, Bell and Romano (2015) found that across studies, children in kinship care experienced greater permanency in terms of lower rates of re-entry to foster care, greater placement stability, and more guardianship placements in comparison to children living with foster families (Bell & Romano, 2015). These findings must be squared, nonetheless, with indications that relatives provide care for less difficult and younger children (Winokur, Holtan, & Batchelder, 2014). There have also been consistent findings that call for continuing to understand how to best match family caregivers with supportive services (Koh & Testa, 2011). In addition, findings for child safety outcomes have been mixed (Bell & Romano, 2015). Nevertheless, despite these challenges, the research on kinship care and guardianship squares relatively well with the social commitment to and policy value of reinforcing family ties (Bell & Romano, 2017).

Federal Guardianship Policy

In 2008, Congress passed the *Fostering Connections to Success and Increasing Adoptions Act or "Fostering Connections Act."* An important purpose of the Act was to incentivize the use of relative guardianships to help children in foster care achieve permanency. The Act established the Title IV-E Guardianship Assistance Program (GAP), which allows federal funds to be used as subsidies for eligible children and relative guardians who are committed to caring permanently for their children. The *Fostering Connections Act* allows states to pay relative guardians a subsidy up to the same rate as the state's monthly foster care subsidy, but no more than this.

The Act includes a number of important provisions that are intended to shape state-subsidized guardianship policies. In order to use federal IV-E funds to support kinship guardianship, the Act requires that:

- The potential guardian be a relative of the child (although the law does not define "relative").

- The guardian has a strong commitment to caring permanently for the child and has cared for the child in a licensed foster care home for at least six consecutive months.

- The guardian be licensed as a foster parent and pass criminal record and child abuse registry checks.

- The child meets current eligibility for Title IV-E funds.

- A child over the age of 14 be consulted about the guardianship.

- Reunification and adoption must be ruled out as appropriate permanency options for the child.

- The state match federal funds with state dollars (see 42 U.S.C. §§ 671(a)(20)(C) & 673(d); Fostering Connections to Success and Increasing Adoptions Act of 2008 § 101(b)-(c)).

If states are not able to meet these requirements, they may – at their discretion – fund a guardianship program with their own funds. Although the Act allows states to pay relative guardians up to the same rate as the state's foster care subsidy, the Act does not allow states to pay relative caregivers a rate greater than the foster care subsidy.

Variance in Guardianship Policies and Legal Frameworks

A comprehensive review of guardianship law and policy was conducted in 2016 (Vesneski et al., 2017). This study found a number of areas where states have used their discretion to create different legal frameworks to support guardianships. For example, some states have sought to make guardianship appealing to families by setting relatively expansive eligibility criteria, at least when compared to those identified in the Fostering Connections Act. Specifically, a number of states have extended the maximum age for receiving a subsidy and they enable some families to have financial and social service supports beyond monthly subsidy payments. In addition, states vary in how they address parental rights after guardianship. One of the major appeals of guardianship to relatives is that it explicitly does not require the termination of parental rights. Nevertheless, states have discretion in how they shape the nature of these rights. This study indicates variation among the states on issues like parental visitation, child support, and parents' ability to set aside the guardianship at a later date. Finally, states differ in the use of fictive kin. Many – but not all – allow the use of fictive kin to serve as guardians. This includes family friends, foster parents, and other allies of the child (Killos et al., 2018).

Despite the apparent benefits to children and families involved in the CW system, some states do not have a Title IV-E Guardianship Assistance Program. One national study found four reasons why states made this policy choice: (1) they believed that guardians and children in the state will not meet Title IV-E eligibility criteria due to licensure and other requirements; (2) there was a lack of local legislative support for the program (evidenced by no funding or other resources to implement the program); (3) the belief that guardianship is not considered a permanent option for children; and (4) a preference for using state-funded guardianship because it is believed to be more flexible (Killos et al., 2018).

State Innovations and Strategies to Maximize the Effectiveness of Guardianship Assistance Programs

As researched by Generations United and Casey Family Programs (e.g., Generations United et al., 2016; Killos et al., 2018), six potential strategies for maximizing the effectiveness of any state guardianship program emerge from the research:

1. Build a community of support so that the public CW agency can develop strong relationships and referral processes with organizations that provide services to guardians and their children.

2. Educate state legislators, judges, parents, guardians, CW staff, practitioners, and leaders on the benefits of guardianship and the allowance of fictive kin to serve as guardians.

3. Enact standards for waiving non-safety-related licensure requirements. (In general, state CW agencies determine licensure regulations and not the federal government.)

4. Set guardianship subsidy rates to be equal to foster care and adoption rates.

5. Create concise and colorful non-technical brochures with brief checklists to help relatives and fictive kin understand the differences between legal guardianship, adoption, and foster care.

6. Use both federal Title IV-E GAP funds and state funds as needed to support guardians and children.

Adoption

Adoption as a Key Form of Legal Permanence

Children deserve willing and able families to love them, protect them, and to help them grow in a healthy manner. In previous chapters, we described community supports and services to help parents fulfill their child-rearing responsibilities. But when those efforts are not successful and serious threats to a child's physical safety or emotional well-being remain, children are placed in out-of-home care. While children are increasingly placed with relatives, tribal clan members, or fictive kin, those placements and non-relative foster care placements are often not permanent; and, while guardianship is one form of legal permanence, guardianship agreements expire when children reach the age of majority. Thus, adoption is often recommended when family reunification is not possible. This section describes the various forms of adoption, who is adopted, the outcomes of this service, current policy issues, and program design challenges surrounding adoption.

The use of adoption varies widely across countries. Although national and international adoption statistics are imprecise, Americans almost certainly adopt more children than all other countries combined. Since the early part of this century, the largest group of children adopted in the U.S. has come from foster care. Adoption is widely accepted in the United States and has lost much of the stigma that once shadowed it. Ninety-five percent of children under 18 live with one or two biological parents, but children may also live with adoptive parents or step-parents (see Table C9, "Children by Presence and Type of Parent(s), Race, and Hispanic Origin: 2012," retrieved from www.census.gov/hhes/families/files/cps2012/tabC9-all.xls).

According to the 2010 Census, more than 2 million U.S. children are adopted, comprising 2.3 percent of the total child population in the country (Kreider & Lofquist, 2014). The percentage of adopted children in families varies considerably at the state and local level with census data showing the percentages ranging from 2.0 percent in California, New Jersey, and Texas to 4.2 percent in Alaska (Kreider & Lofquist, 2014).

Adoption creates a legal family for children when the birth family is unable or unwilling to parent. Yet, adoption is not only a program for children. Adoption creates new families, expands existing families, and engages adoptive parents in the priceless costs and benefits of parenting. Birth parents who voluntarily place their child with adoptive parents may also benefit from adoption because it frees them from the parenting role, which they judge themselves unready to assume. Those who involuntarily relinquish children may experience relief as well as loss (Fessler, 2006). Adoption also offers birth parents the hope for a better life for their child. At its best, adoption meets the hopes of the child, the adoptive parents, and the birth parents. American adoption law and practice have developed to address the needs of this adoption triangle.

Communities also have an interest in the policies and practices of adoption. The future of our communities and society depends on our children, and their future requires an adequate family life. Many communities within our society, especially Native American tribes, ethnic communities, and other self-defined communities such as foster parents and gay men and lesbians, are asserting their right to adopt or to have first claim on children available for adoption. Because adoption occurs at the intersection of love and law, it evokes a powerful response from these communities. Adoption is a social and legal institution that reflects the status, interests, and moral views of nearly every social entity.

History of American Adoption

Early on in U.S. history children were more likely to be indentured than to be adopted. The end of indentured servitude was followed by the growth of orphanages; and individual states first began to legislate and regulate adoption practices at that time (Whitmore, 1876). Regulations emerged to protect birth parents' rights to give or withhold permission for the child's adoption, adopting parents' rights not to have their child reclaimed, and children's rights to be cared for by suitable adopting parents. By 1929, every state had adoption statutes. Statutes varied on several accounts, but all reflected concern that adoption promoted the welfare of the child. The first regulations required social investigations of prospective adoptive parents and trial placement periods in prospective adoptive homes (Heisterman, 1935). A few states also required home visits by agents of the state CW department, the precursor to today's home study, although the rationale for the visits was rarely clarified (a legacy with influence today in the home-approval process).

The nation's involvement in adoption in the middle part of this century was primarily through placement of infants by young unmarried women who were often not so voluntarily having their newborns placed with decidedly middle-class married couples. Adoption was firmly controlled by private and, then, public agencies that made the arrangements and screened and chose the parents. The dominance of this form of adoption began to wane with the passage of *Roe v. Wade* in 1974, although infant adoptions of a typically more open and voluntary form continue. Adoption of older children began to re-emerge after World War II. In 1949 the Children's Home Society began a "new type of child care program in North Carolina to provide ways and means of placing older children in institutions, in family homes for adoption" (Weeks, 1953, p. i). This effort was partly in response to waiting lists to place children in orphanages. Today, all American orphanages are closed or converted to residential treatment care, and foster care is the typical setting for older children awaiting adoption.

Types of Adoption

Overview. Adoption occurs through a variety of means involving different types of agencies and auspices, each with unique procedures and requirements. Taken together, approximately 119,000 children were adopted in 1990 (Flango & Flango, 1993). This number increased slightly to 127,000 children in 2000 and 2001 (Flango & Caskey, 2005), and with 133,737 adoptions in 2007. By 2014 adoptions had dipped to 110,373 (41,023 related adoptions and 69,350 unrelated adoptions) (Jones & Placek, 2017). The year 2007 is likely to have been the peak of adoption's growth, although more recent data are not readily available. In 2014, the largest number of unrelated domestic adoptions was handled by public agencies (47,094), and the rest were handled by private agencies (16,312) or were independent adoptions handled by private individuals, usually attorneys (5,944). In 2014, infants comprised about a quarter (18,329 or 26.5 percent) of unrelated domestic adoptions, and special needs children (some may have been infants) comprised almost nine-tenths (61,341 or 88.5 percent) of unrelated domestic adoptions (Jones & Placek, 2017). Generally, adoptions are grouped into five categories, which are described in the next sections.

Step-parent adoptions. Step-parent adoptions refer to the adoption of children by the spouse of a parent. Step-parent adoptions differ from other adoptions because the adoption involves a child who is already legally in the family. In most states, step-parent adoptions are about twice as common as non-step-parent adoptions. Step-parent adoptions are typically administered separately from non-step-parent adoptions and, because of their impact upon the distribution of family property, are often overseen in superior court or probate court rather than in a juvenile court (which typically hears CW cases). Approximately half a million children are adopted by step-parents but note that the U.S. Census Bureau cannot distinguish children adopted by their step-parents (Kreider & Lofquist, 2014, p. 1).

Independent adoptions. Independent adoptions occur when parents place children directly with adoptive families of their choice without an agency serving as an intermediary.

Intermediaries are most often counselors or attorneys. In the 1950s, agency adoptions and independent adoptions were about equal in number and primarily involved infants. Independent adoptions held steady at about 20 percent of all adoptions in the 1960s and 1970s (Meezan, Katz, & Russo, 1978) but have increased to nearly one-third (National Committee for Adoption, 1989). Currently, there were an estimated 16,000 independent adoptions in 2014 (Jones & Placek, 2017). As of 2017, only five states do not permit independent adoption (Colorado, Connecticut, Delaware, Massachusetts, and North Dakota), although they do offer a form of direct adoption via agencies which is close to independent adoption (Adoption101.com, 2017).

Agency or relinquishment adoptions. Agency or relinquishment adoptions are those that follow the voluntary or involuntary legal severance of parental rights to the child and are overseen by a public or private agency providing foster care and adoption. The intent of the Adoption Assistance and Child Welfare Act of 1980 and of the Adoption and Safe Families Act of 1997 was to increase the number of relinquishment adoptions. This has occurred. Although good national data have only recently emerged, data from AFCARS show a doubling of the number of children adopted from foster care from approximately 25,693 in 1995 to a high of 57,200 in 2009, and 56,507 in 2016 – the highest number since 2010 (U.S. DHHS, 2017). The growth in adoptions of children from foster care has been dramatic. The increase from the baseline years of 1995 to 1998 to 2005 was 69 percent. This growth appears to have been leveling off since about 2002 as fewer children enter foster care, more remain with relatives, and more states begin to support kinship guardianships in addition to adoption. This may be an important respite for adoption services, as it will allow adoption agencies to focus on the quality of adoptions done and allow for a greater focus on the needs of the more than 350,000 children who have been adopted in recent years, and are still being raised by their parents (post-permanency services).

Intercountry adoptions. Intercountry adoptions involve the adoption of foreign-born children by adoptive families. In the United States, intercountry adoptions are a small but significant proportion of adoptions. Federal law requires a satisfactory home study. Private adoption agencies assist families by conducting family assessments for Latin American, Pacific Rim, or Eastern European adoptions. In addition, children who are adopted must clearly be orphans. These adoptions raise a number of policy issues such as proper safeguarding of birth parent rights, cultural genocide, and resolving citizenship for the child. The nature and use of international adoptions merit careful review and analysis. More than 9,000 foreign-born children were adopted in the United States in 1991 (Immigration and Naturalization Service, 1991), growing to nearly 18,000 in 2000, increasing from approximately 5 percent of all adoptive placements to 15 percent (Flango & Caskey, 2005).

Recent trends, however, indicate a substantial decrease in the number of adoptions. According to the U.S. State Department, there were 5,370 international adoptions in 2016 – down notably from 2004 when the number peaked at nearly 23,000 (U.S. Department of State, 2016). Children adopted internationally most frequently were born in China, Ethiopia, Russia, South Korea, and Ukraine (U.S. Department of State, 2017). In 2014, there were a total of 5,987 unrelated intercountry adoptions. Intercountry adoptions comprised 7.9 percent of total unrelated adoptions in 2014, down from 20.3 percent since 2007 (Jones & Placek, 2017). Over the years, adoptions from Russia and China have decreased owing to growing concerns about the safety of children adopted into the U.S. and rejection of the notion that these countries are unable to care for their own children.

Special needs adoptions. Federal law describes special needs adoption as indicating that a child in foster care cannot or should not be returned to the home of his or her birth parents; and that the child has a specific factor or condition (such as ethnic background; age; membership in a minority or sibling group; or the presence of factors such as medical conditions or physical, mental, or emotional handicaps) which make it reasonable to conclude that the child cannot be placed with adoptive parents without providing adoption assistance or medical assistance. In addition, the state must find that a reasonable but unsuccessful effort has been made to place a child with appropriate adoptive parents without providing adoption or medical assistance. This latter requirement can be, and often is, waived if it would be against the best interests of the child. State regulations vary widely in their interpretations of the Adoption and Safe Families Act but generally identify special needs adoptions as involving the adoption of children age 3 or older, ethnic children, handicapped children, emotionally or intellectually impaired children, or sibling groups of three or more. Almost all (88%) of the children adopted from foster care are judged to be special needs: the proportion of these children ranged from 16 percent (CT) to 100 percent (SC) in FY 2001 (Dalberth, Gibbs, & Berkman, 2005).

Between 1982 and 1986, the number of special-needs adoptions showed little or no growth (National Committee for Adoption, 1989), but the foster care population grew by 7 percent (Tatara, 1994). In contrast, by 2000, the growth of the foster care population was flat and adoptions were growing. Special needs adoption of foster children accounted for about 10 percent of all exits from foster care in the early to mid-1980s (Barth & Berry, 1988), and in 2015 the ratio was 22 percent. In 2016, the AFCARS data show that 56,507 children left care by adoption in 2016 and 250,248 left in all, so the ratio would be 23 percent (U.S. DHHS, 2016b). Basically, virtually all (92%) foster care adoptions are special needs adoptions – typically indicated by whether or not they receive a subsidy (see www.acf.hhs.gov/sites/default/files/cb/afcarsreport23.pdf).

Infant and Older Child Adoptions

Adoptions may also be classified across types as either infant or older child adoptions. In 2016, across the United States, 56 percent of children adopted through the CW system were infants to 5 years old at the time of adoption with a median age for all adoptees of 5.2 years (U.S. DHHS, 2018). Infant adoptions (whether private, independent, or intercountry) are popular but somewhat controversial programs because they are sometimes perceived as principally for parents rather than for children and often provide more privileged parents with the babies of mothers from marginalized communities. Infant adoptions are perceived as requiring little social commitment on the part of parents; yet adoptive parents do provide a vital service to newborns and their parents when reunification is simply not possible.

In contrast, older child adoptions – of abused, neglected, or abandoned children who cannot go home – are considered children's programs because the decision to place a child with a family is to address the child's welfare most and because parents' needs are secondary. The pathway for older child adoption is summarized in Table 6.2.

The Child Welfare League of America's *Standards for Adoption Services* (CWLA, 1998) asserts that adoption is a means of finding families for children, not finding children for families. Yet, this dualistic appraisal of adoptions is somewhat unfortunate and makes it all too easy to ignore the multiple needs of everyone involved in an adoption, including the needs of the child or infant, the needs of the parents, and the needs of consenting parents or abandoned children residing in a range of countries and communities. The future of improved adoption services rests on renewed attention to meeting the needs of all these parties to the adoption.

Use of Adoption by Various Countries

Countries vary in their use of adoption as a form of legal permanence for children. In-country adoptions, including adoptions from foster care, are rare in European jurisdictions other than the four United Kingdom nations (personal communication, June Thoburn, December 3, 2016). For example, in Norway in 2012/2013, 36 children (0.03 per 10,000) were adopted from the CW system as compared to 4,010 children (3 per 10,000) in England (Skivenes & Thoburn, 2016, p. 155). Policy variations across countries can result in different program emphases: a growing emphasis on children's rights in Norway has led to a degree of questioning of the dominance of the family preservation principles that have traditionally informed policy and practice there. In England there have also been moves toward a more diversified understanding of the alternative routes to permanence

Table 6.2 The Path to Older Child Adoption

Steps	Adoptive Parent(s)	Child	Birth Parent(s)
1	Parent contacts agency requesting information or home study	Child enters CW system via abuse, abandonment, or relinquishment	Parent is determined to be neglecting or abusing child
2	Group or individual home study begins	Child is determined unsafe at home and enters foster care	Parent should receive all reasonable efforts to prevent placement
3	Parents and agency identify type of child most suited to family	Child begins to be involved in counseling to address the possibility that child will be adopted. Older children have their rights to influence this decision explained	Parent is determined to be likely to continue to endanger child or child is removed to enable correction of health or behavior
4	Agency completes home study and approves family		Parents should be offered to participate in reunification services (e.g., drug treatment, public housing provision, parent training)
5	Parents review possible children for adoption		
6	Available children presented by social worker		
7	Visits with child begin	Child is determined unlikely to return home and enters foster/adoption home	
8	Parents may be linked to adoption support group (developed during home study or after)	Child is determined to be unable to return home	Parents' progress in rehabilitating home and self is reviewed and found inadequate with no allowance for additional time
9		Child is transferred to the adoption program	Birth parents' rights are terminated by law
10		Adoption placement begins with supervision	
11		Adoption is legalized	Birth parents may be offered opportunity for open adoption or provided with post-TPR services

for children of different ages and with differing needs, including a shift toward support for long-term foster care and having children stay with their foster parents (albeit with *modest* government support) after the age of 18 (Skivenes & Thoburn, 2016).

In many countries that allow adoption, the majority of adults wishing to adopt a child express a preference for adopting young children. For example, the majority of those adopted in England had not yet had their first birthday when they came into out-of-home care, and were under the age of 2 at the time of placement with their adoptive family.

> So, leaving aside government policies or professional practices, it is therefore unsurprising that larger numbers of English children leave care via adoption than is the case in Norway where fewer children enter care when under the age of 2. Young children entering care in England are likely to leave care quickly via adoption, whereas similar children in Norway, who cannot return safely to birth parents, are likely to remain in care for many years.
>
> (Skivenes & Thoburn, 2016, p. 155)

Despite the documented problems of foster care placement change and the resulting trauma and poor outcomes that result (see Chapter 5), in both of these countries and in many other countries, long-term foster care remains acceptable (although not especially beneficial; see Brannstrom et al., 2017).

Conclusion

Regardless of the type, adoptions follow certain general guidelines based on the premises that every child has a right to a family and that the child's needs are paramount. Arising from this fundamental right are other agency principles: that finality of adoption be made as soon as possible (after a sufficient trial of the placement's viability); that every party have options and assistance in weighing these options; that confidentiality be ensured as far as possible; and that agency services be available before and after placement.

Major Adoption Legislation

Indian Child Welfare Act

For the first 200 years, American adoption was legislated locally. The first major piece of national legislation influencing adoption was the Indian Child Welfare Act (ICWA) of

1978. The legislation provides legal guidelines to promote the stability and security of Native American tribes and families, and to prevent the unwarranted removal of Native American children from their homes. The passage of ICWA was fueled by the recognition that as many as 30 percent of Native American children were not living in their homes but were residing in boarding schools, foster homes, or adoptive homes. Founders of the Act asserted that the viability of Native American tribes was dissipating in the face of the removal of its children. The Act emphasizes protecting tribal communities and institutions (about half of Native Americans are members of tribes).

Within this broad Act are protections specific to adoption. Most notably, termination of a Native American's parental rights requires the highest standard of proof. CW authorities must show beyond a reasonable doubt that the continued custody of the child by the parent or Native American custodian is likely to result in serious emotional or physical damage to the child. Thus, the court must find with virtual certainty that the child will be seriously harmed in the future before he or she is freed for adoption. This high standard protects tribal rights but leaves little latitude for overseeing the child's right to be safe.

Section 1915 of the Act legislates the adoptive placements of Native American children after termination of parental rights. Preference is given to placement with a member of the child's extended family, other members of the child's tribe, or other Native American families. The act places the rights of the tribe above those of the birth parent. For example, Native American parents who are tribal members cannot place their children for adoption with non-Native American families off the reservation; placement of tribal children is governed by the tribe.

As a result of these stringent provisions, ICWA has never been without controversy. Fischler (1980) argued that the greater sovereignty for Native American adults places Native American children in jeopardy. Further, by regarding children as the property of parents, families, and tribes, some believe that ICWA does not protect children adequately. Defenders of ICWA argue that a child's right to a lifelong cultural affiliation deserves at least as much protection as the right to household permanency (Blanchard & Barsh, 1980). They propose that the choice to protect culture is what tribal CW professionals have made explicit in their support of ICWA.

The impact of the Act has undergone little evaluation. The only assessment of ICWA implementation indicates that, as envisioned by the framers of the Act, an increasing proportion of Native American children are being placed in foster and adoptive homes with Native American parents. Yet, Native American children in care are less likely than other children to have a case plan goal of adoption (Plantz et al., 1989). When they are adopted, this is very often by aunts and uncles or by other relatives (Barth, Webster, & Lee, 2002). State and federal courts have yet to achieve a consistent balance between the interests of tribal survival, CW, and parental authority. The conflict is especially vexing when the parents of a Native American child want to place the child in a non-Native American family, or a tribe seeks to place a child on an unfamiliar reservation in which the child has no close family (Hollinger, 1989). These cases continue to be contested (National Council on State Legislatures, 2013). The relationship between ICWA – which contains a very high standard for termination of parental rights – and subsequent CW legislation that requires time limits on foster care placements and termination of parental rights when those time limits are exceeded is only now being explored.

Adoption Assistance and Child Welfare Act and Adoption and Safe Families Act

The Adoption Assistance and Child Welfare Act (AACWA) was passed in 1980, followed by the Adoption and Safe Families Act in 1997. The broad mandates in the AACWA are that CW agencies implement pre-placement preventive services, programs to reunify placed children with their biological families, subsidized adoption, and periodic case reviews of children in care. Perhaps most importantly, AACWA instituted a timeline of 18 months for reunification or a decision to free a child for adoption. To facilitate adoption, a federal subsidy program was included that allows federal dollars to be used to match state contributions made to give subsidies – which could not be larger than the prior foster care payment – to families adopting children with special needs. In 1997, Congress passed the Adoption and Safe Families Act (ASFA) to strengthen these provisions. The time frame for making permanency decisions was shortened to 12 months and the expectations that a child would be free for adoption, even if there was not an immediately available adoptive family, were added to the law, along with many other provisions.

The changes in the focus and completion of adoption have, subsequently, been dramatic. In 1982, more than 50,000 children were legally free from their parents and waiting to be placed (Maza, 1983). About 17,000 of these children had the specific permanent plan of adoption and approximately 14,400 older children were placed for adoption in the United States (Maximus, 1984). By 2004, more than 118,000 children were legally free for adoption and more than 52,000 children were adopted, almost all of whom were given adoption subsidies. The massive increase since 1975 in the placement of older foster children and special needs children for adoption has greatly changed the historic purpose and scope of CW services.

The Adoption Assistance and Child Welfare Act encouraged states to develop adoption subsidy programs for special needs adoption and reimburses the state for 50 percent of the subsidy costs. The intent was to ensure that families were not penalized financially for adopting. Reforms to make subsidies available to families that adopt special needs children passed, over the objections that sentiment should be the only consideration in adoption. Instead, the law acknowledged subsidies as a means to facilitate the adoption of special needs foster children and promote new adoptions. Subsidies are meant to encourage families to adopt. Families that adopt special needs children are entitled to subsidies without a means-test, although their financial condition can be taken into account.

Adoption assistance payments are now provided in all states, and state adoption subsidy programs operate in virtually every state. Nationwide, adoption assistance payments rose from $442,000 in 1981 to an estimated $100 million in 1993 to more than $2.3 billion in 2014 (U.S. Senate, 1990; U.S. DHHS, 2007; Rosinsky & Connelly, 2016). It was projected that more money will be be spent by the federal government, each day, on adoption subsidies than on foster care payments. Concerned about the growing number of children receiving adoption subsidies, some states have endeavored to cut adoption subsidies, despite the fact that they are already lower than foster care or group care payments and are much less expensive than paying for children who grow up in out-of-home care (Barth et al., 2006). Court challenges to cuts in existing subsidies have successfully argued that they could not make such cuts to families that had accepted children into their families with the understanding of a higher subsidy payment (Eckholm, 2006).

Multiethnic Placement Act and Interethnic Adoption Provisions

The passage of the Howard M. Metzenbaum Multiethnic Placement Act of 1994 prohibits any agency or entity that receives federal assistance:

> to categorically deny to any person the opportunity to become an adoptive or a foster parent, solely on the basis of race, color, or national origin of the adoptive or foster parent, or the involved child; or delay or deny the placement of a child for adoption or into foster care, or otherwise discriminate in making a placement decision, solely on the basis of race, color, or national origin of the adoptive or foster parent, or the child involved.
>
> (S. 553[a]I[A&B])

Initially identified as a "permissible consideration," agencies could consider the cultural ethnic or racial background of the child and the capacity of the prospective parents to meet the needs of the child as one of a number of factors in determining the best interests of the child. This clause was later stricken in the Interethnic Adoption Provisions, which amended the Multiethnic Placement Act and added penalties for failing to comply with this Act as a violation of the Civil Rights Act of 1964. The Acts also require that states provide diligent recruitment of potential adoptive and foster families that reflect the ethnic and racial diversity of children in the state for whom foster and adoptive homes are needed.

The passage of this Act may have increased the likelihood of adoption for African American children; however, this is not a clear result of the law. The U.S. DHHS has done little else to try to study the impact of the law. Shaw (2006) found no change in the proportion of multiethnic adoptions in California since the law. Several states have now been successfully sued by the Office of Civil Rights for failing to implement the law; Ohio received a $1.8m fine (U.S. DHHS, Departmental Appeals Board, 2006) At the same time, the lengths of stay in foster care for African American children are declining because of more movement into guardianship and kinship adoptions (Wulczyn, 2003).

Other Laws and Policies

Tax cuts. In 1994 tax cuts were passed for all families who adopted and submitted their adoption expenses. This was the beginning of a steady series of actions that have endeavored to balance the national goal of placing children from foster care into adoption, and the interests of adoptive parents (and private agencies and attorneys) who seek to defray the costs of independent, agency, and international adoptions. In more recent iterations, the tax cuts were changed to tax credits and made larger for families adopting from public agencies. Research then showed that these families were not using the credits because they did not have many expenses or much income. The *Economic Growth and Tax Relief Reconciliation Act* (P.L. 107–16) of 2002 includes provisions to extend permanently the adoption credit; increased the maximum credit to $10,000 per eligible child, and created a flat tax credit for special needs adoptions so that parents do not need to document expenses for special needs adoptions.

As part of the President's Adoption 2002 Initiative, which was an administrative program developed in 1996 by President William Clinton to double the number of adoptions in six years, an adoption incentive program was developed to give states a bonus for increasing the number of adoptions of foster children above their baseline. Although the effects of this program are unknown – as the bonuses are relatively small and the short-term cost of an adoption is high – this was established as federal policy, as part of the Adoption Promotion Act (P.L. 108–145) of 2003. This law provided additional incentives to states for increasing the number of children aged 9 and older who are adopted from foster care. P.L. 110–351 renews the Adoption Incentive Program for an additional five years. Somewhat perversely, the Act updates to FY 2007 the adoption baseline above which incentive payments are made (which usually raises the baseline) but then doubles the incentive payments for adoptions of children with special needs and older children adoptions above that baseline. The Act also permits states to receive an additional payment if the state's adoption rate exceeds its highest recorded foster care rate since 2002.

Most recently, the advances in support for college tuition and expenses for former foster youth has caught the attention of the adoption community. The College Cost Reduction and Access Act (P.L. 110–84) was passed to ensure that there would be no disincentives for adoption of older children from foster care, and that they could continue to be eligible for any federal assistance given to emancipated foster youth. This legislation thus makes it possible for adolescents in foster care to be adopted without losing access to college financial aid.

A recent change is that the Federal government is no longer providing bonuses to the states for increasing the number of children adopted but for increasing the rate of children judged as needing adoption and legal guardianship:

> The Adoption and Legal Guardianship Incentive Payments program (formerly called the Adoption Incentive Payments program) recognizes improved performance in helping children and youth in foster care find permanent homes through adoption and legal guardianship. The program was originally established as part of the Adoption and Safe Families Act of 1997 and has been reauthorized and revised several times since, most recently as part of the Preventing Sex Trafficking and Strengthening Families Act, signed into law in September 2014. A key change in this reauthorization is the renaming of the program to reflect that incentives will be paid to jurisdictions for improved performance in both adoptions and legal guardianship of children in foster care.
>
> (www.acf.hhs.gov/cb/focus-areas/adoption)

Current Adoption Practice

Overview

Recruitment of adoptive parents for foster children is arguably the most important element of adoption practice because, once adoptive placements are made, adoptions generally require few ongoing services. Recruitment is especially critical for African American children because they remain strikingly overrepresented in foster care. Although adoption practices vary broadly, practitioners struggle to decide how to keep pace with emerging trends in a way that fits their agency and is in the best interests of children, families, and the community.

Adoption Planning for the Child

Permanency planning legislation provides grounds to free many children for adoption, but agencies have been slow to implement the specifics of the legislation, and many barriers to placement and permanence remain. Determining a child's eligibility for adoption continues to be a confused mixture of answers to three questions. Is the child (1) interested in adoption, (2) likely to be adopted, or (3) likely to remain adopted? Adjusting practice to the needs of these older children includes recognizing that some disruption is inevitable (see Box 6.2 for definitions). But, as Cole (1986) conceptualized this, "The only failed adoption is the one you didn't try" (p. 4). Workers who recognize and accept the possibility of disruption in adoption find creative ways to facilitate adoptions for all waiting children and support the placement in accordance with the risk involved. Recent innovations in adoption practice are resulting in children getting adopted even though they are over the age of 21 (Barth & Chintapalli, 2009).

Box 6.2   Definitions

- **Disruption** is used to describe an adoption process that ends after the child is placed in an adoptive home and before the adoption is legally finalized, resulting in the child's return to (or entry into) foster care or placement with new adoptive parents.

- **Dissolution** is generally used to describe an adoption in which the legal relationship between the adoptive parents and adoptive child is severed, either voluntarily or involuntarily, after the adoption is legally finalized. This results in the child's return to (or entry into) foster care or placement with new adoptive parents.

Source: Gateway (2012, p. 1).

Not every child will be better off adopted than in long-term foster care or guardianship. Although many adoptive families struggle and may need post-adoption assistance, the general evidence of positive adoption outcomes is powerful (Barth, 2002; Malm et al., 2011; Triseliotis, 2002). The value of adoption and the relatively modest disruption rates of about 11 percent (Gateway, 2012) make adoption an excellent alternative over foster care. Experienced CW workers have lower adoption disruption rates for families that had been in their care. At the same time, children who are not adopted but who have had their parental rights terminated are likely to experience a variety of significant legal and personal disadvantages (Barth & Chintapalli, 2009).

Speedy efforts to place children while they are young and better able to fit into an adoptive family's home represent the starting point for successful adoption. Adoption delayed is often adoption denied. Efforts to terminate parental rights more quickly when reunification is improbable and to move children into foster-adopt situations deserve full support and dissemination. At the same time, older children whose parent's rights have been terminated are too often unable to be adopted and are, therefore, suffering the legal consequences of having no legal family ties.

Recruitment of Adoptive Parents

Agencies continue to engage in a variety of methods to find adoptive families. Recent years have seen advances in search methods that involve information provided by the youth who will be adopted. In these procedures, social workers help youth identify people who they have known and cared about and who might consider adopting them. In addition, there is a growing use of people-finder firms to seek relatives of children in foster care.

In addition to exchanges, parent recruitment also occurs through community education. Broad education in the community can reach groups of potential parents who may never have previously considered adoption. Beginning in 1979, Father George Clements, a priest in Chicago, challenged every African American church in Chicago through the *One Church, One Child* program to accept the responsibility and opportunity to have one member of each congregation adopt an African American child (Veronico, 1983). Federal and state governments subsequently provided years of support to *One Church, One Child* to encourage its replication. Many states now have a version of *One Church, One Child* and focus on the recruitment of families from other ethnic groups. The program has continued to be used (Gibson, 2003; National One Church, One Child, 2016) but has not yet been evaluated.

Another recruitment strategy that has shown promise involves using special features on television or in newspapers to present a particular child and a description of his or her strengths and needs (e.g., "Tuesday's child"). These media campaigns are modestly successful and inexpensive. Ethnic adoption fairs also bring interested parents and eligible children together in a picnic situation. Internet services are a growing tool for identifying children in need of adoption.

Pre-placement Services

Home studies are a nearly 150-year-old tradition and continue to serve the primary function of screening adoptive families to protect children from harmful situations (Crea,

Barth, & Chintapalli, 2007). A well-established but secondary function is to help adoptive families clarify their intentions and flexibility regarding the characteristics of children they seek to adopt. Developments have been made in the use of situation-based questions and scenarios that can better draw out if the adoptive parent has key traits of flexibility, equitable approaches to problem-solving, empathy, and communication (Duehn, 2014).

During the past decade, there has also been a greater use of the group process for training and support of pre-adoptive families so that they are more able to parent special needs children successfully. Many of these groups prepare participants to become either adoptive or foster parents. Groups may last for as long as ten sessions and include guest presentations by current foster and adoptive parents. Prospective foster parents are told that they may change their minds and become adoptive parents instead. People who expressly want to adopt (and they usually outnumber those who want only to provide foster care) are oriented to the social services system, and the legal and moral responsibility to facilitate the child's reunification with the birth family when that is the case goal. Adoptive families that begin the process in such multi-family groups often maintain contact with peers well beyond their time of contact with the social worker. Although group-based home studies have not been well evaluated, some evidence suggests that they strengthen high-risk placements (Barth & Berry, 1988), whereas other evidence suggests that they have little benefit (Puddy & Jackson, 2003).

Social workers try to provide adopting parents with all pertinent information about the child during pre-placement services. Because of the inevitable coordination problems and some confidentiality concerns, much valuable background information is not shared. This inefficiency could be redressed by rethinking the type of information collected and how it is summarized and transmitted to the families. However they accomplish it, social workers with more years of experience are more effective in supporting families so that they succeed in their adoptions – for each year of worker experience the adoption disruption rate decreases by 2 percent (Smith et al., 2006).

Researchers have confirmed importance of information-sharing calls for prompt action (Barth and Berry, 1988). Better information is associated with better outcomes. Also, the success of a few "wrongful adoption" lawsuits is forcing agencies to change their information-sharing practices and states to change their laws to reduce liability. Nonetheless, some social workers continue to withhold information to increase the likelihood of adoption.

Some families have taken legal action when the child's history and current functioning have not been disclosed fully. These "wrongful adoption cases" rest on an assertion that the adoptive parents would not have pursued the adoption if they had received all the pertinent information about the child (including possible mental health issues or other critically important details). While these lawsuits are rare events, they can be quite demoralizing to agencies and workers – but can be prevented when agencies prepare an information-sharing checklist and packet of information for each child for use by social workers and adoptive parents. Despite the risk of disruption, overall, adoption has proven to be a very successful strategy for achieving permanence.

Open Adoption

The practice of open adoption, or the continuance of contact or correspondence between the adopted child and birth parents, is increasingly common. In a study using data from the National Survey of Adoptive parents, 39 percent of adoptive families who adopted through the foster care system reported having had contact with birth families (Faulkner & Madden, 2012). Henney and colleagues (2003) examined the practices of 31 adoption agencies from 1987 to 1999 and showed that only 36 percent of agencies offered fully disclosed arrangements in 1987 but that, by 1999, 79 percent offered fully disclosed arrangements. At the end of that time, not one agency only offered confidential adoptions.

The benefits of open adoption are becoming more accepted, but remain controversial. On ideological grounds, because outcome data on open adoptions are scarce, Pannor and Baran (1984) called for "an end to all closed adoptions" (p. 245). They view the secrecy of conventional adoptions as an affront to the rights of adopted children. Kraft and colleagues (1985) countered that open adoptions may interfere with the process of bonding between the adoptive parent and child. Other evidence suggests that the adoptive parents' control over their child's contact with birth parents is critical to the success of the placement (Barth & Berry, 1988) and the parents' comfort with the placement (Berry, 1991; Dunbar et al., 2006). Berge and colleagues (2006) examined adolescents' feelings on openness and found that "adolescents desired and benefited from having openness in their adoption arrangements" (p. 1036). Berge and colleagues (2006) also found that adolescents desired more contact with birth moms, which demonstrated that the contact with the birth mothers was not harmful.

Von Korff, Grotevant, and McRoy (2006) examined whether the degree of openness between adoptive and birth family members was associated with the behavioral and emotional adjustments of adolescents who had been adopted as babies: "The adoptive parents' reports indicate no significant association between openness and adolescent adjustment" (p. 531). "Adoptee reports suggested that externalizing behavior is higher in confidential as compared with ongoing fully disclosed arrangements" (p. 534), but the authors make no claims that openness causes better outcomes. They recommend that openness arrangements be voluntary and that openness decisions be made on a case-by-case basis.

Whereas most open adoptions continue to be voluntary on the adoptive parents' part, recent case law has added stipulations to adoption decrees that provide birth parents with visitation rights (Hollinger, 1993). A few countries (for instance, New Zealand) have made open adoptions the requirement for all adoptions on the grounds that it is in the child's best interest. These changes are in stark contrast to the historical notion of adoption as a parent–child relationship equivalent to the birth parent–child relationship and without conditions. This change occurred despite the absence of noteworthy evidence that children in open adoptions have better outcomes than other children.

The potential benefit of open adoption is that it provides a resource for coping with the typical transitions in the child's understanding about adoption as he or she moves toward adulthood. The danger for older children is that continued contact with birth parents may disrupt the development of the child's relationship with the new family. The older adoptive child and parent are trying to become a family and need a structure to do so. It may seem that the older a child, the less detrimental and more natural it is to retain ties to former caretakers. The danger in this logic is that older children have a more difficult time developing ties to their new family because they are also pushing toward independence, and this development may be pre-empted by contact with birth families. Open adoption may perhaps best be viewed as enrichment to a stable placement, not a necessity for all placements or a palliative for a troubled one.

Non-traditional Adoptions

The traditional requirement that adoptive parents be married couples who own a home with a full-time mother at home severely narrowed the field of possible adoptive parents. Although these requirements may have been helpful in reducing the field of applicants during the infant adoption boom, they were also erroneously promulgated to protect children from unsuitable parents. Instead, they limited the placement of special needs children. The bigger pool of parents needed for these waiting children is not attainable without flexible requirements. Requirements for adoptive parents have typically been more flexible in public agencies than in private ones.

Modest changes in agency policy and practice have opened up opportunities for adoption by gay and lesbian parents (Mallon, 2015; Pace, 2005; Ryan, Pearlmutter, & Groza, 2004). In 2015, more than 13,000 children were adopted by single females (U.S. Health and Human Services, 2016). These statistics do not indicate what percentage of these children live with same-sex partners or opposite-sex partners. Gay, lesbian, and bisexual foster parents face multiple challenges when beginning the adoption process, as it frequently begins by becoming foster parents. Despite being a valuable resource for our nation's foster children, Downs and James (2006) found that many gay, lesbian, and bisexual foster parents were met by lack of support, inappropriate social workers, and even legal resistance. Results of a study by Leung, Erich, and Kanenberg (2005) indicated that for children who were adopted by gay/lesbian-headed families, there were no negative effects for their parenting. In addition, higher levels of family functioning were found in gay/lesbian-headed households with adopted children who were older, non-sibling grouped, and had more foster placements. These results indicate that gay/lesbian adoptions should be encouraged. Indeed, agency personnel have a clear understanding that gay and lesbian families are a vitally important resource for achieving social goals of ensuring that children have loving, legal, lifetime families (Brodzinsky, Patterson, & Vaziri, 2002). A new generation of work is clarifying important considerations in the assessment and support of gay and lesbian foster and adoptive parents (e.g., Mallon & Wornoff, 2006; Mallon, 2007, 2015).

Adoption of children by kin who cared for them as foster parents has increased in recent years. Kinship foster care has become the most common type of foster care in many urban areas, and kinship adoptions have also grown in recent years. This is partially responsible for their finding that African American children are more likely than other children to be adopted even though their rate of adoption is slower than other children (Wulczyn, Chen, & Hislop, 2007). Although this is generally a more protective legal arrangement for children than foster care, kinship adoptions are more likely to be by older, less educated, poorer, single parents than other adoptions.

Post-permanency/After-care Supports

Overview

According to AFCARS follow-up data, nearly one in five children currently in care was in care previously. A significant number of families are fractured and re-fractured when children come in and out of foster care. Stable and nurturing families can bolster the resilience of children and ameliorate negative impacts upon their developmental outcomes, which, in time, can ensure that these children will grow up to be healthy, contributing members of society (Roberts, O'Brien, & Pecora, 2017). These protective factors cannot be nurtured sufficiently with the instability that accompanies re-entry into foster care.

One way for foster care agencies to continue to support the development of these protective factors and ensure that they endure over time is to improve services and programs dedicated to supporting families as they transition out of care. Successful programs help strengthen families by preventing child abuse and neglect and by improving well-being. Currently, the evidence base and access to services are weak for post-permanency services and consequently, a significant number of children re-enter care after achieving reunification, adoption, or guardianship.

Although there has been a recent upward trend in the number of children in care, overall there has been a significant decline in the out-of-home care population since 2000. This decline has resulted in nearly 25 percent fewer children in care, with total numbers of such children under the age of 18 just over 424,000. What remains unchanged is the rate of re-entry, which, if addressed effectively, has the potential to keep families together and reduce the number of children in care even further. What is more, while recent trends have seen an increase in the number of children coming into care, the percentage in care who are re-entries has not changed. Between 2000 and 2015, almost 97,000 fewer children were in out-of-home care in the U.S. (Figure 6.1). Meanwhile, the percentage of children in care who are re-entries has remained stable at nearly 20 percent. In other words, 80,000 children who are currently in out-of-home care have previously been in care. These re-entry numbers clearly demonstrate that community conditions and service delivery systems are not providing the supports necessary for a significant number of children and families to remain together safely (Roberts et al., 2017).

More detailed information about which kinds of placements have re-entries in Maryland (Goering & Shaw, 2017) shows that children who achieved guardianship with kin had the lowest odds of reentry overall, followed by guardianship with non-kin, and reunification with family of origin. Children reunifying against the recommendations of the Children and Family Services Department had the highest odds of re-entry. The authors also found substantially higher re-entry rates when they included youth who had gone home from foster care and came back into juvenile services. These findings need replication in other states.

Although Figure 6.1 depicts a stable national re-entry rate, it also represents a significant opportunity. Even modest progress made to improve programs dedicated to supporting families through their transition from the foster care system could result in (1) a significant increase in children's safety and well-being; and (2) a significant reduction in the number of children and families who re-enter care.

Need for Post-placement Support

Agency support following placement may be needed for some children. Any placement will have challenges. The goal for the agency is to stay close enough to the family to be

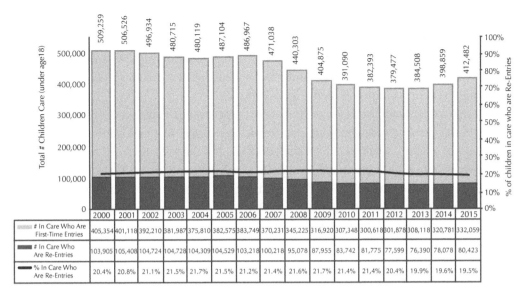

	2000	2001	2002	2003	2004	2005	2006	2007	2008	2009	2010	2011	2012	2013	2014	2015
# In Care Who Are First-Time Entries	405,354	401,118	392,210	381,987	375,810	382,575	383,749	370,231	345,225	316,920	307,348	300,618	301,878	308,118	320,781	332,059
# In Care Who Are Re-Entries	103,905	105,408	104,724	104,728	104,309	104,529	103,218	100,218	95,078	87,955	83,742	81,775	77,599	76,390	78,078	80,423
% In Care Who Are Re-Entries	20.4%	20.8%	21.1%	21.5%	21.7%	21.5%	21.2%	21.4%	21.6%	21.7%	21.4%	21,4%	20.4%	19.9%	19.6%	19.5%

Figure 6.1 The Number of Children In Out-Of-Home Care and the Percent Who Have Been in Care Before

Source: AFCARS National File; available from NDACAN at Cornell University; data pulled April 21, 2017 by Data Advocacy, Casey Family Programs.

aware of these problems and guide the family to resources to aid in their resolution. However, many families are reluctant to seek services until it is too late because they are afraid they will lose their child.

Both the child and the parents have needs in post-placement services. Agencies typically maintain contact with the family during the first three to six months to reassure the child of continuity with his or her past, and to enable the family to explore uncertainties without feeling lost. The goal is to catch problems early in the placement before they escalate into unsalvageable disasters. The evidence is unequivocal that the needs of adoptive families for support and services last well beyond the first year (Festinger, 2006).

To meet these ongoing needs, CW agencies must establish ways to provide services for high-risk placements throughout adolescence. Post-adoption services may be useful but they are specifically geared toward preserving placements on the verge of disruption. Rather, they tend to serve adoptees placed as infants, not older child adoptees, and help them reconcile their adoptions, make decisions about searching for birth parents, and deal with their concerns as they become adolescents and young adults.

Many agencies have introduced support groups of adoptive families for parents and children. It is often helpful for new adoptive parents and children to talk to fellow adopters and adoptees about what is normal in adoption and to share realistic expectations and feelings about the process. These groups also facilitate supportive relationships that parents and children can fall back on when they need to. Support groups probably operate best when started during the home study, but successful versions have been developed following placement to support high-risk placements.

There is a clamor for the development of post-placement and post-legalization services that meet the demands of supporting older child adoptions. The call is for something far more than mandatory visits soon after the adoption and the availability of crisis intervention services. Although the principles underlying this demand are sound, a few concerns arise. First, post-adoption services should not be staffed at the expense of recruitment and home study efforts. Resources spent on conventional post-placement services are not as valuable to agencies and families as dollars spent on recruitment because most adoptions succeed with no significant agency effort following placement. Second, although referral to outside services is often useful, social workers or other adoptive families involved with the family should be available to assess the situation and coordinate post-placement services from other providers. Families are less likely to ask the agency for help when they lose contact with the worker who did their home study. The home study is a poignant process that builds strong bonds between the worker and family. The organization of services should facilitate a continuous relationship among the family, social worker, and other adoptive families who can assist in times of duress.

Adjusting to older child adoptions is often difficult for both parents and child. At times, the future of the adoption may be in doubt. With so much riding on the outcome of such a crisis, it is unwise to rely on conventional social casework counseling or office-based psychotherapy. Adoption preservation services are needed. Although some early efforts to apply short-term and intensive methods of family preservation were not successful, derivative models have emerged and been reported by parents to be very valuable (Zosky et al., 2005) and have been accompanied by changes in adoptive parents' depression and children's behavior problems. Since permanency planning, family preservation services have emerged in most states. They have been used primarily to keep children out of the CW or mental health systems and not to help preserve adoptive placements.

Relatively few adoptive families now have the benefit of intensive home-based, family preservation services to prevent adoption disruption, an observation that has not changed in the past 20 years. Yet, many states have developed at least some post-adoption services. For families in crisis, in-home interventions reduce the likelihood of alienation that can occur during out-of-home care. The specific presenting problems that precipitate adoption disruptions are those that signal the breakdown of other families, especially assault, running away, and non-compliance of latency and teenage children. Intensive services are costly, but if they are successful, their costs can be favorably weighed against the lifelong benefits that follow adoption. To date, there are no models of post-adoption services that have been shown to be effective – admittedly a difficult evaluation challenge because these services tend to respond to families with a wide range of backgrounds and concerns. Despite the limitations in post-adoption services, there appears to be no greater risk of disruption in recent years than during the period when the adoption rate was only half as high (Smith et al., 2006).

Post-permanency Programs

Although promising post-permanency programs exist, the evidence base is sparse, in part because of the limited focus by the federal government and by philanthropy targeting this critical area of practice. What we do know is that most children in foster care have physical, emotional, and/or behavioral challenges that can create significant ongoing concerns, which are often a result of the parent's and/or child's unmet needs. These challenges require services and supports while the child is in care as well as after he or she leaves the system. To date, programs and services offered to families have focused on preventing maltreatment in the first place or addressing issues that have prevented permanent placement (e.g., child problem behaviors, parenting competencies). They may or may not provide services that can be associated with sustained positive child and family functioning and permanency.

Most research has focused on post-permanency programs that address one or a few specific behavioral characteristics of children/families that either support (e.g., parenting skills) or deter (e.g., conduct problems, parental substance use) successful family reunification. Existing post-permanency programs have included the following components (Roberts et al., 2017):

- *Basic family resources*, including housing, employment, and income support.

- *Safety-focused practices*, which must become a major component of every service program to ensure that children are not put at further risk of maltreatment.

- *Clinical child supports*, including programs that address (1) the trauma that led to the child's entry into foster care; (2) the trauma associated with removal itself; and (3) the stresses associated with transition either back to the home from which they were removed, or to a new home, separated from their biological families.

- *Caregiver supports and services*, including counseling/other clinical services, skills training, childcare, healthcare services, advocacy training, educational services, parenting skills training, and substance abuse treatment.

- *Support networks*, including support groups, childcare referrals, and respite care.
- *Navigation services*, including a point-person for families to connect to resources, supports, and services.

While it is unlikely that any one program is going to address all the components above, to be effective, these components must be provided in the right amount for the circumstances of each child and family. For example, a family may have basic family resources and caregiver services, but what they are lacking are support networks. This is a critical part of the intervention process – assessment and individual service planning – which must be part of any effective intervention strategy. CW agencies can strive to provide services that meet each child's need and the programs listed in Box 6.3 could help some children avoid coming back into foster care.

Box 6.3   Looking for Inspiration?

Programs across the U.S. are providing a range of post-permanency services, including those that focus on basic family resources, safety-focused practices, clinical child supports, caregiver supports and services, support networks, and navigation services. Explore the links below to learn about some of these programs.

- ADAPT (A program offering post-adoption supports has been implemented in North Carolina to assist families with older children adopted from foster care. See www.aecf.org/blog/a-resource-for-strengthening-adoptive-families-with-older-kids/?utm_source=eblast&utm_medium=email&utm_campaign=Evidence-Based-Practice.

- Kinship Navigator Program: dshs.wa.gov/kinshipcare/

- Homebuilders: institutefamily.org/programs_IFPS.asp/

- The Incredible Years: incredibleyears.com/

- Treatment Foster Care Oregon (formerly Multidimensional Treatment Foster Care for Preschoolers): tfcoregon.com.

- Nurturing Parenting Program: nurturingparenting.com.

- On the Way Home: cehs.unl.edu/ccfw/way-home/.

- Oregon Post Adoption Resource Center: orparc.org.
- Shared Family Care: http://calswec.berkeley.edu/sites/default/files/uploads/pdf/CalSWEC/san_francisco_cft_shared_family_care_planning_and_shared_coaching_manual_final_7-7-15.pdf.

Source: Adapted from Roberts, Y.H., O'Brien, K., & Pecora, P.J. (2017). *Supporting Lifelong Families Ensuring Long-Lasting Permanency and Well-Being.* Seattle, WA: Casey Family Programs. wwww.casey.org/supporting-lifelong-families/. For a research brief with action strategies see: www.casey.org/supporting-lifelong-families-action-plan/

Policy Issues and Challenges

Previous sections of this chapter have highlighted a number of policy issues, such as how should reunification, kinship care, guardianship, and adoption be incentivized with the right balance of emphasis? Will GLBTQ persons or couples be allowed to adopt children or teens without added scrutiny or being prohibited from doing so? What is the right balance of international versus domestic adoptions of unrelated children?

Another issue is how to set policies that encourage high-quality integration of services and effective early services – so that the "downstream services" are not hindered. For example, the CW services "system" is an amalgam of programs. The outcomes of efforts to prevent out-of-home placements, to reunify families, and to provide long-term care all depend on the quality of the programs that have previously worked with the children. Each program must work if the other programs are to do what they are intended to do. If older children receiving CW services are not adopted or able to stay adopted, then the rationale for moving quickly to terminate the rights of birth parents (after a determination that children cannot go home) is weakened.

Indeed, the pressure to leave children in or return them to unsafe birth families is intensified when permanent adoptive homes are unavailable, because social workers fear that children will experience more harm in a lifetime of foster care than at home. Many agencies will not free children from foster care until a stable home is all but guaranteed. Without confidence that terminating parental rights and freeing children for adoption will ultimately result in an adoption, judges lose their conviction to do so, time limits on foster care are rendered unattainable, and mandates for speedy permanency planning become moot. Successful older child adoption services may not be the hub of effective CW services, but they are critical.

Conclusion

Future Directions

Family reunification, adoption, and guardianship remain viable permanency options for children in out-of-home care. Yet major gaps in the stability and outcomes of kinship care and guardianship remain. Adoption is also facing increasing scrutiny by all interested adult parties. Birth mothers and fathers, adopting parents, and adoption agencies and centers are developing new and more rigorous procedures for trying to ensure that their needs are met. Given the relative lack of research, it is unclear how well these approaches will work to support the interests of children who need adoptive homes. Despite the general success of adoption for all parties involved, a considerable tightening of adoption regulation and more procedural barriers to adoption may occur.

These procedures – which lead to greater legal uncertainty for people pursuing adoption – may result in diminished interest on the part of potential adoptive parents who will instead choose to pursue surrogacy arrangements or fertility treatments with lower success rates. Such strategies will not lead to the adoption of children in need of placement. Of the utmost importance is the public policy goal of increasing adoptive placements. In addition, a substantial challenge exists to find ways to make adoption a way to create and affirm family ethnic, and community relationships in all their manifestations. This involves supporting a range of adoptive arrangements that allow the child to recognize the significance of birth parents and siblings, racial and ethnic make-up, and cultural origins, and give the child opportunities to act on that recognition.

Discussion Questions

1. How have strategies for helping children placed in out-of-home care achieve legal and emotional permanency evolved over the years?

2. What do you see as the major barriers to helping youth find permanence?

3. What funding changes would most enhance the effectiveness of adoption and guardianship programs?

For Further Information

Children's Defense Fund, Child Trends, American Bar Association Center on Children and the Law, Casey Family Programs, Child Focus, & Generations United. (2012). *Making it work: Using the Guardianship Assistance Program (GAP) to close the permanency gap for children in foster care*. Seattle, WA, and Washington, DC: Authors. Retrieved from www. childrensdefense.org/library/data/making-it-work-using-the.pdf. A concise but informative summary of kinship care and why guardianship should be a key program component.

Kerman, B., Maluccio, A.N., & Freundlich, M. (2009). *Achieving permanence for older children and youth in foster care*. New York: Columbia University Press. Excellent compendium of essays regarding the research related to permanency planning for youth in foster care.

Mallon, G.P. (2006). *Toolbox No. 3: Facilitating permanency for youth*. Washington, DC: Child Welfare League of America. Practical strategies, case review prototypes, and other resources for helping youth achieve permanency.

For useful adoption resources, visit the following websites:

- www.adoptioninstitute.org/index.php
- www.childwelfare.gov/adoption/index.cfm
- www.nacac.org.

Bibliography

Adoption101.com. (2017). *Independent adoption*. Retrieved from www.adoption101.com/ independent_adoption.html.

Ahn, H., DePanfilis, D., Frick, K., & Barth, R.P. (2018). Estimating minimum adequate foster care costs for children in the United States. *Children and Youth Services Review, 84*, 55–67. doi:10.1016/j.childyouth.2017.10.045.

Barth, R.P. (1988). Disruption in older child adoption. *Public Welfare, 46*, 23–29.

Barth, R.P. (2002). Outcomes of adoption and what they tell us about designing adoption services. *Adoption Quarterly, 6*, 45–60.

Barth, R.P., & Berry, M. (1988). *Adoption and disruption: Rates, risks, and responses*. Hawthorne, NY: Aldine de Gruyter.

Barth, R., & Chintapalli, L. (2009). Permanence and impermanence for youth in out-of-home care. In B. Kerman, M. Freundlich, & A. Maluccio (Eds), *Achieving permanence for older children and youth in foster care* (pp. 88–108). New York: Columbia University Press.

Barth, R.P., Webster, D. II, & Lee, S. (2002). Adoption of American Indian children: Implications for implementing the Indian Child Welfare and Adoption and Safe Families Acts. *Children and Youth Services Review, 24*, 139–158.

Barth, R.P., Courtney, M.E., Berrick, J.D., & Albert, V. (1994). *From child abuse to permanency planning: Child welfare services pathways and placements*. New York: Aldine de Gruyter.

Barth, R.P., Lee, C., Wildfire, J., & Guo, S. (2006). Estimating costs of foster care vs. adoption using propensity score matching. *Social Service Review, 80*, 127–158.

Bell, T., & Romano, E. (2015). *Permanency and safety among children in foster family and kinship care: A scoping review, Trauma, Violence, and Abuse, 1*, 9. Retrieved from http://tva. sagepub.com/content/early/2015/10/09/1524838015611673.

Bell, T., & Romano, E. (2017). Permanency and safety among children in foster family and kinship care: A scoping review. *Trauma Violence, and Abuse, 18*(3), 268–286. doi:10.1177/1524838015611673.

Berge, J.M., Mendenhall, T.J., Wrobel, G.M., Grotevant, H.D., & McRoy, R.G. (2006). Adolescents' feelings about openness in adoption: Implications for adoption agencies. *Child Welfare, 85*(6), 1011–1039.

Berrick, J.D., Choi, Y., D'Andrade, A., & Frame, L. (2008). Reasonable efforts? Implementation of the reunification bypass provision of ASFA. *Child Welfare, 87*(3), 163–182.

Berry, M. (1991). Open adoption in a sample of 1296 families. *Children and Youth Services Review, 13,* 379–396.

Berzin, S.C., Thomas, K.L., & Cohen, E. (2007). Assessing model fidelity in two family group decision-making programs: Is this child welfare intervention being implemented as intended? *Journal of Social Service Research, 34*(2), 55–71, doi:10.1300/J079v34n02_05.

Blanchard, E.L., & Barsh, R.L. (1980). What is best for tribal children: A response to Fischler. *Social Work, 25,* 350–357.

Brannstrom, L., Vinnerljung, B., Forsman, H., & Almquist, Y.B. (2017). Children placed in out-of-home care as midlife adults: Are they still disadvantaged or have they caught up with their peers? *Child Maltreatment, 22,* 205–214.

Brodzinsky, D., Patterson, C., & Vaziri, M. (2002). Adoption agency perspectives on lesbian and gay prospective parents: A national study. *Adoption Quarterly, 5,* 5–23.

Casey Family Programs. (2016). *Rapid permanency reviews: Key elements.* Seattle, WA: Technical Services Unit, Casey Family Programs.

Chapman, M.V., Wall, A., & Barth, R.P. (2004). Children's voices: The perceptions of children in foster care. *American Journal of Orthopsychiatry, 74*(3), 293.

Child Welfare League of America. (1998). *Standards for adoption services.* Washington, DC: Child Welfare League of America.

Children's Defense Fund, Child Trends, American Bar Association Center on Children and the Law, Casey Family Programs, Child Focus, & Generations United. (2012). *Making it work: Using the Guardianship Assistance Program (GAP) to close the permanency gap for children in foster care.* Seattle, WA, and Washington, DC: Authors. Retrieved from www.childrensdefense.org/library/data/making-it-work-using-the.pdf.

Cole, E.S. (1986). Post-legal adoption services: A time for decision. *Permanency Report, 4*(1), 1, 4.

Committee on Supporting the Parents of Young Children; Board on Children, Youth, and Families; Division of Behavioral and Social Sciences and Education; National Academies of Sciences, Engineering, and Medicine. (2016). *Parenting matters: Supporting parents of children ages 0–8.* Washington, DC: The National Academies Press. Retrieved from www.nap.edu/21868.

Crea, T.M., Barth, R.P., & Chintapalli, L.K. (2007). Home study methods for evaluating prospective resource families: History, current challenges, and promising approaches. *Child Welfare, 86*(2), 141–159.

Crea, T.M., Barth, R.P., Chintapalli, L.K., & Buchanan, R.L. (2009). The implementation and expansion of SAFE: Frontline responses and the transfer of technology to practice. *Children and Youth Services Review, 31*(8), 903–910. doi:10.1016/j.childyouth.2009.04.005.

Cross, S.L. (2006). Indian family exception doctrine: Still losing children despite the Indian Child Welfare Act. *Child Welfare, 85*(4), 671–690.

Dalberth, B., Gibbs, D., & Berkman, N. (2005). *Understanding adoption subsidies: An analysis of AFCARS data final report.* Research Triangle Park, NC: RTI International. Prepared for Office of the Assistant Secretary for Planning and Evaluation, U.S. Department of Health and Human Services, January.

D'Andrade, A. (2009). The differential effects of concurrent planning practice elements on reunification and adoption. *Research on Social Work Practice, 19*, 446–459.

D'Andrade, A., Frame, L., & Duerr-Berrick, J. (2006). Concurrent planning in public child welfare agencies: Oxymoron or work in progress? *Children and Youth Services Review, 28*(1), 78–95.

Davis, C.W., O'Brien, K., Rogg, C.S., Morgan, L.J., White, C.R., & Houston, M. (2013). 24-month update on the impact of roundtables on permanency for youth in foster care. *Children and Youth Services Review, 35*(12), 2128–2134.

Dijkstra, S., Creemers, H.E., Asscher, J.J., Dekovi , M., & Stams, G.J.J. (2016). The effectiveness of family group conferencing in youth care: A meta-analysis. *Child Abuse & Neglect, 62*, 100–110.

Downs, A.C., & James, S.E. (2006). Gay, lesbian, and bisexual foster parents: Strengths and challenges for the child welfare system. *Child Welfare, 85*(2), 281–298.

Duehn, W.D. (2014). "Let's get it right": Interactional methods in assessing adoptive families and in post adoptive services. *Ontario Association of Children's Aid Societies Journal, 58*(2), 34–41.

Dunbar, N., Van Dulmen, M.H., Ayers-Lopez, S., Berge, J.M., Christian, C., Gossman, G., Henney, S.M., Mendenhall, T.J., Grotevant, H.D., & McRoy, R.G. (2006). Processes linked to contact changes in adoptive kinship networks. *Family Process, 45*(4), 449–464.

Eckholm, D. (2006). Judge bars subsidy cuts in adopting foster children. *New York Times,* May 2, p. 1.

Faulkner, M., & Madden, E.E. (2012). Open adoption and post-adoption birth family contact: A comparison of non-relative foster and private adoptions. *Adoption Quarterly, 15*(1), 35–56.

Fessler, A. (2006). *The girls who went away: The hidden history of women who surrendered children for adoption in the decades before* Roe vs. Wade. New York: Penguin.

Festinger, T. (2006). Adoption and after: Adoptive parents service needs. In M.M. Dore (Ed.), *The postadoption experience: Adoptive families service needs and service outcomes.* Washington, DC: Child Welfare League of America.

Fischler, R.S. (1980). Protecting American Indian children. *Social Work, 25*, 341–349.

Flango, V.E., & Caskey, M.M. (2005). Adoptions, 2000–2001. *Adoption Quarterly, 8*(4), 23–43.

Flango, V.E., & Flango, C.R. (1993). Adoption statistics by state. *Child Welfare, 72*, 311–319.

Fraser, M.W., Walton, E., Lewis, R.E., & Pecora, P.J. (1996). An experiment in family reunification: Correlates of outcomes at one-year follow-up. *Children and Youth Services Review, 18*(4–5), 335–361.

Gateway. (2012). *Adoption disruptions and dissolutions.* Washington, DC: ACYF, US Children's Bureau. Retrieved from www.childwelfare.gov/pubPDFs/s_disrup.pdf#page=2&view=Disruptions.

Generations United. (2016). *Raising the children of the Opioid Epidemic: Solutions and support for grandfamilies.* Washington, DC: Author. Retrieved from www.gu.org/Portals/0/documents/Reports/16-Report-State_of_Grandfamiles.pdf.

Gibson, T.J. (2003). One church one child: Targeting churches for adoption and foster care ministries in the Washington, DC area. *The Clergy Journal,* October, pp. 10–14.

Goering, E.S., & Shaw, T.V. (2017). Foster care reentry: A survival analysis assessing differences across permanency. *Child Abuse & Neglect, 68*, 36–43.

Heisterman, C. (1935). A summary of legislation on adoption. *Social Service Review, 9*, 269–293.

Henney, S.M., McRoy, R., Ayers-Lopez, S., & Grotevant, H.D. (2003). The impact of openness on adoption agency practices. *Adoption Quarterly, 6*(3), 31–51. doi:10.1300/J145v06n03_03.

Hollinger, J.H. (1989). Beyond the interests of the tribe: The Indian Child Welfare Act and the adoption of Indian Children. *University of Detroit Law Review, 66*, 452–491.

Hollinger, J.H. (1993). Adoption law. *The Future of Children, 3*(1), 43–62.

Howard, J.A., Smith, S.L., Zosky, D.L., & Woodman, K. (2006). A comparison of subsidized guardianship and child welfare adoptive families served by the Illinois Adoption and Guardianship Preservation Program. *Journal of Social Services Research, 32*, 123–134.

Immigration and Naturalization Service, Statistical Analysis Branch. (1991). *Statistical year book.* Washington, DC: Author.

Jones, J., & Placek, P. (2017). *Adoption by the numbers.* Washington, DC: National Council for Adoption. Retrieved from www.adoptioncouncil.org/publications/2017/02/adoption-by-the-numbers.

Katz, L. (1999). Concurrent planning: Benefits and pitfalls. *Child Welfare, 78*, 71–87.

Kerman, B., Maluccio, A.N., & Freundlich, M. (2009). *Achieving permanence for older children and youth in foster care.* New York: Columbia University Press.

Killos, L., Vesneski, W. Rebbe, R., Pecora, P.J., & Christian, S. (2018). *Guardianship assistance policy and implementation: A national analysis of Federal and State Policy and Programs.* Seattle, WA: Casey Family Programs. Retrieved from www.casey.org/guardianship-assistance-policy-and-implementation-a-national-analysis-of-federal-and-state-policies-and-programs/.

Koh, E. (2010). Permanency outcomes of children in kinship and non-kinship foster care: Testing the external validity of kinship effects. *Children and Youth Services Review, 32*, 389–398.

Koh, E., & Testa, M.F. (2011). Children discharged from kin and non-kin foster homes: Do the risks of foster care re-entry differ? *Children and Youth Services Review, 33*, 1497–1505.

Kraft, A.D., Palombo, J., Woods, P.K., Mitchell, D., & Schmidt, A.W. (1985). Some theoretical considerations on confidential adoptions: Part I. The birth mother. *Child and Adolescent Social Work, 2*, 13–21.

Kreider, R.M., & Lofquist, D.A. (2014). *Adopted children and stepchildren – 2010.* U.S. Census Bureau. Report No. P20–572. Retrieved from www.census.gov/prod/2014pubs/p20-572.pdf.

Leung, P., Erich, S., & Kanenberg, H. (2005). A comparison of family functioning in gay/lesbian, heterosexual and special needs adoptions. *Children and Youth Services Review, 27*(9), 1031–1044.

Liao, M., & Testa, M. (2016). Postadoption and guardianship: An evaluation of the adoption preservation, assessment, and linkage program. *Research on Social Work Practice, 26*, 675–685.

Mallon, G.P. (2007). *Lesbian and gay foster and adoptive parents: Recruiting, assessing, and supporting an untapped resource for children and youth in America's child welfare system.* Washington, DC: Child Welfare League of America.

Mallon, G.P. (2015*). Lesbian, gay, bisexual and trans foster and adoptive parents: Recruiting, assessing, and supporting untapped family resources for children and youth* (2nd edn). Washington, DC: Child Welfare League of America.

Mallon, G.P., & Wornoff, R. (2006). Busting out of the child welfare closet: Lesbian, gay, bisexual, and transgender-affirming approaches to child welfare. *Child Welfare, 86*(2), 115–122.

Malm, K., Vandivere, S., Allen, T., DeVooght, K., Ellis, R., McKlindon, A., Smollar, J., Williams, E., and Zinn, A. (2011). *Evaluation Report Summary: The Wendy's Wonderful Kids Initiative.* Washington, DC: Child Trends. Retrieved from https://dciw4f53l7k9i.cloudfront.net/wp-content/uploads/2012/10/Evaluation_Report_Summary.pdf.

Maluccio, A.N., Warsh, R., & Pine, B.A. (1993). Family reunification: An overview. In B.A. Pine, R. Warsh., & A.N. Maluccio (Eds), *Together again: Family reunification in foster care* (pp. 3–19). Washington, DC: Child Welfare League of America.

Maximus, Inc. (1984). *Child welfare statistical fact book: 1984: Substitute care and adoption.* Washington, DC: Office of Human Development Series.

Maza, P.L. (1983). Characteristics of children free for adoption. *Child Welfare* (Research Notes #2). Washington, DC: Children's Bureau, Administration for Children, Youth and Families.

Meezan, W., Katz, S., & Russo, E.M. (1978). *Adoptions without agencies: A study of independent adoptions.* New York: Child Welfare League of America.

National Committee for Adoption. (1989). *Adoption fact-book: United States data issues, regulations, and resources.* Washington, DC: Author.

National Council on State Legislatures. (2013). *The U.S. Supreme Court and the Indian Child Welfare Act.* Denver, CO: Author. Retrieved from www.ncsl.org/research/state-tribal-institute/the-supreme-court-and-the-indian-child-welfare-act.aspx.

National One Church, One Child (2016). *The National One Church, One Child Working Document 2016–2021 Strategic Plan.* Retrieved from www.nationalococ.org/pdf/OCOC-Strategic-Plan-nonrestricted-updated-october-2016.pdf.

Pac, J. (2017). The effect of monthly stipend on the placement instability of youths in out-of-home care. *Children and Youth Services Review, 72*, 111–123. doi:10.1016/j.childyouth.2016.10.019.

Pace, P.R. (2005). Court upholds gay foster parents. *NASW News, 2*(5).

Pannor, R., & Baran, A. (1984). Open adoption as standard practice. *Child Welfare, 63*, 245–250.

Pine, B.A., Spath, R., & Gosteli, S. (2005). Defining and achieving family reunification. In G. Mallon & P.M. Hess (Eds), *Child welfare for the 21st century: A handbook of children, youth, and family services: Practices, policies, and programs* (pp. 378–391). New York: Columbia University Press.

Plantz, M.C., Hubbell, B.J., Barrett, B.J., & Dobrec, A. (1989). Indian child welfare: A status report. *Children Today, 18*(1), 24–29.

Puddy, R.W., & Jackson, Y. (2003). The development of parenting skills in foster parent training. *Children and Youth Services Review, 25*(12), 987–1013.

Research Triangle Institute. (2017). *The understanding post-adoption and guardianship instability for children and youth who exit foster project* (Project Summary). Chapel Hill, NC: Author.

Roberts, Y.H., O'Brien, K., & Pecora, P.J. (2017). *Supporting lifelong families ensuring long-lasting permanency and well-being.* Seattle, WA: Casey Family Programs. Retrieved from www.casey.org/supporting-lifelong-families/Research.

Rolock, N., Pérez, A.G., White, K.R., & Fong, R. (2017). From foster care to adoption and guardianship: A 21st century challenge. *Child & Adolescent Social Work Journal.* doi:10.1007/s10560-017-0499-z.

Rosinsky, K., & Connelly, D. (2016). *Child welfare financing SFY 2014: A survey of federal, state, and local expenditures.* Washington, D.C.: Child Trends.

Ryan, S.D., Pearlmutter, S., & Groza, V. (2004). Coming out of the closet: Opening agencies to gay and lesbian adoptive parents. *Social Work, 49*(1), 85–95.

Shaw, T.V. (2006). *The Multi-ethnic Placement Act.* Unpublished paper, School of Social Welfare, University of California at Berkeley.

Skivenes, M., & Thoburn, J. (2016). Pathways to permanence in England and Norway: A critical analysis of documents and data. *Children and Youth Services Review, 67*, 152–160.

Slingerland, W.H. (1919). *Child-placing in families.* New York: Russell Sage Foundation.

Smith, S.L., Howard, J.A., Garnier, P.C., & Ryan, S.D. (2006). Where are we now? A post-ASFA examination of adoption disruption. *Adoption Quarterly: Innovations in Community and Clinical Practice, Theory, and Research, 9*(4), 19–44.

Tatara, T. (1994). Some additional explanations for the recent rise in the U.S. child substitute care flow data and future research questions. In R.P. Barth, J.D. Berrick, & N. Gilbert (Eds), *Child welfare research review* (pp. 126–145). New York: Columbia University Press.

Triseliotis, J. (2002). Long-term foster care or adoption: The evidence examined. *Child & Family Social Work, 7*, 23–33.

U.S. Department of Health and Human Services, Administration for Children and Families, Children's Bureau. (2015). *The AFCARS Report – Preliminary FY 2014 estimates as of (23).*

Washington, DC: U.S. Department of Health and Human Services. Retrieved from www. acf.hhs.gov/sites/default/files/cb/afcarsreport23.pdf.

U.S. Department of Health and Human Services. (2016a). *Child Welfare Outcomes 2010–2013: Report to Congress*. Retrieved from www.acf.hhs.gov/programs/cb/resource/cwo-10-13 (accessed July 4, 2016).

U.S. Department of Health and Human Services, Administration for Children and Families, Administration on Children, Youth and Families, Children's Bureau. (2016b). *The AFCARS report No. 23*. Washington, DC: Author. Retrieved from www.acf.hhs.gov/cb/resource/afcars-report-23.

U.S. Department of Health and Human Services, Administration for Children and Families, Administration on Children, Youth and Families, Children's Bureau. (2016c). *Trends in foster care and adoption*. Washington, DC: Author. Retrieved from www.acf.hhs.gov/cb/resource/trends-in-foster-care-and-adoption-fy15.

U.S. Department of Health and Human Services, Administration for Children and Families, Children's Bureau. (2016). *The AFCARS Report – Preliminary FY 2015 estimates as of June 2016 (23)*. Washington, DC: U.S. Department of Health and Human Services. Retrieved from www.acf.hhs.gov/sites/default/files/cb/afcarsreport23.pdf.

U.S. Department of Health and Human Services, Administration for Children and Families, Administration on Children, Youth and Families, Children's Bureau. (2017). *Preliminary FY 2016 estimates as of October 20, 2017. No. 24*. Washington, DC: Author. Retrieved from www.acf.hhs.gov/sites/default/files/cb/afcarsreport24.pdf.

U.S. Department of Health and Human Services. (2007). *Fiscal Year 2007 Budget in brief*. Retrieved from www.hhs.gov/budget/parts.html (accessed April 19, 2007).

U.S. Department of Health and Human Services. (2015). www.acf.hhs.gov/sites/default/files/cb/final/age2014.pdf.

U.S. Department of Health and Human Services, Departmental Appeals Board. (2006). *Case of Ohio Department of Job and Family Services*. Retrieved from www. hhs.gov/dab/decisions/dab2023.htm.

U.S. Department of State (2016). *Annual report on intercountry adoption*. Washington, DC: Author. Retrieved from. https://travel.state.gov/content/adoptionsabroad/en/about-us/statistics.html.

U.S. Department of State. (2017). *Adoption statistics*. Retrieved from https://travel.state.gov/content/travel/en/Intercountry-Adoption/adopt_ref/adoption-statistics.html.

U.S. Senate, Committee on Finance. (1990). *Foster care, adoption assistance, and child welfare services*. Washington, DC: U.S. Government Printing Office.

Veronico, A. (1983). One church, one child: Placing children with special needs. *Children Today, 12*, 6–10.

Vesneski, W., Killos, L., Pecora, P.J., & McIntire, E. (2017). An analysis of state law and policy regarding subsidized guardianship for children: Innovations in permanency. *Journal of Juvenile Law & Policy, 21*(1), 26–75.

Von Korff, L., Grotevant, H.D., & McRoy, R.G. (2006). Openess arrangements and psychological adjustment in adolescent adoptees. *Journal of Family Psychology, 20*(3), 531–534.

Wald, M.S. (2015). *Beyond CPS: Developing an effective system for helping children in neglectful families.* Stanford, CA: Stanford University, Stanford Law School. Retrieved from http://ssrn.com/abstract=2554074.

Walton, E. (1998). In-home family-focused reunification: A six-year follow-up of a successful experiment. *Social Work Research, 22*(4), 205–214.

Warsh, R., Maluccio, A.N., & Pine, B.A. (1994). *Teaching family reunification: A sourcebook.* Washington, DC: Child Welfare League of America.

Warsh, R., Pine, B.A., & Maluccio, A.N. (1996). *Reconnecting families – A guide to strengthening family reunification services.* Washington, DC: CWLA Press.

Weeks, N.B. (1953). *Adoption for school-age children in institutions.* New York: Child Welfare League of America.

Whitmore, W.H. (1876). *The law of adoption in the United States.* Albany, NJ: J. Munsell.

Winokur, M., Holtan, A., & Batchelder, K. (2014). Kinship care for the safety, permanency, and well-being of children removed from the home for maltreatment. Cochrane Database of Systematic Reviews: CD006546. doi:10.1002/14651858.CD006546.pub3.

Wulczyn, F. (2003). Closing the gap: Are changing exit patterns reducing the time African American children spend in foster care relative to Caucasian children? *Children and Youth Services Review, 25*, 431–462.

Wulczyn, F.H., Chen, I., & Hislop, K. (2007). *Foster Care Dynamics 2000–2005: A report from the Multistate Foster Care Data Archive.* Chicago, IL: University of Chicago, Chapin Hall Center for Children.

Xu, Y., Ahn, H., & Bright, C.L. (2017). Family involvement meetings: Engagement, facilitation, and child and family goals. *Children and Youth Services Review, 79*, 37–43. doi:http://dx.doi.org/10.1016/j.childyouth.2017.05.026.

Zosky, D.L., Howard, J.A., Smith, S.L., Howard, A.M., & Shelvini, K.H. (2005). *Adoption Quarterly, 8*(3), 1–24.

Juvenile Justice and Crossover Youth in Child Welfare

The incarceration rate in the U.S. is the highest in the world. There are more than 2.3 million people behind bars in federal and state prisons and local jails, including 34,000 youth who are detained in 901 juvenile detention centers and approximately 4,500 youth incarcerated as adults (Wagner & Rabuy (2017), using data sources from 2013–2015). People of color are overrepresented in the U.S. criminal justice system and comprise more than half of the incarcerated population where Black and Native American males have a greater likelihood of incarceration followed by Latino males compared to their White counterparts (The Sentencing Project, 2017). Similarly, although juvenile incarceration rates have declined since 1999 (Figure 7.1) (Sickmund et al., 2017), youth of color remain disproportionately represented and are more likely to receive harsher punishment where Black youth experience a greater likelihood of incarceration for simple assault (Rovner, 2017). In addition to the enduring racial disparities in the juvenile justice system, the overlap between child maltreatment and delinquent behavior is a cause for concern.

In the past four decades, multiple studies have demonstrated the link between child maltreatment and involvement with the juvenile justice system (Bilchik & Nash, 2008; Lansford et al., 2007; Ryan & Testa, 2005; Smith & Thornberry, 1995; Stewart, Livingston, & Dennison, 2008). Over time, maltreated children are more likely to engage in delinquent behavior than children who have never experienced maltreatment. For some youth, the likelihood of delinquency increases by 7 percent and juvenile arrest by 59 percent. Historically, conservative estimates of youth involved in the child welfare (CW) system who are also engaged in delinquency are between 9 to 29 percent, but recent estimates could be as high as 50 percent (Smith & Thornberry, 1995; Hockenberry & Puzzanchera, 2015). Probation data further reveal that about 42 percent of youth under probation also had

Number of Youth Committed to Juvenile Facilities, 1999–2013

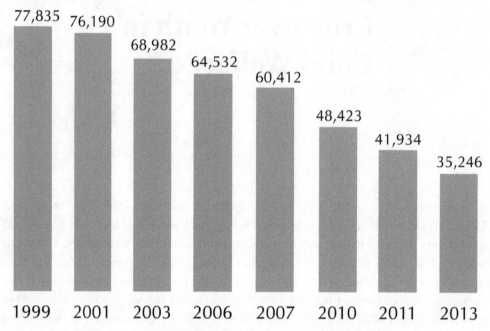

Figure 7.1 Declining Rates of Incarcerated Youth
Source: Reprinted by the Sentencing Project (2017, p. 6).

contact with the CW system (Bilchik & Nash, 2008). These studies have strengthened our understanding of the intersection of the CW system and juvenile justice services (JJS) where many children and youth find themselves wedged in between.

This chapter focuses on this intersection and explores the multiple challenges of addressing the needs of a subgroup of youth often referred to as crossover youth, dual contact youth, and dually adjudicated youth. We will provide clarification of these terms and suggest the use of "crossover youth" as an overarching term to encompass multiple subgroups of youth impacted by the two systems in various ways. As the intersection between CW and JJS is now widely recognized, there is also an increased recognition that policy and practice must respond to this overlap. This chapter will discuss some of the challenges inherent in these intersecting but siloed systems, and some promising policy and practice responses in various settings.

Definitions

Various terms have been created to refer to youth who are involved in the CW and JJS systems. "Dual-status youth" has been used for decades to refer to youth who have been involved in the CW system and the juvenile system. Use of this term, however, glosses over other segments of this population who may have experienced maltreatment but were not formally receiving services through CW or those who may have engaged in delinquent behavior but have never been adjudicated. The term "dually adjudicated youth" is limited in scope as it only encompasses youth whose case has been adjudicated in both systems. Herz, Ryan, and Bilchik (2010) suggested the term "crossover youth" to refer to youth who are engaged in delinquent behavior and have experienced some form of child abuse and neglect regardless of whether or not they have a formal case with either the CW system or JJS system. They also provided clarification on other subgroups of youth referred to as "dually involved youth" and "dually adjudicated youth" (Box 7.1). In this chapter, "crossover youth" is used to refer to all youth who experienced maltreatment at some point and engaged in delinquency, and may include those who belong to the other two subgroups of dually involved and dually adjudicated youth. Moreover, crossing over is often not concurrent, as many youth who have experienced child maltreatment early in their life course may only come into contact with JJS later on. One common pattern is that youth exiting foster care subsequently receive services through JJS.

Box 7.1   Definitions

- *Crossover Youth:* Youth who experience maltreatment and engage in delinquency and who may or may not be known to the CW and/or juvenile systems.

- *Dually Involved Youth:* Crossover youth who have some level of involvement (diversionary, formal, or a combination of both) with both the CW and JJS.

- *Dually Adjudicated Youth:* Dually involved youth who are formally involved (sustained dependency court allegation) and are adjudicated by the delinquency court.

Source: Herz, D.C., Ryan, J.P. & Bilchik, S. (2010). Challenges facing crossover youth: An examination of juvenile-justice decision making and recidivism. *Family Court Review, 48,* 305–321. (Definitions from pp. 305–306.)

An Overview of Pathways Leading to Identification as a Dually-Involved Youth

	Starting Point	Occurrence	Result
Pathway 1	Youth has an open child welfare case	Youth is arrested	Youth enters the delinquency system
Pathway 2	Youth is arrested	Youth has a previously closed child welfare case	Referral is made to child welfare
Pathway 3	Youth is arrested— no previous contact with child welfare	Upon investigation, maltreatment is discovered	Referral is made to child welfare
Pathway 4	Youth is arrested, adjudicated, and placed in a correctional placement	Time in correctional placement ends, but there is no safe home to return to	Referral to child welfare

Figure 7.2 Pathways Leading to Identification as a Dually Involved Youth

Source: Herz et al. (2012, p.3). Reprinted with permission.

There are various ways that maltreated youth engaged in delinquency become known to CW and/or JJS and become dually involved. Herz et al. (2012, p. 3) identified four major pathways (shown in Figure 7.2).

One pathway begins when a youth is receiving services through the CW system. A typical example is when a youth who resides in congregate care runs away and engages in delinquency. Once arrested, the youth comes into contact with the juvenile justice system and may start receiving care in both systems. Another pathway begins on the other end of the spectrum where a youth is involved in the juvenile justice system through an arrest, but the child has already had contact with the CW system. Thus, the youth is subsequently referred to CW. Another scenario is when a youth is arrested but does not have prior contact with CPS. However, if experiences of maltreatment become known, the case may be referred to CPS. The final pathway could begin from juvenile correction when a youth is released and they do not have a suitable home for their reintegration post-release. They are then referred to the CW system for further services. Other related paths are possible in which children or youth are dismissed from one system and, later, re-enter the other system.

Estimating the number of crossover youth has been a challenge for some time. CW and JJS are separate entities with a distinct mission and functions. They are silos by design. Further, administrative data are shared rarely between these agencies. This makes it difficult to estimate the population of youth impacted by maltreatment who are also engaged in some form of delinquent behavior. Variations in estimates of the crossover youth population are also influenced by the lack of consensus in categories used to identify crossover youth. Recent prevalence estimates in Los Angeles indicate that 79 percent of crossover youth arrests happened in out-of-home placements through the CW system while 67 percent of JJS-involved youth had been in contact with the CW system at some point in their lives (Halemba & Siegel, 2011; Herz & Ryan, 2008). These estimates do not include youth who never came into contact with either CW or JJS but have histories of child maltreatment and have engaged in delinquency at some point. These youth fall under a more liberal definition of "crossover youth" where they are considered crossover regardless of their system involvement. The majority are male and have existing mental health, substance use, and school problems (Herz et al., 2012).

Why Crossover Youth Matter

The evidence regarding the negative effects of child maltreatment on development is well established. Engagement in delinquency further worsens these outcomes and multiplies developmental risks for crossover children and youth. Those with a history of maltreatment who become involved with JJS are more likely to recidivate than those who have never been involved in CW (Halemba & Siegel, 2011). Moreover, a larger proportion recidivate in the long term (e.g. about 72 percent of crossover youth compared to about 60 percent of those without histories of maltreatment) (Lee & Villagrana, 2015). Youth who have been involved with CW services and JJS are also more likely to experience arrest and incarceration as adults (Thornberry, Huizinga, & Loeber, 2004). In a study of young adult outcomes in Los Angeles county (see results in Figure 7.3), 18 percent of crossover youth were later under adult probation compared to approximately 7 percent of those who did not have any earlier contact with the juvenile justice system (Culhane et al., 2011; Tam et al., 2016). Many crossover youths are also vulnerable to commercial sex trafficking or exploitation (CSE), especially those with histories of running away and those who were placed in out-of-home care (Casey Family Programs, 2014). Recent estimates of CSE among children with histories of contact with CW range from 78 to 98 percent (Connecticut Department of Children and Families, 2012; Feldman, 2007; Walker, 2013).

Crossover youth have also often experienced trauma that can have a devastating impact upon their health and well-being. The prevalence of traumatic experience among youth who have committed offenses is high, with a majority having been exposed to at least one traumatic event and 70 percent reporting experiences of physical or sexual abuse or exposure to violence (Abram et al., 2004, 2007; Dierkhising et al., 2013; Ford et al., 2007, 2013). Also, poly-victimization is a major concern, especially for girls involved with the JJS (Ford et al., 2013). Traumatic experiences are likely to worsen outcomes for youth and increase their vulnerability to various mental and socio-behavioral problems (Briere, Agee, & Dietrich, 2016; Kendall-Tackett, 2003). Insofar as JJS fails to address these traumatic experiences, or exacerbates them, the outcomes are likely to be adverse.

Outcomes across multiple domains are also compromised. Crossover youth are more likely to have worse economic outcomes as adults. In the Los Angeles County study (Figure 7.3) (Culhane et al., 2011), half of crossover youth experienced extreme poverty compared to one-third of those who were involved only in CPS. They were also more likely to receive drug and alcohol treatment, mental health services, and health services. A greater cause for concern is that these negative outcomes begin even before crossover youth transition into adulthood. A study by Herz and Ryan (2008) revealed that 80 percent of crossover youth from Arizona had issues related to substance abuse and 61 percent had mental health issues. The majority of crossover youth grew up in families impacted by criminal justice involvement, domestic violence, and mental health problems. The family environments of these youth are also uncommonly compromised by adversities related to parental incarceration, domestic violence, and mental health problems (Herz et al., 2012).

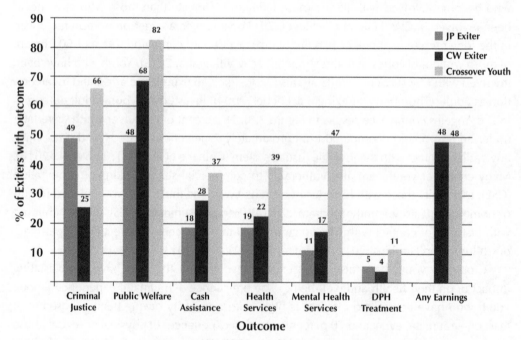

Figure 7.3 Services Used and Outcomes for Crossover Youth Compared to Child Welfare Only and Juvenile Probation Only Youth in Los Angeles County

Source: Culhane et al. (2011, p. 10). Reprinted with permission.

The above threats to the short-term and long-term outcomes of crossover youth are a cause for concern. In addition, the magnitude of these threats is possibly underestimated due to the challenges of determining the true prevalence of crossing over. Many youth are possibly not accounted for, and their needs remain unassessed. More alarming is the racial disproportionality that exists in these systems. African American children are overrepresented in the CW system and JJS, as are Latinx children in some areas of the United States. (Note that we use this term because it is a gender-inclusive term that departs from the masculine-centric term "Latino" and the binary nature of alternative terms Latino/a and Latina. See Scharrón del Río & Aja, 2015.) Given their overrepresentation, the prevalence of crossing over could be much higher for African American youth than children of other racial or ethnic backgrounds as the CW system becomes a pathway toward juvenile services receipt. Consequently, children of color could be at higher risk for worse outcomes over their life course.

Despite the odds that are seemingly stacked against crossover youth, identification of early poor outcomes across multiple domains points to a window of opportunity for preventive efforts to stop or slow down their cascade into adulthood. Prevention is about investing in future outcomes by targeting current conditions (Stagner & Lansing, 2009). The challenge of this approach lies in the identification of risk factors that matter most for crossover youth and the protective factors that would have the strongest impact in promoting resilience. This is particularly important for crossover youth, as they possess more risk factors and fewer protective factors than their non-crossover counterparts (Herz et al., 2012).

The overrepresentation of children of color in these systems should also compel us to craft our practice and policy responses to reduce their involvement in these systems. Further, we must acknowledge that the disproportionality could be rooted in larger structural issues that must be understood and addressed. For example, racial biases have been well documented, with research indicating that youth of color are both more likely to be arrested than White youth and are more likely to receive longer sentences (Lowery, Burrow, & Kaminski, 2016; Andersen, 2015; Cochran & Mears, 2015; U.S. Department of Justice, Civil Rights Division, 2015). There is some evidence that interventions aimed at addressing such disproportionality can be successful (see, e.g., Annie E. Casey Foundation, 2009; Center on Juvenile and Criminal Justice, 2004).

The Role of Protective Factors

The preceding discussion shows the well-established link between multi-systems involvement and worse life course outcomes. Nevertheless, there are variations in these outcomes where some crossover youth defy the odds, achieve positive outcomes, and live productive lives. Many crossover youths do not recidivate. Some achieve educational success through community colleges and four-year courses at universities (Culhane et al., 2011). While assessment of risk factors that contribute to many negative outcomes is important, assessing protective factors is just as important. What helps crossover youth rise above adversities? What factors help them overcome the likelihood of adult incarceration? What helps them escape the pipeline to prison and divert to the pipeline to educational success instead?

Focusing on risk factors alone could lead to missed opportunities to make a positive impact in improving youth outcomes. Practitioners and researchers need to incorporate protective factors in intervention design and implementation, as these factors can promote resilience and their strengthening could help prevent the cascading negative outcomes of child maltreatment (Afifi & MacMillan, 2011; Developmental Services Group, 2013; Jenson & Fraser, 2016).

Look at the picture shown in Figure 7.4. We see a scale of risk and protective factors. If protective factors are not taken into account, there would not be anything to counterbalance the effects of risk factors. However, as we introduce protective factors into the scale, the beam slowly balances out. While the diagram does not represent the complexities at work here, it illustrates how we must strive to strengthen protective factors to the point that

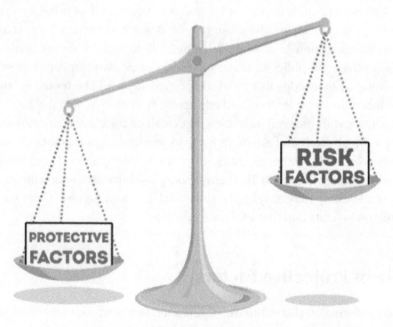

Figure 7.4 The Need to Account for Protective and Risk Factors
Source: www.centerforresilientchildren.org/wp-content/uploads/scales.gif. Reprinted with permission.

this side of the beam becomes heavier than the risk factor side. Increasing protective factors has implications toward fostering resilience and countering the adverse effects brought on by risk factors.

As discussed in Chapter 3 and in one of the textbook resource papers (Pecora, 2018), a helpful approach to identifying protective factors is the use of a systems lens where we examine the different contexts within which youths are nested. Protective factors at the individual level are personal characteristics and traits. Family-level factors could include resources available within the family and supportive relationships. At the community level, research has identified various positive relationships that could strengthen resilience and promote positive development. Table 7.1 presents a summary of some of these factors across systems. The table may also serve as a template for strengths-based assessment in social work practice in CW and JJS settings. When engaging with crossover youth and their families, this simple template could help direct assessment questions toward discovering their strengths and the positive relationships they have with their families and communities. Recognizing a lack of these factors also allows for identifying where more cultivation of protective elements may be done to promote resilience.

Table 7.1 Top Ten Protective Factors that Reduce Risk for Children in Child Welfare Systems

Individual Level

Relational skills: Relational skills encompass two main components: (1) a youth's ability to form positive bonds and connections (e.g., social competence, being caring, forming positive attachments and prosocial relationships); and (2) interpersonal skills such as communication skills, conflict resolution skills, and self-efficacy in conflict situations.

Self-regulation skills: Self-regulation skills refer to a youth's ability to manage or control emotions and behaviors. This skill set may include self-mastery, anger management, character, long-term self-control, and emotional intelligence.

Problem-solving skills: Includes general problem-solving skills, self-efficacy in conflict situations, higher daily living scores, decision-making skills, planning skills, adaptive functioning skills, and task-oriented coping skills.

Involvement in positive activities: Refers to engagement in and/or achievement in school, extracurricular activities, employment, training, apprenticeships or military.

Relationship Level

Parenting competences: Parenting competences refers to two broad categories of parenting: (1) parenting skills (e.g., parental monitoring and discipline, prenatal care, setting clear standards, and developmentally appropriate limits); and (2) positive parent–child interactions (e.g., close relationship between parent and child, sensitive parenting, support, caring).

(Continued)

Table 7.1 (Continued)

Relationship Level

Positive peers: Refers to friendships with peers, support from friends, or positive peer norms.

Caring adult(s): This factor most often refers to caring adults beyond the nuclear family, such as mentors, home visitors (especially for pregnant and parenting teens), older extended family members, or individuals in the community.

Community Level

Positive community environment: Positive community environment refers to neighborhood advantage or quality, religious service attendance, living in a safe and higher quality environment, a caring community, social cohesion, and positive community norms.

Positive school environment: A positive school environment is primarily defined as the existence of supportive programming in schools.

Economic opportunities: Refers to household income and socioecomic status; a youth's self-perceived resources; employment, apprenticeship, coursework, and/or military involvement; and placement in a foster care setting (from a poor setting).

Source: Development Services Group, Inc. (2013). *Protective factors for populations served by the administration on children, youth, and families. A literature review and theoretical framework: Executive summary.* Washington, DC: U.S. Department of Health and Human Services, Administration for Children and Families, Children's Bureau, p. 6. Retrieved from www.dsgonline.com/acyf/DSG%20Protective%20Factors%20 Literature%20Review%202013%20Exec%20Summary.pdf (accessed May 20, 2014).

Program Design Challenges

Multiplicity of Youth Needs

The multiplicity of the needs of crossover youth reflects their exposure to multiple risk factors. They have been exposed to various adversities in their families. Many have witnessed domestic violence and have traumatic experiences of victimization. They have mental health and substance use problems that cascade into other life domains, including school and social relationships. In addition, they have behavioral issues that brought them to the attention of either CW and/or JJS. This array of issues speaks to the need for Wraparound and other integrated systemic approaches and services to improve future life outcomes of crossover youth (see Chapter 8). However, given that in most states CW and juvenile justice systems operate as separate entities, there are several challenges that need to be addressed.

Services Coordination

The siloed nature of these systems means there is a lack of coordination in the case of dually involved youth. During the past decade some efforts have been made to improve care coordination following the ground-breaking work of Shay Bilchik and the Georgetown Center for Juvenile Justice Reform (CJJR). CJJR developed the Crossover Youth Practice Model (CYPM), aiming to achieve systemic change toward reducing the prevalence of crossing over and strengthening collaborative relationships across agencies serving crossover youth. Current practice in many counties in the United States encourages multidisciplinary teams to work together in certain CW cases. This typically includes case coordination across systems, provision of multi-systemic therapy, establishing crossover units in CW and developing crossover courts. Bexar County in Texas has implemented some of these practices through its One Family/One Judge Crossover Court and a crossover unit that focuses on crossover youth with open cases in both CW and JJS (Kolivoski, Barnett, & Abbott, 2015).

Despite these advances, the adaptation of structure across systems that require interaction between CW and JJS staff has been moderate. The continued lack of coordination extends to the mental health and education systems where staff members do not have access to information relevant to a student or client who may also be receiving services from CW or JJS. There has been slow acknowledgment that dually involved cases must be responded to and in some places there is still a lack of recognition that such cases exist and warrant integrated solutions (Herz et al., 2012; Kolivoski et al., 2017). This lack of coordination could lead to possible duplication of services or even lack of services when one system assumes that services are already being provided through another service provider.

The lack of coordination may be due, in part, to the lack of a cross-system data-sharing platform. Currently, there are no central databases where staff could cross-check the services already being rendered. Data sharing would facilitate the sharing of information, and staff could easily find out whether a youth is already receiving services to avoid potential duplication of service (Chuang & Wells, 2010). Lack of coordination could also result in contradictory services, especially when systems fail to collaborate regarding a family case plan that outlines permanency goals for youth.

Recognizing that youth of color are often disproportionately represented in CW and JJS systems, the efforts of JDAI to utilize data and encourage members of the initiative to address racial equity in juvenile justice work are noteworthy. Below is an excerpt from *JDAIconnect* regarding how some organizations are responding to racial and ethnic disparities in the juvenile justice system by beginning the work from within the partnership. The collaborative partnership between Meghan Harrah and Albino Garcia demonstrates the importance of addressing structural inequalities across alliances:

> On paper, Meghan Harrah and Albino Garcia had a shared goal: to reduce racial and ethnic disparities in the juvenile justice system. They also had a shared

349

title: Co-chair of the working group within the Juvenile Detention Alternatives Initiative® (JDAI) in Bernalillo County, New Mexico. But their different perspectives and unaddressed pain and anger, which stemmed from decades of racial and ethnic tensions, threatened to undermine this work.

Today, Harrah and Garcia are not just professional partners – they're friends. They made a conscious effort to address hidden fissures caused by structural racism, and their story illustrates both the challenges and opportunities JDAI partners face when working with their counterparts in the community to improve racial and ethnic equity. Garcia is executive director of La Plazita Institute in Albuquerque, a nonprofit that engages youth, elders and communities through a philosophy of "la cultura cura," or "culture heals." Garcia and those he represented felt resentment and pain toward a juvenile justice system that they felt locked their kids up while disrespecting their culture and history. Harrah, a juvenile probation supervisor for the New Mexico Children, Youth and Families Department, represented that system. She and her staff felt under attack – and a target of hate – by the local community.

When Garcia and Harrah became co-chairs of the reducing racial and ethnic disparities working group a few years ago, distrust and negative assumptions clouded their work. Cultural differences in body language and communication norms led to unintended insults. At one point, the divide between the two leaders grew so wide that they flat-out refused to work together.

Ultimately, through external mediation, Garcia and Harrah talked through the assumptions that each had made and confronted their own personal feelings and biases. Equally important: The leaders acknowledged how they, their communities and their employees fit into the larger societal dynamic of structural racism. Structural racism reinforces or perpetuates inequity among racial groups through public policies, institutional practices and cultural norms. It operates at the societal level and is not caused by individuals. Garcia recalls a pivotal moment in his relationship with Harrah: "I saw tears come out of my enemy's [Harrah's] eyes – I thought, "There's a human inside there. [.] At least they are making an effort."

Now, the leaders are taking steps to bridge the divide between their respective communities. The probation department has developed two trainings for managerial and line staff. The first engages community members to educate staff members about structural racism and internal bias. More than 100 employees working in probation and detention have attended the four-hour training. Harrah says that she and her probation officers are learning to engage in more of a dialogue with community members, creating a safe space for anger and sadness and recognizing and respecting cultural traditions. The second training, to start in January 2018, digs into local data on decision points. It will help probation and detention staff members examine how their decisions can influence racial disparities within the system.

(Annie E. Casey Foundation, 2017a. Reprinted with permission)

Other suggested approaches to improve services for crossover youth are listed below:

- *Agency communication and collaboration.* The needs of crossover youth are complex. Agency collaboration is necessary to address the problems and conditions these youth face. These collaborations should include mental health departments, health services, and educational systems, in addition to the two major agencies that serve crossover youth. Such partnerships could be formalized through Memoranda of Understanding that facilitate identification of crossover youth, avoid duplication services, and in some cases result in diversion of youth from JJS (Haight et al., 2014).

- *Comprehensive and coordinated case assessment and planning.* Joint assessment by CW and JJS is central to the success of crossover services. Case coordination and planning are shared between systems from intake to disposition and continues throughout the life of a case based on the changing needs of youth and their families (Herz et al., 2012).

- *Data sharing.* One file per case across agencies could facilitate information sharing. Case files should record assessment information, case plans, program activities, and progress reports. Databases could also be linked across various systems to facilitate case tracking and synchronize delivery of services.

- *Partnering with families and communities.* Family members and community members have a wealth of strengths and expertise that could be tapped and built upon as soon as a youth comes into contact with CW or JJS. Their meaningful participation in case planning and assessment is vital in creating a community of people that could offer support in various ways. Community members may include representatives from schools, recreational youth programs, spiritual communities, and other service providers who could come together during decision-making meetings, case staffing, and multidisciplinary meetings (Herz et al., 2012).

- *Evidence-based programs.* Evidence-based programs such as Dialectical Behavior Therapy, Functional Family Therapy, and Multi Systemic Therapy should be used when available to support crossover youth and their caregivers (see Chapter 8).

In addition, trauma-informed interventions could potentially address the impact of trauma. Programs for crossover youth must respond to the high rates of trauma exposures among juvenile offenders, mainly since traumatic experiences could compromise the ability of young people to self-regulate. Finally, cultural adaptation is essential in program planning and implementation. Evidence-based interventions must be adapted to fit local culture, so that it aligns with their values and worldviews (see Box 7.2).

Box 7.2

"My judge now, she's nice, real nice. She took me in the back room and talked to me. To get my life story, and she was real supportive when I was pregnant and she helped me out the most. She helped me get in a foster home instead of placement [in a group home]. If I wanted to meet with a family she would try that too, to see if that works, instead of just throwing me in placement or in a detention center."

(Participant, A 100 Percent Pittsburgh Pilot Project)

There may be no equivalent substitute for a healthy and thriving family that is free from maltreatment; however, we can certainly do better in preventing youth from crossing over from child welfare to juvenile justice. [.] After considering and listening to the stories of the crossover youth, we are left with little doubt that many of their problems that occurred in adolescence and young adulthood could have been prevented by receiving higher quality foster care and sustained supportive child welfare services. Prevention through child welfare systems means that these young people are not tossed from one abusive setting to another; that they are given a chance to thrive by improving child welfare systems, quality of placements, and permanency planning.

(Abrams & Terry, 2017, p. 192)

Promising Responses

In the past few years, CW and JJS have made big strides in addressing the issue of crossover youth. Some of the more notable developments are information and data sharing adapted by some counties in states such as Maryland, South Carolina, and Indiana. The Juvenile Law Center and the Child Welfare League of America (now with the Robert F. Kennedy

National Resource Center for Juvenile Justice) developed a toolkit that could be used by stakeholders to facilitate information sharing (see www.infosharetoolkit.org). Although the adaption of data-sharing approaches such as the creation of central databases that could track crossover and dually involved youth has been slow, researchers have used innovative ways to match administrative data from different systems to estimate the prevalence of crossing over.

Knowledge about risk and protective factors has added another layer of the foundation upon which promising models and practices have anchored their approaches. Researchers and government agencies including the court systems recognize the complexity of needs of crossover youth and have, in the past decade, worked together to develop models for stronger collaborations. One such model is the Crossover Youth Practice Model (CYPM), highlighted next for its specific focus on crossover youth and its innovative multi-agency collaborative approach. In recognition of the structural issues that influence crossover youth outcomes, a coalition that is working toward racial equity in the juvenile justice system is also highlighted here.

The Crossover Youth Practice Model

The CYPM is a multi-system practice model that targets youth who are involved in the CW and/or juvenile justice system. It seeks to reduce dual involvement; reduce out-of-home placement and congregate care; and address racial disproportionality. The Georgetown University Center for Juvenile Justice Reform and Casey Family Programs developed the model. It has been implemented in 103 counties in 21 states across the United States (see Figure 7.5) (Center for Juvenile Justice Reform, 2014).

The CYPM emphasizes the importance of data collection, particularly the use of cross-system data to inform program and policy decisions. It also provides a structure for multi-agency collaborations that encourages consistency and resource sharing. As described in Table 7.2, the CYPM is divided into three phases (Herz et al., 2012). Phase One refers to a point in time when youth is identified, arrests take place, and youth is placed in detention. Joint assessment and planning take place during Phase Two where youth needs are identified, family and service providers are engaged, and joint assessment is conducted. Phase Three is focused on coordinated case management and planning towards permanency, transition, and case closure. Family engagement is central, and inter-agency information sharing is expected across the three phases.

Inter-system collaboration is fundamental to the CYPM. A team is organized from the beginning when a delinquency referral is made. The collaboration includes various stakeholders, including representatives from the probation department, CW agency, school,

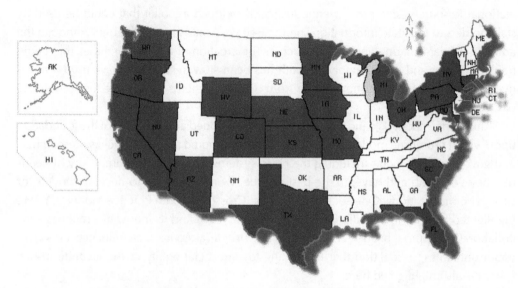

Figure 7.5 States that Adopted the Crossover Youth Practice Model (in grey shading)
Source: Center for Juvenile Justice Reform (2014). Reprinted with permission.

Table 7.2 Practice Phases and Process Measures of CYPM

Practice Phases	Process Measures
Phase One: Arrest, Identification, and Detention	• Increasing family engagement and voice in decision making • Increase cross-agency communication and collaboration • Reducing the use and length of stay in pre-adjudication detention • Increasing the use of diversion • Increasing interagency information sharing
Phase Two: Joint Assessment and Planning	• Increasing family engagement and voice in decision making • Increasing interagency information sharing • Increasing the use of a joint assessment process • Increasing the timely identification of a youth's needs • Increasing the identification of appropriate services and treatment • Increasing the number of youth in appropriate placement settings

Practice Phases	Process Measures
Phase Three: Coordinated Case Management and Planning for Permanency, Transition, and Case Closure	• Increasing the satisfaction of youth and parents with the process • Increasing interagency information sharing • Increasing the number of youth achieving permanency • Reducing the number of youth re-entering CW from juvenile justice placements • Reducing the number of foster youth penetrating the juvenile justice system • Reducing the use of congregate care • Reducing recidivism

Source: Center for Juvenile Justice Reform. (2018). Crossover Youth Practice Model. Retrieved from http://cjjr.georgetown.edu/our-work/crossover-youth-practice-model/. Reprinted with permission.

mental health agency, parents or guardians, and the youth. The model also requires that the probation officer and CW social worker assigned to the case work closely together and jointly inform the court regarding critical issues and recommendations.

Program evaluation results show promise. Findings revealed lower rates of recidivism among youth served within the CYPM (Haight et al., 2016). In Philadelphia, Pennsylvania, the CYPM team diverted almost 900 youth from the juvenile justice system by creating a single court process (Herz et al., 2012). Staff across CW, juvenile justice and legal systems also evaluated the model positively and described improved procedures and services (Haight et al., 2014).

Systems Integration Initiative

The Child Welfare League of America developed the Systems Integration Initiative (SII) (now implemented by the Robert F. Kennedy Children's Action Corps) to support jurisdictions in developing a more integrated juvenile justice and CW system, and to encourage a collaborative approach to policy and program development and implementation (Herz et al., 2012). Through this initiative, CW and JJS formalize agreements to collaborate, integrate information systems, and share fiscal responsibility.

Recognizing the rising needs of crossover youth in Washington State, King County adapted the SII model in 2003. Since then, the King County Uniting for Youth Program has created and sustained collaborative leadership; developed and disseminated a resource guide; established and implemented procedures for coordinated case planning and service delivery; conducted regular cross-system trainings; improved screening and assessment for mental health and substance abuse; and developed a program to help school dropouts (Halemba & Siegel, 2011).

The Juvenile Detention Alternatives Initiative

The Juvenile Detention Alternatives Initiative (JDAI) model pioneered by the Annie E. Casey Foundation aims to reduce the rates of juvenile detention (see www.aecf.org/work/juvenile-justice/jdai/). They have been working toward this goal for more than two decades worldwide. While this model specifically targets youth offenders, it promotes the same core strategies from the CYPM and SII. It encourages inter-agency collaboration among stakeholders, including staff from probation departments, juvenile courts, lawyers, schools, and community organizations. Decision making is informed by rigorously analyzed data. The JDAI has also launched an online platform, *JDAIConnect,* where information is shared, thus facilitating dissemination of effective strategies and success stories. The JDAI's attention to racial and ethnic disparities sets it apart from the other models with its intentional approach to identifying policies and practices that disadvantage youth of color, and its results show the value of that approach (Annie E. Casey Foundation, 2017a).

Within CW, promising responses include providing support for foster families who have children in their care who may have broken the law. Internal emergency response protocols could help address incidents such as property destruction in foster homes to avoid unnecessary police reports and prevent youth from crossing over from the CW system to JJS. We also need policies that consider what the minimum age should be for referral to JJS when it is a punitive system. Should we not restrict referral to JJS to children below 10 years old? What are some important developmental factors to consider?

Finally, the recent enactment of Justice for Victims of Trafficking Act (JVTA) of 2015 is a big step toward addressing the sexual exploitation of minors in the U.S. The JVTA was enacted to provide services to victims of trafficking through state grants. The Act made specialized training programs possible for professionals who could come into contact with CSE victims (e.g., law enforcement officers, first responders, child welfare works, juvenile justice staff, court personnel). The State of Georgia was a front-runner in responding to the needs of CSE youth through infrastructure development, task force creation, victim services provision, and tracking of victims who come into contact with CW and JJS (Walker, 2013). The Connecticut Department of Children and Families (CDCF) has developed and implemented practice strategies to screen and track children who come into contact with their office and has established protocols for coordinated care that includes mental health services, mentoring, safety planning, and job preparation (Connecticut Department of Children and Families, 2012). In Los Angeles, the county government created a specialty court for CSE youth, the Succeeding Through Achievement and Resilience (STAR) Court, with an ultimate goal of re-enrolling CSE youth in school, engaging youth in counseling to address trauma, and assisting them in safely transitioning back to their families and communities (California Courts, the Judicial Branch of California, n.d.).

Conclusions

In this chapter, we have explored the intersection between the CW system and the juvenile justice system. We examined the landscape of youth traversing these two systems and saw that the odds are seemingly stacked against them. The impacts of their experiences of trauma and involvement in multiple systems upon their health, mental health, and life chances are significant. However, we also noted that these effects are possibly not inexorable. There are protective factors at every level of a youth's ecology that we could strengthen to mitigate some of the adverse effects of earlier negative experiences. We also made a case for prevention and why investing in today's crossover youth could bring substantial returns in the long term.

We considered the challenges inherent to serving youth at risk for or who are involved in multiple systems. Many of these challenges are linked to the reality that the CW and juvenile justice systems operate in silos. Cross-system coordination is complex and requires commitment from various stakeholders who are invested in promoting crossover youth success and well-being. Data sharing is an important part of the collaborative process. There are many programs and models that are working toward cross-system partnerships to provide coordinated care to crossover youth and their families. In this chapter, we highlighted CYPM, SII, and JDAI whose cross-cutting core strategies facilitate the establishment of effective cross-system collaboration.

In closing, in the years ahead, two of the most pressing policy challenges that remain to be addressed for crossover youth are the perpetuation of the overrepresentation of youth of color, and the development of institutional practices that acknowledge personal and collective histories and cultural strengths. There is wisdom in reflecting upon institutional practices that further disadvantage youth of color and perpetuate long-standing structural inequities. Systemic and individual biases need confronting to help address the continued racial disparities in CW and juvenile justice systems. Individual and collective histories also need acknowledgment. Part of this work is to recognize the resilience of communities of color and the many strengths of their cultural practice and traditions. Policies intended to shape practice could further invest in the discovery of how we could leverage these strengths in improving crossover youth outcomes.

Discussion Questions

1   What do you see as the greatest challenge to establishing collaborative services between CW and JJS?

2   What policy changes at the federal, state, and local level could improve case tracking, needs assessment, and coordinated service planning?

3   What are some steps to take to ensure that crossover youths become active participants in the formulation of services and interventions?

References

Abram, K., Teplin, L.A., Charles, D.R., Longworth, S.L., McClelland, G.M., & Dulcan, M.K. (2004). Posttraumatic stress disorder and trauma in youth in juvenile detention. *Archives of General Psychiatry, 61*(4), 403–410.

Abram, K., Washburn, J., Teplin, L., Emanuel, K., Romero, E., & McClelland, G. (2007). Posttraumatic stress disorder and psychiatric comorbidity among detained youths. *Psychiatric Services, 58*, 1311–1316.

Abrams, L.S., & Terry, D. (2017). *Everyday desistance: The transition to adulthood among formerly incarcerated youth.* Rutgers University Press.

Afifi, T.O., & MacMillan, H.L. (2011). Resilience following child maltreatment: A review of protective factors. *The Canadian Journal of Psychiatry, 56*(5), 266–272.

Andersen, T. (2015). Race, ethnicity, and structural variations in youth risk of arrest. *Criminal Justice and Behavior, 42*(9), 900–916.

Annie E. Casey Foundation. (2009). *An effective approach to reduce racial and ethnic disparities in juvenile justice.* Retrieved from www.aecf.org/resources/an-effective-approach-to-reduce-racial-and-ethnic-disparities-in-juvenile-j/ (accessed December 27, 2017).

Annie E. Casey Foundation. (2017a). *JDAI at 25: Juvenile Detention Alternatives Initiative – Insights from the annual results reports*. Retrieved from www.aecf.org/m/resourcedoc/aecf-jdaiat25-2017.pdf.

Bilchik, S., & Nash, J.M. (2008). Child welfare and juvenile justice: Two sides of the same coin. *Juvenile and Family Justice Today, 17*.

Briere, J., Agee, E., & Dietrich, A. (2016). Cumulative trauma and current PTSD status in general population and inmate samples. *Psychological trauma: Theory, research, practice, and policy*.

California Courts, the Judicial Branch of California. (n.d.). Succeeding Through Achievement and Resilience (STAR) Court – Los Angeles Superior Court. Retrieved from www.courts.ca.gov/27693.htm (accessed January 19, 2018).

Casey Family Programs. (2014). *Addressing child sex trafficking from a child welfare perspective (Rep.)*. Retrieved from www.casey.org/media/child-sex-trafficking.pdf.

Center for Juvenile Justice Reform. (2018). Crossover Youth Practice Model. Retrieved from http://cjjr.georgetown.edu/our-work/crossover-youth-practice-model/.

Center on Juvenile and Criminal Justice. (2004). *Reducing disproportionate minority confinement: The Multnomah County Oregon success story and its implications*. Retrieved from www.cjcj.org/portland/portland_main.html (accessed January 3, 2006).

Chuang, E., & Wells, R. (2010). The role of inter-agency collaboration in facilitating receipt of behavioral health services for youth involved with child welfare and juvenile justice. *Children and Youth Services Review, 32*(12), 1814–1822.

Cochran, J., & Mears, D. (2015). Racial, ethnic and gender divides in juvenile court sanctioning and rehabilitative intervention. *Journal of Research in Crime and Delinquency, 52*(2), 181–212.

Connecticut Department of Children and Families. (2012). *A child welfare response to domestic minor sex trafficking*. Retrieved from www.ct.gov/dcf/lib/dcf/humantraficing/pdf/response_to_domestic_minot_sex_trafficking.pdf.

Culhane, D.P., Byrne, T., Metraux, S., Moreno, M., Toros, H., & Stevens, M. (2011). Young adult outcomes of youth exiting dependent or delinquent care in Los Angeles County. In *The selected works of Dennis P. Culhane* (pp. 3–22), Los Angeles County: County of Los Angeles, Chief Executive Office.

Development Services Group, Inc. (2013). *Protective factors for populations served by the administration on children, youth, and families. A literature review and theoretical framework: Executive summary*. Washington, DC: U.S. Department of Health and Human Services, Administration for Children and Families, Children's Bureau, p. 6. Retrieved from www.dsgonline.com/acyf/DSG%20Protective%20Factors%20Literature%20Review%20 2013%20Exec%20Summary.pdf (accessed May 20, 2016).

Dierkhising, C.B., Ko, S.J., Woods-Jaeger, B., Briggs, E.C., Lee, R., & Pynoos, R.S. (2013). Trauma histories among justice-involved youth: Findings from the National Child Traumatic Stress Network. *European Journal of Psychotraumatology, 4*(1), 20274.

Feldman, C. (2007). Report finds 2,000 of state's children are sexually exploited, many in New York City. April 23. Retrieved from www.nytimes.com/2007/04/24/nyregion/24child.html (accessed January 2, 2018).

Ford, J.D., Chapman, J.F., Hawke, J., & Albert, D. (2007). Trauma among youth in the juvenile justice system: Critical issues and new directions. *National Center for Mental Health and Juvenile Justice*, 1–8.

Ford, J.D., Grasso, D.J., Hawke, J., & Chapman, J.F. (2013). Poly-victimization among juvenile justice-involved youths. *Child Abuse & Neglect, 37*(10), 788–800.

Haight, W., Bidwell, L., Choi, W.S., & Cho, M. (2016). An evaluation of the Crossover Youth Practice Model (CYPM): Recidivism outcomes for maltreated youth involved in the juvenile justice system. *Children and Youth Services Review, 65*(Supplement C), 78–85. Retrieved from https://doi.org/10.1016/j.childyouth.2016.03.025.

Haight, W.L., Bidwell, L.N., Marshall, J.M., & Khatiwoda, P. (2014). Implementing the Crossover Youth Practice Model in diverse contexts: Child welfare and juvenile justice professionals' experiences of multisystem collaborations. *Children and Youth Services Review, 39*, 91–100.

Halemba, G., & Siegel, G. (2011). *Doorways to delinquency: Multi-system involvement of delinquent youth in King County (Seattle, WA)*. Pittsburgh: National Center for Juvenile Justice.

Herz, D.C., & Ryan, J.P. (2008). Exploring the characteristics and outcomes of 241.1 youth crossing over from dependency to delinquency in Los Angeles County. *Center for Families, Children & the Courts Research Update*, 1–13.

Herz, D.C., Ryan, J.P., & Bilchik, S. (2010). Challenges facing crossover youth: An examination of juvenile-justice decision making and recidivism. *Family Court Review, 48*, 305–321.

Herz, D., Lee, P., Lutz, L., Stewart, M., Tuell, J., & Wiig, J. (2012). *Addressing the needs of multi-system youth: Strengthening the connection between child welfare and juvenile justice*. Retrieved fromhttps://cjjr.georgetown.edu/wp-content/uploads/2015/03/MultiSystemYouth_March2012.pdf.

Hockenberry, S., & Puzzanchera, C. (2015). *Juvenile court statistics 2013*. Pittsburgh, PA: National Center for Juvenile Justice.

Jenson, J., & Fraser, M. (Eds) (2016). *Social policy for children and families: A risk and resilience perspective* (3rd edn). Newbury Park, CA: Sage.

Kendall-Tackett, K. (2003). *Treating the lifetime health effects of childhood victimization*. Kingston, NJ: Civic Research Institute.

Kolivoski, K.M., Barnett, E., & Abbott, S. (2015). *The crossover youth practice model (CYPM) CYPM in brief: Out-of-home placements and crossover youth*. Washington, DC: Center for Juvenile Justice Reform.

Kolivoski, K.M., Shook, J.J., Kim, K.H., & Goodkind, S. (2017). Placement type matters: Placement experiences in relation to justice system involvement among child welfare-involved youth and young adults, *Journal of Human Behavior in the Social Environment, 27*(8), 847–864.

Lansford, J.E., Miller-Johnson, S., Berlin, L.J., Dodge, K.A., Bates, J E., & Pettit, G.S. (2007). Early physical abuse and later violent delinquency: A prospective longitudinal study. *Child Maltreatment, 12*(3), 233–245.

Lee, S-Y., & Villagrana, M. (2015). Differences in risk and protective factors between crossover and non-crossover youth in juvenile justice. *Children and Youth Services Review, 58*, 18–27.

Lowery, P., Burrow, J., & Kaminski, R. (2016). A multilevel test of the racial threat hypothesis in one state's juvenile court. *Crime & Delinquency, 64*(1), 1–35.

Pecora, P.J. (2018*). Risk and protective factors for child abuse and neglect: A resource paper*. New York: Taylor and Francis, Routledge.

Rovner, J. (2017). Still increase in racial disparities in juvenile justice. October 19. Retrieved from http://amsterdamnews.com/news/2017/oct/19/still-increase-racial-disparities-juvenile-justice/ (accessed December 29, 2017).

Ryan, J.P., & Testa, M.F. (2005). Child maltreatment and juvenile delinquency: Investigating the role of placement and placement instability. *Children and Youth Services Review, 27*(3), 227–249.

Scharrón-del Río, M.R., & Aja, A.A. (2015). The case for "Latinx": Why intersectionality is not a choice. *Latino Rebels, 5*.

Sickmund, M., Sladky, T.J., Kang, W., and Puzzanchera, C. (2017). Easy access to the Census of Juveniles in Residential Placement. Retrieved from www.ojjdp.gov/ojstatbb/ezacjrp/.

Smith, C., & Thornberry, T.P. (1995). The relationship between childhood maltreatment and adolescent involvement in delinquency. *Criminology, 33*(4), 451–481.

Stagner, M.W., & Lansing, J. (2009). Progress toward a prevention perspective. *The Future of Children, 19*(2), 19–38.

Stewart, A., Livingston, M., & Dennison, S. (2008). Transitions and turning points: Examining the links between child maltreatment and juvenile offending. *Child Abuse & Neglect, 32*(1), 51–66.

Tam, C.C., Abrams, L.S., Freisthler, B.F., & Ryan, J.P. (2016). Juvenile justice sentencing: Do gender and child welfare involvement matter? *Children and Youth Services Review, 64*, 60–65.

The Sentencing Project. (2016). *Trends in U.S. corrections*. Retrieved from https://sentencing-project.org/wp-content/uploads/2016/01/Trends-in-US-Corrections.pdf (accessed January 18, 2018).

Thornberry, T.P., Huizinga, D., & Loeber, R. (2004). The causes and correlates studies: Findings and policy implications. *Juvenile Justice, 9*, 3.

U.S. Department of Justice, Civil Rights Division. (2015). Investigation of the St. Louis County Family Court, St. Louis, Missouri. Retrieved from www.justice.gov/sites/default/files/crt/legacy/2015/07/31/stlouis_findings_7-31-15.pd.

Wagner, P., & Rabuy, B. (2017). *Mass incarceration: The whole pie 2017* (press release). Prison Policy Initiative. Retrieved from www.prisonpolicy.org/reports/pie2017.html.

Walker, K. (2013). *Ending the commercial sexual exploitation of children: A call for multi-system collaboration in California*. Child Welfare Council, 2012. Retrieved from www.chhs.ca.gov/Child%20Welfare/Ending%20CSEC%20-%20A%20Call%20for%20Multi-System%20Collaboration%20in%20CA%20-%20February%202013.pdf.

Specialized Treatment Services for Children and Families

Learning Objectives

1. Understanding characteristics, selected data sources, and proportions of youth with persistent and complex needs and their families served by child welfare and in need of specialized treatment services.

2. Understand core values and components of "system of care" as a framework for understanding specialized treatment services.

3. Understand selective evidence-based treatment exemplars and useful data sources for identifying evidence-based resources such as the California Evidence-Based Clearinghouse for Child Welfare (CEBC).

4. Understand the role and value of group homes and residential treatment centers as part of the continuum of care.

5. Understand future challenges for policy, research, and practice in identifying and implementing evidence-based specialized treatment services for children, youths, and families served by child welfare.

Introduction

Throughout each of the three previous editions of *The Child Welfare Challenge* the focus of the chapter on specialized treatment services has evolved from an almost exclusive emphasis on residential group treatment to what is best described as a suite of intensive, evidence-based services for children and youth with persistent and complex needs and their families (Pecora et al., 1992, 2000, 2009). Some of these interventions focus on delivery of needed treatment directly within the family of origin, while others use specialized foster family care or residential group treatment as the primary locus of helping others combine them artfully. In part, this shift has come about due to increasing concerns about the overuse of residential treatment services, as well as the strong desire on the part of advocates to identify effective service alternatives closer to families and communities of origin. This chapter will briefly explore: (1) the continuing need for specialized treatment services within child welfare (CW), including some of the forces that have initiated and sustained the cause of identifying a range of intensive service alternatives; (2) some promising service exemplars, and (3) take-away messages for policy development, practice enhancement, and future research in this critical sector of CW.

What Do We Know About the Population of Children Served by Child Welfare Who Require Some Level of Intensive Treatment Services?

To answer that question, we turn to a recent policy brief from the Chadwick Center and Chapin Hall (2016) commissioned by the Annie E. Casey Foundation and issued by two of the leading CW research centers in the U.S. Together, these two institutions with senior researchers John Landsverk (Chadwick at Rady Children's Hospital, San Diego) and Fred Wulczyn (Chapin Hall Center for Children at the University of Chicago) and their teams drew upon analyses from three rich data sources, including the following:

- The *Multistate Foster Care Data Archive* (FCDA). Chapin Hall Center for Children, The University of Chicago is a longitudinal archive containing the foster care records of approximately 3 million children in 25 states (including approximately 60 percent of the youth in foster care in the U.S.). The FCDA contains both child and spell data that allow us to identify the characteristics of CW spells, including placement changes, types of placement including congregate care, and spell duration. For the purpose of this research, congregate care includes group home, shelters, and residential treatment (all non-family settings) (Chadwick Center & Chapin Hall, 2016, p. 9).

- The *National Survey of Child and Adolescent Well-being* (NSCAW II). A longitudinal study of youth referred to U.S. CW agencies for whom an investigation of maltreatment was completed between February 2008 and April 2009. Initial interviews were collected within approximately four months of completed investigations. NSCAW II used a national probability sampling strategy. Analyses used data from interviews with caregivers and CW workers about children ≥18 months of age (Chadwick Center & Chapin Hall, 2016 p. 4).

• The *California Evidence-Based Clearinghouse for Child Welfare* (CEBC). Funded by the California Department of Social Services, the CEBC is a registry of programs that can be utilized by professionals serving children and families involved with the CW system. The programs, organized by topic area, are described in detail and rated using the Scientific Rating Scale to determine the level of research evidence supporting each practice. As such, the CEBC serves as a key resource for identifying evidence-based alternatives to congregate care (Chadwick Center & Chapin Hall, 2016, p. 5).

In their analyses for this policy brief, the authors note that based on the Chapin Hall Foster Care Archive Data (FCDA) the number of children in congregate care in FCDA states declined by nearly 20 percent between 2009 and 2016 but that "state level changes vary dramatically from nearly 80% fewer to 60% more young people living in congregate care" (Chadwick Center & Chapin Hall, 2016, p. 8). This is illustrated in Figure 8.1.

Additional analysis by Chadwick Center and Chapin Hall using the Child Behavior Checklist (CBCL) (Achenbach & Rescorla, 2001) suggests that children and youth in out-of-home settings with presumed higher service intensity – such as therapeutic foster care and group or therapeutic residential care – present with higher CBCL clinical cut scores than those in family foster care or emergency shelter care. The authors note that in the higher end settings children tend to be older (ages 11+) and likely to exhibit externalizing behaviors (51–57%) (Figure 8.2).

Several NSCAW II findings underscore the idea that youth with comparable clinical characteristics are more likely to be placed in congregate rather than therapeutic foster care to manage their behavioral risk. Among those youth requiring higher levels of care, those with internalizing problems (e.g., depression and anxiety) are more likely to be placed in therapeutic foster homes than in congregate care settings (Chadwick Center & Chapin Hall, 2016, pp. 4–5). Cognizant of the continuing interest in CW to increase home-based placements but with the support of powerful interventions like Functional Family Therapy, Dialectic Behavior Therapy, or Cognitive Behavioral Therapy (CBT), the authors conclude:

> This suggests that investments in interventions focused on stabilizing affect and behavior, de-escalating conflict and promoting mindfulness and stress reduction could be used to make more home-based placements available to youth with externalizing behaviors.
>
> (Chadwick Center & Chapin Hall, 2016, p. 5)

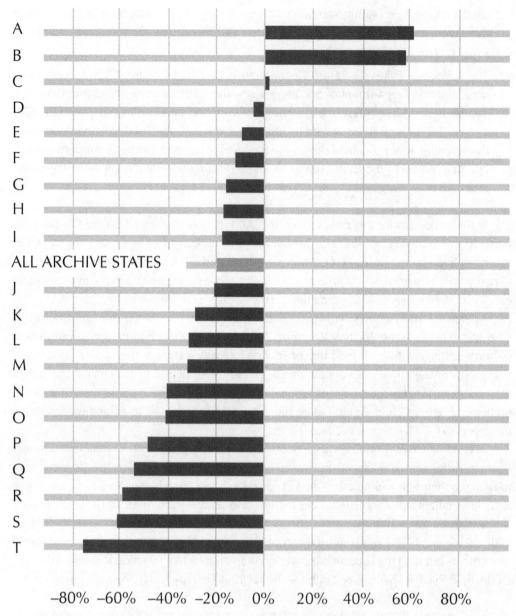

Figure 8.1 Percent Change in the Number of Children In Congregate Care By Archive State:
2009 to 2015

Source: Chadwick Center & Chapin Hall. (2016, p. 4). Reprinted with permission.

This figure shows the change in congregate care use between 2009 and 2015. States to the left of the center line lowered line lowered their use of congregate care; states to the right increased their use of congregate care. The average of all the states combined is displayed in orange. (Data Source: FCDA)

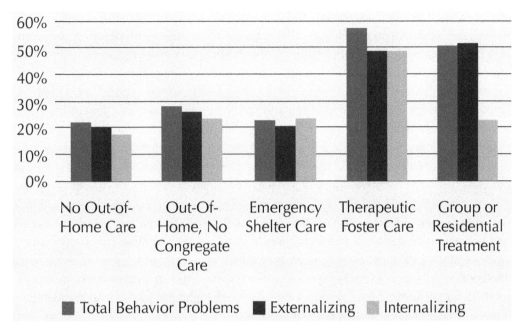

Figure 8.2 Percent of Youth Above the CBCL Clinical Cut Point by Placement Type

Source: Chadwick Center & Chapin Hall (2016., p. 4). Reprinted with permission. Note that the CBCL data were obtained from the NSCAW study.

This figure shows that youth in group or residential treatment settings are clinically similiar to youth in therapeutic foster homes, and have nearly twice the rate of clinical problems as those in traditional out-of-home care. Youth placed in emergency shelter care more closely resemble their home-based (no out-of-home care) counterparts. (Data source: NSCAW II)

Recent research by Briggs et al. (2012) and others confirms that children in residential (congregate) settings present challenging mental health and behavioral issues:

- Children in congregate care settings are almost three times as likely to have a DSM diagnosis compared to children in other settings. (Note that this is not wholly unexpected because a DSM diagnosis is required for payment in most of these congregate care settings.)
- Children in congregate care settings are more than six times more likely than children in other settings to have "child behavior problems" as a reason for removal from home. (Briggs et al. (2012, p. 8) defined behavior problems as including violent, aggressive, destructive, dangerous, or illegal behaviors at school, home, or in the community.)

Perspectives from practitioners in the field confirm the severity of problems of children and youth typically referred for intensive services, often including a combination of mental and behavioral health, educational, and substance abuse issues (Thompson et al., 2014). Indeed, the intensity and duration of challenges posed by youth with persistent and complex behavioral health problems are part of the stimulus for identifying an array of service responses to meet their needs.

Many of the forces referenced throughout this text have also spurred the search for innovative service solutions for children and youth with persistent complex needs. These include the increasing importance of finding evidence-based service approaches, the felt desire to deliver services in culturally appropriate and competent ways, greater awareness of cost considerations, and the importance of family connections, to name a few. In our view, the transformative vision of services contained in systems of care thinking has played a major role in the quest for intensive service alternatives. The classic contribution of Stroul and Friedman (1986) in setting forth a system of care framework for mental and behavioral health services for children, youth, and their families has also provided a powerful stimulus for seeking out service solutions that engage families in all facets of intervention, and seeks to embed services in the familiar lived environment where families reside. A recent update of the system of care approach highlights some of the key elements in design of service arrays. This is presented next.

System of Care Definition and Philosophy

Definition

A *system of care* is a spectrum of effective, community-based services and supports for children and youth with or at risk for mental health or other challenges and their families, that is organized into a coordinated network, builds meaningful partnerships with families and youth, and addresses their cultural and linguistic needs, in order to help them to function better at home, in school, in the community, and throughout life. (For a definition that may be more in tune with CW, see https://gucchd.georgetown.edu/products/PRIMER_ChildWelfare.pdf.)

Core Values

A system of care is:

- Family driven and youth guided, with the strengths and needs of the child and family determining the types and mix of services and supports provided.

- Community based, with the locus of services, as well as system management, resting within a supportive, adaptive infrastructure of structures, processes, and relationships at the community level.

- Culturally and linguistically competent, with agencies, programs, and services that reflect the cultural, racial, ethnic, and linguistic differences of the populations they serve to facilitate access to and use of appropriate services and supports.

Practice Should be Guided by Principles from System of Care and Trauma-informed Care

A system of care is designed to:

1. Ensure availability of and access to a broad, flexible array of effective, evidence-informed, community-based services and supports for children and their families that addresses their physical, emotional, social, and educational needs, including traditional and non-traditional services as well as informal and natural supports.

2. Provide individualized services in accordance with the unique potential and needs of each child and family, guided by a strengths-based, individualized care coordination and planning process in true partnership with the child and family.

3. Deliver services and supports within the least restrictive, most normative environments that are clinically appropriate.

4. Ensure that families, other caregivers, and youth are full partners in all aspects of the planning and delivery of their own services, and in the policies and procedures that govern care for all children and youth in their communities, states, territories, tribes, and nation.

5. Ensure cross-system collaboration, with linkages between child-serving agencies and programs across administrative and funding boundaries, and mechanisms for system-level management, coordination, and integrated care management.

6. Provide care management or similar mechanisms to ensure that multiple services are delivered in a coordinated and therapeutic manner, and that children and their families can move through the system of services in accordance with their changing needs.

7. Provide developmentally appropriate mental health services and supports that promote optimal social and emotional outcomes for young children and their families in their homes and community settings.

8. Provide developmentally appropriate services and supports to facilitate the transition of youth to adulthood and to the adult service system as needed.

9. Incorporate or link with mental health promotion, prevention, and early identification and intervention to improve long-term outcomes, including mechanisms to identify problems at an earlier stage and mental health promotion and prevention activities directed at all children and adolescents.

10. Incorporate continuous accountability mechanisms to track, monitor, and manage the achievement of system of care goals; fidelity to the system of care philosophy, and quality, effectiveness, and outcomes at the system level, practice level, and child and family level.

11. Protect the rights of children, youth, and families and promote effective advocacy efforts.

12. Provide services and supports without regard to race, religion, national origin, gender, gender expression, sexual orientation, physical disability, socioeconomic status, geography, language, immigration status, or other characteristics; services should be sensitive and responsive to these differences (Stroul, Blau, & Friedman, 2010).

The core values of system of care thinking – particularly the idea of family engagement, partnership, and delivery of services in culturally competent ways – resonates deeply with CW practitioners. While some specific interventions, such as Wraparound (to be discussed later in this chapter), can claim direct lineage to system of care thinking, the goals, values, and principles of system of care has had a salutary effect across the entire CW service array. Similarly, in the next section we highlight the elements of a child and family services system attuned to childhood *trauma* – an increasingly important dimension in treatment planning – and offer useful summaries of selected trauma-focused interventions.

Trauma-Oriented Treatment Resources

All areas of CW and behavioral health services should more fully implement trauma-informed care approaches, including those addressing trauma caused by system factors such as poorly handled initial child placement, maltreatment by foster parents and ***complex trauma*** (see Figure 8.3). Typically, complex trauma exposure involves the simultaneous or sequential (long-term) occurrence of child maltreatment; it may include psychological maltreatment, neglect, physical and sexual abuse, poly-victimization

(Finkelhor, Ormrod, & Turner, 2007), and witnessing domestic and community violence. Complex trauma is associated with the following:

- chronic exposure;

- early childhood occurrence;

- occurrence within the child's primary caregiving system and/or social environment.

Exposure to these initial traumatic experiences, the resulting emotional dysregulation, and the loss of safety, direction, and the ability to detect or respond to danger cues may impact a child's development and behavior over time and may lead to subsequent or repeated trauma exposure in adolescence and adulthood without supports that might buffer the negative effects (Center for Early Childhood Mental Health Consultation, adapted from Blumenfeld et al., 2010; /www.ecmhc.org/tutorials/trauma/mod1_2.html). In essence, a trauma-informed treatment approach begins not by asking the child "Why are you doing that?" but "What has happened to you?" The focus is on endeavoring to help dampen the intense reflex reactions to others that impede adjustment and often prevent a child from making progress. The National Child Traumatic Stress Network has developed a wide array of interviewing and assessment resources to help children's services professionals know how to work with children exposed to trauma and those who have trauma symptoms. They have also developed extensive protocols on how to help modify children's services agencies (see below) so that they are more trauma-informed and reduce trauma rather than add to it (see http://nctsnet.org/).

A number of researchers have noted that individuals who suffered severe, long-lasting, interpersonal trauma, especially in early life, frequently suffer from symptoms that span the domains of attachment, biology, affect regulation, disassociation, behavior, cognition, and self-concept, including the following:

- Increased propensity to seek out experiences and relationships that mirror their original trauma.

- Severe difficulties in controlling emotions and regulating moods.

- Identity problems, including the loss of a coherent sense of self.

- Marked inability to develop trusting relationships.

- Sometimes, adoption of the perpetrator's belief system (Cook et al., 2005; Hosier, 2014).

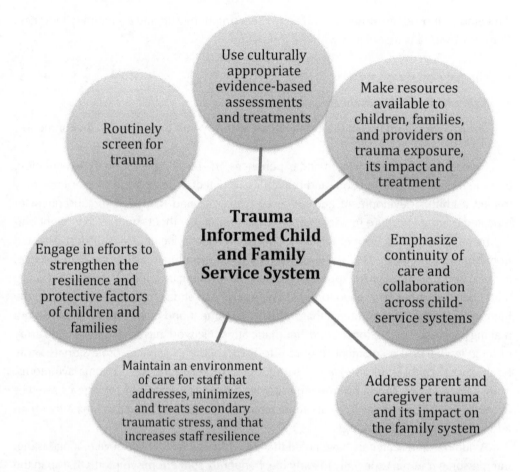

Figure 8.3 Elements of a Trauma-informed Child and Family Service System According to the National Child Traumatic Stress Network

Source: National Child Traumatic Stress Network (NCTSN). (n.d.). *What is a Trauma-informed Child- and Family-service System?* Retrieved from http://nctsn.org/resources/topics/creating-trauma-informed-systems and re-formatted by Pecora & English (2016).

These consequences of exposure to traumatic experiences suggest a need for comprehensive assessment, not just of the presenting problem, but of youth experiences across time. This kind of assessment will more accurately reflect youth trauma and risk behaviors, as well as the service array needed to address identified needs. In addition to offering targeted services based on youth need, services targeting caregiver need and further examination of the provision of these services at the community level to prevent the need for a higher level of care, or to support successful transition back to the community, should be considered.

(Pecora & English, 2016, p. 16)

What Are Some Promising Treatment Resources to Meet the Needs of Children and Youth with Persistent and Complex Needs?

A number of recent publications analyze a broad array of research-based treatment alternatives including in-home, specialized foster family and therapeutic residential care options:

- Chadwick Center & Chapin Hall (2016).

- Conradi, Landsverk, & Wotring (2014).

- Pecora & English (2016).

- The preventing emotional and behavioral disorders in adolescents report from the National Academies of Sciences, Engineering, and Medicine (O'Connell, Boat, & Warner, 2009).

- The National Quality Improvement Center for Adoption and Guardianship Support and Preservation (2017) Intervention and Program Catalog.

For more than 100 years an array of programs have emerged (and they continue to do so) that appear to be based on an important idea (like the importance of attachment or of trauma) but have not been rigorously tested or replicated. With respect to treatments appropriate for intervening with disruptive behavior – a common occurrence in children and youth needing intensive services – the Chadwick Center and Chapin Hall (2016, p. 6) report identifies nine interventions well supported by research as rated by the California Evidence-Based Clearinghouse (CEBC). The effectiveness of children's services programs for our most challenging youth is gaining greater clarity and documentation. The California Evidence-Based Clearinghouse (CEBC) for Child Welfare (cebc4cw.org), while state-funded, is an internationally recognized resource which helps identify programs that have been rigorously and positively evaluated as having a sustained benefit; are highly relevant to the population of children receiving CW services; and have had some measure of replication. The highest ranking is a 1, indicating that the intervention is *well supported by research evidence*, which requires that at least two randomized controlled trials have shown the practice to be effective and that sustained effect has been seen 12 months after the end of services, as compared to a control group. The CEBC also helps link to the peer-reviewed papers that provide the justification for their rating. We provide some additional perspectives about some of the highly ranked programs that address children with the most significant behavioral challenges.

Multi-systemic Therapy (MST)

Among the treatments identified, Multi-Systemic Therapy (MST) has perhaps the longest record of use and the widest application in the population of children and youth referred to CW (see Chapter 3). The origins of MST may be traced to some early work in the 1970s in Virginia when Scott Henggeler was a Ph.D. candidate in psychology at the University of Virginia:

> He was hired by the state's Department of Pediatrics to work with antisocial children and was given some of the most difficult cases. After working with them for a while – and making little progress – Dr. Henggeler decided to visit the adolescents in their homes. "It took me 15 to 20 seconds," he recalls, "to realize how incredibly stupid my brilliant treatment plans were." He saw that he needed to treat the children in the full context of their lives, to see them where they lived, went to school, hung out.
>
> (http://mstservices.com/what-is-mst/what-is-mst)

More than 100 peer-reviewed studies have been done of MST and many have been independent (Henggeler & Schaeffer, 2016). Eventually an institute – MST Services – was developed to continue to refine the MST model, explore its application to different populations and service settings, and aid in the dissemination, training, and evaluation of new programs. Presently, MST Services may be found in 34 states and 15 international applications. The California Evidence Based Clearinghouse for Child Welfare lists three adaptations of MST that have high ratings for research support: MST Child Abuse and Neglect (MST-CAN), and MST for Youth with Problem Sexual Behavior (MST-YPSB).

Another important development with direct CW application is the development of the MST-Building Stronger Families program (Schaeffer et al., 2013). MST-BSF is an integrated treatment model for the co-occurring problem of parental substance abuse and child maltreatment among CWS-involved families. MST was developed by psychologists but has always had social workers involved and relies heavily on social ecological theory, in-home services, family work, and consultation with schools and other entities (e.g., juvenile services or CW) that are also involved with the family. The flexibility of MST – which has shown its effective reach across a range of problems – makes this one of the leading interventions for children and families with the most complex and enduring problems.

Many child, youth, and family service agencies have incorporated MST into their repertoire of interventions with the goal of keeping families engaged in the helping process and increasing their delivery of evidence-based interventions. For example, Youth Villages, a large, multi-state, multi-site agency headquartered in Tennessee, offers a succinct rationale for its selection of MST as an intervention in selective states:

> MST is built on the principle and scientific evidence that a seriously troubled child's behavioral problems are multidimensional and must be confronted using multiple strategies. The serious behavior problems of a child typically stem from a combination of influences, including family factors, deviant peer groups, problems in school or the community, and individual characteristics. The MST model calls for simultaneously addressing all of those inter-related areas.
>
> Therapy is intensive and is conducted in the child's home by a single counselor. The counselor typically works with the child and family over a three- to five-month period. As part of the process, the counselor typically works closely with teachers, neighbors, extended family, even members of the child's peer group and their parents. A counselor on the MST team is available to the family 24 hours a day, seven days a week.
>
> Youth Villages' MST Program features elements of successful trials of MST that have been demonstrated to transport to diverse communities:

- Low caseload (four to six families)
- High level of supervision, training, and clinical consultation, all conducted in accordance with MST specifications
- Thorough, on-going assessment of each family's strengths, needs, and barriers to progress
- Individually designed treatment plans to address specific drivers of antisocial behavior
- Monitoring of adherence through implementation of MST's Quality Assurance protocols.

The average cost of MST treatment for a child is much less expensive than traditional hospital-based treatment or other out-of-home placements. Savings result not only from less expensive services, but also from reduced future costs to the community due to successful treatment outcomes. MST is one of only a handful of models to be listed as highly effective in comprehensive reviews of randomized clinical trials for treating seriously troubled youth. (For further information, see www.youthvillages.org/what-we-do/intensive-in-home-treatment/mst#sthash.d487UE0q.dpbs.)

This particular application of MST from Youth Villages is significant, as it comes from an agency that has been selected as one of a dozen service programs nationally in a project entitled Blue Meridian Partners – a unique collaboration of private philanthropy and model service programs initiated by the Edna McConnell Clark Foundation in New York. The goal of the partnership is to invest $1 billion in total – approximately $200 million in each partner agency – over a five- to ten-year period to make a national impact upon economically disadvantaged children and youth. Tracing the progress of what the partnership terms its "Big Bets," like the one on Youth Villages, will be of particular interest to CW researchers and planners – both in terms of overall effects and identifying key components of future service strategies. (For further information on Blue Meridian, see www.emcf.org/our-strategies/blue-meridian-partners/.)

Treatment Foster Care Oregon-Adolescents (TFCO-A)

One additional program has achieved a top-tier evidence rating: Treatment Foster Care Oregon-Adolescents (TFCO-A). While not nearly as widely disseminated as MST, TFCO-A is well worthy of note as a potential remedy in meeting the needs of high-resource-using youth in CW. This specialized treatment foster care program – developed by Dr. Patty Chamberlain and colleagues at the Oregon Social Learning Center – builds on a long and distinguished empirical tradition of applied behavior analysis with a wide range of family and child problems. Formerly known as Multidimensional Treatment Foster Care (MTFC), TFCO-A presents a richly detailed and precise model of intervention applied in a wide variety of sites both nationally and internationally. While space limits our description here, the reader is highly encouraged to seek a more detailed description in the CEBC as well as from the TFCO-A website at www.cebc4cw.org/program/treatment-foster-care-oregon-adolescents/detailed and www.tfcoregon.com/what-is-tfco/.

MTFC-A has spun off into a version that is less costly on an individual family basis and requires far fewer trained and specialized staff. KEEP (**Keep**ing Foster and Kin Parents Supported and Trained) has simplified some of the requirements of TFCO-A while maintaining the use of parental reports, positive coaching of foster parents, and basic anticipatory guidance and contingency management as core program elements (Greeno et al., 2016; Price et al., 2009). The results have been excellent in reducing placement disruptions, generating lower levels of positive behaviors, and increasing positive exits from foster care.

Recently KEEP has been combined with other related interventions, including one for reunification and one that teaches supervisors and resource parents to better apply social learning principles in all of their interactions. These have been piloted in New York City (Chamberlain et al., 2016) and, now, in Tennessee, and promise a more coherent approach to service delivery.

Wraparound

Of course, not all intervention programs for youth with persistent and complex behavioral health needs in CW have as yet attained the highest rating from the CEBC. To complete this brief review, we choose the Wraparound process and the Teaching-Family Model (TFM) as exemplary programs that have achieved a level 3, indicating "promising research results" in the CEBC reviews. Moreover, each of these programs achieves the designation of "high relevance for the CW system" in the same CEBC reviews.

Wraparound grew in the 1980s out of the recognition that children and youth with complex behavioral health needs were being placed in long-term institutions. In 1982, Jane Knitzer released the report, *Unclaimed children: The failure of public responsibility to children in need of mental health services*, which further documented that this population of youth did not have access to much-needed services. This report, as well as family advocacy, led to a national push for deinstitutionalization of children and a move to comprehensive service arrays that would support youth in their communities. We deliberately chose to provide additional detail on Wraparound, as it illustrates some of the ways in which developers are dealing with issues of fidelity in their attempts to bring programs to scale.

As a result, Congress appropriated funds in 1984 for the Child and Adolescent Service System Program (CASSP) through the National Institute of Mental Health and, shortly after, Wraparound was developed and implemented in places such as Alaska, Michigan, Maine, Wisconsin, Vermont, and Kansas based primarily on the key principles of individualization, unconditional care, strengths-based planning, and increasing family voice and choice. While the term *Wraparound* came to be more and more widely used throughout the 1990s, there was still no formal agreement about exactly what Wraparound was. Many Wraparound programs shared common features, but consensus about essential components for Wraparound existed. Some programs were able to document extraordinary successes, but it also became apparent that many teams and programs were not operating in a manner that reflected the Wraparound principles. Toward the early 2000s, it became increasingly clear that without a common and concise definition of what Wraparound was (and was not), any practice or group of services could be called "Wraparound," regardless of quality or practice components. Furthermore, it would be impossible to establish evidence for Wraparound's effectiveness without a clear definition of the practice (see NWI, "Mission and History" at http://nwi.pdx.edu).

Over the years since then and owing to the efforts of many practitioners, parents, youths, and researchers, those basic questions of definition, critical components, and implementation requirements have moved closer to having answers. Wraparound is in the process of building an impressive body of efficacy and implementation studies that will inform the next generation of demonstrations. This includes very promising work to help all Wraparound sites set expectations and utilize tools to answer four basic questions:

1. What types of youth and families are enrolling in Wraparound and what are their needs?

2. Are the Wraparound services being delivered of high quality?

3. Are the overall systems involved in delivering the services and the programs themselves adequately hospitable to allow for high-quality Wraparound implementation?

4. Are youth and families experiencing positive outcomes?

Over 30 years later, Wraparound has moved beyond the initial foundation principles into a practice model that is an intensive, holistic method of engaging with individuals with complex needs and typically multi-system involvement (most typically children, youth, and their families) so that they can live in their homes and communities and realize their hopes and dreams. Now operating in nearly every state in the United States, this intensive, individualized, care planning and management process builds on the collective action of a committed team comprising family, friends, community, professional, and cross-system supports mobilizing resources and strengths from a variety of sources resulting in the creation of a plan of care. It is important to note that Wraparound is not a treatment or a service, but rather a process through which services and supports across child-serving systems are brainstormed, coordinated, and managed. (As of 2017, 25 states were using the Wraparound Fidelity Assessment System (WFAS) in at least some sites – a multi-method approach to assessing the quality of individualized care planning and management for children and youth with complex needs and their families. See http://depts.washington.edu/wrapeval/.)

The Wraparound process aims to achieve positive outcomes by providing a structured, creative, and individualized team planning process that, compared to traditional treatment planning, results in plans that are more effective and relevant to the child and family. In addition, Wraparound plans are more holistic than traditional care plans in that they are designed to meet the identified needs of caregivers and siblings, and to address a range of life areas. Wraparound also aims to develop the problem-solving skills, coping skills, and self-efficacy of young people and family members. Finally, there is an emphasis on integrating the youth into the community and building the family's social support network.

The values of Wraparound, as expressed in its core principles, are fully consistent with the system of care framework. Youth and their families are at the center of the process and their perspectives must be given primary importance. In Wraparound there are ten principles that are operationalized throughout the process:

1. Family Voice and Choice

2. Team Based

3. Natural Supports

4. Collaboration

5. Community Based

6. Culturally Competent

7. Individualized

8. Strengths Based

9. Persistence

10. Outcome Based.

More specifically, what distinguishes Wraparound from other value and team-based models are four key elements: (1) Grounded in a strengths perspective, (2) Driven by underlying needs, (3) Supported by an effective team process, and (4) Determined by families. *Grounded in a strengths perspective* means that strengths should be reflected through all four phases of Wraparound and should guide all activities with families and for teams. One thing distinguishing the strength approach in Wraparound from other strength-based approaches is the ecological nature of strengths work within the Wraparound process. Strengths of the identified youth and their family are not the only strengths that are the focus of service delivery and decision making. Strengths of the family, all team members, the service environment, and the community are purposefully and transparently used in all decision-making and service delivery options.

Driven by underlying needs is a core concept in effective Wraparound implementation. The notion of underlying need means that the process will be organized to create agreement about the root cause of behaviors or situations. Rather than focusing on surface needs, the effective Wraparound practitioner will lead a team inclusive of and centered on the family in developing a common understanding of underlying need. This step of reaching agreement will be followed by an organized approach to constructing strengths-based responses to address those underlying causes. The concept of underlying need is used because it avoids judging people or families for current conditions and all Wraparound activity is focused on meeting needs rather than containing problems.

Supported by an effective team process means that Wraparound is not a process that can be done by a single individual or family. The process is predicated on the notion that a group of people working together around common goals, objectives, and team norms are likely to produce more effective outcomes. All wraparound inputs (underlying needs, functional strengths, strength-based strategies, etc.) have to be sorted, synthesized, and shared with team members who are acting collectively. Teams do not just happen to become high functioning. Within Wraparound certain steps are taken to assure that the gathered group moves toward a target of working as a high-functioning team.

The final key element is that of *Family determination* – which means that the family's perspective, preferences, and opinions are, first, understood; second, considered in decision making; and finally, influential in how the team makes decisions. It is not as simple as choosing activities because the "family says so" but within Wraparound all team members are expected to have enough depth of understanding so that they not only know what the family want but why they want it and how those choices relate to unique family strengths, culture, and needs.

The Wraparound process occurs over four phases: (1) engagement and team preparation, (2) initial plan development, (3) implementation, and (4) transition. In the engagement and team preparation process, a care coordinator meets with the family and may be joined by a parent and/or youth peer-support partner. The care coordinator engages the family to share their family story and listens carefully for functional strengths as well as potential team members and underlying needs. The care coordinator will work with the family to create an initial crisis plan and addresses any urgent safety concerns. The care coordinator begins to contact possible team members and explains their role in the Wraparound process, and schedules a time and location for the initial team meeting. The phase is short, typically one to two weeks.

During phase 2, initial plan development, the team comes together comprised of both formal and informal supports. During this phase the team comes together in one or two meetings to create the initial plan of care. A plan of care consists of a family vision statement, team mission, functional strengths list, underlying needs, and individualized strategies, brainstormed and selected to address underlying needs. The family should feel that they are being heard and a plan is being developed that will support them in meeting their needs.

In phase 3, implementation, the initial Wraparound plan is implemented, progress is continually reviewed, and the team is working toward needs met. During this stage traditional treatment services, including evidence-based practices, are put into place as well as non-traditional supports such as dance classes, football camp, etc. The plan of care is reviewed and changes are made through the team process with the mantra, "families don't fail, plans fail." This phase is the longest – typically lasting for around one year or less. The final phase of Wraparound is the transition phase and during this phase there is a team focus on purposeful transition out of formal Wraparound. Although this is the final phase, transition planning occurs throughout the process so that everyone is aware that Wraparound is an intensive intervention with a goal for a family to move to a less intensive support system. Many of the services and support included in Wraparound continue with the family after Wraparound has ended. The National Wraparound Initiative developed the Theory of Change for Wraparound (Figure 8.4) to explain how this process works to create change in a family's life.

The present emphasis of Wraparound is supported and disseminated through the National Wraparound Implementation Center (NWIC). The NWIC is a partnership between the University of Maryland, School of Social Work (UMSSW), University of Washington (UW), and Portland State University (PSU). The NWIC supports states, communities, and organizations to implement Wraparound as part of broader health reform strategies. The NWIC uses innovative approaches grounded in implementation science and spanning the policy, financing, evaluation, and workforce development areas to comprehensively support Wraparound implementation and related system reform efforts. They provide support that is intensive and individualized; and focused on building sustainable local capacity to provide model-adherent, high-quality Wraparound, thereby increasing positive outcomes for children, youth, and their families.

As with most of the more established evidence-based practices described in this chapter, the NWIC offers an electronic fidelity-support tool as well as online and face-to-face coaching to help sites maximize the possibility of achieving positive outcomes. To support implementation, the NWIC utilizes specific tools such as the Wraparound Fidelity Assessment System (WFAS) and the Wraparound Practice Improvement Tools. The Wraparound Fidelity Index, version 4 (WFI-4) is a set of four interviews that measure the nature of the Wraparound process that an individual family receives. The interviews are completed with four types of respondents: caregivers, youth (11 years of age or older), Wraparound

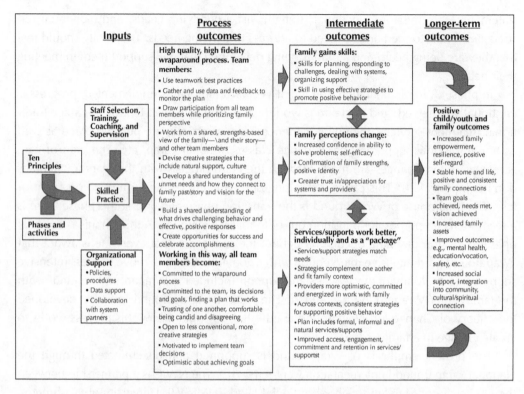

Inputs	Process outcomes	Intermediate outcomes	Longer-term outcomes

Ten Principles

Phases and activities

Staff Selection, Training, Coaching, and Supervision

Skilled Practice

Organizational Support
• Policies, procedures
• Data support
• Collaboration with system partners

High quality, high fidelity wraparound process. Team members:
• Use teamwork best practices
• Gather and use data and feedback to monitor the plan
• Draw participation from all team members while prioritizing family perspective
• Work from a shared, strengths-based view of the family—\and their story—and other team members
• Devise creative strategies that include natural support, culture
• Develop a shared understanding of unmet needs and how they connect to family past/story and vision for the future
• Build a shared understanding of what drives challenging behavior and effective, positive responses
• Create opportunities for success and celebrate accomplishments

Working in this way, all team members become:
• Committed to the wraparound process
• Committed to the team, its decisions and goals, finding a plan that works
• Trusting of one another, comfortable being candid and disagreeing
• Open to less conventional, more creative strategies
• Motivated to implement team decisions
• Optimistic about achieving goals

Family gains skills:
• Skills for planning, responding to challenges, dealing with systems, organizing support
• Skill in using effective strategies to promote positive behavior

Family perceptions change:
• Increased confidence in ability to solve problems; self-efficacy
• Confirmation of family strengths, positive identity
• Greater trust in/appreciation for systems and providers

Services/supports work better, individually and as a "package"
• Service/support strategies match needs
• Strategies complement one aother and fit family context
• Providers more optimistic, committed and energized in work with family
• Across contexts, consistent strategies for supporting positive behavior
• Plan includes formal, informal and natural services/supports
• Improved access, engagement, commitment and retention in services/supportst

Positive child/youth and family outcomes
• Increased family empowerment, resilience, positive self-regard
• Stable home and life, positive and consistent family connections
• Team goals achieved, needs met, vision achieved
• Increased family assets
• Improved outcomes: e.g., mental health, education/vocation, safety, etc.
• Increased social support, integration into community, cultural/spiritual connection

Figure 8.4 Wraparound Theory of Change

Source: National Wraparound Initiative Workforce Advisory Group (2013). Reprinted with permission.

facilitators, and team members, with each unique perspective important to fully understand how Wraparound is being implemented.

The WFI-4 interviews are organized by the four phases of the Wraparound process (Engagement and Team Preparation, Initial Planning, Implementation, and Transition), and are keyed to the ten principles of Wraparound. In this way, the WFI-4 interviews are intended to assess both conformance to the Wraparound practice model as well as adherence to the principles in service delivery. There is also a shortened version of the WFI-4 that may be used online called the WFI-EZ. In addition, the WFAS also includes the Team Observation Measure (TOM 2.0), Community Supports for Wraparound Inventory (CSWI), Document Assessment and Review Tool (DART), and Wraparound Structured Assessment and Review (WrapSTAR). The TOM is designed to assess adherence to standards of high-quality Wraparound observed during team meeting sessions. It consists of 36 indicators, organized into 7 subscales. The CSWI is a 40-item research and quality improvement program intended to measure how well a local system supports the implementation of the Wraparound process and assesses the system context for Wraparound as opposed to the fidelity to the practice model for an individual child and family. The DART is a revised version of the Document Review Measure that may be used by supervisors, coaches, and external evaluators to assess adherence to standards of high-quality Wraparound as noted in youth/family documentation (such as intake and assessment documentation, team meeting notes, plans of care, crisis plans, and other records). Finally, the WrapSTAR process combines WFAS tools into comprehensive fidelity and outcomes scores based on key practice elements of the NWI Wraparound model. It produces additional information on implementation supports (e.g., leadership, organizational climate), community conditions, and system conditions – which provides invaluable context and information for developing meaningful quality improvement initiatives.

In addition to the WFAS, the NWIC uses Wraparound Practice Implementation Tools (WPITs) designed to assess quality practice versus fidelity to the model. The WPITs include the Coaching Observation Measure for Effective Teams (COMET), Supportive Transfer of Essential Practice Skills (STEPS), Coaching Response to Enhance Skill Transfer (CREST), and Supervisory Assessment System (SAS). The COMET is a practice-level implementation tool utilized by supervisors and coaches to assess Wraparound practitioners' mastery of the skills necessary to ensure a high fidelity and quality Wraparound process. STEPS is designed to be a supervisory tool to assist supervisors and coaches to stay on track about the necessary Wraparound elements and guide the dialogue with staff to focus on adherence to implementing the model. CREST is a proactive supervision tool used to build and reinforce skill development around quality Wraparound practice. Lastly, the SAS is a system by which a coach would assess a supervisor's ability to support staff skill development as well as collect and analyze data around staff skill sets to identify effective practice skills and linking those skills to the broader practice of Wraparound. NWIC leverages the use of the full continuum of the tools listed above to ensure that practice is not only a fidelity practice but also to ensure quality and consistency of implementation and workforce development.

The Teaching Family Model

The CEBC offers the following brief description of the Teaching Family Model (TFM): the TFM is a unique approach to human services characterized by clearly defined goals, integrated support system, and a set of essential elements. The TFM has been applied in residential group homes, home-based services, foster care and treatment foster care, schools, and psychiatric institutions. The model uses a married couple or other "teaching parents" to offer a family-like environment in the residence. The teaching parents help with learning living skills and positive interpersonal interaction skills. They are also involved with children's parents, teachers, and other support networks to help maintain progress (www. cebc4cw.org/program/teaching-family-model/detailed).

In its original configuration, TFM, then called Achievement Place, resulted from some pioneering experiments at the University of Kansas Bureau of Child Research to extend the principles and techniques of Applied Behavior Analysis to a wide range of childhood problems in a variety of community settings. As an early review notes:

> Achievement Place [.] grew out of the joint efforts of a group of concerned citizens, juvenile court professionals and behavioral psychologists [.] [its] goal was to teach youths the basic skills – social, academic, self-help and prevocational – that will help them out of trouble with their families, their teachers and the law (Phillips et al., 1973). Central to the model is the teaching interaction created between the youths and their "teaching parents" – a professional couple specially trained in the techniques of behavior analysis and intervention.
>
> (Whittaker, 1979, pp. 58–59)

Ellery "Lonnie" Phillips, then a Masters student at the University of Kansas (KU), and his wife Elaine were the original "teaching parent" couple under the mentorship of Professor Montrose Wolf (one of the pioneers of Applied Behavior Analysis), and other members of the KU faculty and graduate student community. In a great many ways, Achievement Place, which was later renamed the Teaching Family Model (TFM), flew in the face of conventional wisdom at that time about services planning for difficult-to-manage youth. It used *house parents* – albeit specially trained ones – at a time when the field was moving toward shift staff. It made the locus and focus for change the home milieu, as opposed to office-based therapy. It measured precisely the effects of behavioral interventions, and used those findings to inform and improve a continuously changing training regimen. It also measured the behavior of the teaching parents to make sure that they were consistently positive and offering more praise than correction. For further details on the genesis and early development of TFM, including the contribution of Dean Fixsen and Karen Blasé, see Fixsen and Blasé (2008: https://teaching-family.org/wp-content/uploads/2013/10/tfabibli ography.pdf). That publication provides details about the challenges and breakthroughs in developing a coherent and replicable treatment model.

The TFM model soon attracted national attention both in its replications and many contributions to the professional applied behavior analysis literature. The National Institute of Mental Health through its Center for Studies in Crime and Delinquency provided early support for model development and in 1975 a Teaching Family Association (TFA) was founded to "ensure the quality of care provided by professionals who actively pursue the goals of humane, effective, individualized treatment for children, families, and dependent adults using the common framework of the Teaching-Family Model for treatment and support" (https://teaching-family.org/association-information/).

In 1974, the iconic Boys Town in Nebraska became the largest site (and "headquarters") for TFM programs in Omaha and other states. They also developed an in-home model that builds on their parenting program and helps birth parents create some of the positive and effective characteristics of their group living model. Boys Town (which includes a multi-site/multi-service operation, a national research institute, and an extensive outreach effort) describes the critical elements of TFM:

- Multiple layers of safety system for youth and staff

- Positive short-term and long-term outcomes

- Manualized training, supervision, and staff certification system

- Evidence-based practices that are embedded in the program

- Youth experience the program in a normalized family environment; they attend school and participate in family, school, and community activities

- There is a focus on supporting youth transition from the program to a permanent family.
(Thompson et al., 2014, p. 9).

Through the member agencies of the National Teaching Family Association (TFA), TFM is presently being delivered in multiple sites in 11 U.S. states as well as two international applications (TFA, 2017). For further specific information, please consult the detailed report on this program in the CEBC.

While differences exist between MST, Wraparound, and TFM, all three programs share a common origin: they were forged in the crucible of real-world, contemporary practice, have a strong basis in social learning theory, and recognize the strengths of family relationships. This is important to remember as we conclude this chapter with a section on therapeutic residential care and the emergent issues in policy, practice, and research that will guide the development of new and improved specialized services for children and youth with persistent and complex needs who are involved with the CW system.

Therapeutic Residential Care[1]

Overview

Historically, group homes and residential treatment centers have been an important but controversial part of the child welfare continuum of services. As of September 30, 2016, 437,465 youth were in out-of-home care, 21,649 (5%) placed in group homes, and 31,679 (7%) were placed in residential treatment and other institutions of some kind. This is 12 percent (53,328) of those in out-of-home care in the United States (UDHHS, 2017).

Frequently, some or all of these facilities, including shelter care and juvenile justice facilities, are referred to as "congregate care." For example, there are only two categories in the Adoption and Foster Care Analysis and Reporting System (AFCARS) that combine to form the congregate care placement option: group home and institution. In AFCARS, group homes are licensed or approved homes providing 24-hour care for children in a setting that generally has 7 to 12 children. An "institution" is a childcare facility operated by a public or private agency that provides 24-hour care and/or treatment for children who require separation from their own homes and a group living experience. These facilities may include childcare institutions, residential treatment facilities, and maternity homes (U.S. Children's Bureau, 2015).

As illustrated in Figure 8.5, states vary substantially in how extensively they use congregate care and for which groups of children and youth. Some believe that TRC and other forms of congregate care were developed and "entrenched" during a time when child welfare practice ideology and interventions were very different. So, it is an industry that delivers a product that is no longer required at the same scale and was not adequately efficacy tested (personal communication, Nadia Sexton, November 5, 2015).

Many states are focusing on more carefully using this form of care, including some as part of their Title IV-E waiver (e.g., Arizona, Delaware, Massachusetts, Rhode Island, and West Virginia). Group homes and residential treatment centers have been challenged to better define and standardize their intervention models and the youth they are best suited to serve. They have been asked to shorten lengths of stay, involve family members more extensively in treatment, help youth learn skills for managing their emotions and behaviors that they can use in the community, and conduct more extensive evaluation studies (Annie E. Casey Foundation, 2010; Jenson & Whittaker, 1987; Kerman, Maluccio, & Freundlich, 2009; Libby et al., 2005; Murray, 2017). This is a call to be more specific and targeted in order to better meet the needs of the children, youth, and families that receive services at this level of care.

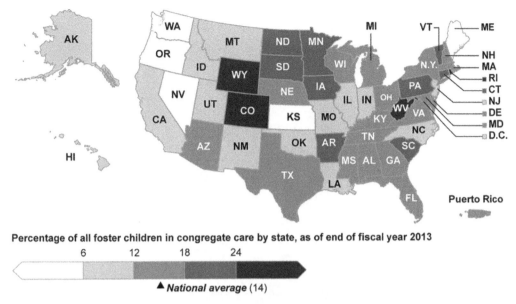

Percentage of all foster children in congregate care by state, as of end of fiscal year 2013

6   12   18   24

▲ *National average* (14)

Figure 8.5 Children in Congregate Care (September 30, 2013)
Source: Map abstracted from Government Accountability Office (2015).

The group care field has responded by improving many aspects of intervention design, implementation, staff development, and evaluation, including providing more aftercare services – support services that follow youth into the community transition (Courtney & Iwaniec, 2009; Whittaker et al., 2006; Whittaker, del Valle, & Holmes, 2015). But there is not yet consensus on transformation, and, as with any systems change, these agencies will need a method of funding to support these transformations. In addition, states are working to determine what kinds of program models, funding mechanisms, and performance monitoring will make those reforms possible (The American Association of Children's Residential Care Agencies, 2011; Annie E. Casey Foundation, 2010). Both the rate of use and length of time in care have decreased in many states.

There has been a significant decrease in the percentage of children placed in congregate care settings in the past decade (34 percent from 2004 to 2013), and this reduction is at a greater rate than the overall foster care population (21%) (see Figure 8.6). According to the most recent data available, children spend an average of eight months in congregate care (34 percent spent more than nine months). While these trends suggest that child welfare practice is moving toward more limited use of congregate care, the depth of

The percentage of children placed in congregate care settings has decreased by 34% from 2004 to 2013.

Figure 8.6 Percentage Decrease in the Use of Congregate Care Between 2004 and 2013
Source: Data taken from U.S. Children's Bureau (2015).

improvement is not consistent across states, and some cohorts of children and youth have fared better than others (Wulczyn, Alpert, Martinez, & Weiss, 2015).

Rather than "congregate care," we will use a more precise term for these services and centers: *therapeutic residential care* (TRC). As mentioned before, this term refers to group homes serving seven or more children, residential treatment centers, and psychiatric residential treatment facilities (PRTFs). PRTFs provide non-acute inpatient facility care for recipients who have a mental illness and/or substance abuse/dependency and need 24-hour supervision and specialized interventions. (For PRTF service requirements, coverage criteria, and limitations, refer to Clinical Coverage Policy #8D-1, Psychiatric Residential Treatment Facilities.) We will not focus on shelter care because it is designed to serve as temporary housing for children and it has few therapeutic components, and because some states intend to significantly reduce shelter care by using other strategies to care for children in crisis situations. Psychiatric hospital programs will also not be a focus because they are a very intense and restrictive use of group care, limited to a very small group of youth with acute and severe problems. This chapter also does not focus on secure detention and other forms of juvenile corrections placements.

Data Limitations

Before reporting some of the key characteristics of youth served in TRC and the broader programs of congregate care, we will highlight a few of the major data limitations in this program area. First, there are limitations in the clinical diagnoses of youth placed in these programs in that case records occasionally do not include the proper data. Second, there are little comparable data in relation to the demographic characteristics of the families of origin of the young people served by TRC programs. Yet in designing TRC programs for specific populations, it is important to have demographic data for the families of the young people to be served, as well as for the young people themselves (personal communication, Frank Ainsworth, October 20, 2015). Finally, there is little information about the trauma/risk behavior trajectories and adequacy of interventions utilized prior to entry of these youth into this higher level of care.

There is some research indicating that a worrisome proportion of youth enter TRC directly, without other, less restrictive treatment efforts being tried first (James et al., 2006). In a few cases, this may be appropriate rather than having the child "fail up" into higher and higher levels of care instead of being placed in the most appropriate level of care at the outset. For most children, however, we should be focusing on helping to serve them successfully, in less restrictive (and less costly) settings.

Therapeutic Residential Care Outcomes Research

A number of studies have shown positive effects of TRC, including improvements in child behavior, and reductions in trauma symptoms, and increased optimism, life satisfaction, and other emotional health improvements while in care and during 3- to 12-month follow-up periods (for an international review see Harder & Knorth, 2015). For example, the Boys Town studies have been consistently strong and positive in most respects, including a recent study of the Family Home Model that showed continuing effects post-treatment (Farmer, Murphy, & Wonnum, 2013; Gilman & Handwerk, 2001; Lee & Thompson, 2008; Lyons, Terry, Martinovich, Peterson, & Bouska, 2001; Ringle et al., 2012). Two California studies of other models also demonstrated treatment effects: one study of 8,933 children found that when properly assessed and placed into the appropriate level (intensity) of care upon entry, the majority of children exit the residential care system altogether, and return home or to home-like settings sooner and at a lower cost. Furthermore, in this particular study, high-level (intensive) residential therapeutic care programs achieved the greatest placement stability, with reduced placement stability with less intensive TRC (Sunseri, 2005). This is an important finding because placement stability is associated with more positive outcomes for children placed in out-of-home care (See, e.g., Pecora et al., 2010; Ryan & Testa, 2004). A more recent study of TRC in four counties in California as part of a services reform project provided preliminary evidence of improvement in behavioral functioning and more youth stepping down to less restrictive placements (McDowell et al., 2014).

Finally, a recent analysis of the Midwest Study data of youth in foster care as they aged out of care found that when a wide range of demographic and life experience variables were controlled for, the only outcome differences between youth who had been in foster care without residential treatment experience and those with residential treatment experience were not being in the labor force in the past 12 months and not owning a car. The researchers commented:

> Youth who enter residential care are likely to be more troubled and have more problematic histories and experiences than youth placed in other out-of-home settings. The drastic reduction in statistical significance that was observed in the second set of regression models once these characteristics were accounted for suggests that it is these characteristics, and not just the residential care setting per se, that contribute to the bleak outcomes observed later in life. This represents both an opportunity for and places an onus on the future of residential care. Knowing that more troubled children will enter these settings, and that their time in placement could potentially solidify or disrupt the trajectories toward unfavorable outcomes, more intentional and data-driven approaches to residential care are called for.
>
> (Okpych & Courtney, 2015, pp. 185–186)

Thus while there is clearly evidence of effective programming in general, the models studied and the rigor of the evaluations vary significantly. For example, there has been an underinvestment in intervention design, service quality monitoring, and outcomes research in TRC. The field needs intervention studies using randomly selected control groups, rigorous quasi-experimental designs, and longitudinal outcome studies that use common measures across studies (for a concise analysis and set of practical strategies to improve TRC research, see Lee & Barth, 2015). With those limitations in mind and with some study exceptions, it appears that although many youth improve in some areas of functioning during the course of TRC, gains are frequently lost following their return to the community. A number of studies have found significant treatment gains that have been maintained post-placement in group home and residential treatment care (see, e.g., Briggs et al., 2012; Larzelere et al., 2001, p. 10; Lee et al., 2011; Lee & Thompson, 2008; Little, Kohm, & Thompson, 2005; Ringle et al., 2012). Further, improvement during the course of treatment has not been a reliable predictor of long-term outcomes. However, the likelihood of maintaining some gains after discharge can be increased by at least three factors ("common elements of treatment"):

1. Involving the resident's family in the treatment process before discharge (for example, in family therapy).
2. Achieving stability in the place where the child or youth goes to live after discharge.
3. Ensuring that aftercare support for the child or youth and their families is available (Hair, 2005, p. 556).

Treatment Principles

While there has been no formal concurrence or agreement, the following treatment principles and areas of clinical focus appear to be important for high-quality TRC, as highlighted by early studies of TRC and the United States General Accounting Office 1994 study:

- Individualize child-specific treatment to address trauma and risk behavior in residential settings as well as step-down community services.
- Help youth learn skills for managing their emotions and behaviors that they can use in the community (adaptation skills) (Leichtman et al., 2001).
- Address other areas of child functioning, such as social/peer, academic, and life skills, including community linkages upon transition.
- Support a trauma-centered therapeutic milieu and positive working relationships between staff and youth (Trieschman, Whittaker, & Brendtro, 1969).

- Minimize lengths of stay, whenever possible, including the use of brief, repeatable TRC episodes, if needed (for more information about how many gains can be made in the first six months of TRC when the child psychopathology is less severe, see Hoagwood & Cunningham, 1992; Hussey & Guo, 2002; Seifert et al., 1999).

- Collaborate with others to facilitate the achievement of legal and emotional permanency, including carefully approaching discharge/transition planning with permanency in mind.

- Integrate family while youth is in residence as well as part of step-down planning; with the child's case manager, and identify and link the child to a caring adult who will be there for the child after treatment (U.S. General Accounting Office, 1994).

- Provide timely aftercare/post-permanency services to the family as needed, including treatment foster care.

The National Child Traumatic Stress Network (NCTSN) study of those served in TRC, and the Knoverek et al. (2013) and Underwood et al. (2004) reviews, highlight the need to address specific areas of treatment: reduced mental health symptoms, aggressive behaviors, cognitive distortions leading to delinquent behavior, cognition impairment, complex trauma, criminal activity, deviant sexual fantasies (applicable to a very small proportion of youth), disassociation, running away, substance abuse, suicidality and other forms of self-injury; elimination of trauma re-victimization; improved attitude, self-concept, self-esteem/self-worth, academic achievement, affect regulation, and attachment; and improved readiness to live in the community.

Program Models and Interventions That Are Effective or Relevant for Therapeutic Residential Treatment and Group Care

In a 24/7 environment childcare workers can be powerful members of a treatment team because they manage the living environment, including crucial times of the day such as early morning and bedtime. But these staff need specialized training and coaching to do that well, as emphasized by a book about "the other 23 hours" and the CARE approach (personal communication, Frank Ainsworth, October 20, 2015. See, e.g., Holden et al., 2015; Polsky, 1962; Trieschman, Whittaker, & Brendtro, 1969). Seven TRC program models have received more careful scrutiny and they are listed by CEBC evidence rating level in Table 8.1, followed by individual clinical interventions (see also James, 2011).

Table 8.1 Program Models and Interventions That Appear to Be Effective or Relevant For Therapeutic Residential Treatment and Group Care

TRC Program Models

Supported	• Positive Peer Culture (PPC)
Promising	• Boys Town Family Home Program^SM and Teaching Family Model (TFM) • The Sanctuary Model • The Stop-Gap Model
Not Able to Be Rated Because of Insufficient Research Evidence At This Time	• Menninger Clinic Residential Treatment Program Model (CRTP) • Multifunctional Treatment in Residential and Community Settings (MultifunC) • Re-ED (originally called Re-Education of Children with Emotional Disturbance)

TRC Interventions (CEBC, Blueprints, OJJDP, or SAMHSA NREP Ratings)

Well-supported

- Attachment Biobehavioral Catch-up (ABC)
- Cognitive Behavioral Therapy (CBT)
- Cognitive Processing Therapy
- Coping Cat
- Ecologically Based Family Therapy
- Eye Movement Desensitization and Reprocessing (EMDR)
- Multisystemic Therapy (MST) for Youth with Problem Sexual Behavior
- PAX Good Behavior Game (PAX GBG)
- Trauma-focused Cognitive Behavioral Therapy

Supported

- Adolescent Community Reinforcement Approach
- Aggression Replacement Therapy (ART) (OJJDP rated it as effective)
- Brief Strategic Family Therapy
- Cognitive Behavioral Therapy (CBT) for Adolescent Depression (NREP ratings 3.4–3.7)
- Dialectical Behavior Therapy (DBT)
- Ecologically Based Family Therapy
- Functional Family Therapy
- Moral Reconation Therapy (NREP ratings 1.9–2.0)
- Structured Sensory Intervention for Traumatized Children, Adolescents and Parents – At-risk Adjudicated Treatment Program (SITCAP-ART)(NREP 2.5 rating)
- Trauma Affect Regulation: Guide for Education and Therapy (TARGET)(NREP ratings 3.0–3.2)

Promising

- Anger Replacement Training® (ART®)
- Adolescent Coping with Depression (NREP ratings: 3.6–3.8)
- Interpersonal Psychotherapy for Depressed Adolescents (IPT-A)
- Residential Student Assist Program (RSAP) (OJJDP rated it as effective)
- Solution-Focused Brief Therapy (SFBT)(OJJDP rated it as promising)
- Theraplay

(Continued)

Table 8.1 (Continued)

Not Able to Be Rated Because of Insufficient Research Evidence At This Time

- Anger Management Group Treatment Model
- Applied Behavior Analysis (ABA) approaches with Individualized Intensive Behavioral Interventions (IBI)
- Attachment, Regulation, and Competency (ARC)
- Biofeedback and Neurofeedback
- Complex Trauma Treatment
- Equine Therapy
- Focused ABA interventions
- Music Therapy
- Real Life Heroes
- Sensorimotor techniques
- Structured Psychotherapy for Adolescents Responding to Chronic Stress (SPARCS)
- Therapeutic Crisis Intervention (TCI)
- Trauma Systems Therapy (TST)
- Trust-Based Relational Intervention (TBRI®) Therapeutic Camp

Source: Pecora, P.J. & English, D.J. (2016). *Elements of effective practice for children and youth served by therapeutic residential care.* Seattle, WA: Casey Family Programs. Retrieved from www.casey.org/residential-care/, pp. 24–25. Reprinted with permission.

The Future Of Specialized Services for Children and Youth With Persistent And Complex Treatment Needs: Challenges for Policy, Practice, and Research

We conclude this brief introduction to intensive treatment service options for children and youth served by CW with the overarching question: Where do we go from here? What challenges confront us as we seek to:

1. Improve our service outcomes with more effective interventions?

2. Measure our results with more accuracy and precision?

3. Insure that our policy initiatives reflect the very best that we know how to do?

Inevitably, this reminds us of the critical interplay among the spheres of practice, research, and policy that inform and inscribe the architecture of this text. With this in mind, the following questions identify some of the key issues and challenges that will confront us in our search for effective intensive treatment options whether our particular role in CW is as practitioner, researcher, or policy planner.

What Constitutes an Adequate "Suite of Intensive Services" to Meet the Needs of High-Resource Using Children, Youths, and Their Families?

Over the past decade or so, the field has gained considerable experience in the adoption of evidence-based alternatives (e.g., MST, TFCO-A) to various forms of residential care services such as residential treatment and group homes and other traditional placement-based services such as family foster care. Among other things, this has raised the issues of *breadth, accessibility*, and *cultural synchrony* with respect to the services offered to children and families.

Recognizing the clear preference for serving children in their own families, should the principle of honoring consumer choice compel us to have at least *some* service options which utilize therapeutic residential care or specialized therapeutic foster care in the mix of choices available to families? Writing from the perspective of over 40 years of research and service delivery at Boys Town in Nebraska and elsewhere in the previously cited Teaching Family Model (TFM), Thompson et al. (2014) make a strong case for some high-quality therapeutic residential care options in the array of needed intensive services provided within states and localities. Buttressed by recent research on discerning quality in therapeutic residential care by Farmer et al. (2017), the Boys Town team with public and voluntary community partners in Florida worked to produce both an assessment tool and practice manual which recent legislation (HB1121) identifies as major elements of an effort to improve TRC performance statewide (Group Care Quality Standards Workgroup, 2015; see also Daly et al., in press).

This initiative aligns with sentiments expressed in a recently published consensus statement developed by an international work group comprising researchers, clinicians, service providers, and others representing 11 countries. The consensus statement – now published in professional journals in Dutch, Italian, Spanish, and Hebrew as well as English – sets forth a working definition for therapeutic residential care, as well as a set of principles and a strong call for needed research in identifying the critical elements in quality TRC programs (for further information, see Whittaker et al., 2016; Whittaker, 2017).

While clearly "one size doesn't fit all" in working with families in CW, what other factors should be considered in choosing an array of service options: for example, costs and efficacy? A closely related issue has to do with the *accessibility* of a desired specialized treatment option in a given state or locality. For example, many of the innovative service interventions identified in the CEBC, while showing saturation in some areas of the country, are either unavailable or are extremely limited in other areas. Moreover, to the extent that certain interventions are trademarked and require up-to-date training for full certification, one finds that the list of available, fully certified sites – say, in MST – is simultaneously expanding in some areas while shrinking in others. For example, see the comments by Whittaker on an excellent cross-national review of child protection systems by Gilbert, Parton, and Skivenes:

> How do differing societies interpret their mandate to protect vulnerable children while supporting the families of those children? How are commonly accepted best practices in child protection, including evidence-based model interventions, subtly shaped to fit the niches of differing cultural, social, and political contexts? How are variations in service provision (e.g., rates of children in various forms of out-of-home care) to be understood among progressive, industrialized countries?
>
> (Whittaker, 2012a, 358)

Lastly, as was referenced in the preceding section on system of care (Stroul, Blau, and Friedman, 2010), services should be "responsive" to differences in race, ethnicity, sexual orientation, language, and other forms of diversity. How *synchronous* are various specialized treatment resources with the diverse communities they seek to serve? Are materials available in translation for use in language-diverse communities? Do staff reflect the communities and cultures from which children are referred? Are special needs of LGBTQ youths adequately met both in the service context and in training schemes? In a diverse, multicultural, multiethnic society, one should expect nothing less than a full and constantly improving mechanism for meeting diverse client needs as part of the boiler-plate of any specialized treatment service options.

What Resources are Available to Us as Practitioners to Identify Truly High-quality Service Options for Children, Youths, and Their Families?

This chapter has made frequent reference to the California Evidence-Based Clearing House for Child Welfare (CEBC) as a rich source of detailed information on a wide range of programs and interventions and their current evidence base. In addition to efficacy, the CEBC rates all interventions with respect to their relevance to CW services. Moreover, programs in the CEBC are routinely updated as new information becomes available. Procedures for review are clearly explained, with excellent oversight from leading CW researchers. We strongly suggest that all CW practitioners and program managers make the CEBC a frequently used tool in their search for up-to date evidence-based intervention information.

As with the Chapin Hall/Chadwick research brief (2016), the CEBC is not infrequently used as a point of reference in research reviews of particular sectors of practice like therapeutic residential care (James, 2011; James et al., 2013). Similarly, the Multi-State Data Archive at Chapin Hall Center for Children at the University of Chicago provides an excellent series of "big picture" CW snapshots with its database of over 3 million children in 25 states within the foster care system. Researchers are constantly generating new studies on particular topics relevant to CW and the Chapin Hall website contains detailed information on reports and issues briefs on their findings (www.chapinhall.org).

As previously noted, program-specific websites for many of the programs and interventions reviewed in the CEBC also provide a rich source of information, particularly on scaling-up of their respective interventions as well as research in progress. Research reviews such as those by the Campbell Collaboration (www.campbellcollaboration.org) and the Washington State Institute for Public Policy (WSIPP) (www.wsipp.wa.gov) provide comparative reviews on various interventions of interest to CW. Cross-national CW researchers are also adding to a growing database on how present trends – such as the movement toward evidence-based practice – are playing out in different countries and regions (Shlonsky and Benbenishty, 2013).

How Should We Think About The Role and Function of Our Teams – Whether in Public or Voluntary Agencies – With Respect to Adopting More Evidence-based Practices?

All three of the previously discussed intensive interventions – MST, TFM, and Wraparound – were created in the crucible of intimate direct practice. In fact, even after many years of expanded implementation, they continue to be refined and improved from practice-based research and through the ongoing analysis of data from current applications. That is why we think it important to view CW practitioners not solely as recipients of the best available evidence-based interventions developed elsewhere. Rather, we think of agencies – public or private – as incubators of practice innovation and the practitioners within them as co-creators of new and improved interventions designed to meet specific needs.

For example, California has recently embarked on a major statewide initiative to better meet the needs of youth with complex treatment needs: California Continuum of Care Reform (AB 403 Fact Sheet, 2015). Among other things, the initiative seeks to rely less on residential service provision and more on community- and family-centered programs to meet client needs. Presently, key voluntary service agencies with long histories of commitment to serve California's children are engaged in a process of transformation to determine the proper mix of service alternatives, identify achievable outcomes, and monitor and evaluate results. In the process, agencies such as Casa Pacifica (www.casapacifica.org), Hathaway Sycamores (www.hathaway-sycamores.org), and Seneca Family of Agencies (www.senecafoa.org) will be transforming their service programs as well as identifying potentially useful service interventions – which could one day benefit children and families far beyond California's borders if supported by rigorous evaluation.

In the meantime, their efforts at discerning the right mix of services – in-home, foster family based and residential – as well as the training and other support structures required to implement them will provide fruitful insights on how one state or region goes about implementing a major reform effort. These efforts have, in part, influenced the national debate which was heading toward federal legislation to significantly curtail federal financing for residential care and was opposed by members of the California legislative group which wanted not to interfere with the current path toward a more complete and rational service array for youth with the greatest behavioral health challenges.

Is The Process of Building An Evidence-based Service Approach Essentially Additive or Integrative?

Recent research by James, Thompson, and Ringle (2017) from the field of therapeutic residential care sheds light on both the progress and challenges in adopting evidence-based practices (EBPs) in this important sector of intensive service. First, the authors identified only a relatively small number of milieu wide evidence-based program models. These models tended to be guided by an overall treatment philosophy, may rely on a theory of change, and generally involve a "package" of case management, psychosocial, and pedagogical elements. (The authors note that: *"introducing a new program model into an agency may require substantial systemic and organizational change and potentially a reconceptualization of the mechanisms of change"* (James, Thompson, & Ringle, 2017, p. 5, emphasis added).

In contrast, the authors note that almost 90 percent of residential agencies surveyed were incorporating *client-specific EBPs* into their regular practice: These are treatments or interventions that are meant to augment "residential care as usual" to address specific client-level problems, such as aggression or trauma. Many of these psychosocial interventions have not been developed for or in residential care, and some have in fact been created as alternatives to residential or inpatient care (e.g., Dialectical Behavior Therapy (DBT)). There is evidence (James et al., 2015) that a growing number of residential care settings are transporting such interventions into residential care. Adopting a client-specific EBP may not require the reorganization or restructuring of an entire therapeutic or pedagogical concept of a facility, making it a less resource-intensive option for introducing EBPs into a setting (James, Thompson, & Ringle, 2017, p. 5).

Whatever the potential benefits for individual clients, a strategy of simply adding more EBPs without addressing their potential interactions and their impacts upon the overall treatment program carries risks. As long ago as the late 1950s, pioneering research in applied behavior analysis in an adult mental health inpatient setting demonstrated how the positive effects of individual interventions could be canceled out by the unintended effects of parallel interventions (Ayllon & Michael, 1959).

Fortunately, two researchers with considerable experience in conducting research in Therapeutic Residential Care (TRC) have recently proposed four promising approaches for incorporating EBPs into TRC settings (Lee & McMillen, 2017). If implemented, these could greatly increase our understanding of how discrete interventions might be combined systematically to improve program and client outcomes. These include using the "Common Elements Approach" described by Lee and McMillen. Thus, instead of focusing on an evidence-based intervention's treatment manual as the unit of analysis, the common elements approach unbundles manualized treatments into actual practice techniques or building blocks frequently found across interventions with known effectiveness (Lee & McMillen, 2017, p. 20; see also Barth et al., 2012, 2014; Chorpita, Daleiden, & Weisz, 2005).

This particular strategy appears most promising for all of CW, as it lends itself to the identification of critical skill and knowledge components for a high-quality social work curriculum in preparation for child and family practice. Other strategies identified by the authors specific to TRC include (1) building a home-grown program and its evidence base, (2) changing an EBP to fit a group care setting, and (3) adapting a group care model to incorporate an EBP (Lee & McMillen, 2017).

A related issue for EBPs includes how interventions or programs known to be effective are most efficiently brought to scale so that their benefits may be widely shared across populations in need of effective services. This issue of how EBPs are best brought to scale has stimulated a new field of research on its own – implementation science – as well as an association of researchers and planners – The Society for Implementation Research Collaboration (SIRC) interested in examining successful implementation strategies across a wide range of health, welfare, and behavioral health fields (https://societyforimplementationresearchcollaboration.org).

How Do We Mobilize Stakeholders – Consumers, Fellow Professionals, Advocates, Researchers – to Work Together to Build a More Effective Community-wide Response?

How do we influence public policy in CW at the local, state, and federal levels? In the U.S., certain major foundations have played a key role both in identifying system change goals within the broad CW sector and implementing multifaceted system change efforts on a local, state, regional, and national level. Chief among them are the previously cited Annie E. Casey Foundation in Baltimore (AECF) and Casey Family Programs in Seattle (CFP) whose collective efforts generate numerous policy and research briefs, research studies, and action guidelines pertinent to CW reform. Taken together with their highly qualified professional staffs and assets measured in the billions, they represent a major force in initiating and shaping CW policy (see www.aecf.org and www.casey.org).

Similarly, national and regional professional associations like the National Association of Social Workers offer multiple resources on CW practice, policy, and research (see www.socialworkers.org/Practice/Child-Welfare.aspx). Finally, many schools of social work offer multiple pathways and specialized resources for students interested in pursuing careers in CW practice, research, and policy.

In conclusion, the search for effective and humane intensive service options for children and youths served by CW continues apace. Seeking out effective and evidence-based intensive services will of necessity involve scanning an ever-widening horizon of research and practice exemplars, including from sister disciplines to social work like psychology, and from cross-national projects where societies approach similar problems in CW in differing ways (see, e.g., Gilbert, Parton, & Skivenes, 2011; Whittaker, 2012b; Fernandez & Barth, 2010; Whittaker, del Valle, & Holmes, 2015). Understanding the sometimes only slightly nuanced differences between service provision in otherwise largely similar societies will be an expanding field for U.S. child welfare researchers and practitioners as we seek to answer the perennial and elusive question of "What Works?"

Note

1   This chapter section is adapted from Pecora & English (2016).

References

Achenbach, T.M., & Rescorla, L. (2001) *Manual for the ASEBA school-age forms and profiles*. Burlington, VT: University of Vermont, Research Center for Children, Youths and Families.

Annie E. Casey Foundation. (2010). *Rightsizing congregate care: A powerful first step in transforming child welfare systems*. Retrieved from www.aecf.org/~/media/Pubs/Topics/Child%20Welfare%20Permanence/Foster%20Care/RightsizingCongregateCareAPowerfulFirstStepin/AECF_CongregateCare_Final.pdf.

Ayllon, T., & Michael, J. (1959). The psychiatric nurse as a behavioral engineer. *Journal of the Experimental Analysis of Behavior, 2*(4), 323–334. Available at https://doi.org/10.1901/jeab.1959.2-323, and retrieved from https://onlinelibrary.wiley.com/doi/abs/10.1901/jeab.1959.2-323.

Barth, R.P., Kolivoski, K.M., Lindsey, M.A., Lee, B.R., & Collins, K.S. (2014). Translating the common elements approach: Social work's experiences in education, practice, and research. *Journal of Clinical Child and Adolescent Psychology, 43*(2), 301–311. doi:10.1080/15374 416.2013.848771.

Barth, R.P., Lee, B.R., Lindsey, M.A., Collins, K.S., Strieder, F., Chorpita, B.F., Becker, K.D., & Sparks, J.A. (2012). Evidence-based practice at a crossroads. *Research on Social Work Practice, 22*(1), 108–119.

Blumenfeld, S., Groves, B.M., Rice, K.F., & Weinreb, M. (2010). *Children and trauma: A curriculum for mental health clinicians.* Chicago, IL: The Domestic Violence & Mental Health Policy Initiative.

Briggs, E.C., Greeson, J.K.P., Layne, C.M., Fairbank J.A., Knoverek, A.M., & Pynoos, R.S. (2012). Trauma exposure, psychosocial functioning, and treatment needs of youth in residential care: Preliminary findings from the NCTSN Core Data Set. *Journal of Child and Adolescent Trauma, 5,* 1–15.

Chadwick Center & Chapin Hall. (2016). *Using evidence to accelerate the safe and effective reduction of congregate care for youth involved with child welfare.* San Diego, CA; Chicago, IL. Retrieved from www.chapinhall.org/sites/default/files/effective%20reduction%20 of%20congregate%20care_0.pdf.

Chamberlain, P., Feldman, S.W., Wulczyn, F., Saldana, L., & Forgatch, M. (2016). Implementation and evaluation of linked parenting models in a large urban child welfare system. *Child Abuse & Neglect, 53,* 27–39. doi:10.1016/j.chiabu.2015.09.013.

Chorpita, B.F., Daleiden, E.L., & Weisz, J.R. (2005). Identifying and selecting the common elements of evidence based interventions: A distillation and matching model. *Mental Health Services Research, 7*(1), 5–20.

Conradi, L., Landsverk, J., & Wotring, J.R. (2014). *Screening, assessing, monitoring outcomes and using evidence-based interventions to improve the well-being of children in child welfare.* Washington, DC: U.S. Department of Health and Human Services, Administration for Children and Families, Children's Bureau. Retrieved from www.acf.hhs.gov/sites/default/ files/cb/wp2_screening_assesing_monitoring.pdf.

Cook, A., Spinazzola, J., Ford, J., Lanktree, C., Blaustein, M., Cloitre, M. et al. (2005). Complex trauma in children and adolescents. *Psychiatric Annals, 35*(5), 390–398.

Courtney, M.E., & Iwaniec, D. (Eds) (2009). *Residential care of children: Comparative perspectives.* New York: Oxford University Press.

Daly, D.L., Bender, K., Davis, J., Whittaker, J.K., & Thompson, R. (in press). Quality care in therapeutic residential programs: Definition, evidence for effectiveness, and quality standards. *Residential Treatment for Children and Youth.*

Farmer, E., Murphy, M., & Wonnum, S. (2013). Comparing treatment processes and outcomes between Teaching-Family and Non-Teaching-Family Group Homes. Paper presented at Teaching-Family Association 36th Annual Conference, Salt Lake City, UT, cited in R.W. Thompson & D.L. Daly (2015), The Family Home Program: An adaptation of the Teaching Family Model at Boys Town. In J.K. Whittaker, J.F. del Valle, & L. Holmes (Eds), *Therapeutic residential care for children and youth: Developing evidence-based international practice* (pp. 113–123). London: Jessica Kingsley.

Farmer, E., Murray, M.L., Ballantine, K., Rautkis, M.B., & Burns, B. (2017). Would we know it if we saw it? Assessing quality of care in group homes for youth. *Journal of Emotional and Behavioral Disorders, 25*(1), 28–36.

Fernandez, E., & Barth, R.P. (Eds) (2010). *How does foster care work? International evidence on outcomes.* London: Jessica Kingsley.

Finkelhor, D., Ormrod, R.K., & Turner, H.A. (2007). Poly-victimization: A neglected component in child victimization. *Child Abuse & Neglect, 31*, 7–26.

Fixsen, D., & Blasé, K. (2008). *The evidence bases for the Teaching-Family model.* Tampa, FL: Louis de la Parte Florida Mental Health Institute. Retrieved from http://teaching-family.org/wp-content/uploads/2013/10/tfabibliography.pdf.

Gilbert, N., Parton, N., & Skivenes, M. (Eds) (2011). *Child protection systems: International trends and orientations.* Oxford: Oxford University Press.

Gilman, R., & Handwerk, M.L. (2001). Changes in life satisfaction as a function of stay in a residential setting. *Residential Treatment for Children & Youth, 18*(4), 47–65.

Government Accountability Office. (2015). *FOSTER CARE: HHS could do more to support states' efforts to keep children in family-based care* (Report No. GAO-16-85, p. 9). Washington, DC: Author.

Greeno, E.J., Uretsky, M.C., Lee, B.R., Moore, J.E., Barth, R.P., & Shaw, T.V. (2016). Replication of the KEEP foster and kinship parent training program for youth with externalizing behaviors. *Children and Youth Services Review, 61*, 75–82. doi:10.1016/j.childyouth.2015.12.003.

Group Care Quality Standards Workgroup. (2015). *Quality standards for group care.* Boystown, NE: Author. Retrieved from www.boystown.org/quality-care/Documents/quality-standards-for-residential-group-care.pdf.

Hair, H.J. (2005) Outcomes for children and adolescents after residential treatment: A review of research from 1993–2003. *Journal of Child and Family Studies, 14*(4), 551–575.

Harder, A.T. & Knorth, E.J. (2015). Uncovering what is inside the "black box" of effective therapeutic residential youth care. In J.K. Whittaker, J.F. del Valle, & L. Holmes (Eds), *Therapeutic residential care for children and youth: Developing evidence-based international practice* (pp. 217–228). London: Jessica Kingsley.

Henggeler, S.W., & Schaeffer, C.M. (2016). Multisystemic Therapy®: Clinical overview, outcomes, and implementation research. *Family Process, 55*(3), 514–528. doi:10.1111/famp.12232.

Hoagwood, K., & Cunningham, M.P.A. (1992). Outcomes of children with emotional disturbance in residential treatment for educational purposes. *Journal of Child and Family Studies, 1*, 129–140.

Holden, M.J., Anglin, J.P., Nunno, M.A., & Izzo, C.V. (2015). Engaging the total therapeutic residential care program of quality improvement: Learning from the CARE model. In J.K. Whittaker,

J.F. del Valle, & L. Holmes (Eds), *Therapeutic residential care with children and youth: Developing evidenced-based international practice* (pp. 247–272). London: Jessica Kingsley.

Hosier, D. (2014). *The difference between PTSD and complex PTSD.* Retrieved from http://childhoodtraumarecovery.com/tag/ptsd-triggers/ (accessed September 9, 2015).

Hussey, D.L., & Guo, S. (2002). Profile characteristics and behavioral change trajectories of young residential children. *Journal of Child and Family Studies, 11*, 401–410.

James, S. (2011). What works in group care? A structured review of treatment models for group homes and residential care. *Children and Youth Services Review, 33*, 301–321.

James, S., Alemi, Q., & Zepeda, V. (2013). Effectiveness and implementation of evidence-based practices in residential care settings. *Children and Youth Services Review, 35*(4), 642–656.

James, S., Thompson, R.W., & Ringle, J.L. (2017). The implementation of evidence-based practices in residential care: Outcomes, processes and barriers. *Journal of Emotional and Behavioral Disorders, 25*, 4–18.

James, S., Leslie, L.K., Hurlburt, M.S., Slymen, D.J., Landsverk, J., Davis, I. et al. (2006). Children in out-of-home care: Entry into intensive or restrictive mental health and residential care placements. *Journal of Emotional and Behavioral Disorders, 14*(4), 196–208.

James, S., Thompson, R., Sternberg, N., Schnur, E., Ross, J., Butler, L., & Muirhead, J. (2015). Attitudes, perceptions and utilization of evidence-based practices in residential care. *Residential Treatment for Children & Youth, 32*, 144–166.

Jenson, J.M., & Whittaker, J.K. (1987). Parental involvement in children's residential treatment: From pre-placement to aftercare. *Children and Youth Services Review, 9*, 81–100.

Kerman, B., Maluccio, A.N., & Freundlich, M. (2009*). Achieving permanence for older children and youth in foster care.* New York: Columbia University Press.

Knoverek, A.M., Briggs, E.M., Underwood, L.A., & Hartman, R.L. (2013). Clinical considerations for the treatment of latency age children in residential care. *Journal of Family Violence, 28*, 653–663.

Larzelere, R.E., Dinges, K., Schmidt, M.D., Spellman, D.F., Criste, T.R., & Connell, P. (2001). Outcomes of residential treatment: A study of the adolescent clients of Girls and Boys Town. *Child and Youth Care Forum, 30*, 175–185.

Lee, B.R., & Barth, R.P. (2015). Improving the research base for therapeutic residential care: Logistical and analytic challenges meet methodological innovations. In J.K. Whittaker, J.F. del Valle, & L. Holmes (Eds), *Therapeutic residential care for children and youth: Developing evidence-based international practice* (pp. 231–242). London: Jessica Kingsley.

Lee, B.R., & McMillen, J.C. (2017). Pathways forward for embracing evidence-based practice in group care settings. *Journal of Emotional & Behavioral Disorders, 25*, 19–27.

Lee, B.R., & Thompson, R. (2008) Comparing outcomes for youth in treatment foster care and family style group care. *Children and Youth Services Review, 30*(7), 746–757.

Lee, B.R., Bright, C.L., Svoboda, D.V., Fakunmoju, S., & Barth, R.P. (2011). Outcomes of group care for youth: A review of comparative studies. *Research on Social Work Practice, 21*(2), 177–189. doi:10.1177/1049731510386243.

Leichtman, M., Leichtman, M.L., Barber, C., & Neese, D.T. (2001). Effectiveness of intensive short-term residential treatment with severely disturbed adolescents. *American Journal of Orthopsychiatry, 71*(2), 227–235.

Libby, A.M., Coen, A.S., Price, D.A., Silverman, K., & Orton, H.D. (2005). Inside the black box: What constitutes a day in a residential treatment centre? *International Journal of Social Welfare, 14,* 176–183.

Little, M., Kohm, A., & Thompson, R., (2005). The impact of residential placement on child development: Research and policy implications. *International Journal of Social Welfare, 14,* 200–209.

Lyons, J.S., Terry, P., Martinovich, Z., Peterson, J., & Bouska, B. (2001). Outcome trajectories for adolescents in residential treatment: A statewide evaluation. *Journal of Child and Family Studies 10, 3,* 333–345.

McDowell, D., Ortiz, M.J., Stevenson, A.M., Lichtenstein, C., & Pecora, P.J. (2014). *Final evaluation report for the California Residentially Based Services (RBS) Reform Project.* Sacramento, CA: Walter R. McDonald and Associates. Retrieved from http://c.ymcdn.com/sites/www.cacfs.org/resource/resmgr/Advocacy/RBS_Year_3_Outcomes_Evaluati.pdf.

Murray, M. (2017). Does model matter? Examining change across time for youth in group homes. *Journal of Emotional and Behavioral Disorders, 25*(2), 119–128.

National Quality Improvement Center for Adoption and Guardianship Support and Preservation (QIC-AG). (2017). *QIC-AG Intervention and Program Catalog.* Retrieved from http://qic-ag.org/logs.

National Wraparound Initiative Workforce Advisory Group. (2013). *Theory of change for Wraparound.* Portland, OR: Portland State University, National Wraparound Initiative.

O'Connell, M.E., Boat, T., & Warner, K.E. (Eds) (2009). *Preventing mental, emotional, and behavioral disorders among young people: Progress and possibilities.* Committee on Prevention of Mental Disorders and Substance Abuse among Children, Youth, and Young Adults: Research Advances and Promising Interventions. National Research Council and Institute of Medicine. Board on Children, Youth, and Families, Division of Behavioral and Social Sciences and Education. Washington, DC: The National Academies Press. Retrieved from www.nap.edu/catalog.php?record_id=12480.

Okpych, N.J., & Courtney, M.E. (2015). Relationship between adult outcomes of young people making the transition to adulthood from out-of-home care and prior residential care. In J.K. Whittaker, J.F. del Valle, & L. Holmes (Eds), *Therapeutic residential care for children and youth: Developing evidence-based international practice* (pp. 173–186). London: Jessica Kingsley.

Pecora, P.J., & English, D.J. (2016). *Elements of effective practice for children and youth served by therapeutic residential care.* Seattle, WA: Casey Family Programs. Retrieved from www.casey.org/residential-care/ (accessed May 23, 2016).

Pecora, P.J., Whittaker, J.K., & Maluccio, A.N. (with R.P. Barth & R. Plotnick). (1992). *The child welfare challenge.* Hawthorne, NY: Walter de Gruyter.

Pecora, P.J., Whittaker, J.K., Maluccio, A.N., & Barth, R.P. (2000). *The child welfare challenge* (2nd edn). Hawthorne, NY: Walter de Gruyter.

Pecora, P.J., Whittaker, J.K., Maluccio, A.N., Barth, R.P., & DePanfilis, D. (2009). *The child welfare challenge* (3rd edn). Piscataway, NJ: Aldine-Transaction Books.

Pecora, P.J., Kessler, R.C., Williams, J., Downs, A.C., English, D.J., White, J., & O'Brien, K. (2010). *What works in family foster care? Key components of success from the Northwest Foster Care Alumni Study.* New York; Oxford: Oxford University Press.

Phillips, E.L., Phillips, E.A., Wolf, M.M., & Fixsen, D.L. (1973). Achievement place: Development of the elected manager system. *Journal of Applied Behavior Analysis, 6*(4), 541–561.

Polsky, H. (1962). *Cottage six: The social system of delinquent boys in residential treatment.* New York: Wiley.

Price, J.M., Chamberlain, P., Landsverk, J., & Reid, J. (2009). KEEP foster-parent training intervention: Model description and effectiveness. *Child & Family Social Work, 14*(2), 233–242. doi:10.1111/j.1365-2206.2009.00627.x.

Ringle, J.L., Huefner, J.C., James, S., Pick, R., & Thompson, R.W. (2012). 12-month follow-up outcomes for youth departing an integrated residential continuum of care. *Children and Youth Services Review, 34*, 675–679.

Ryan, J., & Testa, M. (2004). *Child maltreatment and juvenile delinquency: Investigating the role of placement and placement instability.* Champaign-Urbana, IL: University of Illinois at Urbana-Champaign School of Social Work, Children and Family Research Center.

Schaeffer, C.M., Swenson, C.C., Tuerk, E.H., & Lenggeler, S.W. (2013). Comprehensive treatment for co-occurring child maltreatment and parental substance abuse: Outcomes from a 24-month pilot study of the MST-Building Stronger Families program. *Child Abuse & Neglect, 37*(8), 596–607. doi:10.1016/j.chiabu.2013.04.004.

Seifert, H., Shapiro, J.P., Welker, C.J., & Pierce, J.L. (1999). An evaluation of residential treatment for youth with mental health and delinquency-related problems. *Residential Treatment for Children & Youth, 17*, 33–48.

Shlonsky, A., & Benbenishty, R. (2013). *From evidence to outcomes in child welfare.* Oxford: Oxford University Press.

Stroul, B.A., & Friedman, R.M. (1986) *A system of care for seriously emotionally disturbed children and youth.* Washington, DC: CASSP Technical Assistance Center, Georgetown University Child Development Center.

Stroul, B., Blau, G., & Friedman, R. (2010). *Updating the system of care concept and philosophy.* Washington, DC: Georgetown University Center for Child and Human Development, National Technical Assistance Center for Children's Mental Health.

Sunseri, P.A. (2005). Children referred to residential care: Reducing multiple placements, managing costs and improving treatment outcomes. *Residential Treatment for Children & Youth, 22*(3), 55–66.

Teaching Family Association. (2017). Accredited agencies. Retrieved from https://teaching-fam ily.org/agencies/.

The American Association of Children's Residential Care Agencies. (2011). *Redefining residential series: One through eight.* Milwaukee, WI. Retrieved from http://aacrc-dc.org/page/ aacrc_position_paper_first_series_redefining_role_residential_treatment.

Thompson, R.W., Huefner, J.C., Daly, D.L., & Davis, J.L. (2014). *Why quality group care is good for America's at-risk kids: A Boys Town initiative.* Boys Town, NE: Boys Town Press.

Trieschman, A., Whittaker, J., & Brendtro, L. (1969). *The other 23 hours: Child-care work with emotionally disturbed children in a therapeutic milieu.* Oxford: Aldine.

U.S. Children's Bureau. (2015). *A national look at the use of congregate care in child welfare.* Washington, DC: U.S. Department of Health and Human Services, Administration for Children and Families, Children's Bureau. Retrieved from www.acf.hhs.gov/programs/cb/resource/congregate-care-brief (accessed August 23, 2015).

U.S. Department of Health and Human Services, Administration for Children and Families, Administration on Children, Youth and Families, Children's Bureau. (2017). *The AFCARS Report No. 24. Preliminary FY 2016 estimates as of October 20, 2017.* Washington, DC: Author. Retrieved from www.acf.hhs.gov/sites/default/files/cb/afcarsreport24.pdf.

U.S. General Accounting Office. (1994). *Residential care: Some high-risk youth benefit, but more study needed.* Washington, DC: Author.

Underwood, L.A., Barretti, L., Storms, T.L., & Safonte-Strumolo, N. (2004). A review of clinical characteristics and residential treatments for adolescent delinquents with mental health disorders: A promising residential program. *Trauma, Violence, & Abuse, 5*(3), 199–242.

Whittaker, J.K. (1979). *Caring for troubled children: Residential treatment in a community context.* San Francisco, CA: Jossey Bass.

Whittaker, J.K. (2012a). A review of *Child protection systems: International trends and orientations*, by N. Gilbert, N. Parton, & M. Skivenes. *Social Service Review, 86*(2), 356–358. doi:10.1086/667366.

Whittaker, J.K. (2012b). What works in residential treatment: Strengthening family connections residential treatment to create an empirically based family support resource. In A.P. Curtis & G. Alexander (Eds), *What works in child welfare* (2nd edn). Washington, DC: CWLA.

Whittaker, J.K. (2017). Pathways to evidence-based practice in therapeutic residential care: A commentary. *Journal of Emotional and Behavioral Disorders, 25*, 57–61. doi:10.1177/1063426616686345.

Whittaker, J.K., del Valle, J.F., & Holmes, L. (Eds) (2015). *Therapeutic residential care for children and youth: Developing evidence-based international practice.* London: Jessica Kingsley.

Whittaker, J.K., Holmes, L., del Valle, J.F., Ainsworth, F., Andreassen, T.H., Anglin, J.P., & Zeira, A. (2016). Therapeutic residential care for children and youth: A consensus statement of the international work group on therapeutic residential care. *Residential Treatment for Children & Youth, 33*, 89–106. doi:10.1080/0886571X.2016.1215755.

Whittaker, J.K., Greene, K., Schubert, D., Blum, R., Cheng, K., Blum, K., Reed, N., Scott, K., Roy, R., & Savas, S.A. (2006). Integrating evidence-based practice in the child mental health agency: A template for clinical and organizational change. *American Journal of Orthopsychiatry, 76*(2), 194–201.

Wulczyn, F., Alpert, L., Martinez, Z., & Weiss, A. (2015). *Within and between state variation in the use of congregate care.* Chicago, IL: Chapin Hall Center for Children, The Center for State Child Welfare Data.

Leadership, Staffing, and Other Organizational Requisites for Effective Child and Family Services[1]

Learning Objectives

1. Understand key organizational requisites for success, including clear goals, specific outcomes, strong leadership, and positive organizational climate.

2. Explore major workforce organizational environment and other design challenges in child welfare and possible strategies for addressing them.

3. Review current workforce challenges in child welfare.

4. Understand what innovations are being developed or implemented.

Introduction

The preceding chapters have outlined the major concepts and principles for providing effective CW services and clarified that CW does not operate in isolation and is affected by local community characteristics such as employment, housing, racial segregation, police and fire protection, public transportation, recreation programs, and other forms of community investment or disinvestment. The availability and quality of other health and human services is also critical, such as health and mental health, education, vocational development, and juvenile justice. Community history and current levels of racism, sexism, and other forms of discrimination also affect the ability of CW to succeed in protecting children and strengthening families. Because agency capacity will be affected by these factors, supplemental agency supports are almost certain to be needed if the community infrastructure is not adequate for supporting families.

CW practice today requires specialized skills. The essential practice skills for CPS, family-based services, foster care, reunification and adoption services cannot be learned quickly. If 10,000 hours are required to excel at complex tasks (Gladwell, 2008) this is certainly a minimum for learning to be an effective CW caseworker. The CW "clinical toolbox" has evolved to a point where fundamental practice skills are required such as safety/risk assessment, motivational interviewing, behaviorally specific case planning, and permanency planning. CW workers require expert training and support from their supervisors to succeed. Recent advances in implementation of CW practices, as well as supervision and management training programs, are bringing new capacity and support to CW agencies. Some evidence now indicates that this is making a difference in supporting the CW workforce's engagement over time (Dickinson & Perry, 2002) (see Box 9.1).

Box 9.1

The importance of the work can't be exaggerated. Studies that consider why child welfare workers remain in the field indicate that the work is "exciting, challenging, and unpredictable.'" Furthermore, satisfied staff point to the importance of the work and the personal value they derive from engaging, every day, in work that is meaningful.[a] But there is so much more to child welfare. If it were simply a question of the heart, then many passions would be stirred and countless college graduates would flock to the field. Instead, the work is emotionally satisfying at the same time that it is emotionally taxing. It can be deeply intellectually engaging, but the bureaucratic rules that govern the work sometimes stifle workers' most creative thinking. Child welfare workers help children and families daily, but in order to help, they must first determine how. Much of their work involves consequential decision making.[b] Is this child eligible for services? Is this child safe? What will happen to this child tonight, if I walk away? What type of service can best help this family? Can we provide the services that this family needs? Where should this child live, if not with parents? Can this child safely return home?

Source: Berrick (2018, p. 4).

Notes:
[a]Ellett, A., Ellis, J.I., Westbrook, T.M., & Dews, D. (2007, p. 274); Westbrook, Ellis, & Ellett (2006).
[b]Gelles (in press).

Components of Organizational Excellence

Attention to Leadership

When we think about working for an excellent organization, what qualities spring to mind? What aspects of that organization differentiate it from others? Is excellence related to the presence of a clear focus on the service being delivered? Is it because staff members understand management's expectations and have a clear idea of what constitutes excellence? Are staff members acknowledged for increasing those identified elements of success? Are service recipients and staff valued by the organization?

CW organizations operate in turbulent and challenging organizational environments that demand a clear organizational mission and strong leadership to be effective. To deliver effective services and be considered an excellent place to work, an organization must have a number of components in place. Workers and supervisors need to be supported in specific ways that complement the agency's mission and program objectives. The *workforce*, *workplace*, and the *practice model* must all be working well to achieve overall effectiveness. One cannot address just one without addressing the others (personal communication, Hal Lawson, February 5, 2008).

Recent demands for system improvement in CW, public health, and behavioral health necessitate increased leadership attention to staffing, career ladders, and staff development because the new practice models and evidence-based interventions require a more highly skilled workforce. In addition, a small number of state and county CW agencies are seeking accreditation from the Council on Accreditation (COA) or another organization to provide them with information about whether they adhere to nationally recognized organizational components, quality improvement, and results. This information can then be used to enhance services and staffing. But high worker turnover wastes much of the funds invested in recruiting, onboarding, training, and mentoring new staff. So some leaders of public and private CW agencies are paying greater attention to finding and keeping their staff, and how the following organizational, managerial, and structural components support staff retention as well as the effective delivery of human services. These are described in more detail in the sections that follow.

1. A clear organizational mission and program philosophy is widely disseminated throughout the organization.

2. Benchmarks for organizational excellence are in place for particular service areas (organizational standards of quality and expected results are clear).

3. A positive interorganizational and organizational climate exists.

4. Workforce challenges are addressed.

5. Effective interventions and other practice-related strategies are implemented carefully and nurtured over time.

6. High-quality ongoing coaching and monitoring of staff activities, and a strong system of supervisory capacity and supports is in place.

7. There is wise use of technology.

8. Community-based services and proactive interaction with the media are used to build political support and protection.

The interrelationships between many of these factors are illustrated in Figures 9.1, 9.2, 9.3, and 9.4. As depicted in Figures 9.1 and 9.2, many leaders of public and private CW

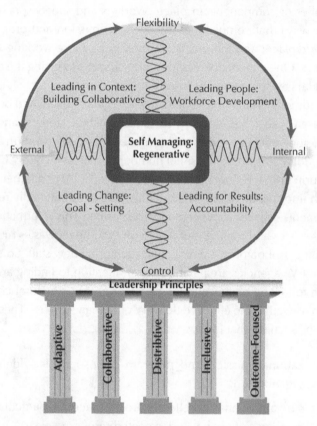

Figure 9.1 National Child Welfare Workforce Institute Leadership Model
Source: National Child Welfare Workforce Institute (2011).

(Note how these human services management competencies include a robust array of interpersonal, intellectual, and technical skills.)

DOMAIN: **EXECUTIVE LEADERSHIP**

• Interpersonal skills	• Communication skills
• Analytical and critical thinking skills	• Cross-cultural understanding
• Professional behavior	• Advocates for social justice
• Maintains stakeholder relationships	• Facilitates innovative change

These interpersonal skills are necessary to motivate others to successfully communicate the organizational mission and vision at all levels of management.

DOMAIN: **RESOURCE MANAGEMENT**

• Effectively manages human resources	• Ensures transparency, protection and accountability
• Effectively manages and oversees the budget and other financial resources	• Manages all aspects of information technology

The competencies delineated under the domain of Resource Management list the intellectual skills that provide for a clear perspective on the organization in its environment and are essential to possessing the capacity to think and act strategically.

DOMAIN: **STRATEGIC MANAGEMENT**

• Fundraising	• Manages risk and legal affairs
• Marketing and public relations	• Ensures strategic planning
• Designs and develops effective programs	

The competencies delineated under the domain of Strategic Management provide a selection of technical skills that are essential to successfully managing organizational functions such as budget and finances, human resources and technology.

DOMAIN: **COMMUNITY COLLABORATION**

• Builds a relationship with complementary agencies, institutions and community groups and is an amalgamation of all the skills needed in social work management that are employed at the senior level.

Figure 9.2 The Network for Social Work Management Framework of Human Services Management Competencies

Source: Network for Social Work Management (2015, p. 2). Reprinted with permission.

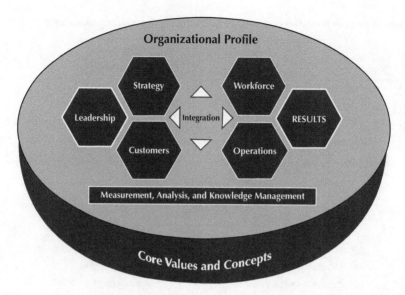

Figure 9.3 The 2015–2016 Baldrige Excellence Framework

Source: www.nist.gov/baldrige/publications/baldrige-excellence-framework/businessnonprofit.

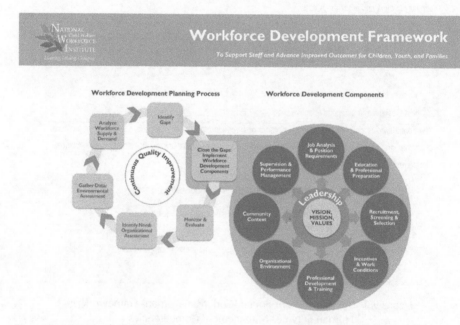

Figure 9.4 National Child Welfare Workforce Institute Workforce Development Framework

Source: National Child Welfare Workforce Institute (n.d.). Reprinted with permission.

agencies are paying greater attention to how leadership and managerial competencies support the effective delivery of human services. Then, as depicted in Figure 9.3, these factors are illustrated by the Baldrige Criteria for Performance Excellence Framework used to assess many corporations and other kinds of organizations. We follow this with the National Child Welfare Workforce Institute's (NCWWI) "workforce development framework" (see Figure 9.4). There is also an entire toolkit to support these kinds of innovations on the NCWWI website at http://ncwwi.org/index.php/myncwwi-home (see also Austin & Hopkins, 2004; Pecora et al., 2010). Note that while agency leaders and front-line supervisors may not be primarily responsible for all of these areas, they work within this larger context – and within two to four years of graduation many student readers of this book may become supervisors or agency leaders.

Clear Agency Mission, Philosophy, and Program Objectives

One of the most common characteristics of effective human service organizations is their use and commitment to a clear, well-defined, value-driven organizational mission (Peters & Waterman, 1983). A simple yet effective mission and philosophy statement that captures the organization's dedication to its services and those served provides clear direction and purpose for the agency and its leaders and staff. An effective agency organizes itself from the customer inward through the creation of customer-driven agency outcomes, services, and quality improvement processes ensuring that the most efficacious interventions are being provided (Testa & Poertner, 2010).

Growing numbers of CW agencies have been able to define and sustain their mission in ways that promote staff, client, and public understanding of what it is that they do. This image and clear sense of mission is bolstered by a supportive ideology: a particular set of values and beliefs about the organizational mission, service technology, and the clients served. Patti, Poertner, and Rapp (1987, p. 378) believe that organizational excellence is dependent upon:

> not only clear objectives, structured roles, competent personnel, and adequate resources to perform well, but more importantly, the organization needs values, symbols, and beliefs that attach a social significance to the organization's outcomes and processes, and that help to reconcile ever present ambiguity and uncertainty.

As with virtually all human service programs, CW agencies function within a political and organizational context that heavily influences their organizational mission and philosophy. For example, a variety of family-centered CW services such as family support services, special needs adoption family counseling, and post-adoption support have expanded during the past ten years. This occurred, in part, because it was recognized that permanency planning was a necessary but insufficient way to minimize the number of children being placed in substitute care.

As we discussed in Chapters 1 and 3, placing a priority on a family-centered approach is also being promoted because of the "ideological fit" of such an agency mission with the standards of the Federal Child and Family Services Review (CFSR) and of allied agencies involved with children's mental health. Many CW agencies are also reconsidering the agency mission in order to respond to the requirements of the CFSR to deepen their community partnerships so that they can show that they are working with education, juvenile justice, mental health, and the courts to achieve services to promote child well-being (see Chapters 3 and 8).

While this process often requires changes in state law, administrators and line staff feel it is worth the effort in terms of more effective targeting of services and lowering unreasonably high worker caseloads. These administrators may believe that CW staff should not act as public health enforcers, school attendance enforcement agents, or family therapists for local school systems for cases that do not very clearly involve child abuse or neglect. Other agencies are attempting to limit the types of child protection cases because of concern for abrogating parental rights and the need to try to allocate scarce resources to primary and secondary prevention programs rather than to the administrative costs of pursuing court-supervised interventions. A variety of innovative program designs have been proposed along those lines, along with a call for client-centered and outcome-oriented services (Testa & Poertner, 2010; Wulczyn, Orlebeke, & Haight, 2009).

Benchmarks for Organizational Excellence

As mentioned above and in Chapter 1, according to professional and federal standards, CW agencies need to achieve a critical set of outcomes in three broad outcome domains: *child safety*, *child permanence*, and *child well-being* (U.S. Department of Health and Human Services, 2016). Wulczyn and colleagues (2009) suggest that the mandate for the CW system should be expressed as *achieving* safety and permanency outcomes and *ensuring* that the CW system engages the education, health, and mental health systems. This approach helps the CW system rightfully take credit for working to create safe and stable families for children without creating an unrealistic expectation of improving a wide range of indicators of well-being. (Child well-being will be enhanced, naturally, with greater safety and permanency.)

Organizational excellence is rooted in administrators being expert in implementing interventions or services that will be most effective for meeting their customers' needs. Many CW agencies are building "logic models" that depict the key elements of interventions necessary to accomplish the desired service results. After outlining the philosophical principles, outcomes, and performance measures of their CW programs, logic models identify the community resources, organizational capacity, and funding needed to achieve those results. Logic models reflect a theory of change for the specific intervention or program that outlines the key short-term, intermediate, and long-term results to be achieved; essential activities that may lead to those results; staff, equipment, and other resources necessary to achieve results; and the cost of attaining those outcomes. Logic models are part of a continuous quality improvement approach, backed by concise practice protocols or guidelines where possible, within a management philosophy where leaders "manage to outcomes rather than to process."

This also involves paying attention to strategic planning, understanding the agency's service catchment area, being focused on the well-being and skills of staff, and paying attention to program performance outcomes. Balancing service capacity and quality is a hallmark of a successful organization.

Organizational Standards of Quality and Expected Results are Clear

Specify, measure, and use agency performance data to improve services. Performance data should be brought to bear to establish benchmarks and track improvement or make corrections to stimulate improvement over time using a Continuous Quality Improvement approach. When feasible, agencies should establish trend lines that repeatedly compare achieved standards of quality and key program expectations. Trend data help clarify patterns and counteract distraction that might otherwise result from an occasional tragic event, bad quarter, or extraordinary year. This is made easier by software and performance dashboards such ChildStat or Safe Measures. For example, ChildStat is an internal management accountability and quality improvement process initially developed in New York City. ChildStat was modeled after the police debriefing and management tool, CompStat, and has been adapted for use in New Jersey's CW agency, as well as Pennsylvania and others. In 2017, ChildStat was revamped and revitalized in New York City to reflect the following essential components:

- An emphasis on weekly, rigorous review of randomly selected high-risk cases, including ongoing investigations, and a deep analysis of critical performance data.

- Elevation of ChildStat to include regular participation of executive leadership – Commissioner and senior ACS staff to demonstrate the priority placed on the process.

- A focus on accountability at all levels of the agency.

- Continuity from session to session to ensure that change results from each meeting.

- Building a more unified culture of excellence in practice that reaches across the five boroughs (see www1.nyc.gov/assets/acs/pdf/PressReleases/2017/0510.pdf).

When bolstered by sophisticated geo-mapping (including "heat mapping"), and multivariate analyses (including predictive analytics), greater understanding of the true dynamics of system performance occurs. But we also need to go beyond these approaches if we want to make the kinds of major systems reforms and intervention breakthroughs that are needed. For example, Liebman (2017), based on the Harvard University Performance Center work with 50 jurisdictions spanning 24 states, offers two strategies for achieving those goals: First, we need to help state and local social services agencies to use data more effectively as a management tool with **much faster cycles of using data** to generate innovation, systems re-engineering, and continuous improvement. And second, we need to launch, structure, and fund purposeful data-driven community-level efforts to tackle difficult social problems in a way that breaks down funding silos and introduces accountability for *population-wide* outcomes. Thus we need to move from static evaluation of programs to real-time improvement in outcomes and to systemic-focused solutions to challenging social problems. To help do that, LeMahieu (2017) has advocated moving beyond being satisfied with interventions with moderate to high effect sizes to determining *how* that success was achieved, and *how* variation toward the negative performance zone could be minimized through the use of Improvement Science and Networked Improvement Communities.

Staff want to achieve positive outcomes and celebrate those achievements. Another organizational requisite for CW that supports effective practice is the systematic collection and use of program evaluation data by program planners, supervisors, and line staff. Any quality organization achieves success by delineating and meeting performance expectations. This is not done without a vibrant and practical management information enterprise that has the commitment of leadership, supervisors, and staff. This system enables regular collection and use of program performance data, including performance measurement, analysis, and knowledge management. Many organizations are drowning in data but thirsty for usable information. Both service output and client outcomes data are important, as well as consumer perceptions about the quality of the service delivery process. But these data need to be organized and analyzed in ways that provide meaningful and timely information to affect decision making at multiple organizational levels.

Performance measurement should ultimately also be tied to a strong process management system, including ongoing assessment of program quality, model fidelity, outputs, and outcomes. In setting or examining program performance levels, it is essential to monitor multiple criteria. For example, family reunification programs that are poorly designed (e.g., where reunifications occur too quickly or without sufficient aftercare) may result in shorter lengths of stay in foster care, but may also result in more children re-entering foster care.

Now more than ever, CW agencies are being asked to increase the amount of evaluation effort in all program areas to refine prevention, treatment, and administrative efforts in this field. Many federal funders require "evaluation," which has typically meant clients served, but now federal programs – and many local ones – also ask for follow-up trend data on outcomes. Research efforts must, however, be realistic, empower communities, be carefully fitted to the program objectives, and incorporate a variety of approaches – quantitative and/or qualitative. Experts are urging that a more consumer-oriented management and service delivery system be adopted within an *"Improvement Science"* evaluation framework, where steadily improving service quality and client outcomes becomes more of the program focus rather than how much service was provided (Christie, Lemire, & Inkelas, 2017).

The extent to which the agency management information system can support program evaluation depends on whether they support turning data into information that can be used by supervisors and workers. Organizational integrity is increased when programs are validated through achievement of positive client outcomes. Cost-effectiveness data allow organizations to more clearly advocate for program funding. Standardized assessment instruments (such as the Child and Adolescent Needs and Strengths (CANS) scale, Family Assessment Form (FAF), North Carolina Family Assessment Scales (NCFAS), the Achenbach suite of checklists, the Strengths and Difficulties Questionnaire (SDQ), and the Treatment Outcome Package (TOP)) are increasingly in use. But some of these instruments may not be scored until much later, and so the information is not provided to workers or families in a timely manner. Management information systems and required paperwork in many CW agencies are being redesigned to reduce duplication and provide more useful information regarding both client outcomes and worker performance – but unfortunately often with considerable initial disruption of office work.

Some cautions about performance assessment: The need to focus on quality and understand what indicators of outcome and quality mean. Outcomes assessment should not be pursued at the cost of ignoring the quality of the services provided. There is a danger in overreliance on outcomes, given the present state of the field. For example, some state or local governments have transferred many CW services to a private provider, with minimal process guidelines or standards of quality, but are instead using a few outcome measures to guide agency practice and to govern their level of payment to the private agency. This may be especially likely to occur when there are capitated payments and few process requirements governing placement and service delivery. Using outcome measures as a wholesale substitute for requirements governing such things as staff qualifications, case planning, fidelity assessment, and review procedures and due process protections can be literally very dangerous to children.

Another danger in the wholesale substitution of outcome measures for quality standards or process requirements (such as licensure, qualifications, protocols for service selection, or required arrays of services) is that this prevents CW from becoming a mature field of practice. If there is no consistency in training or qualifications of staff, service selection, and available services, then we do not develop expertise in our field; for this reason many organizations such as the American Public Human Services Association and the Child Welfare League of America have undertaken major efforts to identify key indicators of quality CW services delivery so that every state will have access to such information.

Finally, one of the challenges ahead is to link the daily activities and observable outcomes of CW services to their impact upon the lives of children when they are no longer under the supervision of these services. A focus on outcomes must never be allowed to become a narrow focus on certain service outcomes; vulnerable children need our vigilance and assurances that we care about them as whole individuals, across all life domains.

Interorganizational and Organizational Climate and Supports

A team approach of providing services to children and families requires that participating agencies demonstrate that they each have economic or other incentives to communicate, cooperate, and coordinate activities so that collaboration can occur. Integrating essential CW and ancillary services may also include integrating behavioral health services. Interorganizational coordination can have mixed results in improving service quality and outcomes if organizational climate and treatment of staff are not also considered (Glisson & Hemmelgarn, 1998; Glisson & James, 2002). Since collaborative efforts are seldom successful based solely on participants' goodwill or intentions, a team approach of providing services to children and families requires that participating agencies have incentives to communicate, cooperate, and coordinate activities so that collaboration may occur.

Additional mechanisms for promoting collaboration include: (1) funding and accountability criteria based on outcomes achieved; (2) setting program goals across disciplines; (3) encouraging the use of informal ties among managers to get things done across organizational lines; and (4) working together on outcomes with no single organization having control over all the processes involved. State performance-based contracting refinements and other initiatives such as the Harvard Government Performance Lab (https://govlab.hks.harvard.edu/) are striving toward these breakthroughs to achieve new gains in program effectiveness.

Factors within the organization are also important for effectiveness. For example, the Tennessee Safety Culture initiatives have shown that careful attention to establishing a supportive workplace where "workers are not thrown under the bus" when a casework crisis arises can have an impact upon the perceived psychological safety of staff and turnover of CW caseworkers (Vogus et al., 2016). Glisson, Dukes, and Green (2006) designed an intervention at the agency level entitled ARC (Availability, Responsiveness, and Continuity) that involved consistent consultation with agency management about the way they led their organization and responded to the needs of their staff. Using an experimental design, 10 urban and 16 rural case management teams were randomly assigned to either the ARC organizational intervention condition or to a control condition. The ARC organizational intervention reduced the probability of CW workers quitting their jobs during the year by two-thirds and improved organizational climate in urban and rural case management teams.

In a follow-up study, Glisson, Green, and Williams (2012) examined the association of organizational climate, casework services, and youth outcomes in CW systems. Building on preliminary findings linking organizational climate to youth outcomes over a three-year follow-up period, this study extended the follow-up period to seven years and tested main, moderating, and mediating effects of organizational climate and casework services on outcomes by analyzing all five waves of the National Survey of Child and Adolescent Well-being (NSCAW) with a U.S. nationwide sample of 1,678 maltreated youth aged 4 to 16 years and 1,696 caseworkers from 88 CW systems.

They found that maltreated youth served by CW systems with more engaged organizational climates have significantly better outcomes. Moreover, the quantity and quality of casework services neither mediate nor interact with the effects of organizational climate on youth outcomes. While this is a key finding that organizational climate is associated with youth outcomes in CW systems, a better understanding is needed of the mechanisms that link organizational climate to outcomes. In addition, there is a need for evidence-based organizational interventions that can improve the organizational climates and effectiveness of CW systems.

In an unusual study to see whether organizational supports can boost the effectiveness of an evidence-based intervention, Glisson et al. (2010) assessed the effectiveness of a 2-level strategy for implementing evidence-based mental health treatments for delinquent youth in 14 rural Appalachian counties and they included 2 factors: (1) the random assignment of delinquent youth within each county to a multi-systemic therapy (MST) program or usual services; and (2) the random assignment of counties to the ARC (availability, responsiveness, and continuity) organizational intervention for implementing effective community-based mental health services.

The study design created four treatment conditions (MST plus ARC, MST only, ARC only, control). An analysis of six-month treatment outcomes found that youth total problem behavior in the MST plus ARC condition was at a nonclinical level and significantly lower than in other conditions. Total problem behavior was equivalent and at nonclinical levels in all conditions by the 18-month follow-up, but youth in the MST plus ARC condition entered out-of-home placements at a significantly lower rate (16%) than youth in the control condition (34%). They concluded that two-level strategies which combine an organizational intervention such as ARC and an evidence-based treatment such as MST are promising approaches to implementing effective community-based mental health services. More research is needed to understand how such strategies may be used effectively in a variety of organizational contexts and with other types of evidence-based treatments.

Workforce Challenges are Addressed

There is no single answer to the question of how to address the CW workforce challenges, including recruitment issues and low worker retention. An agency that implements just one strategy (e.g., reducing direct service worker caseloads but not improving supervision and agency supports or having staff with the professional commitment to do the job) will probably not be very successful in the long run. It is a combination of organizational conditions, targeted and cohesive workforce strategies, and personal factors which current and prospective staff bring to their job that will result in improved retention, in some cases even when emotional exhaustion is high (Kruzich, Mienko, & Courtney, 2014; Stalker et al., 2007).

If a family-centered approach to service delivery is to be implemented, part of that approach involves empowering clients. Workers also need to be empowered if they are expected to aid in the empowerment of others. Basic office and clerical supports are two important components of this support. (Workforce challenges and strategies are discussed more thoroughly in the next major chapter section, such as how to increase staff retention, as described in Figure 9.6.)

As discussed earlier, Williams and Glisson (2013) hypothesized that reducing staff turnover is not enough and that we need proficient organizational cultures to support positive youth outcomes in CW. In their study, the association between caseworker turnover and youth outcomes was moderated by organizational culture. Youth outcomes were improved with lower staff turnover in proficient organizational cultures and the best outcomes occurred in organizations with low turnover and high proficiency. To be successful, efforts to improve CW services by lowering staff turnover must also create proficient cultures that enable the development of worker competence and hold staff accountable for being responsive to the needs of the youth and families they serve.

Strategies for improving staffing requirements and results involve forming realistic career ladders with positions for technicians, mid-level practitioners, and family intervention and CPS specialists, as well as developing pay grades that do not require people to move to supervisory positions to obtain equitable salary increases. Workforce development also involves implementing and publicizing job validation or job effectiveness studies that document the knowledge and skills required for particular positions in CW. Policy makers need to be made aware of the increased costs involved in hiring and supervising under-educated or under-trained workers, as well as the agency's increased vulnerability to and expenses incurred in defending charges of malpractice as well as high levels of turnover.

Agencies can encourage individuals with social work degrees to apply for CW positions by partnering with universities to educate BSW and MSW students for CW careers and by using special recruitment campaigns and job announcements that specify that social work degrees are preferred. But staff retention can also be enhanced by hiring staff with professional commitment and previous job-related experience, as well as the maturity to address the complex needs of the children and families served by the system. Staff professional degree and post-degree certification programs have been recognized as useful (Barbee et al., 2012). Support for staff attaining professional degrees has been enabled in about 40 states through Title IV-E training funds, where BSW and MSW partner with state CW agencies to provide degrees for current or prospective staff (Zlotnik & Pryce, 2013).

Effective Interventions and Other Practice-related Strategies are Implemented Carefully and Nurtured Over Time

As CW agencies move to implement more fully a family-centered approach, service approaches based on neighborhood offices, service delivery teams, community development specialists, and use of informal helping networks are being emphasized (e.g., Daro et al., 2005). In addition, administrators recognize that "maximizing productivity through people" is critical for human services. This requires a concentration of effort, and the use of a well-formulated treatment technology. Despite limitations in our knowledge of human behavior there is a growing body of empirical research and practice wisdom that some agencies are aggressively tapping to provide their staff with the most powerful change technologies available (see, e.g., the California Evidence-Based Clearinghouse (www. cebc4cw.org/).

CW administrators and workers, in designing their service approach, should be making careful decisions about the intervention technology to be used. The empirical evidence and practice wisdom supporting various approaches should be carefully examined before implementation occurs. Indeed, studies of policy and program implementation have emphasized the need to carefully choose and systematically implement an effective service technology (Blase et al., 2015; Fixsen et al., 2005; Walsh, Reutz, & Williams, 2015).

Unfortunately, determining which theoretical models should guide treatment interventions is complicated by the lack of evaluative research in the CW field. It is sobering to consider how relatively few evidence-based interventions are suitable for CW (Barth, 2008). Fortunately, despite some limitations (e.g., Jensen et al., 2005), there is growing use of EBP models such as Trauma-focused Cognitive Behavior Treatments, Functional Family Therapy, Parent Child Interaction Therapy, Multi-dimensional Foster Family Treatment, and others (see Chapters 3 and 8 for a discussion of some of these interventions; Clara, Garcia, & Metz, 2017; Pecora, O'Brien, & Maher, 2015). Ancillary services essential for success must also be identified and provided. For example, what specific kinds of mental health, healthcare, education, vocational development, juvenile justice, and other services are needed? What kinds of integrated behavioral health services are essential?

High-quality Ongoing Coaching and Monitoring of Staff Activities, and a Strong System of Supervisory Capacity and Supports Is In Place

Attention to human resource issues includes a positive organizational climate, supervisor availability, "responsiveness continuity" (Glisson et al., 2006), treating staff with dignity, maximizing professional discretion to the extent possible, and development of staff through regular training opportunities. Ongoing staff coaching and group/team supervision are also important for practice model implementation (e.g., American Public Human Services Association, 2012).

Staff professional degree and post-degree certification programs have been recognized as useful (Barbee et al., 2012). Support for staff attaining professional degrees has been supported in about 40 states by Title IV-E training funds, where BSW and MSW partner with state CW agencies to provide degrees for current or prospective staff (Zlotnik & Pryce, 2013). Finally, specialized training, peer support, and recognition of CW *managers* should not be overlooked (e.g., New Jersey *management fellows* and *data fellows* programs, Title IV-E training support of states and universities) (Webb & Carpenter, 2011).

There Is Wise Use of Practice-related Technologies

Because technology can be an expensive distraction from the difficult and non-glamorous work of day-to-day service delivery and supervision, it is important to adopt a balanced approach to the use of technology. In other words, a wise leader and supervisor carefully balances what kinds of technology staff really need versus the kinds of technology that staff want or that management thinks will improve productivity (e.g., tablets that enable quick access to the internet and have the ability to display and store hand-drawn notes and diagrams like genograms, social network maps, and other diagrams, teleconference facilities, easy-to-use management information systems, data-capturing whiteboards, voice–text software, and dial-in web-based assessment measures). See, for example, CaseAIM (www.chsfl.org/services/caseaim/) and Casebook (http://ncwwi.org/index.php/link/239-mind-the-gap-5-transforming-child-welfare-decision-making-through-modern-technology-data-analytics).

For examples of web-based, free instant-scoring assessment tools for human services see www.caseylifeskills.org. Finally, there is an annual publication called *CW360* that in 2011 devoted an entire issue to the use of technology in CW (www.cascw.org/wp-content/uploads/2013/12/CW360_2011.pdf).

Community-based Services and Proactive Interaction with the Media Are Used to Build Political Support and Protection

Many strong agency leaders have been brought down by a tragic event that was not well managed in the media – resulting in a loss of confidence in the upper reaches of the agency or community. Agencies need a carefully designed communications plan, including a crisis management plan for such predictable exigencies (Turnell, Murphy, & Munro, 2013). Development of prior political and media support is also essential to buffer human services administrators and staff from the day-to-day controversies of this work. Despite best efforts, children will occasionally be harmed during service delivery, and agencies need to be supported by a network of university and community-based partners. Ensuring active, meaningful ways to engage external audiences about the value and impact of the work that staff do every day can help provide an essential buffer and shore up essential support for the agency and its staff during times of crisis. What can help staff feel supported and increase effectiveness are community partnerships. Community collaborations are a way to understand that the whole community has a stake in CW outcomes and should support their CW agencies. However, the focus on the media should ensure that the agencies and universities are educating the media about what CW does and how difficult it is to do it, including having a crisis management plan. Agency directors meeting with editorial boards of local newspapers is just one strategy (personal communication, Joan Levy Zlotnik, July 21, 2017).

For example, in Fort Lauderdale, the Calvert Church took on the special role of supporting foster families in their community. In Spokane, a local car dealer provided used cars to a social service agency at a reduced cost to help needy families. In other cities, United Parcel Service and other employers have stepped up to hire youth in foster care to help provide them with employment experience. The point here is that workers need to feel that they are not alone in this work; they need to feel that they are part of a *larger collaborative*.

Media coverage about CW agencies is often controversial and unfair. For example, CW workers are sometimes criticized for removing children from their homes, but are also criticized for leaving children at home whom the public believes should have been placed in shelter or foster care. CW agencies have also earned a low public image in some areas because of poor services, overloaded telephone systems and receptionists, "inaccessible" workers, terrible office facilities, and other service delivery problems. Professionally trained workers, like other professional groups, prefer to work in agencies with strong public support and a solid reputation for delivering effective services. Everyone wants to be part of an effective team. So we need to negotiate reasonable but high-reaching expectations for success and then to relentlessly drive toward achieving them – celebrating milestones of success along the way. This requires paying attention to how we design our organizational performance dashboards and what we do with the information on them.

To the extent possible, agencies must strive to have an organizational identity that is positive and proactive around key practice issues, so that staff will feel they are part of an effective team – even though the work is challenging and some of our most important child success indicators may not be immediately visible. Strategies for addressing this problem include improving CW agency use of the media through special public relations campaigns, publication of "success stories," newspaper columns authored by CW personnel, and talk show appearances. In addition, agency ombudspersons or constituent affairs representatives should listen and respond to client complaints or recommendations. Focused legislative efforts with state and local policy makers are essential to implementing and publicizing family preservation service and adoption programs to emphasize that public CW agencies preserve families and find permanent homes for children, rather than merely investigate reports of maltreatment and place children in foster care. Finally, it is helpful to promote attitudes among social work practitioners and faculty that emphasize CW as a vital and exciting area of practice, one that is often more challenging than private practice specialties.

Key Workforce Challenges in Child Welfare

Overview

One of the most critical components of organizational excellence is attracting and maintaining a stable, motivated, and skilled workforce. CW agencies, along with many other health and human service agencies, experience much difficulty in this area – although this is uneven. Some states and counties can tout a highly trained, largely Masters-level workforce, with significant staff member retention levels.

CW researchers have identified specific barriers against, and accelerators toward, the development of a high-quality professional workforce. Some of these issues include the existence of clear organizational strategic objectives and clear articulation and understanding of priorities. The availability of quality supervision is another key ingredient, as is peer support (DePanfilis & Zlotnik, 2008; Kruzich et al., 2014). In addition, when organizational quality and outcomes are monitored regularly, positive outcomes can be recognized and rewarded. Challenges such as maintaining realistic caseload sizes, workplace safety, low salaries, and confusing or nonexistent career ladders that don't allow for advances other than acceptance of administrative promotions must be addressed (American Public Human Services Association, 2010).

Privatization of some CW responsibilities to staff at contract agencies must be accompanied by an emphasis on service quality and careful monitoring and incentivizing of positive outcomes. Staff deployment should be strategic (e.g., careful use of generic versus specialized workers, strategic deployment of professional and paraprofessional staff). The current fiscal environment of resource scarcity or large fluctuations in funding from year to year has also hindered progress in addressing workforce issues. New Jersey and Tennessee are among the states that have been refining this approach over time; and the Harvard Business Review published a case study of one of the Tennessee agencies (Youth Villages) that benefited from the performance incentives (Grossman, Foster, & Ross, 2008). See the

Government Performance Lab at Harvard University for some of the most current materials (https://govlab.hks.harvard.edu/).

The sections that follow provide an overview of some of the key workforce challenges that public and private CW agencies face every day, including those summarized in Box 9.2.

Box 9.2   Key Workforce Challenges in Child Welfare

- Caseloads and workloads frequently spike or are too high.
- Unreasonable requirements for flexibility in work hours to cover evenings and weekend shifts.
- Insufficient job-related education and training.
- Lack of ongoing staff supervision, coaching, and training for key aspects of practice.
- Lack of pay differential for key positions that require experienced and skilled staff.
- Low rates of staff retention/high staff turnover that impact the workloads of remaining staff.
- Low salaries and insufficient benefits.

- Perceived or actual lack of supportive organizational climate and culture.
- Secondary trauma for staff.
- Staff recruitment that doesn't reflect the key competences and values required for effective practice.
- Onerous documentation of casework actions in the agency management information system that leaves too little time for direct work with children and families.
- Workplace safety issues, including working in the homes of families without sufficient staff back-up and a process for accessing support.

Workforce Minimum Qualifications and Characteristics

Excellent service quality and outcomes can only be achieved with a fundamental organizational commitment to hiring staff with the necessary prerequisite values, knowledge, and skills; and providing staff with appropriate and adequate resources to accomplish their jobs. And yet the public CW agency workforce in many states too often comprises staff in the very early stages of their careers and those who have no preparation for CW work prior to the pre-service training that the agency may offer. More than 60 percent are without social work degrees (Dolan et al., 2011) which would have brought them a broad under-standing of the place of CW work and systems of care in the human services landscape and basic skills for working with families and children.

Fortunately, much progress has been made in specifying the worker characteristics of successful CW staff, including specifying the competences necessary for workers (and super-visors) to possess – both at the time when they are initially hired and later as full-fledged or "journeyman" staff members (see, e.g., http://ncwwi.org/index.php/child-welfare-competen cy-model; Collins-Camargo & Royse, 2010; Social Work Policy Institute, 2011).

Lack of these data has contributed in some state agencies to the weakening of educa-tional standards for CW positions. In fact, given changes in state-hiring standards for CW that weaken hiring requirements ("reclassification" or "declassification"), poor working conditions, and high staff turnover, the number of CW staff with undergraduate and grad-uate degrees in social work remains low (Institute for the Advancement of Social Work Research, 2005; Social Work Policy Institute, 2010a, 2010b). Furthermore, the hiring reg-isters in many states lack BSW or MSW applicants, especially for rural areas. Thus, CW services are being provided by personnel with a wide variety of educational backgrounds; some that are job related such as social work, psychology, or marriage and family coun-seling, and many that are not.

This trend of underutilization of social work-trained staff is ironic in light of a small but growing number of studies that document the job relevance or superior job performance of workers with social work degrees or specialized CW training as part of a social work degree (Institute for the Advancement of Social Work Research, 2005). However, there still remains a need for more research that assesses the differential effectiveness of BSWs, MSWs, and other types of educated personnel in CW. And the continuing lack of profes-sionally trained CW staff is to be expected, given high caseloads, de-emphasis in some states on worker provision of treatment-oriented services, fiscal pressures to keep salaries low, reduction in agency programs for tuition reimbursement and administrative leave, friction between unions and professional organizations, fewer social workers in policy and management positions, and other factors (e.g., IASWR, 2005; U.S. GAO, 2003).

The second National Survey of Child and Adolescent Well-being (NSCAW II) is a longitudinal study intended to answer a range of fundamental questions about the func-tioning, service needs, and service use of children who come into contact with the CW system. But this landmark study also gathered data about the CW workforce in 2008/2009.

The majority of the 5,052 investigative caseworkers interviewed were female (79.3%). Approximately 70 percent (72.1%) of caseworkers were 25 to 44 years old, with fewer caseworkers younger than 25 years old (7.8%), 45 to 54 years old (14.3%), or 54 years old or older (5.8%). Over half were White (57.5%), 23.7 percent were Black, 14.9 percent were Hispanic, and 4.0 percent described their race/ethnicity as "Other." Caseworkers representing children in the NSCAW II cohort were experienced in their positions, with an average of 5 years of tenure at their assigned agency (median = 3.0) and 7.1 years of tenure in the CW system (median = 5.0). The majority of caseworkers reported attaining a Bachelor's degree (52.3%) or Bachelor of Social Work degree (21.9%), while nearly 25 percent had attained a Master's-level degree. Few caseworkers reported having less than a Bachelor's degree (0.5%) or a Doctorate (0.4%) (Dolan et al., 2011, p. 7). Staff profiles from California and Washington are presented below to give a general sense of the workforce in a particular state.

California. A total of 363 people working in public CW were anonymously surveyed either online or during professional development training classes that took place in Northern California during 2013/2014. While not a random sample of the workforce, this study had a large sample size and adds important information to the field. Most (80%) of the respondents were female, and 64 percent identified as White. Close to 60 percent held a Master's degree or higher (44 percent were MSWs and 14 percent held a Master's degree in another field), 34 percent had a Bachelor's degree and 7 percent had no college degree. Nearly 32 percent of the staff had experienced four or more adverse childhood experiences (ACES), signifying significant trauma in their own childhoods. Indicative of the difficult nature of CW work, many staff in this same study reported poor health outcomes and exhibited the impacts of significant stressors. On average, workers reported carrying over 30 cases. A total of 45 percent of staff identified as having post-traumatic stress disorder (PTSD) due to experiencing secondary traumatic stress. Three-quarters of the staff reported having fair or poor health, and 47 percent reported not getting enough sleep because of the emotional stress they felt at work (Hatton Bowers, Brooks, & Borucki, 2014, pp. 1, 4).

Georgia. Without such a strong network among the university social work programs and the state CW agency, in 2003 fewer than 20 percent of CW caseworkers in Georgia had social work degrees (Ellett, Ellett, & Rugutt, 2003).

Washington State. A 2008 survey of the workforce found that 76 percent were female and 73 percent identified as White. About half of the workforce had earned a Bachelor's degree, 14 percent held a Master of Social Work (MSW) degree, and 32 percent had earned a Master's degree in another field. Washington is similar to many other states in that neither a social work degree nor a Master's degree is required for entry into the field.

Maintaining Reasonable Caseload Sizes and Workloads Helps Ensure Worker Capacity

Some jurisdictions around the country struggle to identify and maintain casework levels that feel manageable to their CW staff. This can become a particularly critical issue in the aftermath of a high-profile tragedy such as that experienced by the Administration for Children's Services (ACS) in New York City in late 2016, when morale was low, attrition increased, and front-line CW positions appeared less appealing to job candidates. During these challenging times, there can be a lot of pressure to find fault with individual staff, add layers of accountability that further restrict staff judgment, and add new initiatives. All these combined can overwhelm the staff, and put pressure on the system. ACS resisted most of these traps and the managers there have since worked to make a series of core improvements, including beginning a new prevention unit in 2017.

In general, the CW field is finding that *workload* – meaning the sum of all job-related duties, including direct contact with children and families, case documentation, court appearances, time required for supervisory and clinical consultations, etc. – provides a more useful metric than *caseload* for assessing the human impact of staffing levels. This is not easy to measure. However, some jurisdictions are approaching this in innovative and promising ways. For example, Nebraska has been developing and testing a weighted case assignment tool to assign cases based on various case characteristics that are weighted for factors such as travel, family size, and risk level. Historically, they used a caseload approach to distribute work among front-line CW staff. This common approach involved a simple count of the number of children and families assigned, with each child or family given the same weight. Under the premise that all children and families do not require equal work, and that there are circumstances whereby a caseworker is required to devote more time to a child/family, the workload approach to work distribution assigns points for certain case conditions. Early results indicate that modest progress in lowering caseloads is being made both in Nebraska (personal communication, Doug Beran, July 25, 2017), and in medium-sized counties like Waupaca in Wisconsin (Meyer et al., 2017).

Staff Retention Rates

Many state and county CW agencies strive to achieve their mission by supporting positive worker morale and maximizing worker retention rates. *Design teams* (representative groups of department of human services CW employees working together to solve specific organizational issues affecting staff retention in a solution-focused manner) are being used (Strolin-Goltzman et al., 2009; Strolin-Goltzman, 2010).

Others struggle, as summarized in Figure 9.5, which reports the results of a recent analysis by Partners for Our Children at the University of Washington. They examined retention in Washington State and found that the one-year attrition rate among newly hired Social Service Specialist 2 and 3 field positions fluctuated between 20 and 41 percent from fiscal years 2007 through 2014, with a rate of 32 percent in 2014, the most recent year in which data were available (Partners for Our Children, 2016).

The turnover rates among CW workers in some other states is also very high, estimated at between 25 and 40 percent annually nationwide, with the average tenure being less than two years (Stewart, 2016; The Center for Advanced Studies in Child Welfare and the Minnesota Association of County Human Services Administrators, 2016; U.S. GAO, 2003). And yet some states and counties are making focused efforts and investments in their workforce and achieving significantly better outcomes; New Jersey reported an attrition rate of just 7 percent in 2015 and a rural Wisconsin County, Waupaca, has been experiencing very high rates of staff retention (Meyer et al., 2017).

This section and Figure 9.6 present the reasons why we should be very concerned about staff retention. First, staff turnover costs money. Turnover results in delays in finding children permanent homes (Figure 9.7), which result in increased foster care caseloads and more funds being spent overall, as foster care is more expensive than adoption or other permanency options. The U.S. Department of Labor estimates that the cost of worker turnover is approximately one-third of a worker's annual salary. It takes more than

12 Month Attrition Among Newly Hired
Social Service Specialists

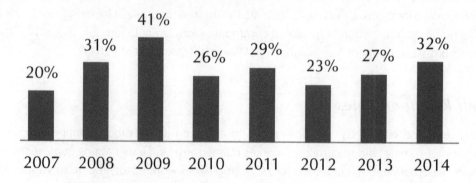

Figure 9.5 Newly Hired Line Staff Turnover in Washington State Over a Seven-Year Period
Source: Partners for Our Children (2016, p. 1). Reprinted with permission.

Figure 9.6 Why We Should Care About Worker Retention Rates

Source: National Child Welfare Workforce Institute (2011). References at https://ncwwi. org/_les/Why_the_Workforce_Matters_References.pdf.

six months to advertise for, recruit, and train new employees to assume a full caseload (CDF, 2007, p. 10). Thus it should come as no surprise that it costs anywhere from $45,000 to $79,000 to replace a staff person – when recruitment, screening, orientation, training, and extra supervision costs are fully monetized.

Researchers found that the average cost of replacing a CW worker was $27,000 in 2003 when including separation, replacement, local, and state training costs (Dorch, McCarthy, & Denofrio, 2008). The average cost of replacing an employee who received tuition subsidy for a MSW degree was $50,000. In another state, attrition of CW professionals translates to an annual cost of more than $6.2 million in separation, recruitment, staff training, lost productivity, certification, and supervision (minus staff salary savings: Florida Senate, 2014). CW leaders in Georgia, New Jersey, and Waupaca, Wisconsin are inspiring us to take a creative look at how to address the workforce issues of staff morale and worker retention in CW (Meyer et al., 2017). The stakes are very high for the reasons described in the following section.

From the above discussion it becomes clear that staff turnover hurts children and families. Yet many states report difficulty hiring and retaining qualified staff. The average tenure of CW workers is less than two years. Why does this occur? Studies indicate that dissatisfaction with supervision is one of the primary reasons for worker turnover (Ellett et al., 2007; Kruzich et al., 2014). High caseloads get in the way of effective work with children and families. High caseloads result in workers not having enough time to make adequate face-to-face contact with children and families, prepare appropriate case plans and reports, receive adequate supervision, and make thoughtful decisions that affect children's lives. High caseloads contribute to poor relationships between workers and families, and to the re-entry of children into foster care. Continued staff unhappiness can occur with increased caseloads, burnout, and mental health stress (See AFCSME report at www.afscme.org/pol-leg/dj01.htm).

Caseworker turnover is associated with children's multiple placements in foster care, longer lengths of stay for children in foster care, and lower rates of finding permanent homes for children. Worker turnover results in families' receipt of fewer services and is a major factor in failed efforts to reunify children with their families. For example, a powerful study in Milwaukee demonstrated how, with every change in staff person, a child's likelihood of achieving permanency was drastically reduced. For 659 children who entered care from January 1, 2003 through September, 2004 in Milwaukee, and exited to permanency within the same time period, the numbers of worker changes were strongly correlated with a lower chance of achieving permanency. See Figure 9.8 for how the child's chances of achieving legal permanency plummets from 74.5 percent with one worker to 17.5 percent for children who had two case managers, and 5.2 percent for children who had three workers (Flower, McDonald, & Sumski, 2005). While the research design used has limitations, it is one of the few studies available in this area.

As part of the study, the impact of staff turnover was aptly illustrated by a situation where a staff member was a child's *tenth* worker within a five-year period. When that

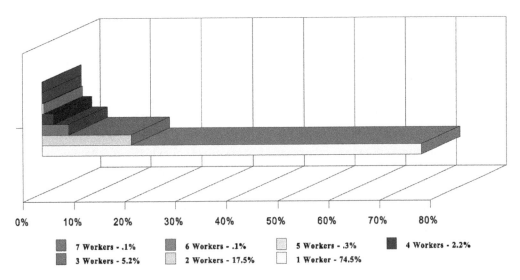

0%   10%   20%   30%   40%   50%   60%   70%   80%

■ 7 Workers - .1%	■ 6 Workers - .1%	□ 5 Workers - .3%	■ 4 Workers - 2.2%
■ 3 Workers - 5.2%	□ 2 Workers - 17.5%	□ 1 Worker - 74.5%	

Figure 9.7 How Worker Turnover is Associated with Reduced Levels of Achieving Permanency

Note: Data reported represent 679 children who entered care in calendar year 2003 through September, 2004 and exited within the same time period. Data reported to review staff by the Bureau of Milwaukee Child Welfare.

Source: Flower, McDonald, & Sumski (2005, p. 4).

most recent staff transfer happened, the child did not want to know the worker's name and instead referred to the worker as *Number Ten*: "Good afternoon No. 10. What do want from me today No. 10?" Changes in case managers force youth and parents to start over in building trust and a working relationship. This often results in a lack of trust and delays in moving ahead with the service plan and other activities necessary to achieve permanency. In addition, worker changes may result in delays in court hearings, which produce docket delays as cases are rescheduled. It becomes a travesty to not act more quickly.

Workplace Safety

Too many front-line caseworkers have been victims of violence or received threats of violence. For example, over 70 percent of the affiliates of American Federation of State, County and Municipal Employees (AFSCME) reported that front-line workers in their agencies have been victims of violence or threats of violence in the line of duty. Less than 15 percent reported that violence was not a problem (AFSCME, 2016). One state found that 90 percent of its child protective services employees had experienced verbal threats; 30 percent experienced physical attacks; and 13 percent were threatened with weapons

(U.S. GAO, 2003). When the group being surveyed had more voluntary agency staff participating, the number dropped substantially. Nineteen percent of NASW CW section members report having been victims of violence, although 63 percent say they have been threatened at some point in their CW practice.

One interesting note in this study was how many social workers cited violent acts by children. *However, 94 percent of section members say they generally feel safe making home visits. The overwhelming majority (98 percent) of these members make home visits alone.* Ninety-two percent say they are "somewhat" or "very comfortable" making home visits alone (NASW, 2004). In response to concerns about social worker safety, the National Association of Social Workers (2013) developed workplace safety guidelines, and more recently, bipartisan legislation was proposed: the Social Worker Safety Act of 2017 (H.R. 1484) introduced in March, 2017 by Representatives Kyrsten Sinema and Elise Stefanik.

Workplace Psychological Safety and Other Supports Can Make a Difference

Kruzich and her colleagues, based on extensive reviews of literature in other fields and some new research, are finding that workplace psychological safety is very important for maintaining high levels of staff retention (Kruzich, Mienko, & Courtney, 2014). Other factors can ease the burdens of the CW workforce. One factor relates to implementation of evidence-based practices – and the expectation that workers need to have a certain level of competency and critical thinking to implement evidence-based interventions – especially clinical judgment. Thus we believe that the U.S. Children's Bureau should be supporting the use of Title IV-E training funds for clinical training.

In addition, strong collaborative processes with other service agencies help CW, Juvenile Probation, and Behavioral Health avoid fighting among themselves instead of focusing on how best to serve the family. As we saw in Kansas, privatization of human services, if handled poorly, can result in huge shifts in staff allocations without sufficient planning or adjustment time (Myslewicz, 2010). Thus Texas, Washington, and other states are planning carefully and implementing in stages.

A meta-analysis of 22 studies by Kim and Kao (2014) identified 36 variables that most impacted CW caseworkers' intention to leave and those factors are summarized in Figure 9.8. Factors related to *perceptions of the organizational climate* explained significantly more variance in types of organizational withdrawal than personal or job characteristics. *Employees' reports of "stress"* (captured by emotional exhaustion, role overload, and role conflict) contributed more to job withdrawal, work withdrawal,

HIGH EFFECT
Stress
Emotional exhaustion
Organizational commitment
Job satisfaction

MEDIUM EFFECT
Well-being
Safety concerns
Depersonalization
Role conflict
Inclusion
Role ambiguity
Organizational support
Perceptions of fairness
Organizational culture
Police
Supervisor support
Professional commitment
Organizational climate
Human caring

MODERATE EFFECT
Age
Tenure
Education level
Job demand
Coping
Autonomy
Financial reward
Co-worker support
Professionalism
Salary
Career development
Work self-efficacy

LOW EFFECT
Racial group
Gender
Social Work degree
Other degrees
Caseload Size
Spouse/other support

Figure 9.8 Factors that Predict CW Caseworkers Intention to Leave Their Job

Source: Diagram from National Child Welfare Workforce Institute. Retrieved from https://ncwwi.org/files/Retention/Kim__Kao_2015.pdf. Findings are drawn from Kim & Kao (2014).

job search behavior, and exit from the organization than any other factor (Hopkins et al., 2010, p. 1380).

Salaries predict retention (Dickinson & Perry, 2002), and if employees believe that pay, security and fringe benefits are adequate, staff are more likely to remain in their position (Kim & Kao, 2014). In the U.K., *high workloads* are a key factor in the decision to leave teaching (House of Commons, 2004) and nursing (Royal College of Nursing, 2001). In social work, *excessive policy changes and paperwork* can be sources of job dissatisfaction (Dressel, 1982). Landsman (2001), among others, found *job stress* closely related to the retention of CW workers (Webb & Carpenter, 2011, p. 5). In summary, it appears that multiple factors affect worker job satisfaction and retention, as illustrated in Figure 9.8.

Summary

The National Child Welfare Workforce Institute, the researchers we have cited in this chapter, and leaders in Missouri, New Jersey, and Wisconsin have spoken up about what they are learning to improve staff retention in their communities. The above sections have presented what we know can make a difference in this area, including aspects of organizational excellence from the business, organizational psychology, and social work literature.

Additional Workforce Supports

What Else Can be Done to Support the Child Welfare Workforce?

A 20 percent or more annual staff turnover will cripple nearly any industry – except possibly very simple jobs where training may take only a day. It is a form of "system insanity" that needs to be urgently addressed. We have a lot to learn but have some insights now that can be considered by any CW system. A combination of personal factors that current and prospective staff bring to their job results in improved retention: professional commitment, previous experience, skills, and maturity to address the complex needs of the children and families served by the system, coupled with an organizational environment that values and supports these staff.

As mentioned earlier, some, but not all, CW agencies have been plagued by high rates of worker turnover, which undermines these agencies at a time when they are implementing increasingly more sophisticated practice models and intervention methods. Very little research has been conducted about the effectiveness of certain strategies – which leaves the field with ideas but relatively little data about what actually makes a difference. Some of the following strategies might be considered unconventional but are worth considering because of how they may break through some persistent and serious barriers.

Caseworker teaming. Caseworker teaming is a CW staffing model and organizational approach that supports the sharing of casework functions on certain cases among more than one caseworker and the use of group supervision to make case decisions as well as assess and address child and family needs. It is designed to (1) reduce caseworker isolation and workload; (2) strengthen workforce retention; and (3) improve casework decision making and service delivery to children, youth, and families. As Judge James Payne (2014, p. 6) explains:

> The issue of teaming or dual caseload assignments has been piloted in a number of jurisdictions over the last few years. The most prominent of these may be the pilot begun under Harry Spence, former Commissioner of the Massachusetts Department of Children and Families, [.] but also implemented in New York State [New York State Child Welfare Training Institute, 2010] and other jurisdictions. The concept has a number of philosophical and theoretical underpinnings, but the bottom line is that having a second caseworker on a case provides the opportunity for alternative evaluation and assessment of the needs of the child and family. In

addition, the issue of safety for an individual case manager is an important element, often acknowledged but not directly addressed in the organizational structure [Sioco, 2010]. Compare child welfare caseworkers with law enforcement agencies, fire departments, and emergency medical technicians – none of which appear alone on scene for their professional services. They are always with a co-worker, teaming to provide the best service possible and to ensure the safety of their colleagues. Caseworkers visit those same locations at the same evening or weekend hours and under the same emotional conditions, but do so alone. In addition, the concept of dual caseload assignment or teaming provides a better opportunity to address the issue of case transfer (particularly with millenials who tend to be team-oriented and work well in group styles). With dual caseload assignment or teaming, should one of the caseworkers assigned to a particular case leave the agency, or at least at some point not have a caseload because of promotion or FMLA, the remaining assigned caseworker is already familiar with the case and can continue the trust relationship as well as the direction and focus of the case without having to review and reevaluate the circumstances and facts of the case. All of this provides a better opportunity to appropriately serve children and families and avoid the issues associated with case transfer.

A number of states and progams send out a team of two staff for key service appointments. For example, the nationally recognized Homebuilders family preservation services program teams up workers whenever necessary. Worker teaming can not only improve assessment and decision making but also potentially reduce staff stress and boost staff retention rates.

Multidisciplinary teaming. As Los Angeles, Georgia, and other systems are considering, we must recognize that many aspects of CW require multidisciplinary teaming to be effective. CW leaders (and their stakeholders) should appreciate and highlight that the latest practice science in safety and risk management in CPS, case planning and functional assessment, and treatment are all more effective with strategic use of specialists such as public health nurses and home visitors, pediatric consultants, substance abuse experts, behavioral health clinicians, and family conflict and domestic violence specialists. Fully utilizing a *team* of specialists (if competent) should result in more effective and efficient assessment, case planning, and services provision. Decision-making and risk management science also support the use of teams, as recently emphasized by the Federal Commission on Child Fatalities that recommended multidisciplinary teaming for reports of suspected abuse in children ages 3 and under (Commission to Eliminate Child Abuse and Neglect Fatalities, 2016).

In addition, this approach has the potential for building public will, as well as boosting worker morale and retention, in one of the most high-pressure, high-stakes job settings imaginable. Also consider how a public will-building communications campaign and a staff recruitment campaign might each be more successful if the pictures and staff structure featured teams – and not the solo practice aspects of CW services delivery.

Reform human resources practices, and job/salary classifications systems because they hold agencies back. What effective industry takes six to nine months to screen and hire to fill a position? In some systems the minimum qualifications for some CW positions are set so low that many applicants are truly not qualified to do the work and will not be able to withstand the pressures and skill demands of the job. Why do we continue to interview a stream of non-qualified candidates? Why do we allow the job replacement process to drag on for months and months? If we would not tolerate this in business, why should this be allowed to continue in many government agencies? *Without reforms, we are pairing twenty-first-century CW practice models with nineteenth-century Human Resource systems to staff them.*

Major reform of these systems may not be easy, and it may take some political pressure, but it is essential for addressing the larger workforce issues. Low-cost, high-impact, and feasible strategies need to build from the data about who is leaving quickly and why. Agencies can do *Business Process Mapping* to specify what the steps are to get hired and the time needed for each step to detect where there are delays or problems. Business process mapping involves the charting out of specific processes for a program or aspect of work to identify problems (see Dias & Saraiva, 2004; Graham, 2004; Lucero et al., 2017). We also need to pay attention to the degree to which an agency might have an aging workforce (e.g., a CW leader recently discussed how 500 workers left a large state CW agency within a two-month period).

Worker pay must be commensurate to the KSAs. The knowledge, skills and abilities (KSAs) required by CW practice are considerable. We referenced a small section of the worker toolbox of KSAs above – documentation about that can and should be used to reclassify the positions in CW so that the pay matches the actual job.

Are we recruiting the wrong people who will not stay? Many CW agencies hire young college graduates and the turnover rates among these young people are high. Is it time to consider also recruiting older professionals with job-related educational degrees, more mature "first career retirees," and transfers from other fields such as education, the military, law enforcement, and business? To do that, the HR departments will need to consider new outlets, as some of these potential employees will be reached through non-traditional advertising outlets.

Are we screening job applicants effectively? We need to show job applicants the realities of the job so that they can select themselves in or out (e.g., Homebuilders). The

National Child Welfare Workforce Institute (NCWWI) has a one-page summary and actual videos of realistic job previews, as well as competency-based selection processes that screen applicants for attitudes and characteristics that are not amenable to training.

Is it time to consider job-sharing, teleworking for some tasks, and alternative schedules in CW to boost retention rates? Some of the most effective staff in CW may be "first career retirees" or transfers from other fields. But a small but substantial proportion of these competent people will want to work *part-time*. The added administrative costs of job-sharing should be dwarfed by the savings from increasing worker retention rates. Is this not worth testing?

Reward the high-performing workers who want to remain in direct practice. Review and revise salary policy in terms of who is paid what, and allocate funds for rewarding experienced staff so that they do not feel pressured to apply for a promotion just to get a raise. These experienced staff can coach and mentor new staff, or help with training, to add to their leadership skills and feelings of value/meaning of giving back, as well as a way to justify higher pay (personal communication, Sara Munson, November 7, 2017).

Career ladders and succession planning through leadership development. This is becoming a key area as the baby boomers begin to retire from CW organizations. We must mentor, train, and develop younger staff for specialist and leadership positions (Austin & Hopkins, 2004), but there are relatively few programs available to do so other than some of the university-based continuing education management certificate or executive MBA programs,.

Additional Strategies to Boost Staff Retention Rates

The NASW CW specialty staff survey had three key findings related to worker motivation and retention: (1) social workers in CW, at least those who are also members of NASW, are more satisfied with their jobs than the general population of CW workers; (2) issues confronting children and families were the most challenging aspect of the job, *not* the workplace issues confronting the social workers; and (3) the single most satisfying aspect of the work of social workers in CW is "successes with children and families."

Competitive wages, valuable benefits, and job security are very important in attracting staff with MSWs and other job-relevant degrees to public CW. To retain them, however, states and counties need to take additional actions such as the following:

1. Review the job expectations of workers, and whether the caseloads and paperwork expectations indeed permit these workers to achieve the core objectives of the CW system.

2.   Develop institutionalized mechanisms of support for staff members, recognizing that CW work, by its very nature, is intense and emotionally draining. Establishing regular case conferences and promoting close collaboration between workers within the same program unit or across units would provide opportunities for sharing experiences and responsibilities. Fostering development of informal support networks among staff would also do much to enhance worker morale and prevent burnout. This includes promoting, to the extent possible, a reasonable approach to life–work balance.

3.   Recognize the increased likelihood of worker burnout after about two years on the job and offer greater flexibility in movement from one program area to another.

4.   Set up institutionalized mechanisms for regular two-way communication between workers and administration (beyond supervisors) for each group to hear at first-hand about the realities of the other and to develop a collaborative, rather than adversarial, work environment (Curry, McCarragher, & Dellmann-Jenkins, 2005; Smith, 2005).

5.   Recognize the increased likelihood of worker burnout due to supervisory, organizational, and peer support contexts and create workplace, staffing, and support structures to decrease burnout (e.g., Kruzich et al., 2014).

6.   Agency leaders and supervisors, to the extent that they are identified as aligned with the organization's mission and strategies, contribute to employee perceptions of positive organizational support, and ultimately to job retention (Eisenberger et al., 2002).

Policy and Program Design Challenges

The challenges associated with recruiting, selecting, and retaining qualified CW staff are formidable but must be addressed, because effective CW services require personnel capable of providing skilled interventions. Low worker turnover is essential for providing a consistent level of service. Furthermore, the importance of adequate salaries (which require not only political advocacy, but also thorough documentation of the worker competences necessary for effective job performance) has been highlighted by studies as an important factor not only for minimizing worker turnover, but also for increasing job satisfaction (Kim & Kao, 2014).

This chapter has highlighted some of the organizational requisites for CW services. Many challenges remain to be addressed, such as adequate program funding, clear mission statements, strong leadership, supportive work environments, powerful intervention technologies, reasonable caseload sizes, and supervision strategies that promote "best practice." If CW agencies are to effectively implement the service strategies described in the previous chapters, key organizational components must be in place. Family-centered approaches involve certain strategies for supporting parents and children. But in order to empower families, practitioners must first be empowered by the organizations within which they work.

In closing, we need more real-time information from CW human resources and quality assurance units about the reasons why staff are leaving CW agencies. And we need rigorous evaluations of the staff selection, training, coaching, recognition, and other strategies that are being implemented – what works best for what kinds of CW agencies?

Discussion Questions

A number of key questions remain to be addressed more definitively:

1. What factors are most important to sustain a strong CW workforce?
2. What are the most effective strategies for assigning and organizing various CW caseloads?
3. How many workers, *of what kinds*, are needed to provide effective CW services?
4. How do variations in staff minimum qualifications for CW positions relate to positive child and family outcomes (e.g., how do we best determine the value of social work, psychology, and other work-related degrees)?
5. What new training partnerships need to be fostered between universities and CW agencies; and how can these be paid for? (adapted from Zlotnik et al., 2005; Zlotnik, 2009).

Note

1   Special thanks to the following experts who shared ideas and resources: Jean Kruzich, Nancy McDaniel, Sara T. Munson, Fred Simmens, Sue Steib, and Joan Zlotnik.

For Further Information

American Public Human Services Association. (2012). *Building workforce capacity through a child welfare practice model: Lessons from the field.* Washington, DC: Author. Retrieved from www.aphsa.org/content/dam/aphsa/pdfs/OE/2012-10-Build-Workforce-Capacity-Child Welfare-Practice-Model-Lessons.pdf. Provides real-world state examples of innovative uses of practice models and other strategies.

Austin, M.J., & Hopkins, K.M. (Eds) (2004). *Supervision as collaboration in the human services: Building a learning culture.* Thousand Oaks, CA: Sage. A wide-ranging collection of chapters addressing the major functions of supervision.

Berrick, J.D. (2018). *The impossible imperative: Navigating the competing principles of child protection.* New York: Oxford University Press. Using case stories from MSW-level child welfare workers, this book illustrates the challenges of implementing current child welfare policy.

Harvard University Government Performance Lab for a variety of current contracting and other performance-enhancing strategies for human services organizations (https://govlab.hks. harvard.edu/).

Kruzich, J.M., Mienko, J.A., & Courtney, M.E. (2014). Individual and work group influences on turnover intention among public child welfare workers: The effects of work group psychological safety. *Children and Youth Services Review, 42,* 20–27.

Potter, C.R., & Brittain, C.R. (Eds) (2009). *Child welfare supervision: A practical guide for supervisors, managers and administrators.* Oxford: Oxford University Press. A book filled with practical articles about child welfare supervision.

The National Workforce Webinar Series is designed to showcase feasible strategies for strengthening the quality and capacity of the child welfare workforce. All of the recordings and handouts are located here at www.ncwwi.org/events/archive.html.

Bibliography

American Federation of State, County and Municipal Employees (AFSCME). (2016). *Violence in the workplace.* Washington, DC: Author (website article). Retrieved from www.afscme. org/news/publications/workplace-health-and-safety/double-jeopardy-caseworkers-at-risk-helping-at-risk-kids/violence-in-the-workplace.

American Public Human Services Association. (2010). *Workforce guidance.* Part of the Positioning Public Child Welfare Guidance series. Washington, DC: Author. Retrieved from http:// ncwwi.org/files/Job_Analysis__Position_Requirements/PPCW_Workforce_Guidance.pdf.

American Public Human Services Association. (2012). *Building workforce capacity through a child welfare practice model: Lessons from the field.* Washington, DC: Author. Retrieved from www. aphsa.org/content/dam/aphsa/pdfs/OE/2012-10-Build-Workforce-Capacity-ChildWelfare-Practice-Model-Lessons.pdf.

Austin, M.J., & Hopkins, K.M. (Eds) (2004). *Supervision as collaboration in the human services: Building a learning culture.* Thousand Oaks, CA: Sage. A wide-ranging collection of chapters addressing the major functions of supervision.

Barbee, A.P., Antle, B.F., Sullivan, D., Dryden, A.A., & Henry, K. (2012). Twenty-five years of the Children's Bureau Investment in Social Work Education. *Journal of Public Child Welfare, 6,* 376–389.

Barth, R.P. (2008). The move to evidence-based practice: How well does it fit child welfare services? *Journal of Public Child Welfare, 2*, 145–172.

Blase, K.A., Fixsen, D.L., Sims, B.J., & Ward, C.S. (2015). *Implementation science – Changing hearts, minds, behavior, and systems to improve educational outcomes*. Paper presented at the Wing Institute's Ninth Annual Summit on Evidence-based Education, Berkeley, CA.

Children's Defense Fund. (2009). *Summary of CW retention research for the CDF 2009 Webinar presentation on the R&R Grants*. Retrieved from www.nrcpfc.org/teleconferences/9-30-09/Retention%20Research.doc.

Children's Defense Fund. (2011). *Summary of literature on child welfare demographic trends*. Retrieved from www.ncwwi.org/docs/Workforce_Demographic_Trends_May2011.pdf.

Children's Defense Fund & Children's Rights, Inc. (2006a). *Components of an effective child welfare workforce to improve outcomes for children and families: What does the research tell us?* Cornerstones For Kids. Retrieved from www.childrensrights.org/wp-content/uploads/2008/06/components_of_effective_child_welfare_workforce_august_2006.pdf.

Children's Defense Fund & Children's Rights, Inc. (2006b). *Supporting and improving the child welfare workforce: A review of program improvement plans (PIPs) and recommendation for strengthening the Child and Family Services Reviews (CFSRs)*. Cornerstones For Kids. Retrieved from www.childrensrights.org/wp-content/uploads/2008/06/supporting_and_improving_child_welfare_workforce_2006.pdf.

Children's Defense Fund & Children's Rights, Inc. (2007). *Promoting child welfare workforce improvements through federal policy changes*. The Human Service Workforce Initiative. Cornerstones For Kids. Retrieved from www.childrensrights.org/wp-content/uploads/2008/06/promoting_child_welfare_workforce_improvements_2007.pdf.

Children's Defense Fund Compelling Facts. Retrieved from www.childrensdefense.org/child-research-data-publications/data/promoting-child-welfare-workforce-improvements.pdf, p.5.

Children's Defense Fund Components & Framework. Retrieved from www.childrensdefense.org/child-research-data-publications/data/components-of-an-effective-child-welfare-workforce.pdf.

Christie, C.A., Lemire, S., & Inkelas, M. (2017). Understanding the similarities and distinctions between improvement science and evaluation. In C.A. Christie, M. Inkelas, & S. Lemire (Eds), Improvement science in evaluation: Methods and uses. *New Directions for Evaluation, 153*, 11–21.

Clara, F., Garcia, K., & Metz, A. (2017). *Implementing evidence-based child welfare: The New York City experience*. Seattle, WA: Casey Family Programs. Retrieved from www.casey.org/media/evidence-based-child-welfare-nyc.pdf.

Cohen-Callow, A., Hopkins, K., & Kim, H. (2009). Retaining workers approaching retirement: Why child welfare needs to pay attention to the aging workforce. *Child Welfare, 5*, 209 228.

Collins-Camargo, C., & Royse, D. (2010). A study of the relationships among effective supervision, organizational culture promoting evidence-based practice, and worker self-efficacy in public child welfare. *Journal of Public Child Welfare, 4*, 1–24. doi:10.1080/15548730903563053.

Commission to Eliminate Child Abuse and Neglect Fatalities. (2016). *Within our reach: A national strategy to eliminate child abuse and neglect fatalities*. Washington, DC: Government Printing Office. Retrieved from www.acf.hhs.gov/programs/cb/resource/cecanf-final-report.

Curry, D., McCarragher, T., & Dellmann-Jenkins, M. (2005). Training, transfer and turnover: Exploring the relationship among transfer of learning factors and staff retention in child welfare. *Children and Youth Services Review, 27*(8), 931–948.

Daro, D., Budde, S., Baker, S., Nesmith, A., & Harden, A. (2005). *Creating community responsibility for child protection: Findings and implications from the evaluation of the community partnerships for protecting children initiative*. Chicago, IL: University of Chicago, Chapin Hall Center for Children.

DePanfilis, D., & Zlotnik, J. (2008). Retention of front-line staff in child welfare: A systematic review of research. *Children and Youth Services Review, 30*(9), 995–1008.

Department for Children, School and Families (DCSF). (2009). *Building a safe, confident future: The final report of the Social Work Taskforce*, London: DCSF.

Dias, S., & Saraiva, P.M. (2004). Use basic quality tools to manage your processes. *Quality Progress, 37*(8), 47–53. Retrieved from http://sharpthinkers.info/articles/Basic_Tools.pdf.

Dickinson, N.S., & Perry, R.E. (2002). Factors influencing the retention of specially educated public child welfare workers. *Evaluation Research in Child Welfare, 15*(3/4), 89–103.

Dolan, M., Smith, K., Casanueva, C., & Ringeisen, H. (2011). *NSCAW II Baseline Report: Caseworker characteristics, child welfare services, and experiences of children placed in out-of-home care*. OPRE Report #2011–27e. Washington, DC: Office of Planning, Research and Evaluation, Administration for Children and Families, U.S. Department of Health and Human Services. Retrieved from www.acf.hhs.gov/sites/default/files/opre/nscaw2_cw.pdf.

Dorch, E., McCarthy, M., & Denofrio, D. (2008). Calculating child welfare separation and replacement costs. *Social Work in Public Health, 23*(6), 29–54.

Dressel, P.L. (1982). Policy sources of worker dissatisfactions: The case of human services in aging. *Social Service Review, 56*(3), 406–423.

Eisenberger, R., Stinglhamber, F., Vandenberghe, C., Sucharski, I.L., & Rhoades, L. (2002). Perceived supervisor support: Contributions to perceived organizational support and employee retention. *Journal of Applied Psychology, 87*(3), 565–573.

Ellett, A.J. (2009). Intentions to remain employed in child welfare: The role of human caring, self-efficacy beliefs, and professional organizational culture, *Children and Youth Services Review, 31*(1), 78–88.

Ellett, A.J., Ellett, C.D., & Rugutt, J.K. (2003). *A study of personal and organizational factors contributing to employee retention and turnover in child welfare in Georgia*. Retrieved from www.uh.edu/socialwork/_docs/cwep/national-iv-e/ExecSummary.pdf.

Ellett, A.J., Ellis, J.I., Westbrook, T.M., & Dews, D. (2007). A qualitative study of 369 child welfare professionals' perspectives about factors contributing to employee retention and turnover. *Children and Youth Services Review, 29*, 264–281. doi:10.1016/j.childyouth.2006.07.005.

Fixsen, D.L., Naoom, S.F., Blase, K.A., Friedman, R.M., & Wallace, F. (2005). *Implementation research: A synthesis of the literature.* Tampa, FL: University of South Florida, Louis de la Parte Florida Mental Health Institute, The National Implementation Research Network (FMHI Publication #231).

Florida Senate. (2014). *Bill analysis and fiscal impact statement* (Cs/SB 1666). Retrieved from www.flsenate.gov/Session/Bill/2014/1666/Analyses/2014s1666.ap.PDF.

Flower, C., McDonald, J., & Sumski, M. (2005). *Review of turnover in Milwaukee County private agency child welfare ongoing case management staff.* Milwaukee, WI: Milwaukee County Department of Social Services.

Gelles, R. (in press). *Out of harm's way.* New York: Oxford University Press.

Gladwell, M. (2008). *Outliers: The story of success.* New York: Little Brown.

Glisson, C. (2015). The role of organizational culture and climate in innovation and effectiveness. *Human Service Organizations: Management, Leadership & Governance, 39*(4), 245–250.

Glisson, C., & Hemmelgarn, A. (1998). The effects of organizational climate and interorganizational coordination on the quality and outcomes of children's service systems. *Child Abuse & Neglect, 22*(5), 401–421.

Glisson, C., & James, L.R. (2002). The cross-level effects of culture and climate in human service teams. *Journal of Organizational Behavior, 23*, 767–794.

Glisson, C., Dukes, D., & Green, P. (2006). The effects of the ARC organizational intervention on caseworker turnover, climate, and culture in children's service systems. *Child Abuse & Neglect, 30*(8), 855–880.

Glisson, C., Green, P., & Williams, N.J. (2012). Assessing the organizational social context (OSC) of child welfare systems: Implications for research and practice. *Child Abuse & Neglect, 36*, 621–632.

Glisson, C., Schoenwald, S.K, Hemmelgarn, A., Green, P., Dukes, D., Armstrong, K.S., & Chapman, J.E. (2010). Randomized trial of MST and ARC in a two-level evidence-based treatment implementation strategy. *Journal of Consulting and Clinical Psychology, 78*(4), 537–550.

Graham, B. (2004). *Detail process charting: Speaking the language of process.* Hoboken, NJ: Wiley.

Grossman, A., Foster, W., & Ross, C. (2008). *Youth Villages case study.* Boston, MA: Harvard University Business School. Retrieved from https://hbr.org/product/youth-villages/an/309007-PDF-ENG.

Hatton Bowers, H., Brooks, S., & Borucki, J. (2014). *Associations between health, workplace support, and secondary traumatic stress among public child welfare workers: A practice brief.* Northern California Training Academy, University of California Davis.

Hopkins, M., Cohen-Callow, A., Kim, H., & Hwang, J. (2010). Beyond intent to leave using multiple outcome measures for assessing turnover in child welfare. *Children and Youth Services Review, 32*, 1380–1387.

House of Commons Education and Employment Committee. (2004) *Secondary education: Teacher retention and recruitment, Volume 1: Fifth Report of Session 2003–2004, HC 1057–I.* London: The Stationery Office.

Institute for the Advancement of Social Work Research (IASWR). (2005). *Factors influencing retention of child welfare staff: A systematic review of research.* Retrieved from www.iaswresarch.org.

James, L.R. (1982). Aggregation bias in estimates of perceptual agreement. *Journal of Applied Psychology, 67*, 219–229.

Jensen, P.S., Weersing, R., Hoagwood, K.E., & Goldman, E. (2005). What is the evidence for evidence-based treatments? A hard look at the soft underbelly. *Mental Health Services Research, 7*(1), 53–74.

Kim, H., & Kao, D. (2014). A meta-analysis of turnover intention predictors among US child welfare workers. *Children and Youth Services Review, 47*, 214–223.

Kruzich, J.M., Mienko, J.A., & Courtney, M.E. (2014). Individual and work group influences on turnover intention among public child welfare workers: The effects of work group psychological safety. *Children and Youth Services Review, 42*, 20–27.

Landsman, M.J. (2001). Commitment in public child welfare. *Social Service Review, 75*(3), 387–419.

LeMahieu, P. (2017). *Networked improvement communities – What? Why? And a little how[.].* Presentation to Casey Family Programs, November 8.

Liebman, J.B. (2017). Using data to make more rapid progress in addressing difficult U.S. social problems. *Annals of the American Academy of Political and Social Science, 675*(1), 166–181.

Lucero, N., Leake, R., Scannapieco, M., & Hansen, S. (2017). Evaluating the cultural fit of an approach for practice model development for tribal child welfare. *Journal of Public Child Welfare, 11*(1), 91–107. doi:10.1080/15548732.2016.1242446.

McDaniel, N. (2010). *Connecting the dots: Workforce selection and child welfare outcomes.* National Child Welfare Workforce Institute. Presented at the 2010 Florida Coalition for Children Annual Conference.

Meyer, A.F., Norbut, C., Price, C., Miller, K., & Kelly, S. (2017). *Becoming a trauma informed agency: The Waupaca story.* Waupaca, WI: Department of Health and Human Services. Retrieved from www.aliainnovations.org/recentlyreleased/.

Mind the Gap No. 6. (Webinar). Retrieved from http://ncwwi.org/index.php/link/256-mind-the-gap-6-becoming-a-trauma-informed-child-welfare-agency-the-waupaca-county-journey.

Mor Barak, M.E., Nissly, J.A., & Levin, A. (2001). Antecedents to retention and turnover among child welfare, social work and other human service employees: What can we learn from past research? A review and metanalysis. *Social Service Review* (December), 625–661.

Myslewicz, M. (2010). *An analysis of the Kansas and Florida privatization initiatives.* Seattle: Casey Family Programs. Retrieved from www.washingtongrp.com/wp-content/uploads/2013/04/Privatization-Review-of-Kansas-and-Florida-by-Casey-Family-Programs-2010.pdf.

National Associaion of Social Workers (NASW). (2004). *"If you're right for the job, it's the best job in the world": The National Association of Social Workers' Child Welfare Specialty Practice Section members describe their experiences in child welfare*. Washington, DC: Author. Retrieved from www.socialworkers.org/LinkClick.aspx?fileticket=Mr2sd4diMUA%3D&portalid=0.

National Association of Social Workers (NASW). (2013). *Guidelines for social worker safety in the workplace*. Washington, DC: Author. Retrieved from www.socialworkers.org/practice/naswstandards/safetystandards2013.pdf.

National Child Welfare Workforce Institute. (2011). *The National Child Welfare Workforce Institute Leadership Competency Framework*. Albany, NY: Author, p. 4. (A Service of the U.S. Children's Bureau.) Retrieved from http://ncwwi.org/files/LeaderCompFrame5-31-2011.pdf.

National Child Welfare Workforce Institute. (n.d.). *Workforce development framework*. Retrieved from http://ncwwi.org/index.php/special-collections/workforce-development-framework.

Network for Social Work Management. (2015). *Human services management competencies*. Author. Retrieved from https://socialworkmanager.org/wp-content/uploads/2016/01/Competency-Brochure-4-19-15-With-Forms.pdf.

New York State Child Welfare Training Institute. (2010). *Teaming in child welfare: A guidebook*. In State of New York, Office of Children and Family Services. Retrieved from www.ocfs.state.ny.us/main/cfsr/Teaming%20in%20Child%20Welfare%20A%20 Guidebook%202011.pdf (accessed April 8, 2014).

Partners for Our Children. (2016). *Employment retention among CWTAP graduates*. Unpublished. Seattle: University of Washington.

Patti, R.J., Poertner, J., & Rapp, C.A. (1987). Managing for service effectiveness in social welfare organizations. *Social Work, 32*(5), 377–381.

Payne, J. (2014). *Beyond quick fixes: What will it really take to improve child welfare in America? Paper One: Want to improve child welfare outcomes? Reduce case transfers!* Retrieved from www.publicconsultinggroup.com/humanservices/library/white_papers/documents/Reduce_case_transfers_whitepaper2_fs.pdf.

Pecora, P.J., O'Brien, K., & Maher, E. (2015). *Levels of research evidence and benefit-cost data for Title IV-E waiver interventions: A Casey research brief* (3rd edn). Seattle, WA: Casey Family Programs. Available at www.casey.org/media/Title-IV_E-Waiver-Interventions-Research-Brief.pdf.

Pecora, P.J., Cherin, D., Bruce, E., & Arguello, T. (2010). *Administrative supervision: A brief guide for managing social service organizations*. Newbury Park, CA: Sage.

Peters, T.J., & Waterman, R.H. (1983). *In search of excellence: Lessons from America's best run companies*. New York: Harper and Row.

Royal College of Nursing. (2001). *Time to deliver*. London: Royal College of Nursing.

Sioco, M. (2010). Safety on the job: How managers can help workers. CWLA *Children's Voice* (March–April), 20–23. Retrieved from https://mariacarmelasioco.carbonmade.com/projects/3259343#1.

Smith, B. (2005). Job retention in child welfare: Effects of perceived organizational support, supervisor support, and intrinsic job value. *Children and Youth Services Review, 28*(2), 153–169.

Social Work Policy Institute. (2010a). *High caseloads: How do they impact delivery of health and human services?* Washington, DC: The National Association of Social Workers, Social Work Policy Institute. Retrieved from www.socialworkpolicy.org/wp-content/uploads/2010/02/r2p-cw-caseload-swpi-1-10.pdf.

Social Work Policy Institute. (2010b). *Professional social workers in child welfare work: Research addressing the recruitment and retention dilemma*. Washington, DC: The National Association of Social Workers, Social Work Policy Institute. Retrieved from www.socialworkpolicy.org/research/child-welfare-2.html.

Social Work Policy Institute. (2011). *Supervision: The safety net for front-line child welfare practice*. Washington, DC: National Association of Social Workers.

Sorensen, J.B. (2002). The strength of corporate culture and the reliability of firm performance. *Administrative Science Quarterly, 47*, 70–91.

Stalker, C.A., Mandell, D., Frensch, K.M., Harvey, C., & Wright, M. (2007). Child welfare workers who are exhausted yet satisfied with their jobs: How do they do it? *Child & Family Social Work, 12*(2), 182–191.

Stewart, C. (2016). High staff turnover, burnout puts child welfare system in crisis. *MyDayton Daily News*, December 9, 2016. Retrieved from www.mydaytondailynews.com/news/local/high-staff-turnover-burnout-puts-child-welfare-system-crisis/lDxydAqvyWqr3INdDikMWM/.

Strolin-Goltzman, J. (2010). Improving turnover in public child welfare: Outcomes from organizational intervention. *Children and Youth Services Review, 32*, 1388–1395.

Strolin-Goltzman, J., Lawrence, C., Auerbach, C., Caringi, J., Claiborne, N., Lawson, H., McCarthy, M., McGowan, B., Sherman, R., & Shim, M. (2009). Design teams: A promising organizational intervention for improving turnover rates in the child welfare workforce. *Child Welfare, 88*(5), 149–168.

Testa, M.F., & Poertner, J. (2010). *Fostering accountability: Using evidence to guide and improve child welfare policy*. Oxford; New York: Oxford University Press.

The Center for Advanced Studies in Child Welfare and Minnesota Association of County Human Services Administrators. (2016). *Minnesota Child Welfare workforce stabilization study*. Minneapolis, MN: Author. Retrieved from http://cascw.umn.edu/wp-content/uploads/2016/09/WFSS_Summary.WEB_.pdf.

Turnell, A., Murphy, T., & Munro, E. (2013). Soft is hardest: Leading for learning in child protection services following a child fatality. *Child Welfare, 92*(2), 197–214.

U.S. Department of Health and Human Services, Administration for Children and Families, Administration on Children, Youth and Families, Children's Bureau. (2016). *Executive summary of the final notice of statewide data indicators and national standards for child and family services reviews* (amended May, 2015). Washington, DC: Author. Retrieved from www.acf.hhs.gov/sites/default/files/cb/round3_cfsr_executive_summary.pdf.

U.S. General Accounting Office (GAO). (2003). *Child welfare: HHS could play a greater role in helping child welfare agencies recruit and retain staff.* Retrieved from www.cwla.org/programs/workforce/gaohhs.pdf (accessed August 18, 2009).

Vogus, T.J., Cull, M.J., Hengelbrok, N.E., Modell, S.J., & Epstein, R.A. (2016). Assessing safety culture in child welfare: Evidence from Tennessee. *Children and Youth Services Review, 65*, 94–103.

Walsh, C., Reutz, J.R., & Williams, R. (2015). *Selecting and implementing evidence-based practices: A guide for child and family serving systems.* San Diego, CA: California Evidence-Based Clearinghouse. Retrieved from www.cebc4cw.org/files/ImplementationGuide-Apr2015-online linked.pdf.

Webb, C.M., & Carpenter, J. (2011). What can be done to promote the retention of social workers? A systematic review of interventions. *British Journal of Social Work*, 1–21.

Westbrook, T.M., Ellis, J., & Ellett, J. (2006). Improving retention among public child welfare workers. *Administration in Social Work, 30*(4), 37–62.

Williams, N.J., & Glisson, C. (2013). Reducing turnover is not enough: The need for proficient organizational cultures to support positive youth outcomes in child welfare. *Children and Youth Services Review, 35*(11), 1871–1877.

Wulczyn, F.H., Orlebeke, B., & Haight, J. (2009). *Finding the return on investment: A framework for monitoring local child welfare agencies.* Chicago, IL: Chapin Hall at the University of Chicago. Retrieved from www.chapinhall.org/sites/default/files/Finding_Return_On_Investment_07_20_09.pdf.

Zlotnik, J.L. (2009). *Social work and child welfare: A national debate.* Fauri Lecture, University of Michigan School of Social Work. Paper presented October 27. Ann Arbor, MI: University of Michigan.

Zlotnik, J.L., & Pryce, P. (2013). The status of the use of Title IV-E funding in BSW & MSW programs. *Journal of Public Child Welfare, 7*, 430–446.

Zlotnik, J.L., DePanfilis, D., Daining, C., Lane, L., & Weschler, J. (2005). *Factors influencing retention of child welfare staff: A systematic review of research.* Retrieved from www.family.umaryland.edu/ryc_research_and_evaluation/publication_product_files/final_reports/finalreport.pdf and www.uh.edu/socialwork/_docs/cwep/national-iv-e/5-CW-SRR-FinalExecSummary.pdf.

10 International Innovations in Child and Family Services

Learning Objectives

1. Explain how the concept of globalization affects social work and child welfare policy and practice.

2. Highlight some child welfare policies and interventions that were created in countries other than the United States and are being implemented in various countries, including the U.S.

3. Describe in more detail a small subset of these interventions.

Introduction

Globalization – and the ways in which it brings people together, both in person and virtually – is having a profound impact upon social work in general, and it presents critical challenges for the field (Dominelli, 2010). In particular, globalization has exacerbated both wealth and income inequality and has contributed to the migration of large numbers of people, including children, across international borders. Coupled with the rise of neoliberalism, globalization has also led to the devolution of social welfare programs and supports for children, youth, and families. Neoliberalism is a politico-economic theory that underscores the importance of entrepreneurial freedom in order to advance human well-being and social development. More specifically, it proposes that the primary role of the state is to preserve private property rights, ensure free markets, and facilitate free trade (Harvey, 2005, p. 3).

Globalization also means that social work practices and interventions that may have been developed and implemented solely within one nation can now cross borders and be diffused internationally more easily. A result of this shift in the global order is a challenge to fundamental assumptions about child welfare practice. In particular, personal and community relationships have taken on greater importance, and there is heightened attention to implementing integrated and internationally coordinated responses to social problems (Kennett, 2001, p. 2).

Shifts in thinking, spurred by globalization, also align with long-standing intellectual currents in child welfare (CW). Fifteen years ago, our colleagues challenged the CW field to "rethink" what was meant by child placement (Whittaker & Maluccio, 2002). Through historical analysis, they showed that our understanding of a seemingly fixed CW practice, such as child placement, is actually fluid and subject to contemporary influences and policy priorities. They encouraged the field to take a number of actions, including: experimenting with different models of kinship placement, developing creative approaches to short-term residential services, exploring new models of whole-family care, personalizing out-of-home care, and in general, stretching our collective thinking about what ecologically focused, cross-setting, and developmentally appropriate placement might look like (Whittaker & Maluccio, 2002, p. 127). Sixteen years later – as the American CW system grapples with problems of nearly 50 years' standing, many of which are described in this volume – Whittaker and Maluccio's prescription for creative thinking remains not only relevant, but essential to forward progress in the field.

One way to respond to our colleagues' challenge is to study CW practices that now traverse the globe. In this sense, globalization – and its ability to "lift up" local practices and move them to other regions – allows us to learn from the successes and challenges faced by other countries as they tackle challenges posed by child poverty, neglect, and abuse. At the same time, we can also look to see how countries respond to particular responses, like migration, catalyzed by globalization.

Learning from other nations' CW experiences, as well as their innovative practices, is especially important in the United States. Because of the federal nature of U.S. policy development and governance, CW practice tends to be relatively insular. The majority of CW work is highly influenced by local custom, state law, county court rules, and local policy directives and tends not to look either internationally, or even across the United States, for inspiration. In short, the practice is, by its very nature, highly localized. While this insularity facilitates the growth of local knowledge and expertise, it also runs the risk of reifying local practice in ways that limit innovation and development.

Through thoughtful reflection on international developments in the field, U.S. CW practitioners may be better able to question some of the certainty of local practices and answer Whittaker and Maluccio's call for greater practice innovation, especially in relation to child placement. In short, an understanding of how things are done differently "over there" can facilitate a deeper understanding for how and why things are done "right here." More specifically, such comparative analysis can yield a better appreciation of the policy and political contexts surrounding particular practices, greater interrogation of the meanings associated with these practices, expanded knowledge about the ways these practices manifest power and social inequity, and, ultimately, guidance about how to move CW casework toward a place that is more closely aligned with social justice work (Finn & Jacobson, 2003). Ultimately, we live in an era where child welfare practices, like other social work methods, are frequently being contested and transformed (Parton, 1998). Attention to international developments helps us become more intentional about the transformation of local practice and grow more nimble when navigating the complexity of modern CW work.

With this in mind, this chapter reviews practices that have crossed international boundaries and respond to fundamental – and vexing – questions about the nature of child placement and permanency practice within the CW field. Three of the practices we address originated outside the United States: social pedagogy (originating in Germany), family group decision making (originating in New Zealand), and Signs of Safety® (originating in Australia). One of the practices, the Mockingbird Family Model, originated in the United States but has attracted considerable attention in the United Kingdom, making it as widely implemented there – if not more so – than in the United States. Thus, we include it in this chapter because it is both currently "globalizing" and because it is strongly aligned with our interest in family-based service delivery, concern for youth in transition, and establishing permanency for all youth in care. Alongside these four practices, we address a fifth topic of increasing importance to CW: migration and transnational families. While effective practices are just beginning to be developed in relation to migration, it is of increasing importance to the field, not only in Europe but also in the United States. Ultimately, by examining international practices and globalized challenges, our goal in this chapter is to help current practitioners spot opportunities for innovation within their own work. In sum, international insights and developments can help us advance the cause of safe, empowering, family-centered practice within the field.

Social Pedagogy

We begin our examination of international CW practices by focusing on social pedagogy. While most U.S. child welfare workers are unfamiliar with this approach, it is one of the primary theoretical underpinnings for residential care in Germany and lies at the heart of much CW practice in that country. Just as important, in recent years social pedagogy has crossed European borders and has been integrated into practice in Denmark, Ireland, the Netherlands, Norway, and the U.K. (Kyriacou et al., 2009; Petrie et al., 2009; Hallstedt & Hogstrom, 2005).

Pedagogy typically refers to educational methods and practices. However, in the context of social welfare practice with youth in the countries where it is rooted, the term is more expansive. In these countries, social pedagogy concerns an individual child's relationship to society and the use of strategies to "promote people's social functioning, inclusion, participation, social identity and social competence as members of society" (Hämäläinen, 2003, p. 76). Thus, social pedagogy takes an expansive view of youth development and individual maturation, and places it more closely within the center of social work's focus on the person-in-environment. It also provides a theoretical container for deeper integration of ideas about place (including the natural and built environments), place disruption, and processes of place attachment in children's lives (Lewicka, 2011; Morgan, 2010; Hidalgo & Hernández, 2001; Unrau et al., 2010). Thus, social pedagogy facilitates insights about child welfare practice which challenge more linear and staged models of child development and attachment that are dominant in the United States CW system. It also provides a practice framework that aligns with Whittaker and Maluccio's call for greater personalization of out-of-home care and a redesign of group care practices (2002, pp. 127–128). A brief summary of the evolution of social pedagogy in Germany – and comparisons to the rise of social work in the Anglo-American world – helps shed light on this practice approach.

Historical Context of Social Pedagogy

In the U.S. and U.K., social work – arising in the context of the Charity Organization Society (COS) movement – began initially as an intervention focused on individuals. COS workers – typically volunteer "friendly visitors" – aimed to prevent destitution among their clients through the provision of charitable assistance. These workers did this by identifying those individuals who were most deserving of aid.

Friendly visitors employed a relatively systematic strategy for "assessing" the needs of these individuals, determining the reasons for their suffering, and guiding the provision of assistance. Beneath this approach was a "hardy belief" that the poor had a "moral responsibility" for their own circumstances (Kemp, Whittaker, & Tracy, 1997, p. 26). Although the growth of the Settlement House movement disrupted this narrative – by directing workers to the social and environmental causes of urban poverty and individual suffering – the preoccupation with individual character has remained a persistent theme in child welfare practice. This is especially true in American CW practice where service has traditionally focused on the shortcomings of individual parents and promoted racialized constructions of their deservingness and undeservingness (Kemp et al., 2009; Reich, 2005; Rodenborg, 2004; Roberts, 2002).

This focus on individual morality in American social work and child welfare practice stands in contrast to early methods of social welfare assistance in Germany, where social pedagogy both arose and remains vibrant today. Here, social welfare methods and policies emerged within a "public framework" where there was a greater drive to "transcend individualism" than in the U.K. and the U.S. (Lorenz, 2008, p. 630). Key to this socially rooted framework was the idea of "subsidiarity" which envisioned society as a "system of mutual obligations between 'smaller' and 'larger' units" and where the state maintained a strong cultural and educational presence, often described in parental terms (i.e., "the fatherland)" (Lorenz, 2008, p. 632). Ultimately, this context-rich, social welfare ethic became manifest in early twentieth-century German social policy and practice with children and youth, culminating in the Youth Welfare Act of the Weimar Republic (additional details may be found in Box 10.1). This Act not only guaranteed every child's right to an education but the right "to participate as a citizen in the overall processes of forming a society as a community of 'learners'" (Lorenz, 2008, p. 633). It is this view of society as an educational community – where children are nested within interconnected social units – that undergirds social pedagogy in Germany today.

Box 10.1 The Youth Welfare Act

To best understand social pedagogy in Germany it is helpful to have an appreciation for the political and ideological origins of this unique social welfare framework. The Youth Welfare Act (*Reichsjugen-wohlfahrtsgesetz*) of 1922 was a landmark legislative achievement of the Weimar Republic that deeply reflects pedagogical thinking. While this period of German history (1919 and 1933) was characterized by significant economic crises, which ultimately contributed to the rise of the Nazi party, it is also noted for its wide-ranging social progressivism, including the adoption of workers' rights policies, extensions of health insurance, and support for veterans. The Youth Welfare Act was among these progressive reforms. Included among its various provisions were the recognition of daycare as a public responsibility and the provision of childcare services for families that could not provide them. The Act also included advances in child protection. Similarly, the Youth Court Act, also passed in 1922 as part of the same Weimar-era reforms, included new standards for determining criminal responsibility and a stronger focus on basing criminal sanctions on children's psychological development (Stolleis, 2013, p. 110). Together, these and other pieces of legislation helped direct German social welfare policy toward more ecologically rooted and contextualized solutions to social problems which remain embedded in that country's social welfare landscape today.

Overall, the different histories of social welfare assistance in Germany, the U.K., and the U.S. led to critical differences in how such assistance is provided today, particularly in relation to vulnerable children, youth, and families. Social pedagogy – and its roots in communal responsibility for children – helps mitigate against the risk of pathologizing individual children (and their parents) that can be evident in American CW practice (Bruskas, 2008; Kemp et al., 2009; Samuels & Pryce, 2008; Dumbrill, 2006). From a social pedagogy perspective, youth have the capacity for "always developing themselves further," despite the challenges they have faced, if sufficient resources are made available to them (Lorenz, 2008, p. 636).

Overall, social pedagogy assumes that children have the capacity for healthy development and that society has a collective responsibility for providing them with the critically needed education and supports necessary to become successful adults (Petrie et al., 2006, p. 21). This pedagogical value undergirds both formal educational services, but also informal social supports like sports programs, out-of-school time services, clubs, and recreational activities. Included among these programs is residential care work.

Current Practice Approach

Recent studies on pedagogical approaches to residential care in Europe have articulated its unique values and benefits. For example, Claire Cameron (2004) has helped describe the pedagogic method in both Germany and Denmark. (In fact, in both countries residential care workers typically have higher education training in social pedagogy.) The specific practices associated with social pedagogy in these and other countries vary, as do lists of principles associated with the approach. The principles identified in Box 10.2 are adapted from Cameron and Moss's (2011, p. 9) examination of the field in Denmark. While not exhaustive, they succinctly summarize pedagogic principles that frequently appear in the literature.

> **Box 10.2   Practice Principles Associated with Social Pedagogy**
>
> 1. There is a focus on the whole child and support for a youth's overall development.
> 2. Practitioners view themselves in relationship to the youth.
> 3. Youth inhabit the same "lifespace" as practitioners; they do not exist in separate domains.
> 4. Practitioners constantly reflect on their practice and apply theoretical understanding and self-knowledge to their work.
> 5. Practitioners are practically minded and involved in many aspects of a youth's everyday life.
> 6. The groups youth live in are essential to their development, and practitioners should foster and make use of them.
> 7. Pedagogy builds on an understanding of children's rights that is not limited to procedural requirements.
> 8. Teamwork is emphasized and all team members make a contribution to youth.
> 9. A practitioner's relationship with a youth is central and requires deep listening and ongoing communication.
>
> *Source:* Adapted from Cameron and Moss (2011, p. 9).

While all of these principles are important, three are worth highlighting because they point to ways that CW practice care in the U.S., particularly residential care, might be enhanced through a social pedagogic approach.

1. Practitioners in relationship to youth. Social pedagogy is sometimes referred to as "heart, heads and hands" working in combination (Cameron, 2004, p. 144). This view is quite distinct from the ways in which youth/social worker relationships are frequently envisioned in the U.S. For example, in a review of emotional intelligence and its implications for social work practice, Morrison (2007) explains that client assessment and practice frameworks with youth involved in public systems (in the U.K., which bears marked similarities to the U.S. system) tend to minimize children's emotional and traumatic experiences, including loss and bereavement. Similarly, in an assessment of effective practices in residential care, James (2011, p. 319) underscores that care facilities vary considerably in their practice approaches and that they tend to "stuff" a broad array of treatments and services into their practice framework. Thus, beyond a focus on licensure and minimal safety, there is considerable divergence in the kinds and quality of services provided by care facilities (Whittaker, 2004). This diversity is unlike practice in countries where social pedagogy is the guiding orientation.

In countries utilizing social pedagogy, the relationship between a "pedagogue" and the youth they work with is both personal and requires deep attention to a child's "wants, feelings, interests, fears, and pleasures" in much the same way that parents attend to their children's care (Petrie et al., 2006, p. 23). This close attention to a child's emotional and inner life leads to a "good upbringing" (Petrie et al., 2006, p. 31). Workers in a pedagogical context must also be able to deploy relational skills, operate from a basis of compassion, and respond intuitively to the emotional needs of youth. Such emotional intelligence is viewed as a core function of social pedagogical practice.

Moreover, this approach necessitates a relatively sophisticated understanding of not only children's feelings but also the meanings attached to these feelings and the fact that children – like all of us – often feel multiple and conflicting things at once. The complicated emotional demands of care based in social pedagogy are best summarized by Cameron (2004, p. 145):

> Care within pedagogy is about recognizing feelings, putting feelings into words in an empathetic way, allowing for the spaces between feelings and words and actions, containing the difficult, perhaps distressing, emotions of self and others, being prepared to give of the self, but also to preserve oneself, to manage closeness and distance.

Such complex emotional work – particularly coupled with a perception that the care worker plays a significant role in a child's "upbringing" – creates deep ties between workers and the youth they serve. Interestingly, these relationships are so close that even the "considered and careful use of physical contact" to offer comfort and reassurance to children is viewed as "normal practice" from a pedagogical perspective (Cameron, 2004, p. 144). Such physical contact is likely quite atypical within practice in residential care facilities in the U.S.

2. Constant reflection: Connected to the deeply relational nature of social pedagogy work, is the practice's anchoring in individual reflection and praxis. Praxis, in this context, refers to the link between dialog and action and the "active process of learning/theorizing and acting/changing at the same time" (Ife, 2008, p. 158; Freire, 1993). For social pedagogues, their practice is dynamic and requires continuous self-reflection and self-inquiry. Workers using the approach are committed to asking themselves questions about their work and their relationships with the children they serve. This ongoing inquiry serves as the basis for continuous adjustment of one's practice in order to best meet a child's individual needs and maximize the child's potential for growth. Put another way, care workers who subscribe to a social pedagogic approach are always interrogating their work, assessing its impact, and reconciling it with theoretical ideals (Cameron, 2004, p. 146).

This form of deep self-reflection not only strengthens the quality of care provided by individual workers, but also enables workers to model healthy adult behavior for youth. Ongoing self-reflection and modeling, in turn, serves as a template for youth to learn how to reflect upon their own behavior, the consequences of their decisions, and the impact their actions have upon themselves as well as upon those around them (Petrie et al., 2006, p. 28). Social pedagogic practice offers other benefits for youth. For example, when youth have transgressed against others – such as bullying or committing a micro-aggression – the modeling of praxis and self-reflection by a worker helps the youth explore the ways in which they and others experience oppression and privilege (Ginwright & Cammarota, 2002). In short, social pedagogy, and its emphasis on praxis and self-reflection, helps workers and youth grapple with the complex and challenging issues of growing up in a residential care setting (Cameron, 2004, p. 140).

3. Children's rights. According to social pedagogy practice, children are perceived as active agents and citizens who have the right to take responsibility for themselves (Cameron, 2004, p. 144). To ensure that this happens, youth are involved in all decisions concerning them, as developmentally appropriate. Thus, in residential care settings, children's views and opinions are not only important, but are critical and must be taken into account when decisions are made about their care (Cameron, 2004, p. 144). Not only does this approach center children's preferences and desires, it requires that children's individual circumstances and unique contexts be taken into account during the decision-making process (Petrie et al., 2006, p. 31). This approach differs from that of typical residential care in the U.S. which tends to minimize children's involvement in their own care. For example, while research has found that nearly all residential care facilities in the U.S. develop individualized treatment plans for youth that prioritize collaboration with a youth's family, only 12 percent of family members play major roles in their children's care and only 17 percent of youth serve "as the primary decision makers in the development of the plan" (Brown et al., 2010, p. 153). While strides are being made to increase children's voices in their own care in the U.S., there remains a wide gap between current practice and the general orientation to inclusion from the perspective of social pedagogy.

Summary

Social pedagogy is an important feature of social welfare practice with youth in a variety of European countries, especially in residential care environments. It emphasizes the individual betterment of youth in the context of deeply relational work. Key to this approach is an ongoing commitment to self-reflection and praxis on the part of the care worker as well as an emphasis on children's rights. The prevalence of social pedagogy in German practice with youth is the result of a different historical and developmental trajectory for social welfare assistance, compared to the U.K. and the U.S. Nevertheless, social pedagogy provides a model for innovating and transforming troublesome aspects of U.S. CW practice, including a tendency to focus on individual deficits. Greater utilization of social pedagogic approaches in the U.S. would enable us to respond to Whittaker and Maluccio's call for greater innovation in residential care and enhanced personalization of these services.

Family Group Decision Making

As highlighted in Chapter 3, Family Group Decision Making (FGDM) has gained significant traction as a CW practice both in the United States and elsewhere since the 1990s, and like social pedagogy it aims to rebalance relationships between child welfare workers and those they serve. FGDM generally includes a number of practices, in a CW setting, where family members come together to make decisions about how to care for their children and to develop a plan for ensuring this care. A variety of names have been used for this type of intervention over the years, including family team conferencing, family team meetings, family group conferencing, family team decision making, family unity meetings, and team decision making (Child Welfare Information Gateway, 2017).

Family Group Decision Making has evolved from the cultural practice of *whanau hui* among the Maori of New Zealand. *Whanau hui* refers to a gathering of immediate and extended kin in order to address and resolve a crisis or critical problem facing a family (Love, 2000). Such family meetings were mandated in New Zealand following the introduction of the 1989 Children, Young Persons and Their Families Act. The purpose of this mandate was to help build a more culturally embedded model of CW practice in the country and to help ensure that a family's unique strengths and resources were fully leveraged when addressing any challenges they faced.

Over the years, FGDM has crossed international borders and taken root in a number of different countries. For example, it was initially introduced into the United Kingdom in the early 1990s. The use of FGDM in the U.K. was spurred by a desire for more empowering professional–family relationships, driven in part by the 1989 Children Act (Morris & Connolly, 2012). Since then, FGDM has been modified and put to use throughout Europe and North America as well as in Australia, Israel, Spain (see Box 10.3), and South Africa. In the U.S., FGDM is practiced in at least 150 communities in 35 states (Merkel-Holguin, 2003).

> **Box 10.3   Long-term Family Care in Spain**
>
> Family Group Decision Making seeks to leverage the strengths of family networks and kin resources in order to ensure the stability and safety for children in care. Research has shown that perhaps no European country leverages family strengths and resources more than Spain in ensuring long-term permanence for children. Studies indicate that more than 85 percent of Spanish children involved in the child welfare system, and who are not placed in residential care, live with relatives (primarily with grandparents), and that many of these placements exist over the long term – in fact, they last an average of nearly five years with nearly half of the placements ending only after the child reaches adulthood (del Valle et al., 2009). In general, placement disruptions are less likely to occur in Spain if the child is placed with relatives because kin appear to have greater personal commitments and investments in the children (López et al., 2011). The permanence of these placements is also notable because nearly 90 percent of the children involved continue to reside with their relatives after reaching majority. Just as important is visitation with parents, common in Spanish kinship placement with visits typically taking place in the caregiver's home. Like U.S. child welfare cases involving FGDM, there are higher levels of cooperation between parents and caregivers when children are placed with kin (del Valle et al., 2009). The lasting nature of Spanish kinship placements is also significant given that these relatives generally receive very little governmental support and financial assistance (del Valle et al., 2009).

General Model for Family Decision-making Meetings

In general, wherever FGDM is implemented, the New Zealand approach serves as the benchmark against which other local models are assessed. In short, the New Zealand approach has been described as both a "gold standard" (Adams & Chandler, 2004) and "best practice model" (Gill, Higginson, & Napier, 2003). According to this approach, family decision-making meetings have three stages (Walton et al., 2003).

First, family conferences begin with a formal gathering of kin, CW authorities, and professional service providers during which a detailed report on a maltreated child's circumstances is presented to all attendees. Second, although family members are very likely to differ in their views about the nature, cause of, and solution to their child's maltreatment, they are asked to come together during "private time" to develop a unified comprehensive plan for the child's care (Merkel-Holguin, 2000; Pennell, 2004). During private time, family members are able to speak honestly with one another, air out differences, and find common ground away from the watchful eye of social workers and court personnel. The family's plan often includes details about the child's placement (whether with kin or strangers in foster care), the therapeutic services needed by the child and other family members, and the timelines for service completion.

Third, the plan is reviewed by all in attendance, and appropriate benchmarks and individual responsibilities for achieving the plan are identified (Lupton, 1998). Because it assumes that families have the resources, abilities, and skills to make sound decisions about their children, FGDM places far greater emphasis on the family's role in ensuring the safety of an abused and neglected child than does "service as usual" CW practice in most countries (Nixon, 2000). The FGDM approach also reflects the deeply held commitment among many child welfare workers to empowering, family-centered practice. Finally, and most importantly, FGDM addresses a family's unique needs and, thus, avoids a "one-size-fits-all" strategy in the commissioning and delivery of CW services.

Partnership between families and CW workers lies at the core of FGDM work. Morris and Connolly (2012, p. 42) stressed this aspect of FGDM when they wrote, "partnership work and sharing power with families is a universal human right that has the potential to strengthen the safety net for children at risk." They further explain that along with its roots in indigenous cultural practice, FGDM is embedded within a human rights-based paradigm, reflecting concepts of social justice and cultural responsiveness (Morris & Connolly, 2012).

Alongside its emphasis on partnership and human rights, FGDM is also deeply reflective of family support practice principles. Such services are strengths based and aim to "enable and empower people by enhancing and promoting individual and family capabilities that support and strengthen family functioning" (Dunst, Trivette, & Deal, 1994, p. 31). One potential reason why Family Group Decision Making has grown in use over the past two decades is because it enables CW systems to effectively meet both the need for accountability as well as provide family support. Theoretically, FGDM provides an authentic and constructive space for families to come together, leverage their strengths, and meet their children's needs. At the same time, it provides a meaningful role for CW workers, keeps them actively involved in a case, and ensures that they remain ultimately responsible for key safety concerns.

In 2010, the American Humane Association – a leader in promoting the use of FGDM in the United States CW system – articulated guidelines to help inform its local implementation (American Humane Association, 2010). These guidelines are rooted in empowerment-oriented, strengths-based values, and are summarized in Box 10.4.

Box 10.4   Practice Values for Family Group Decision Making

- Children have a right to maintain their kinship and cultural connections throughout their lives.

- Children and their parents belong to a wider family system that both nurtures them and is responsible for them.

- The family group, rather than the agency, is the context for child welfare and child protection resolutions.

- All families are entitled to the respect of the state, and the state needs to make an extra effort to convey respect to those who are poor, socially excluded, marginalized, or lacking power or access to resources and services.

- The state has a responsibility to recognize, support, and build the family group's capacity to protect and care for its young relatives.

- Family groups know their own histories, and they use that information to construct thorough plans.

- Active family group participation and leadership is essential for good outcomes for children, but power imbalances between family groups and child protection agency personnel must first be addressed.

- The state has a responsibility to defend family groups from unnecessary intrusion and to promote their growth and strength.

Source: American Humane Association. (2010). *Guidelines for family group decision making in child welfare.* Washington, DC: Author, p. 9. Retrieved from www.harriscountytx.gov/Cmp Documents/107/Misc/Fam%20Group%20Decision%20Making%20in%20Child%20Wel fare%20guidelines.pdf.

Research on FGDM

There is a considerable body of literature analyzing the theoretical and practice implications of FGDM as well as its impact upon child welfare outcomes. We briefly summarize both lines of research.

Process and theory research. Included in this scholarship are various process and implementation studies of conferencing. These empirical examinations underscore the ways that FGDM reflects family practice principles and they support its alignment with a rights-orientation to CW services. Specifically, parents and family members who participate in FGDM generally find the experience to be a positive one and they are typically satisfied with this aspect of their CW service involvement (Crampton, 2007; Marsh & Crow, 2003). Moreover, the plans that families develop to protect their children through FGDM are typically approved and implemented by CW authorities (Merkel-Holguin, Nixon, & Burford, 2003; Marsh & Crow, 2003). Similarly, parents and other family members involved with FGDM feel respected and valued for their participation (Lohrbach & Sawyer, 2004; Merkel-Holguin, 2003). These findings underscore the empowering nature of conferences.

One Australian study, in particular, reflects the general trend within this body of research. Specifically, Darlington and colleagues (2012) completed interviews with ten parents who were involved in FGDM in Brisbane. They found that parents who had positive views of conferencing felt respected by CW professionals, felt that their opinions were heard during the case, and felt supported at the conference event. Those with negative views did not feel respected or heard. In reflecting upon their findings, the authors emphasize the importance of the FGDM facilitator:

> In particular, the convenor role is pivotal for negotiating a successful family group conference [.] part of this role involves ensuring adequate pre-meeting preparation; hence, professionals require a clear understanding of the meeting's purpose so that this can be conveyed to parents. Adequate attention to preparation and planning before the meeting may alleviate parents' fear and uncertainty and promote positive outcomes. It is also crucial that facilitators support parents in active decision-making throughout the meeting.
>
> (Darlington et al., 2012, p. 336)

Thus, the success of a family group decision-making meeting is linked to the preparation and skill of the facilitator. Collectively, these studies emphasize the empowering nature of FGDM and the ways it reflects family-centered and supportive services for youth.

Outcomes research. Outcomes and impact studies are relatively scarce and it remains somewhat unclear how FGDM affects core CW outcomes, such as permanence and safety. Those outcome studies that do exist have frequently focused on small samples and individual programs within particular geographies; and they have not followed conference participants over the long term. In addition, where outcome findings exist, they have been inconsistent in supporting FGDM's value over traditional CW practice.

For instance, in a widely cited study from Sweden, Sundell and Vinnerljung (2004) compared the outcomes for nearly 100 children who were the focus of family conferences against the outcomes flowing from 104 child protection investigations using traditional methods. All of the children were followed for three years to determine how often subsequent maltreatment reports were filed. The researchers found that the families who had participated in a conference had higher satisfaction levels with CW service provision than the comparison group. These children were also more often placed with kin, compared to those children receiving traditional services. However, children who were involved with FGDM experienced *higher* rates of re-referral for abuse or neglect. Interestingly, these referrals were frequently made by extended kin. The children who were involved in conferences also experienced longer out-of-home placements relative to the comparison group. While the researchers noted that FGDM accounted for only a very small amount of the variance in the outcomes between the two groups of children, they cautioned against the uptake of FGDM without more rigorous examination. In contrast to the Swedish research, a later study by Berzin et al. (2008) used a randomized control study to compare children receiving FGDM (without private time) in California to those who did not. While the sample sizes were small, that study found no significant differences between the two groups based on the number of cases closed or reasons for closure.

Similarly, research has also yielded mixed results in the areas of child maltreatment re-reports and out-of-home placements: some studies have found positive effects (Crampton & Jackson, 2007; Hollinshead et al., 2017; Pennell & Burford, 2000; Pennell, Edwards, & Burford, 2010; Sheets et al., 2009); and other studies have identified negative or neutral effects (Berzin et al., 2008; Sundell & Vinnerljung, 2004). Meta-analyses have documented various impacts of family meetings beyond these traditional outcomes (Merkel-Holguin, Nixon, & Burford, 2003).

Some evaluations have also examined the effects of family meetings by family race/ethnicity. For example, in Texas, research indicated that FGDM involvement led to higher rates of reunification or placements with relatives for minority children (Sheets et al., 2009). But in Washington State, a three-year study showed that Family Team Decision Making (FTDM) did not affect the time to permanency for African American or American Indian children, but did enable Asian and Latino children to achieve permanency more quickly (Miller, 2011). These FTDMs reduced the rate of out-of-home placement for Latino children, but failed to reduce disparities between White children and African American or American Indian children with respect to removals and length of stay in out-of-home care (Miller, 2011).

Mixed results have also been obtained when FGDM is used with children in group care. A study in two Maryland counties showed that "Family Involvement Meetings (FIMs)" for children in group settings resulted in higher rates of family reunification in the FIM counties than in the comparison counties (Lee et al., 2013). Even so, the results indicate a relatively modest positive effect in terms of actual reunifications. Families and youth reported very positive reactions to these meetings even when no reunification occurred.

Lastly, one meta-analysis of FGC effectiveness found that minority children who received a FGC experienced higher rates and longer durations of out-of-home placements compared to those who did not receive FGC (Dijkstra et al., 2016).

Summary

Family Group Decision Making has become an increasingly widespread practice within CW services in the U.S., Australia, New Zealand, and the U.K. FGDM reflects core family support and empowerment principles, and helps facilitate CW practice that identifies and then leverages core family strengths. In this sense, it is well aligned with Whittaker and Maluccio's call to redouble our efforts at engaging parents in the care nurture of their children when they are placed outside the home (2002, p. 127). Alongside evidence that FGDM shifts the tone and nature of traditional practice, there remains "a vital need" for evaluation research, using random assignment, that rigorously examines long-term impacts of FGDM participation on key CW outcomes (Sundell & Vinnerljung, 2004).

Mockingbird Family Model

The Mockingbird Family Model (MFM) is an innovative approach to delivering foster care services that, like family group decision making, is anchored in family support. The Mockingbird Family Model was developed in 2001 by The Mockingbird Society, a private nonprofit agency based in Seattle, Washington. The organization's mission is to improve foster care and end youth homelessness. In 2003, the organization received federal funding to implement the MFM, beginning with a partnership with UJIMA Community Services/One Church One Child of Washington, the first African American child placing agency in Washington State. Currently, the MFM has been implemented widely in Washington State, as well as in Fresno, California; Queens, New York, and in the United Kingdom.

While developed in the United States, we include the MFM in this chapter because of its growing presence within child welfare practice in the U.K. The MFM first gained ground in the U.K. in 2015, beginning with seven different sites, and was expanded to ten additional sites in 2017. It is also undergoing the most rigorous evaluation to date in the U.K. (to be completed over three years). All of this arguably means that the MFM is now more widely implemented in the United Kingdom than it is in the United States. Given this significant uptake, the model will likely experience significant customization and adaptation as it moves from the U.S. to Europe. The results of the U.K. evaluation will, in turn, inform American development and implementation of the model. Consequently, the

MFM is truly a globalizing practice approach which exemplifies our interest in CW practices that rapidly cross international boundaries and that undergo iterative, multinational transformation.

The Mockingbird Family Model^tm Approach

The MFM is specifically designed to be holistic and avoid multiple placement changes for children in foster care. It also helps minimize the separation of siblings in care and seeks to reduce the sense of isolation frequently experienced by children in care as well as by their caregivers. The model rests upon an MFM Constellation which is comprised of six to ten satellite families that "orbit" a single hub foster home. Satellite homes are foster, kinship, foster-to-adopt, or birth families who live in close proximity to the central hub which is also a licensed foster care provider. Children residing in the satellite families are between birth and 21 years old. A Host Agency is responsible for the overall implementation of MFMs. Figure 10.1 depicts the hub/satellite home arrangement. Each of the components of the MFM approach is described below.

Satellite homes. The satellite home is a licensed foster care provider with children placed in their home and the caretakers at the satellite are willing to be active and engaged members of an MFM Constellation. The goal of the satellite home is to provide high-quality care to children, and care providers must actively engage in MFM activities, meetings, and events. Satellite carers communicate regularly with hub homes and proactively seek assistance from hubs in order to avoid unnecessary placement disruptions and caregiver burnout. As the MFM training manual states:

> The overall goal is for the Satellite Home families to participate in a mutually supportive micro-community as a means to improve relationships and outcomes for children and youths in their care and to support the achievement of each child's or youth's permanency plan.
>
> (Mockingbird Family Model Constellation Training and Resource Manual, 2014, p. 11)

In general, the hub/satellite network is intended to function like an extended family.

Hub homes. The hub home is charged with providing core support to satellites, including helping them navigate complicated CW systems, providing peer support for children in their care as well as the children's parents, offering impromptu and scheduled social supports, and delivering crisis assistance. Hub homes also organize monthly events and gatherings for families in the Constellation (such as movie nights, parties, and outings). Families that serve in the hub role are experienced foster care providers who are deeply

Figure 10.1 Hub and Satellite Homes in Mockingbird Family Model[tm]
Source: The Mockingbird Society. (2010, p. 1). Reprinted with permission.

knowledgeable about the issues and challenges faced by foster families. In general, hub home parents function as extended family members to satellite homes – they serve the roll of a grandparent or aunt/uncle and they do what it takes to meet the needs of children in the satellites through creativity and resourcefulness.

One of the most critical roles hub homes play is providing respite care and serving as a mediator in any disputes that may exist among members of the satellite family. Children often come into foster care at times of serious familial conflict and this can affect their ability to transition into the satellite home. In addition, crises may arise over the course of a child's time in care, which can lead to conflict between children and foster parents or with other children in the home. Hub homes play an essential role during these sensitive times because they provide support to satellite parents, as well as children, and help reduce stress, foster the growth of trusting relationships, and ease transitions during difficult times. Put differently, hub homes help resolve conflicts, serve as a liaison, and enable children to remain in a satellite home or return to it as quickly as possible if they have to leave. One

467

of the major strategies for achieving these goals is through the provision of respite care to satellite families.

Respite care in the Mockingbird Family Model can take one of three different forms:

1. *Planned respite.* Satellite homes can sign up for planned respite care on a monthly calendar provided by the hub. Hub homes are transparent about when they cannot provide such care and, during these times, the satellite and Host Agency may find an alternative. There is no set limit to the amount of time a satellite can obtain planned respite from the hub home. Planned respite includes overnight care.

2. *Brief respite.* Brief respite allows Satellite caregivers to attend regular activities or meetings, or to visit friends and relatives.

3. *Emergent respite care.* During a crisis, a satellite home can call hub parents directly and secure immediate help. This aspect of the MFM increases the capacity of everyone in the Constellation to effectively respond to a crisis within one of the families. Crises may involve either a child or other members of a satellite family and may include emergency medical appointments, a sick or injured child, or, less urgently, simply the need for a few hours to regroup after a child has acted out or exceeded the patience of a caregiver.

Host agency. The MFM is implemented by individual "host" agencies that provide family support, foster care licensing, or other child placement assistance. The Mockingbird Society in Seattle does not supervise children in care; it only provides technical support and capacity-building assistance to those agencies that take on the MFM. Host Agencies are responsible for children living within Constellations. These agencies have typically directed significant resources to implementing MFM, including bringing a variety of professionals together for planning (including social workers, licensors, and placement coordinators) as well as community stakeholders (Mockingbird Society, 2010, p. 33). Once a Constellation is launched, the Host Agency staff members work together to ensure successful implementation of the model.

Core Practice Principles

The MFM model is anchored in a mix of family support, strengths-based, and empowerment-oriented practice principles. It is specifically intended to address inefficiencies in the foster care system, including disconnections among its various components, as well as high caseloads and burnout faced by child welfare workers. The eight core principles of MFM are summarized in Box 10.5.

Box 10.5 Mockingbird Family Model[tm] Core Practice Principles

Principle	Definition
1. Unconditional Care	All children deserve safe, nurturing environments in which to live and thrive.
2. Normalization	Children in care must receive the same opportunities, supports, and challenges as their peers for full development and growth.
3. Community Based	Children should be in the least restrictive environment possible and should grow up in communities that are familiar to them and close to their families.
4. Continuity	Children should benefit from consistency and continuity in their lives – the same school, friends, and out-of-school activities.
5. Safety	Trusting relationships with adults invested in children's safety are essential; with more adults watching out for them, the lower the chance that abuse or neglect will go undetected.
6. Family Support	Biological families and kin are resources and children should have the skills and boundaries needed to develop and maintain positive relationships with their families.
7. Culture	Children do best when closely connected to their cultures and placed in homes that reflect it.
8. Caregiver Support	The people who take care of children must also be taken care of. Caregiver support leads to healthy, effective adults with the energy to provide unconditional care to children.

Source: Adapted from The Mockingbird Society (2010). *The Mockingbird Family Model approach: An innovative approach to child welfare reform.* Retrieved from https://bettercarenet work.org/sites/default/files/MFM_Brochure_2010.pdf.

Impact of the Mockingbird Family Model

Evaluations of the Mockingbird Family Model in both Washington State and the U.K. underscore the ways in which it provides emotional and social support to caregivers and potentially facilitates positive outcomes for youth (McDermid et al., 2016; Northwest Institute for Children and Families, 2007). It is believed that the provision of such support can, in turn, facilitate the growth of conditions that are positively associated with improved placement stability and the retention of foster care providers over time (McDermid et al., 2016). Overall, these and several other important themes have emerged from evaluations of the Mockingbird Family Model over recent years. Five of these key themes are discussed in the following sections.

1. *Supportive relationships.* A British study of 16 MFM Constellations showed that children and their caregivers develop supportive relationships with one another and are able to access one-to-one support from caregivers from within Constellations. Hub families are viewed as "extremely responsive" to requests for help and support from satellites and, when provided, this assistance is customized to meet the unique needs of the satellite family. In a review of the U.K. pilot of the MFM, all of the Constellations came together in group meetings with up to 11 Constellation families in attendance. Conversations during these meetings focused on the day-to-day challenges of providing foster care in a non-judgmental environment. Satellite families learned about one another's experiences during these meetings and felt supported by hearing others discuss similar challenges. Along with these larger meetings, hub families also held social events, including Christmas parties, walks, and bowling outings which were attended by all members of the satellite families (McDermid et al., 2016, p. 19). Such inclusive activities were particularly helpful to satellite families who had birth children and foster children living together. Both children and caregivers in the U.K. pilot also reported that they enjoyed attending these events and that members of the Constellation got along with one another (McDermid et al., 2016, p. 22).

2. *Respite care.* Research shows that the ability to secure respite care is a critical feature of the MFM. This finding is likely linked to the fact that the MFM helps normalize and redefine respite care so that it is no longer viewed as problematic or the "last option" before a crisis (McDermid et al., 2016, p. 21). Satellite families indicate that respite care is easily accessed and that there is continuity in who provides such care. As a result, both children and their caregivers feel comfortable seeking respite care and find the experience less stressful than seeking respite from someone they do not know.

3. *Safety.* Multiple evaluations of MFM in Washington State (conducted by the University of Washington) indicate that children remain safe while placed within a Constellation. Specifically, there were no founded child abuse or neglect referrals to the state's Child Protection Services for MFM caregivers during the most recent study period (Northwest Institute for Children and Families, 2006, 2007). This finding exceeds federal standards for safety while in care.

4. *Birth family connections*. In Washington, children in MFM Constellations maintain relationships with their birth families. In fact, 94 percent of children in the most recent evaluation sample were placed in the same Constellation as their siblings (Northwest Institute for Children and Families, 2007). In addition, hub parents organized visits with birth parents or other adults from birth families for 12 percent of the children in the Constellations with 10 percent of children being reunified with their birth parents. Birth families were also invited to join Constellation-wide events. Somewhat in contrast, however, in the U.K., researchers found that there was "limited evidence" that MFM activities helped maintain contact and relationships with birth families during the study period (McDermid et al., 2016, p. 23). The percentage of children with siblings in the same Constellation (18%) was lower than for the Washington sample.

5. *CW outcomes*. Washington evaluations indicate that 21 percent of children cared for by a Constellation achieve their permanency plan over the course of a year (Northwest Institute for Children and Families, 2007). Permanency includes reunification with birth families, adoption, movement to kinship care, or transition to adulthood. Overall, 90 percent of children achieving permanency were discharged to permanent homes. In the United Kingdom, the MFM model is not sufficiently developed to make definitive statements about the impact upon CW outcomes. There was little evidence that the MFM affected children's educational outcomes or permanence. Within the U.K. sample, six children experienced placement disruptions, one of which was planned, and in two cases the child moved to a different satellite home. Overall, 4 percent of the children in the British MFM study experienced disruptions compared to 8 percent nationwide (McDermid et al., 2016, p. 28). None of the caregivers stopped providing care during the British study, in contrast to a 6 percent attrition rate nationally. In Israel, a model similar to the MFM produced some positive outcomes (see Box 10.6).

Box 10.6 Cluster Family Care in Israel

The Family Cluster Program was a unique approach to providing foster care to children in Israel that was described in child welfare literature in the late 1990s and early 2000s; it shares similarities with the Mockingbird Family Model. In particular, in a cluster approach, up to eight foster families live in community with one another – alongside children's parents – in order to provide a supportive, therapeutic framework for care. Relationships between parents and foster parents are anchored in mutual respect, empowerment, and the acquisition of useful, effective parenting skills (Mosek, 2004, p. 329). Children living in such environments essentially inhabit "two worlds" – one with their foster parents and the other with their biological parents (Colton & Williams, 1997). Children placed in such "cluster" models are better positioned to negotiate their futures with both foster and biological parents, all caregivers work together in partnership for the best interests of the child, and foster parents have access to more information and resources in caring for the children (Mosek, 2004). Just as important, the child welfare worker is perceived as actively involved and concerned with the care of the child in this family-to-family model. Overall, like the Mockingbird Family Model, such an approach aims to surround vulnerable youth with ecologically oriented and community-based supports and resources.

Summary

The Mockingbird Family Model (MFM) is a community-based model of foster care delivery that builds and facilitates empowering relationships between six to ten satellite families that live in close proximity to one another. These households, in turn, are supported by a hub home that provides peer support, social activities, and offers ongoing respite care. In this regard, the practice closely aligns with Whittaker and Maluccio's (2002, p. 127) call to expand the use of "whole-family" care models as well as the need to expand our models of respite care. Beginning with its development in Washington State, the MFM has been utilized in several additional states and is currently being taken up by CW practitioners in the United Kingdom. Research on the model suggests that it helps build supportive relationships, offers valuable assistance to satellite homes, and potentially lays the groundwork for positive CW outcomes. Like other examples of current and innovative globalizing practices, there remains work to be done to build an evidence base that explains how, and under what circumstances, the MFM yields the greatest impact, including spurring positive outcomes for youth.

Signs of Safety

In the 1990s Andrew Turnell and Steve Edwards (1999) helped develop the *Signs of Safety* approach to CW work in Western Australia. While the approach is now used in the United States, with the First Nations people in Canada, other communities in Canada, in England,

Ireland, Sweden, the Netherlands, and other countries, it has been most widely adopted by the Department for Child Protection in Western Australia. Like other globalizing practices, this practice framework challenges traditional models of CW practice that can force families and child welfare workers into adversarial relationships. Instead, it seeks to build constructive partnerships between workers and parents when child abuse or neglect is either suspected or substantiated.

Practice Values

Signs of Safety is grounded in three key values, which in turn are anchored in strengths-based practice, empowerment, and collaboration with families. The three principles are as follows:

1. *Working relationships.* Involvement in CW services is typically involuntary. Consequently, parents often feel powerless and they may lack the knowledge and skills needed to effectively navigate the competing demands and conditions imposed upon them by the CW system. Parents also feel that their perspectives and views do not really count in service design and planning; in fact, they are frequently only informed of case decisions, rather than playing significant roles in the decision-making processes that affect them (Kemp et al., 2009, p. 107). The Signs of Safety approach acknowledges that mutually constructive relationships between workers and families are at the heart of successful CW practice. Similarly, the approach works to build connections and solidify relationships across professional silos and among child welfare workers within highly bureaucratic agencies. Focusing on communication is essential because research indicates that miscommunication and poorly functioning professional relationships are often implicated in the deaths of children in care (Government of Western Australia, 2011, p. 5; Munro, 2011). Overall, creating effective relationships among professionals and with families, and facilitating communication among all of these stakeholders, is not easy. It requires that both workers and families understand and appreciate the complex and "typically messy lived experience" of all those involved in a CW case, including professionals, family members, and children (Government of Western Australia, 2011, p. 5).

2. *Inquiry and curiosity.* Despite the many challenges families in the CW system face, they remain far more knowledgeable about their children than do professionals. In short, they are the experts on their families. With this in mind, workers using Signs of Safety orient their practices toward a greater sense of curiosity than might be typical

in the field. They are self-reflective and seek to check their initial judgments about families. Nigel Parton (1998, p. 23) has explained that this attitude of "uncertainty" is critical to effective practice in the current age. He writes:

> Rather than seeing a commitment to uncertainty as undermining and lying at the margins of practice, I would suggest it lies at the heart, and that its recognition provides an opportunity for valuing practice, practitioners and the people with whom they work.

In the context of Signs of Safety, cultivating a sense of uncertainty means that social workers deploy both their professional knowledge and expertise while – simultaneously – recognizing the contingent nature of their judgments and assumptions about the families they serve. Thus, they reconcile what they believe they know about a family against the reality of what they learn from the family. Through this inquiry-based practice, some of the workers' preconceptions will be validated and others will be challenged and dropped. Failure to cultivate such an inquiry-based approach to practice means that workers may erroneously be convinced that they "know the truth" about a case or situation. This rigid and limiting view can lead to the fracturing of relationships – both with colleagues and family members – all of whom may hold different views. It can also lead to blind spots in practice or disregard of critical information that does not align with faulty assumptions (Government of Western Australia, 2011, p. 5).

3. *Everyday practice.* Signs of Safety is grounded in the workaday realities of CW practice. The approach has been developed with "an acute sensitivity to the lived-experience of those at the sharp end of the child protection business, the service deliverers and clients" (Government of Western Australia, 2011, p. 5). Consequently, much of the knowledge base supporting its use is anchored in the experiences of practitioners and families. This practice-focused approach to research aligns with calls for greater use of critical social theory in examinations of social work services. Specifically, Finn and Jacobson (2003, p. 67) tell us that social work (or, as they encourage us to think of it, social justice work) must recognize the ways in which both workers and clients make meaning of their lives and navigate the "lived, material reality of human pain and possibility." By prioritizing applied research, gathering data from on-the-ground practice (rather than large datasets), and using what is learned to inform the development of the model, Turnell and colleagues have sought to build Signs of Safety into a worker-informed and family-centered approach to CW services.

Implementation

Signs of Safety is primarily implemented through the use of an assessment protocol or "mapping tool." Turnell has stated that this is the only formal protocol used in the model (Signs of Safety, 2017). The protocol is presented in Figure 10.2.

The protocol is intended to help child welfare workers and family members clearly articulate the threats that a child faces, the family's strengths, and the factors that contribute to the child's safety. The protocol also helps facilitate the mutual development of goals for the case as well as indicators of progress that may be used to guide decision making in the future. The protocol is completed in dialog with the family so that the worker and caregivers can come to a shared understanding of what has happened in the past and what needs to happen in the future. Ultimately, the protocol is designed to spur collaborative assessment and planning between workers and families and to encourage workers to "dig deeper" into family strengths and resources rather than to rely solely upon initial reactions and judgments.

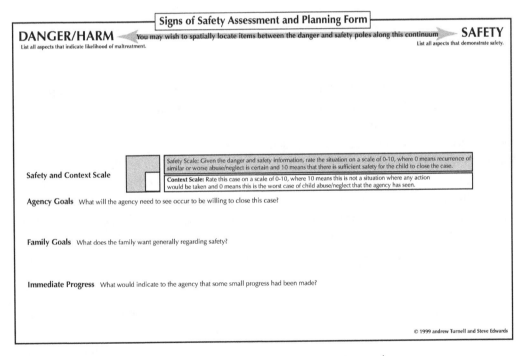

Figure 10.2 Signs of Safety Assessment Protocol

Source: Turnell & Edwards (1999). Reprinted with permission.

When We Think About the Situation Facing this Family:		
What are we Worried About?	**What's Working Well?**	**What Needs to Happen?**
HARM **DANGER STATEMENTS** **Complicating factors**	**Existing strengths** **EXISTING SAFETY**	**SAFETY GOALS** **Next steps**
On a scale of 0 to 10 where 10 means everyone knows the children are safe enough for the child protection authorities to close the case and zero means things are so bad for the children they can't live at home, where do we rate this situation? (If different judgements place different people's number on the continuum).		

0 ◄――――――――――――――――――――――――――――――――――――――► 10

Figure 10.3 Streamlined Signs of Safety Protocol
Source: Resolutions Consultancy. (2018). Reprinted with permission.

The version of the mapping tool presented in Figure 10.3 has been further adapted by a number of local CW agencies. Turnell and others have also worked to simplify the protocol and hone in on its three core components: risks (including potential harms, dangers, and complications), strengths (safety assets and benefits), and goals (agency goals and family goals). This alternate version of the tool is presented in Figure 10.3.

A further version of the tool has been developed for direct work with children, whose voices are often marginalized from CW practice and safety planning. This child-oriented model has been described as the "Three Houses" approach which relabels the columns in Figure 10.4 as "House of Good Things," "House of Bad Things," and "House of Dreams." When using the Signs of Safety model with children, workers may employ both words and pictures to help ensure their understanding.

In keeping with its focus on everyday practice, much of the evaluation and empirical literature about Signs of Safety has addressed its implementation and use in the field. For instance, the Department of Child Protection in Western Australia, where the approach is extensively used, has reported a variety of results. Specifically, the government indicates that Signs of Safety has helped slow the increase in the number of children in care and has contributed to the increased use of intensive family support services (Turnell, 2013). Just as important, a survey of staff indicated that the approach yielded more positive casework experiences for workers and families, including the following:

- Better family understanding of issues and expectations.
- More collaboration with partner agencies.
- More open, transparent, and honest practice.

Similar improvements in practice have been found in other countries. In New Zealand, Keddell (2011) reported improvements in relationships between workers and families following use of the approach as well as greater attention to family strengths. In the Netherlands, where Signs of Safety has been used since 2006, child welfare workers reported fewer feelings of isolation, stronger collegial relationships with one another, better family understanding of case developments, and more efficient practice (Turnell, 2013). Fidelity to the model is currently being measured via parent and supervisor ratings of workers (Roberts et al., 2016).

Despite these positive reports, the evidence base surrounding child-level outcomes remains provisional. Like other innovative practices, there continue to be gaps in our understanding of how Signs of Safety facilitates long-term safety and permanence for children and how it might reduce rates of recidivism. Nevertheless, even if these outcomes parallel those of traditional practice, there are important indications that Signs of Safety shifts the nature and tone of CW practice toward a more collaborative and empowering approach (Turnell et al., 2017).

Summary

The Signs of Safety approach, developed in Western Australia, provides a practice framework for CW workers to build collaborative and empowering relationships with families involved in the system. By spurring an inquiry-based and curious attitude toward practice, and conducting research that is anchored in everyday practice, Signs of Safety seeks to facilitate effective worker/client and worker/worker communication. In this regard, it also meets Whittaker and Maluccio's (2002, p. 127) focus on greater involvement of families in the care and nurture of their children when placed in out-of-home care. More specifically, Signs of Safety asks workers to identify threats to children's safety, family strengths, and factors that contribute to safety. Like other innovative approaches, the research base for Signs of Safety has shown that it enhances worker's relationships with clients but more data are needed about its impact upon achieving CW outcomes.

Migration and Transnational Families

An important feature of globalization has been the rise of immigrant and refugee families whose members are increasingly separated from one another by national borders. Families now cross international boundaries under a variety of circumstances – ranging from highly traumatic escapes from persecution and oppression to relatively routine changes in a parent's job location. When these changes occur, family members may remain in their new destination country for short or extended periods. These trends have given rise to "transnational families" whose family and kin relationships extend across international boundaries. Such families are more complex and more difficult to classify when contemplating the provision of social welfare assistance (Zentgraf & Chinchilla, 2012). The growth of transnational families poses a challenge for CW systems across the world and is the final area of exploration in this chapter.

In the United States, migration has led to an increase in the number of immigrant families – many from Latin America – who come into contact with CW services. These families may face a number of barriers and can become stressed and challenged as they navigate a variety of social and economic hurdles (Finno-Velasquez, 2014). Similarly, in Europe, CW systems are challenged to meet the needs facing migrant children and their families, some of whom are refugees (Barn et al., 2015). In light of these significant demographic changes, CW practitioners and scholars in both Europe and the United States are developing practice frameworks that help ensure children's safety, while also leveraging family strengths, maintaining family ties, and providing culturally embedded services to families whose members cross international boundaries. In doing so, they raise critical considerations for work in this area. We address three of these concerns in this chapter: family relationships, cross-system collaboration, and culturally embedded trauma-informed practice.

Family Relationships

A number of scholars have called for more flexible and fluid definitions of family and familial relationships so that they may better reflect the complicated nature of human relationships in an age of globalization and migration. Migration separates parents from their children and, especially in relation to mothers, it challenges dominant (Euro-American) discourses about attachment (Falicov, 2007). More specifically, while parents and children may not be in close physical proximity, they may be in regular contact, and thus maintain strong and ongoing ties, or as Parreñas (2005, p. 317) describes it: "intimacy across great distances." Such transnational parenting is now aided by a variety of technologies, including phone calls, videos, gifts, remittances, text messages, letters, and visits (Madianou & Miller, 2012; Parreñas, 2005; Asis, Huang, & Yeoh, 2004). The nature and extent of parent/child contact is also mediated by larger economic and structural forces. These forces, in turn, may prevent parents from achieving the kind of relationship they desire with their children.

In a CW context, children who have either emigrated or been a refugee may come to the attention of CW authorities when their parent is not physically present. While such a separation may typically be viewed as a problem – or even the initial cause of child protection attention – practitioners must be careful not to assume that the separation is traumatizing. Workers must also guard against assuming that a parent has abandoned a child, especially when the parent has left the child in the care of a trusted adult. Instead, workers should aim to understand how the child and the adults in the child's life understand the separation, interpret it, and react to it. They should also seek to assess the degree to which the child and parent remain connected and attached over distance, and the steps a parent takes to ensure a child's safety and ongoing stability, despite their presence (Zentgraf & Chinchilla, 2012). At the same time, CW workers will likely need to devote additional effort to searching for family members, both domestically and internationally, who may be able to serve as kin placements. Such effort will require the development and implementation of new trans-border family search techniques and greater patience with the complexity of working across international boundaries and language barriers.

Cross-system Collaboration

CW systems working with transnational families are likely to interact with a variety of national and international governmental agencies. At the same time, workers may find themselves at the intersection of conflicting policy mandates reflecting varied political values and priorities, including immigration enforcement, criminal justice directives, asylum policies, and CW standards (Earner & Križ, 2015). Undoubtedly, as migration continues and transnational families grow in numbers, CW workers in the U.S. will also be forced to grapple with conflicting timeframes for achieving permanency. This means reconciling policy pressure to resolve CW cases relatively swiftly under the Adoption and Safe Families Act with the complexity – and lengthy process – of navigating cross-border practice. Collaboration with outside agencies, possibly located in another country, is often necessary to effective practice in this arena but may be time-consuming and cumbersome (Finno & Bearzi, 2010).

Effective collaboration across boundaries also means that CW staff should be aware of the legal and policy tools that may be available to them to help manage and resolve a case. Perhaps the most important of these is the Special Immigrant Juvenile Status (SIJS), which is available to children in the U.S. who have been abused, abandoned, or neglected. Under the SIJS, children can obtain a green card that enables them to live and work permanently in the United States if they meet the following conditions (U.S. Department of Homeland Security, 2017):

- The child is under 21 years old, not married, and currently living in the United States.
- A state court has declared the child a dependant.
- It is not in the child's best interests to return to their home country (or the last country they lived in).
- The child cannot be reunited with a parent.

States are becoming increasingly sophisticated about SIJS and some, like New Mexico, have streamlined their court procedures so that children can take advantage of the status (Finno & Bearzi, 2010). Navigating legal procedures like SIJS and casework, in general, with children who have immigration issues can be both complex and demand a higher degree of cross-system collaboration than is typical (Križ & Skivenes, 2012). The Texas Child Protective Services Handbook provides some indication of this higher level of collaboration when children are not U.S. citizens (Texas Department of Family and Protective Services, 2017). It indicates that caseworkers working with children who have complicated citizenship and immigration statuses may need to:

- Obtain a child's birth records.
- Coordinate with an Immigration Specialist from within the CW department.
- Notify and work collaboratively with foreign consulates.
- Request and help coordinate a home study in a foreign country.
- Place a child in a foreign country and arrange necessary monitoring and safeguards.

While CW staff in this practice area are certainly not expected to be experts on the intricacies of immigration law, they must be sufficiently knowledgeable about the facts of their cases to collaborate effectively with CW workers and attorneys with such specialized knowledge. Using this knowledge to help resolve issues of citizenship and immigration status is essential to establishing permanency for vulnerable children and to effectively working with children's transnational families. If CW workers do not attend to these issues, children with unresolved citizenship, and who age out of foster care, run the risk of an uncertain legal status and potential forced return to their country of origin upon reaching majority.

Culturally Embedded and Trauma-informed Practice

In the United States, CW workers must contend with the consequences of increased immigration enforcement under the direction of the Immigration and Customs Enforcement (ICE) agency. ICE's local practices – including raids at home and the workplace – can exacerbate the already fraught relationship between child protection workers and families by diminishing trust of government, traumatizing family members, and separating families through deportation or detention (Finno & Bearzi, 2010). In fact, parents involved in the CW system, and who are not U.S. citizens, may face deportation while their U.S.-born children may be able to remain in the country. This forces parents into inhumane and untenable choices between leaving their children behind or uprooting them from their homes (Zayas & Bradlee, 2014). Such difficulties only compound those already faced by many immigrant children in the U.S., some of whom have fled exceedingly dangerous and violent situations in their home countries (Child Welfare Information Gateway, 2015). Given these emotionally charged contexts, CW practice with transnational families should incorporate trauma-informed practice principles, including cognitive behavioral approaches that help children address post-traumatic stress disorder symptoms, anxiety, and depression (Kataoka et al., 2003).

In addition to recognizing and addressing trauma, CW practice with transnational families requires caseworkers to have an understanding of the cultural, racial, and ethnic diversity of their clients (Maiter & Leslie, 2015, p. 187). This means that social workers should, minimally, have fundamental knowledge of the history, values, and beliefs of their client's culture (Tan, 2012, p. 129). It also means that caseworkers respect a family's culture, faith, and rituals (Texas Department of Family and Protective Services, 2017).

Summary

Globalization has fostered an increase in the number of transnational families. For U.S. workers, this means that children who come to the attention of CW systems may be separated from their parents, but remain connected and attached to them. A variety of legal complexities are inherent in practice with transnational families, including the possibility that parents and children may have different citizenship statuses and that children should be provided with Special Juvenile Immigrant Status. Collaborative, culturally embedded practice and use of trauma-informed care principles are essential to working with families who cross borders during this era of globalization and migration.

Conclusions

This chapter has sought to describe the ways in which globalization has affected child welfare policy and practice by showing how interventions and approaches created in one country can traverse the globe and take root elsewhere.

> Child and family welfare systems mirror the cultural and institutional contexts in which they have evolved. These local cultural and institutional environments impose strong constraints on the choices any child and family welfare project will be allowed to try (O'Hara, 1998). Nonetheless, despite such barriers, looking at our own realities in light of experiences elsewhere highlights a range of possibilities, and underscores the fact that our current arrangements are neither inevitable nor universal. Both to generate hope as well as to stimulate creativity, it is worthwhile to examine our existing systems of child and family welfare in light of a continuum of existing and suggested alternatives.
>
> (Freymond & Cameron, 2006, p. 4)

We focused our analysis on five such developments: social pedagogy, family group decision making, the Mockingbird Family Model, Signs of Safety, and migration and transnational families. All of these interventions help advance and stretch child welfare practice in ways that make it more ecologically focused and developmentally appropriate for youth. Or, as Whittaker and Maluccio (2002) call for, they are innovative strategies for providing whole-family care. Perhaps more importantly, none of the interventions and approaches we review is static: they are, in fact, growing and changing as research and practice experience yields new insights about them. In a very real sense, all of them are nascent and evolving. By including these still-developing practice models in this chapter, we seek to reinforce the notion that continued developmental research is not only necessary, but critical to achieving positive outcomes for youth. We also hope to underscore that interventions and approaches that have positive impacts in one context may also prove valuable under different local conditions and at different moments if they are sensitively adapted and deployed. In the end, this chapter suggests that child welfare is a dynamic and global phenomenon that is shaped by local conditions and which seeks to ensure children's safety and permanence in a wide variety of international contexts.

References

Adams, P., & Chandler, S. (2004). Responsive regulation in child welfare: Systemic challenges to mainstreaming the family group conference. *Journal of Sociology and Social Welfare, 31*(1), 93–116.

American Humane Association. (2010). *Guidelines for family group decision making in child welfare.* Washington, DC: Author. Retrieved from www.harriscountytx.gov/CmpDoc uments/107/Misc/Fam%20Group%20Decision%20Making%20in%20Child%20Wel fare%20guidelines.pdf.

Asis, M., Huang, S., & Yeoh, B. (2004). When the light of the home is abroad: Unskilled female migration and the Filipino family. *Singapore Journal of Tropical Geography, 25*(2), 198–215.

Barn, R., Križ, K., Pösö, T., & Skivenes, M. (2015). Migrant children and child welfare systems: A contested challenge. In M. Skivenes, R. Barn, K. Križ, & T. Pösö (Eds), *Child welfare, systems and migrant children.* Oxford: Oxford University Press.

Berzin, S., Cohen, E., Thomas, K., & Dawson, W. (2008). Does family group decision making affect child welfare outcomes? Findings from a randomized control study. *Child Welfare, 87*(4), 35–54.

Brown, J.D., Barrett, K., Ireys, H.T., Allen, K., Pires, S.A., & Blau, G. (2010). Family-driven youth-guided practices in residential treatment: Findings from a national survey of residential treatment facilities. *Residential Treatment for Children & Youth, 27*(3), 149–159.

Bruskas, D. (2008). Children in foster care: A vulnerable population at risk. *Journal of Child and Adolescent Psychiatric Nursing, 21*(2), 70–77.

Cameron, C. (2004). Social pedagogy and care. *Journal of Social Work, 4*(2), 133–151.

Cameron, C. & Moss, P. (2011). *Social pedagogy and working with children and young people.* London: Jessica Kingsley.

Child Welfare Information Gateway. (2015). *Immigration and child welfare.* Retrieved from www.childwelfare.gov/pubPDFs/immigration.pdf (accessed December 26, 2017).

Child Welfare Information Gateway. (2017). *Family group decision-making.* Retrieved from www.childwelfare.gov/topics/famcentered/decisions/ (accessed November 11, 2017).

Colton, M., & Williams, M. (1997). Global trends in foster care. *Community Alternatives, 9*(1), 21–32.

Crampton, D. (2007). Research review: Family group decision-making: A promising practice in need of more programme theory and research. *Child & Family Social Work, 12*(2), 202–209.

Crampton, D., & Jackson, W. (2007). Family group decision making and disproportionality in foster care: A case study. *Child Welfare, 86*(3), 51–69.

Darlington, Y., Healy, K., Yellowlees, J., & Bosly, F. (2012). Parents' perceptions of their participation in mandated family group meetings. *Children and Youth Services Review, 34*(2), 331–337.

del Valle, J., López, M., Montserrat, C., & Bravo, A. (2009). Twenty years of foster care in Spain: Profiles, patterns and outcomes. *Children and Youth Services Review, 31*, 847–853.

Dijkstra, S., Creemers, H., Asscher, J., Dekovi , M., & Stams, G. (2016). The effectiveness of family group conferencing in youth care: A meta-analysis. *Child Abuse & Neglect, 62*, 100–110.

Dominelli, L. (2010). Globalization, contemporary challenges and social work practice. *International Social Work, 53*(5), 599–612.

Dumbrill, G. (2006). Parental experience of child protection intervention: A qualitative study. *Child Abuse & Neglect, 30*(1), 27–37.

Dunst, C., Trivette, C., & Deal, A. (1994). *Supporting & strengthening families, Vol. 1. Methods, strategies and practices*. Cambridge, MA: Brookline Books.

Earner, I., & Križ, K. (2015). The United States: Child protection in the context of competing policy mandates. In R. Barn, K. Križ, T. Pösö, & M. Skivenes (Eds), *Child welfare systems and migrant families*. New York: Oxford University Press.

Falicov, C. (2007). Working with transnational immigrants: Expanding meanings of family, community and culture. *Family Process, 46*(2), 151–171.

Finn, J., & Jacobson, M. (2003). Just practice: Steps toward a new social work paradigm. *Journal of Social Work Education, 39*(1), 57–78.

Finno, M., & Bearzi, M. (2010). Child welfare and immigration in New Mexico: Challenges, achievements, and the future. *Journal of Public Child Welfare, 4*(3), 306–324.

Finno-Velasquez, M. (2014). Barriers to support service use for Latino families reported to child welfare: Implications for policy and practice. Published by Migration and Child Welfare National Network. Retrieved from http://cimmcw.org/wp-content/uploads/2013/03/Barriers-to-Support-Service-Use-for-Latino-Immigrant-Families-Reported-to-Child-Welfare.pdf (accessed December 26, 2017).

Freire, P. (1993). *Pedagogy of the oppressed: New revised 20th anniversary edition*. New York: Continuum.

Freymond, N., & Cameron, G. (Eds) (2006*). Towards positive systems of child and family welfare: International comparisons of child protection, family service and community caring systems*. Toronto: University of Toronto Press.

Gill, H., Higginson, L., & Napier, H. (2003). Family group conferences in permanency planning. *Adoption & Fostering, 27*(2), 53–63.

Ginwright, S. & Cammarota, J. (2002). New terrain in youth development: The promise of a social justice approach. *Social Justice, 29*, 92–95.

Government of Western Australia. (2011). *The signs of safety: Child protection practice framework* (2nd edn). Retrieved from www.dcp.wa.gov.au/Resources/Documents/Policies%20and%20Frameworks/SignsOfSafetyFramework2011.pdf (accessed December 26, 2017).

Hallstedt, P., & Hogstrom, M. (2005). *The recontextualisation of social pedagogy: A study of three curricula in the Netherlands, Norway and Ireland*. Doctoral thesis. Retrieved from http://muep.mau.se/handle/2043/7231.

Hämäläinen, J. (2003). The concept of social pedagogy in the field of social work. *Journal of Social Work, 3*(1), 69–80.

Harvey, D. (2005). *A brief history of neoliberalism*. Oxford: Oxford University Press.

Hidalgo, M., & Hernández, B. (2001). Place attachment: Conceptual and empirical questions. *Journal of Environmental Psychology, 21*(3), 273–281.

Hollinshead, D., Corwin, T., Maher, E., Merkel-Holguin, L., Allan, H., & Fluke, J. (2017). Effectiveness of family group conferencing in preventing repeat referrals to child protective services and out-of-home placements. *Child Abuse & Neglect, 69*, 285–294.

Ife, J. (2008). *Human rights and social work: Towards rights-based practice.* Cambridge: Cambridge University Press.

James, S. (2011). What works in group care? – A structured review of treatment models for group homes and residential care. *Children and Youth Services Review, 33*, 308–321.

Kataoka, S., Stein, B., Jaycox, L., Wong, M., Escudero, P., Tu, W., Zaragoza, C., & Fink, A. (2003). A school-based mental health program for traumatized Latino immigrant children. *Journal of the American Academy of Child and Adolescent Psychiatry, 42*(3), 311–318.

Keddell, E. (2011). Reasoning processes in child protection decision making: Negotiating moral minefields and risky relationships. *The British Journal of Social Work, 41*(7), 1251–1270.

Kemp, S., Whittaker, J., & Tracy, E. (1997). *Person-environment practice: The social ecology of interpersonal helping.* New York: Aldine de Gruyter.

Kemp, S., Marcenko, M., Hoagwood, K., & Vesneski, W. (2009). Engaging parents in child welfare services: Bridging family needs and child welfare mandates. *Child Welfare, 88*(1), 101–126.

Kennett, P. (2001). *Comparative social policy: Theory and research.* Buckingham: Open University Press.

Križ, K., & Skivenes, M. (2012). How child welfare workers perceive their work with undocumented immigrant families: An explorative study of challenges and coping strategies. *Children and Youth Services Review, 34*(4), 790–797.

Kyriacou, C., Ellingsen, I.T., Stephens, P., & Sundaram, V. (2009). Social pedagogy and the teacher: England and Norway compared. *Pedagogy, Culture & Society, 17*(1), 75–87.

Lee, B., Hwang, J., Socha, K., Pau, T., & Shaw, T. (2013). Going home again: Transitioning youth to families after group care placement. *Journal of Child and Family Studies, 22*(4), 447–459.

Lewicka, M. (2011). Place attachment: How far have we come in the last 40 years? *Journal of Environmental Psychology, 31*(3), 207–230.

Lohrbach, S., & Sawyer, R. (2004). Family group decision making: A process reflecting partnership-based practice. *Protecting Children, 19*(2), 12–15.

López, M., del Valle, J., Montserrat, C., & Bravo, A. (2011). Factors affecting foster care breakdown in Spain. *Spanish Journal of Psychology, 14*(1), 111–122.

Lorenz, W. (2008). Paradigms and politics: Understanding methods paradigms in an historical context: The case of social pedagogy. *The British Journal of Social Work, 38*(4), 625–644.

Love, C. (2000). Family group conferencing: Cultural origins, sharing and appropriation – A Maori reflection. In G. Burford & J. Hudson (Eds), *Family group conferencing: New directions in community-centered child and family practice* (pp. 15–30). Hawthorne, NY: Aldine de Gruyter.

Lupton, C. (1998). User empowerment or family self-reliance? The family group conference model. *British Journal of Social Work, 28*, 107–128.

Madianou, M., & Miller, D. (2012). Polymedia: Towards a new theory of digital media in interpersonal communication. *International Journal of Cultural Studies, 16*(2), 169–187.

Maiter, S., & Leslie, B. (2015). Child welfare systems and immigrant families: Canada. In M. Skivenes, R. Barn, K. Križ, & T. Pösö (Eds), *Child welfare systems and migrant children* (pp. 179–198). Oxford: Oxford University Press.

Marsh, P., & Crow, G. (2003). Family group conferencing: A national process and outcome study in England and Wales – 1997. *Protecting Children, 18*, 129–130.

McDermid, S., Baker, C., Lawson, D., & Holmes, L. (2016). The evaluation of the Mockingbird Family Model: Final evaluation report. Retrieved from www.gov.uk/government/uploads/system/uploads/attachment_data/file/560625/DFE-RR528-Mockingbird_family_model_evaluation.pdf (accessed December 26, 2017).

Merkel-Holguin, L. (2000). Diversions and departures in the implementation of family group conferencing in the United States. In G. Burford & J. Hudson (Eds), *Family group conferencing: New directions in community-centered child and family practice* (pp. 224–231). Hawthorne, NY: Aldine de Gruyter.

Merkel-Holguin, L. (2003). Promising results, potential new directions: International FGDM research and evaluation in child welfare. *Protecting Children, 18*(1), 2–11.

Merkel-Holguin, L., Nixon, P., & Burford, G. (2003). Learning with families: A synopsis of FGDM research and evaluation in child welfare. *Protecting Children, 18*(1), 2–11.

Miller, M. (2011). Family team decision making: Does it reduce racial disproportionality in Washington's child welfare system? (Document No. 11–03–3901). Olympia, WA: Washington State Institute for Public Policy. Retrieved from www.researchgate.net/profile/Marna_Miller/publication/286450531_family_team_decision-making_does_it_reduce_racial_dispropor tionality_in_washington%27s_child_welfare_system/links/5669ff7a08ae1a797e378870/family-team-decision-making-does-it-reduce-racial-disproportionality-in-washingtons-child-welfare-system.pdf (accessed January 4, 2018).

Mockingbird Family Model Constellation Training and Resource Manual. (2014). Unpublished manual. The Mockingbird Society, Seattle, WA.

Mockingbird Society. (2010). Mockingbird Family Model. 2009 Management Report on Program Outcomes. Retrieved from www.mockingbirdsociety.org/images/info/2009_mgmt_report_final_fullreport.pdf (accessed December 26, 2017).

Morgan, P. (2010). Towards a developmental theory of place attachment. *Journal of Environmental Psychology, 30*(1), 11–22.

Morris, K., & Connolly, M. (2012). Family decision making in child welfare: Challenges in developing a knowledge base for practice. *Child Abuse Review, 21*(1), 41–52.

Morrison, T. (2007). Emotional intelligence, emotion and social work: Context, characteristics, complications and contributions. *The British Journal of Social Work, 37*(2), 245–263.

Mosek, A. (2004). Relations in foster care. *Journal of Social Work, 4*(3), 323–343.

Munro, E. (2011). *Munro review of child protection. Interim report: The child's journey*. Retrieved from http://dera.ioe.ac.uk/1915/1/Munrointerimreport.pdf (accessed December 26, 2017).

Nixon, P. (2000). Family group conference connections: Shared problems and solutions. In G. Burford & J. Hudson (Eds), *Family group conferencing: New directions in community-centered child and family practice* (pp. 15–30). Hawthorne, NY: Aldine de Gruyter.

Northwest Institute for Children and Families. (2006). Mockingbird family model project evaluation. Year two evaluation report. Retrieved from www.mockingbirdsociety.org/images/info/nwicf_2006-4_report.pdf (accessed December 26, 2017).

Northwest Institute for Children and Families. (2007). Mockingbird family model project evaluation. Year three evaluation report. Retrieved from www.mockingbirdsociety.org/images/info/nwicf_2007-5_report.pdf (accessed December 26, 2017).

O'Hara, K. (1998). *Comparative family policy: Eight countries' stories*. Ottawa: Renouf Publishing.

Parreñas, R. (2005). Long distance intimacy: Class, gender and intergenerational relations between mothers and children in Filipino transnational families. *Global Networks, 5*(4), 317–336.

Parton, N. (1998). Risk, advanced liberalism and child welfare: The need to rediscover uncertainty and ambiguity. *The British Journal of Social Work, 28*(1), 5–27.

Pennell, J. (2004). Family group conferencing in child welfare: Responsive and regulatory interfaces. *Journal of Sociology and Social Welfare, 31*, 117–135.

Pennell, J., & Burford, G. (2000). Family group decision making: Protecting children and women. *Child Welfare, 79*(2), 131–158.

Pennell, J., Edwards, M., & Burford, G. (2010). Expedited family group engagement and child permanency. *Children and Youth Services Review, 32*(7), 1012–1019.

Petrie, P., Boddy, J., Cameron, C., Simon, A., & Wigfall, V. (2006). *Working with children in Europe*. Buckingham; Open University Press.

Petrie, P., Boddy, J., Cameron, C., Heptinstall, E., McQuail, S., Simon, A., & Wigfall, V. (2009). *Pedagogy – A holistic, personal approach to work with children and young people, across services: European models for practice, training, education and qualification*. Retrieved from http://eprints.ioe.ac.uk/58/1/may_18_09_Ped_BRIEFING__PAPER_JB_PP_.pdf (accessed November 11, 2017).

Reich, J. (2005) *Fixing families: Parents, power, and the child welfare system*. New York: Routledge.

Resolutions Consultancy. (2018). *The Signs of Safety approach to child protection casework*. East Perth: Author. Retrieved from www.signsofsafety.net/signs-of-safety/.

Roberts, D. (2002). *Shattered bonds: The color of child welfare*. New York: Basic Civitas Books.

Roberts, Y.H., Caslor, M., Turnell, A., Pecora, P.J., Pearson, K. et al. (2016). *Signs of Safety® Supervisor Fidelity Assessment Tool: Field Test and Evaluation Report*. Seattle, WA: Casey Family Programs, and East Perth Australia: Resolutions Consultancy. Retrieved from www.casey.org/signs-of-safety/.

Rodenborg, N. (2004). Services to African American children in poverty: Institutional discrimination in child welfare? *Journal of Poverty, 8*(3), 109–130.

Samuels, G., & Pryce, J. (2008). What doesn't kill you makes you stronger: Survivalist self-reliance as resilience and risk among young adults aging out of foster care. *Children and Youth Services Review, 30*(10), 1198–1210.

Sheets, J., Wittenstrom, K., Fong, R., James, J., Tecci, M. Baumann, D., & Rodriguez, C. (2009). Evidence based practice in family group decision-making for Anglo, African American and Hispanic families. *Children and Youth Services Review, 31*(11), 1187–1191.

Signs of Safety. (2017). Website. Retrieved from www.signsofsafety.net/signs-of-safety/.

Stolleis, M. (2013). Origins of the German Welfare State: Social policy in Germany to 1945. In *Origins of the German Welfare State. German social policy,* vol. 2. Berlin, Heidelberg: Springer.

Sundell, K., & B. Vinnerljung, B. (2004). Outcomes of family group conferencing in Sweden: A 3-year follow-up. *Child Abuse & Neglect, 28*(3), 267–287.

Tan, N. (2012). Cultural conflict and conflict resolution. In L. Healy & R. Link (Eds), *Handbook of international social work* (pp. 128–133). Oxford: Oxford University Press.

Texas Department of Family and Protective Services. (2017). *Child protective services handbook.* Section 6700: International and Immigration Issues. Retrieved from www.dfps.state.tx.us/handbooks/CPS/Files/CPS_pg_6700.asp (accessed December 26, 2017).

Turnell, A. (2013). *Signs of Safety: International use and data.* Published by Resolutions Consultancy. Retrieved from http://cssr.berkeley.edu/cwscmsreports/LatinoPracticeAdvisory/PRACTICE_EB_Child_Welfare_Practice_Models/Safety%20Organized%20Practice/Turnell%202012.pdf (accessed December 26, 2017).

Turnell, A., & Edwards, S. (1999). *Signs of Safety: A safety and solution oriented approach to child protection casework.* New York: W.W. Norton.

Turnell, A., Pecora, P.J., Roberts, Y.H., Caslor, M., & Koziolek, D. (2017). Signs of Safety as a promising comprehensive approach for reorienting CPS organizations' work with children, families and their community supports. In M. Connolly (Ed.), *Beyond the risk paradigm in child protection* (pp. 130–146). London: Palgrave Macmillan Education. Retrieved from https://he.palgrave.com/page/detail/beyond-the-risk-paradigm-in-child-protection-marie-connolly/?sf1=barcode&st1=9781137441300.

Unrau, Y., Chambers, R., Seita, J., & Putney, K. (2010). Defining a foster care placement move: The perspective of adults who formerly lived in multiple out-of-home placements. *Families in Society, 91*(4), 426–432.

U.S. Department of Homeland Security. (2017). Green card based on Special Immigrant Juvenile classification. Retrieved from www.uscis.gov/green-card/sij (accessed December 26, 2017).

Walton, E., Roby, J., Frandsen, A., & Davidson, A. (2003). Strengthening at risk families by involving the extended family. *Journal of Family Social Work, 7,* 1–21.

Whittaker, J.K. (2004). The re-invention of residential treatment: An agenda for research and practice. *Child and Adolescent Psychiatric Clinics of North America, 13*(2), 267–278.

Whittaker, J., & Maluccio, A. (2002). Rethinking "child placement": A reflective essay. *Social Service Review, 76*(1), 108–134.

Zayas, L., & Bradlee, M. (2014). Exiling children, creating orphans: When immigration policies hurt citizens. *Social Work, 59*(2), 167–175.

Zentgraf, K., & Chinchilla, N. (2012). Transnational family separation: A framework for analysis. *Journal of Ethnic and Migration Studies, 38*(2), 345–366.

Index

Locators in **bold** refer to tables and locators in *italics* refer to figures.